ABBREVIATIONS COMMONLY USED

tsp. = teaspoon	oz. = ounce or ounces
tbsp. = tablespoon	lb. = pound or pounds
c. = cup	sq. = square
pt. = pint	min. = minute or minutes
qt. = quart	hr. = hour or hours
pk. = peck	mod. = moderate or moderately
bu. = bushel	doz. = dozen

SIMPLIFIED MEASURES

dash = less than ⅛ teaspoon	2 pints (4 cups) =1 quart
3 teaspoons = 1 tablespoon	4 quarts (liquid) =1 gallon
16 tablespoons =1 cup	8 quarts (solid) =1 peck
1 cup =½ pint	4 pecks =1 bushel
2 cups =1 pint	16 ounces =1 pound

If you want to measure part-cups by the tablespoon, remember:

4 tablespoons =¼ cup	10⅔ tablespoons =⅔ cup
5⅓ tablespoons =⅓ cup	12 tablespoons =2/4 cup
8 tablespoons =½ cup	14 tablespoons =⅞ cup

OVEN TEMPERATURES

Slow	250 to 300°
Slow moderate	325°
Moderate	350°
Quick moderate	375°
Moderately hot	400°
Hot	425 to 450°
Very hot	475 to 500°

CONTENTS OF CANS

Of the different sizes of cans used by commercial canners, the most common are:

Size	Average Contents
8-oz	1 cup
picnic	1¼ cups
no. 300	1¾ cups
no. 1 tall	2 cups
no. 303	2 cups
no. 2	2½ cups
no. 2½	3½ cups
no. 3	4 cups
no. 10	12 to 13 cups

BETTY CROCKER'S

PICTURE

COOK BOOK

Rodale Inc.
and
General Mills, Inc.

Minneapolis

We're excited to bring this treasured first edition of Betty Crocker's Cook Book. The recipes are exactly as they appear in the original cookbook to reflect the heritage of American cooking. Eating habits may have changed since 1950, but the fond memories of sharing delicious recipes from this cookbook remain the same.

Mom or Grandma may have used more salt, sugar and fat in her cooking than we do today, and some ingredients and food safety concerns have changed over the years. So you may want to try these recipes using today's ingredients and methods. Or ask Mom or Grandma how they make these recipes still taste so good today!

Printed in China

2 4 6 8 10 9 7 5 3 direct mail hardcover

Home of Betty Crocker Service

Where visitors are welcomed. The office section beyond the curved glass screen is light and cheery, with colorful walls and blonde book shelves. Through the wide view window straight ahead you look into a lovely blue kitchen.

Kamera Kitchen With three complete working units, where foods that are to have their pictures taken are "made up." Appropriate dishes and colorful fabrics to set them off are kept in the commodious cabinets.

Terrace Kitchen Has every known home-type convenience. General recipe testing goes on here and guest luncheons are prepared. Visitors in the patiolike terrace outside, with its garden furniture, can look in on the hum of activity.

Polka Dot Kitchen Gayest, most colorful of all . . . with stainless steel counters and a laundry unit for experimental work with appliances.

Kitchen of Tomorrow Two kitchens in one. Light walls with amusing Swedish figures and mottos give gay atmosphere. One is for important experimental baking, to develop new methods and new products for the future. The other for Products Control, to test our products daily.

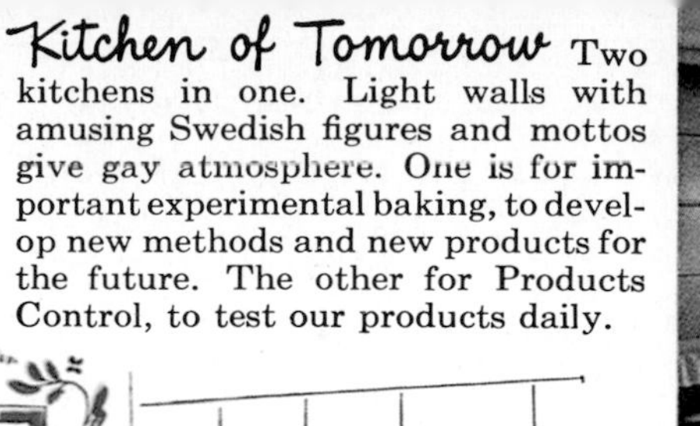

Tasting Bar Planned for taste tests . . . a practical demonstration center too.

Early American Dining Room Surprising contrast to the up-to-the-minute kitchens, this spacious room boasts mellow old panelling from a New England home of 1750. The wide fireplace with old-time cooking utensils reveals how women used to labor. Antique chairs . . . dough box . . . and old pewter convey the charm of old-time peace.

HOME OF BETTY CROCKER SERVICE

Won't you let me take you on a tour of our Department to see each one of our kitchens and the members of our Staff in action? From this hostess desk you can see the library of cook books . . . rows of recipe files . . . and the section where correspondence is handled. As we walk past these book shelves, you'll want to stop a moment to see our miniature kitchen!

It is an authentic reproduction of a kitchen of about 1880 when GOLD MEDAL FLOUR was first milled. See the "God Bless Our Home" motto . . . the pump in the dry sink . . . the churn in the corner . . . the old range with the woodbox to be filled and the kerosene lamps. Yes, it's one of those big old kitchens where women walked *miles* a day.

KITCHENS OF 1950

What a contrast to our modern kitchens! First, here's the Kamera Kitchen where the Staff works with the foods to be photographed to make sure they will look their most beautiful. It's been the scene of the special testing of recipes for the cook book. Now let's step across the terrace to this view window and watch the girls at work in our lovely *blue* kitchen. It's really like a large home kitchen with all the latest time-saving, step-saving features. It is used for recipe testing and for preparing the frequent guest luncheons.

KITCHEN OF 1750

Where are those luncheons served? Right here in our Early American dining room. Most of our visitors seem to like this room the best of all. They come back to gaze at the wide old fireplace . . . the mellow pine paneling from a New England house of 1750 . . . the tall clock and other antiques which give the old-time cozy charm. Some of the early cooking utensils . . . the heavy iron kettles, and spiders and long handled waffle iron around the fireplace . . . are evidence of the heavy labor that went into cooking in early days. Notice the old dough box for making bread . . . the spice box . . . and the pewter plates and measures in the open cupboard.

NEW AIDS TO HOMEMAKING

But let's go into the gay Polka Dot Kitchen where appliances are tested. The history of one household is told by these irons of different periods. First, there is the very early handmade "sadiron." And well named it is, when you lift it! Then these others, down to one of the *first* electric irons. It seems almost a monstrosity compared to our beautiful streamlined Tru-heat iron.

You know, this iron was developed by General Mills from the specifications of what women want for ease in ironing. The work with appliances such as toasters, waffle irons, and coffee makers is handled on the stainless steel counters.

ASSURING SUCCESS

In this next kitchen, with its amusing wall paintings in gay Swedish colors, we carry on the daily testing of products. Samples of our flour from the Gold Medal mills in different parts of the country are baked to make sure they will perform right for you with all our recipes.

The other kitchen, or section of this double kitchen, lives up to the name "Kitchen of Tomorrow." For special new experimental baking projects go on here to develop new methods and new products.

FOUNDATION OF SERVICE

And here we are at the door of the supply room and at the Tasting Bar. Whenever any of the Staff want to get other members to taste test the foods they've been working on, it's easy to call them together here. The fate of many a recipe, and even the fate of new food mixes, has been decided here. Showings of food ideas for ads and demonstrations are from this tasting center.

Does this give you an idea of how we carry on the careful testing and checking, experimenting and planning that has been the sound foundation of our service? I think it *does* make anyone appreciate all the care and thought and science which is back of our products.

Dear Friend,

This book seems like a dream come true for us. And we hope it will be for the thousands of you who have requested a cook book full of our famous tested recipes! And to those who have asked for a successor to that old brown-covered Gold Medal Cook Book which their mothers and grandmothers treasured, —here it is at last, a new and different cook book for a new age!

We dedicate it to homemakers everywhere, —to all of you who like to minister to your dear ones by serving them good food. That's the age-old way to express love and concern for their welfare. And it's just as important today when we make use of the latest short cuts, equipment and prepared foods as it was when women made their own bread, butter, cheese, —all the foods their families ate.

We have tried to include extra tips, pointers, and secrets. Our radio friends have always loved stories of the origin of recipes and the fascinating bits of food history, and we hope you will enjoy all these features. But most important of all, we want you to feel as we do that this is a collection of basic cooking information and "first choice" recipes, —those you will need for every type of cooking.

You see, we first checked all those we have put out in our many years of service, and compared them with recipes from other sources. Then we retested and perfected them with *new and simplified methods*. When we fitted them onto the pages we chose the most popular and interesting of all, and sent them out to representative homes across the country to be tested again. Only those that passed the home testing with a top score for perfect results and eating enjoyment were included.

Home testers say they love this new plan of recipes with variations. It saves having to read the same directions over and over. Yet we give additional aids to perfect results. Don't miss the recipes marked with a ★! They are special favorites with our Staff, and are served often in our own homes. And don't forget that in our service we are continually offering new recipes and food ideas in magazines, over the radio, and in television.

We hope this book will bring you more fun in cooking and deeper joy in your homemaking.

Betty Crocker

How to Get PERFECT *Results from Recipes in this Book . . .*

1 Read Recipe Carefully! Every word of it. And do be *sure* to see if there's anything to be done before you start mixing . . . like chopping nuts or melting chocolate.

2 Look at the Pictures! They give you "know how" you need for every step.

3 Turn on the Heat! If the cookies are to be baked immediately after mixing, see that the oven is heated to correct temperature.

4 Get Your Ingredients Together! Saves time and steps to have them all in one place.

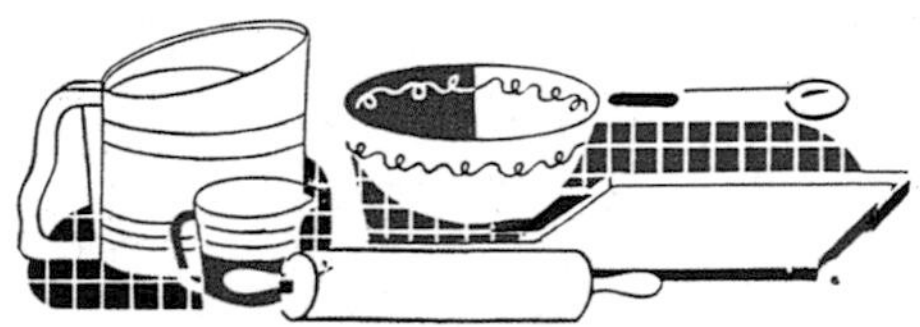

5 Collect Utensils, Too! Gather together all you'll need . . . from the flour sifter to the baking pan.

6 Measure as Exactly as a Druggist follows a doctor's prescription! Two minutes spent measuring carefully may save you hours of grief.

7 Mix Carefully as Directed (cream or stir or beat or fold in, etc.). Follow every step exactly as described in the recipe and pictures.

8 Bake or Cook or otherwise prepare correctly as the recipe indicates. Correct cooking or baking is necessary for complete success.

HOW TO MEASURE *to be Sure of Results . . .*

Use squares of paper when sifting, measuring, etc.

Cooking success is up to you!
If you'll take pains to measure true,
Use* Standard *cups and spoons all the way.
And then level off—it'll always pay!

Use straight-edged knife for "leveling off."

Dry Measuring Cup has no rim . . . 1-cup line is even with top.

Use for any dry ingredients or shortening.

Liquid Measuring Cup . . . has rim above the 1-cup line.

Use for measuring any liquid ingredients.

Graduated Measuring Cups . . . ¼, ⅓, ½, 1 cup.

Use for part-cups of any dry ingredients or shortenings.

Measuring Spoons . . . ¼, ½, and 1 teaspoon, 1 tablespoon.

Use for less than ¼ cup of any ingredient.

FLOUR

1 Sift flour through large open sifter (to aerate it) onto square of paper before measuring.

2 Then spoon sifted flour lightly into a "dry" measuring cup . . . heaping it up.

3 Level off cup with straight-edged knife. Don't shake cup. This is important!

SUGAR

1 White Granulated Sugar needs sifting only if lumpy. Spoon lightly into "dry" measuring cup. Level it off with a straight-edged knife. Don't knock or tap cup.

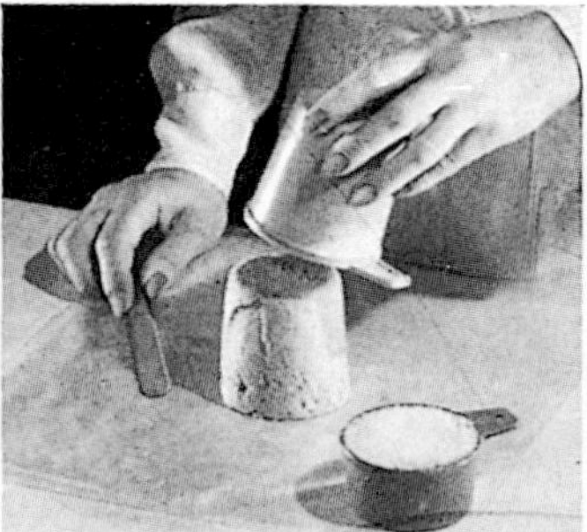

2 Brown Sugar. If it's lumpy, press through coarse sieve; or heat in slow oven; or crush lumps with rolling pin. Pack into "dry" measuring cup just enough to hold its shape. Level off.

3 Confectioners' Sugar. Press through sieve to remove lumps. Spoon lightly into "dry" measuring cup. Level off with straight-edged knife. Don't shake or knock cup.

HERE'S HOW WE MEASURE

Baking Powder, Soda, Salt, Cornstarch, Cream of Tartar, Spices, Etc.

Fill measuring spoon. Level off with straight-edged knife.

SHORTENING

Use Graduated Measuring Cups. Have shortening at room temperature. Pack shortening firmly into measuring cup. Level off with straight-edged knife.

In measuring less than ¼ cup, use a tbsp. (hold fingers under bowl to prevent breaking it).

BUTTER

To measure: 1 cup (½ lb.), cut one *lb.* brick in two . . . ½ cup (¼ lb.), cut *half* brick in two . . . ¼ cup (⅛ lb.), cut the *quarter* brick in two.

EGGS

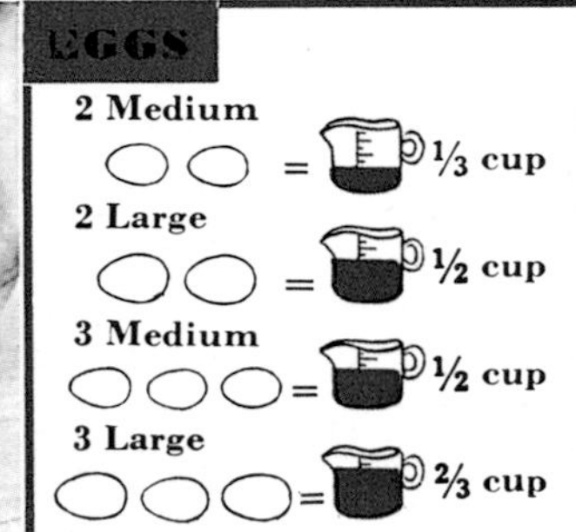

Eggs vary in size . . . so be sure to measure them. Never use less than the minimum amount specified in recipe.

LIQUIDS

Use "liquid" measuring cup to prevent spilling. Pour liquid into cup on table. Have measuring line on eye level.

MOLASSES OR SYRUP

Fill cup (previously used for shortening). It rounds up, so level off. Scrape out with rubber spatula.

DRIED FRUIT

Pack raisins, dates, figs., etc., lightly into measuring cup. Press gently to level off top.

NUTS AND COCONUT

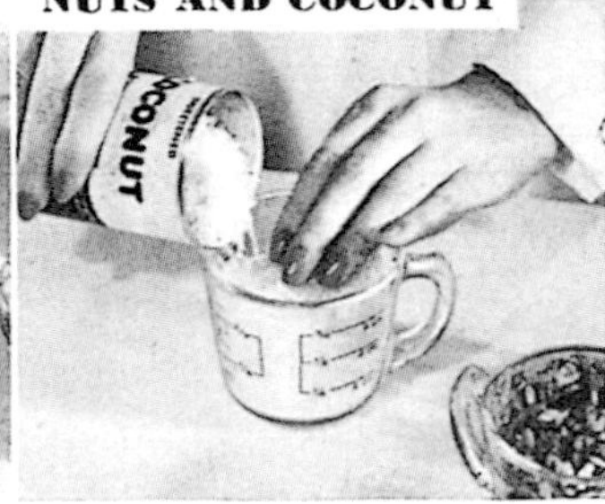

Pack coconut or nuts lightly into measuring cup. Level off.

SOFT BREAD CRUMBS

Pack lightly into measuring cup. Do not press down hard. Level off.

SHREDDED OR GRATED CHEESE

Pack lightly into measuring cup. Level off.

FINE DRY BREAD CRUMBS

Spoon lightly into measuring cup. Level off. Don't shake cup.

MEANING OF TERMS

This page gives the meaning of terms in this book! It's here just to help you to be a Prize Cook!

SUGAR
Fine white granulated sugar, unless otherwise specified in recipe.

SALT
Cooking salt in cloth sacks. It is cheaper and stronger than table salt.

CHOCOLATE
Unsweetened baking chocolate. If sweet chocolate or bits or pieces are required, recipe will so state.

GOLD MEDAL FLOUR
Gold Medal *"Kitchen-tested"* Enriched Flour—the country's most popular brand of all-purpose flour. *Recipes in this book, except cake recipes, have been perfected for Gold Medal only.*

SOFTASILK CAKE FLOUR
Specially milled from selected "soft" winter wheats to make exceptionally delicate, fine-textured cakes.

MILK
Fresh, sweet milk, unless otherwise indicated.

BUTTERMILK and SOUR MILK
May be used interchangeably. Too old milk has disagreeable flavor!

MOLASSES
Dark molasses . . . for rich flavor, dark color. Light molasses gives more delicate color and flavor.

SPICES and FLAVORINGS
High quality always, for flavor and dependability.

WHEATIES
The crispy, whole-wheat flakes nationally known as the "Breakfast of Champions."

ROLLED OATS
Either quick-cooking or regular (uncooked).

MOIST SHREDDED COCONUT
Shredded coconut that's moist . . . either from a can or a package . . . or shredded from a fresh coconut.

BAKING POWDER
Any of the well known nationally distributed brands of double-action baking powder give good results with the recipes in this book.

EGGS
Large fresh eggs (2 oz.) or equivalent amounts from smaller eggs.

SHORTENING
Any fresh, mild-flavored solid fat . . animal or vegetable, such as those at right. Butter is indicated in certain recipes for flavor.

MEANING OF TERMS (cont.)

MUSTARD

Dry mustard: ground mustard seed in powdered form.

Prepared mustard: paste made of dry mustard blended with vinegar, sometimes especially seasoned.

CHEESE

American (Cheddar) cheese: "unaged" (green) or "aged;" the greener cheese is mild, the aged cheese sharper in flavor. It ranges from firm to crumbly in texture . . . from pale to deep yellow in color.

White cream cheese: of smooth creamy consistency. **Note:** 3-oz. and 8-oz. pkg.

PEPPERS

Black pepper: ground from whole peppercorns.

White pepper: from peppercorns with outer bark removed.

[**Paprika:** mildly pungent.
Red pepper: sharper.
Cayenne: hottest of all.]
All ground from red pepper pods.

PLAIN GELATINS

Plain unflavored gelatin: each envelope contains 1 tbsp.

FLAVORED GELATINS

Gelatin with sugar, color, and flavoring added.

MUSHROOMS (2 forms)

Both should be sautéed in butter before using.

COFFEE

The beverage—not uncooked ground coffee.

YEAST

Compressed yeast: in cake form—keeps about 2 weeks in refrigerator.

Dry yeast: in granular form in packages, needs no refrigeration. Keeps fresh for weeks (see expiration date on pkg.).

MASHED POTATOES and POTATO WATER

Freshly mashed potatoes: no milk or seasoning added.

Potato water: in which potatoes have been boiled.

RYE FLOUR

Flour made from rye. Usually blended with wheat flour to give it rising power.

WHOLE WHEAT or GRAHAM FLOUR

The fine or coarsely ground kernels of wheat including bran, germ, and all.

CORN MEAL

The coarsely ground kernel of the corn (either white or yellow corn meal).

HERBS

Garden Fresh. Dried Crushed. Powdered: Must be fresh, full-bodied. Keep in tightly covered jar in cold place. Replace when freshness is gone.

MEANING OF TERMS

HERBS

Herb authorities claim there are six simple herbs basic to all seasoning.

Mint: For tea, iced drinks, ices, pea soup, cottage cheese, salads, salad dressings, meat broths, and potatoes.

Thyme: Common thyme of the many varieties of this herb is the general kitchen herb that glorifies such varying foods as soups, sauces, stuffings, cheeses, meats, hare, fish, and salad dressings. It is particularly delicious with tomatoes either in a salad or in cooked dishes.

Sage: Fresh sage is more satisfactory than dried. The gray pointed leaves should be added sparingly to beans, cottage cheese, salt fish, stews, duck, or geese. Although traditional in stuffing for turkey, herb authorities claim it is too strong for turkey or chicken. They recommend a blend of savory, thyme, and sweet basil for a more pleasing and subtle flavor.

Marjoram: Two kinds . . . sweet marjoram, one of the "big six," and wild marjoram, often called by its Spanish name, oregano. It is used in all Spanish and Mexican dishes, and is excellent with lamb or fresh mushrooms. The Italians call it the "mushroom herb." Sweet marjoram can be used successfully too in all of these. The Germans use sweet marjoram in making sausage and call it "Wurstkraut" . . . the sausage herb. Its general uses are in sauces, soups, salads, meats, stuffings, and fish.

Rosemary: Fragrant as a flower, this delightful herb gives subtlety to meat, poultry, sauces, greens, and stuffings. Some prefer it to garlic in a roast.

Basil: Adds distinction to soups, ragouts, salads, cottage cheese, meats, sauces, and fruit drinks.

ADDITIONAL HERBS FREQUENTLY USED

***Anise:** Seeds used in cookies, breads, cheese; the leaves used in salads.

Bay: Bay leaf for meats, soups, relishes, poultry, and stuffings.

***Caraway:** Seeds used in cookies, breads, sauerkraut, cream cheese, and over roasting pork.

Chervil: A salad herb par excellence. Combines well with other herbs. Good in soups, eggs, cheese, and some meats.

Chives: For potatoes, potato salads, omelettes, sauces, and cheese.

**Keep herb seeds in the refrigerator to prevent becoming rancid.*

Curry Powder: Not truly an herb, but a powdered combination of herbs and spices including green ginger, coriander seeds, cumin seeds, garlic, turmeric, chili, and peppercorns. Used with lamb and chicken.

Parsley: When used as a tasty, nutritious addition to sauces, soups, stews, meats.

Savory: Both leaves and flowers give flavor to poultry stuffings, salads, peas, pork, green beans, rice, horseradish sauce.

Tarragon: Crumbled leaves are used sparingly in salads, soups, fish sauces, dressings, meats, stews, and sprinkled over fish.

Winter Savory: A milder herb, can be used in larger amounts. Good in fish dishes.

HERB BOUQUETS

The Herb Bouquet is the first thing Europeans throw into the soup, stew, casserole, or roasting pan to impart the subtle flavor average American cooking lacks.

Fines Herbes: French term for a combination of 3 or 4 herbs used to flavor certain dishes—such combinations as parsley, basil, and chives. They are mixed together, chopped fine, and tossed into the food just before serving. They are used in tartar sauce, cream soups, and cream cheeses. When used in omelettes, they are mixed with the eggs before cooking.

Bouquet Garni: French term for a tablespoon of powdered herbs (such as 2 sprigs parsley, 1 sprig marjoram, 2 sprigs thyme, and ½ bay leaf) tied in a muslin bag, and left in a roast or soup for the last hour of cooking, then removed. For canned soups, it should be left in for the entire cooking time. In cold foods, fruit juices, cocktails, or cottage cheese, it takes several hours to draw out the flavor.

MEANING OF TERMS often found in Recipe Directions

bake. To cook by dry heat in an oven.

batter. A mixture of flour and liquid . . . usually in combination with other ingredients . . . thin enough to pour.

beat. To mix with a vigorous over-and-over motion, with a spoon, wire whip, or rotary beater. To enclose air in the food.

blend. To mix very thoroughly two or more ingredients.

boil. To cook in boiling water or other liquid in which bubbles are breaking on the surface and steam is given off.

broil. To cook directly under a red hot heating unit, or over an open fire or grill.

brush. To spread thinly, as with a brush or finger.

caramelize. To melt sugar to a golden brown "caramel"-flavored syrup.

chill. To allow to become thoroughly cold, but not frozen.

chop. To cut into coarse or fine pieces with a sharp knife or chopper.

combine. To mix unlike ingredients.

cream. To soften fat by rubbing it against the bowl with a spoon, or beating with electric mixer until it is light and creamy.

cream together. To blend two ingredients together, such as creaming fat with sugar, until the mixture is light and fluffy.

cube. To cut into solids of 6 equal square sides (usually ¼ to ½" in size).

cut in. To combine fat with dry ingredients using two knives, a fork, or pastry blender.

dice. To cut into small cubes about ¼" in size.

dust. To sprinkle or coat lightly with flour or sugar.

flake. To break lightly into small pieces with a fork.

fold in. To mix by a gentle motion: cutting down through and bringing up close to bowl, then folding over before cutting down through again. Proper folding in prevents loss of air.

fry. To cook in hot fat. *French fry.* To cook in hot fat deep enough to float the food. *Pan-fry.* To cook in a small amount of fat. Often called sauté.

grate. To rub against a grater to tear food into bits or shreds of various sizes.

grind. To change a food into tiny particles by cutting and crushing in a food grinder.

mince. To cut with knife or scissors into *very* fine pieces.

mix. To combine two or more ingredients, usually by stirring.

parboil. To boil food in water until partially cooked.

pare. To cut off the outside covering . . . with a knife, as from a potato or apple.

peel. To remove outside covering by stripping off, as from a tomato, a peach, or a banana.

poach. To cook by surrounding with simmering (not boiling) water or other liquid.

preheat. To turn on heat in oven and heat to desired temperature before putting in food.

sauté. To cook in a small quantity of hot fat. See "pan-fry."

scald. To heat to just below boiling point.

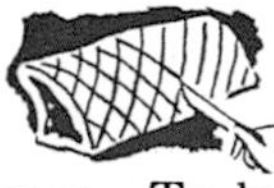

score. To cut narrow grooves or gashes.

sear. To brown the surface quickly with intense heat.

shred. To tear or cut into small, long, narrow pieces.

sift. To pass through a sieve.

simmer. To cook in liquid just below boiling point on top of stove.

slice. To cut into slices.

sliver. To cut or shred into long pieces.

steam. To cook in the steam which arises from a pan of boiling water or other liquid.

steam-bake. To cook in the oven . . . the utensil being set first in a pan having water reach well up on the outside of it.

stew. To cook slowly in a small amount of liquid for a long time.

stir. To mix, usually with a spoon, by rotary motion.

A DICTIONARY OF SPECIAL AND FOREIGN TERMS

A

à la king. Food served in rich cream sauce usually containing mushrooms, green pepper, pimiento,—often flavored with sherry.

angelica. The candied leafstalk of a European herb . . . used in decorating cakes, candies, desserts, etc.

antipasto. Italian for assorted appetizers of fish, cold cuts, or vegetables.

aspic. A jelly made from concentrated vegetable, meat, or fish stock . . . with gelatin.

au gratin. With a crust; usually fine bread crumbs. Sometimes with cheese.

B

baba. A French cake, made with a yeast dough, and usually soaked in rum.

barbecue. Roast meat on a rack over coals basted with highly seasoned sauce.

bar-le-duc. A jam originally made in Bar-le-duc, France, from currants and honey. The seeds were laboriously pushed out with a needle. Popularly made in the United States with the seeds left in.

baste. To moisten food while cooking (as meat while roasting) to add flavor and prevent dryness.

beurre noir. Browned butter sauce.

bind. To thicken slightly, usually with flour mixed with melted fat (as to bind soup). Commonly applied to soup.

bisque. 1. A rich cream soup (usually of vegetables or shellfish). 2. Or a frozen dessert, usually ice cream, with nuts in it.

blanch. 1. To remove skins from fruit or nuts by dipping into boiling water (1 to 5 minutes). 2. To whiten or set color of food by plunging into boiling water.

bombe. A round or melon-shaped frozen dessert, combining two or more frozen mixtures.

borsch. A Russian soup containing beets.

bouillabaisse. A French chowder of several varieties of fish and other ingredients.

bouillon. A clear soup made from lean beef.

braise. *See* "MEATS."

bread. To dredge with fine dry bread crumbs.

brioche. A slightly sweetened rich bread which originated in France.

brochette. 1. French word for skewer. 2. **en brochette.** Cooked on a skewer.

C

café au lait. *See* "BEVERAGES."

canapé. *See* "APPETIZERS."

candy. 1. A confection. 2. To cook in sugar or syrup.

caramel. 1. Burnt sugar syrup used for coloring and flavoring. 2. A candy flavored with burnt sugar syrup.

caviar. Prepared and salted roe (eggs) of the sturgeon and other large fish. Black or red, they are served as an appetizer.

chantilly. A dish in which whipped cream is one of the ingredients. Name derived from that of a castle north of Paris.

charlotte. A gelatin dessert containing flavored whipped cream, molded in a form lined with sponge cake or lady fingers.

chutney. A spicy, somewhat sweet relish, made from several fruits and vegetables.

coat. To cover with a thin film, such as flour on meat or flour on greased pans.

cobbler. *See* "DESSERTS."

cocktail. *See* "APPETIZERS."

coddle. To cook gently in liquid just below the boiling point.

condensed milk. Whole milk concentrated by evaporating part of the water, then sweetened.

compote. 1. A stemmed dish. 2. A mixture (as of fruits) served in a stemmed dish.

condiment. Something to give relish to food,—usually a pungent substance such as catsup, chutney, mustard, etc.

consommé. A light colored clear meat soup.

cracklings. The crisp residue of fat after the lard has been removed.

cream sauce. "*See* SAUCES."

Creole. Highly seasoned food typical of that prepared by the Creoles, descendants of early French and Spanish settlers of Louisiana.

crisp. To make firm and brittle . . . by placing in very cold water or in a moist cold place (as for vegetables), or in a moderate oven (as for crackers or potato chips).

croquette. *See* "MEATS."

croustade. A toast case. *See* p. 26.

croutons. *See* "HOW TO PREPARE."

curry. A stew cooked or flavored with curry.

cutlet. A small piece of meat, cut from leg or ribs, for broiling or frying. Or a mixture, usually of fish, shaped and cooked like a meat cutlet.

D

demitasse. The French for "half cup." A small cup for or of after-dinner coffee.

devil. To prepare with hot seasonings, such as pepper, mustard, etc.

dissolve. To cause a dry substance to pass into a solution in a liquid.

dot. To scatter small bits (such as butter) over surface of food.

dredge. To sprinkle or cover lightly with flour, or sugar, or other fine substances.

drippings. Fat and juice dripped from roasting meat.

E

eclair. Cream puff paste baked in oval shape filled with whipped cream or custard.

entrée. In formal dinners, a small "made" dish that is served as a separate course between the heavy courses. In informal meals, the chief dish of the main course . . . of meat, poultry, fish, or meat substitute.

A DICTIONARY OF SPECIAL AND FOREIGN TERMS (cont.)

evaporated milk. Whole milk from which 60% of its water has been evaporated.

F

fillet. Long, thin, boneless strip of lean meat or fish,—usually a choice cut.
filet mignon. Small, tender fillet, usually from beef tenderloin.
fondant. Sugar syrup cooked to the soft ball stage (234°), cooled, and kneaded to creaminess.
fondue. A light, fluffy baked food made with eggs, cheese, and milk and thickened with bread or cracker crumbs.
frappé. Diluted sweetened fruit juice, frozen to a mushy consistency.
fricassee. Properly, to cook by braising. For chicken, etc.,—it means stewing . . the browning process may be omitted.
fritter. *See* "QUICK BREADS."
frizzle. To pan-fry until the edges curl.
fromage. French word for cheese.
frosting. *See* "FROSTINGS."

G

garnish. To decorate with small portions of colorful food.
glacé. 1. Coated with a sugar syrup cooked to the "crack" stage. 2. Frozen.
glaze. To coat with a thin sugar syrup which has been cooked to the "crack" stage . . . or with melted jelly or thin aspic.
goulash. A thick Hungarian beef or veal stew flavored with vegetables and paprika.
grits. Coarsely ground corn, a breakfast food.
gumbo. 1. West Indian plant used to flavor rich, thick Creole soup. 2. The soup.

H

herb bouquet. *See* "HERBS."
hollandaise. *See* "SAUCES."
hors d'oeuvre. *See* "APPETIZERS."

I

ice. 1. *See frozen* "DESSERTS." 2. To cover with frosting.
icing. Same as "frosting."
infusion. The liquid extract obtained by steeping a substance, such as tea, coffee, herbs, etc., in a liquid.

J

julienne. To cut food into match-like strips.
junket. A dessert of milk coagulated by rennet, sweetened and flavored.

K

kisses. Small meringues.
knead. *See* "YEAST BREADS."

L

lard. To insert strips of fat into or on top of uncooked meat to give flavor or prevent dryness.
leek. Onion-like bulb, smaller, more pungent.
legumes. Vegetables which bear their fruit or seeds in pods, such as peas, beans, lentils.
Lyonnaise. Seasoned with onions, parsley.

M

macaroons. Small cakes made from egg whites, sugar, and almond paste of powdered almonds.
macédoine. A mixture of fruits or vegetables.
marguerite. A salty cracker covered with a mixture of boiled frosting and nuts or coconut . . . baked in the oven until browned.
maître d'hôtel. 1. A French term meaning "head steward or cook." 2. A sauce: *See* "SAUCES."
marinade. An oil-acid mixture used to give flavor to meats or salads.
marinate. *See* "SALADS."
meringue. A stiffly beaten mixture of egg whites and sugar (1) used to cover the top of a pie and usually browned in the oven, or (2) made in small cakes and baked.
mignon. 1. A French term meaning "favorite, delicate, darling." 2. A meltingly tender cut of boneless tenderloin beef.
minestrone. Italian for thick vegetable soup.
mocha. A flavor from coffee infusion or a combination of coffee and chocolate.
mousse. 1. *See frozen* "DESSERTS."
2. Certain hot dishes of smooth texture.

P

pan-broil. To cook uncovered in a hot frying pan, pouring off fat as it accumulates. No liquid.
pan-fry. To cook in small amount of hot fat, salad oil, or drippings in skillet.
parch. To brown with dry heat.
parfait. *See frozen* "DESSERTS."
paste. A smooth mixture of two ingredients, usually flour and water, used as thickening.
Pasteurize. To partially sterilize a liquid at a temperature (140–180°) which destroys certain pathogenic organisms and arrests fermentation (as for pasteurized milk).
pâté de foie gras. Goose liver paste.
patty. A patty shell filled with a creamed mixture of chicken, or fish, etc.
petits fours. Little fancy iced cakes, made by cutting sheet cakes into special shapes (squares, diamonds, etc.). Frosting is poured on and decorations added.
pilau. Rice stewed with meat, poultry, or fish, spices, etc.
pit. To remove pits or stones from fruit.
polenta. Italian for a corn meal or farina mush to which cheese is often added.

A DICTIONARY OF SPECIAL AND FOREIGN TERMS (concl.)

purée. 1. To press fruit or vegetables through a fine sieve or ricer. 2. A heavy, smooth, very thick liquid mixture made by rubbing cooked foods through a sieve.

R

ragout. A highly seasoned thick meat and vegetable stew.

ramekin. An individual baking dish.

ravioli. Small shapes of Italian or noodle paste spread with a meat or vegetable filling folded over and poached in meat stock.

relish. A highly flavored food used with other foods to stimulate appetite.

render. To melt fat to free it from connective tissue.

rissole. A savory meat mixture enclosed in rich pastry and fried in deep fat.

roast. Commonly applied to meats. To cook by dry heat, usually in an oven.

roe. Eggs of fish. Roe Herring means herring with the eggs.

roll. 1. To place on a board and spread thin with a rolling pin. 2. A small shape made from a dough and baked.

roux. *See* "SAUCES "

S

salt. To apply salt. Or to season or cure with salt.

scallion or shallot. A bulbless onion.

scallop. To bake in a casserole a food usually cut in pieces and mixed with a sauce.

sear. To brown the surface quickly with intense heat.

seasoning. A pungent substance used to give relish to food.

sherbet. *See* "DESSERTS."

shortening. A fat suitable for baking.

skewer. 1. A long pin of wood or metal on which food is placed and held in shape while cooking. 2. To fasten meat with skewers to keep it in shape during cooking.

soak. To immerse in liquid for a time.

soufflé. A delicate baked custard containing cheese, fruit, minced meat, or vegetables... made light by stiffly beaten egg whites.

sponge. A batter made with yeast in it.

steep. To extract flavor, colors, or other qualities from a substance by allowing it to stand in liquid just below the boiling point.

sterilize. To destroy microorganisms by boiling in water, by dry heat, or by steam.

stock. The liquid in which meat, poultry, fish, or vegetables have been cooked.

T

tamale. A highly seasoned Mexican dish of ground meat, seasonings, cooked corn meal, beans, ripe olives, and fat, rolled in oiled cornhusks, steamed or boiled.

timbale. An *un*sweetened custard combined with minced vegetable, chicken, or fish, molded and baked.

timbale case. *See* "QUICK BREADS."

toast. To brown by direct heat.

torte. A rich cake, usually made from crumbs, eggs, and nuts . . . or a hard meringue baked in the form of a cake (*p. 232*).

tortilla. A thin round Mexican cake . . . made of corn meal and hot water and baked on a griddle. Mexican hot mixtures are often rolled in them.

toss. To lightly mix ingredients without mashing them.

truss. To tie a fowl or other meat so that it will hold its shape.

try out. To fry solid fat or fat meats, cut in small pieces, until fat is separated from membrane.

tutti-frutti. Mixed fruit.

U

until set. Until a liquid has become firm . . . often refers to a gelatin or custard mixture.

W

whip. To beat rapidly to produce expansion through the incorporation of air, as in egg whites, and heavy cream.

Z

zwieback. A kind of toasted biscuit or rusk.

USEFUL KITCHEN UTENSILS A GUIDE FOR SELECTING

Just as every carpenter must have certain tools for building a house, every woman should have the right tools for the fine art of cooking. The size and needs of each household determine the kind and quantity that may be used for a number of purposes. Colorful utensils add a cheery note to the kitchen.

For Measuring

For top-stove cooking

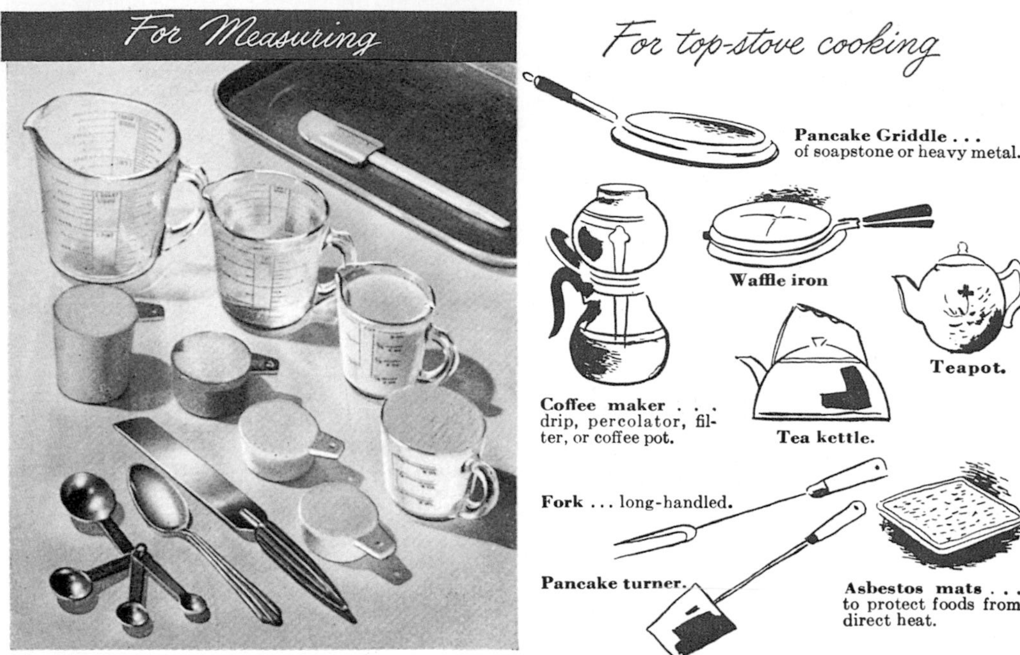

Pancake Griddle . . . of soapstone or heavy metal.

Coffee maker . . . drip, percolator, filter, or coffee pot.

Waffle iron

Teapot.

Tea kettle.

Fork . . . long-handled.

Pancake turner.

Asbestos mats . . . to protect foods from direct heat.

Set of standard measuring spoons.
Big spoon . . . for spooning into cup.
Straight knife . . . for "leveling off."
Nest of measuring cups: with lip for liquids . . . plain rim for dry ingredients.
Pint and quart measures.
Utility tray.
Rubber spatula . . . to scrape out cups.

For top-stove cooking

3 saucepans with close-fitting covers (2 to 4-qt. sizes).

2 lipped saucepans for heating liquids.

A double boiler (1½-qt. if you have only one).

A large kettle with steamer to fit . . . for steamed puddings, etc. Used without steamer for doughnuts, etc.

Deep fat frying basket . . . to fit into large kettle . . . for French fried potatoes, etc.

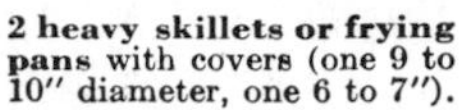

2 heavy skillets or frying pans with covers (one 9 to 10″ diameter, one 6 to 7″).

For Mixing

Kitchen fork and knife . . . for many uses.
Flat wire whip . . . beats more air into egg whites.
Pastry blender . . . for cutting in shortening.
Wooden spoon . . . for creaming, stirring sauces, etc.
Blending fork . . . for thorough mixing.
Rotary egg beater (sturdy) . . . for icings, etc.
Flour sifter (large open) containing a fine wire screen . . . sifting and aerating *white* flour.
Mixing bowls . . . a set of convenient sizes.

KITCHEN UTENSILS (cont.)

Measure that Pan!

Do keep a ruler handy,
To measure pans it's dandy.
Place the rule across the top,
Right size pan prevents a flop!

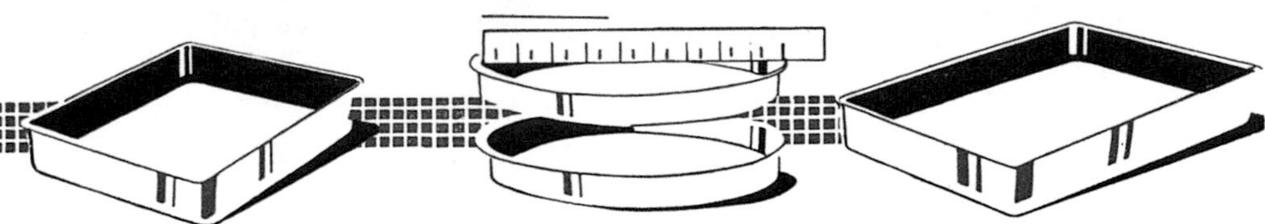

Square Pan 9″ sq.—2″ deep.

Round Layer Pans (2) at least $1\frac{1}{4}$″ deep for 8″ pan; $1\frac{1}{2}$″ deep for 9″ pan.

Oblong Pan . . . 13x9″—2″ deep.

Tube-center Pan 10″ diam.—4″ deep.

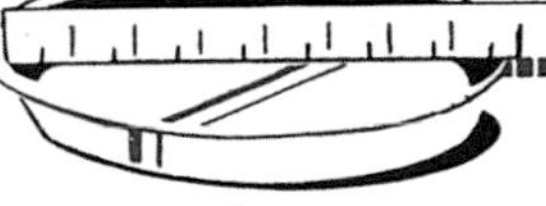

Pie Pan 1″ deep, measured from inside rim to outside rim, they measure evenly 8″ or 9″.

Bread Loaf Pan 9x5″—3″ deep.

Cooky Sheet or Baking Sheet . . . without sides.

Ring Mold for puddings, breads, salads, etc.
Wire Rack for cooling cakes, cookies, breads, etc.
Oven Thermometer for checking oven temperature.

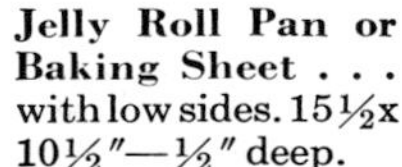

Jelly Roll Pan or Baking Sheet . . . with low sides. $15\frac{1}{2}$x $10\frac{1}{2}$″—$\frac{1}{2}$″ deep.

Muffin Pan . . . large, medium, or small cups.

Casserole with cover. Round, oval, or square 1 qt., $1\frac{1}{2}$ qt., or 2 qt. size.

Individual Custard Cups . . . set in shallow pan to bake.

Fluted Pudding Mold . . . for steamed puddings, for breads, etc. 1 qt. (7″diam.) or 2 qt. (8″ diam.).

Roasting Pan . . . with rack. In size suitable for family.

Round Pudding Mold (1 or 2 qt.) . . . for brown bread, plum puddings, and other steamed puddings.

KITCHEN UTENSILS (cont.)

FOR FOOD PREPARATION

2 or 3 sharp **paring knives** . . . for paring, cutting vegetables, fruits, etc.

Vegetable parer with floating blade . . . for paring potatoes and other vegetables thinly.

Several **straight-edged knives.**

French pattern knife . . . for quickly mincing and cutting nuts, celery, green pepper, etc.

Bread knife with saw-tooth edge . . . for cutting breads, fruit cake, etc., neatly.

Long slicer . . . for evenly slicing roasts.

Limber **spatulas**—large and small . . . for removing cakes from pans, icing cakes, etc.

Grapefruit knife—with a curved blade . . . for cutting under grapefruit section.

Small **ball cutter** . . . for cutting out melon balls, potato balls, butter balls.

Chopping bowl and knife . . . for chopping meat for hash, giblets for gravy, etc.

Ice crusher . . . to crush ice easily.

Apple corer . . . to remove apple cores.

Strawberry huller . . . for hulling strawberries, picking pin feathers from poultry, etc.

Sturdy pair of **kitchen scissors** . . . an essential for many uses.

Food choppers—with fine and coarse cutters . . . for grinding meats, vegetables, nuts, etc.

Several tablespoons . . . for general use.

Wire strainers—fine, coarse, and very fine . . . for straining foods, sieving them, etc.

Funnel . . . for filling jars and bottles.

Large spoon with holes or slots . . . for scooping food out of a liquid (as a poached egg).

Ladle—with long handle . . . for soups, jams.

Tongs . . . for lifting vegetables, meats, etc. out of liquid or pan.

Pastry brush . . . for greasing pans, brushing dough with melted butter, etc.

Potato ricer . . . for ricing potatoes or other vegetables, perhaps preliminary to mashing.

Potato masher—of solid wood or heavy wire . . . for mashing potatoes and other foods.

Set of graters . . . to grate food to different degrees . . . from very fine to coarse.

Lemon squeezer . . . for extracting juice from lemons, oranges, grapefruit.

Can opener. Jar opener. Bottle opener. Corkscrew.

Molds—such as ring, melon, or fluted-shaped molds for puddings, salads, etc. Fancy shaped individual molds for single serving. (Custard and muffin cups may be used.)

Timer—with an alarm . . . to let you know when a dish has finished cooking.

Cutters of various shapes and sizes . . . for cookies, biscuits, doughnuts, etc.

Bread or **pastry board** . . . for kneading dough and rolling out cookies, pastry, etc. Also a canvas or heavy crash **cover** for the board.

Rolling pin—and, for a **cover**, a child's white ribbed cotton stocking with foot cut off.

Pastry set . . . a canvas or heavy crash cover for the board and a white jersey tube cover for the pin.

Colander (a perforated metal pan) . . . for straining coarse foods or puréeing vegetables.

FOR STORAGE

Canister set (cans for sugar, flour, etc.).

Bread box (if not part of cabinet).

Cake safe (if not part of cabinet).

Cooky jar.

Set of refrigerator dishes with covers.

Plastic refrigerator covers and bags.

Waxed paper, cheesecloth, rubber bands.

Aluminum foil.

FOR SINK AND CLEANING

Rubber scraper . . . for scraping dishes clean.

Dish pans . . . when sink not used for pan.

Rubber mats for drain boards.

Small scrub brush . . . bottle brush . . . vegetable brush.

Dish mop . . . dish cloths.

Pot holders . . . dish towels.

Paper towels with holder.

Sink strainer.

Waste basket.

Garbage can (if no incinerator or disposal).

Soap, steel wool, cleaning powder, etc.

STORING FOODS

SHORTENINGS

Keep *lard* and *butter* closely covered in refrigerator. Strain *drippings* directly into container and store in refrigerator.

MILK, CREAM, AND EGGS

Keep *milk* and *cream* covered, and *eggs* (unwashed until ready to use) near freezing unit in refrigerator.

CHEESE

Tightly cover *soft cheese;* wrap *hard cheese* in waxed paper; store covered in refrigerator. Grate leftover cheese; keep in covered jar.

SUGARS

Keep *granulated* and *confectioners' sugar* covered in dry place. Keep *brown sugar* in airtight container with slice of apple or orange on waxed paper to add moisture (change fruit often to insure freshness). Hard brown sugar can be softened by placing crisp lettuce leaf or slice of fresh bread in container or by heating the sugar a few min. in slow oven. (If heated, use immediately.)

STAPLE SUPPLIES

Keep tightly covered in cool, dry place. Replace herbs and spices as soon as they lose their freshness. After dried fruit package has been opened, wrap fruit in waxed paper.

COFFEE AND TEA

Keep tightly covered in cool, dry place. After opening, keep in refrigerator . . . and keep only week's supply on hand.

FLOUR AND CEREALS CAKE MIXES, ETC.

Keep tightly covered in *cool*, dry place. Do not keep whole wheat or other coarse flours or cereals near white flour. (Damp flour may be dried by sifting before an open oven. Breakfast foods may be crisped by heating in oven.) For long keeping, store whole wheat, corn meal, and rye flours in tightly covered glass jars. In hot weather, place in refrigerator.

NUTS AND COCONUT

Keep *shelled nuts* and *coconut* tightly covered in refrigerator. Renew softness of coconut by heating over hot water.

MARSHMALLOWS

Keep tightly sealed in bread box or glass jar. Soften by heating in damp bag in oven.

STORING FOODS (cont.)

FRESH FRUIT

Keep *unripe fruit* at room temperature to ripen. Store *ripe fruit* (except pineapple, bananas) in cool place.

PARSLEY, WATER-CRESS, LETTUCE

Keep washed *parsley* and *watercress* (with water shaken from them) in tightly covered jar in refrigerator. For storing *lettuce,* see "SALADS."

CUT ONIONS AND GARLIC

Place cut-side-down in jelly glass or cardboard carton. Cover, store in refrigerator.

CUSTARD MIXTURES

Very perishable. A chemical change may make these egg mixtures dangerous; so cool, then cover, and store them in refrigerator **not more than 24 hr.** Never eat custard mixtures that have been kept overnight without careful refrigeration.

HULLED AND SWEETENED BERRIES AND SLICED PEACHES

Keep *fresh berries* wrapped in paper in refrigerator; wash and hull shortly before using. Keep leftover *hulled berries* in tightly covered glass jar in refrigerator.

POTATOES, ONIONS, BEETS, CARROTS, OTHER ROOT VEGETABLES

Keep in cool, dry, well ventilated place. For other vegetables, *see* "VEGETABLES."

CUT LEMONS, ORANGES, MELONS

Place cut-side-down on plate or in covered container and store in refrigerator.

SALAD DRESSINGS

Cover tightly and keep at room temperature or in refrigerator (*not* coldest part). Never freeze!

CONDIMENTS, also SALAD OILS, SYRUPS, MOLASSES, ETC.

Keep tightly covered in refrigerator or kitchen cupboard.

SLICED BREAD

If not to be used right away, wrap in waxed paper or place in moisture-proof bags and store in freezing tray of refrigerator or in home freezer. Take out and use as desired. To freshen dried bread slices, place them in paper bag, sprinkle with water, twist top, and heat in mod. hot oven (400°) 5 to 8 min.

SUBSTITUTIONS THAT ARE SAFE

It's best to use ingredients
The recipe recommends;
But if you have to substitute,
This list solution lends.

For	*Use*
1 cup *sifted* all purpose flour (GOLD MEDAL)	1 cup plus 2 tbsp. *sifted* cake flour (SOFTASILK)
1 cup *sifted* cake flour (SOFTASILK)	1 cup minus 2 tbsp. *sifted* all-purpose flour (GOLD MEDAL)
1 tbsp. cornstarch (for thickening)	2 tbsp. flour (approximately)
1 tsp. baking powder	¼ tsp. soda plus ½ tsp. cream of tartar
1 whole egg	2 egg yolks plus 1 tbsp. water (in cookies, etc.)
1 whole egg	2 egg yolks (in custards and such mixtures)
1 cup fresh sweet milk	½ cup evaporated milk plus ½ cup water
1 cup fresh sweet milk	½ cup condensed milk plus ½ cup water (reduce sugar slightly in recipe)
1 cup fresh sweet milk	4 tbsp. powdered milk plus 1 cup water
1 cup fresh sweet milk	1 cup sour milk or buttermilk plus ½ tsp. soda (decrease baking powder 2 tsp.)
1 cup sour milk or buttermilk	1 cup fresh sweet milk with 1 tbsp. lemon juice or vinegar stirred in
1 sq. unsweetened chocolate (1 oz.)	3 to 4 tbsp. cocoa plus 1 tbsp. shortening
1 cup honey	¾ cup sugar plus ¼ cup liquid
1 cup sugar	1 cup honey or syrup and reduce liquid in recipe ¼ cup (in cakes substitute honey for only ½ the sugar)
1 cup brown sugar (*firmly* packed)	1 cup granulated sugar
1 cup canned tomatoes	about 1⅓ cups cut-up fresh tomatoes, simmered 10 min.

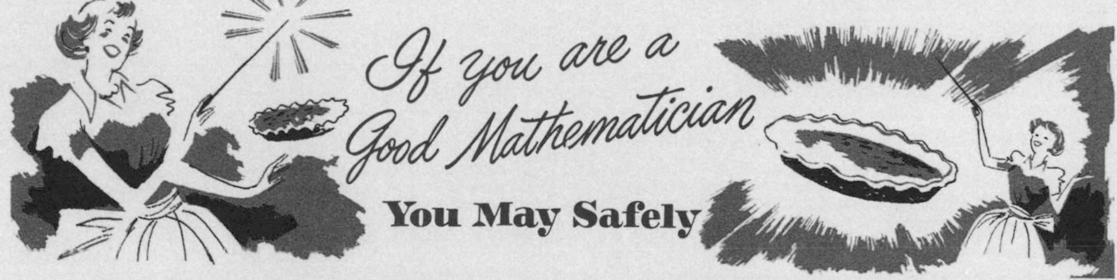

REDUCE RECIPES

To make half a recipe:

Use exactly *one-half the amount of each ingredient.* (See Equivalents, p. 22, and How to Measure, pp. 7–8, for help in dividing or multiplying ingredients.)

If the divided recipe calls for less than 1 egg, beat up a whole egg. Measure with a tbsp. Divide. (Use egg that is left, in scrambled eggs, sauces, etc.)

Baking pans used for half recipes of muffins, pies, etc. should measure about half the area of those for the whole recipe. Approximate baking time and oven temperature the same.

INCREASE RECIPES

To double a recipe:

Use exactly *twice the amount of each ingredient.*

If the increased recipe calls for uneven amounts of flour, liquid, eggs, etc. *see p. 123,* for diagrams on measuring fractions.

Use 2 pans of the same size indicated for the original recipe or a pan double in area . . . so that the batter will be the same depth in the pan and same baking time and temperature may be maintained.

COMMON FOOD EQUIVALENTS

(See bottom of page for nuts and dried fruits most frequently used in baking)

	UNIT	APPROXIMATE MEASURE
Apples	1 lb.	3 medium (3 cups sliced)
Bananas	1 lb.	3 medium (2½ cups sliced)
Butter and Other Fats	1 lb.	2 cups
Cheese, American or Cheddar	1 lb.	4 cups grated
Cheese, Cottage	1 lb.	2 cups
Cheese, White Cream	3-oz. pkg	6 tbsp.
	½-lb. pkg	16 tbsp. (1 cup)
Chocolate, Unsweetened	½-lb. pkg	8 1-oz. squares
Coconut, Shredded	1 lb.	5 cups
Coffee, Ground	1 lb.	80 tbsp.
Cream, Heavy	1 pt.	2 cups (4 cups whipped)
Flour		
All-Purpose	1 lb.	4 cups (*sifted*)
Cake	1 lb.	4½ cups (*sifted*)
Whole Wheat	1 lb.	3½ cups
Rye	1 lb.	4½ to 5 cups
Lemon, Medium-sized		
Juice	1	2 to 3 tbsp.
Rind, lightly grated	1	1½ to 3 tsp.
Marshmallows	¼ lb.	16
Orange, Medium-sized		
Juice	1	⅓ to ½ cup
Rind, lightly grated	1	1 to 2 tbsp.
Sugar		
Granulated	1 lb.	2 cups
Brown	1 lb.	2¼ cups (firmly packed)
Confectioners'	1 lb.	3½ cups (*sifted*)
Powdered	1 lb.	2⅓ cups

EQUIVALENT WEIGHTS AND MEASURES

Nuts and Fruits Most Commonly Used

	NUTS IN SHELL	SHELLED NUTS
ALMONDS	1 lb. = 1 to 1¾ cups nut meats	1 lb. = 3½ cups nut meats
PECANS	1 lb. = 2¼ cups nut meats	1 lb. = 4 cups nut meats
PEANUTS	1 lb. = 2¼ cups nut meats	1 lb. = 3 cups nut meats
WALNUTS	1 lb. = 1⅔ cups nut meats	1 lb. = 4 cups nut meats

1 CUP WHOLE SHELLED NUTS = broken = cut-up = coarsely chopped 1 cup minus 1 tbsp. = finely chopped ⅞ CUP

	WHOLE	PITTED	CUT-UP	FINELY CUT
DATES	1 lb. = 2¼ cups	2 cups	1¾ cups	1½ cups
PRUNES	1 lb. = 2⅓ cups	4 cups (cooked)	3 cups (cooked)	2⅞ cups (cooked)
FIGS	1 lb. = 2¾ cups	———	2⅔ cups	2½ cups
RAISINS	15-oz. pkg. = 3 cups	———	2¾ cups	2½ cups
CANDIED FRUIT	½ lb. = ———	———	1½ cups	
CANDIED PEELS	½ lb. = ———	———	1½ cups	

HOW TO PREPARE some special ingredients the quick, easy way!

MELTING CHOCOLATE

Place it on waxed paper set in bowl over boiling water.

or

Place it in a small bowl set in a wire strainer over boiling water.

Remove melted chocolate from bowl or paper with rubber scraper.

PREPARING NUTS Some foods look and taste their best if the nuts in them are in big chunks. In others, the nuts should be in smaller pieces. The recipes tell you just how.

Broken Nuts: It's quick and easy to break nuts with fingers into about 1/3-inch chunks.

Cut-Up Nuts: Cut with scissors (works better than knife) into about 1/4-inch pieces.

Coarsely Chopped Nuts: Chop with long, straight knife. Hold point against cutting board, chop crisply through spread-out nuts—swinging handle around in quarter circle.

TOAST NUTS: to be sure they will taste fresh. Heat through in moderate oven.

Finely Chopped Nuts: Chop same as for Coarsely Chopped, but into finer pieces.

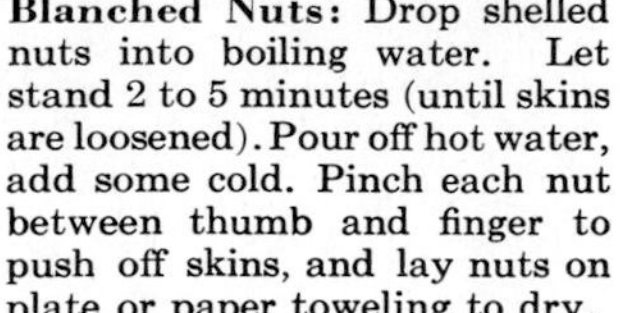

Blanched Nuts: Drop shelled nuts into boiling water. Let stand 2 to 5 minutes (until skins are loosened). Pour off hot water, add some cold. Pinch each nut between thumb and finger to push off skins, and lay nuts on plate or paper toweling to dry.

Sliced or Slivered Nuts: First blanch . . . then cut with very sharp knife while nuts are moist and warm.

To brown blanched almonds, etc., spread in pan. Heat in mod. oven until delicately browned. *Watch carefully.*

Ground Nuts: Use fine knife of food grinder for finely ground . . . coarse knife for coarsely ground. Nuts should be dry.

HOW TO PREPARE some special ingredients.

KNOW YOUR RAISINS

Seeded raisins are the large variety from which seeds have been removed. The sweetness released when they were slit open makes them sticky.

Seedless raisins are the small variety, both dark and light . . . dried from seedless grapes. Cut them to get the full sweetness and flavor.

Plump seedless raisins by washing and spreading them out in a flat pan. Cover. Heat slowly in mod. oven (350°) until they puff up and wrinkles come out.

DATES

Cut up dates and other sticky fruits with wet scissors. Dip scissors in water occasionally.

CANDIED FRUIT

To cut citron or candied orange or lemon peel, first *slice it thinly*—then cut slices into ½ or ¼″ squares.

GRATED RIND

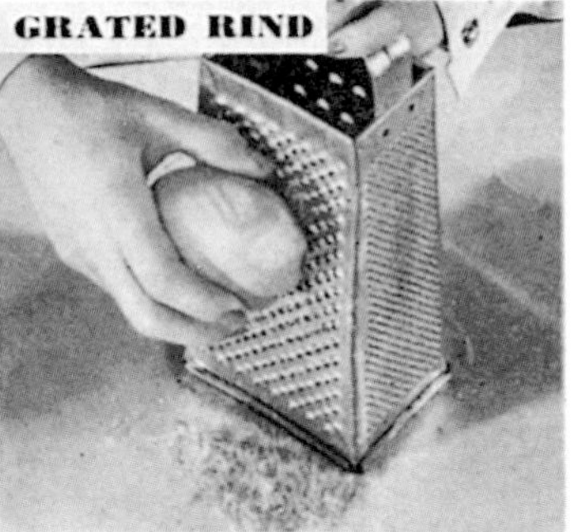

Rub washed fruit diagonally across grater in *long* strokes (peel won't stick to grater). Grate only outermost colored rind.

FRESH COCONUT

Pierce 3 holes at one end. Drain out milk. Heat in mod. oven 30 min. Cool.

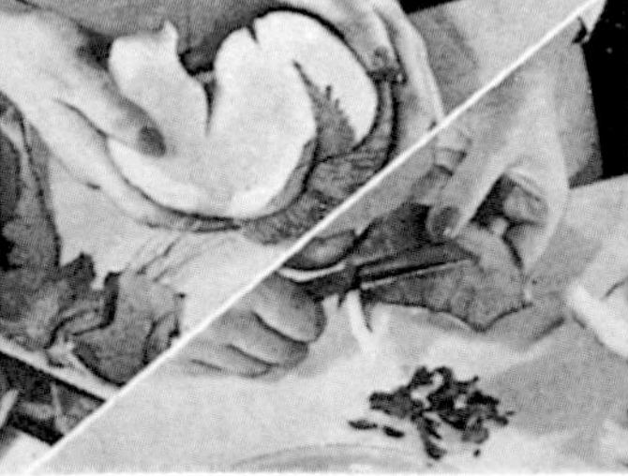

Break shell with hammer or chisel, remove. Break the meat in pieces. Pare off brown skin.

Grate or shred white meat. (Keep any not used, in refrigerator, tightly covered.)

PREPARING COCONUT

Snip through long shreds of coconut. The shorter shreds blend into doughs more evenly.

To tint coconut: Soak in little milk or water, add a few drops of food coloring. Drain, dry.

To toast coconut: Heat in shallow pan in mod. oven until golden brown, stirring frequently.

HOW TO PREPARE special ingredients.

CARAMELIZING SUGAR

Melt sugar in heavy pan over low heat, stirring constantly; or shake pan gently.

Heat until melted to a golden brown syrup, stirring constantly.

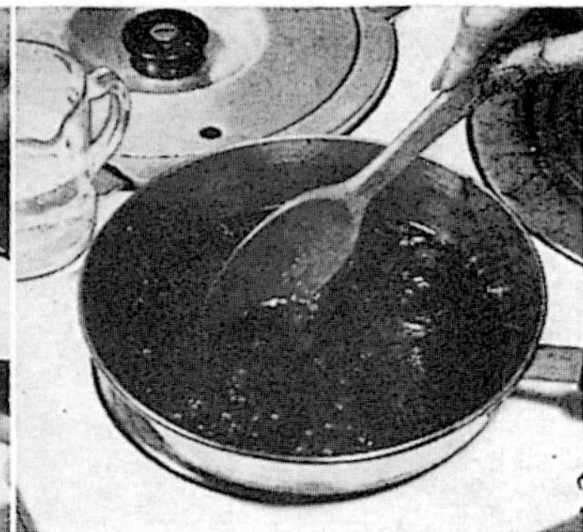
Stir in hot water (amount recipe indicates). Be careful steam does not burn hand.

DISSOLVING GELATIN

For gelatin puddings, Bavarian creams, etc.: soften gelatin in cold water. Dissolve *in* boiling liquid.

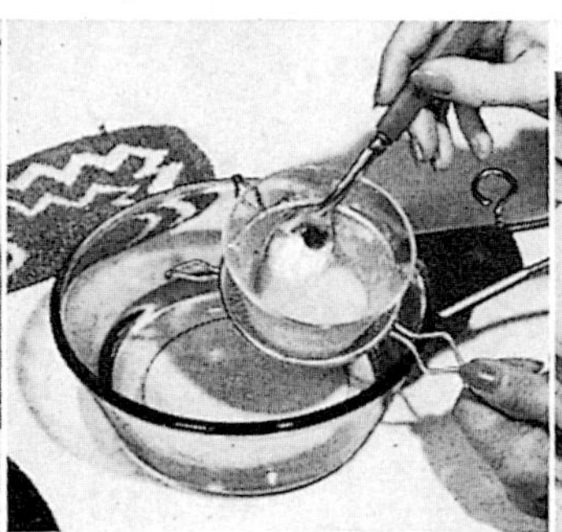
Keep 1 c. whipped cream stiff; beat in 1 tsp. gelatin softened in 1 tbsp. milk, dissolved over hot water.

WHIPPING CREAM

Beat chilled cream (at *least* 25% butterfat) in chilled *deep* bowl with cold rotary beater until fluffy.

OILING MOLD

Brush molds for Bavarian creams, or any gelatin cream puddings, with salad oil to prevent sticking.

SALTING NUTS

To 1 cup nuts in pan, add 1 tsp. salad oil. Stir. Brown in mod. oven, stir often. Drain. Salt.

SOURING MILK OR CREAM

Add 1 tbsp. vinegar or lemon juice to 1 cup sweet milk or cream. Let stand few minutes.

PREPARING CREAM OR CUSTARD FILLING

Mix sugar, salt, cornstarch or flour. Gradually stir in liquid. Cook over low heat, stirring until mixture boils.

Boil 1 min., stirring constantly. Remove from heat. Stir a little of the hot mixture into the beaten eggs.

Blend into hot mixture. Boil 1 min. more, stirring. Remove from heat. Blend in butter and flavoring. Cool . . . stir occasionally.

HOW TO PREPARE bread for various uses.

SOFT BREAD CRUMBS

With fork, pull day-old bread into crumbs. Or tear it into small pieces with fingers.

FINE DRY CRUMBS

Remove crusts from stale bread. Dry bread in slow oven. Crush. Or put through food grinder.

CUBES

Trim and cut bread into cubes. For *croutons,* butter bread first, toast the buttered cubes in oven.

MELBA TOAST

Remove crusts from day-old bread. Slice thin (1/8″). Bake in slow oven until crisp, light brown (20 min.). Serve hot or cold.

Brush thinly sliced bread (crusts removed) with melted butter. Press into muffin cups. Toast in mod. oven.

TOAST CASES

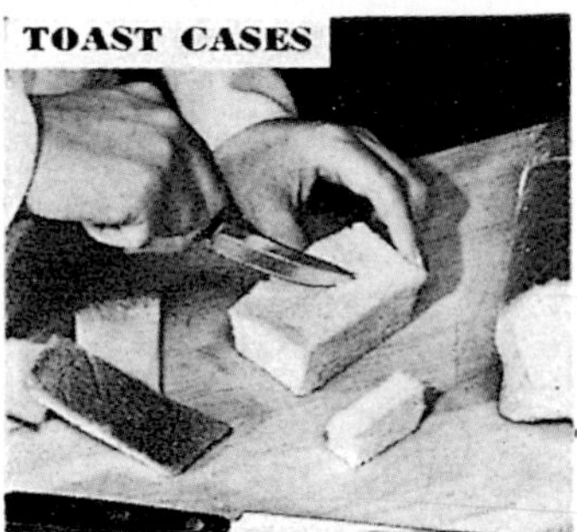

Cut bread 2″ thick. Remove crusts. Cut into squares or oblongs. Hollow out. Brush with melted butter. Toast in oven.

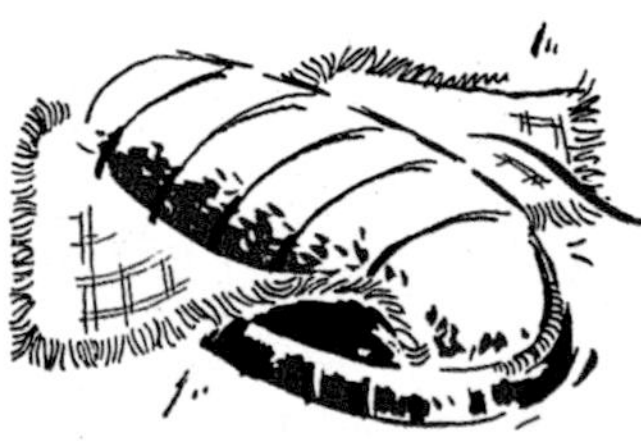

Slice diagonally (thick, not through bottom crust). Spread soft butter on 1 side each slice (try garlic or chives in butter). Heat in mod. oven 10 min. Serve.

BUTTERING THIN PARTY SANDWICHES

Spread softened butter on bread before cutting each slice.

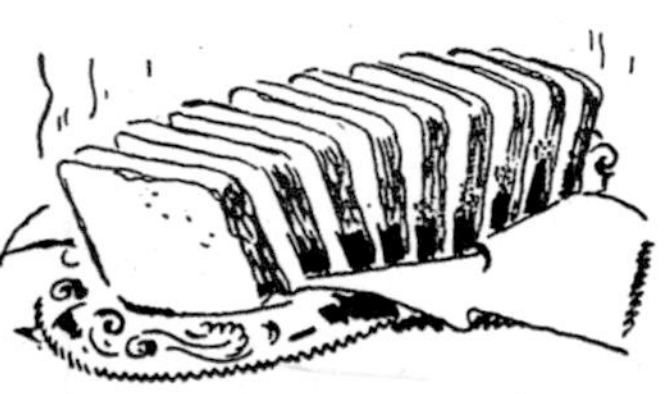

Slice loaf, but not through bottom crust. Pour melted butter over slices, distributing evenly. Cover with paper bag. Heat in mod. oven 15 to 20 min. Serve hot.

CUTTING SANDWICH LOAF

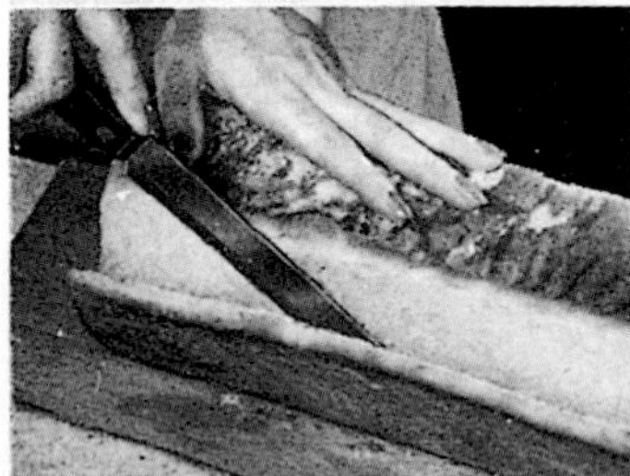

Remove crusts from loaf of sandwich bread . . . leaving bottom crust until last. A long, very sharp knife is needed.

SLICING SANDWICH LOAF

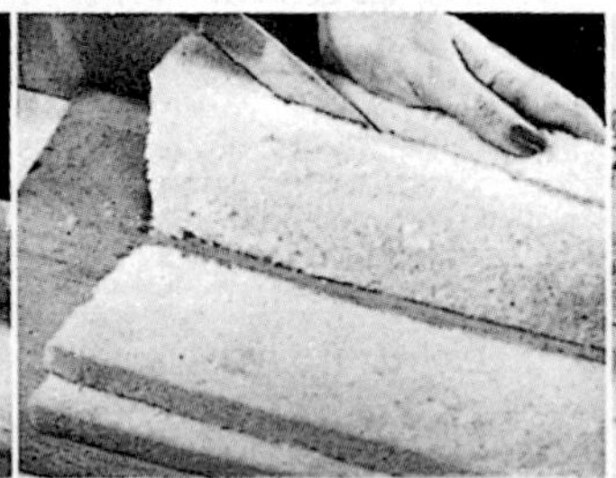

For sandwich loaf or pinwheel sandwiches, slice into long layers of thickness desired. Lay each slice aside, keeping in order.

CLUB SANDWICH LOAF

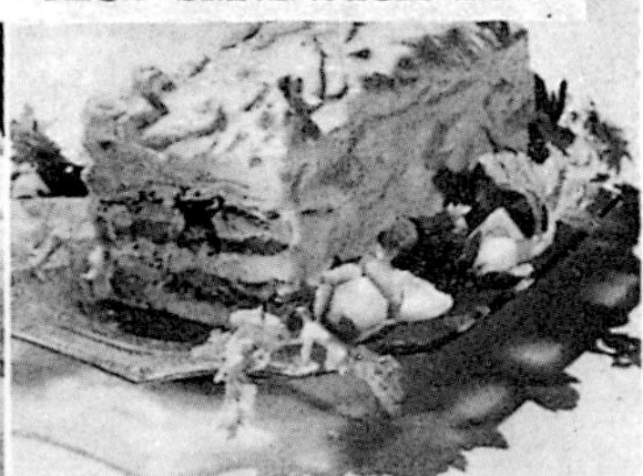

Filling: chicken, lettuce, bacon, tomato. Covered with mild mayonnaise with chopped hard-cooked eggs in it (*recipe, p. 401*).

HOW TO PREPARE some special ingredients.

FRESH MUSHROOMS

Wash mushrooms gently under cold running water. (Never soak.) Trim off spots.

Cut off stems. Use caps for baking, broiling. Mince stems, sauté for sauces and soups.

Slice whole mushrooms down through stems. Sauté in butter. Use for sauce, stuffing, etc.

CANNED MUSHROOMS

To sauté: add mushrooms and liquor to melted butter in hot pan. Cook 'til liquor is absorbed.

BROWNING FLOUR

Spread in thin layer in pan. Heat on range or in mod. oven, stirring until golden brown.

GRATING CHEESE

Firm cheese: rub over grater or shredder. *Soft cheese:* rub through coarse sieve.

CHOPPING OR MINCING ONION

Cut end slice trom peeled onion. Discard. Cut exposed surface into tiny squares to any desired depth. Cut crosswise in thin slices.

ONION JUICE

Cut end slice from peeled onion. Discard. Squeeze out juice on lemon squeezer. Or scrape cut side of onion with back of knife.

DICING CELERY (or Rhubarb)

Place several stalks of cleaned celery together on board. Slash through all at once. (Dice rhubarb stalks the same way.)

PEELING A TOMATO

Hold over flame or heat 1 min.

Or place in boiling water 1 min.

Skin will slip off easily.

HOW TO PREPARE some special fruits for salads, etc.

CANDIED FRUIT GARNISH

Cut candied cherries and citron into shapes of flowers and leaves to decorate icings, etc.

PARING GRAPEFRUIT

Cut thin slice from top . . . then pare the grapefruit 'round and 'round like an apple.

GRAPEFRUIT SECTIONS

To section: cut along each dividing membrane. Lift out sections whole.

PINEAPPLE SLICES AND WEDGES

Cut washed pineapple into slices.

Cut away rind, remove "eyes."

Remove core, cut into wedges.

PINEAPPLE BOAT

Cut in two lengthwise. Cut around edge with curved knife, remove fruit. Discard core.

MELON BALLS

Use a ball cutter or a rounded measuring spoon. Cut into melon with circular motion.

POMEGRANATE SEEDS

Cut washed pomegranate in two. Remove seeds with fork.

AVOCADO

Cut through avocado to seed . . . twist slightly to pull halves apart. If using only half, leave seed in other half.

Run knife down center back of each half . . . cut through center of thin outer rind only. Pull off sections of skin.

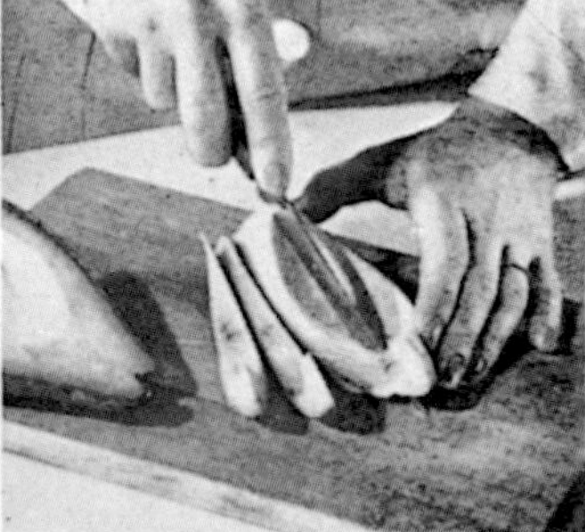

Place avocado half on board. Slice as thick as desired. Drench slices with lemon or lime juice to prevent darkening.

Easy confections for the children.

ELSIE'S NOUGAT BARS

From Elsie Martinson Allison whose children love it.

Melt over hot water . . .

3 tbsp. butter
½ lb. marshmallows

Remove from heat. Fold in . . .

4 cups KIX (or CHEERIOS)
¼ cup coarsely chopped nuts
½ cup moist shredded coconut
½ tsp. salt

Turn into buttered 9″ sq. pan. With hand, protected by piece of waxed paper, pat out mixture evenly in pan. Pour over top 4 oz. sweet or semi-sweet chocolate, melted . . . spreading it in thin layer with rubber scraper or spatula. Chill until set (45 to 60 min.). Cut into bars.
AMOUNT: 2⅔ doz. 1″x2″ bars.

WHEATIES TING-A-LINGS

More delicious than the originals.

Melt over hot water . . .

2 7-oz. pkg. semi-sweet chocolate pieces (or ½ lb. sweet chocolate with 2-oz. unsweetened)

Cool at room temperature. Gently stir in until well coated . . .

*4 cups WHEATIES (½ of 8-oz. box)

Drop by tablespoonfuls onto waxed paper. Place in refrigerator until chocolate is set, dry, and hard (about 2 hr.).
**Peanut Ting-A-Lings:* Use 1 cup large salted peanuts with 3 cups WHEATIES.

All you have to do—

For Hurry-Up Popcorn: melt in heavy skillet 2 to 4 tbsp. butter. Add 4 cups KIX (or CHEERIOS). Sprinkle with ½ tsp. salt. Mix well. Stir over mod. heat 5 min. Serve like popcorn or salted nuts.

PEANUT SQUARES

Mix together . . .

1 cup peanuts, finely ground
1 tsp. salt
¼ tsp. soda

Stir over low heat until sugar is dissolved . . .

1 cup brown sugar
1 cup granulated sugar
⅔ cup water
2 tbsp. white corn syrup

Cook without stirring to 290° (drops in cold water become brittle). Remove from heat *immediately*. *Quickly* add peanuts . . . stirring only once or twice. Pour into greased warmed 18x12″ pan . . . and spread thinly. As it begins to harden, mark into squares.
AMOUNT: 12½ doz. 1½″ pieces.

CARAMEL APPLES

Every youngster loves these!

Wash, dry thoroughly, and chill . . .

8 to 10 medium-sized apples

Insert a sturdy wooden skewer into stem end of each apple. Mix together in deep 2-qt. saucepan . . .

2 cups sugar
1 cup brown sugar
⅔ cup white corn syrup
⅔ cup butter
1 cup cream
1 tsp. salt
2 tsp. vanilla

Cook to 246° (a little dropped into cold water forms a firm ball) . . . stirring constantly toward end of cooking period to prevent scorching. Remove from heat; cool until mixture thickens slightly. Quickly dip each apple into the caramel mixture and twist until evenly and completely covered. Drain on waxed paper.

CHOCOLATE COCONUT DROPS

Melt over hot water . . .

2 sq. unsweetened chocolate (2 oz.), cut-up

Stir in . . .

1 can sweetened condensed milk
½ lb. coconut, chopped
½ cup walnuts, cut-up

Drop by teaspoonfuls onto baking sheet in shape of bonbons. Place in mod. oven (350°); turn off heat. Leave until candy has glazed appearance (15 to 20 min.).

MOLASSES PATTIES

Like Caramel Corn.

Measure into greased large bowl . . .

4 cups CHEERIOS (or KIX)
1½ cups salted peanuts

Mix together in large saucepan . . .

1½ cups brown sugar
¾ cup light molasses
½ cup water
4 tsp. vinegar
⅛ tsp. cream of tartar

Cook over low heat, stirring occasionally, to 250° (a little dropped into cold water forms a hard ball). Blend in . . .

1½ tsp. soda

(Mixture becomes fluffy and porous.)

Pour syrup over peanut mixture. Mix with greased spoon. Cool slightly to thicken. With greased hands, form into patties. Cool on greased baking sheet.
AMOUNT: 3 doz. 2″ patties.

CONFECTIONS Candies . . . a few favorites.

CHOCOLATE FUDGE (🔑 Recipe)

Marcella Meier of Minneapolis, who makes the best fudge we ever ate, gave us this recipe.

Place over low heat, stirring until chocolate is melted and mixture smooth . . .

2/3 cup milk
1 to 2 sq. unsweetened chocolate (1 to 2 oz.), cut-up, or 3 to 4 tbsp. cocoa

Stir in . . .

2 cups sugar
1 tsp. corn syrup
dash of salt

Cook gently, stirring from the bottom occasionally, to 236° (a little dropped into cold water forms a soft ball). Remove from heat. Add . . .

2 tbsp. butter

Cool, without stirring, to lukewarm. Add . . .

1 tsp. vanilla

Beat until thick and no longer glossy. If desired, stir in . . .

1 cup broken nuts

Turn onto waxed paper and shape into a 12″ roll; chill, and slice. Or spread in buttered pan and cut into squares.

AMOUNT: About 1¼ lb.

WHITE FUDGE

Follow 🔑 recipe above—*except* omit chocolate (but scald the milk).

PENUCHE

Follow 🔑 recipe above—*except* omit chocolate (but scald the milk) and, in place of half the sugar, use 1 cup brown sugar. *For Coconut Penuche:* add 2 cups chopped shredded coconut with the sugar.

CREAM CARAMELS

Bring slowly to a boil, stirring constantly . . .

2 cups sugar
3/4 cup light corn syrup
1/2 cup butter
1 cup cream

Then stir in gradually . . .

1 more cup cream

Stir frequently as mixture begins to thicken . . . constantly as it darkens. Cook to 254° (a little dropped into cold water forms a hard ball). Pour into buttered 7″ sq. pan with ½ cup broken nuts scattered over the bottom. When cold, cut into squares.

AMOUNT: 5 doz. caramels.

UNCOOKED FONDANT

Measure into bowl . . .

2/3 cup sweetened condensed milk (1/2 can) (*not* evaporated)

Add gradually . . .

4 1/2 cups *sifted* confectioners' sugar

Blend well. Then add . . .

1 tsp. vanilla
1 tsp. almond extract

Knead until smooth and creamy. Cover tightly with a damp cloth, and store in refrigerator 24 hr. Then mold as desired.

FRUIT FONDANT

Into one-half the Uncooked Fondant (*above*), knead ¼ cup *each* finely chopped nuts, cut-up candied cherries and candied pineapple (also enough additional confectioners' sugar to make easy to handle). Shape into a roll, slice as desired, and chill until ready to use. *Makes 32 pieces.*

COCONUT FONDANT

Shape one-half the Uncooked Fondant (*above*) into a roll. Dip roll into well beaten egg white, then in tinted coconut (*p. 24*). Slice, and chill. *Makes 16 pieces.*

WALNUT CREAMS

Shape one-half the Uncooked Fondant (*above*) into balls ½″ in diameter. Then press half a walnut meat on each side of each ball. *Makes 18 creams.*

DIVINITY

Place in saucepan over low heat . . .

2 cups sugar
1/2 cup white corn syrup
1/2 cup water

Stir until sugar is dissolved; then cook without stirring to 252° (a little dropped into cold water forms a hard ball). Remove from heat and pour, beating constantly, in a fine stream into . . .

2 egg whites, stiffly beaten

Continue beating until mixture holds its shape and loses its gloss. Add . . .

1 tsp. vanilla
1/2 cup broken nuts

Drop quickly from tip of spoon onto waxed paper in individual peaks . . . or spread in greased shallow pan and cut into 1″ squares when firm.

AMOUNT: About 1¼ lb.

Good Nutrition Brings Double Happiness

GOOD EATING brings happiness two ways. First, there is the joy and satisfaction of eating delicious, well-prepared food. Then there's the buoyant health, vitality, and joy of living that comes from a wise choice of foods. Both are important to good nutrition.

Betty Crocker

Be sure that these BASIC SEVEN FOODS appear on your table daily to fill in the circle of Good Nutrition

GROUP 1

Green and Yellow Vegetables . . . some raw—some cooked, frozen, or canned

one serving a day

GROUP 2

Oranges, Tomatoes, Grapefruit . . . or raw cabbage or salad greens

one serving a day

GROUP 3

Potatoes and Other Vegetable and Fruits . . . raw, dried, cooked, frozen, or canned

two or more servings a day

GROUP 4

Milk and Milk Products . . . fluid, evaporated, dried milk, or cheese

1½ pints to 1 quart milk a day for each child

1 qt. a day for nursing mothers.
1 pt. a day for all others.*

GROUP 5

Meat Poultry, Fish, or Eggs . . . or dried beans, peas, nuts, peanut butter

3 or 4 eggs each week

1 serving of meat, poultry, or fish each day. Occasionally dried beans or peas instead.

GROUP 6

Bread, Flour, and Cereals . . . natural whole-grain or enriched or restored

three or more servings a day

GROUP 7

Butter and Fortified Margarine . . . (with added Vitamin A)

If supplies are limited or unattainable for you, you can still give your family an adequate diet when you learn how to use the Basic 7.

*In addition, all growing children and expectant mothers should have 400 units a day of Vitamin D—Vitamin D milk, fish liver oil, or Vitamin D concentrate.

PROTEIN

Builds and repairs body tissues. When we eat more protein than our bodies need, it becomes a source of calories. There are two kinds of protein . . . complete and incomplete. About half our needs should be provided by eggs, meat, fish, poultry, milk, and cheese. The rest are obtained from cereal products and vegetables.

PROTEIN CONTRIBUTIONS

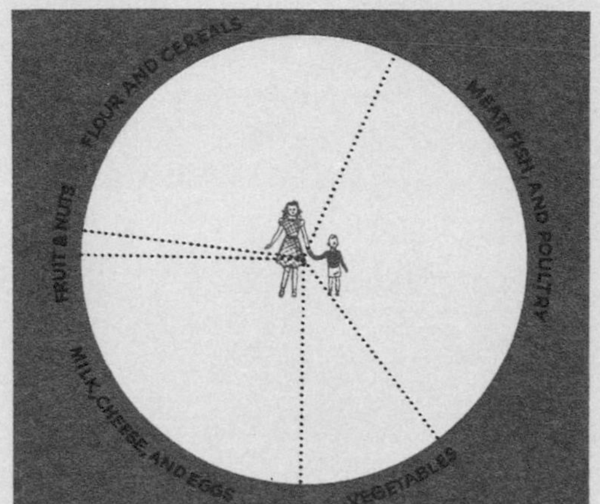

CARBOHYDRATES and FATS

(SUGARS, STARCHES) Supply our bodies with heat and energy. We measure the energy value of food in CALORIES. These elements, chief source of calories, are called caloric foods. Fats give more than twice as many calories (per gram) as carbohydrates (1 tbsp. butter or 2 tbsp. sugar = 100 calories).

CALORIC CONTRIBUTIONS

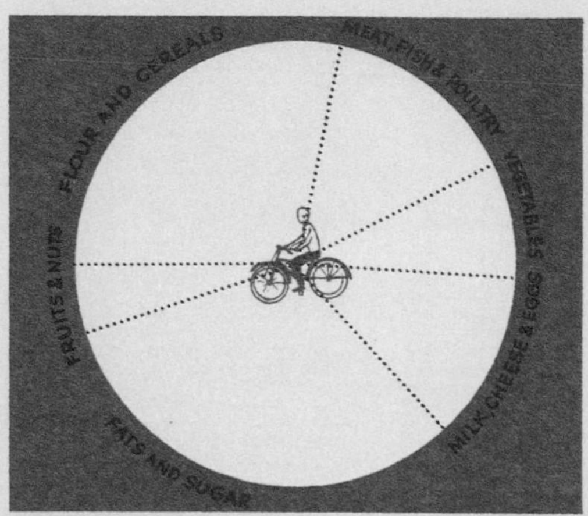

VITAMINS and MINERALS

Why we need them. Best food sources.

Vitamin A

Helps to resist colds, to maintain health of mucous membranes and skin.

Dark green leafy and yellow vegetables (spinach, squash, carrots, etc.), fish liver oils, liver, whole milk, butter or fortified margarine, and yellow fruits (peaches, etc.).

Vitamin B_1 (Thiamine)

Necessary for nervous system, for proper utilization of carbohydrates and fat; promotes growth in children, stimulates appetite.

Lean pork and beef, poultry, milk, eggs, enriched bread, enriched flour, restored breakfast cereals, peanuts, green peas, potatoes, dried legumes, some fruits, such as bananas, apples, and citrus.

Vitamin B_2 (Riboflavin)

Needed for healthy skin and hair, good digestion, sound nerves.
Same sources as thiamine. Milk especially important.

Another B Vitamin (Niacin)

Chief factor in cure and prevention of pellagra. Deficiency results in poor mental state and poor skin condition.

Same sources as thiamine.

Vitamin C (Ascorbic Acid)

Essential for normal body growth and maintenance, very important for upkeep of bones and teeth.

Grapefruit, oranges, lemons, tomatoes, green leafy vegetables, such as cabbage and broccoli, and potatoes.

Vitamin D

Essential for growth, normal development, and promoting best use of phosphorus and calcium for bones and teeth.

Only adequate sources are Vitamin D milk, fish liver oil, Vitamin D concentrate, exposure of body to sun's rays or other source of ultra violet light.

Calcium and Phosphorus

For strength and rigidity of teeth and bones. Needed in soft tissues, too.

Milk. Green leafy vegetables for calcium; breakfast cereals, meat, eggs, fish, for phosphorus.

Iron

Blood builder; regulates other body functions, too. Liver, lean meat, eggs, enriched bread, dried fruit and beans, green vegetables.

Iodine

Necessary for normal function of thyroid.

Salt-water fish, iodized salt.

ENRICHMENT is one of the most dramatic food contributions of recent years. When surveys revealed that the Vitamin B group was alarmingly lacking in our American diet . . . nutritionists tried to find a way to insure everyone's getting his daily requirement of these vitamins.

Bread and baked foods are our most common foods in all parts of the country; therefore, it was decided to add these important nutrients to white flour.

The chart below shows what advantages "Enriched Flour" offers you.

Be sure the flour you buy is "Enriched!"

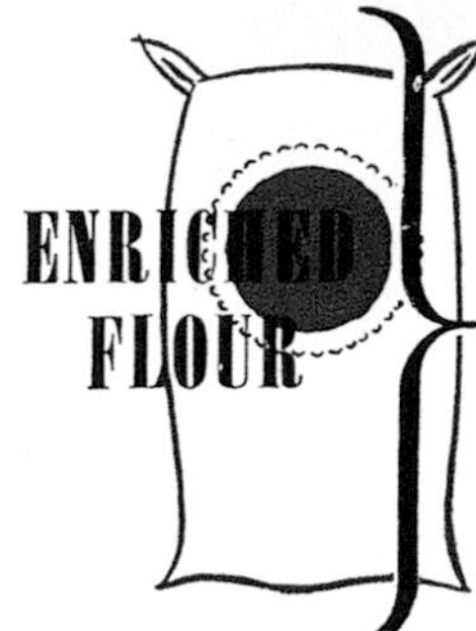

Same Protein as
Same Calories as
Almost 6 times more Thiamine than
Almost 3 times more Niacin than
Seven times more Riboflavin than
Over 3 times more Iron than

THE BASIC SEVEN IS EASY IF YOU FOLLOW THIS PATTERN

	A good breakfast for a good start.	A satisfying lunch for a satisfying afternoon.	A good dinner after a full day.
	BREAKFAST	**LUNCH**	**DINNER**
FOR ADEQUATE MEALS	Fruit Cereal and Milk Bread and Butter	Main Dish Vegetables Bread and Butter Fruit	Meat and Potatoes Green or Yellow Vegetables Salad (raw vegetable) Bread and Butter Fruit
Milk for children at every meal.			
FOR COMPLETE OR ABUNDANT MEALS	Fruit Cereal and Milk Egg or Meat Bread and Butter	Main Dish Vegetables Bread and Butter Fruit Cake or Cookies or Pudding	Appetizer or Soup Meat and Potatoes Green or Yellow Vegetables Salad (raw vegetable) Fruit Bread and Butter Dessert (Pie or Cake)

The same basic pattern should be used for all members of the family. Simply adjust it to meet individual needs of age, work, activity, and special diets.

GROWING CHILDREN (1 to 16 years)	ADOLESCENTS (14 to 20 years)	ADULTS (20 to 100 years)
Need more food for size than grownups.	Need more food than at any time in their lives. A few pounds overweight at this period is an asset for health.	Need food according to size and activity. Women during pregnancy and lactation require additional food for certain elements.
Serve according to size and age of child.	Double and triple servings.	Small servings for inactive. Medium for moderately active. Large for very active.

MEAL-PLANNING

Check Your Daily Meals For:

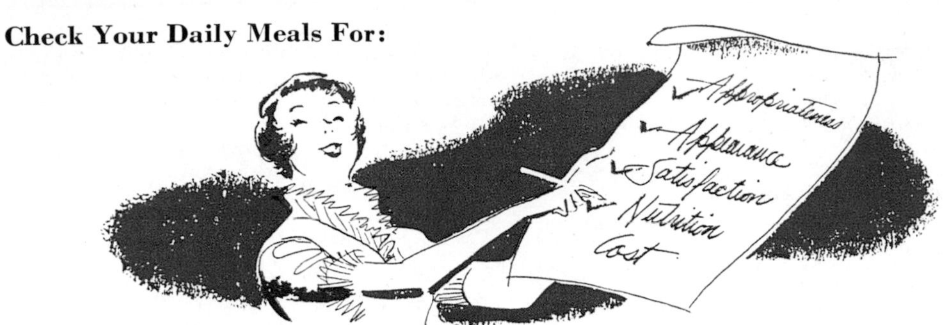

SMART HOMEMAKERS SAY:

Planning, preparing, and serving meals is an *art* which develops through inspiration and thought. And meal-planning is really fun! It may look difficult to the beginner, but like driving a car, swimming, or anything we learn to do without thought or conscious effort, it is a skill which grows easier with the doing

It's important to plan a *variety* of foods for well balanced meals to keep your family well nourished. But above all, be sure those meals are appetizing, attractive, and delicious to eat. For mealtime should help build happy home life.

"My meals are more nutritious since I've been planning them ahead. I check in advance the basic foods and the daily needs of my family."

"Planning meals ahead helps me to save time and energy."

"I have made the cooking of meals a pleasure and a study rather than a job, and so I enjoy planning each day's menus."

"My meals are more interesting since I started planning ahead, because I avoid repetition and plan for variety in color, texture, and flavor."

I. APPROPRIATENESS

Cut your meal pattern to fit:

Your situation

The occasion

The family needs

"I always remember birthdays and holidays with a special dessert or color scheme."

"I plan the meals to be healthful for the children, first, and then interesting to adults, without cooking separate menus."

"We have a five-room bungalow with limited dining space and no help at all; this requires simplicity and informality."

"I plan my meals with the needs of my young son in mind. I never cook separately for him, but prepare simple foods appropriate for him and then dress them up for grown-up tastes and add to the menu to meet adult needs."

II. APPEARANCE

Prepare
Serve
Present } **each food attractively for greater appetite appeal**

"I think each meal out in detail, so there will be color appeal as well as good eating."

"When I was a child my father used to say, 'We should feast the eye as well as the appetite.' And it has become a tradition with me."

"In my kitchen windows I have many plants and I alternate them in decorating the table at mealtime."

III. SATISFACTION

Good cooking and seasoning

Right combinations of food

Follow tested recipes carefully

Something soft and something crisp
Should always go together,
And something hot with something cold
No matter what the weather;
Something bland needs the complement
Of something with tang and nip.
Follow these rules and all your meals
Will have taste appeal and zip.

"I use a variety of seasonings—sage, thyme, marjoram, flavored salts; and I keep pots of fresh parsley and chives."

"I always try to have a crisp vegetable with a definite shape with one that's creamed or mashed."

IV. NUTRITION

Serve a wide variety of foods

Balance meals by including foods from the 7 basic groups

Breakfast should give about 1/3 of the day's food supply

"I have a list of menus for balanced meals which is a helpful guide in insuring good nutrition in my meals."

"I have a chart of how much vitamins, minerals, and proteins each member of my family needs according to age and activity."

"I've always tried to balance meals for the whole day. If some factor of the Basic 7 is left out of one meal, I get it into one of the other two."

V. COST

A food budget will help you

Buy the basic food needs for the family first

Buy less of the more expensive foods and more of the less expensive foods

Grow your own fruits and vegetables, if possible

"We buy the foods we must have for good nutrition first. Then if we feel we can spend more we buy the things that are not so important, but give our meals a lift."

"I find a semi-monthly budget economical, because bulk buying of staples is a worthwhile saving; and if funds are budgeted over longer periods I can take advantage of sales and special values."

"I've always had to consider the cost but have learned to manage by buying in season, taking advantage of sales, and by raising quantities of vegetables which we eat in abundance in summer and can for winter use."

DRESS UP FOOD FOR EYE APPEAL

TOMATO FLOWER

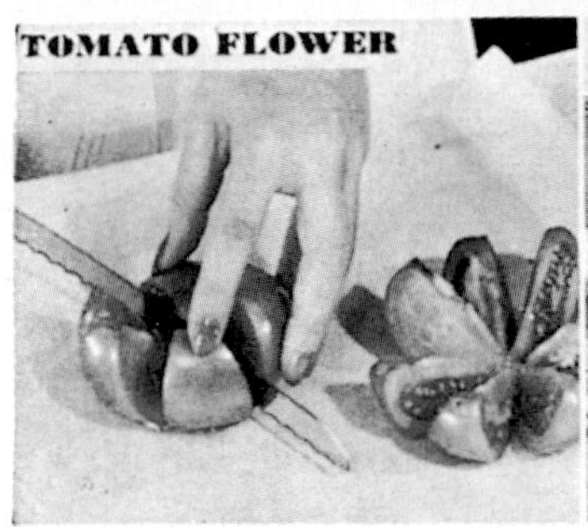

Cut tomato into wedges, leaving base uncut. Press open slightly. (Fill with salad or other mixtures.)

FRINGED CUCUMBER SLICES

Cut off ends. Pare, if desired. Then pull sharp fork firmly down lengthwise surface. Repeat around cucumber. Slice thinly. Chill.

GREEN PEPPER RINGS

Slice firm green pepper thinly crosswise . . . cut out all white portions and remove seeds. Crisp in ice water.

CELERY STICKS WITH HEARTS

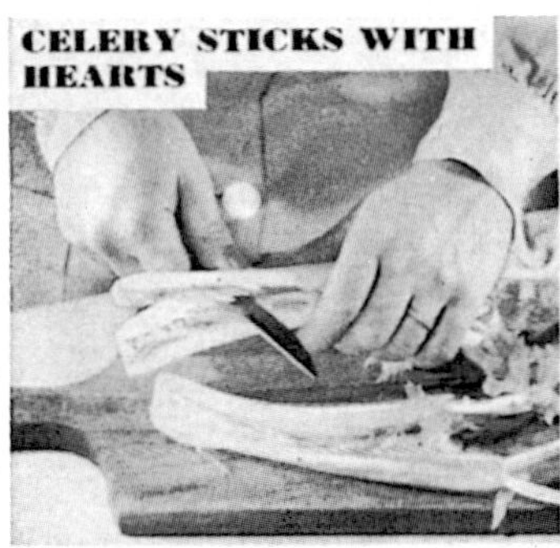

To include choice heart with each piece, slice through entire stalk from one end to the other.

CELERY CURLS

Cut into short lengths. Slit ends in narrow strips (can slit both ends). Ends will curl in ice water.

CARROT CURLS

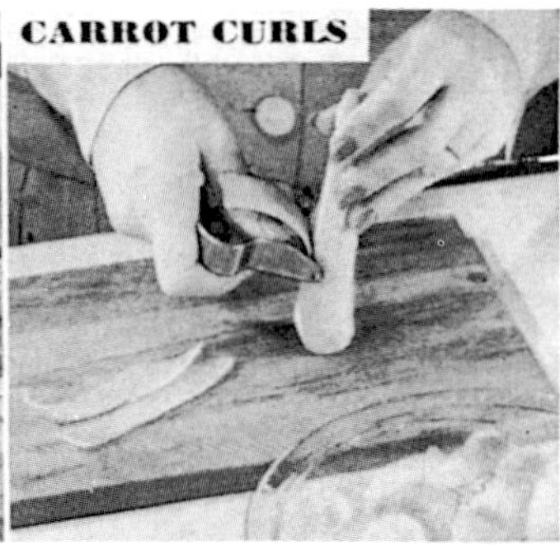

Slice the length of scraped raw carrots paper-thin with slicer. Crisp in ice water until curled.

ONION RINGS

Slice Bermuda or Spanish onions thinly *crosswise* and separate into rings. Crisp in ice water.

CAULIFLOWERETS

Cut away green leaves and woody base of cauliflower. Wash and break head into tiny flowerets. Chill.

MINCED PARSLEY

Fold leaves of several stalks (washed). Hold together . . . cut fine with scissors.

MINCED GREEN PEPPER

Wash pepper. Cut out stem and seeds. Rinse with cold water. Cut into strips. Cut several strips together into tiny pieces.

RADISH ROSES

Cut off root end, leave bit of stem, leaf. Cut *thin* petals from stem to root end around radish. Place in ice water to blossom.

LATTICED VEGETABLES

Use lattice cutter to cut attractive lattice slices and sticks from raw vegetables (carrots, potatoes, turnips, etc.).

IT'S THE FINISH THAT COUNTS

It may be only a ruffle of lettuce to set off a salad; a bunch of purple grapes for an accent note on a platter of roast chicken; a few tiny pimiento bells to add color to a bowl of oyster stew at Christmastime. Whatever the finishing touch, be sure to make it just as good to eat as it is to see. Best garnishes are simple, too.

Each should add contrast of shape, color, crispness, or flavor to the food it adorns. Notice the finishing touches suggested in many of our recipes . . . and shown in the color pictures in this book and in magazines. Take time to add that one little frill that can bring out color and appetite appeal of a special dish.

A Few Simple Examples

For FRUIT CUPS

Just before serving, top with:
- A whole berry
- A sprig of mint
- A dip of fruit ice or sherbet

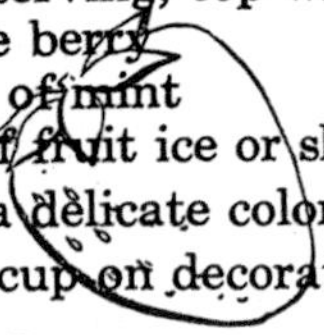

Tint syrup a delicate color.

Set sherbet cup on decorative leaf.

For SOUPS

Just before serving, top with:
- A spoonful of salted whipped cream . . . minced parsley, chives, pimiento, etc. may be added
- A sprinkling of minced parsley, chives, watercress, fresh herbs
- Thin slice of lemon
- Vegetables julienne

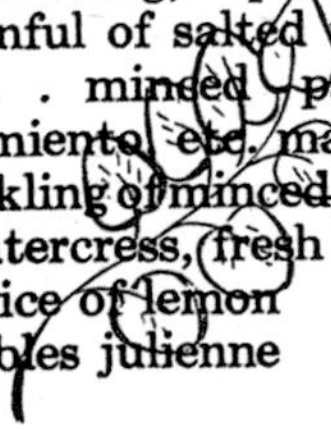

For FISH

Surround fish on platter with:
- Lemon wedges or slices sprinkled with:
  - parsley — minced pimiento
  - paprika — minced green pepper
- Bright orange slices
- Grapefruit sections
- Thick slices of cucumber
- Tomato slices topped with thin slices of lemon and stuffed olive

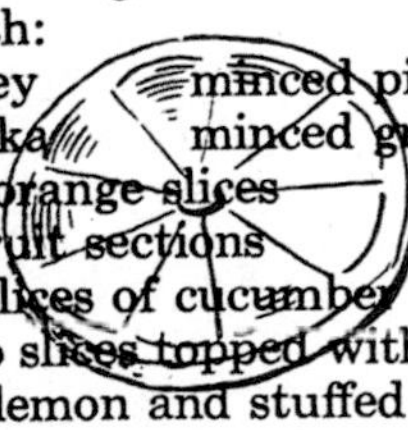

For VEGETABLES

Combine contrasting colors:
- Red beets and green Brussels sprouts
- Yellow carrots and green peas

Combine contrasting shapes:
- Carrot strips and round peas
- Little round onions with slivered beans

Sprinkle grated cheese on white cauliflower

Sprinkle sieved hard-cooked eggs on:
- Asparagus broccoli spinach

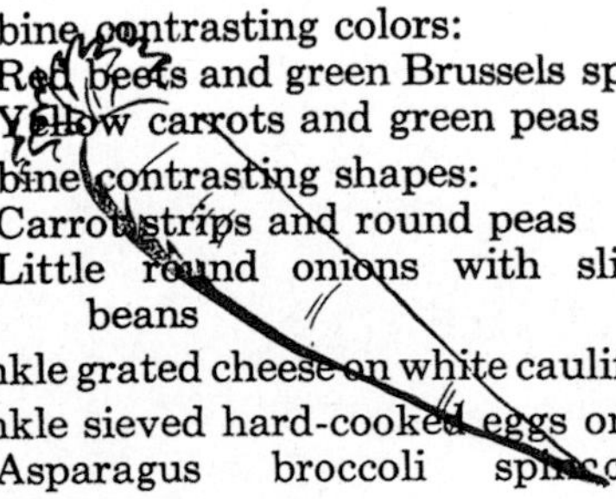

All you have to do—

To make flower garnishes for meats: shape daffodils from carrot curls and slices cut like petals; turnips can be cut to form daffodils or calla lillies, etc.

For MEATS

Surround meat on platter with:
- Broiled Fruits (*p. 361*)
- Pink Cinnamon Apples (with pork)
- Stuffed black prunes (with pork)
- Slices of orange decorated with watercress or parsley (with duck)
- Bunches of red, green, or purple grapes (with chicken)
- Molded cranberry cutouts on orange slices (with turkey and chicken)
- Canned pear halves filled with green mint jelly (with lamb)
- Spiced peach halves and watercress (with ham)
- Sautéed mushroom caps (with steak)
- French fried onion rings (with steak)
- Glazed onions and buttered carrot strips (with beef)
- Tiny scooped-out tomatoes filled with horseradish (with pot roast)

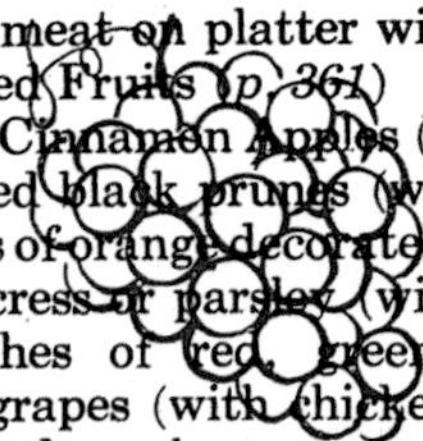

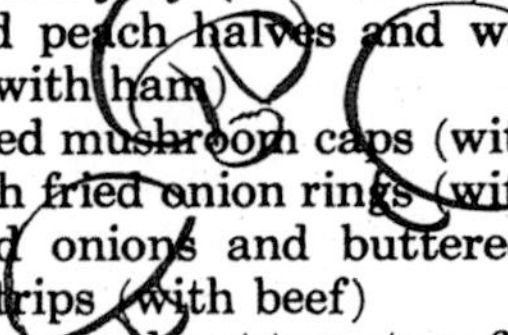

For SALADS

Add gaily the last minute:
- Sprays of watercress, mint, or parsley
- Thin strips of pimiento or green pepper
- Cream cheese balls . . . may be rolled in nuts or chives
- Prunes, dates, figs, or cherries stuffed with seasoned cream cheese or nuts

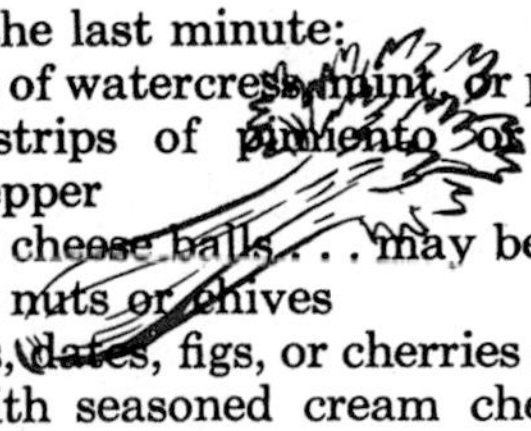

For DESSERTS

Top plain puddings with:
- Whole or sliced fresh berries . . . cherries
- Cubes of bright colored gelatin

Surround creamy or frozen desserts with:
- Bright colored fresh fruits or berries

Decorate dessert plates with:
- Clusters of berries or grapes
- Ivy or grape leaves
- A single fresh flower
- Ring of berries at base of sherbet glass

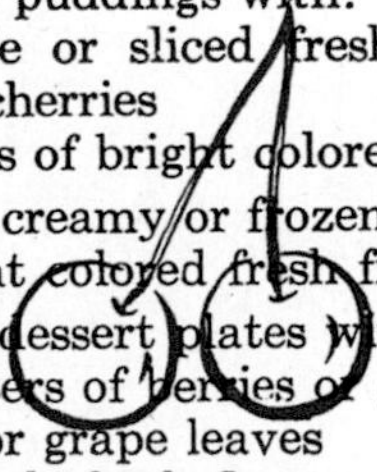

IS YOUR TABLE ATTRACTIVE AT MEALTIME?

Linen spotless? Silver and china shining? Glassware sparkling? Table neat and orderly?

HOW TO SET THE TABLE

1. For formal dinners: use all-over cloth of white or pastel colored damask or lace. For informal dinners and luncheons: lace or linen mats or runners. For breakfasts: gay, colorful cloths or mats.

2. Place napkins, folded in squares or rectangles, at left, as near silver as possible without touching it, or on the service plate. If no service plate is used, napkin may be placed in center of cover. Place open corner of napkin at lower right.

3. Place silver 1″ from edge of table in straight line even when edge of table is curved. Place no more than 3 pieces of silver on each side of plate.

4. Place all forks (except cocktail fork) at left of plate with prongs up. (Cocktail fork is placed on plate or at extreme right.) Place knives at right of plate with sharp edges toward plate. Place spoons at right of knives.

5. Each piece of silver should be placed in order of use, beginning at outside. (When salad accompanies main course, dinner fork may be used for both meat course and salad.)

6. At informal dinners, dessert silver is usually on the table at beginning of the meal. For more formal service, dessert silver is brought on with the dessert.

Table Set for Formal Afternoon Tea

7. Place beverage spoon on saucer, if desired. The tiny after-dinner coffee spoon is *always* placed on saucer.

8. Place water glass or goblet just above point of knife,—bread-and-butter plate just above forks. Place small butter spreader across butter plate either parallel to edge of table or in line with rest of silver and perpendicular to edge of table. (Bread-and-butter plates are not usual at very formal dinners, though they may be placed to hold relishes and hard rolls.)

9. Place salt and pepper shakers (well filled) between each two covers on a line with tip of knife. If individual salts and peppers are used, place above each plate.

10. Service plates .are used always at formal dinners, often at informal dinners and luncheons to add finish . . . usually 10″ plates with handsome decorative border. Place them 1″ from edge of table, in exact center of each place. Leave on table during appetizer and soup courses; remove just before placing main course plates.

11. Always observe neatness, order, and balance. Avoid crowding center of table. Bread or relishes may be placed on table with serving fork or spoon *beside* them at convenient points—such as at the corners.

The outside area is reserved for the centerpiece and candles.

12. The centerpiece for informal family meals may be a few well arranged flowers, a growing plant, or colorful fruit in a low bowl. Even for more elaborate dinners, the bouquet or pyramid of fruit should be low enough so guests may see across the table. The soft glow of candles lends a festive air to the evening meal. Candles should never be used for daylight parties.

13. Place cards may be used for seating a large number of guests. Write names simply on white or ivory cards. Place them directly in front of each "cover" between the service plate and centerpiece.

SETTING TABLE FOR TEAS AND BUFFET SUPPERS

For teas and receptions: Arrange the table with simple elegance, tea service at one end, coffee service at the other . . . with cups, plates, and spoons. Accompaniments for each should be nearby . . . the food placed conveniently for passing to guests who may stand or be seated. A hostess pours the tea or coffee. Guests may be invited to help themselves to the sandwiches, cookies, etc.

For buffet suppers and luncheons: Main dishes are usually placed at ends and sides of table, with serving silver, the stacks of plates, rows of forks, etc. around them. The order should be whatever is most natural . . . and makes it easiest for guests to serve themselves. Coffee and dessert are usually placed on a side table or are served from the kitchen by the hostess and her helpers.

TABLE SERVICE

ANSWERS TO QUESTIONS ON HOW TO SERVE

1. There are a number of approved methods for placing and removing dishes. The main thing is to do it unobtrusively without interrupting conversation.

2. It is correct to remove and place all dishes except those for beverages from the left. Foods passed must be offered from the left so the guest may use his right hand in serving himself.

3. Always serve coffee and tea, fill water glasses, from the right.

4. Some prefer to serve the hostess first, so that she may lead the way, and remove her plate first at the end of each course. Others serve the honor guest first, continuing in order around the table.

5. A cold appetizer course may be on the table when dinner or luncheon is announced; or placed on service plate (at formal occasion) after guests are seated. When removing service plate, take it up from right as the dinner plate is set before each guest.

6. Just before serving dessert, clear table of everything except centerpiece which, beside flowers or fruit and candles, may include silver or glass compotes of candies or nuts or both. Remove crumbs with folded napkin and small plate. Dessert silver may then be put in place or served directly on individual dessert plates. At a formal dinner, finger bowls are brought in on dessert plates (small lace doily under bowl), with dessert fork on plate at left of bowl and dessert spoon at right. Each guest places finger bowl and doily aside, above plate at left, and places fork at left and spoon at right of plate.

7. Coffee may be served with main course as well as dessert course at informal dinners or luncheons. At formal dinners serve it last, either at table or in living room. If the latter, always use small demitasse cups. Popular taste demands that we offer both cream and sugar with after-dinner coffee, although it is more correct to drink after-dinner coffee black.

ANSWERS TO QUESTIONS ON TYPES OF SERVICE

1. English or Family Service: Most suitable for the average family. Food is served at table by host or hostess. Host serves meat and vegetables from serving dishes placed before him. Hostess serves dessert and coffee. Served plates are passed to the guests.

2. Russian Service: More formal, not adaptable to servantless household. Host and hostess have no part in this service. Food is arranged on the individual plates in the kitchen and placed before each guest, or it is placed on platters in the kitchen and offered to each guest to help himself.

3. Compromise or Mixed Service: A combination of English and Russian service. The main course is usually served at the table; the soup, salad, and dessert Russian style, directly from kitchen to guest.

Be flexible! Make mealtime a real pleasure for the family!

Surprise them with a Sunday supper on trays in the living room—pamper a house guest with Sunday breakfast in bed—let the children plan a picnic supper on the porch—or serve breakfast outdoors. Make mealtime a time of gay surprises!

Off to a good start

"WELL BEGUN IS HALF DONE" *is true when you serve appetizers before a meal! The entire atmosphere brightens when food appears. It may be the simplest fruit juice cocktail,—for a tired husband just home from work . . . or it may be a tray of colorful canapés offered guests as soon as they arrive. Fatigue and formality vanish. Success of the meal or party is assured.*

Betty Crocker

Fruit and Vegetable Cocktails

Seafood Cocktails

Canapés

Favorite Appetizer Spreads

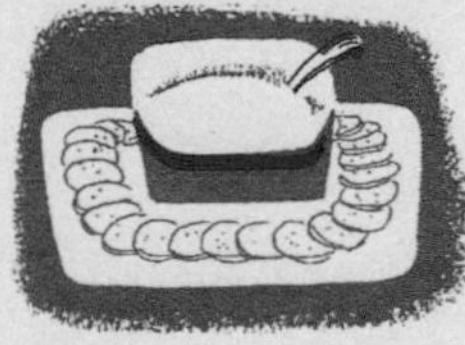

Hors d'Oeuvres

Olive-and-Bacon	.50	Garlic Olives	.50
Wrapped Sweet Pickles	.50	Green Balls	.50
Cornucopias	.50	Burning Bush	.50
Dried Beef Rolls	.50	Triple Treat	.50
Wedgies	.50	Savory Dill Franks	.50

COLORFUL RELISHES FOR DECORATING APPETIZER TRAY

Attractive relishes and garnishes that give colorful appeal to the Appetizer Tray are: radish roses or accordions, celery curls, tomato flowers, bouquets of parsley, carrot or turnip lilies, etc. Stuffed Cucumber, Celery Trunks, and Stuffed Celery are interesting additions.

STUFFED CUCUMBER

Remove center from pared cucumber with apple corer. Stuff tightly with a firm cheese mixture. Chill and slice ¼″ thick.

CELERY TRUNKS

Fill matching stalks of celery with well seasoned cream cheese. Then fit the stalks back together (the way they were grown). Tie with string and chill. When firm, slice ½″ thick. The celery curls around the cheese in attractive form.

STUFFED CELERY

Fill stalks with Roquefort cheese softened with cream cheese and seasoned with a drop or two of Worcestershire sauce. Or fill with a mixture of 1 cup mashed avocado, 2 tbsp. grated horseradish, and ½ tsp. tabasco sauce. Sprinkle with paprika. Chill.

All you have to do –

"To have a delicious appetizer on hand for holiday entertaining," says Valentine Thorson, long-time friend and Director of Home Service, Northern States Power Company, Minneapolis, "make a Green Cheese Ball. It's so easy!"

GREEN CHEESE BALL

Soften equal amounts of sharp American, white cream, and Roquefort type cheese. Season well. Mix in chopped pecans and minced parsley. Form into a large ball. Roll in minced parsley and chopped nuts.

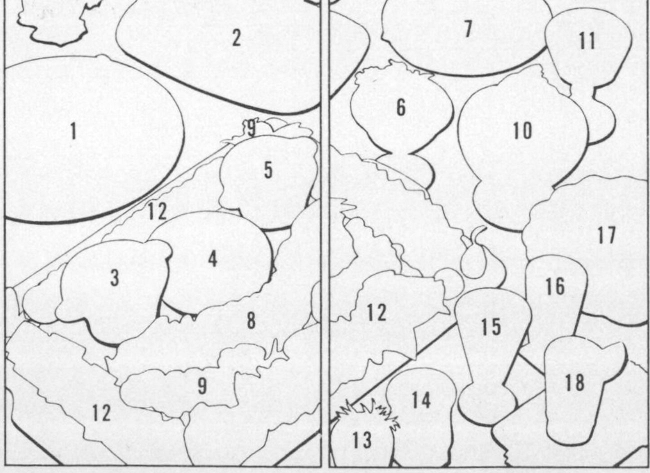

Where to find recipes for Appetizers in color photograph, pp. 44 and 45:

APPETIZERS

Appetizers are comparative newcomers in our American cuisine. Yet these "small portions of food or drink served before the first course of a meal," as the dictionary describes them, have been served in Europe for centuries. The custom seems to have started in Ancient Greece and Rome. In the days of their fabulous feasts, the Romans munched on chicory, endive, or celery, to excite hunger.

Later, nations of Europe picked up the custom and elaborated on it. They have passed on to us the elegance of Russian caviar, Italian antipasto, French hors d'oeuvres, and the Scandinavian smorgasbord with all its countless items.

During the rugged formative period of our country, hunger was the natural and best appetizer. But with the refinements of later years, we have wholeheartedly adopted European appetizers, and even added some innovations of our own. We serve them not only at formal dinners, but for informal hospitality like simple dinners, buffet suppers . . . even party refreshments.

It is "high style" to serve these tiny portions of food with beverages in the living room before a meal. The informality of moving around and helping themselves to the tidbits starts conversation and puts guests at ease. It's also a help to the hostess without a maid. While her guests are enjoying themselves, she can slip out and put the main course on the table.

Some appetizers,—fruit cups, seafood cocktails, individual plates of hors d'oeuvres, etc. are more conveniently served at the table. In this chapter you will find the different types explained, and recipes for the most familiar and popular. We have featured those that are simplest to prepare. We hope they will make your entertaining easier and more fun.

FAMILIAR COCKTAILS

Popular curtain-raisers to the dinner.

Fruits—seafoods—or vegetables usually make their appearance as appetizers in "cocktails." They are served in small individual dishes, such as sherbet glasses, or small cups sometimes set in a compote of crushed ice.

A highly seasoned cocktail sauce is poured over seafood or vegetables to add zest. Fruits are served in their own juice. The simplest form of cocktails are fruit or vegetable *juices* served in small fruit juice glasses. (*See picture, pp. 44 and 45.*)

FRUIT CUP

Fresh or whole frozen fruits are ideal because they are less sweet than canned fruit. Serve whole, halves, or cut in attractive sizes (not too small). Add lemon or lime juice for a refreshing tartness. To blend the flavors, prepare in advance and chill. Serve cold. Eat with spoon.

In Orange Cups: Serve any combination of fruit in hollowed-out orange halves. Garnish with watercress or mint.

Frozen Fruit Cocktail: Pour cold gingerale over cut-up fruit and tiny sweet green grapes. Freeze to a mush. Serve in sherbet glasses.

FRUIT PLATE

Arrange attractively on leaves of lettuce, watercress, or endive on individual plates any colorful combination of fruits. Dark glossy prunes or dates stuffed with cream cheese add color accent. Eat with fork.

FRESH STRAWBERRY PLATE

Place large red strawberries (with green hulls and stems left on) in a ring around a mound of snowy confectioners' sugar, on individual plates. Dip berries into sugar and eat.

BROILED GRAPEFRUIT

Remove seeds from grapefruit halves. Cut around sections, remove center. Sprinkle with a bit of sugar (brown or maple). Broil slowly until heated (15 to 20 min.). Add a little maraschino cherry juice or sherry flavoring. Serve hot.

COCKTAIL SAUCE

For seafood and vegetable cocktails.

Combine and chill thoroughly . . .

- **½ cup chili sauce**
- **⅓ cup catsup**
- **⅓ cup prepared horseradish**
- **1½ tsp. Worcestershire sauce**

NOTE: For a sharper sauce, add ¼ tsp. salt, 2 tbsp. lemon juice, dash of pepper, and a few drops of tabasco sauce.

OYSTERS ON THE HALF SHELL

Blue Point oysters are best. Clean oysters, chill. Wash oyster shells and serve oysters in the deepest halves of the shells. Arrange 5 to 7 on a plate of crushed ice. Place a tiny cup of cocktail sauce in the center and add a wedge of lemon.

SEAFOOD COCKTAIL

Fresh seafood preferably, or frozen or canned.

Combine large flakes or pieces of cooked shrimp, crabmeat, and lobster. Season, add minced onion, finely diced celery. Serve ice cold in a sherbet glass with Cocktail Sauce and a wedge of lemon.

SHRIMP COCKTAIL

Clean cooked shrimp, removing black line from back. Chill. Mix in finely chopped celery. Season. For each serving, place 4 to 6 shrimps in a lettuce-lined cocktail cup set in ice. Add Cocktail Sauce.

CRABMEAT COCKTAIL

For each serving, use ¼ cup flaked or larger pieces of cooked crabmeat with Cocktail Sauce. Or combine crabmeat with pineapple sections or chopped celery or diced avocado, and serve ice cold with seasoned mayonnaise and Cocktail Sauce.

Saviche (favorite in Mexico): shred raw Red Snapper (or Sieva). Soak 3 hr. in lemon juice. Drain. Add minced onion, tomato, parsley, "hot" cocktail sauce.

Easiest of all to make and serve. **COCKTAILS**

The clever wife has a simple appetizing cocktail (cold in summer, hot in winter) ready for her weary husband when he comes home at night. Vegetable or fruit juices are at their best when two or three tart flavors are chilled and served ice cold in appropriate glasses.

TOMATO JUICE

Add a little salt, lemon juice, a few drops of Worcestershire sauce, and onion juice to tomato juice. Serve cold or hot.

TOMATO BOUILLON

Combine equal parts tomato juice and bouillon (dilute canned bouillon or use cubes with boiling water). Serve hot.

TOMATO-SAUERKRAUT JUICE

Combine two parts tomato juice and 1 part sauerkraut juice. Serve hot or cold.

TOMATO-CLAM JUICE

Combine equal parts clam juice and tomato juice; season to taste with onion, salt, and pepper. Serve hot.

BOUILLON OR CONSOMMÉ

Dilute canned bouillon or consommé with water, season to taste. Serve hot in bouillon cups. Garnish with minced parsley.

JELLIED BOUILLON

For hot weather. (*See p. 366.*)

VEGETABLE JUICE COCKTAILS

Combine the juice extracted from crushed fresh vegetables with bouillon, tomato, or clam juice. Season to taste.

SIMPLE ACCOMPANIMENTS

Spread crackers lightly with butter, and sprinkle with celery seeds or paprika, etc. Crisp the crackers (heat in a mod. oven).

Sprinkle potato chips with grated Parmesan-type cheese. Toast in mod. oven.

VEGETABLE COCKTAIL

Drain 4 cups cooked tomatoes, chop the tomato pulp finely and mix with . . .

- **¼ cup finely chopped celery**
- **⅓ cup minced green pepper**
- **1 tbsp. grated onion**

Add the tomato juice and . . .

- **1 tbsp. grated horseradish**
- **2 tbsp. sugar**
- **¼ cup vinegar**
- **1 tbsp. salt**
- **dash of red and black pepper**

Chill several hr. Serve cold in sherbet glasses. Eat with spoon. *Serves 6.*

CRANBERRY COCKTAIL

Cook 2 cups cranberries in 3 cups water until skins pop; strain. Cook ½ cup sugar with juice until dissolved (about 2 min.). Chill and add a little lemon juice, half as much ginger ale, or unsweetened pineapple juice (to taste). Serve cold in glasses. *Serves 8.*

SPICED CIDER

Simmer 2 qt. cider with 1 tsp. whole allspice, 1 stick cinnamon, and a few whole cloves for 15 min. Strain. If desired, just before serving, add ¼ cup lemon juice and 2 tbsp. orange juice. *Serves 10.*

MINTED CITRUS JUICE

Combine equal parts lemon and orange juice and water. Add one sprig of mint, crushed. Chill 2 hr. Serve cold.

All you have to do—

For fruit juice cocktails: combine two or three flavors to taste, such as pineapple, grape, and lime.

BUTTERED OR CHEESE KIX

Each taste calls for another.

Melt in heavy skillet 5 tbsp. butter. Remove from heat. Stir in 5 tbsp. grated Parmesan-type cheese, if desired. Add ¼ box KIX (4 cups). Sprinkle with ½ tsp. salt. Stir well.

CANAPÉS, APPETIZERS Midget open-faced sandwiches.

Canapés . . . designed to be eaten gracefully from the fingers . . . are savory little morsels of food on a toast or cracker base. A variety, served in the living-room with cocktails, starts the dinner party off on a gay, happy note. They are equally smart for party refreshments.

Often hors d'oeuvres, which are also dainty finger foods, are served with canapés. It is important that the canapé tray look "as pretty as a picture" . . . irresistible to the eye as well as the taste. Small cocktail napkins, and sometimes small plates, are offered for these appetizers.

FIRST, PREPARE TOAST BEDS FOR CANAPÉS

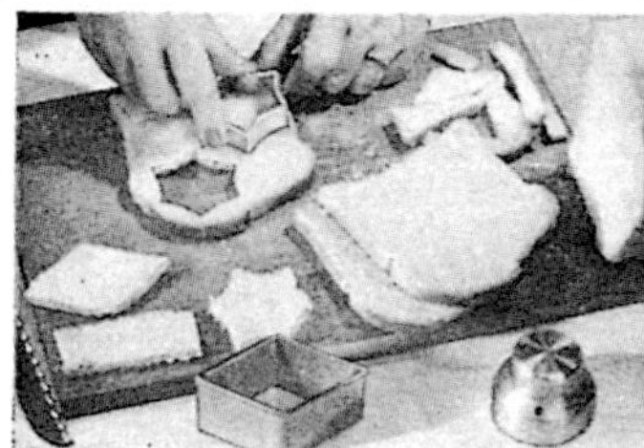

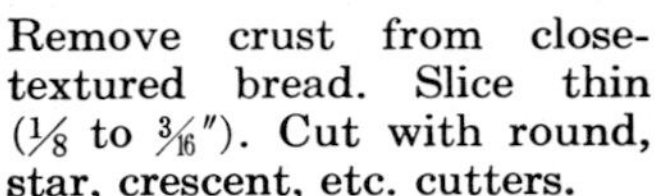

Remove crust from close-textured bread. Slice thin ($\frac{1}{8}$ to $\frac{3}{16}$″). Cut with round, star, crescent, etc. cutters.

Toast *on one side only* by sautéing in a little butter in hot skillet over low heat until nicely browned.

About $\frac{1}{2}$ hr. before serving, spread *untoasted side* lightly with mayonnaise, then with appetizer. Standing ruins them.

CANAPÉS THAT ARE POPULAR—EASY TO FIX

PEANUT BUTTER-AND-BACON

Spread prepared toast bed with crunchy peanut butter. Sprinkle with crumbled crisp bacon. Trim with minced parsley.

CHUTNEY-AND-BACON

Mix bits of crumbled crisp bacon into chutney. Spread on prepared toast bed. Trim with minced pimiento.

MINCED CLAM-CHEESE

Mix drained, minced clams with white cream cheese. Season. Spread on toast bed.

CAVIAR

Mix together $\frac{1}{4}$ cup caviar, 1 tsp. lemon juice, and $\frac{1}{4}$ tsp. minced onion. Spread on toast bed with tiny pearl onions. Trim with sieved hard-cooked egg yolks and egg whites.

TOMATO-AND-SHRIMP

Cut a thin slice from a small red tomato. Place slice on a frill of lettuce on a prepared round toast bed. In the center, a dab of mayonnaise. Press in a shrimp.

DEVILED HAM

Mash deviled ham with a little horseradish, grated onion, and coarse black pepper to taste. Spread on toast beds.

ANCHOVY OR SARDINE

Place a small anchovy or sardine on a long narrow prepared toast bed. Decorate edge with finely chopped stuffed olives.

SMOKED TURKEY OR GOOSE LIVER PASTE

Mash the paste and, if necessary, blend in a little mayonnaise to make easy to spread. Spread on prepared toast beds. Dip the edges all around in mayonnaise, then in minced parsley or pimiento.

SMOKED OYSTERS

Place a smoked oyster on each tiny round prepared toast bed. Heat, if desired.

CUCUMBER-AND-ANCHOVY

Cut thin slices from a scored cucumber. Place each slice on a prepared round toast bed. In the center of the cucumber, squeeze a small circle of anchovy paste. Press a stuffed olive slice into the paste.

SAVORY MUSHROOM CANAPÉS

Chop mushrooms fine. Pan-fry in butter with a hint of onion. Season with garlic salt. Blend in 1 tbsp. flour and 1 tbsp. cream. Pile on toast beds. Heat 1 min., if desired. Garnish with minced parsley.

HOT CHEESE PUFFS

Beat 2 egg whites until stiff. Beat in ½ tsp. baking powder, ¼ tsp. salt, ¼ tsp. paprika. Fold in ½ cup grated sharp American cheese. Heap on 1½" rounds of prepared toast beds. Broil about 5 min. until delicately browned.

HOT CRABMEAT PUFFS

A specialty at open house after the football games, at the home of Mrs. Harold Whittaker, Minneapolis, Minnesota.

Whip 2 egg whites until stiff. Fold in 1 cup mayonnaise and 1 cup flaked crabmeat (7-oz. can). Season and pile on toast beds. Sprinkle with paprika. Broil 3 min. until puffy, lightly browned.

MINIATURE PIGS IN BLANKETS

Wrap Vienna sausage halves in thinly rolled pastry or rich biscuit dough. Let ends show. Bake at 450° (hot oven) 8 min. Serve hot.

CHILI-SARDINE SNACKS

Brush oblong toast beds with sardine oil. Spread with chili sauce. Top with a sardine, and sprinkle with grated Parmesan cheese. Broil until lightly browned.

CHEESE-BACON ROLLS

Place thin slices of cheese on slices of bread. Roll up. Wrap in a strip of bacon. Broil slowly until bacon is done.

Favorite Appetizer Spreads

It's easy, informal, and fun for everyone to place a bowl of some nippy spread in the center of a tray with a suitable knife for spreading. Surround with crisp crackers, potato chips, corn or cheese chips, etc. Garnish the tray with colorful relishes (see p. 42). Place it on a convenient table in the livingroom. Let everyone spread his own.

CREAM CHEESE-AND-CHIVES

Soften white cream cheese by beating in cream or top milk. Season to taste with salt, pepper, and a few drops of onion juice. Add finely minced chives to taste.

CHEESE-ANCHOVY SPREAD

From Mrs. Ward H. Olmsted of Minneapolis, Minnesota, who says it's good and so easy!

Mix together three 3-oz. pkg. white cream cheese softened with cream, anchovy paste to taste (about ½ tube), 1 tbsp. lemon juice, a dash of cayenne pepper, 1 tsp. Worcestershire sauce, 1 tsp. scraped onion, ¼ bottle capers, ¼ tsp. paprika.

CHEESE-OLIVE-ANCHOVY

Same as above—*except* use minced chives in place of onion, and chopped stuffed olives in place of capers.

HOLLYWOOD DUNK

Combine 4 tbsp. deviled ham with 4 tbsp. horseradish, 1 tbsp. grated onion, 2 tbsp. minced chives, and stiffly whipped cream to taste. (Whip about 1 cup cream.)

ROQUEFORT SPREAD

Soften ⅓ cup Roquefort or blue cheese, ¼ cup white cream cheese; blend with 2 tbsp. mayonnaise, ¼ to 1 tsp. Worcestershire sauce, and onion and lemon juice. A perfect dip for cauliflowerettes.

HERRING-APPLE SPREAD

Virginia Safford—newspaper columnist, delightful hostess, and connoisseur of good food, serves this as a "different" appetizer when friends gather at her lovely home on the Minnesota River.

Place in shallow serving dish (such as glass pie plate) alternate layers of pieces of pickled herring, thinly sliced apple (pared), and Bermuda onion. Use skinless and boneless pickled herring soaked in wine, then drained. Season each layer with salt, pepper, and mustard. Sprinkle layers with capers and chives. Cover layers thinly with whipped thick sour cream. Chill. Serve coarse wheaty crackers with it.

All you have to do—

To serve shrimps as an appetizer: place bowl of Cocktail Sauce in center of serving plate. Surround with large cooked cleaned shrimps on wooden picks. Place crackers around them.

HORS D'OEUVRES APPETIZERS Good starters to mellow the mood.

Colorful and varied in size and shape. Exciting, too! That's your platter of hors d'oeuvres. These finger morsels may be plain, stuffed, or decorated. Prepare ahead of time. Serve on wooden picks thrust into a holder of wood or a grapefruit or eggplant, etc. so that guests can help themselves. Or place them on a tray to pass. Canapés and relishes are often served on the same tray.

OLIVE-AND-BACON

Roll ½ strip of bacon around large stuffed green olive. Broil 5 min. Serve hot.

WRAPPED SWEET PICKLES

Wrap sweet pickles in fillets of smoked salmon or anchovy. Secure with a pick.

CORNUCOPIAS

Roll salami slices into cornucopias, fasten with a pick. Fill with white cream cheese seasoned with horseradish.

DRIED BEEF ROLLS

Spread slices of dried beef with white cream cheese with horseradish to taste mixed into it. Roll up, chill.

WEDGIES

Spread 4 slices of large bologna or minced ham with softened cream cheese seasoned with onions or chives and mustard. Place slices together (like a layer cake). Spread cheese over top and sides, decorate with sliced olives. Chill. Cut into wedges.

GARLIC OLIVES

Add a cut garlic clove to the brine of large black olives. Soak several hours.

GOOSELIVER BONBONS

Mash gooseliver to a paste, add bits of crumbled crisp bacon; roll into a tiny ball. Roll in chopped ripe olives. Serve in little paper bonbon cases.

All you have to do—

To serve hors d'oeuvres as a first course: arrange a few on individual plates to be eaten with a fork.

GREEN BALLS

Mix together ½ cup grated Swiss cheese, ½ cup minced cooked ham, ½ tsp. prepared mustard, 1 egg yolk, ¼ tsp. salt, dash of pepper. Form into balls. Roll in minced chives or parsley.

BURNING BUSH

Form softened, seasoned white cream cheese into balls. Roll in minced dried beef.

TRIPLE TREAT

Place on one pick a maraschino cherry, a pickled onion, a gherkin. Happy surprise!

SAVORY DILL FRANKS

Spread two ¼″ slices cooked frankfurts with a mustard-horseradish-mayonnaise spread. Put together with slice of dill pickle between. Fasten with wooden pick.

PECANS WITH ANCHOVY

Place 2 large pecan halves together with anchovy paste between.

SIMPLE HORS D'OEUVRES

Smoked white fish fillets, deviled eggs, frankfurts (1″ lengths), smoked salmon, shrimp or lobster, Vienna sausages.

FLAMING CABBAGE

An exciting, spectacular feature at a cocktail party in Mr. and Mrs. Phil Hindley's charming home, Oakland, California.

Clean a large cabbage. Curl outer leaves back from top. Cut out center; hollow it out about 6″ deep. Place a sterno lamp in the cavity (lamp hidden, but flame should come almost to top of cabbage). Place cabbage on serving plate. Surround with a frill of parsley. Thrust wooden picks through cocktail sausages, and stick into the cabbage. Stick an olive onto end of each (to protect fingers from flame). Guests broil their own sausages.

Our Favorite Beverages Are an Aid to Gracious Living

"CUPS O' KINDNESS" *bring to mind the heart-warming sociability of friends over fragrant, steaming cups of coffee or tea. If the weather is warm, tall frosty glasses of chilled fruit juice take their part in pleasant hospitality.*

Betty Crocker

Chilled Fruit Drinks

Chocolate and Cocoa

Coffee

Egg and Milk Drinks

Tea

SERVING BEVERAGES

CHOCOLATE AND COCOA

Hot Chocolate or Cocoa

Special chocolate cups are small and narrow.

Top each cup with a swirl of whipped cream or a marshmallow, or serve plain. Cinnamon may be sprinkled over the cream.

If pouring chocolate or cocoa at the table, use a regular chocolate pot or a covered pitcher (preheated), but do not attempt to use a teapot. It will be next to impossible to get the spout cleaned.

Iced Chocolate

Top with sweetened whipped cream.

Set tall glass of iced chocolate on a saucer or in a special holder. A long handled iced tea spoon usually accompanies iced chocolate.

COFFEE

Hot Coffee

Coffee cups are larger and wider than teacups.

Offer rich cream and sugar (either loaf or granulated). Arrange sugar bowl and cream pitcher on a small tray covered with a white linen doily or small napkin.

After-Dinner Coffee

Served black and strong in tiny "after-dinner coffee" cups. On the saucer beside the cup is a tiny after-dinner coffee spoon. Usually served in the living room.

Some hostesses, however, do serve it at the end of the dinner at the dining table. Some offer sugar and cream, as for hot dinner coffee.

Tiny cups of this extra-strong coffee are sometimes offered before breakfast as an "eye-opener."

Iced Coffee

Serve in tall glasses with ice and offer sugar and cream, as with hot coffee.

TEA

Hot Tea

Regular teacups are smaller than coffee cups.

Offer thin cream or milk and sugar (either loaf or granulated).

Or offer thin lemon slices and sugar. The lemon slices are sometimes studded with whole cloves. Arrange a tray covered with a white linen doily or small napkin, and have on it the plate of lemon slices as well as the sugar and creamer.

A pitcher or a small silver jug of hot water or another teapot filled with hot water should also accompany the tea service, since some like a much milder flavored tea than others. Those who want the less strong tea can dilute it with hot water.

Iced Tea

Finely granulated sugar and lemon wedges are offered with iced tea. Serve in tall glasses on coasters or in special holders.

Garnish with a sprig of mint.

"... cups that cheer ... welcome peaceful evening in."

BEVERAGES TEA

The glamor of centuries surrounds tea. Serving and drinking it has long been a ceremony in both China and Japan. It made its debut in England in 1666 as "tay." The London coffee houses which first served it soon became "tea" shops. "There are few hours of life more agreeable than the hour dedicated to afternoon tea," wrote an American novelist on his visit to England. Tea-drinking in this country had received a setback at the Boston tea party. However, in the earlier days it had been a popular custom in the American colonies. In New York, the Dutch housewife usually made several different kinds of tea in different teapots (pewter, china, and silver) to please the tastes of her guests. The tea table, teapot, sugar bowl or shaker, and strainer were the pride of the Dutch housewife. "Bite-and-stir" sugar boxes were special Dutch pieces. On one side, was loaf sugar to nibble with the tea; and on the other, the granulated sugar to stir into the tea.

*THREE KINDS OF TEA

Black Tea: from India, Ceylon, Java, and Sumatra. The leaves are first fermented, then heated and dried.

Green Tea: from China and Japan. The leaves are not fermented. "Gunpowder" is a type of green tea.

Oolong Tea: from Formosa. The leaves are fermented only a short time.

**Flower-scented teas* have flower petals added. Jasmine is the most popular. Others are gardenia or yulan.

WHEN BUYING TEA REMEMBER

Orange Pekoe is not a kind of tea. It refers to the size of the tea leaf. "Pekoe" indicates a larger leaf than "orange" pekoe.

Tea bags of parchment or cloth are a convenience for making 1 or 2 cups of tea. It is more economical to buy tea in bulk.

Buy tea in small amounts. It loses flavor in long storage. 1 lb. yields from 150 to 200 cups. Unless one serves a great deal of tea, ¼ lb. is enough to buy at a time.

Keep tea in an airtight container.

A GOOD CUP OF TEA ... *Soothing, refreshing. Follow these simple rules for making.*

1. The Teapot: Should be china, pottery, or heat resistant glass. Keep spotlessly clean. Wash with soap and hot water after each using.

2. Scald Teapot: Heat the teapot just before making tea by filling it with boiling water. Let it stand a few minutes. Then pour off water and put the tea leaves in the heated pot.

3. How Much Tea: Allow 1 to 1½ tsp. tea for each cup of water.

4. Pour Fresh Boiling Water over Tea Leaves: "Until the kettle boiling B, Filling the pot will spoil the T." It is important to have freshly drawn water boiling furiously when it is poured over the tea. "Take the teapot to the kettle, never the kettle to the pot."

5. Cover Pot and Let Tea Steep: 3 to 5 min. will bring tea to desired strength. Then strain it into another heated pot or into cups. Tea becomes bitter if it steeps too long.

Iced Tea

Strain freshly made *double strength* tea over ice in pitcher or in iced tea glasses. (Fill glasses with ice.)

To Insure Clear Iced Tea: Because tannin and caffein are less soluble in cold than hot water, iced tea often looks cloudy. A "clear tea" can be made thus: Allow 3 tsp. tea for each ¾ cup cold water. Let this tea stand covered in refrigerator 12 to 24 hr. Strain before serving.

COFFEE BEVERAGES The All-American beverage.

Centuries ago in Abyssinia, a herdsman noticed his goats were unusually lively after eating the berries of a certain shrub. He took some of the berries to the abbot of a nearby monastery who dried and boiled them. He and his monks were delighted with the new black drink which they called "kaffia" (the name of the shrub). The use of coffee spread to Arabia, thence by caravan trade to India, Egypt, and Syria. By the seventeenth century, "coffee houses" and clubs were flourishing in England and colonial America. The coffee shop was a gathering place for literary and business men who gossiped and discussed politics over their coffee cups. Gradually the American people adopted the custom of drinking coffee at home. Now the art of making good coffee is an asset to successful homemaking.

SIX ESSENTIALS FOR A CUP OF GOOD COFFEE . . . easy to follow.

1. Fresh Coffee: It loses flavor quickly when exposed to air. Keep it tightly covered and buy it often.

2. The Right Grind for the Coffee Maker: "Drip" grind for glass vacuum makers and dripolators. "Regular grind" or "steel cut" for percolators or for steeped (boiled) coffee.

3. A Clean Coffee Maker: Wash with soap and water after each use. Stains in coffee pot can ruin the taste. Boiling water with soda in the pot removes stains. Follow directions for cleaning your type of coffee maker.

4. Start with Fresh Cold Water: Not *hot* water from the tap or tea kettle. Bring to a full rolling boil before putting the coffee container in the coffee maker.

5. Use Enough Coffee for Desired Strength:
For *weak* coffee . . .
1 tbsp. to ¾ cup water;
For *medium* coffee . . .
2 tbsp. to ¾ cup water;
For *strong* coffee . . .
3 or 4 tbsp. to ¾ cup water.

6. Serve Coffee as soon as Possible: If necessary to let it stand, remove grounds. Keep hot on asbestos pad over very low heat; or in pan of hot water. Cooled coffee loses flavor if reheated.

Caution: For best results brew coffee at full capacity of coffee maker.

Leftover Coffee: If you want to use it, pour into glass jar. Cover. Keep in refrigerator. Reheat over low heat.

CAFÉ AU LAIT

French, meaning "coffee with milk."

Make coffee double strength. Heat an equal amount of milk to scalding. Pour hot coffee and milk into serving cups at the same time (use equal amounts of each).

AFTER-DINNER COFFEE

Served in small after-dinner cups. It is called demitasse . . . French word for "half cup."

Make stronger than usual. Use 3 to 4 tbsp. coffee to ¾ cup water for each serving.

VIENNA COFFEE

Demitasse with whipped cream.

COFFEE FOR THE CROWD

For *48 cups* of coffee: mix 1 egg (shell and all) into 1¼ lb. coffee. Add 1 cup cold water. Tie coffee in cheesecloth bag large enough to allow room for coffee to swell. Measure 9 qt. cold water into large coffee pot. Immerse coffee bag in water, bring to boil. Remove pot from heat. Leave bag of coffee in water 3 to 4 min., remove and stir. Keep hot. If preferred, use boiling water to start, bring to boil. Stir. Remove from heat. Let stand 10 min. Remove coffee and serve.

MAKING COFFEE IN DIFFERENT TYPES OF COFFEE MAKERS

Drip Coffee

Measure coffee (drip grind) into filter section. Measure fresh boiling water into upper container, then cover. Set coffee maker over very low heat. When all the water has dripped through the coffee, remove upper section immediately. Stir brew and serve.

Flask Filter Coffee

Follow manufacturer's directions, using special filter paper made for the coffee maker. Measure coffee and place in top compartment. Measure water. Bring to a simmer (not a full boil). Pour over coffee. When water has dripped through, it is ready to serve. Do not put coffee maker over direct heat at any time. To keep hot, place on asbestos mat or in hot water over low heat.

Vacuum-Type Coffee

Follow manufacturer's directions for use of coffee maker. Measure coffee (drip or pulverized grind) and water. If cloth filter is used, keep it immersed in cold water when not in use. Never allow it to dry, and never wash with soap.

Percolated Coffee

Measure fresh cold water and coffee (regular grind). Place coffee in percolator basket, and water in bottom of container. Let water boil until it has "perked" about 5 to 10 min., depending on strength desired, or until bubbles appear foamy.

Steeped Coffee

(Commonly called "boiled.")

Allow 2 tbsp. coffee (regular grind) to each ¾ cup water. Pour fresh boiling water over it. Place over heat. Stir well. Bring just to boil. Stir again. Remove from heat. Add dash of cold water to settle grounds. Let stand over low heat about 5 min. Strain and serve. If coffee is allowed to boil, flavor and aroma are lost.

"Boiled" Coffee with Egg: Stir ½ tbsp. beaten egg or egg white into 5 to 6 tbsp. of the coffee before adding the water.

ICED COFFEE

Make coffee as usual, but use twice as much coffee. Pour over crushed ice in glasses.

CHOCOLATE BEVERAGES Delicious and nourishing.

Cortez, the Spanish conquistador, was the first European to taste chocolate. Montezuma, the Aztec emperor of Mexico, gave a big feast and served "chocolatl" to his guest in a golden goblet. It was really a bitter mush, served stone cold. Cacao beans had been roasted and ground, then mixed with corn meal, vanilla, peppers, spices, and herbs. Cortez learned that the cacao beans were used as money among the Indians. He procured some. Soon the Dutch, Italians, Austrians, and French were experimenting with these beans. In 1657, a notice in a London newspaper announced that a Frenchman in Bishopgate street was offering an excellent West Indian drink, "jacolatte." Chocolate houses sprang up where society gathered afternoons to gossip and drink the new delicacy. Soon chocolate was being served by English colonists in America.

TYPES OF COCOA AND CHOCOLATE AVAILABLE TODAY

Unsweetened Chocolate: made from cocoa beans with no fat removed.

Semi-Sweet Chocolate: just enough sweetening added to give a partially sweet flavor. More cocoa butter is also added.

Cocoa: made from cocoa beans with varying amounts of cocoa butter removed.

Breakfast Cocoa: has a minimum of 22% cocoa fat.

Dutch Process Cocoa: made from special cocoa beans processed to make them more soluble.

Ready-to-Serve Cocoa: needs only addition of hot or cold water or milk to be ready to serve.

HOT COCOA

For each cup cocoa, mix together 1 tsp. sugar, 2 tsp. cocoa, and ¼ cup cold water. Cook over *low* heat (boil about 4 min.). Add 1 cup milk. Heat until scalded, but do not boil. Add a pinch of salt (a drop of vanilla, too, if desired). Just before serving, stir until smooth. Serve hot. Pour over a marshmallow in each cup.

HOT CHOCOLATE

For 6 servings, heat over *low* heat 2 sq. unsweetened chocolate (2 oz.) and 1 cup water, stirring until chocolate melts. Add a pinch of salt and 3 to 4 tbsp. sugar. Boil 4 min., stirring. Then slowly stir in 3 cups milk. Heat until scalded. Do not boil. Just before serving, beat with rotary beater until smooth. Top with whipped cream. Serve hot.

SOUTH AMERICAN CHOCOLATE

Melt over hot water ½ lb. sweet cooking chocolate (or a 7-oz. pkg. chocolate pieces). Add 1 cup strong hot coffee. Stir well and cook over *low* heat 1 min. Scald 6 cups milk (1½ qt.). Add to chocolate. Simmer until very hot. Beat with rotary beater until frothy on top. Set over hot water 10 min. to blend flavors. Just before serving, beat again with rotary beater. *Serves 8.*

ICED CHOCOLATE

Make cocoa or chocolate your favorite way. Cool. Serve in glasses with chopped ice. Top with sweetened whipped cream.

MARTHA WASHINGTON'S COLONIAL CHOCOLATE

George Washington's favorite hot chocolate. From a radio friend who wrote, "It came from my cousin whose husband is a direct descendant of Martha Washington."

Mix to a smooth paste in a saucepan . . .
- **4 tbsp. cocoa**
- **a little cold water**

Stir in . . .
- **2 cups water**
- **⅓ cup sugar**
- **2 cups milk**

Bring to a boil and blend in . . .
- **2 tbsp. cornstarch dissolved in a little cold milk**

Boil 3 min. longer. Remove from heat and set in warm place.

Beat until light and foamy . . .
- **1 egg with ½ cup hot water**

Pour half of egg mixture into a pitcher.

Blend in . . .
- **½ tsp. vanilla**

Add hot chocolate slowly. Pour remaining egg mixture over top. Serve at once.
AMOUNT: 6 servings.

EGGNOG (🔑 Recipe)

Beat together . . .
1 egg, well beaten
2 tbsp. sugar

Beat in . . .
1 cup chilled rich milk
***¼ tsp. vanilla**

Serve cold in tall glass sprinkled lightly with . . .
nutmeg

***1½ tbsp. sherry flavoring and 1 tbsp. either brandy or rum flavoring may be substituted for vanilla.*

FRUIT EGGNOG

Make 🔑 recipe above—using 2 tbsp. fruit or 1 tbsp. fruit juice (grape, orange, cherry juice, etc.) instead of vanilla and nutmeg.

CHOCOLATE EGGNOG

Make 🔑 recipe above with 2 tbsp. Chocolate Syrup and omit sugar.

ORANGE EGGNOG

To . . .
1 egg, well beaten

Add . . .
1 tbsp. lemon juice
½ cup orange juice
1 tbsp. light corn syrup

Mix thoroughly. Chill. Serve ice cold.
AMOUNT: 1 glass.

GRAPE JUICE WITH EGG

Appetite-tempter for convalescents.

Pour into a tall glass . . .
3 tbsp. orange juice
½ cup grape juice

Add . . .
2 tsp. sugar
dash of salt

To . . .
1 egg white, beaten stiff

Add egg white to fruit juice and stir just enough to mix well.
AMOUNT: 1 tall glass.

FRUIT MILK SHAKES

After-school treats for children, refreshing for invalids.

Have milk thoroughly chilled. Shake or beat with fruit until well blended. Use *2 cups of milk* and add various flavors as desired. The beverage may be topped with a bit of whipped cream and sprinkled with nutmeg, if desired.

Banana: Add 1 mashed banana.

Prune: Add 1 cup prune juice.

Orange Blossom Milk Shake: Add 2 cups orange juice, ¼ tsp. almond flavoring, and sugar to taste.

Strawberry Milk Shake: Add ½ cup crushed sweetened strawberries.

Molasses: Stir in 4 tbsp. molasses.

CHOCOLATE SYRUP

Combine in saucepan . . .
1 cup cocoa or 4 sq. unsweetened chocolate (4 oz.)
2 cups sugar
¼ tsp. salt

Stir in . . .
2 cups cold water

Simmer until smooth and thick (about 5 min.), stirring or beating with rotary beater.

Cool and add . . .
1 tbsp. vanilla

Stir well. Pour into jar. Seal. Store in refrigerator.

CHOCOLATE MILK SHAKE

Add 1½ to 2 tbsp. Chocolate Syrup to 1 cup milk. Beat with rotary beater.

FROSTED CHOCOLATE

Beat a small spoonful of ice cream into each chocolate milk shake.

MALTED MILK DRINKS

There are 2 kinds . . . the plain unflavored malted milk, and the sweetened milk with the addition of malt extracts and chocolate or cocoa. Simply add hot or cold water. Mix well and serve.

CHILLED FRUIT BEVERAGES For the good old summertime.

LEMONADE (🔑 Recipe) *As American as circus day . . . saves lemons, gives flavor.*

Combine in saucepan.............. 1 cup sugar, 1 cup water, rind of 2 lemons, cut into pieces

Stir over *low* heat until sugar is dissolved. Boil about 7 min. Cool.

Add.............................. 1 cup lemon juice (5 to 6 lemons), 4 cups ice water

Pour over ice in pitcher or tall glasses. AMOUNT: 6 to 8 servings.

Minted Lemonade: Place bruised mint leaves in bottom of glasses before adding Lemonade (🔑 recipe above). Garnish each glass with a sprig of mint.

Pink Lemonade: Follow 🔑 recipe above—and add a little grenadine syrup.

Pineapple Lemonade: Follow 🔑 recipe above—but use 1 qt. water and 1½ cups sugar for the syrup. Add 2 cups crushed pineapple with 1½ cups lemon juice. Garnish each glass with a sprig of mint. *Serves 10.*

All you have to do— *To make lemonade quickly:* squeeze lemons, add sugar and water to taste.

Limeade: Follow 🔑 recipe above—using lime juice instead of lemon juice. Add a little green food coloring, if desired.

Orangeade: Follow 🔑 recipe above—*except,* in place of lemon juice, use 2 cups orange juice and ¼ cup lemon juice.

RASPBERRY SHRUB

An old-time favorite from grandma's day.

Mix, cook together in saucepan 10 min. . . .
- 3 pt. raspberries (washed and hulled)
- 1½ cups sugar
- 2 cups water

Strain and cool. Add . . .
- 1 cup lemon juice
- 2 qt. water

Serve with crushed ice.

AMOUNT: 10 SERVINGS (about 2½ qt.).

PINK RHUBARB REFRESHER

Cook to a mush in 5 cups boiling water 2 lb. tender pink rhubarb (cut, but not peeled). Press through sieve. Measure juice. For each cup, add ⅓ cup sugar. Stir until dissolved. Chill. For each cup rhubarb juice, add ½ cup grapefruit juice. Add ¼ cup lemon juice to entire mixture. Just before serving, add 1 qt. ginger ale. *Serves 24.*

All you have to do—

To make an interesting WASSAIL BOWL for holiday entertaining: stud 3 oranges with whole cloves and bake 30 min. in a mod. oven (350°). Heat 2 qt. sweet cider until it steams. Pour into a punch bowl and float the baked oranges on top. Serve in mugs, using cinnamon sticks for stirring. *Serves 10.*

RED FRUIT PUNCH

Mix together . . .
- ½ cup sugar
- 1 cup lemon juice
- 1 cup cherry juice
- 2 cups pineapple or pear juice

Cover and chill until flavors are well blended. Just before serving, add . . .
- 1 qt. carbonated water or ginger ale

AMOUNT: 10 servings.

PUNCH FOR BIG AFFAIRS

Sounds odd, but is unusually delicious.

Make syrup by boiling together 10 min. . . .
- 4 cups sugar
- 2 cups water

Add . . .
- 2 cups strong black tea
- juice of 10 lemons (about 2 cups)
- juice of 10 oranges (about 2½ cups)
- 2 #2 cans pineapple juice (5 cups)

Chill 2 to 3 hr. Strain, if desired. Add
- 12 oz. maraschino cherries with juice
- 3 gal. water
- 2 qt. dry ginger ale

Pour over block of ice in punch bowl or over ice cubes. Serve.

AMOUNT: 75 servings.

Breads-Quick and Hot
A Conversation Piece

HOT QUICK BREADS in their many delightful forms help tell the story of civilization. Notice the bits of history tucked into these pages and serve them up as table conversation. They'll make cooking, and eating, more fun.

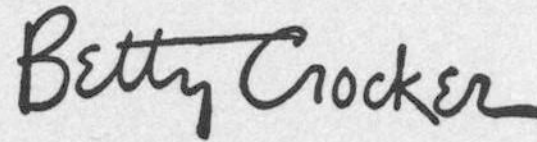

For Quick Morning Wake-Ups

For Charming Lunches

For Leisure Breakfasts or Brunches

Accompaniments for Dinner

Meal-Finishers

Late Afternoon or Evening Snacks

Hints and Quick Tricks

The beauty of hot breads is to have them served piping hot from the oven. Snuggle them in a napkin in serving dish to retain the heat. Place on plate just enough to go around. Then replenish from the oven for seconds or thirds.

To avoid that last minute rush just before the meal, measure all ingredients for muffins, biscuits, corn breads, etc. ahead of time—sift dry ingredients together and then it takes only a jiffy to mix and pop into the oven.

If more convenient to make up dough for quick breads an hour or two ahead of time, keep it in cold place until time to bake.

If muffins get done a little ahead of the rest of the meal, loosen them, tip them slightly in the pans, and keep them in the warm oven.

When the batter does not fill all the cups in the muffin pan, don't grease the muffin cups that are not to be filled. Wipe out the grease from unfilled cups before putting in oven so grease will not brown onto pan.

Muffins can be baked in little paper baking cups for attractive serving.

Cut square biscuits quickly by using the ice cube divider from a refrigerator tray.

Serve second-day rolls, muffins, biscuits, or corn bread split, spread with a little butter, and toasted in broiler.

To make doughnuts without a doughnut cutter, cut the dough with a biscuit cutter. Stick forefinger (floured) through the center of each plain round of dough and twirl finger quickly to make a $\frac{3}{4}''$ hole.

Where to find recipes for Quick Breads in color photograph of Kitchen Breakfast Buffet, p. 64

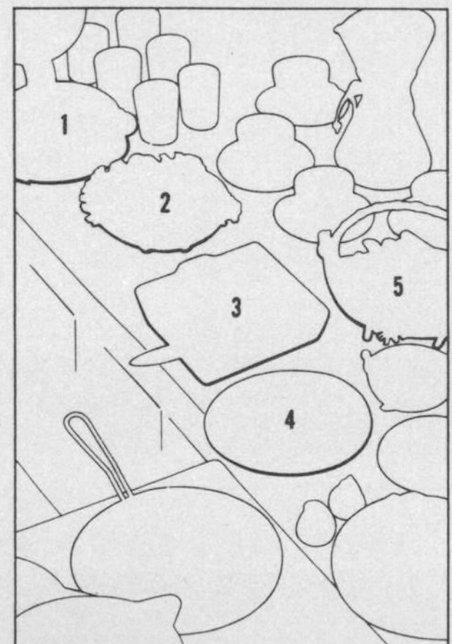

QUICK BREADS

May we introduce to you breads with a story? You see, the families of quick breads go way, way back into history. Our delicious American hot breads are the lineal descendants of the crude hearth cakes of primitive people. The famous "cakes" which King Alfred forgot to watch, as he sat in a peasant hut, were early ancestors of our present day quick breads. Others were the "bannocks o' barley" that Robert Burns wrote about. You will find that the bits of history given in these pages make interesting table conversation when you serve hot breads at your table.

These popular breads are classified as *quick* because they are made with quick-acting leavening,—baking powder, or soda and sour milk, or steam, etc., instead of the slower acting yeast. They include many different types of *baked* breads, — biscuits, muffins, nut loaves, corn breads, etc. Some are cooked on a griddle, — the pancakes, waffles, etc. Then there are those cooked by steam, such as dumplings and brown breads. And, last of all, the old favorites fried in deep fat, — doughnuts and fritters. All of them can be made at the last minute and served piping hot and fresh from the oven, griddle, or kettle.

Our Staff has found the easiest, quickest ways to make each and every type. You can now make most of these recipes by the one-bowl double-quick method. No longer need you fuss with that bothersome extra step of melting the shortening!

Here are recipes for pancakes, waffles, or muffins for lovely leisurely breakfasts, — popovers or nut breads for a luncheon to be long remembered! The scones and coffee cakes are ideal for the tea or coffee hour. And do try surprises like the crunchy corn sticks for special dinners. There are delicious fruit breads for sandwiches and savory cheese biscuits just right for those important evening snacks. And they are quicker than ever to make!

MUFFINS QUICK BREADS Quick, easy way of mixing.

Off on the right foot in muffin-mixing:

First of all

Read through the recipe.

Preheat oven to 400° (mod. hot oven).

Assemble ingredients.

Assemble utensils and grease muffin cups.

Sift flour and measure all dry ingredients into sifter.

1 Sift dry ingredients into mixing bowl.

2 Measure and add *soft* shortening, unbeaten egg, and milk.

3 Mix together with pastry blender (or blending fork). Use a cutting-in motion at first to divide shortening into small pieces (about 8 strokes).

5 Fill well greased muffin cups ⅔ full.

4 Stir (in a circular motion) with blender *just until* flour is moistened and ingredients blended. The batter will look lumpy.

6 Bake until golden brown. Loosen with spatula and serve immediately. Keep those not served hot until ready to eat.

MUFFINS (🔑 Recipe) *The name means "little muffs" . . . to warm the fingers.*

Make either type desired.	*Popular Muffins*	*Sweeter Muffins*
Sift together into mixing bowl	2 cups *sifted* GOLD MEDAL Flour	1½ cups
	¼ cup sugar	½ cup
	3 tsp. baking powder	2 tsp.
	½ tsp. salt	½ tsp.
Add	¼ cup soft shortening	¼ cup
	1 egg	1 egg
	1 cup milk	½ cup

Mix together with blending fork or pastry blender. Then stir *just until* ingredients are blended. Fill greased muffin cups ⅔ full. Bake until golden brown. Serve hot with butter and with jam, marmalade, honey, or any desired spread.

TEMPERATURE: 400° (mod. hot oven).

TIME: Bake 20 to 25 min.

AMOUNT: 12 medium-sized muffins.

WHOLE WHEAT MUFFINS

(Graham Gems) And they *are* gems!

Follow 🔑 recipe for Popular Muffins above—*except* use only 1 cup flour and 2 tsp. baking powder. Add 1 cup whole wheat (Graham) flour to the *sifted* dry ingredients *in the mixing bowl.*

SOUR MILK MUFFINS

Follow 🔑 recipe for Popular Muffins above—*except* use only 2 tsp. baking powder, and add ½ tsp. soda; substitute sour milk for sweet milk.

★ WHEATIES MUFFINS

An ideal hot bread for dinner.

Follow 🔑 recipe for Popular Muffins above—*except* use only 1 cup flour and ½ cup milk and carefully fold in 2 cups WHEATIES at the last.

PRUNE MUFFINS

Studded with the glossy dark fruit.

Follow 🔑 recipe for Popular Muffins above—*except* add ¼ cup brown sugar and ¼ tsp. nutmeg to flour mixture, and at the last fold in ¾ cup cut-up well drained cooked prunes.

SURPRISE MUFFINS

The secret's inside.

Follow 🔑 recipe for Popular Muffins above. Fill muffin cups half full of batter. Drop scant teaspoonful of jelly on center of batter. Add more batter to fill cup ⅔ full. Discovering the jelly inside the baked muffin is the surprise.

★ BLUEBERRY MUFFINS

Deliciously moist with luscious blue fruit.

Follow 🔑 recipe for Sweeter Muffins above—and at the last blend in carefully 1 cup well drained fresh blueberries. If canned berries are used, ¾ cup.

ORANGE HONEY MUFFINS

Follow 🔑 recipe for Sweeter Muffins above—*except* use 2 eggs. Place in bottom of each well greased muffin cup 1 tsp. honey, then a thin slice of unpeeled orange, cut in quarters. Spoon batter on top. Serve orange slice up.

APPLE MUFFINS

A Sunday breakfast or supper treat.

Follow 🔑 recipe for Sweeter Muffins above—*except* sift ½ tsp. cinnamon with dry ingredients. Add 1 cup grated raw tart apple (unpared) with shortening. Bake 25 to 30 min. If desired, sprinkle top with:

NUT-CRUNCH TOPPING

Mix together ⅓ cup brown sugar, ⅓ cup broken nuts, and ½ tsp. cinnamon.

MAPLE SYRUP MUFFINS

Follow 🔑 recipe for Popular Muffins above—*except* substitute ½ cup maple syrup for ½ cup of the milk.

DATE, FIG, OR RAISIN MUFFINS

Follow 🔑 recipe for Popular Muffins above—and add 1 cup finely cut-up dates or figs or raisins.

★ "LIGHT-AS-FEATHER" MUFFINS

One of the specialties of Mrs. K's Toll House, Silver Springs, Maryland, famous for its wonderful food and charming atmosphere.

Mix together thoroughly . . .
- **1/4 cup sugar**
- **1/4 cup soft shortening**

Blend in . . .
- **1 egg**

Sift together . . .
- **1 3/4 cups *sifted* SOFTASILK Cake Flour**
- **4 tsp. baking powder**
- **1/2 tsp. salt**

and stir in alternately with . . .
- **1 cup milk**

Fill greased muffin cups 2/3 full. Bake until golden brown. Serve hot.

TEMPERATURE: 375° (quick mod. oven).

TIME: Bake 20 to 23 min.

AMOUNT: 14 to 16 small muffins.

★ OATMEAL MUFFINS

They're marvelous! So moist and rich.

Soak together for 1 hr. . . .
- **1 cup rolled oats**
- **1 cup buttermilk or sour milk**

Mix together thoroughly . . .
- **1/3 cup soft shortening (part butter)**
- **1/2 cup brown sugar**
- **1 egg**

Sift together . . .
- **1 cup *sifted* GOLD MEDAL Flour**
- **1 tsp. baking powder**
- **1/2 tsp. soda**
- **1 tsp. salt**

and stir in alternately with rolled oats and buttermilk.

Fill greased muffin cups 2/3 full. Bake until golden brown. Serve hot.

TEMPERATURE: 400° (mod. hot oven).

TIME: Bake 20 to 25 min.

AMOUNT: 12 medium-sized muffins.

BEST BRAN MUFFINS

Follow recipe for Oatmeal Muffins above —*except* omit rolled oats. No soaking. Begin with mixing shortening, etc. *After* sifting together dry ingredients, mix with 3 cups bran, stir into shortening mixture alternately with the 1 cup buttermilk.

★ FRENCH BREAKFAST PUFFS

Like delicate, glorified doughnuts. Miss Esoline Beauregard of Fort Lauderdale, Florida said, "Please try my mother's recipe."

Mix together thoroughly . . .
- **1/3 cup soft shortening**
- **1/2 cup sugar**
- **1 egg**

Sift together . . .
- **1 1/2 cups *sifted* GOLD MEDAL Flour**
- **1 1/2 tsp. baking powder**
- **1/2 tsp. salt**
- **1/4 tsp. nutmeg**

and stir in alternately with . . .
- **1/2 cup milk**

Fill greased muffin cups 2/3 full. Bake until golden brown. Immediately roll in...
- **6 tbsp. melted butter**

then in mixture of . . .
- **1/2 cup sugar**
- **1 tsp. cinnamon**

Serve hot.

TEMPERATURE: 350° (mod. oven).

TIME: Bake 20 to 25 min.

AMOUNT: 12 medium-sized muffins.

★ COUNTRY BREAKFAST MUFFINS (Sour Cream)

With that so good flavor and tenderness.

Beat until light . . .
- **1 egg**

Beat in . . .
- **2 tbsp. sugar**
- **1 tbsp. soft shortening**
- **1 cup thick sour cream**

Sift together and stir in . . .
- **1 1/3 cups *sifted* GOLD MEDAL Flour**
- **1 tsp. baking powder**
- **1/2 tsp. soda**
- **1/2 tsp. salt**

Fill greased muffin cups 2/3 full. Bake until golden brown. Serve hot.

TEMPERATURE: 400° (mod. hot oven).

TIME: Bake 20 to 25 min.

AMOUNT: 12 medium-sized muffins.

All you have to do—

To serve muffins piping hot from the oven: mix and fill muffin cups ahead. Let stand in refrigerator until about to serve, then bake. Or get ingredients all measured . . . mix and bake at the last.

DO'S AND DON'TS WITH BISCUITS

First of all

Read through recipe.

Turn on oven so it will preheat to 450° (hot oven).

Assemble ingredients.

Assemble utensils.

Sift flour and measure all dry ingredients into sifter.

1 Sift dry ingredients into mixing bowl. Measure shortening and cut into flour mixture with pastry blender or blending fork until finely blended. Mixture should look like "meal."

2 Stir in almost all the milk. If dough does not seem pliable, add the rest. Use enough to make a soft, puffy dough easy to roll out. Too much milk makes dough sticky, not enough makes biscuits dry.

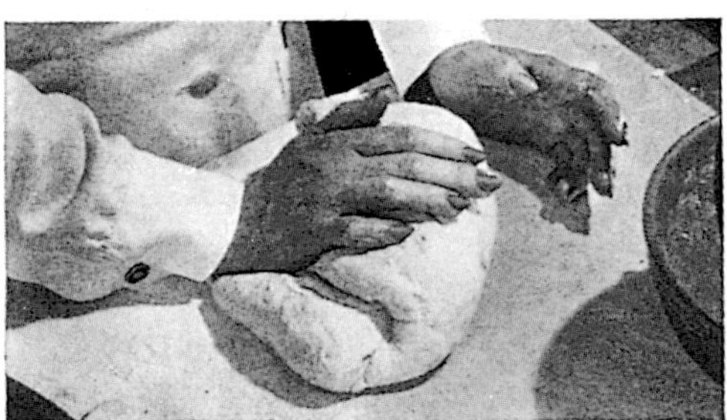

3 Round up on lightly floured cloth-covered board. Knead (fold dough over and press lightly with heel of hand about six times). Handle lightly. Too much handling makes biscuits tough.

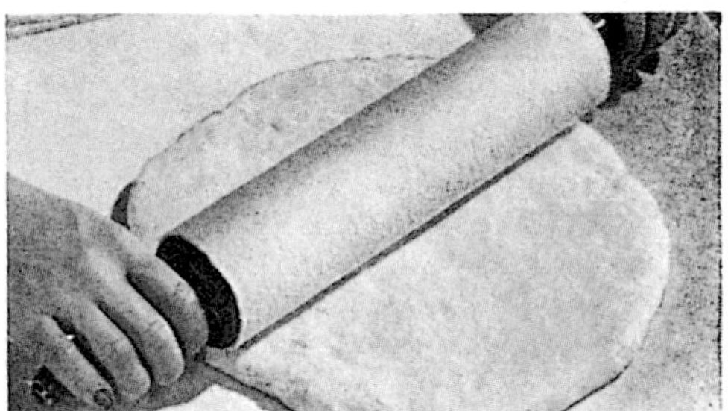

4 Roll dough or pat out (with floured hand) ¼″ thick for thin, crusty biscuits . . ½″ for thick, soft biscuits. "Southern" type are thin and rich; "northern" type are thick, plainer biscuits.

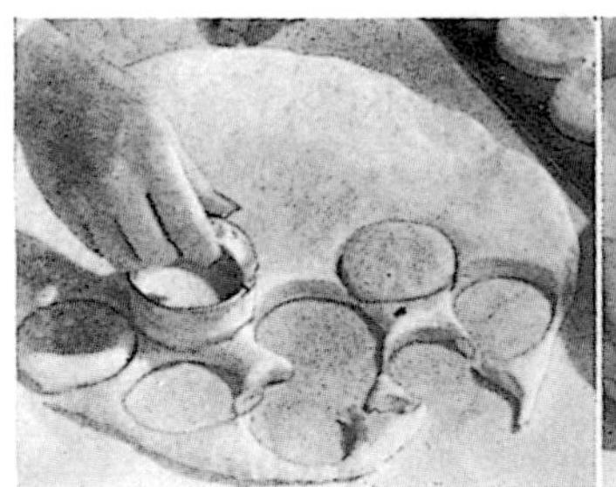

5 Cut close together with floured biscuit cutter. For speed, cut in squares with knife. Fit leftover bits together. Do not reknead. Pat out, roll smooth, and cut as desired.

6 Place close together for soft sides, an inch apart for crusty sides, on ungreased baking sheet. If using pan with sides, invert; bake on bottom.

7 Bake in middle of oven A heavy or shiny pan helps prevent overbrowning biscuits on bottom. Bake until golden brown. Serve immediately. Keep extras hot until needed.

BISCUITS (🔑 Recipe) *The daily bread of earlier days.*

Make either type desired.	*Typical Biscuits*	*Richer Biscuits*
Sift together	2 cups *sifted* GOLD MEDAL Flour	2 cups
	2½ tsp. baking powder	3 tsp.
	1 tsp. salt	1 tsp.
Cut in finely	¼ cup shortening	6 tbsp.
Stir in (to make soft dough)	¾ cup milk	⅔ cup

Round up on lightly floured cloth-covered board. Knead lightly. Roll or pat out about ½″ thick. Cut. Place on ungreased baking sheet. Bake until golden brown. Serve piping hot with butter and also jelly, honey, syrup, etc.

TEMPERATURE: 450° (hot oven).

TIME: Bake 10 to 12 min.

AMOUNT: 20 1¾″ biscuits.

For easy Stir-N-Roll Biscuits, see p. 433.

BUTTERMILK BISCUITS

Follow 🔑 recipe above—*except*, in place of milk, use buttermilk. Use only 2 tsp. baking powder, and add ¼ tsp. soda.

BACON BISCUITS

Perfect with eggs.

Follow 🔑 recipe above—adding ⅓ cup drained cooked bacon bits (about 4 strips) to flour and shortening mixture.

★ CHEESE BISCUITS

Golden and savory . . . with salads.

Follow 🔑 recipe above—adding ½ cup grated dry sharp American cheese to flour and shortening mixture.

CHIVES BISCUITS

A dash of green and taste supreme.

Follow 🔑 recipe above—adding 4 tbsp. minced chives to flour mixture.

HERB BISCUITS

Gourmets' delight . . . with roast meats.

Follow 🔑 recipe above—adding ¼ tsp. dry mustard, ½ tsp. dry sage, and 1¼ tsp. caraway seeds to flour mixture.

CURRY BISCUITS

Super with veal, lamb, chicken, eggs, etc.

Follow 🔑 recipe above—adding ¼ tsp. curry powder to dry ingredients.

To save lighting oven: bake biscuits on lightly greased hot griddle . . . covered. Brown on 1 side 5 min., turn, and bake on other. Or bake in waffle iron.

All you have to do—

To save time and work: make Drop Biscuits.

DROP BISCUITS

Follow 🔑 recipe above—*except* increase milk to 1 cup. Drop from spoon on greased pan or into greased muffin cups.

★ ORANGE TEA BISCUITS

Follow 🔑 recipe above—*except* add grated rind of 1 orange to dry ingredients. Before baking, press ½ cube of loaf sugar, dipped in orange juice, into top of each biscuit.

FILLED BISCUITS

Quick, easy snack for the young people.

Follow 🔑 recipe above—*except* roll dough only ¼″ thick. Place a piece of cheese or a pitted date or a bit of deviled ham, etc. on each biscuit. Fold it over, press edges together. Bake.

WHOLE WHEAT BISCUITS

Follow 🔑 recipe above—*except* substitute ½ cup whole wheat flour for ½ cup of the white flour.

SCONES

A tea-time favorite in the British Isles.

Follow 🔑 recipe above—*except* add 2 tbsp. sugar to dry ingredients; use only ½ cup milk, and add 1 slightly beaten egg. Roll dough ¼″ thick. Cut into triangle and diamond shapes. Place slightly apart on baking sheet. Brush with milk and sprinkle with sugar. Bake

PIGS IN BLANKETS

The "pigs" are sausages wrapped in blankets of fluffy biscuit dough.

Follow recipe for Typical Biscuits (*p. 67*)–*except* roll dough only ¼" thick. Cut into oblong pieces 3"x4". Roll each piece around a wiener or frankfurter, letting tip show at each end. Seal well by pinching edge of dough into roll. Bake with sealed edge underneath, about 15 min. Serve hot with mustard, catsup, or relishes.
AMOUNT: 12 Pigs in Blankets.

TINY PIGS IN BLANKETS

Follow recipe for Pigs in Blankets above —*except* roll dough thinner (⅛"). Cut into 2" squares and wrap around tiny cooked Vienna sausages. Bake 10 min.
AMOUNT: 48 tiny rolls.

RING BISCUITS FOR SHORTCAKES

New twist for an old idea.

Follow recipe for Richer Biscuits (*p. 67*) —*except* cut out half the dough with biscuit cutter, half with doughnut cutter the same size. Bake. Butter plain rounds, cover with creamed chicken, meat, or fish, etc. and place ring-shaped biscuits on top. Garnish center with parsley or jelly.

HOT PIMIENTO CHEESE BISCUITS

Rich golden cheese melting on biscuits makes these special for snacks or salads.

Follow recipe for Typical Biscuits (*p. 67*). Place biscuits a little apart on lightly greased baking sheet. Melt over hot water soft-spreading pimiento cheese (6 to 8 oz. glass) with 2 tbsp. butter. Place a spoonful on each biscuit. Bake. The cheese will run down over it. Serve hot.

SAUCY SUSANS

Pretty pink biscuits savory with cheese.

Follow recipe for Typical Biscuits (*p. 67*)—*except* use tomato juice in place of milk. Roll dough ⅓" thick and put biscuits together in pairs with a round slice of cheese between. Place these double biscuits close together on pan, and bake. Serve hot.

QUICK CINNAMON ROLLS

Try these hot sweet rolls for breakfast, tea, or supper.

Follow recipe for Richer Biscuits (*p. 67*) —*except* roll dough ¼" thick into rectangle 7" x 16". Spread with 2 tbsp. softened butter. Sprinkle with mixture of ¼ cup sugar and 1 tsp. cinnamon and with raisins, if desired. Roll up tightly as for jelly roll, beginning at the wide side. Seal well by pinching edge of dough into roll. Cut into 1" slices. Place cut-side-down on greased baking sheet or in greased muffin cups. Bake at 425° (hot oven) about 15 min. Serve hot.
AMOUNT: 16 Cinnamon Rolls.

★ QUICK BUTTERSCOTCH ROLLS

Extra delish!

Follow recipe for Cinnamon Rolls above —*except* place the rolls in 16 especially prepared medium muffin cups (1 tsp. melted butter, 1 tsp. brown sugar, and 2 or 3 pecan halves in bottom of each). Bake. Serve hot, bottom-side-up.

PARTY PINWHEELS

Tempting tea or salad accompaniments.

Follow recipe for Cinnamon Rolls above —*except* spread dough with soft-spreading cheese or deviled ham or thick marmalade. (A firm filling stays in the rolls.) Bake at 450° (hot oven) about 12 min.

CHEESE ROLLEMUPS

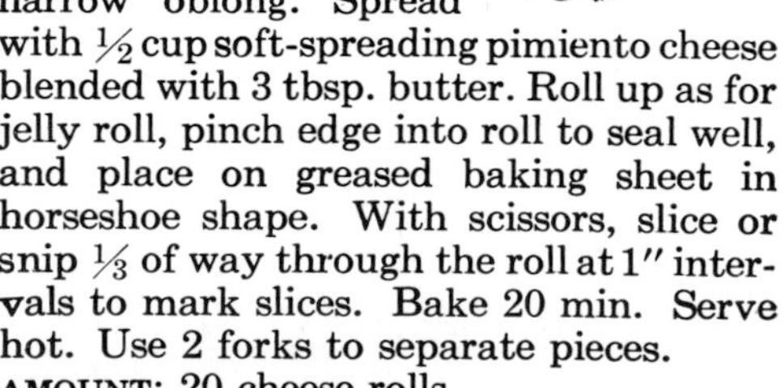

Follow recipe for Richer Biscuits (*p. 67*)—*except* roll dough ¼" thick into narrow oblong. Spread with ½ cup soft-spreading pimiento cheese blended with 3 tbsp. butter. Roll up as for jelly roll, pinch edge into roll to seal well, and place on greased baking sheet in horseshoe shape. With scissors, slice or snip ⅓ of way through the roll at 1" intervals to mark slices. Bake 20 min. Serve hot. Use 2 forks to separate pieces.
AMOUNT: 20 cheese rolls.

YORKSHIRE PUDDING

Follow recipe for Popovers (*p. 69*)—*except* bake in 12x7½x2" baking dish in sizzling hot meat drippings. Cut in squares, serve immediately with roast beef, etc.

POPOVERS

High hat muffins, popped so they are crusty shells, hollow inside.

Beat together just until smooth: 1 cup *sifted* GOLD MEDAL Flour, ½ tsp. salt, 1 cup milk, 2 eggs. Pour into well greased *deep* muffin cups (¾ full) (oven-glass cups make highest popovers). Bake at 425° (hot oven) until golden brown, 35 to 45 min. Serve immediately. AMOUNT: 5 to 9 popovers, depending on size of cup. *It is not necessary to preheat baking cups.*

CORN BREADS QUICK BREADS Truly native to America.

The Indians taught the earliest colonists to parch corn and mix it with boiling water . . . and bake it in thin cakes. These were used by hunters and traders on their long journeys on foot over Indian trails; hence, the name "Journey Cake," later called "Johnny Cake." Almost as many different types of corn bread have been developed as there are different regions in our country. The South prefers white corn meal, the North yellow.

CLUES TO QUICK MIXING OF CORN BREADS

Beat egg. Beat in with rotary beater milk, dry ingredients, soft shortening (bacon fat is good). Beat just until smooth.

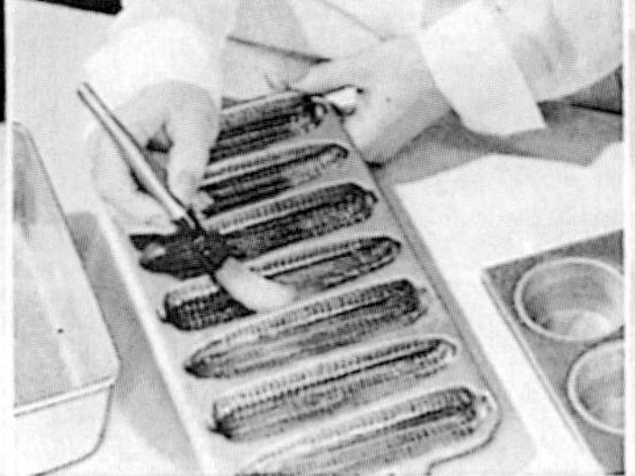

Generously butter 12 corn stick pans, *or* muffin cups, *or* a 9″ square pan (9x9x1¾″). Heat in oven while mixing batter.

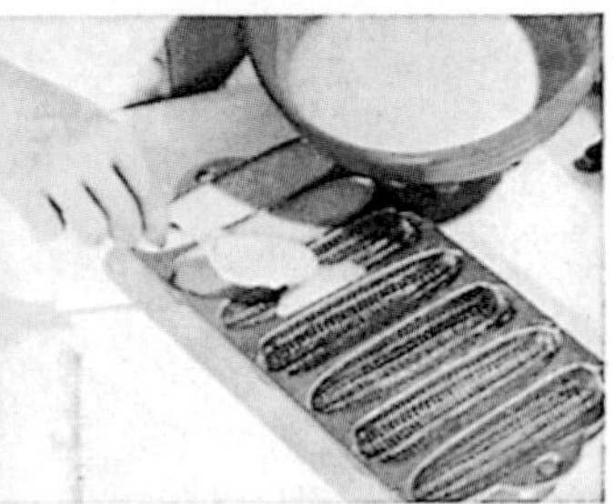

Pour batter into hot pans until *almost* full. If corn breads do not brown, brush with butter, put under broiler a minute.

	★ **Canary Corn Sticks** *From Ohio*	**Corn Cake** *From Kentucky*	**Southern Corn Bread** *From Arkansas*
Beat.......	**1 egg**	**1 egg**	**2 eggs**
Beat in....	**1½ cups buttermilk**	**1⅛ cups milk**	**2 cups buttermilk**
	½ tsp. soda		**1 tsp. soda**
	½ cup *sifted* GOLD MEDAL Flour	**¼ cup *sifted* GOLD MEDAL Flour**	
	1½ cups corn meal	**1¼ cups corn meal**	**2 cups corn meal**
	1 tsp. sugar	**2 tbsp. sugar**	
	3 tsp. baking powder	**3 tsp. baking powder**	
	1 tsp. salt	**1 tsp. salt**	**1 tsp. salt**
	¼ cup soft shortening	**3 tbsp. soft shortening**	

Pour or spoon into buttered hot square pan, muffin cups, or corn stick pans (*see above*). Bake just until set. Serve piping hot with butter. Cut corn breads (baked in square pan) into squares. Keep hot in pan until served.

TEMPERATURE: 450° (hot oven).

TIME: Bake 10 to 15 min. for corn sticks or muffins; 20 to 25 min. for corn bread.

AMOUNT: 12 muffins, corn sticks, or pieces.

BACON CORN BREAD

Follow recipe for Southern Corn Bread above—*except* add ⅓ cup diced crisply cooked bacon at the last, or lay short slices of partially cooked bacon on top of batter in pan (one piece to each serving). Bake.

PLANTATION SHORTCAKE

Serve Creamed Chicken over Corn Bread.

OLD-TIME JOHNNY CAKES

From Rhode Island . . . meal ground on stones.

Beat *1 egg.* Stir in *2 cups water-ground corn meal, 1 tsp. salt, 1¼ to 1½ cups milk* (to make thick batter). Drop spoonfuls of batter onto a well greased hot griddle and fry to a golden brown on each side. Stir batter occasionally to keep well mixed. Serve hot with butter.

AMOUNT: 12 Johnny Cakes.

Hoe Cake and Corn Pone were the first simple forms of corn bread in the South . . . simply corn meal mixed with water, salted, and baked. Hoe Cake was baked on a plank (or the cotton hoe) on hot embers. Pones were the "appones" of the Indians, shaped with the hands into small cakes, baked before the fire. Spoon Bread was evolved when an old-time Virginia cook put a dish of corn meal mush into the oven.

BATTER BREAD

Soft and moist . . . custardy . . . delicious. Upholds the fame of southern cookery. Traditional choice with roe herring.

Beat . . .
- **1 egg**

Beat in . .
- **¾ cup white corn meal**
- **½ tsp. soda**
- **½ tsp. salt**
- **1½ cups buttermilk**

Pour into hot 1-qt. casserole or baking dish with 1 tbsp. butter melted in it. Bake just until set. Serve hot with butter or gravy.

TEMPERATURE: 400° (mod. hot oven).

TIME: Bake 20 to 25 min.

AMOUNT: 6 servings.

HUSH PUPPIES

Toothsome morsels from Florida hunters. When they sat around their camp fish-fries, their hunting dogs would whine for the good smelling food. The men tossed leftover corn patties to them calling, "Hush, puppies!" Satisfied, the dogs hushed. These crispy little corn cakes make a hit at Daytona Beach, Florida, served with fried shrimp and cole slaw.

Beat together . . .
- **3 cups corn meal**
- **2 tsp. baking powder**
- **1½ tsp. salt**
- **1½ cups milk**
- **½ cup water**

Blend in . . .
- **1 egg, if desired**
- **1 onion, finely chopped, if desired**

With hands, mold mixture into little cakes (about 1 tbsp. each) and fry in about 1″ deep fat (*see p. 78*) until well browned (1½ min. on each side). Drain on paper. Serve very hot.

AMOUNT: 2 doz.

★ SPOON BREAD

From a wonderful cook and friend, Mrs. Belle Tedford of Richmond, Virginia. Spooned from the pan, this is served as a breakfast hot bread with butter and maple syrup or with the main course at dinner in place of bread or potatoes. Virginians love it with fried tomatoes.

Pour . . .
- **1 cup boiling water**

over . . .
- **½ cup white corn meal**

Beat in . . .
- **½ cup milk**
- **½ tsp. salt**
- **1½ tsp. baking powder**
- **1 tbsp. soft butter**
- **2 eggs, well beaten**

Pour into buttered 1-qt. casserole or baking dish. Bake just until set. Serve piping hot with butter.

TEMPERATURE: 400° (mod. hot oven).

TIME: Bake 20 to 25 min.

AMOUNT: 6 servings.

SOUTHERN CORN MUFFINS

From Mrs. Virginia McDonald who made her tea room at Gallatin, Missouri, the mecca for travelers from near and far.

Pour . . .
- **1 cup boiling water**

over . . .
- **1 cup white corn meal**

Beat in . . .
- **½ cup milk**
- **½ tsp. salt**
- **2 tsp. baking powder**
- **1 tbsp. soft butter**
- **1 egg, well beaten**

Pour into very *well* greased glass muffin cups. Bake in very hot oven. Serve hot.

TEMPERATURE: 475° (very hot oven).

TIME: Bake 25 to 30 min.

AMOUNT: 9 medium-sized muffins.

PANCAKES QUICK BREADS Griddle Cakes...Wheat Cakes...Pancakes

One of the earliest forms of baking . . . once called "hearth cakes" . . . now known by many names. They vary from hearty buckwheat cakes to the delicate dessert cakes. But whatever the kind, the cakes should be light, tender, and uniformly golden brown. The Dutch settlers brought pancakes to America. Later, the Germans in Pennsylvania served pancakes for breakfast, supper, and noonday meals.

PEEKS AT PANCAKES

A *heavy griddle* is best for even browning of cakes (soapstone is ideal). *Modern* griddles require no greasing . . . follow directions.

Heat griddle while mixing batter. To test, sprinkle with drops of water. If bubbles "skitter around," heat is just right, and cakes will brown immediately.

Pour batter from tip of *large* spoon (one pouring) or from pitcher, in pools a little apart (for perfectly round cakes). If it is necessary, grease griddle very lightly.

MAKE PANCAKES

thick or thin, as desired. It is easy to adjust batter. Make thinner by adding a little liquid; make thicker by adding a little flour.

A thick batter makes thick cakes.

A thin batter makes thin cakes.

Turn pancakes as soon as they are puffed and full of bubbles, *but before they break* . . . important for light cakes. Turn and brown on other side.

If batter has to stand a long time: add a little extra baking powder.

Keep pancakes hot for desserts, etc., place between folds of warm towel in warm oven.

FRENCH TOAST

Dip 6 slices stale bread into mixture of 2 beaten eggs, $\frac{1}{4}$ tsp. salt, $\frac{1}{2}$ cup milk. Brown both sides in butter on griddle.

FAVORITE PANCAKES (🔑 Recipe) *The good old-fashioned kind . . . of sour milk.*

Heat griddle slowly while mixing batter.

Beat well	1 egg
Beat in	1¼ cups buttermilk or sour milk ½ tsp. soda
Then beat in	1¼ cups *sifted* GOLD MEDAL Flour 1 tsp. sugar 2 tbsp. soft shortening 1 tsp. baking powder ½ tsp. salt

Beat with rotary beater until smooth. Bake as directed on p. 72.

AMOUNT: 16 4″ pancakes.

WHEATIES PANCAKES

Follow 🔑 recipe above—and fold in 1 cup WHEATIES at the last.

BLUEBERRY PANCAKES

Follow 🔑 recipe above—and add ½ cup drained fresh or frozen berries to batter, folding in carefully at the last.

NUT PANCAKES

Follow 🔑 recipe above—and add ¼ cup broken or chopped nuts to batter.

The French Colonists of Carolina and Louisiana used rice and hominy as the foundation for many breads and batter foods, such as pancakes. But both North and South claimed Buckwheat Cakes for their own.

SWEET MILK PANCAKES

Follow 🔑 recipe above—*except* substitute sweet milk for buttermilk, add an extra ½ tsp. of baking powder, and omit soda. For extra lightness, beat egg yolks, add milk, etc. Fold in stiffly beaten egg whites.

SOUTHERN CORN CAKES

Follow 🔑 recipe above—*except,* in place of the flour, use ¾ cup corn meal and only ¼ cup flour.

To make George Washington's Mother's Ferry Farm Sauce: heat together slowly over hot water 1 cup strained honey and ½ cup maple syrup. Remove from heat and blend in 1 tsp. cinnamon.

★ OLD-FASHIONED BUCKWHEAT CAKES *From Mary who cooked "with love."*

They bring memories of cozy comfort at the fireside of Hilda and Henry Maust, famous artist in Woodstock, New York . . . who painted so many of our beautiful food pictures.

Dissolve	1 cake compressed yeast
in	½ cup lukewarm water
Add	2 cups cold water
Sift together and stir in	1 cup *sifted* GOLD MEDAL Flour 2 cups buckwheat flour 1½ tsp. salt
Beat vigorously until smooth. Cover, and place in refrigerator overnight. In morning, stir in	1 tbsp. molasses ¼ cup butter, melted 1 tsp. soda dissolved in ½ cup hot water

Let stand at room temperature for 30 min. Bake as directed on p. 72.

AMOUNT: 36 4″ pancakes.

To use batter as a starter for another batch: Save out . . . 1 cup of batter (before adding molasses, butter, soda). Add . . . *1 cup cold water,* cover, and place in refrigerator until night before you wish to use it. Then, pour off water which has risen to top. Blend in the amount of flours and salt as in original recipe. Add . . . *2½ cups cold water,* cover, and let stand that night. In morning, stir in the molasses, butter, soda, and hot water as in original recipe. Let stand 30 min., and bake.

★ DELICATE FLUFFY PANCAKES

Most elegant pancakes you've ever tasted or that we've discovered in years of testing. From a wonderful cook, Mrs. Marian Bucholz of Los Angeles and Omaha.

Beat well with rotary beater . . .
- **3 egg yolks**

Beat in . . .
- **1⅔ cups thick buttermilk**
- **1 tsp. soda**

Sift together and beat in . . .
- **1½ cups *sifted* GOLD MEDAL Flour**
- **1 tbsp. sugar**
- **1 tsp. baking powder**
- **½ tsp. salt**

Beat in . . .
- **3 tbsp. soft butter**

Gently fold in . . .
- **3 egg whites, stiffly beaten**

Bake as directed on p. 72.

AMOUNT: 16 4″ pancakes.

★ OATMEAL PANCAKES

From Mrs. Robert Rypinski of Pasadena, California, who says, "My two boys love them. They're not a bit rich, but they taste so delicious everyone raves about them."

Mix together . . .
- **1½ cups rolled oats**
- **2 cups buttermilk**

Beat in . . .
- **½ cup *sifted* GOLD MEDAL Flour**
- **1 tsp. sugar**
- **1 tsp. soda**
- **1 tsp. salt**
- **2 eggs, beaten**

NOTE: Rolled oats as manufactured these days do not require the soaking often required for old-fashioned oatmeal.

Bake as directed on p. 72. (This is a thin batter, right for oatmeal.)

AMOUNT: 12 4″ pancakes.

WAYS TO SERVE PANCAKES FOR DESSERT

Jelly Roll Pancakes: Thin cakes spread with jelly, rolled up, dusted with confectioners' sugar.

Colonial Cake Stack: Six plate-sized pancakes with butter, sugar, and cinnamon; or butter and jelly between. Sugar on top.

★ FRENCH PANCAKES

Thin but tender. From Mrs. Arden Bucholz, Wheaton, Illinois, who, for years, contributed so much to our service.

Heat together in saucepan . . .
- **1 cup milk**
- **2 tbsp. butter**

When slightly cooled, beat in . . .
- **2 eggs, beaten**
- **½ cup *sifted* GOLD MEDAL Flour**
- **1 tsp. baking powder**
- **½ tsp. salt**

Beat until smooth. Bake (*see below*). Serve as dessert pancakes.

AMOUNT: 30 3″ cakes.

All you have to do—

To bake thin pancakes easily: grease a 4″ or 5″ skillet lightly. Heat, pour in batter to coat bottom. Tilt skillet to cover evenly. Cook 1 min. Loosen with spatula and "flip" onto heated griddle. Turn several times until a delicate brown.

SWEDISH PANCAKES "Plättar" (Little Plates)

Follow recipe for French Pancakes. Bake small cakes (3″) on Swedish griddle (with indentations) *or* see below. Arrange a ring of 6 or 7 overlapping cakes on dessert plate; in center, a spoonful of lingonberries or jam, a fluff of whipped cream.

PANCAKES IN ORANGE SAUCE

Luscious! Idea brought from a resort by Mrs. Norman Mitchell of Minneapolis.

Heat thin pancakes in Orange Sauce: melt ⅓ cup butter, blend in 2 tbsp. sugar, ⅓ cup orange juice, and a dash of grated orange rind. Roll cakes around sweetened strawberries, if desired.

Crepes Suzettes are thin French pancakes heated in a special sauce of butter, sugar, grated orange peel, cointreau, and brandy. The brandy is burned off and the cakes are rolled in the sauce.

The first waffle is said to have been made in 13th century England. A crusader wearing his armor accidentally sat in some freshly baked oat cakes. The cakes were flattened and bore deep imprints of the steel links. However, he spread butter on the cakes and ate them. His wife, delighted with the way butter stayed in the imprints from the armor, made him put it on once a week and sit on fresh oat cakes. They were called "warfres," meaning flat honeycomb-like cakes.

Dutch colonists brought their cherished "waffre" irons to America. They were long handled and very heavy to hold over an open fire.

HOW TO BAKE. Most waffle irons require no greasing after first tempering. Follow directions. Heat while mixing batter. If no automatic heat control, test by sprinkling grids with drops of water. If water "skitters around" before evaporating, iron is just right.

POUR batter from cup or pitcher into center of hot waffle iron. If batter is thick, spread to cover surface. Do not keep iron open longer than necessary. Bake until steaming stops. Lift off waffle carefully with fork. Serve hot with butter and syrup or other spreads.

Nut Waffles . . . special for supper.

WAFFLES (🔑 Recipe) *Crisp pancakes with tucks in them.*

	Typical Waffles	*Richer Waffles*
Heat waffle iron while mixing batter.		
Beat well	**2 eggs**	**3 eggs**
Beat in	**2 cups buttermilk or sour milk**	**1½ cups**
	1 tsp. soda	**1 tsp.**
	2 cups *sifted* GOLD MEDAL Flour	**1¾ cups**
	2 tsp. baking powder	**2 tsp.**
	½ tsp. salt	**½ tsp.**
	***6 tbsp. soft shortening**	**½ cup**

Beat until smooth. This is a thin batter. Bake in hot waffle iron.
*Fresh bacon fat is good in waffles.

AMOUNT: 8 waffles.

SWEET MILK WAFFLES

Follow either 🔑 recipe above—*except* omit soda and use 4 tsp. baking powder; substitute sweet milk for sour milk; and separate eggs. Beat egg whites until stiff and fold in last.

★ NUT WAFFLES

Follow either 🔑 recipe above. Sprinkle 2 tbsp. coarsely cut or broken toasted nuts over batter as soon as it has been poured into iron. Bake.

BLUEBERRY WAFFLES

Follow 🔑 recipe for Richer Waffles above. Sprinkle 2 tbsp. fresh berries or well drained canned berries over batter as soon as it has been poured into the iron. Bake.

CHEESE AND BACON WAFFLES

Follow 🔑 recipe for Typical Waffles above—and fold ½ cup grated American cheese into batter. Pour into iron. Lay short strip of bacon across batter. Bake.

DOUGHNUTS QUICK BREADS How to fry in deep fat.

AFTER MIXING BATTER OR DOUGH . . melt fat for deep fat frying in a heavy kettle or deep fat fryer. Have fat 3″ to 4″ deep. Heat to 390° (*a cube of bread browns in fat in 40 sec.*).

The fat cools some when foods are dropped in—it should be 370° to 380° while foods are frying. If fat is too hot, foods brown before they cook through. If too cool, they become grease-soaked.

DOUGHNUT DIPLOMACY

1 Turn part of dough onto floured cloth-covered board. Keep the rest chilled. Turn dough to lightly cover with flour.

2 Roll out gently ⅓″ thick. Cut with floured sharp doughnut cutter. Take board close to kettle to transfer doughnuts easily.

3 Lift doughnuts on wide spatula, slide quickly into hot fat. Fry as many at a time as can be turned easily.

4 Turn doughnuts as they rise to surface and show a little color. Fry about 3 min. to completely brown on both sides.

5 Lift from fat with long fork. Do not prick doughnuts. Drain over kettle, place on absorbent paper in warm place.

Keep fat to use again:
Clarify fat with raw potato in it (4 slices to 1 qt.). When fat bubbles, strain into jar or can through 2 or 3 thicknesses of cheesecloth, over wire strainer. (The potato absorbs flavors and collects sediment, the remainder settling to the bottom.) Keep in refrigerator in light-proof, tight, covered container.

Known in England in 1536 as "imported doughty cakes," doughnuts were brought to this country by Dutch and English settlers. Originally balls or nuts of yeast dough, the Yankees found a quicker way. Doughnuts were as popular with soldiers of the Revolutionary War as they were with the "doughboys" of World War I. and the G.I.'s of World War II. They are hearty and heartening.

FAVORITE DOUGHNUTS (🔑 Recipe) *The best of old New England recipes.*

Beat well	4 egg yolks (or 2 whole eggs)
Beat in	1 cup sugar 2 tbsp. soft shortening
Stir in	3/4 cup thick buttermilk or sour milk
Sift together and stir in	3 1/2 cups *sifted* GOLD MEDAL Flour 2 tsp. baking powder 1 tsp. soda 1/2 tsp. salt 1/4 tsp. nutmeg 1/4 tsp. cinnamon

Chill dough 2 hr. Heat fat while rolling and cutting doughnuts (*see pictures on opposite page*). Fry until brown. Drain over kettle, then on absorbent paper in warm place. Serve plain, sugared, or glazed.

NOTE: The amount and kind of spice may be varied to suit individual taste. 2 tsp. vanilla may be used in place of spices.
TEMPERATURE OF FAT: 370° to 380°.
AMOUNT: 2 doz. 3" doughnuts.

SWEET MILK DOUGHNUTS

Follow 🔑 recipe above—*except* use sweet milk in place of sour milk; use 4 tsp. baking powder, and omit soda.

★POTATO DOUGHNUTS

Tender and light, with delicious flavor.

No milk; when mashing potatoes, set aside 1 cup. Follow 🔑 recipe above for method but use:

3 eggs
3/4 cup sugar
3 tbsp. soft shortening
2 3/4 cups *sifted* GOLD MEDAL Flour
4 tsp. baking powder
1 tsp. salt
1/4 tsp. nutmeg
1 tsp. mace
1 cup mashed potato (unseasoned)

AMOUNT: 3 doz. 2 1/2" doughnuts.

TO SUGAR DOUGHNUTS: Just before serving, shake doughnuts one at a time in a paper bag with a little confectioners' or granulated sugar.

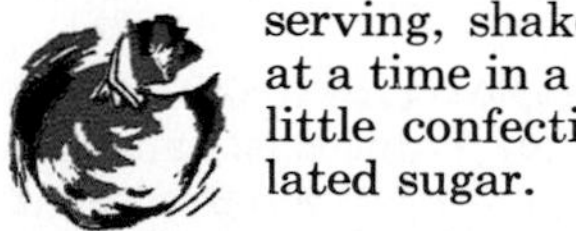

TO COAT WITH NUTS AND SUGAR: Dip warm doughnuts into warm glaze (*see right*), then into mixture of 1/2 cup finely chopped nuts, 1/2 cup sugar, and 1 tsp. cinnamon.

★ORANGE DROP DOUGHNUTS

Exciting and different for "coffee and doughnuts" or afternoon tea.

Beat . . .
2 eggs
Beat in . . .
1/2 cup sugar
2 tbsp. soft shortening
Sift together . . .
2 cups *sifted* GOLD MEDAL Flour
2 tsp. baking powder
1/4 tsp. salt
Stir in alternately with . . .
1/2 cup orange juice
2 tbsp. grated orange rind

Drop by small *tea*spoonfuls into hot fat (375°). Use 2 spoons, dipping them in the fat first to allow dough to slide easily off spoons. Turn to brown evenly. Lift from fat with slotted spoon.

AMOUNT: 3 doz. 1 1/2" doughnuts.

TO GLAZE DOUGHNUTS: Add 1/3 cup boiling water gradually to 1 cup confectioners' sugar. Mix well. Dip warm doughnuts into the warm glaze.

FRITTERS QUICK BREADS Food fantasies fried in deep fat.

FRITTERS (🔑 **Recipe**) *Patties or balls of batter-covered fruit or vegetables, fried in deep fat . . . served as a meat accompaniment.*

Prepare *Fritter Batter* (to bind together fruit or vegetables):

Beat	2 eggs
Stir in	½ cup milk
Sift together and beat in	1 cup *sifted* GOLD MEDAL Flour 1 tsp. baking powder 1 tsp. salt
Beat in	1 tsp. melted fat or cooking (salad) oil

Cut up fruit or vegetables (*see below*). Add to or dip in Fritter Batter. Drop into hot deep fat and fry at 375° until brown. Drain and serve hot with syrup or gravy.

TEMPERATURE OF FAT: 375°.

AMOUNT: 12 to 15 small fritters.

CORN FRITTERS

Follow 🔑 recipe above—adding 1 cup grated-off-cob cooked corn or drained canned whole kernel corn to Fritter Batter. Drop by spoonfuls into hot fat.

APPLE OR BANANA FRITTERS

Follow 🔑 recipe above, dipping apple slices (crosswise) or banana quarters into Fritter Batter. Drop into hot fat.

FRENCH FRIED ONIONS

Follow 🔑 recipe above, dipping rings of *mild* onions (sliced ¼″ thick) into Fritter Batter. Drop rings into hot fat.

★FRENCH FRITTERS (Creole Beignets)

A French delicacy from New Orleans . . . fresh fruits coated with a thin, crisp covering—served for dessert.

Sprinkle cut-up fruits (figs, pears, orange, pineapple, or apple slices) with sugar and grated lemon rind. Let stand 2 to 3 hr. Drain and dip into Thin Fritter Batter (*below*). Fry in deep fat at 375°. Drain and serve hot with confectioners' sugar or a sweet syrup or sauce.

THIN FRITTER BATTER

Beat together with rotary beater . . .
- 2 egg yolks
- ⅔ cup milk
- 1 cup *sifted* GOLD MEDAL Flour
- ½ tsp. salt
- 1 tbsp. butter, melted
- 2 tbsp. lemon juice

Fold in . . .
- 2 egg whites, stiffly beaten

TIMBALE CASES AND ROSETTES

Cases are for creamed meat, fish, or vegetables. Rosettes are for dessert or tea . . . sprinkle with confectioners' sugar.

Sift together . . .
- ½ cup *sifted* GOLD MEDAL Flour
- 1 tbsp. sugar
- ½ tsp. salt

Mix together and stir in . . .
- ½ cup water or milk
- 1 egg, slightly beaten
- 1 tbsp. cooking (salad) oil

Strain mixture. Heat timbale or rosette iron in hot fat (400°) 3″ deep in small saucepan. Tap off excess fat on absorbent paper. Dip into batter until ⅔ covered. Immerse in hot fat. Fry until delicately browned. Remove, tip upside-down to drain. Push off case. Stir batter each time before dipping in iron.

AMOUNT: 18 timbale cases or rosettes.

All you have to do—

If rosettes don't come off iron: fry a little longer. If not crisp, fry a little slower.

CHICKEN, MEAT, OR FISH FRIED WITH BATTER

Dip pieces of cooked meat, fish, frog legs, or chicken into Fritter Batter (*above*) and fry in deep fat until golden brown.

FRENCH FRIED BREAD

Dip slices of bread into Fritter Batter and fry in deep fat until brown.

DUMPLINGS (⚷ Recipe)

Puffs as light as thistledown . . . with flavorful stews, they bring renown. Cooking half time uncovered is the newest and best method.

Sift together	1½ cups *sifted* GOLD MEDAL Flour 2 tsp. baking powder ¾ tsp. salt
Cut in	3 tbsp. shortening
Stir in only until blended	¾ cup milk

Drop by spoonfuls *onto* chicken or meat in boiling meat stock (not in liquid). Cook 10 min. with kettle uncovered, and 10 min. tightly covered.

Remove dumplings and meat to hot platter. Keep hot while making gravy. Pour part of gravy around them. Serve remainder separately.

★ PARSLEY OR CHIVES OR HERB DUMPLINGS

Follow ⚷ recipe above—*except* add 3 tbsp. minced parsley, chives, or herbs, such as fresh sage, thyme, savory, (or a mixture), to the sifted dry ingredients.

CHEESE DUMPLINGS

Follow ⚷ recipe—*except* add ¼ cup grated sharp cheese to sifted dry ingredients.

All you have to do –

If you don't want to steam brown bread: try this modern version—baked:

QUICK BROWN BREAD

Sift together . . .
- 1½ cups *sifted* GOLD MEDAL Flour
- 2½ tsp. soda
- 1½ tsp. salt

Mix in . . .
- 2 cups fine dry bread crumbs

Add, and cut in with pastry blender until mixture looks like meal . . .
- ⅓ cup shortening

Combine and stir in until well blended . . .
- 2 eggs, well beaten
- 2 cups buttermilk or sour milk
- 1 cup molasses
- 1 cup seedless raisins

Pour into well greased 13x9″ oblong pan or three 8½x4½″ bread loaf pans. Bake until wooden pick thrust into center comes out clean. Serve hot with butter to accompany baked beans.
TEMPERATURE: 400° (mod. hot oven).
TIME: Bake 25 to 30 min.

STEAMED BROWN BREAD

Of old—was always served with Baked Beans.

Mix together . . .
- 1 cup rye flour or *sifted* GOLD MEDAL Flour
- 1 cup corn meal
- 1 cup whole wheat flour
- 2 tsp. soda
- 1 tsp. salt

Stir in . . .
- ¾ cup molasses
- 2 cups sour milk or buttermilk

Beat well. Fill greased molds ⅔ full (using two 1-lb. coffee cans or one 7″ tube-center mold). Lay waxed paper over the top. Steam 3 hr. (For method, *see Steamed Puddings, p. 228.*) Serve piping hot with butter.

STEAMING TIPS

If you don't have a steamer, improvise one with large kettle. Place mold above water line by placing it on rack set on cups, etc.

Cover steamer tightly. Do not lift cover until end of steaming unless water must be added, then quickly add boiling water.

CAUTION: Do not use a double boiler as a steamer unless recipe calls for it. It does not allow the steam to circulate completely around the mold of bread or pudding.

SUPPER IN THE GARDEN

When good food and good company meet.

Baked Beans and Steamed Brown Bread   Pigs in Blankets with Piccalilli
Fresh Vegetable Relishes   White Nut Loaf   Doughnuts   Fruit   Coffee

★WHITE NUT LOAF (🔑 Recipe) *Quick, easy to make, inexpensive.*

Mix together thoroughly............... { ¾ cup sugar, 2 tbsp. soft shortening, 1 egg }
Stir in............................... 1½ cups milk
Sift together and stir in............. { 3 cups *sifted* GOLD MEDAL Flour, 3½ tsp. baking powder, 1 tsp. salt }
Blend in.............................. ¾ cup chopped nuts

Pour into well greased 9x5x3″ loaf pan. Let stand 20 min. before baking. Bake until wooden pick thrust into center comes out clean. Serve warm or cold.

NOTE: Cut with thin, sharp knife to prevent crumbling.

TEMPERATURE: 350° (mod. oven)

TIME: Bake 60 to 70 min.

FIG OR DATE NUT LOAF

Follow 🔑 recipe above—*except* substitute brown sugar for white sugar, and add ¾ cup chopped dates or figs with the nuts. Increase baking time about 10 min.

WHOLE WHEAT NUT LOAF

Follow 🔑 recipe above—*except* substitute 2 cups whole wheat flour for 2 cups of the white flour. If desired, add ½ cup chopped figs or dates with nuts.

FRUIT LOAF (🔑 Recipe) *A moist loaf with a delicate fresh fruit flavor.*

Mix together thoroughly............... { ⅔ cup sugar, ⅓ cup soft shortening, 2 eggs }
Stir in............................... { 3 tbsp. sour milk or buttermilk, 1 cup grated apple (unpared) or other fruit }
Sift together and stir in............. { 2 cups *sifted* GOLD MEDAL Flour, 1 tsp. baking powder, ½ tsp. soda, ½ tsp. salt }
Blend in.............................. ½ cup chopped nuts

Pour into well greased 9x5x3″ loaf pan. Let stand 20 min. before baking. Bake until it tests done. Serve warm or cold.

TEMPERATURE: 350° (mod. oven).

TIME: Bake 50 to 60 min.

APPLESAUCE LOAF

Follow 🔑 recipe above—*except* use brown sugar, not white; use applesauce in place of grated apple. Omit sour milk.

ORANGE DATE LOAF

Follow 🔑 recipe for Fruit Loaf above—*except* omit sour milk; in place of the 1 cup apple, use the juice and pulp from 1 orange with enough water to make 1 cup. Add 1 cup cut-up dates.

PRUNE LOAF

Follow 🔑 recipe above—*except* omit sour milk; use ¾ cup prune juice. Substitute 1 cup cut-up drained cooked prunes for apple. Add 2 tsp. grated lemon rind with prunes. Bake about 10 min. longer.

BANANA LOAF

Follow 🔑 recipe above—*except* substitute 1 cup mashed bananas (mashed with fork or pastry blender) for apple.

DATE AND NUT LOAF

Extra moist, delicious. Served by Mrs. Jack Bruce of Winnetka, Illinois, at a buffet supper.

Pour 1½ cups boiling water over . . .
1½ cups cut-up dates and let cool.

Follow 🔑 recipe above for method, but use:
{ ½ cup brown sugar, 1 tbsp. soft shortening, 1 egg }
the dates and water
{ 2¼ cups *sifted* GOLD MEDAL Flour, 1 tsp. soda, ½ tsp. salt }
1 cup broken nuts

COFFEE CAKES QUICK BREADS For breakfast, lunch, or supper.

PRIZE COFFEE CAKE (🔑 Recipe) *The foundation costume for many delightful changes to fit every occasion.*

Mix together thoroughly...............	¾ cup sugar ¼ cup soft shortening 1 egg
Stir in...............................	½ cup milk
Sift together and stir in...............	1½ cups *sifted* GOLD MEDAL Flour 2 tsp. baking powder ½ tsp. salt

Spread batter in greased and floured 9″ square pan. Sprinkle with desired topping (*see below*). Bake until wooden pick thrust into center of cake comes out clean. Serve warm, fresh from the oven.

TEMPERATURE: 375° (quick mod. oven).

TIME: Bake 25 to 35 min.

AMOUNT: 9 3″ squares.

CINNAMON COFFEE CAKE

Tempting, spicy, fragrant, delicious. Brought from Isle Royal by Esther Scarborough (now Mrs. Edgar Chapman) of Minneapolis.

Follow 🔑 recipe above—sprinkling top with a mixture of ½ cup brown sugar and 1½ tsp. cinnamon.

★ STREUSEL-FILLED COFFEE CAKE

The rich cinnamony mixture in the middle makes elegant eating.

Follow 🔑 recipe above—*except* spread only half the batter in pan. Sprinkle with half the Streusel Mixture (*below*). Add the remaining batter, and sprinkle remaining Streusel over top.

STREUSEL MIXTURE

Mix together . . .

- ½ cup brown sugar
- 2 tbsp. flour
- 2 tsp. cinnamon
- 2 tbsp. butter, melted
- ½ cup chopped nuts

HOLIDAY COFFEE CAKE

Gay and colorful with Christmas fruit.

Follow 🔑 recipe above—sprinkling top with ⅓ cup moist cut-up candied fruit, ½ tsp. cinnamon mixed into 3 tbsp. sugar.

QUICK APPLE CAKE

Follow 🔑 recipe above—*except* arrange apple slices in fancy design on top of batter, pressing them slightly into batter, then sprinkle top with 1 tsp. cinnamon mixed with 2 tbsp. sugar. For Christmas, use red cinnamon candies.

★ BLUEBERRY BUCKLE

The best of old-time Blueberry Tea Cakes. Wonderful for summer-time Sunday breakfast. Makes a luscious, fruity, homey dessert.

Follow 🔑 recipe above—*except* use 2 cups flour and carefully blend in at the last 2 cups well drained blueberries. Sprinkle top with *Crumb Mixture:*

Mix together . . .

- ½ cup sugar
- ⅓ cup *sifted* GOLD MEDAL Flour
- ½ tsp. cinnamon
- ¼ cup soft butter

Bake 45 to 50 min.

ORANGE COFFEE CAKE

Refreshing orange flavor, always a favorite.

Follow 🔑 recipe above—*except* use orange juice for half of the milk, and add 1½ tsp. grated orange rind. Sprinkle top with Crumb Mixture (*given just above*), adding to it 1½ tsp. grated orange rind.

MARMALADE COFFEE CAKE

Follow 🔑 recipe above—spreading top with *Marmalade Mixture* of: ½ cup brown sugar, ½ cup *sifted* GOLD MEDAL Flour, 2 tbsp. butter, 1 tbsp. cream, ½ cup orange marmalade. (Topping melts down through the cake during baking.)

PINEAPPLE COFFEE CAKE

Follow 🔑 recipe above—spreading top with mixture of: 2 tbsp. softened butter, 2 tbsp. honey, and ½ cup well drained crushed pineapple.

Bread - the Symbol of Hope, Home, and Hospitality

THE poem below entitled "Our Daily Bread," by Grace Noll Crowell, expresses beautifully just what we would like to say.

Betty Crocker

An ancient rite, as old as life is old:
A woman baking bread above a flame.
Its value is far greater than pure gold,
It is ageless, timeless, and the simple name
Of bread is wholesome as the summer sun
That has lit and warmed the fields that men might eat;
It is as clean as are the winds that run
Their light-foot way across the waving wheat.

A loaf is only half a loaf unless
We share it, and unless we say
Our grace above it, asking God to bless
The bread that He has given day by day.
O women, handle flour as you should!
It is a thing God-given, priceless, good.

Breads

Luncheon and Dinner Rolls

Holiday Breads

Sweet Rolls

Coffee Cakes, Braids, and Fancy Loaves

Doughnuts

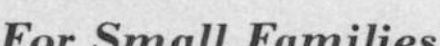

Simplified Yeast Breads

For Small Families

Make *half* of any of these recipes (just take ½ of each ingredient). The rising and baking time will be about the same.

When the half recipe would use just ½ yeast cake, (rather than keeping a half) it is more practical to use the whole cake. It will shorten rising time!

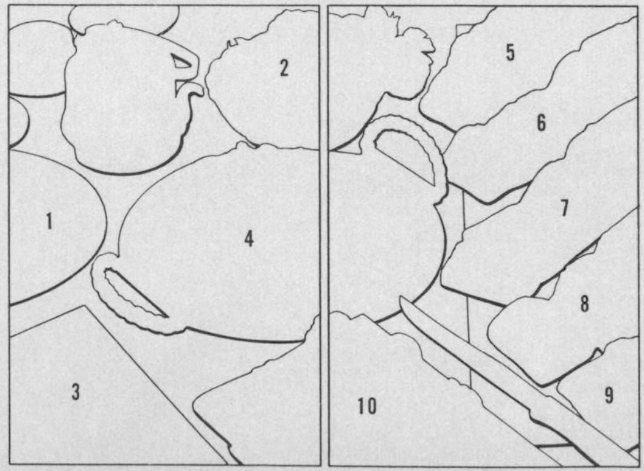

Where to find recipes for Yeast Breads in color photograph, pp. 86, 87

YEAST BREADS

Bread has influenced history more than any other food. It has played an important role in the rise and fall of civilizations, and each nation has its own distinctive breads . . . developed to fit the customs and traditions of the land. The memory of a cozy kitchen filled with the warm fragrance of freshly baked bread *still* means home. It is unforgettable . . . the delight and satisfaction of . . . that tantalizing yeasty aroma . . . the crunch of the golden crust as the knife cuts through . . . the full wheaty flavor of the buttered slice.

Today that warm fragrance of freshly baked bread comes from thousands of modern bakeries that turn out delicious and nutritious breads. And today's homemaker who wants to give her family the cozy comfort of freshly baked bread can make it much more easily and quickly than ever before. We have *pictured and explained for you each special process in handling not only the new quick methods*, but the *Standard Method* for making bread and sweet rolls. The new fast yeasts speed the rising and total time required.

Please notice the recipes of holiday breads from far-away lands. We have simplified and clarified the original recipes, yet kept the special flavor and deliciousness that characterize each one of them. When you make them and serve them, see if you don't sense the festivity and romance that have always surrounded these breads.

Handling yeast dough is more fun than any other "cooking." Members of our Staff always feel this. You are dealing with something alive. The dough springs to life in silky smooth elasticity as you knead it. There's a deep centuries-old satisfaction in molding it into attractive shapes . . . watching the dough rise to a puffy lightness . . . then taking the brown beautiful breads from the oven. Best of all, there's the rich reward of seeing the beaming faces of the family as they enjoy these fruits of your homemaking.

YEAST BREADS

Evolution in Methods.

In the Old Days, women made yeast at home—usually from "hops" or, as some old cook books express it, from the "emptins" of the beer keg!

The strength of the yeast obtained by these methods varied from time to time, so it could not be relied upon for uniform results.

"Yeast Starters." Commercial yeast plus potatoes, water, sugar, and salt. Part of this yeast starter is used in making the sponge. Then some of the sponge is taken out, combined with the remaining yeast starter, and saved for the next breadmaking.

Yeast starters must be stored in a cool place; but even then, bacteria may develop which give the bread a strong flavor. In this case, a new starter has to be made with fresh yeast.

"Sour Dough." Early prospectors and miners were called "Sour Doughs" because of their method of making bread.

A portion of the dough was placed in a stone crock to ferment until ready to bake another batch of bread . . . then a small amount of this "sour dough" was mixed with some water and used in place of yeast.

"Salt-Rising" Bread. Sometimes the supply of homemade yeast or yeast starter ran short, so "Salt-Rising" or "Self-Rising" Bread was made instead. In some sections its distinctive flavor makes it still a favorite.

Corn meal is used in the starter. When it is exposed to the air, bacteria develop which form gas to make the bread rise. (*For recipe for Salt-Rising Bread, write to Betty Crocker.*)

The Sponge Method. In grandmother's day, the cake form of dry yeast was most often used in the sponge or overnight method.

The liquid and yeast are combined with enough flour to make a batter that will drop from the spoon. This batter is set in a fairly warm place (70° to 75°) overnight to become bubbly and "spongy." In the morning, the remaining ingredients are added to make a dough that can be kneaded. (*For Sponge Method recipe, write to Betty Crocker.*)

Modern Methods of Mixing: The two methods most commonly used today are the "straight dough" and the "simplified."

The **"Straight Dough"** used with compressed or dry granular yeast. All the ingredients are combined to make a dough which is kneaded to satiny smoothness. It is then formed into a firm mass, and set to rise in a warm place (85°). It is given two risings before shaping to develop fine texture. It rises again in the pans.

Simplified Methods of Mixing: Quicker and easier than ever before. Specially suited to rolls and coffee cakes.

The **Rich Yeast Batter.** Thorough beating takes the place of kneading. This is the ideal dough for rich tasting tender coffee cake, sweet rolls.

60-Minute Sweet Dough. Mix, shape, let rise, and bake in 60 min. Just mix in the saucepan. A few folds is all the kneading necessary.

Homemade Bread contributes special satisfaction and variety to meals. It is also thrifty if made carefully to prevent any waste of ingredients. It is practical to make several loaves of bread, coffee cake, and sweet rolls. Wrap and store in freezer.

YEAST is a tiny plant which "grows" and multiplies under proper conditions. 80° to 85° is the ideal temperature. It uses the sugar and starch of the dough as food, and forms gas (in the form of tiny bubbles) which makes the dough "rise." It also gives yeast breads their characteristic and delicious flavor. Yeast is available in several forms, especially:

Compressed Yeast (or moist yeast): The plants are alive and active, so they start to grow as soon as food, moisture, warmth, and air are supplied. This yeast is perishable; however, it can be stored in the refrigerator for 1 to 2 weeks, or in a food freezer up to 4 months. It is sold in small cakes (3/5 oz. and 2/3 oz.). Good compressed yeast is grayish tan in color, breaks with a clean edge, and crumbles between the fingers when broken.

Dry Granular Yeast: It can be kept without refrigeration. Note expiration date on package to insure satisfactory results. Use like compressed yeast except follow the package directions *or* add to each pkg., 1/4 cup lukewarm water and let stand 5 min. *without stirring*. Stir thoroughly before adding to liquid mixture. Subtract this 1/4 cup water from the liquid in the dough.

LIQUIDS (used in bread dough). May be milk, water, potato water or a mixture.

Water produces a bread with wheaty flavor and crisp crust.

Milk makes a bread that is more nourishing, has a more velvety grain and creamy white crumb, browner crust, keeps better than that made with water. (Scald raw milk and cool to lukewarm.)

Potato Water adds a characteristic flavor and moisture to bread, gives a little more volume but a slightly coarser product.

FLOUR is the chief ingredient in all breads. Flours milled from Hard Wheats contain ample proteins, which form the elastic pliable substance gluten. The layers of gluten hold the gas produced by the yeast, thus acting as a framework for the rising doughs. Gold Medal "Kitchen-tested" Flour is an all-purpose flour made from a blend of choice selected wheats with high quality gluten for yeast doughs, yet practical for all types of bakings.

Cracked Wheat—entire wheat berry crushed into chunk size.

Whole Wheat (Graham) —entire wheat berry ground into particles.

Bran — purified outer coating of wheat.

Rye Flour — the cream or center of the rye grain.

Rye Meal — entire rye grain ground into several degrees of granulation.

Corn Meal — coarsely ground whole kernel of corn . . . either white or yellow. Water-ground corn meal is ground between rotating stones. The germ is not removed, which means a more moist and deliciously flavorful corn meal . . . but keeping time is limited.

SUGAR adds flavor to the bread and color to the crust. It provides food for the yeast to produce the leavening gas. Too much sugar retards the yeast.

SHORTENING improves flavor, keeping quality, makes the bread more tender, and aids in browning. It lubricates the gluten meshwork so the dough can expand easily. Butter, other shortenings, or a mixture may be used.

SALT gives flavor . . . seems to condition gluten so it expands smoothly without tearing. Too much salt retards the yeast.

YEAST BREADS Mixing-Kneading-Rising

HERE'S THE WAY WE HANDLE THE DOUGH . . .

For Perfect Bread Every Time:
Sift the flour before you measure
Measure level and accurately
Test temperature of liquid

If a drop of liquid on the wrist feels neither hot nor cold, it is the right temperature (*80° or lukewarm*).

CAUTION: *Do not let yeast doughs rise more than double after shaping. They will fall, become coarse and open, and very dry when baked.*

1 Follow directions for mixing according to recipe. Stir well until yeast is dissolved. Mix in the flour, first with spoon, then with hand.

2 When the dough begins to leave the sides of the bowl, turn it out onto a lightly floured board to knead.

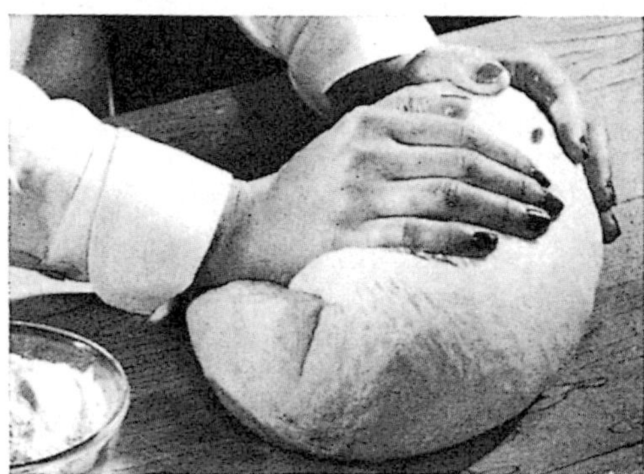

3 Knead: Fold dough over toward you. Then press down away from you with heel of hand. Give dough quarter turn, repeat until it's smooth, elastic, and doesn't stick to board.

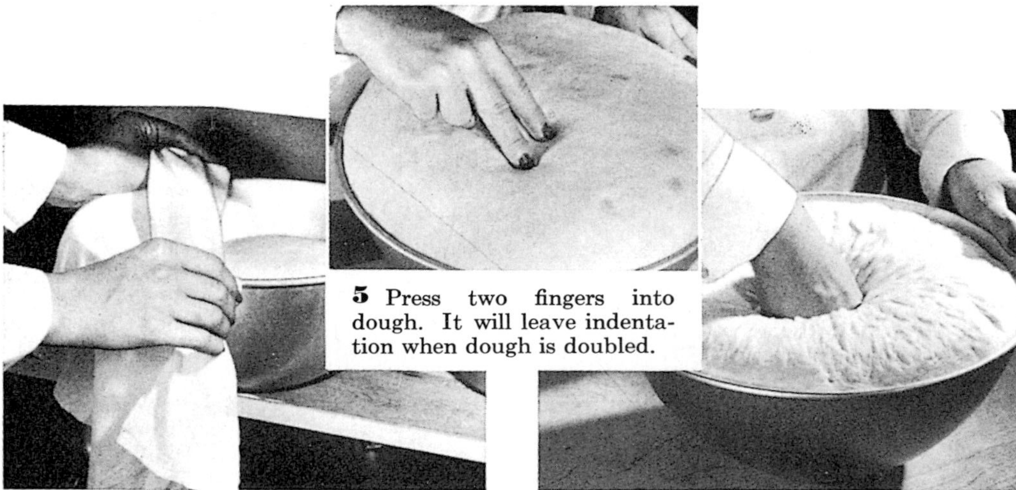

5 Press two fingers into dough. It will leave indentation when dough is doubled.

4 Place in greased bowl, turning once to bring greased side up. Cover with damp cloth and let rise in warm, draft-free spot (80 to 85°) until double (1½ to 2 hr.).

6 Punch down: thrust fist into dough, pull edges into center and turn completely over in bowl. Let rise again until *almost* double in bulk (30 to 45 min.).

WHITE BREAD (Recipe) *The fast Straight Dough method . . .*

	For 2 Loaves	For 4 Loaves
Mix together in large mixing bowl......	*2¼ cups lukewarm liquid	4½ cups
	3 tbsp. sugar	6 tbsp.
	1 tbsp. salt	2 tbsp.
Crumble into mixture..................	**2 cakes compressed yeast	2 cakes
Stir until yeast is well dissolved.		
Add....................................	2 tbsp. soft shortening	4 tbsp.
Mix in with spoon, then with hand....	7 to 7¼ cups *sifted* GOLD MEDAL Flour	14 to 14½ cups

Add the flour in two additions using the amount necessary to make easy to handle. Handle and knead the dough according to directions and pictures on p. 90. Mold the loaves and place in greased 9x5x3″ bread loaf pans. Let rise again and bake. (*See pictures, pp. 92 and 93.*)

**Milk, water, or potato water. If raw milk is used, first scald and cool to lukewarm.*

***For dry yeast, see recipe below.*

TEMPERATURE: 425° (hot oven).

TIME: Bake 25 to 30 min.

All you have to do—

To reduce rising time about 1 hr.: add 1 extra cake yeast. Extra yeast does not give yeasty taste. That results from being too warm during rising.

SPECIAL BREADS FROM A SINGLE DOUGH (*color picture pp. 86, 87*)

Follow recipe for White Bread above. After all the flour is mixed in, take out enough dough for 1 loaf. Flatten out on lightly floured board. Place special ingredients (*see below*) on top of dough and knead or mix in. Shape, let rise, and bake as for White Bread unless indicated.

NUT BREAD

Knead in 1 cup coarsely chopped nuts.

DATE OR RAISIN BREAD

Knead in 1 cup cut-up dates *or* 1 cup raisins. Bake in 400° (mod. hot oven) 30 to 35 min.

CRACKED WHEAT BREAD

Mix in 2 tbsp. honey, 1 cup cracked wheat.

WHOLE WHEAT BREAD

Mix in 4 tbsp. molasses and ¾ cup whole wheat (graham) flour. Bake in 400° (mod. hot oven) 30 to 35 min.

SWEDISH RYE BREAD

Mix in 2 tbsp. molasses, 2 tbsp. dark corn syrup, and ¾ cup rye flour, 1 cup raisins, if desired. Bake at 400° (mod. hot. oven) 30 to 35 min.

All you have to do

To keep bread fresh and free from mold in hot weather: wrap in waxed paper and store in refrigerator. Important for Whole Wheat.

WHITE BREAD MADE WITH DRY GRANULAR YEAST

Follow recipe above—*except* omit ½ cup of the liquid for either number of loaves. In place of compressed yeast, soak 2 pkg. dry granular yeast in ½ cup lukewarm water for 5 min. without stirring. Stir thoroughly before adding.

PAN BISCUITS

Use ½ of recipe "For 2 Loaves" above. Roll into a long roll about 18″ long. Cut off 1½″ pieces and shape into smooth round balls. Place in greased 9″ round pan. Let rise at 80° until light (45 to 60 min.). Bake.

TEMPERATURE: 375° (quick mod. oven).
TIME: Bake 35 to 40 min.
AMOUNT: 1 dozen biscuits.

SALT-FREE BREAD

Sometimes prescribed in special diets.

Follow recipe for White Bread above for mixing and handling dough. Use:

2 cups lukewarm water
6 tbsp. sugar
1 cake compressed yeast
6 tbsp. soft shortening
6 to 6¼ cups *sifted* GOLD MEDAL Flour

Let rise only half the time (without salt it will rise twice as fast). Shape loaves after first rising. Let rise again and bake.

TEMPERATURE: 400° (mod. hot oven).
TIME: Bake 30 to 35 min.
AMOUNT: 2 loaves.

HERE'S THE WAY WE MOLD THE LOAVES . . .

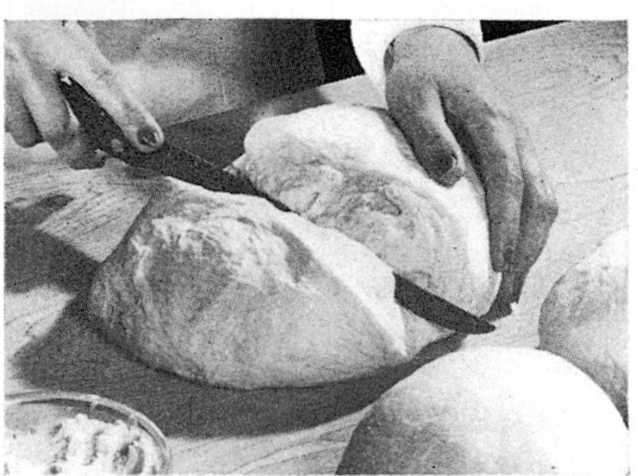

1 Divide dough into portions for molding and shaping *(these vary with size of recipe)*. Let rest covered (10 min.).

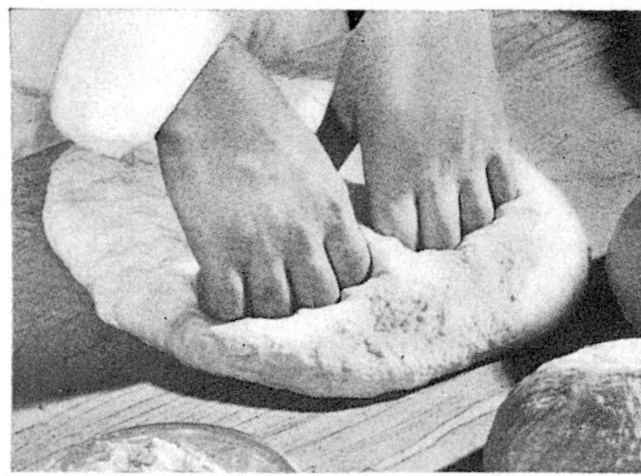

2 Flatten dough into oblong shapes, pressing out all air. (Work with closed fists, back of fingers on dough.)

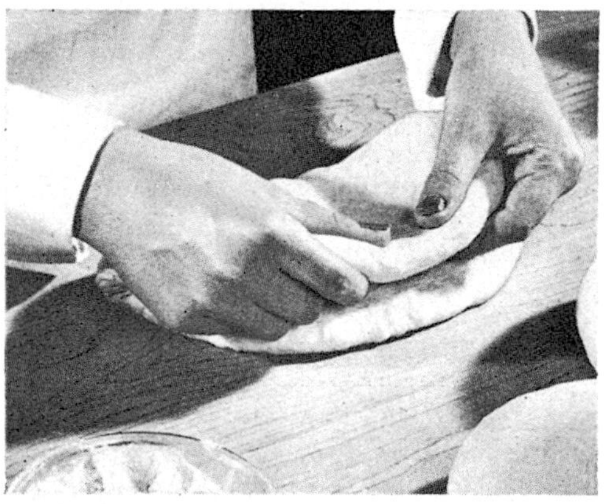

3 Fold dough in half lengthwise. Flatten again to press out air.

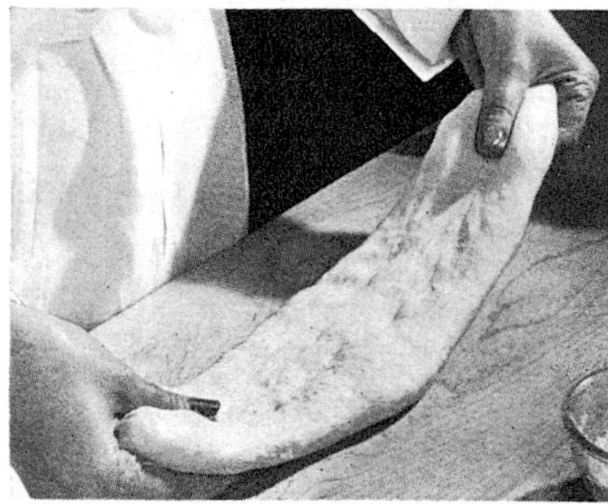

4 Lift dough by ends and pull, slapping table several times to elongate to 15″x5″.

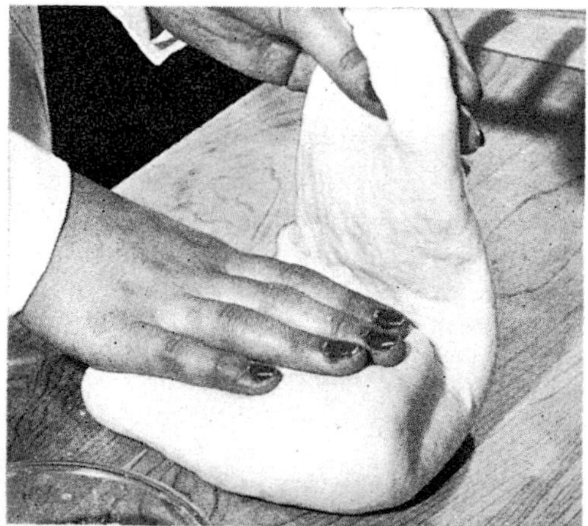

5 Bring the two ends to the center, overlap them, and seal well by pressing down firmly with knuckles.

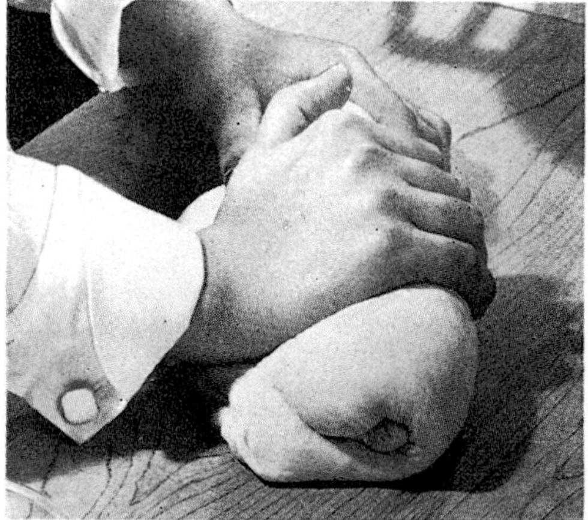

6 Take further edge of long side and fold over toward you, ⅓ of the way at a time, sealing well with heel of hand.

HERE'S THE WAY WE BAKE THE BREAD . . .

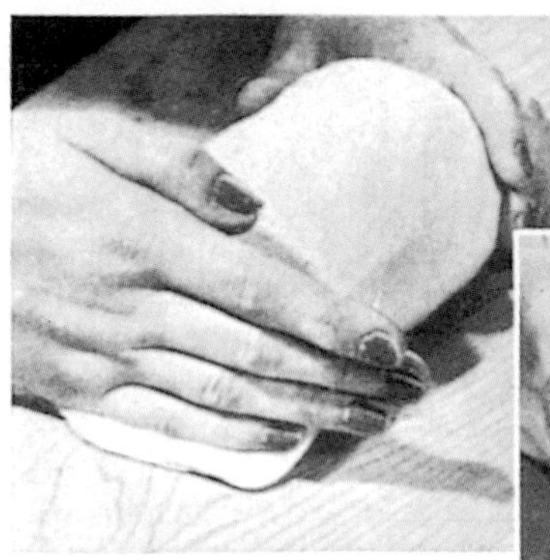

7 Roll back and forth to tighten. Seal each end by pressing with edge of hands.

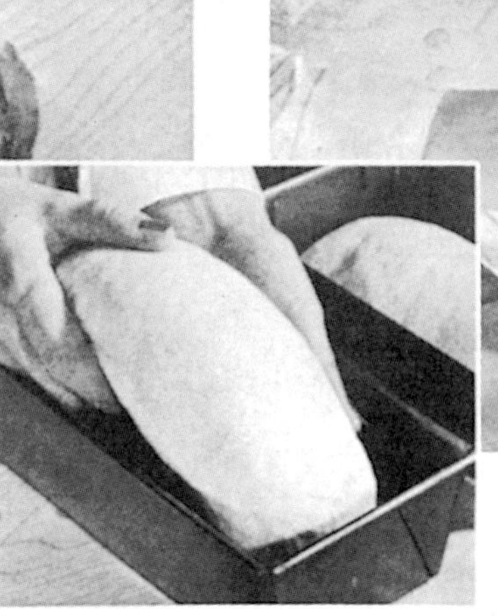

8 Place in pan sealed edge down (*pan ⅔ full*). Cover, let rise until sides of dough reach top of pan and center is well rounded (50 to 60 min.).

9 Test gently with finger. A slight indentation shows loaves are ready to bake.

10 Place the pans in center of hot oven (425°) . . . not touching each other or sides of oven. (*Heat must circulate freely for even baking.*)

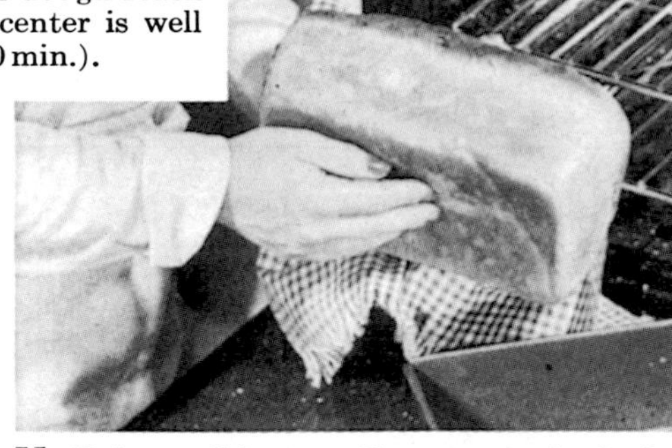

11 Bake until brown. *To test:* tap loaf, tip gently out of pan, tap bottom. It should sound hollow. If not, bake few min. more.

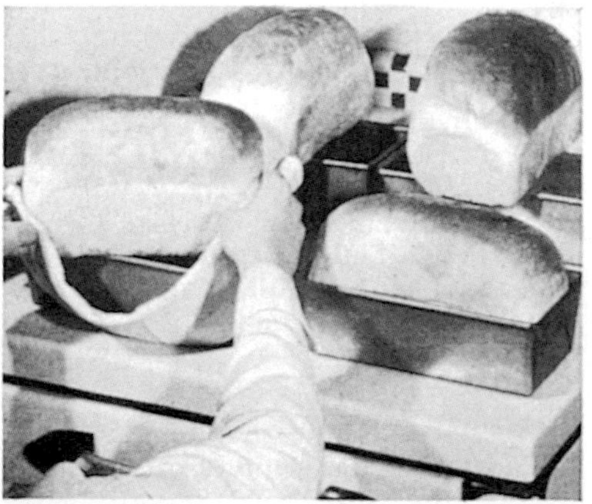

12 Immediately remove bread from pans. Place on wire cooling racks or across top edges of the bread pans. Do not place in direct draft, or crust will crack.

For a **SOFT-BRIGHT-TENDER** crust, brush with soft butter. Cover with a towel for a few minutes to soften crust.

For a **CRISP** crust, do not grease the loaves. Allow them to cool uncovered.

For a **HIGHLY GLAZED** crust, brush with an egg yolk-water mixture before baking.

TO KEEP BREAD AND ROLLS FRESH: store (when cool) in metal covered box . . . ventilated with air holes. (Wrap coffee cakes in waxed paper.) Sterilize bread box occasionally (wash in hot soapy water rinse with boiling water, dry well, air).

All you have to do–

To Reheat Breads or Rolls: place in paper bag, sprinkle bag with water, heat in 400° oven 10 min., or heat in a bun warmer on top of stove.

SPECIAL YEAST BREADS

Unusual breads with unusual appeal.

Perfect for serve-yourself midnight snacks and buffet suppers. Cold ham, sharp cheese, pickles, etc. enhance the flavors of these breads. Bernice Anderson of our Staff likes to serve Swedish Limpa on a shiny Swedish copper tray.

	SWEDISH LIMPA	CARAWAY RYE
Mix together	1½ cups lukewarm water ¼ cup molasses ⅓ cup sugar 1 tbsp. salt finely grated rind of 2 oranges	1½ cups ½ cup —— 1 tbsp. 2 tbsp. caraway seeds
Crumble in	2 cakes compressed yeast	3 cakes
Stir until dissolved. Add	2 tbsp. soft shortening	2 tbsp.
Mix in with spoon, then with hand	2½ cups *sifted* rye flour 2½ to 3 cups *sifted* GOLD MEDAL Flour	2¾ cups 3½ to 4 cups
Add, if desired	1 cup raisins	——

Dough with rye flour will be sticky. Add enough flour so it handles easily.

Knead and let rise twice. (See pictures, *p. 90.*) Shape into 2 round loaves. Place on opposite corners on lightly greased baking sheet. Let rise until double (45 to 60 min.). Bake until brown and tests done.

Pumpernickel Bread is a dense, dark, coarse bread. It requires coarse rye meal (not generally available) instead of rye flour.

NOTE: These breads can be made with only 1 rising before shaping but will have a little heavier and coarser texture.

TEMPERATURE: 375° (quick mod. oven).

TIME: Bake 30 to 40 min.

AMOUNT: 2 loaves.

CHEESE PIMIENTO BREAD

"Marvelous with just butter!" says Jean Banzhaf (Mrs. Christ Banzhaf, Jr.) of Chicago, known for her artistry in table-setting and the selection of properties for photography.

Combine in large saucepan . . .
- 2 tbsp. soft butter
- 3 tbsp. flour
- 1 tbsp. sugar
- 2 tsp. salt

Stir in . . .
- 1¼ cups milk

Cook, stirring over low heat until thickened.

Add . . .
- ⅓ cup grated sharp flavored cheese
- 2 to 3 tbsp. minced pimiento

Stir until cheese is melted. Cool to lukewarm.

Mix together and add . . .
- ¼ cup lukewarm water
- 1 cake compressed yeast

Mix in . . .
- 3 to 3½ cups *sifted* GOLD MEDAL Flour

Knead and let rise twice. Shape into loaf (9x5x3″ pan). (*See pp. 90–93.*) Let rise 1½ times its size (about 30 min.). Bake.

TEMPERATURE: 375° (quick mod. oven).

TIME: Bake 45 to 50 min.

AMOUNT: 1 loaf.

★ HERB BREAD

Serve warm for its delightful aroma. Duncan Hines always asks for it since we served it to him at a guest luncheon a few years ago.

Follow recipe for White Bread (*p. 91*) for mixing and handling dough, but use:

- 1 cup lukewarm milk
- 2 tbsp. sugar
- 1½ tsp. salt
- 1 cake compressed yeast
- 1 egg
- ½ tsp. nutmeg
- 1 tsp. crumbled dried sage
- 2 tsp. caraway seeds
- 2 tbsp. soft shortening
- 3 to 3¾ cups *sifted* GOLD MEDAL Flour

Let rise only once. Shape into loaf (9x5x3″ pan). Let rise double (50 to 60 min.). Bake.

TEMPERATURE: 375° (quick mod. oven).

TIME: Bake 45 to 50 min.

AMOUNT: 1 loaf.

BOHEMIAN RYE BREAD

Follow recipe for Caraway Rye Bread above—*except* use 2 cups water, 3 cups rye flour. Omit molasses, use ¼ cup sugar. Add 2 tbsp. fennel and use 1 tbsp. caraway seeds.

CRESCENT ROLLS

Two delightful favorites . . . both the rich and plainer types.

Rich Crescent Rolls . . . *our recipe for these superb golden crescents has been made famous by Nell and Arthur Palmer of beautiful Lowell Inn, Stillwater, Minnesota.*
Plain Crescent Rolls . . . *ideal for a dinner roll. Easy.*

	★ Rich Crescent Rolls	Plain Crescent Rolls
Mix together until smooth (use rotary beater if desired)	½ cup sugar	2 tbsp.
	½ cup soft shortening	6 tbsp.
	1 tsp. salt	1 tsp.
	2 eggs	—
Stir in	¾ cup lukewarm milk	1½ cups
Crumble into mixture and stir until dissolved.	2 cakes compressed yeast	2 cakes
Beat in with spoon	4 cups *sifted* GOLD MEDAL Flour	4 cups
	Rising Time	
Scrape dough from sides of bowl, cover with damp cloth. Let rise until double	1½ hr.	30 min.
Shape as Crescents or Butterhorns (*see p. 99*). Cover, let rise until double	1 hr.	15 min.
Bake until golden brown.		

TEMPERATURE: 425° (hot oven).
TIME: Bake 12 to 15 min.
AMOUNT: 1⅔ doz. 2 doz.

CELERY CRESCENTS

Brush Plain Crescent Rolls, before baking, with butter, sprinkle with celery seeds, salt.

QUICK ROLLS

Really quick to make. Delicious, too!

	Quick Butter-Milk Rolls	Quick Surprise Rolls
Mix together	1 cup buttermilk (lukewarm, thick)	¾ cup milk (lukewarm)
	—	*½ cup mashed potatoes
	¼ tsp. soda	—
	1 tsp. sugar	2 tbsp.
	1 tsp. salt	1 tsp.
Crumble into mixture	1 cake compressed yeast	1 cake
Stir until dissolved and add	3 tbsp. soft shortening	6 tbsp.
Add just until easy to handle	2½ to 2¾ cups *sifted* GOLD MEDAL Flour	2 to 2¼ cups

**Use unseasoned mashed potatoes*

Mix and knead (*see p. 90*).
Shape into any desired shapes (*see p. 99*).
Let rise until double (45 to 60 min.).
Bake until golden brown.

TEMPERATURE: 400° (mod. hot oven).
TIME: Bake 15 to 20 min.
AMOUNT: 1½ doz. rolls.

WHOLE WHEAT ROLLS

Follow recipe for Plain Crescent Rolls above—*except* substitute whole wheat for 2 cups of the flour.

All you have to do—

For another easy, quick, delicious yeast roll: see recipe on BISQUICK pkg.

FRENCH BREAD

Crusty and delicious outside; open-textured and soft inside. It is an old-time custom in France for the baker's wife, as dawn creeps over the horizon, to peddle through the streets the results of her husband's nocturnal labor. This she does from an apron tied about her waist, or from a pushcart on two wheels. The typical French Bread is a pole-like loaf three to four feet long which people can carry home under their arm.

Follow picture directions for mixing and rising (*p. 90*), but use:

1 cup lukewarm water
1½ tsp. salt
1 cake compressed yeast
1 tbsp. soft shortening
3½ to 3¾ cups *sifted* GOLD MEDAL Flour

When dough is ready for shaping, *after second rising*, follow the picture directions.

TEMPERATURE: 425° (hot oven) . . . then 375° (quick mod. oven).

TIME: Bake 35 to 40 min. (total).

AMOUNT: 1 loaf.

NOTE: This is a heavy dough so requires maximum rising time.

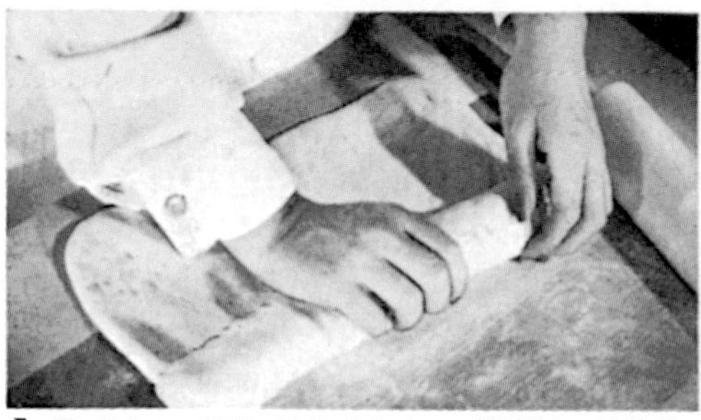

1 Roll into 15″x10″ oblong. Roll up tightly toward you . . . beginning with wide side. Seal edges by pinching together.

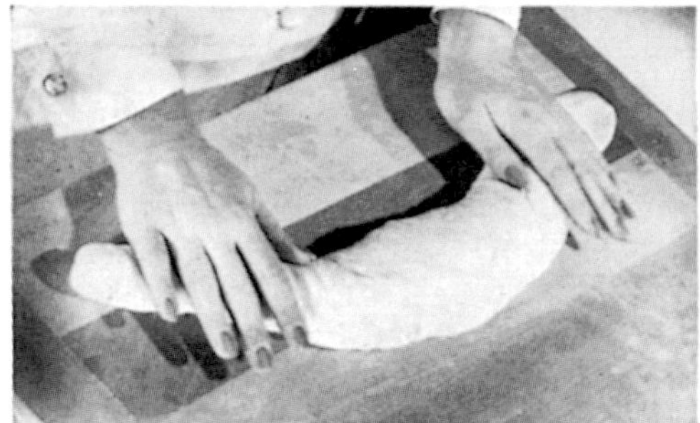

2 With a hand on each end, roll gently back and forth to lengthen loaf and taper ends. Place it diagonally on lightly greased corn meal-sprinkled baking sheet.

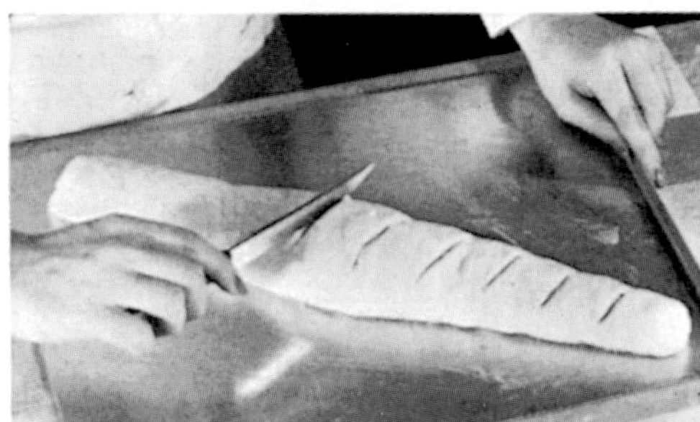

3 Make ¼″ slashes in dough at 2″ intervals, or 1 slash lengthwise. Brush top with cold water. Let stand uncovered about 1½ hr. Brush again, and bake.

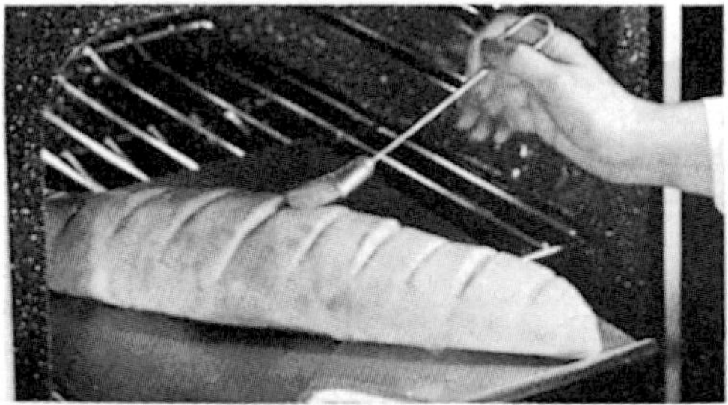

4 Bake 10 min. in hot oven (425°). Remove from oven and brush again. Reduce temperature to 375° and bake 10 min. more. Remove from oven and brush again. Sprinkle with sesame or poppyseeds. Continue baking 15 to 20 min. until golden brown.

All you have to do—

For more glaze, less crustiness: use egg white wash (1 egg white, slightly beaten, with 1 tbsp. water).

FRENCH ROLLS

Crusty, crunchy, . . . like French Bread.

Follow recipe for French Bread (*p. 96*). *After second rising* divide dough into 16 equal parts. Form each into a little bun. Place on greased and corn meal-sprinkled baking sheet.

With scissors, snip rolls in half, then in quarters, cutting through almost to bottom of rolls. Brush with water. Let rise 1 hr. Brush again. If desired, sprinkle with sesame or poppy seeds. (The egg white wash on *p. 96* makes seeds stick better.) Bake until tops are golden, crusty.

TEMPERATURE: 425° (hot oven).

TIME: Bake 10 min. Brush and bake 10–15 min. more.

AMOUNT: 16 rolls.

TWO SUPPER BREADS *So delicious no one should miss them.*

Much more moist and open textured than regular bread. Easy to make, too. The Scotch Oatmeal Bread is from Mrs. Helen Schooley, of Rhinelander, Wisconsin who has always been enthusiastic about our recipes and shared this specialty of hers with us. An amusing story of the origin of Anadama Bread relates— The name ANADAMA comes from a New England fisherman whose lazy wife always served him corn meal mush and molasses for dinner. One day he came home and found the same corn meal and molasses. Tired of it, he mixed it with flour and yeast and baked it as bread, saying: "Anna damn her."

	Anadama Bread	★ Oatmeal Bread
Bring to boil in saucepan	1½ cups water 1 tsp. salt	1½ cups 1½ tsp.
Stir in	⅓ cup yellow corn meal	1½ cups rolled oats
Stir in and cool to lukewarm	⅓ cup molasses 1½ tbsp. shortening	⅓ cup brown sugar 1 tbsp.
Crumble	1 cake compressed yeast	1 cake
in	¼ cup lukewarm water	¼ cup
Blend in the yeast mixture.		
Mix in with spoon, then with hand (The dough will be sticky.)	4 to 4¼ cups *sifted* GOLD MEDAL Flour	3 to 3¼ cups

Cornmeal mixture should be brought to boil, stirring constantly. Immediately remove from heat, pour into large bowl. *Do not boil oatmeal mixture.*

Knead and let rise (*see directions, p. 90*) until double (1½ hr.). Punch down and turn into greased 9x5x3″ loaf pan. Pat into rounded shape. Let rise until double (about 1 hr.). Bake until dark brown.

TEMPERATURE: 375° (quick mod. oven).
TIME: Bake 40 to 45 min.
AMOUNT: 1 loaf.
NOTE: For Anadama Bread, (before baking) brush top with melted butter, sprinkle with a little corn meal and salt.

All you have to do–

To give the birds a treat: a feeding box for birds offers a pleasant way of using leftover bread crumbs, and gives delight to the family.

HONEY CORN MEAL BREAD

Follow recipe for Anadama Bread—*except* use honey in place of molasses. Use milk in place of water. Decrease flour to 3 to 3¼ cups.

SWEET DOUGH YEAST BREADS For delectable rolls and coffee cakes.

SWEET DOUGHS (🔑 Recipes) *Make either type as desired.*

	Sweet Dough	Richer Sweet Dough
Mix together	2 cups lukewarm milk ½ cup sugar 2 tsp. salt	1 cup ½ cup 1 tsp.
Crumble into mixture Stir until yeast is dissolved.	*2 cakes compressed yeast	*2 cakes
Stir in	2 eggs ½ cup soft shortening	2 eggs ½ cup
Mix in first with spoon, then with hand	7 to 7½ cups *sifted* GOLD MEDAL Flour	4½ to 5 cups

For excellent eating and keeping quality, keep doughs as soft as possible, almost sticky . . . just so you're able to handle.

Add flour in 2 additions, using the amount necessary to make it easy to handle. Handle and knead the dough according to directions and pictures on *p. 90.*

After second rising, divide dough for desired rolls and coffee cake. Round up, cover, and let rest 15 min. so dough is easy to handle.
Shape doughs, let rise until light (15 to 30 min.) and bake according to directions for each type of roll or coffee cake.

AMOUNT:	
4 doz. plain rolls	3 doz. rolls
or	*or*
1 large pan rolls	1 large pan
or	*or*
1 coffee cake 2 doz. plain rolls	1 coffee cake 1 doz. rolls

**For dry yeast, see recipe below.*

PLAINER SWEET DOUGH

For plain biscuits or rolls.

Follow 🔑 recipe for Sweet Dough—*except* use only ¼ cup shortening, only 1 egg.

DOUGHS WITH DRY YEAST

Follow either 🔑 recipe above—*except* omit ½ cup of milk. In place of compressed yeast, soak 2 pkg. dry granular yeast in ½ cup lukewarm water for 5 min. without stirring. Stir well before adding.

ROLLS OF ALL SHAPES

Follow either of 🔑 recipes above. Shape dough as desired . . . just follow sketches and directions below. Let rise until light (15 to 20 min.). Bake on lightly greased pan. Serve piping hot.

NOTE: See color pictures on *pp. 86, 87.*

TEMPERATURE: 425° (hot oven).

TIME: Bake 12 to 20 min. (depending on size).

DINNER ROLLS

Roll dough into cylindrical shapes with tapered ends and place on pan.

PARKERHOUSE ROLLS

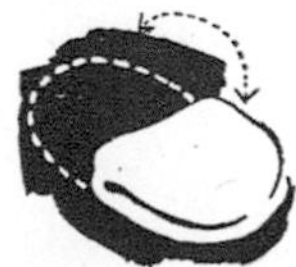

Roll dough ¼″ thick. Cut with biscuit cutter. Brush with melted butter. Make crease across each. Fold so top half slightly overlaps. Press edges together at crease. Place close together on pan.

OLD-FASHIONED BISCUITS

Form dough into balls ⅓ size desired. Place close together in a greased round pan.

CLOVERLEAF ROLLS

Form bits of dough into balls about 1″ in diameter. Place 3 balls in each greased muffin cup. Brush with butter for flavor.

To use egg yolks in these doughs: use 2 yolks plus 1 tbsp. water in place of 1 whole egg.

For all the twisted shapes, roll dough a little less than ½″ thick into a long oblong 12″ wide. Spread with soft butter. Fold ½ of dough over the other half. Trim edges to square the corners. Cut into strips ½″ wide and 6″ long.

FIGURE 8's

Hold one end of strip in one hand and twist the other end . . . stretching it slightly until the two ends when brought together on greased baking sheet will form a figure 8.

TWISTS

Same as Figure 8's, but give strip additional twist just before placing it on baking sheet.

SNAILS

Twist and hold one end of the strip down on baking sheet. Wind strip around and around. Tuck end underneath.

CLOTHESPIN CRULLERS

Wrap strip around greased clothespin so edges barely touch. When baked, twist clothespin and pull out. May be filled with one of Fruit Fillings (*p. 106*).

KNOTS

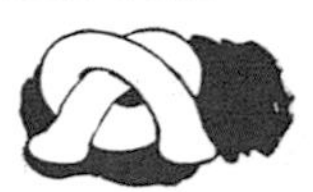

Twist and tie each strip into a knot. Press ends down on greased baking sheet.

TOAD-IN-HOLE (Turk's Cap)

Twist and tie each strip with a knot in one end of strip. Then pull the longer end through center of knot.

BUTTERFLY ROLLS

Roll dough only ⅛″ thick into an oblong 6″ wide. Spread with soft butter, and roll up like jelly roll. Cut into 2″ pieces. Make a deep impression with narrow wooden handle in middle of each roll (to resemble butterfly).

CRESCENTS (Butterhorns)

Roll dough scarcely ¼″ thick into a 12″ circle. Spread with soft butter. Cut into 16 pie-shaped pieces. Beginning at rounded edge, roll up. Place on pan, point underneath.

BUTTER FLUFFS (Fan Tans)

Roll dough ⅛″ thick into a long oblong 9″ wide. Spread with soft butter. Cut into 6 long strips 1½″ wide. Stack 6 strips evenly, one on top of other. Cut into 1″ pieces. Place cut-side-down in greased muffin cups.

SALT STICKS

Roll dough very thin into oblong 8″ wide. Cut into 4″ squares. Starting at a corner, roll each square diagonally to opposite corner. Round the ends. Brush with egg yolk and sprinkle with coarse salt.

PICNIC BUNS

Use ½ of Plainer Sweet Dough (*p. 98*). Divide into 2 parts. Roll each into 7½″ sq. (½″ thick). Cut into 2½″ squares. Place on greased baking sheet. Cover with damp cloth, let rise until double (30 to 45 min.). Bake.

TEMPERATURE: 400° (mod. hot oven).

TIME: Bake 12 to 15 min.

AMOUNT: 1½ doz. buns.

CINNAMON ROLLS (🔑 Recipe) *Pinwheel rolls with fragrant cinnamon-sugar-butter.*

Use ½ Sweet Dough or all Richer Sweet Dough (*p. 98.*). *After second rising:*

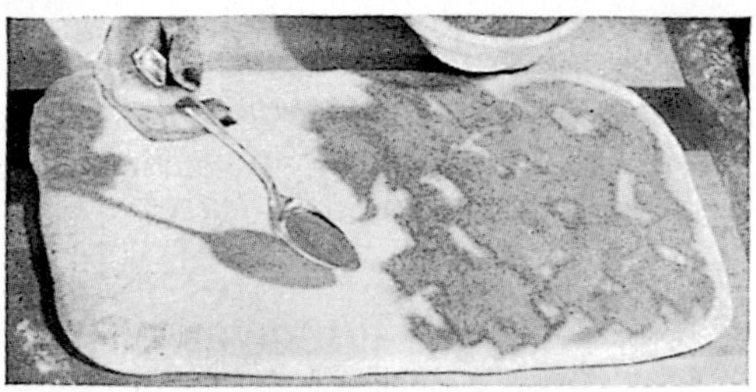

1 Roll dough into oblong 9″x18″. Spread with 2 tbsp. softened butter and sprinkle with ½ cup sugar and 2 tsp. cinnamon.

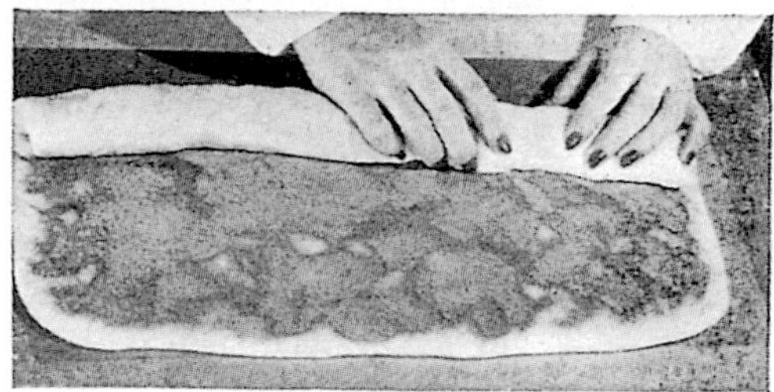

2 Roll up tightly, beginning at wide side. Seal well by pinching edges of roll together.

3 Cut roll into 1″ slices. Place a little apart in greased 13″x9″ pan or 18 muffin cups.

Cover and let rise until double in bulk (35 to 40 min.). Bake until golden brown and completely baked through.

NOTE: To test for doneness . . . separate a roll slightly with fork to see if well baked.

TEMPERATURE: 375° (quick mod. oven).

TIME: Bake 25 to 30 min.

AMOUNT: 1½ doz. rolls.

BUTTERSCOTCH ROLLS

Cinnamon Rolls with butterscotch glaze.

Make *Cinnamon Rolls* as above—*except* place cut slices in baking pan coated with . . .

½ cup melted butter
½ cup brown sugar
½ cup pecan halves

Bake. Immediately turn upside down on a large tray. Let pan stay over rolls a minute so butterscotch runs down over them.

ORANGE ROLLS

Most popular roll of all in tea rooms. Look for them in the color picture, p. 86, 87.

Make as for Cinnamon Rolls above—*except* spread with about 4 tbsp. of orange filling *below.*

Place the rest of filling in the bottom of pan. Let rise and bake as for Cinnamon Rolls. As soon as rolls come from oven, turn upside down on a large tray so filling runs down over rolls. Serve warm.

ORANGE FILLING

Mix, cook 2 min., cool until thick . . .

½ cup sugar
1 tbsp. grated orange rind
¼ cup orange juice and pulp
¼ cup butter

★ HUNGARIAN COFFEE CAKE

Nut encrusted rolls—baked as a cake.

Make ½ Sweet Dough or all Richer Sweet Dough (*p. 98*). *After second rising,* cut dough into pieces the size of walnuts.

Form into balls. Roll each ball in . . .

½ cup melted butter (total amount)

Then roll in mixture of . . .

¾ cup sugar
1 tsp. cinnamon
½ cup finely chopped nuts

Place 1 layer of balls so they barely touch in well greased 9″ tube pan. Sprinkle with a few raisins. Add another layer of balls, sprinkle with more raisins, pressing them in slightly. Let rise 45 min. Bake 35 to 40 min. at 375°. Loosen from pan. Invert pan so butter-sugar mixture runs down over cake (*picture, p. 104*). To serve, break apart with 2 forks.

BUTTER NUT ROLLS

Make as Hungarian Coffee Cake above—*except* place each ball in a greased muffin cup. Let rise until light (20 to 25 min.). Bake. Immediately loosen from cups with spatula. Serve warm.

TEMPERATURE: 375° (quick mod. oven).
TIME: Bake 15 to 20 min.
AMOUNT: 2½ doz. rolls.

★ SWEDISH TEA RING

Spectacular, but easy to make. People used to "OH and AH!" as Elsa Wallin Louis of our Staff made it at our demonstrations and cooking schools. As Mrs. John Louis of Minneapolis, she still makes it for parties.

Follow 🔑 recipe for Cinnamon Rolls (*p. 100*)—*except* sprinkle dough with ½ cup raisins in addition to sugar and cinnamon.

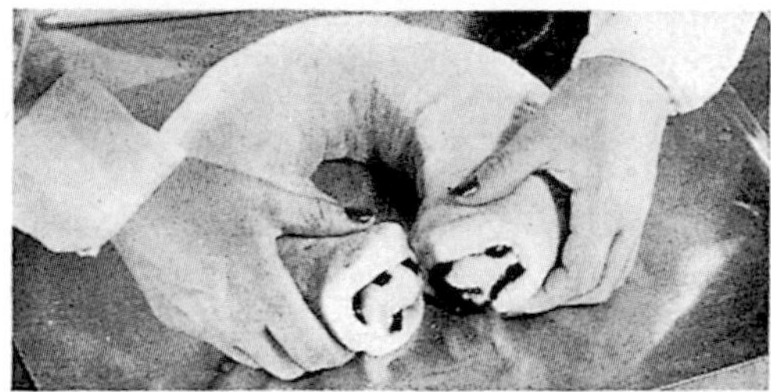

1 Roll up as for Cinnamon Rolls. Then place sealed-edge-down in ring on lightly greased baking sheet. Join ends of ring, seal.

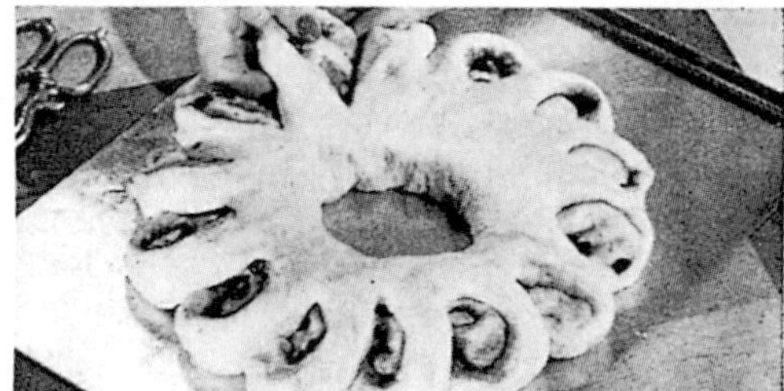

2 With scissors, make cuts ⅔ of the way through the ring at 1″ intervals. Turn each section on its side. Let rise, and bake as for Cinnamon Rolls (*p. 100*).

Frost while warm (*see p. 111*) and decorate with nuts and cherries. Serve warm. *See color picture, pp. 86-87.*

All you have to do–

To cut warm yeast breads: use scissors or hot knife.

STREUSEL COFFEE CAKE

Fluffy coffee cake with crumbly topping.

Use ¼ Sweet Dough (*p. 98*). *After second rising*, mix in ½ cup raisins, if desired. Pat into a greased 9″ round pan. Press into top of dough this crumb mixture

- **⅓ cup sugar**
- **⅓ cup GOLD MEDAL Flour**
- **3 tbsp. butter**
- **1 tsp. cinnamon**
- **½ cup cut-up nuts**

Cover and let rise until double in bulk (25 to 35 min.). Bake. Serve warm.

TEMPERATURE: 400° (mod. hot oven).

TIME: Bake 25 to 30 min.

KAESE KUCHEN (Cheese Cake)

"Just like my mother used to make," says Dr. F. A. Collatz of our company.

Prepare dough in pan as for Apfel Kuchen.→

Fill with a mixture of . . .

- **⅓ cup sugar**
- **1 tbsp. flour**
- **1 cup dry or drained cottage cheese**
- **1 cup cut-up drained pineapple or prunes**
- **¼ cup cut-up nuts**

Sprinkle over top of filling . . .

- **2 tbsp. sugar**
- **1 tsp. cinnamon**

Let rise and bake as for Apfel Kuchen.→ Serve warm.

NOTE: Add fruit and cheese at room temperature.

CINNAMON WHIRLIGIG

Rich loaf with spiral cinnamon filling.

Use ⅓ of Sweet Dough or ⅔ of Richer Dough (*p. 98*). Let rise twice.
Roll dough into an oblong 14″x8″.

Spread with . . .

- **2 tbsp. soft butter**

Sprinkle with mixture of . . .

- **½ cup sugar**
- **2 tsp. cinnamon**

Roll up tight, starting with one end. Place sealed-edge-down in well greased 9x5x3″ loaf pan. Let rise 25 to 30 min.

TEMPERATURE: 375° (quick mod. oven).

TIME: Bake 30 to 35 min.

APFEL KUCHEN (Apple Cake)

An old Dutch Coffee Cake. (*See picture p. 104.*)

Use ¼ Sweet Dough (*p. 98*). *After second rising*, pat into a greased 9″ round pan, forming a ridge around the edge. Arrange thinly sliced apples (1 pared) overlapping one another in a circle over center.

Sprinkle with a mixture of ¼ cup sugar, ¼ tsp. cinnamon, 1 tbsp. soft butter. Cover and let rise until double (25 to 35 min.). Bake, covering the first 10 min. After baking, sprinkle crust with a little extra cinnamon-sugar mixture.

TEMPERATURE: 400° (mod. hot oven).

TIME: Bake 25 to 30 min.

SPECIALTY YEAST BREADS

Festive breads for festive occasions.

★ STOLLEN

Old German holiday bread. Fruity and gay. Mary Madison Wilson (Mrs. Allan B. Wilson), when on our Staff, used to make this for gifts at Christmas.

Use ½ of Sweet Dough or all of Richer Sweet Dough (*p. 98*). *After second rising,* turn dough onto lightly floured board and flatten.

Distribute evenly over dough..........
- **½ cup cut-up blanched almonds**
- **¼ cup *each* cut-up citron, candied cherries**
- **1 cup seeded raisins**
- **1 tbsp. grated lemon rind**

Knead them into the dough. Pat out dough into an oval about 8″x12″. Spread with soft butter. Fold in two the long way. Form into crescent. Press folded edge firmly so it won't spring open. Place on lightly greased heavy baking sheet. Brush top with melted butter. Let rise until double (35 to 45 min.). Bake.

Frost while warm with Confectioners' Sugar Icing (*p. 111*). Decorate with shaved toasted almonds, pieces of citron, cherries. (*See color picture, p. 104.*)

TEMPERATURE: 375° (quick mod. oven).

TIME: Bake 30 to 35 min.

1 Distribute fruit evenly over dough.

2 Knead fruit into dough.

3 Press folded edge firmly so it won't open.

NEW ENGLAND RAISIN BREAD

An old stand-by made for special occasions, such as Town Meeting Day and Fourth of July, in New England.

Follow 🔑 recipe for Richer Sweet Dough (*p. 98*)—*except* use 2 more eggs and 2 extra cups flour.

Mix in . . .
- **2 cups seedless raisins**

Let rise twice.

Shape into 2 loaves (see directions, *p. 92*). Brush tops with butter and sprinkle with sugar. Let rise until double in bulk (1 hr.). Bake until well browned and tests done.

TEMPERATURE: 350° (mod. oven).

TIME: Bake 45 to 50 min.

AMOUNT: 2 loaves (9x5x3″).

FESTIVAL ROLLS

Use ½ of Sweet Dough (*p. 98*). After second rising, roll out ¼″ thick. Cut into rounds with 3″ cutter. Cut *two* 1″ slits in each. Top with ½ tsp. of mixture of. . . .

- **½ cup brown sugar**
- **½ cup shredded coconut**
- **3 tbsp. butter**

Pull outer strand of dough over filling and through slit on other side. Press down strands to form collar around filling. Place rolls 1″ apart on greased baking sheet. Brush with water, sprinkle with sugar. Let rise 35 to 45 min. Bake.

TEMPERATURE: 400° (mod. hot oven).

TIME: Bake 15 to 20 min.

AMOUNT: 2 doz. rolls.

★ OLD VIENNA HOLIDAY WHIRL

Developed from the Slavanian recipe POTICA (Poteetza) brought from Hibbing, Minnesota, by Nielsine Hansen, formerly of our Staff.

Use ½ Sweet Dough or all Richer Sweet Dough (*p. 98*). *After second rising*, roll dough into oblong 8x20″.

Spread (to within 1″ of edge) with filling:

Mix, cook 1 min., cool . . .

- **⅓ cup honey**
- **1 cup finely chopped nuts**
- **⅓ cup butter**
- **⅓ cup cream**
- **2 tsp. cinnamon**
- **1½ cups cut-up raisins**

Roll up dough as for Cinnamon Rolls. Seal in the filling securely by pinching together edges of roll. Elongate roll by slightly stretching and shaping it to even.

Pinch edges. Elongate roll.

Coil it into a huge "snail" to fit into a greased heavy 10″ skillet. Let rise until double in bulk (45 to 55 min.). Brush with egg glaze (*p. 106*). Sprinkle over the top . . . crushed loaf sugar and cut-up unblanched almonds. Bake until well browned. Serve warm (*picture, p. 104*).

TEMPERATURE: 350° (mod. oven).

TIME: Bake 45 to 50 min.

All you have to do—

To prevent overbrowning: cover with brown wrapping paper the last 25 minutes of baking.

All you have to do—

To reheat iced coffee cakes and rolls: place on cooky sheet uncovered, loosely wrap in tin foil, or place in *large* paper bag and heat in 400° oven for about 10 min. Delicious, too, sliced and toasted under broiler

HONEY TWIST

With a "honey of a topping."

Make Richer Sweet Dough (*p. 98*). Let rise twice. Roll dough with hands into a narrow roll (like a broom handle) 1″ thick. Coil, beginning at outside edge, into huge snail, twisting coil to fit into greased 10″ skillet. Leave space between coils. Cover. Let rise until not quite double (35 to 45 min.). Spoon over coils (not on outer edge).

HONEY TOPPING

Mix together . . .

- **¼ cup mild-flavored honey**
- **¼ cup sugar**
- **¼ cup soft butter**
- **¼ cup flour**
- **½ cup cut-up nuts**

Bake. Serve warm or reheated.

TEMPERATURE: 375° (quick mod. oven).

TIME: Bake 20 to 30 min.

FRUIT-FILLED TWIST

Streaks of rich filling . . . pretty as a picture.

Make ½ of Sweet Dough or all of Richer Sweet Dough (*p. 98*). Let rise twice. Roll into oblong 16x11″. Spread with soft butter. Mix.

- **1 cup raisins, ground**
- **½ cup brown sugar**
- **2 tbsp. orange juice**

Spread over dough. Roll up as for Cinnamon Rolls (*p. 100*). Place diagonally on greased baking sheet, sealed edge down. With scissors cut roll into 2 long strips (do not cut through one end). Bring one strip crosswise over the other, *keeping cut side up*. Cross strips several times.

Let rise until double (30 to 45 min.). Bake. Spread thinly with Confectioners' Sugar Icing (*p. 111*). Serve warm.

TEMPERATURE: 350° (mod. oven).

TIME: Bake 30 to 35 min.

CHRISTMAS BREADS FROM MANY LANDS

Hungarian Coffee Cake Old Vienna Holiday Whirl Kulich
Bohemian Christmas Braid Stollen French Coffee Lace
Apfel Kuchen Jule Kage

FRENCH COFFEE LACE *Delicious filling peering through the "lace."*

Make Richer Sweet Dough (*p. 98*). Let rise twice. Prepare fruity filling:

Mix, boil 1 min., then cool . . .

2 cups finely chopped apples
1 cup raisins, ground
1 cup brown sugar
½ tsp. salt
½ tsp. cinnamon

Roll out dough into rectangle 14″x8″. Place on greased heavy baking sheet. Spread fruity filling down center of dough covering space about 3″ wide. At each side of filling, make cuts 2″ apart, making cuts 2″ long into dough. This makes 7 strips on each side.

Take a strip on each side and cross them at center of the filling. Pull strips down, keeping ends inside. Continue to lace opposite strips, tucking last ends underneath. Cover with damp cloth and let rise until double (30 to 45 min.). Bake until rich golden brown. Frost with Confectioners' Sugar Icing (*p. 111*).

NOTE: *See color picture, p. 104.*

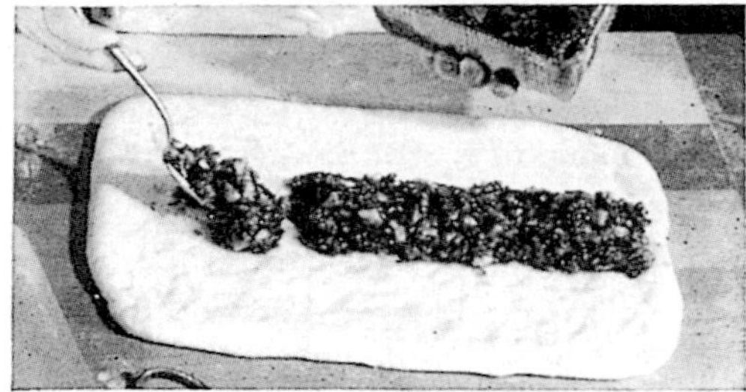

Spread filling down center of dough.

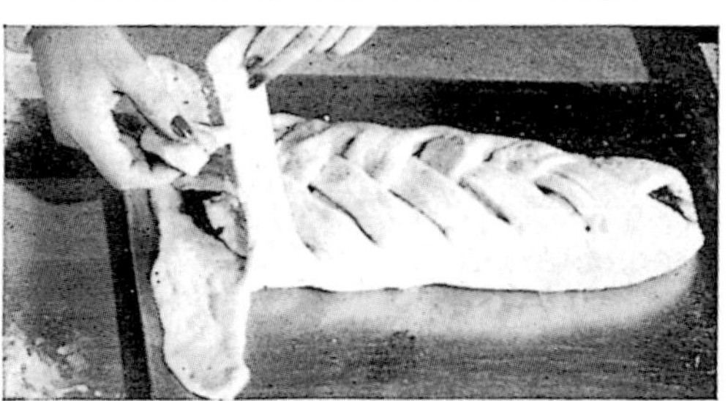

Lace opposite strips of dough across.

TEMPERATURE: 375° (quick mod. oven).

TIME: Bake 30 to 35 min.

JULE KAGE (Christmas Cake)

On the table for a "Glad Jule" in Norway.

Mix together . . .

1 cup lukewarm milk
½ cup sugar
½ tsp. salt
½ tsp. powdered cardamom

Crumble into mixture . . .

1 cake compressed yeast

Stir until dissolved. Add . . .

1 small egg
2 tbsp. soft shortening

Mix in first with spoon, then with hand . . .

3¼ to 3½ cups *sifted* GOLD MEDAL Flour
¼ cup chopped citron
½ cup raisins

Knead and let rise twice (*see p. 90*). Shape into 1 round loaf and place in a greased 9″ round pan. Cover and let rise until double (45 to 60 min.). Bake until brown.

TEMPERATURE: 350° (mod. oven).

TIME: Bake 30 to 40 min.

All you have to do—

To make a golden glaze as in picture, p. 104: brush slightly beaten egg over surface just before baking.

FIG-FILLED SQUARE

For picnics and potlucks . . . take it in the pan.

Use ½ of Sweet Dough (*p. 98*). Let rise twice. Make filling:

Mix, bring to boil, then cool . . .

½ cup cut-up drained soaked figs
¼ cup water
¼ cup sugar
1 tbsp. flour
1 tbsp. lemon juice

Roll out dough into a rectangle 15″x7″. Brush with soft butter. Spread with filling to within 1″ of edge. Roll up, seal edge.

Place roll in greased 9″ sq. pan to form a square. Seal ends together. With scissors, cut almost through the roll at each pan corner. Make 3 more cuts through roll between corner cuts. Turn cut sections so filling shows. Brush with butter and let rise double (30 to 45 min.). Bake.

TEMPERATURE: 350° (mod. oven).

TIME: Bake 30 to 40 min.

KOLACHE ("Ko-latch-ee") *No other nation offers anything quite like these intriguing little fruit buns from Czechoslovakia. Introduced to us by a former Staff member, Mary Lapic, now Mrs. Joseph Boucher of Hopkins, Minnesota. They come in three shapes and with a choice of four different fillings.*

Use ½ of Sweet Dough or all of Richer Sweet Dough (*p. 98*), mixing in . . .

¼ tsp. mace
½ tsp. grated lemon rind

Let rise twice. Prepare any of the fruit fillings below. Shape dough into balls or ovals or squares and fill (*see pictures*). Let rise on greased baking sheet or in muffin cups until light (not quite double), 30 to 40 min. Bake until brown.

TEMPERATURE: 400° (mod. hot oven).

TIME: Bake 20 to 25 min.

AMOUNT: About 2½ doz. buns.

1 Shape dough into 2″ balls. Let rise. When light, make a depression in the center of each ball and fill with fruit filling.

2 Roll balls of dough into ovals. Place a spoonful of filling on half of each oval. Fold other half over. Pinch edges well together.

3 Roll dough ½″ thick. Cut into 3″ squares. Place a spoonful of desired filling on each. Fold corners to center, pinch together.

FRUIT FILLINGS FOR KOLACHE

1. CINNAMON APPLE FILLING: Cook in saucepan until soft . . .

4 small apples, peeled and cut-up
3 tbsp. cinnamon candies
⅓ cup water

Drain and press pulp through sieve.

2. PRUNE FILLING: Soak, cook until soft

30 prunes

Drain, remove pits, mash with fork, add

4 tbsp. sugar
½ tsp. cinnamon

All you have to do—

To make an attractive glaze: mix together 1 slightly beaten egg yolk and ½ cup water. Brush or pat on sweet rolls before baking.

3. APRICOT FILLING: Soak, cook until soft

25 dried apricot halves

Drain, press through sieve, and add . . .

4 tbsp. sugar

4. POPPY SEED FILLING: Mix together . . .

½ cup poppy seeds (crushed or ground)
⅓ cup sour or sweet cream
1 tbsp. butter
1 tbsp. honey or syrup
¼ cup chopped almonds
1 tsp. grated lemon rind
1 tbsp. chopped citron
¼ cup seedless raisins
2 tbsp. sugar
1 tbsp. cornstarch
2 tbsp. red jelly

Boil 1 min. Cool.

★ **KULICH** ***A delicate, sweet, fruity bread rising above tops of cans in mushroom or mosque-like shapes . . . characteristic of old Russia's holiday breads. Perfected by Bernadine Landsberg, formerly of our Staff, now of Red Star Yeast Company.***

Use ½ of Richer Sweet Dough (*p. 98*). Let rise twice.

Distribute over dough and knead in . . . .
- **¼ cup raisins**
- **¼ cup chopped blanched almonds**
- **½ tsp. vanilla**

Divide dough into 2 equal portions. Round up into 2 well rounded bun-like shapes. Place in 2 well greased 1-lb. tin cans. Pat top of dough even. (Cans will be ½ full.) Cover and let rise until double (30 to 40 min.). Place on baking sheet and bake until well browned. Remove from cans. Cool slightly, ice and decorate.

NOTE: The tiny colored decorating candies used for tops of Kulich can be bought at most grocery stores. They are called 100's and 1000's.

TEMPERATURE: 375° (quick mod. oven).

TIME: Bake 30 to 40 min.

AMOUNT: 2 loaves.

To Decorate Kulich

While still warm, drizzle over the tops . . . allowing it to drip over the sides . . .

Confectioners' Sugar Icing

Mix together ½ cup sifted confectioners' sugar, ½ tbsp. warm water, ½ tsp. lemon juice, and a bit of grated rind.

Sprinkle tiny colored decorating candies over the icing.

1 Place dough in cans.

2 Iced and decorated.

HOT CROSS BUNS ***Served in England in the pre-Christian era in honor of the Goddess of Spring. Later, the cross was placed on the bun in a missionary spirit.***

Use ½ of Sweet Dough or all of Richer Sweet Dough (*p. 98*). Let rise twice.

Knead in. . . . .
- **½ cup seedless raisins**
- **¼ cup currants or white raisins**
- **1 tsp. cinnamon**
- **¼ tsp. nutmeg**

Divide dough into 24 pieces and form into balls. Place about 2″ apart on greased baking sheet. Cover and let rise until double (30 to 35 min.). Just before baking, cut a cross in the top of each bun. Bake until brown. Let cool slightly . . . then make cross with Icing (*above*).

Use scissors or sharp knife dipped in flour to cut the crosses.

TEMPERATURE: 400° (mod. hot oven).

TIME: Bake 15 to 20 min.

AMOUNT: 24 buns.

All you have to do—

To glaze buns: a minute before taking them from the oven, brush with milk or slightly beaten egg white, and sprinkle with sugar. Then return to oven a minute to glaze.

All you have to do—

For a Simple Confectioners' Sugar Icing: sift a little sugar into bowl . . . moisten with cream or milk to spreading consistency. Add flavoring, if desired. Spread over slightly warm breads.

Hot Cross Buns ready to serve.

★ BOHEMIAN BRAID *A fruity, nutty, braided elegance for holidays.*

Use ½ of Sweet Dough or all of Richer Sweet Dough (*p. 98*). Let rise twice. Knead in . . .

1 tsp. grated lemon rind
⅛ tsp. mace
½ cup raisins
½ cup chopped blanched almonds

Divide dough into 4 equal parts. Shape 3 of the parts into strands 14″ long. Place them about 1″ apart on lightly greased baking sheet. Braid loosely beginning at middle . . . working toward either end. Seal ends well.

Divide remaining portion of dough into 3 parts and shape into 3 strands each 12″ long. Make another braid as before and place second braid on top of the large braid, pinching ends of small braid into large braid.

Cover and let rise until double in bulk (45 to 60 min.). Bake. Ice while warm (*see p. 111*).
Serve warm.

TEMPERATURE: 350° (mod. oven).

TIME: Bake 40 to 50 min.

NOTE: To give the special holiday touch: decorate with candied cherries and pecan halves. *See color picture, p. 104.*

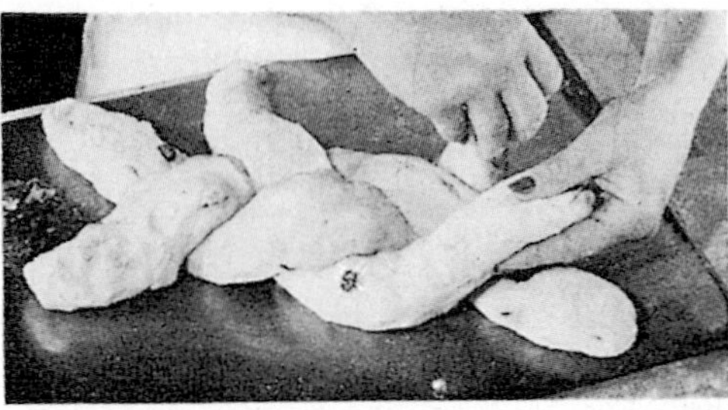

Braid gently and loosely beginning at middle . . . working toward either end. Do not stretch.

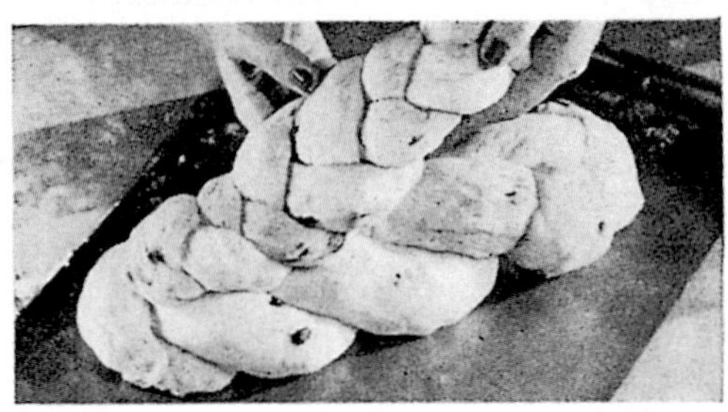

Place second braid on top. Seal braid ends by pressing firmly together and tucking under.

All you have to do—

So braids will be even: elongate dough and divide evenly.

SWEDISH COFFEE BRAID

Flavored with cardamom, reminiscent of afternoon coffee time in old Sweden.

Use ½ of Sweet Dough or all of Richer Sweet Dough (*p. 98*). Mix in . . .

10 cardamom seeds, finely crushed, or 1½ tsp. ground cardamom

Let rise twice. Divide dough into 3 equal portions. Roll each into a 14″ long even strand. Braid as in picture 1. Cover and let rise until light (30 to 45 min.).

Brush on slightly beaten egg and sprinkle with sugar crystals or broken loaf sugar and cut-up unblanched almonds. Bake until rich golden brown. Serve warm.

TEMPERATURE: 350° (mod. oven).

TIME: Bake 35 to 40 min.

FRUIT-FILLED COFFEE BRAID

Each strand in the braid holds a luscious fruit filling.

Use ½ of Sweet Dough or all of Richer Sweet Dough (*p. 98*). Let rise twice.

Divide dough into 3 equal portions. Roll out each into an oblong 13″x6″. Spread oblongs (to within 1″ of edge) with one of the fruit fillings (*p. 106*). Roll up as for Cinnamon Roll. Seal edges of each roll by pinching edges together.

Proceed with braiding as in picture 1. Sprinkle a cinnamon-sugar mixture over top and let rise until light (30 to 45 min.). Bake until a dark brown. Serve warm.

TEMPERATURE: 375° (quick mod. oven).

TIME: Bake 25 to 30 min.

RAISED DOUGHNUTS (🔑 **Recipe**) *Brown and crusty . . . best served warm. New Englanders make them for breakfast and serve them with cheese.*

Use ½ of Sweet Dough (*p. 98*). *After second rising,* roll out dough ⅓″ thick. Cut with floured 3″ doughnut cutter. Let rise on board until very light (30 to 45 min.). Leave uncovered so a crust will form on the dough. Drop into deep hot fat (375°) . . . see directions and pictures (*p. 76*). Drain on absorbent paper. For sugared doughnuts: Place in bag with granulated sugar, and shake.

AMOUNT: 1½ to 2 doz. doughnuts.

FASTNACHTS KUCHEN

Pennsylvania-Dutch fried cakes for the night before Lent.

Follow 🔑 recipe above—*except* increase sugar 2 tbsp., decrease shortening 2 tbsp., and add ¼ tsp. nutmeg.

NANTUCKET DO-NUTS

("Fried Men") Also called "Frogs." After telling on the radio how "Grandmothers" used to make this treat on the day they made bread, this letter came from a little girl in Marshalltown, Iowa.

"My Friend Betty Crocker:
Please register me in your Cooking School. I am only 9 years old, but I want to start learning to cook. I hope I can have the recipe for Fried Men before Hallowe'en. If I can't, I won't be mad, so you don't have to be afraid that I'll unregister."

Pinch off small irregular pieces of raised bread or sweet dough and drop into hot fat as for doughnuts. They bubble and puff up into all sorts of interesting shapes and often look like little brown men or like frogs. Dip quickly into molasses (thinned with a little hot water), or in maple syrup, or honey. Drain. May also be sprinkled with sugar.

★ **CRULLERS**

Old Dutch term for twisted dough.

Follow 🔑 recipe above—*except* shape into twists and slit squares. Fry as for Raised Doughnuts.

TWISTS: Roll dough ½″ thick. Cut in strips ¾″ wide, 10″ long. Shape into twists or figure 8's and drop into hot fat.

SLITSQUARES: Roll out dough ¼″ thick. Cut in 2″ squares. Make 4 slits in each. Then lift by picking up alternate strips between fingers and thumb. Drop into hot fat.

BISMARCKS

Puffy, jelly-filled, crusty, brown balls.

Follow 🔑 recipe for Raised Doughnuts above—*except* roll dough ½″ thick. Cut rounds with a floured 3″ cooky cutter. Fry as for Raised Doughnuts. When cool, cut a *short* slit in the side of each fried ball through the center. Thrust a teaspoonful of jelly into the center and close tightly. Roll in sugar. Serve fresh.

NOTE: To glaze doughnuts, *see p. 77.*

SIMPLIFIED YEAST BREADS Easy . . . quick mixing . . . no kneading.

RICH YEAST BATTER (🔑 Recipe) *Small amount . . . easy to handle.*

One bowl for both mixing and rising. Thorough beating takes the place of kneading. No rolling or cutting. The finished product is more open grained, has thinner crust and less body than kneaded breads. Variations adapted from the old-time Williamsburg Buns recipe by Gladis Schmidt, of Dundee, Minnesota, formerly of our Staff.

Mix together	**3/4 cup lukewarm milk** **1/4 cup sugar** **1 tsp. salt**
Crumble into mixture	**1 cake compressed yeast**
Stir until dissolved. Add	**1 large egg** **1/4 cup soft shortening**
Add	**2 1/4 cups *sifted* GOLD MEDAL Flour** **1/2 tsp. mace** **1/2 tsp. nutmeg**

Beat batter for 1 min. (at least 100 strokes). Scrape down from sides of bowl. Cover with damp cloth and let rise at 85° until double in bulk (about 1 3/4 hr.). Beat well (20 to 30 strokes). Make into coffee cake, buns or puffs as desired. Cover with damp cloth and let rise until very light. Bake (*see directions below*).

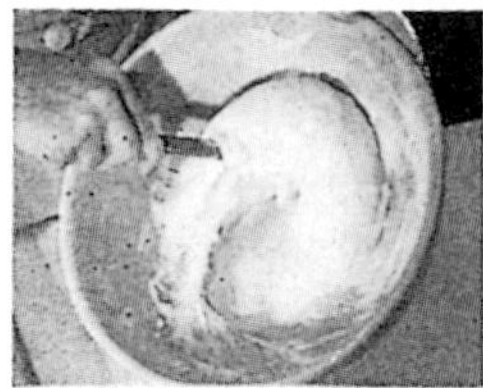
Beat dough.

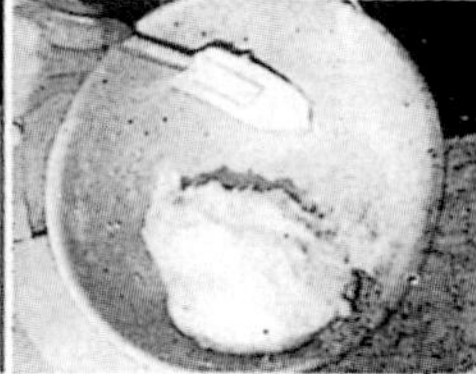
Scrape bowl.

MERRY MORNING RING

A ring of coffee cake . . . gay with cherries.

Follow 🔑 recipe above. After one rising and the beating, spoon batter into greased 9″ ring mold (3″ deep). Cover and let rise (30 to 45 min.). Bake 30 to 35 min. in a mod. oven (350°). Turn onto serving plate and ice (*p. 111*). Decorate with nuts and cherries.

All you have to do—

To improvise a ring mold: Place a greased tin can in center of well greased 9″ round casserole.

YANKEE CLIPPER COFFEE CAKE

With a bubbly brown Streusel topping.

Follow 🔑 recipe above. After one rising and the beating, spread batter in greased 9″ sq. pan.

Mix together and sprinkle over top . . .

1/4 cup sugar
2 tsp. cinnamon
2 tbsp. flour
2 tbsp. butter

Let rise until light (35 to 45 min.). Bake. Serve immediately.

TEMPERATURE: 350° (mod. oven).

TIME: Bake 30 to 35 min.

★ WILLIAMSBURG BUNS

This colonial favorite from Old Virginia was broadcast in our radio series on "Origin of our American Foods." It became a favorite at our guest luncheons!

Follow 🔑 recipe above—*except* original recipe contained 2 tbsp. sherry and omitted 2 tbsp. of the milk. After one rising and the beating, drop by spoonfuls into 12 greased muffin cups . . . each 2/3 full. Let rise until dough rounds slightly above tops of pans (25 to 30 min.).

TEMPERATURE: 400° (mod. hot oven).

TIME: Bake 12 to 15 min.

AMOUNT: 12 medium-sized buns.

SUGAR 'N' SPICE PUFFS

Make Williamsburg Buns above. When baked, remove from pans and quickly dip tops and sides in . . .

6 tbsp. butter, melted

Then roll puffs in a mixture of . . .

1/2 cup sugar
1 tsp. cinnamon

Serve immediately.

TUTTI-FRUTTI BREAD

"Chock" full of fruits and nuts.

Follow 🔑 recipe for Rich Yeast Batter (*p. 110*)—*except* add to the flour . . .

¼ cup cut-up candied cherries
¼ cup cut-up citron
¼ cup raisins
¼ cup cut-up nuts

After one rising and the beating, spread in greased 13x9″ oblong pan.

Sprinkle with . . .

2 tbsp. sugar

Let rise until light (30 to 45 min.). Bake.

TEMPERATURE: 400° (mod. hot oven).

TIME: Bake 15 to 20 min.

FANCY FRUIT BUNS

Make as for Tutti-Frutti Bread above—*except* drop by tablespoonfuls about 3″ apart on greased baking sheet. Brush with milk. Let rise until light (30 to 40 min.). Bake. While still warm, frost.

AMOUNT: 18 buns.

CINNAMON LAYER LOAF

Serve warm for breakfast.

Follow 🔑 recipe for Rich Yeast Batter (*p. 110*)—*except* omit spices. After one rising and the beating, spread half of batter in bottom of greased 9x5x3″ loaf pan. Sprinkle with *half* of . . .

CINNAMON FILLING

½ cup sugar
3 tsp. cinnamon
⅓ cup chopped nuts

Spread the remaining batter and sprinkle with rest of filling. Let rise until light (30 to 35 min.). Bake.

TEMPERATURE: 375° (quick mod. oven).

TIME: Bake 30 to 40 min.

FRESH FOR BREAKFAST

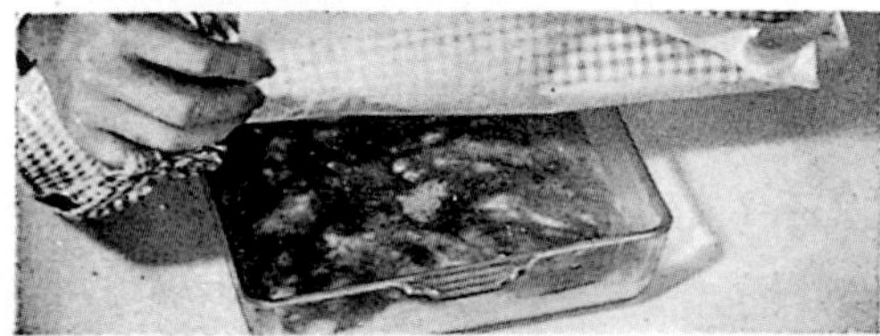

Place the batter for these breads (except the muffin and bun types) in pans as directed in recipes. Cover with waxed paper, then with a damp cloth. Refrigerate overnight. In the morning, bake immediately (no extra rising).

ENGLISH FRUIT BREAD

Very extra special when sliced and toasted.

Follow 🔑 recipe for Rich Yeast Batter (*p. 110*)—*except* omit the spices and add to the flour . . .

2 tbsp. finely cut candied orange peel
2 tbsp. finely cut citron
¼ cup finely cut candied cherries
¼ cup currants
¼ cup raisins
¼ cup chopped nuts

After one rising and the beating, pour into greased 9x5x3″ loaf pan or into 12 large muffin cups (only half full). Let rise until double (45 to 60 min.). Bake. If desired, brush warm bread with icing *below*. Decorate with a few nuts and cherries.

TEMPERATURE: 375° (quick mod. oven).

TIME: Bake 45 min. (loaf),
25 min. (muffins).

★ ALMOND PUFFS

Extra light . . . topped with crunchy almonds.

Follow 🔑 recipe for Rich Yeast Batter (*p. 110*)—*except* omit spices and reduce sugar to 3 tbsp. and flour to 2 cups.

Blanch and chop (for dough and topping) . . .

⅔ cup almonds

Add ⅓ cup of the almonds to the batter. Cover and let rise 45 to 60 min. Drop spoonfuls of batter into greased muffin cups, filling each ½ full. Sprinkle tops with *Almond-Sugar* mixture:

remaining almonds
3 tbsp. sugar

Let rise until double (25 to 30 min.). Bake. Serve warm.

TEMPERATURE: 375° (quick mod. oven).

TIME: Bake 15 to 20 min.

AMOUNT: 24 small or 12 large puffs.

All you have to do—

To frost coffee cakes and other fancy breads make:

CONFECTIONERS' SUGAR ICING

Mix together . . .

1 cup *sifted* confectioners' sugar
1 to 2 tbsp. warm water, milk, or cream (use *amount* for desired thickness)
½ tsp. vanilla or lemon juice (use a bit of grated lemon rind with the lemon)

Spread or drizzle over bread while slightly warm.

SIMPLIFIED YEAST BREADS Two old-time favorites for teatime.

CINNAMON TWISTS *A prize-winning recipe; came to us from a wonderful cook in Ohio.*

Heat to lukewarm in large saucepan...	**1 cup sour cream**
Remove from heat and stir in..........	**3 tbsp. sugar** **1/8 tsp. soda** **1 tsp. salt**
Crumble into mixture................	**1 cake compressed yeast**
Stir until dissolved. Add..............	**1 large egg** **2 tbsp. soft shortening** **3 cups *sifted* GOLD MEDAL Flour**

Mix well (use hand if necessary). Turn dough onto floured board and fold over several times until it is smooth. Then roll into an oblong 24x6″. Follow picture directions below.

TEMPERATURE: 375° (quick mod. oven).

TIME: Bake 12 to 15 min.

AMOUNT: 2 doz. twists.

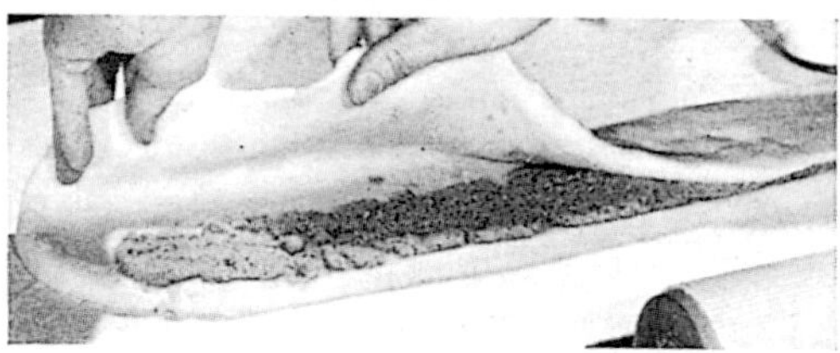

1 Spread with 2 tbsp. soft butter. Sprinkle half of dough with a mixture of 1/3 cup brown sugar and 1 tsp. cinnamon. Fold other half over. Cut into 24 strips 1″ wide.

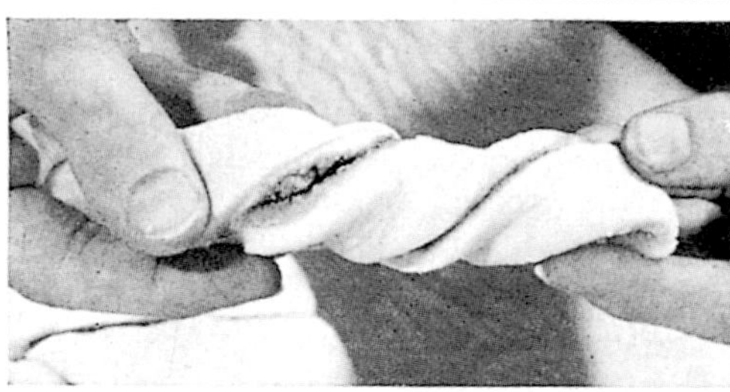

2 Hold strip at both ends and twist (opposite directions).

3 Place on greased baking sheet 2″ apart. Press both ends of twists to baking sheet. Cover and let rise until light (1 hr.). Bake and frost(*p. 111*). Serve warm.

★ SALLY LUNN *Came to America from Bath, England—home of Sally Lunn. The distinctive feature is the shape . . . baked in a tube center pan (originally the Turk's head mold). It has fluffy, porous, sponge-cake-like texture. Serve hot in wedges with butter . . . or serve when a day old . . . toasted.*

Mix together in large bowl............	**2 cups lukewarm milk** **2 tbsp. sugar** **1½ tsp. salt**
Crumble into mixture................	**2 cakes compressed yeast**
Stir until dissolved. Add..............	**2 eggs** **4 tbsp. soft shortening** **5½ cups *sifted* GOLD MEDAL Flour**

Beat until smooth (100 strokes). Cover and let rise until very light (1 hr.). Beat down and pour into greased 10″ tube center pan. Let rise to within 1″ of top of pan (45 min.). Bake until golden brown and crusty. Serve hot.

TEMPERATURE: 350° (mod. oven).

TIME: Bake 45 to 50 min.

AMOUNT: 16 servings.

60-MINUTE SWEET DOUGH (🔑 Recipe) *So quick and easy to make. Gladys Mason, an artist with food, Director of Home Economics of the Sperry Division of General Mills, worked out these delicious recipes.*

Mix in a saucepan . . . a moderately stiff dough that can be rolled out . . . knead only a few turns and shape immediately . . . then set to rise. Bake. Ready to eat in about 60 min.

Heat to lukewarm in medium-sized saucepan	½ cup milk
Remove from heat and stir in	1 tsp. salt 1 tbsp. sugar
Crumble into mixture	1 cake compressed yeast
Stir until dissolved. Stir in	1 egg 2 tbsp. soft shortening
Mix in (just enough to handle easily)	2 to 2¼ cups *sifted* GOLD MEDAL Flour

Mix dough with hand until *moderately* stiff. Turn dough onto floured board and fold it over several times until smooth. Shape, let rise at 85°. Bake. Serve immediately.

TEMPERATURE: 400° (mod. hot oven).

TIME: Bake 20 to 25 min.

PAN ROLLS

Delicious pan biscuits served hot out of oven.

Make 60-Minute Sweet Dough (🔑 recipe.) Divide into 16 equal pieces. Shape each into a ball and place (with a little space between) in a greased 9″ round pan. Cover with damp cloth and let rise until light (25 to 35 min.). Brush with butter.

Bake until golden brown. Serve.

AMOUNT: 16 rolls.

★ FROSTED ORANGE ROLLS

"Luscious is the word for these," says Margaret Doyle Stevning (Mrs. Oliver H.), who was in charge of our first test kitchen.

Make 60-Minute Sweet Dough (🔑 recipe). Roll out dough into a 12x7″ oblong. Spread surface with half of:

CREAMY ORANGE FILLING

Beat until creamy and smooth . . .
- 3 tbsp. soft butter
- 1 tbsp. grated orange rind
- 2 tbsp. orange juice
- 1½ cups *sifted* confectioners' sugar

Roll up as for Cinnamon Rolls. Cut in 12 slices. Place, with a little space between, in greased 9″ round pan. Cover and let rise until light (25 to 35 min.). Bake until golden brown. Remove from pan and spread top with remaining filling. Serve immediately.

AMOUNT: 12 rolls.

CINNAMON SWIRLS

Make 60-Minute Sweet Dough (🔑 recipe). Roll out dough into 12x7″ oblong. Spread surface with . . .

- 1 tbsp. soft butter

Sprinkle with . . .
- ¼ cup sugar
- 1 tsp. cinnamon

Roll up as for Cinnamon Rolls. Cut in 12 slices. Place, with a little space between, in greased 9″ round pan. Cover and let rise until light (25 to 35 min.). Bake until golden brown. Remove from pan. If desired, top with icing (*p. 111*). Serve.

AMOUNT: 12 rolls.

PECAN ROLLS

Make as for Cinnamon Swirls above—*except* place cut slices in a pan coated with ¼ cup *each* melted butter, brown sugar, and pecans. When baked, turn pan upside down onto serving plate for a few min.

All you have to do—

(If your kitchen is cold) To help breads rise within the prescribed time: Place bowl of dough in a closed cupboard with a pan of hot water beside it *or* place bowl of dough on cake rack over bowl of hot water.

REFRIGERATOR YEAST BREADS Handy for "last minute" shaping.

What Doughs Can I Keep in the Refrigerator?
Almost any dough except plain bread dough. Those made with at least ¼ cup sugar and milk, keep about 3 days. Doughs made with water keep about 5 days. (Temperature in refrigerator should be 50° or lower)

When Is the Dough Put in the Refrigerator?
Immediately after mixing. Or it may be allowed to rise once, punched down, and then put into the refrigerator. Then it must be punched down occasionally as it rises.

How Should I Prepare the Dough?
Grease top of dough well and cover with waxed paper or refrigerator cover; then with a damp cloth. Keep cloth damp.

Must I Bake All the Dough at Once?
No, cut off only as much as needed for number of rolls or amounts of coffee cakes. Then return remainder of dough to refrigerator.

How Long to Let Rise Before Baking?
Until doubled (1½ to 2 hr.). The time will vary with coldness of dough, size of rolls, etc.

FAVORITE REFRIGERATOR DOUGH (🔑 Recipe) *Richer and sweeter.*

Mix together	**1½ cups lukewarm water or potato water** **⅔ cup sugar** **1½ tsp. salt**
Crumble into mixture	**1 cake compressed yeast**
Stir until dissolved. Add	**2 eggs** **⅔ cup soft shortening**
Mix in first with spoon, then with hand	**1 cup lukewarm mashed potatoes** **7 to 7½ cups *sifted* GOLD MEDAL Flour**

Knead until smooth (*see p. 90*).

Place in refrigerator (*see above*). About 2 hr. before baking, shape dough into desired rolls, coffee cakes, etc. Cover and let rise until light (1½ to 2 hr.). Bake according to directions with each type.

For Plain Rolls

TEMPERATURE: 400° (mod. hot oven).

TIME: Bake 12 to 15 min.

AMOUNT: 4 doz. medium-sized rolls.

REFRIGERATOR ROLLS

No kneading. Fresh rolls every night.

Mix and handle dough as in 🔑 recipe above—*except do not knead.* Use these ingredients:

2 cups lukewarm water or potato water
½ cup sugar
1½ tsp. salt

2 cakes compressed yeast

1 egg
¼ cup soft shortening

6½ to 7 cups *sifted* GOLD MEDAL Flour

Shape refrigerated dough into desired rolls, etc. Cover, let rise until light (1½ to 2 hr.).

TEMPERATURE: 400° (mod. hot oven).

TIME: Bake 12 to 15 min.

AMOUNT: 3½ doz. rolls.

★ CARAWAY BREAD STICKS

Delicious as salad or soup accompaniment.

Mix and handle dough as in 🔑 recipe above—*except do not knead.* Use these ingredients:

1 cup lukewarm milk or water
1 tbsp. sugar
1½ tsp. salt
½ tsp. nutmeg
1 tsp. leaf sage, crumbled
2 tsp. caraway seed

1 cake compressed yeast

1 egg
¼ cup soft shortening

3 to 3¼ cups *sifted* GOLD MEDAL Flour

Beat vigorously. Cover and refrigerate at least 2 hr. or overnight before forming into sticks. Divide the chilled dough into 3 doz. small pieces. Roll into 8″ pencil-like strips and place 1″ apart on greased baking sheet. Let rise and bake as in 🔑 recipe above.

AMOUNT: 3 doz. bread sticks.

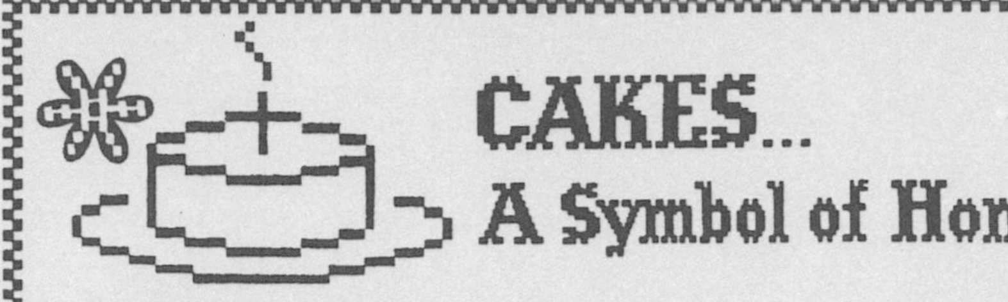

CAKES... A Symbol of Home Life

FROM the beautiful cake for the announcement party—to the triumphantly towering wedding cake—and children's birthday cakes, blazing with candles—to the proud cake celebrating the silver or golden wedding—cakes play an important role in the most significant moments in our lives.

Betty Crocker

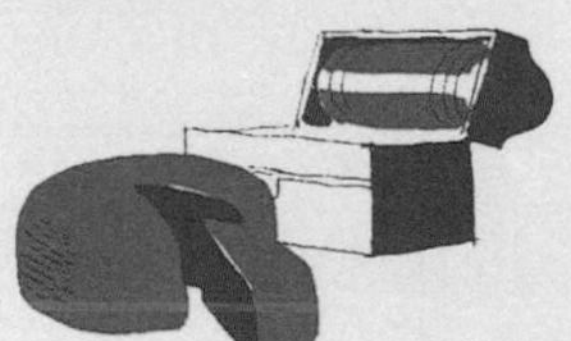

BE A GOOD AR-CAKE-TECHT

FOLLOW THE BLUEPRINT

Each and every recipe has been tested not once but hundreds of times, in our own kitchens and also in representative homes across the country, to insure perfect cakes for each of you who makes them.

CHOOSE GOOD BUILDING MATERIALS

High grade, sweet flavored SHORTENINGS are important in cake-baking. *Hydrogenated* shortenings, such as Crisco, Spry, Swift'ning, and Snowdrift help contribute volume to cakes and give consistently better baking results. Using part butter will add the butter flavor so delicious in white and yellow cakes.

CAUTION: *Do not use oil or melted shortening unless the recipe calls for it.*

CHOCOLATE means *unsweetened* chocolate.

Fine granulated SUGAR is best for cake making, but it may be either cane or beet sugar. If brown or confectioners' sugar is required, it is specified in the recipe.

These recipes are based on *double-action* BAKING POWDER (Calumet, Clabber Girl, Davis OK, K.C.) because more women use this type than any other.

CAUTION: If a tartrate baking powder is used (Royal or Schilling) or a phosphate baking powder (Rumford, Dr. Price, Jewel Tea Co., Davis Phosphate), sprinkle it over batter during last minute of beating. Finish beating and bake *immediately*.

Fresh EGGS. The correct amount of eggs is especially important for success in cakes.

CAUTION: *Always measure eggs for cakes because eggs vary greatly in size.*

LIQUID. It may be milk, buttermilk, coffee, or fruit juice as indicated.

NOTE: Buttermilk and sour milk are interchangeable.

High grade SPICES *and* EXTRACTS are needed for the best flavor. Try interesting combinations, such as almond and vanilla; lemon and orange flower water; almond and rose water.

CHECK THE FRAMEWORK

Flour is particularly important as it is the backbone, 60% of your cake. Our Staff works with and recommends:

As a Cake Flour—SOFTASILK, a super quality Cake Flour—especially milled and designed for cakes. It gives high volume, special tenderness, and a very fluffy delicate cake.

As an all-purpose flour—GOLD MEDAL *Flour*, highest quality all-purpose flour—economical and convenient for every baking purpose. It makes an especially moist, full-flavored cake.

CAUTION: *Use the kind and exact amount of flour indicated in each recipe.*

HAVE THE RIGHT TOOLS

Just as an architect has his slide rule, you must have the right measuring tools to keep proportions correct. Measure level—as exactly as a carpenter measures lumber for the house, if you want perfect cakes. (Cakes are delicately balanced chemical formulas.)

INTERPRET INSTRUCTIONS

Follow the pictures and instructions on the process pages following.

WAIT TILL DONE Have patience.

Don't peek until minimum time is up; then remove cake just as soon as it is done.

Underbaking causes a cake to sink in the middle or have a heavy streak. Sponge, Angel, or Chiffon Cakes may fall out of the pan.

Overbaking dries out the cake and gives thick brown crust. If your cakes do not bake in the time the recipe states, your oven temperature is not correct. Longer baking means the oven is slow; shorter baking time means the oven is hot. Have the oven regulator checked by your utility company or check the temperature yourself with a small oven thermometer.

PROTECT YOUR INVESTMENT

After cake is cool, store, to keep it moist and fresh, in a container with close fitting cover; or invert large bowl over cake plate.

CAKES

We now proclaim you a member of the Society of Cake Artists! And do hereby vest in you all the skills, knowledge, and secrets of the "gentle art" of cake making. Your part is only to heed the directions herein.

For centuries, cake-making changed very little. The 16th century Spice Cake, the 18th century Nun's Cake, even the rich Pound Cake of our colonial days required long hours of labor. Old "receipts" read . . . "take half a peck of fine wheat-flower . . . three pounds of refined sugar . . . dry them by the fire . . . take four pounds of butter, beat it with a cool hand, then beat thirty-five eggs," etc. Later recipes called for smaller amounts but the method of mixing was essentially the same.

Recently our Staff introduced a new cake method to homemakers,—a streamlined method based on precision timing and modern ingredients. It uses only one bowl . . . saves the creaming of shortening and sugar, the separate beating of eggs. It has been given different names, but we call it our *Double-Quick Method.* We have now adapted most of our favorite cakes to it. But knowing that some of you still like to make cakes the old way, we give you the creaming method too, simplified.

Please notice that the left-hand pages give creaming method recipes, the right-hand pages give double-quick method recipes. We hope this *double service* will mean a lot to you! The step-by-step pictures show you just what to do whether you make your cakes by hand or with a cake mixer. And most of the recipes give you your choice of cake flour or all-purpose flour. But the newest and perhaps the most helpful feature of all is the way each cake recipe is "fitted to size" . . . to the size of your family (large or small) . . . and to the size and shape of your cake pans.

Cakes from every land have come to America . . . but none so glamorous as the typically American concoction of richly tender layers, crowned with luscious, creamy icing. Meals are more satisfying, special occasions more festive, with one of these delicious cake creations.

Daffodil
Pink Azalea
Old Kentucky Nut

Brown-Eyed Susan
Chocolate Joy
Bouquet of Flowers

CREAMING METHOD CAKES Conventional way for many years.

THIS IS THE GOOD OLD WAY to mix a "butter" cake.

Read the recipe

Turn on and set the oven

Assemble ingredients

Use ingredients at room temperature (take eggs, milk, etc. out of refrigerator ahead of time).

In *hot* weather, use cold ingredients (liquid and eggs from refrigerator).

Collect utensils

Prepare the pans (p. 123)

Sift flour and measure ingredients. Measure flavoring into liquid. For chocolate cakes, melt chocolate first.

1 Cream softened shortening and sugar together until a smooth, fluffy mass (for fine texture). With mixer, beat at medium speed.

2 Beat in whole eggs or yolks as indicated in recipe. (Chocolate also goes in here when indicated in recipe.) Beat until well mixed. With mixer, use medium speed.

3 Sift together dry ingredients and stir in alternately with the liquid. (Add the flour first and last.) With mixer (low speed), they can be added at the same time.

4 Stir just enough to make batter smooth. When using mixer, be careful not to beat too long. Overmixing reduces volume.

5 In *some* cakes, nuts, raisins, etc. are blended in last. Beaten egg whites are *folded in by hand* at the end. (*Cont. on p. 122.*)

THIS IS THE NEW DOUBLE-QUICK WAY to mix a "butter" cake.

Read the recipe

Turn on and set the oven

Assemble the ingredients

Use ingredients at room temperature (take eggs, milk, etc. out of refrigerator ahead of time). In *hot* weather, use cold ingredients (liquid and eggs from refrigerator).

Collect utensils

Prepare the pans (p. 123)

Sift flour and measure ingredients. Measure flavoring into liquid. For chocolate cakes—melt chocolate first.

CAUTION: Use hydrogenated shortening with this method. See p. 116 for details.

1 Sift dry ingredients into mixing bowl.

2 Add softened shortening, then add a little more than half of liquid (about two-thirds). When using all-purpose flour (GOLD MEDAL), the batter is somewhat heavier, so add all the liquid at once.

3 Beat at medium speed for 2 min., scraping bowl constantly, or beat vigorously with spoon for 2 min. (150 strokes per min.), resting occasionally. Count only actual beating time or strokes.

4 Add remaining liquid and *unbeaten* eggs (or egg yolks or egg whites).

5 Beat 2 min. more, scraping bowl frequently. (*Cont. on p. 122.*)

CAKES FROM CAKE PAN TO CAKE PLATE.

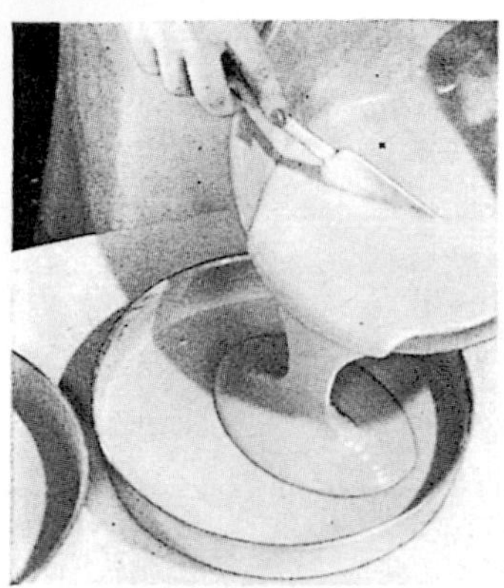

7 Stagger layers in opposite corners, away from oven walls, slightly apart. Top of cake should be at middle of oven.

6 Pour batter into prepared pans of correct size, dividing it evenly. (Batter made by double-quick method is thinner.)

8 When minimum baking time is up, test by lightly touching middle of cake. As soon as no imprint remains, cake is done.

Extra test for oblong or loaf cakes: thrust straw into center. If it comes out clean, cake is done.

10 Turn cake on wire cooling rack so it will not "sweat" and become soggy.

9 Remove from oven. Let stand in pans 10 min. Then carefully loosen from one side with spatula. Tip and turn to let in air.

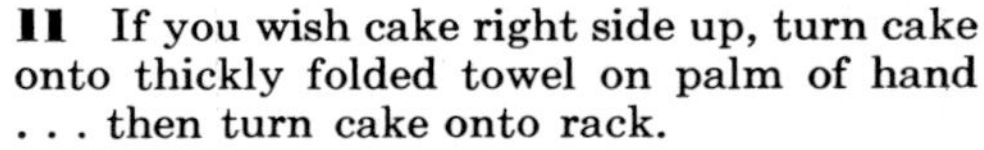

11 If you wish cake right side up, turn cake onto thickly folded towel on palm of hand . . . then turn cake onto rack.

12 As soon as cake is cool, spread frosting or filling between layers to the outer edge. See p. 162.

13 Frost sides and top of cake with light sweeping strokes. Pull frosting from bottom up to top to make cake look well shaped.

PICK THE PROPER PAN

When baking fine layers, loaves, any type cakes,
Choose the size pan the recipe states.

The old-fashioned shallow tin pans are often the cause of batter running over in the oven. Our cake recipes call for modern layer pans 1¼″ to 1½″ deep. Heavy aluminum pans hold heat and distribute it evenly. In heat proof glass pans, cakes should be baked at a temperature 25° lower, as they brown more.

Perfect Cakes promised when you use the right size pan (*see recipes*).

Too *Big* a pan. Cake looks flat and shrunken.

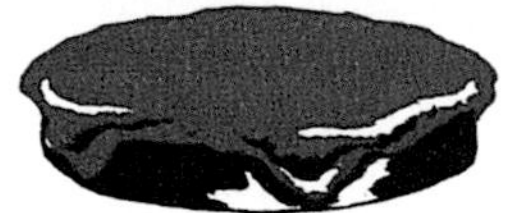

Too *Little* a pan. Cake bulges over and loses contour.

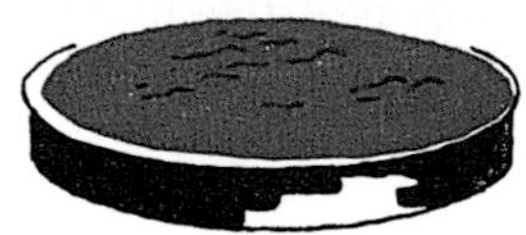

Just the *Right* size pan. Good contour, easy to frost.

PREPARE PANS—For easy removing of cakes.

Grease bottom and sides of layer pans thoroughly.

Dust with flour until well coated on bottom and sides.

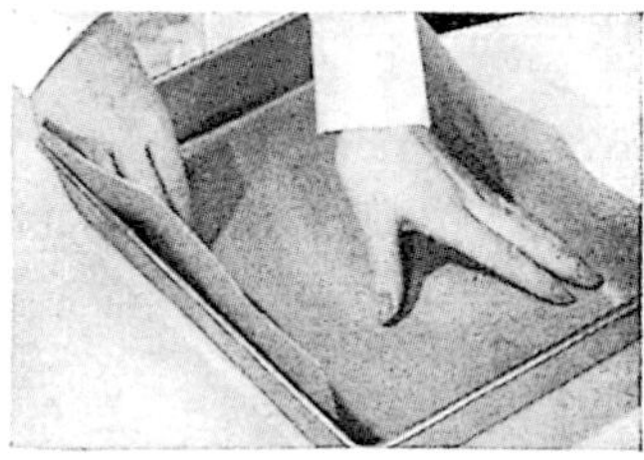

Line bottom of *oblong* pans with brown paper. (Leave "ears.")

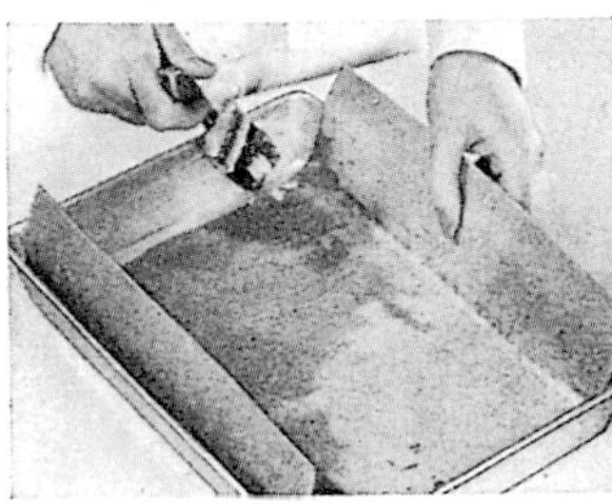

Then grease paper and sides of pan thoroughly.

Cupcakes (especially Double-Quick) hold their shape best if baked in paper cups or liners placed in muffin cups. Saves greasing and washing pan. If not using liners, grease well and flour cups to be filled.

TEMP.: 400° (mod. hot oven).

TIME: Bake 18 to 20 min.

AMOUNT: Small Cake recipe makes 14 medium cupcakes; Large Cake about 20.

Fill cups ⅔ full . . . only ½ full for Double-Quick cakes.

QUESTIONS ON QUANTITIES

Easy to measure fractions if you know your cups. When recipe calls for ⅜, ⅝, or ⅞ cup:

⅜ cup = ¼ cup + 2 tbsp. *or* half way between ¼ cup and ½ cup.

⅝ cup = ½ cup + 2 tbsp. *or* half way between ½ cup and ¾ cup.

⅞ cup = ¾ cup + 2 tbsp. *or* half way between ¾ cup and 1 cup.

HIGH ALTITUDE BAKING

If you live where the elevation is over 2000 feet, follow rules on p. 463. They will help you to make deliciously moist and tender cakes, high in volume, light as clouds,—at any altitude above sea level.

SELF-RISING FLOUR

When using Gold Medal Self-Rising Flour for cakes, follow directions on p. 462.

LIGHT YELLOW CAKE (🔑 Recipe) *Economical for all 'round use.*

	For Large Cake	*Small Cake*
Grease and flour	2 9″ layer pans *or* 13x9″ oblong pan	2 8″ layer pans *or* 9″ square pan
Cream together until fluffy	5/8 cup soft shortening (half butter for flavor)	3/8 cup
	1 7/8 cups sugar	1 1/4 cups
Beat in thoroughly	2 large eggs (1/2 cup)	1 egg (1/4 cup)
Sift together	3 cups *sifted* SOFTASILK *or* 2 3/4 cups *sifted* GOLD MEDAL Flour	1 7/8 cups *or* 1 3/4 cups
	2 1/2 tsp. baking powder	1 1/2 tsp.
	1 tsp. salt	1/2 tsp.
Stir in alternately with	1 1/4 cups milk	7/8 cup
	1 1/2 tsp. vanilla	1 tsp.

Pour into prepared pans. Bake until cake tests done. Cool. Finish with filling and frosting as desired. The oblong or square cake is ideal for the easy topping, p. 169.

TEMPERATURE: 350° (mod. oven).

TIME: Bake layers 30 to 35 min., square or oblong 35 to 40 min.

PINK AND BEIGE CAKE

Children love the marbled colors. The beige part is our old favorite, Cinnamon Cake.

Follow 🔑 recipe above. Divide batter into 2 parts. Blend into one part a few drops of red food coloring. Blend into the remaining part the following spices. Use:

For Large Cake	*Small Cake*
1 tsp. cinnamon	2/3 tsp.
1/8 tsp. cloves	1/8 tsp. (scant)
1/8 tsp. nutmeg	1/8 tsp. (scant)

Drop the 2 batters alternately by spoonfuls into prepared pans. Pull spoon through it to blend colors in "marbled" design. Bake. Cool. Ice with Satiny Beige Frosting with pink coloring drawn through it here and there.

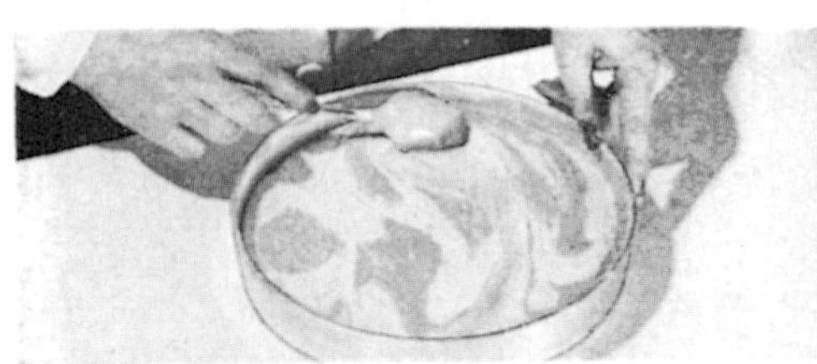

PENUCHE CAKE

You'll admire the beautiful penuche color.

Follow 🔑 recipe above—*except* use brown sugar (lumps removed). Add 1/3 tsp. soda with the baking powder for the Large Cake; 1/4 tsp. (scant) for the Small Cake. Penuche Frosting with toasted pecans brings out the good brown sugar flavor.

BUTTERCUP CAKE (Buttermilk)

The interesting flavor combination of this rich tasting cake was sent us by Mrs. C. Breeden of St. Louis, Missouri.

Follow 🔑 recipe above—*except* use only half the baking powder. To the dry ingredients, add 1/2 tsp. soda for the Large Cake, and 1/3 tsp. soda for the Small Cake. Use buttermilk in place of sweet milk.

For flavoring, substitute for half the vanilla, a combination of orange, lemon, and almond extracts. Frost with Fluffy White Frosting and trim with grated orange or lemon rind to resemble border of buttercups (*see picture on opposite page*).

★ MAPLE SYRUP CAKE

With butternuts (of the walnut family).

Prize-winning recipe for Vermont from Marian Burnes of Montpelier... a recipe from her great grandmother's cook book.

Follow 🔑 recipe for Large Cake above—*except* substitute 1 cup maple syrup for 1 cup of the sugar (use only 7/8 cup sugar). Decrease milk to 5/8 cup (1/2 cup plus 2 tbsp.). Add the syrup with it. Omit vanilla. Blend in 1/2 cup cut-up butternuts or other nuts. Bake. Cool. Frost with Maple Syrup Icing (*opposite page*) or add maple flavoring to a cooked white frosting.

Delicious and not too expensive.

LIGHT GOLDEN CAKE (🔑 Recipe) *High, fluffy, fine-textured.*

	For Large Cake	Small Cake
Grease and flour	2 9″ layer pans *or* 13x9″ oblong pan	2 8″ layer pans *or* 9″ square pan
Sift together	2¼ cups *sifted* SOFTASILK	1½ cups
	1½ cups sugar	1 cup
	3 tsp. baking powder	2 tsp.
	1 tsp. salt	½ tsp.
Add	½ cup soft shortening	⅓ cup
Pour in a little over half of	1 cup milk	⅔ cup
	1½ tsp. flavoring	1 tsp.
Beat 2 min.		
Add remaining milk and	2 eggs (⅓ to ½ cup)	1 egg (¼ cup)
Beat 2 min.		

Pour into prepared pans. Bake until cake tests done. Cool. Finish with filling or frosting as desired. The oblong or square cake is ideal for the easy Broiled Icing, Choc-O-Nut Topping, etc. (see *p. 169*).

NOTE: Small Cake makes *thin* 8″ layers

TEMPERATURE: 350° (mod. oven).

TIME: Bake layers 25 to 30 min., square or oblong 35 to 40 min.

★ NEW BUTTERCUP CAKE

With buttermilk and special flavorings.

Follow 🔑 recipe for Large Cake above—*except* use only half the amount of baking powder. Add ½ tsp. soda to dry ingredients before sifting. Use buttermilk in place of sweet milk.

For flavoring, substitute for half the vanilla, a combination of orange, lemon, and almond extracts. Frost with Fluffy White Frosting. Trim with grated orange or lemon rind to resemble border of buttercups.

MOCK MAPLE NUT CAKE

Follow either 🔑 recipe above or opposite—*except* use maple flavoring and blend in ½ cup cut-up nuts for Large Cake; ⅓ cup for Small Cake. Frost with white icing with maple flavoring added.

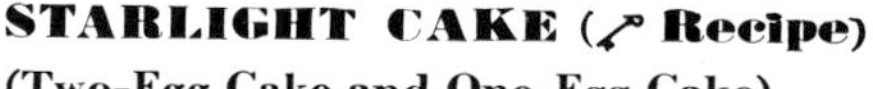

STARLIGHT CAKE (🔑 Recipe)

(Two-Egg Cake and One-Egg Cake)

Prepare pan and use method as given in 🔑 recipe above—*except* add all the milk at once. Makes *thin* 9″ layers. Use:

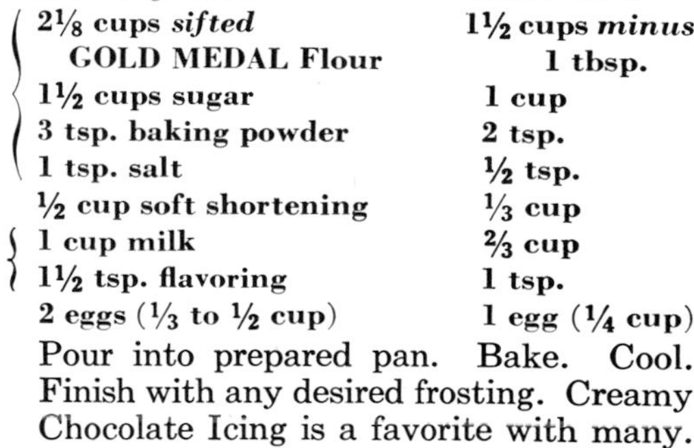

For Large Cake	Small Cake
2⅛ cups *sifted* GOLD MEDAL Flour	1½ cups *minus* 1 tbsp.
1½ cups sugar	1 cup
3 tsp. baking powder	2 tsp.
1 tsp. salt	½ tsp.
½ cup soft shortening	⅓ cup
1 cup milk	⅔ cup
1½ tsp. flavoring	1 tsp.
2 eggs (⅓ to ½ cup)	1 egg (¼ cup)

Pour into prepared pan. Bake. Cool. Finish with any desired frosting. Creamy Chocolate Icing is a favorite with many.

NEW MAPLE SYRUP CAKE

With butternuts (of the walnut family).

Follow either 🔑 recipe for Large Cake above—*except* substitute 1 cup maple syrup for 1 cup of the sugar (use only ½ cup sugar). Decrease milk to ½ cup. Add the syrup with it. Omit vanilla. Blend in ½ cup cut-up butternuts (or other nuts). Bake. Cool. Frost with Maple Syrup Icing or with a cooked white frosting with maple flavoring added.

MAPLE SYRUP ICING

Boil 1¼ cups maple syrup to firm ball stage (242°) and beat gradually into 2 stiffly beaten egg whites.

Old-fashioned yellow cakes.

RICH YELLOW CAKE (🗝 Recipe)

Tender, buttery tasting; will melt in your mouth.

	For Large Cake	*Small Cake*
Grease and flour	2 9″ layer pans or 13x9″ oblong pan	2 8″ layer pans or 9″ square pan
Cream together until fluffy	2/3 cup soft shortening (half butter for flavor)	1/2 cup
	1 1/2 cups sugar	1 1/8 cups
Beat in thoroughly	3 eggs (1/2 to 2/3 cup)	2 eggs (1/3 to 1/2 c.)
Sift together	2 1/2 cups *sifted* SOFTASILK or 2 1/4 cups *sifted* GOLD MEDAL Flour	1 7/8 cups or 1 3/4 cups
	2 1/2 tsp. baking powder	2 tsp.
	1 tsp. salt	3/4 tsp.
Stir in alternately with	1 cup milk	3/4 cup
	1 1/2 tsp. vanilla	1 tsp.

Pour into prepared pans. Bake until cake tests done. Cool. Finish with desired filling and frosting. Especially delicious with a Clear Lemon or Clear Orange Filling and a luscious white coconut frosting.

TEMPERATURE: 350° (mod. oven).

TIME: Bake layers 25 to 30 min., square or oblong 30 to 40 min.

★ DELICATE RICH YELLOW CAKE

Super de luxe version of the Rich Yellow.

Follow 🗝 recipe for the Large Cake above using 2 9″ layer pans and SOFTASILK Cake Flour—*except* use 2 1/4 cups SOFTASILK and reduce milk to 3/4 cup. Delicious with Chocolate Cream Filling between layers and spread thin on top of cake. Finish with Double Boiler Frosting on top and sides. Sprinkle grated chocolate on top for color and taste contrast.

RICH ORANGE CAKE

Follow 🗝 recipe above in layer pans—*except* omit vanilla. In place of the milk, use half water and half orange juice. Add 1 1/2 tsp. grated orange rind for the Large Cake; 1 tsp. for the Small Cake. Put cooled layers together with Clear Orange Filling and frost top and sides with White Mountain Frosting. Decorate with fresh orange sections (membrane removed.)

DAFFODIL (JONQUIL) CAKE

See colored picture on pp. 118 and 119.

Make Rich Orange Cake above. Cool. Spread Clear Orange Filling between layers and over top of cake. Frost sides with a cooked white frosting (tinted yellow) and pull frosting up over filling in the shape of daffodil petals.

BROWN-EYED SUSAN CAKE

Pretty as the picture on p. 119.

Follow 🗝 recipe above in layer pans—*except* omit vanilla. Divide batter into 2 parts. Into one part, blend...

For Large Cake	*Small Cake*
2 sq. chocolate (2 oz.), melted	1 1/2 sq. (1 1/2 oz.)
1/8 tsp. soda	1/8 tsp.
1 tbsp. milk	3/4 tbsp.
Blend into other part...	
1 tsp. orange extract	3/4 tsp.
1 1/2 tbsp. orange rind	1 tbsp.
1/4 tsp. yellow coloring	1/4 tsp. (scant)

Drop the chocolate and orange batters alternately by spoonfuls into prepared pans. Bake. Cool. Fill and frost with Brown-Eyed Susan Frosting (*opposite page*).

Space spoonfuls of 1 batter around pan leaving room to add alternate spoonfuls of other.

★ RICH GOLDEN CAKE (🔑 Recipe) *A delicious rich, tender cake.*

	For Large Cake	*Small Cake*
Grease and flour	2 9″ layer pans or 13x9″ oblong pan	2 8″ layer pans *or* 9″ square pan
Sift together (*See CAUTION in square below*)	2¼ cups *sifted* SOFTASILK *or* 2⅛ cups *sifted* GOLD MEDAL Flour	1⅝ cups *or* 1½ cups
	1½ cups sugar	1 cup
	3 tsp. baking powder	2 tsp.
	1 tsp. salt	½ tsp.
Add	⅔ cup soft shortening	½ cup
*Pour in a little over half of	1 cup milk	⅔ cup
	1½ tsp. vanilla	1 tsp.
Beat 2 min.		
Add remaining milk and	3 eggs (½ to ⅔ cup)	2 eggs (⅓ to ½ c.)
Beat 2 min.		

Pour into prepared pans. Bake until cake tests done. Cool. Finish with desired filling and frosting. This cake is especially delicious with Clear Lemon or Clear Orange Filling and a white icing. Or for a special effect, use the Brown-Eyed Susan Frosting (*below*).

**When using* GOLD MEDAL, *add all the liquid at once.*

TEMPERATURE: 350° (mod. oven).

TIME: Bake layers 30 to 35 min., square or oblong 40 to 45 min.

CAUTION: In our home testing, this cake rated exceptionally high (10) with testers who followed all the directions accurately. Because it is extra rich, it pays to be extra careful (*see page 116 on shortening and baking powder*).

FRESH ORANGE CAKE

Follow 🔑 recipe for Rich Golden Cake above or the Rich Yellow Cake on opposite page—*except* omit vanilla. Use orange extract for flavoring and add 1 to 1½ tsp. grated orange rind to batter. Bake in layers, put cooled layers together with Clear Orange Filling, and ice top and sides with White Mountain Frosting. Decorate with fresh orange sections (membrane removed).

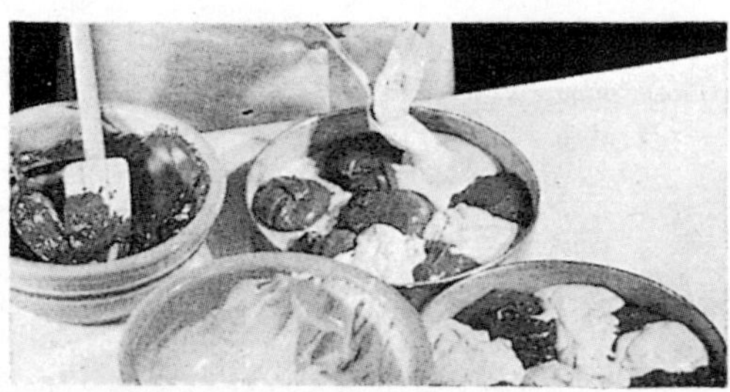

Fill spaces with spoonfuls of other batter. Place baked layers for contrast of colors.

BROWN-EYED SUSAN FROSTING

See the colored picture on p. 119.

For 9″ Layers	*For 8″ Layers*
Heat in saucepan . . .	
4 tbsp. butter	3 tbsp.
3 tbsp. cream	2¼ tbsp.
Stir in . . .	
3 cups *sifted* confectioners' sugar	2¼ cups
Divide frosting about in half. To smaller amount, add . . .	
1 tbsp. grated orange rind	¾ tbsp.
orange juice	orange juice
(just enough to make easy to spread)	
To larger amount, add . . .	
2 sq. chocolate (2 oz.), melted	1½ sq.
rich milk or cream	rich milk, etc.
(to make glossy and easy to spread)	

Spread some of the chocolate frosting between layers and the orange frosting on top of cake. Spread remaining chocolate frosting around sides scalloping the top edge. Sprinkle grated orange rind and clusters of shaved chocolate over the top of the cake to give effect of a field of Brown-Eyed Susans.

SPICE CAKES

Spice, fruit, and nuts add zest.

DUCHESS SPICE CAKE (🔑 Recipe)

Good, old-fashioned flavor . . . rich . . . tender.

	For Large Cake	Small Cake
Grease and flour	2 9″ layer pans or 13x9″ oblong pan	2 8″ layer pans or 9″ squarepan
Cream together until fluffy	3/4 cup soft shortening	1/2 cup
	1 1/4 cups brown sugar	3/4 cup
	1 cup white sugar	3/4 cup
Beat in thoroughly	3 eggs (1/2 to 2/3 cup)	2 eggs (1/3 to 1/2 c.)
Sift together	3 cups *sifted* SOFTASILK *or* 2 3/4 cups *sifted* GOLD MEDAL Flour	2 cups *or* 1 3/4 cups
	1 1/2 tsp. soda	1 tsp.
	1 1/2 tsp. cinnamon	1 tsp.
	3/4 tsp. nutmeg	1/2 tsp.
	3/4 tsp. cloves	1/2 tsp.
	1 tsp. salt	1/2 tsp.
Stir in alternately with	1 1/2 cups buttermilk	1 cup

Pour into prepared pans. Bake until cake tests done. Cool. Finish with White Butter Icing or desired filling and frosting.

TEMPERATURE: 350° (mod. oven).
TIME: Bake layers 35 to 40 min., square or oblong 50 to 55 min.

RAISIN-NUT SPICE CAKE

The extra ingredients "make" the perfect spice cake. Stores well, too.

Follow 🔑 recipe above. Just before pouring batter into pans, fold in a mixture of

For Large Cake	Small Cake
1 cup seeded raisins, cut-up	2/3 cup
1/2 cup nuts, cut-up	1/3 cup
2 tbsp. extra flour	1 tbsp.

Finish with White Butter or Browned Butter Icing.

BLACK WALNUT SPICE CAKE

Follow 🔑 recipe above—*except* omit cinnamon and cloves and add allspice. Fold in black walnuts at the very end. Use:

For Large Cake	Small Cake
1/2 tsp. allspice	1/3 tsp.
1 cup black walnuts, cut-up	2/3 cup

Frost with White Butter Icing and decorate with toasted black walnut halves.

All you have to do–

To make Black Walnut What-nots: cut oblong or square cake into 3″ squares. Split each into 2 layers and put together with Cream Filling. Top with sweetened whipped cream, shaved salted almonds.

LAST-MINUTE FRUIT CAKE

Make large recipe of Applesauce Cake ↗ *except* use only 1/2 cup raisins. At the last mix in 1/4 cup *each* finely cut dates, candied cherries, pineapple, and lemon peel.

★ APPLESAUCE CAKE

Watch this cake disappear!

First, make *thick unsweetened* Applesauce (*p. 129*). Prepare oblong or square pan. Use method as given in 🔑 recipe above—*except* stir in applesauce after egg is beaten in. Use:

For 13x9″ oblong pan	9″ square
1/2 cup soft shortening	1/3 cup
2 cups sugar	1 1/3 cups
1 very large egg (1/3 cup)	1 egg (1/4 cup)
1 1/2 cups applesauce	1 cup
2 7/8 cups *sifted* SOFTASILK *or* 2 1/2 cups *sifted* GOLD MEDAL Flour	1 7/8 cups *or* 1 2/3 cups
1 1/2 tsp. soda	1 tsp.
1 1/2 tsp. salt	1 tsp.
3/4 tsp. cinnamon	1/2 tsp.
1/2 tsp. cloves	1/3 tsp.
1/2 tsp. allspice	1/3 tsp.
1/2 cup water	1/3 cup
Stir in . . .	
1/2 cup walnuts, cut-up	1/3 cup
1 cup seeded raisins, cut-up	2/3 cup

TEMPERATURE: 350° (mod. oven).

TIME: Bake oblong cake 45 to 50 min., square cake 35 to 40 min.

For a decorative effect . . . sift confectioners' sugar through paper doily onto top of cake. *See color picture on p. 138.*

★ NEW DUCHESS SPICE CAKE (Recipe)

A simple spice cake . . . full-flavored and tender.

	For Large Cake	*Small Cake*
Grease and flour	2 9″ layer pans *or* 13x9″ oblong pan	2 8″ layer pans *or* 9″ square pan
Sift together	2½ cups *sifted* SOFTASILK *or* 2⅓ cups *sifted* GOLD MEDAL Flour	1⅞ cups *or* 1¾ cups
	1 cup sugar	¾ cup
	1 tsp. soda	¾ tsp.
	1½ tsp. cinnamon	1 tsp.
	¾ tsp. nutmeg	½ tsp.
	¾ tsp. cloves	½ tsp.
	1 tsp. salt	¾ tsp.
Add	1 cup brown sugar	¾ cup
	⅔ cup soft shortening	½ cup
	1 cup buttermilk	¾ cup
Beat 2 min.		
Add	3 eggs (½ to ⅔ cup)	2 eggs (⅓ to ½ c.)
Beat 2 min.		

Pour into prepared pans. Bake until cake tests done. Cool. Finish with White Butter Icing or any desired frosting.

TEMPERATURE: 350° (mod. oven).
TIME: Bake layers 30 to 35 min., square or oblong 45 min.

NEW RAISIN-NUT SPICE CAKE

Follow recipe above. Just before pouring batter into pans, fold in ½ cup *each* cut-up nuts and cut-up seeded raisins for Large Cake; ⅓ cup *each* for Small Cake.

NEW BANANA CAKE

Follow method as given in recipe above. Add all bananas with *half* of liquid in first 2 min. of beating. Add remaining liquid with the eggs. Fold in nuts at very last.

For Large Cake	*Small Cake*
2½ cups *sifted* SOFTASILK	1⅞ cups
1⅔ cups sugar	1¼ cups
1¼ tsp. baking powder	1 tsp.
1¼ tsp. soda	1 tsp.
1 tsp. salt	¾ tsp.
⅔ cup soft shortening	½ cup
⅔ cup buttermilk	½ cup
1¼ cups mashed ripe bananas (about 3)	1 cup (about 2)
2 large eggs (½ cup)	2 small
⅔ cup chopped nuts	½ cup

NEW BLACK WALNUT CAKE

Make New Duchess Spice Cake above—*except* change as for Black Walnut Spice Cake on opposite page.

NEW APPLESAUCE CAKE

First, make thick unsweetened applesauce (*below*). Then prepare oblong or square pan. Use method as given in recipe above. Add applesauce in last 2 min. of beating. Use:

For 13x9″ Oblong	*9″ Square*
2¾ cups *sifted* SOFTASILK *or* 2½ cups *sifted* GOLD MEDAL Flour	1¾ cups *or* 1⅔ cups
2 cups sugar	1⅓ cups
¼ tsp. baking powder	¼ tsp. (scant)
1½ tsp. soda	1 tsp.
1½ tsp. salt	1 tsp.
¾ tsp. cinnamon	½ tsp.
½ tsp. cloves	⅓ tsp.
½ tsp. allspice	⅓ tsp.
½ cup soft shortening	⅓ cup
½ cup water	⅓ cup
½ cup walnuts, cut-up	⅓ cup
1 cup raisins, cut-up	⅔ cup
1½ cups applesauce	1 cup
1 very large egg (⅓ cup)	1 egg (¼ cup)

TEMPERATURE: 350° (mod. oven).
TIME: Bake oblong cake 45 to 50 min., square cake 35 to 40 min.

All you have to do—

To make 1½ cups applesauce: wash, quarter, and core 6 to 8 tart apples. Add ¼ cup water. Cover and cook to a mush, stirring occasionally. Press through a sieve or food mill.

CARAMEL (Burnt Sugar) CAKE (🔑 Recipe) *Note especially the beautiful color.*

	For Large Cake	*Small Cake*
Grease and flour	2 9″ layer pans *or* 13x9″ oblong pan	2 8″ layer pans *or* 9″ square pan
First, *caramelize the sugar* (*see p. 25*): (Melt in a *heavy* skillet, etc.)	1 cup sugar	¾ cup
Remove from heat.		
Add *slowly*, stirring constantly	½ cup boiling water	⅜ cup
Stir over *low* heat until lumps are dissolved. Pour into measuring cup	*¼ cup caramel mixture	3 tbsp.
and add enough cold water to make	1 cup liquid	¾ cup
Cream together until fluffy	½ cup soft shortening	⅜ cup
	1⅓ cups sugar	1 cup
Beat in thoroughly	3 eggs (½ to ⅔ cup)	2 eggs (⅓ to ½ c.)
Sift together	2½ cups *sifted* SOFTASILK *or* 2⅓ cups *sifted* GOLD MEDAL Flour	1¾ cups *or* 1½ cups
	2½ tsp. baking powder	2 tsp.
	1 tsp. salt	¾ tsp.
Stir in alternately with	caramel mixture	caramel mix.

Pour into prepared pans. Bake until cake tests done. Cool. Finish with Caramel Icing (*see below*).

TEMPERATURE: 350° (mod. oven).
TIME: Bake layers 30 to 35 min., square or oblong 35 to 45 min.

CARAMEL ICING

**Use the remaining caramel syrup. Delicious.*

For Large Cake	*Small Cake*
Heat together . . .	
all the caramel mixture plus cream to equal ½ cup	⅜ cup
6 tbsp. butter	4½ tbsp.
Beat in . . .	
3 cups *sifted* confectioners' sugar	2¼ cups
⅓ tsp. salt	¼ tsp.
1 tsp. vanilla	¾ tsp.

Burnt Sugar Cake—always a prize winner at State and County Fairs.

★ ARABY SPICE CAKE

A rich blend of spices as from the Near East.

Prepare 2 9″ layer pans or 13x9″ oblong. Follow 🔑 recipe above for method. Use:

- ¾ cup soft shortening
- 1½ cups sugar
- 3 eggs (½ to ⅔ cup)

- 2 cups *sifted* SOFTASILK *or* 1⅞ cups *sifted* GOLD MEDAL Flour
- ¼ tsp. baking powder
- ½ tsp. soda
- ¾ tsp. salt
- ¾ tsp. nutmeg
- 1 tsp. cinnamon
- 2 tbsp. cocoa

- ¾ cup buttermilk
- 1 tsp. vanilla
- 1 tsp. lemon extract

½ cup nuts, coarsely cut-up

Finish with ARABY MOCHA ICING

Blend together . . .

- 6 tbsp. softened butter
- 1 egg yolk
- 3 cups *sifted* confectioners' sugar
- 1½ tbsp. cocoa
- 1 tsp. cinnamon
- 1½ tbsp. hot coffee

★ NEW CARAMEL CAKE (Recipe) *Something different in cake flavor.*

	For Large Cake	Small Cake
Grease and flour	2 9″ layer pans *or* 13x9″ oblong pan	2 8″ layer pans *or* 9″ square pan
First, *caramelize the sugar* (*see p. 25*). (Melt in a *heavy* skillet, etc.)	½ cup sugar	⅜ cup
Remove from heat.		
Add *slowly*, stirring constantly	½ cup boiling water	⅜ cup
Stir over *low* heat until lumps are dissolved. Pour into measuring cup and add enough cold water to make	1 cup liquid	¾ cup
Sift together	2¼ cups *sifted* SOFTASILK *or* 2⅛ cups *sifted* GOLD MEDAL Flour	1¾ cups *or* 1⅝ cups
	1 cup sugar	¾ cup
	3 tsp. baking powder	2¼ tsp.
	1 tsp. salt	¾ tsp.
Add	½ cup soft shortening	⅜ cup
*Pour in a little over half of	caramel mixture	caramel mix.
Beat 2 min.		
Add rest of caramel mixture and	2 eggs (⅓ to ½ cup)	1 egg (¼ cup)
Beat 2 min.		

**When using* GOLD MEDAL, *add all the liquid at once.*

Pour into prepared pans. Bake until cake tests done. Cool. Finish with Creamy Caramel Icing (*recipe below*).

TEMPERATURE: 350° (mod. oven).

TIME: Bake layers 25 to 30 min., square or oblong 35 to 40 min.

PEANUT BUTTER CAKE

Prepare pans, bake as in recipe above.

For Large Cake	*Small Cake*
Sift together . . .	
2¼ cups *sifted* SOFTASILK	1½ cups
or 2⅛ cups *sifted* GOLD MEDAL Flour	1⅜ cups
1½ cups sugar	1 cup
3 tsp. baking powder	2 tsp.
1 tsp. salt	½ tsp.
Add . . .	
⅓ cup soft shortening	¼ cup
⅓ cup peanut butter (not oily)	¼ cup
1 cup milk	⅔ cup
Beat 2 min.	
Add . . .	
2 eggs (⅓ to ½ cup)	1 egg (¼ cup)
Beat 2 min.	

Pour into prepared pans. Bake. Cool. Finish with Peanut Butter Broiled Icing for square or oblong or Peanut Butter Fudge Frosting for layers.

All you have to do—

For a Chrysanthemum Cake: make a Caramel (Burnt Sugar) Cake in layers. Frost with Creamy Caramel Icing. Place clusters of garden chrysanthemums around outside edge of cake plate.

CREAMY CARAMEL ICING

For Large Cake	*Small Cake*
Heat together . . .	
⅓ cup cream	¼ cup
6 tbsp. butter	4½ tbsp.

Meanwhile, caramelize 2 tbsp. sugar (*see p. 25*). Add scalded cream and butter, stirring until lumps are dissolved. Gradually stir in . . .

3 cups *sifted* confectioners' sugar	2¼ cups

Beat until icing is smooth, creamy, and of the right consistency to spread. Add more cream if icing becomes too thick.

COCOA CAKES Cocoa colorama of brown, red, and black.

BLACK DEVILS FOOD CAKE (Black Midnight) (Key Recipe) *Very dark—tender.*

	For Large Cake	*Small Cake*
Grease and flour	2 9" layer pans or 13x9" oblong pan	2 8" layer pans or 9" square pan
Cream together until fluffy	2/3 cup soft shortening	1/2 cup
	1 2/3 cups sugar	1 1/4 cups
Beat in thoroughly	3 eggs (1/2 to 2/3 cup)	2 eggs (1/3 to 1/2 c.)
Blend together	2/3 cup cocoa	1/2 cup
	1 1/3 cups cold water	1 cup
Sift together	2 1/4 cups *sifted* SOFTASILK or 2 cups *sifted* GOLD MEDAL Flour	1 3/4 cups or 1 1/2 cups
	1/3 tsp. baking powder	1/4 tsp.
	1 1/4 tsp. soda	1 tsp.
	1 tsp. salt	3/4 tsp.
Stir in alternately with	cocoa-water mixture	cocoa-water
	1 tsp. vanilla, if desired	3/4 tsp.

Pour into prepared pans. Bake until cake tests done. Cool. For a striking color contrast, spread a snowy white frosting between layers and over top and sides.

TEMPERATURE: 350° (mod. oven).

TIME: Bake layers 30 to 35 min., square or oblong 35 to 45 min.

★ CHOCOLATE PECAN CAKE

Perfected from one in the old Williamsburg Cook Book. Its unusual, rich, pecan flavor characterizes the sumptuousness and abundance of the best early Virginia cookery.

Prepare pans, bake as in key recipe above.

For Large Cake	*Small Cake*
Cream together until fluffy . . .	
1/2 cup soft shortening	3/8 cup
2 cups brown sugar	1 1/2 cups
Beat in . . .	
2 large eggs (1/2 cup)	2 eggs (1/3 c.)
Blend together and stir in . . .	
3 tbsp. cocoa	2 tbsp.
2/3 cup water	1/2 cup
Sift together . . .	
2 1/4 cups *sifted* SOFTASILK	1 3/4 cups
or 2 cups *sifted* GOLD MEDAL Flour	*or* 1 1/2 cups
1 tsp. soda	3/4 tsp.
1 tsp. salt	3/4 tsp.
Stir in alternately with . . .	
2/3 cup sour whipping cream (35% butterfat)	1/2 cup
1 1/2 tsp. vanilla	1 tsp.
Stir in . . .	
2/3 cup pecans, cut-up	1/2 cup

Pour into prepared pans. Bake. Cool. Finish with Prize Fudge Frosting.

RED DEVILS FOOD CAKE

To any chocolate cake, add red food coloring: 1 tsp. for Large, 3/4 tsp. for Small Cake. Makes red without tasting of soda.

DUSKY DELIGHT CAKE

(Cocoa Devils Food)

Prepare pans and use method as in key recipe above—*except* stir in cocoa-water mixture after the eggs, and stir in buttermilk alternately with flour mixture. Use:

For Large Cake	*Small Cake*
2/3 cup soft shortening	1/2 cup
1 3/4 cups sugar	1 1/4 cups
3 eggs (1/2 to 2/3 cup)	2 eggs
1/2 cup cocoa	1/3 cup
1/2 cup water	1/3 cup
2 1/4 cups *sifted* SOFTASILK	1 1/2 cups
or 2 1/8 cups *sifted* GOLD MEDAL Flour	*or* 1 1/3 cups
1 tsp. soda	3/4 tsp.
1 tsp. salt	1/2 tsp.
3/4 cup buttermilk	1/2 cup

Pour into prepared pans. Bake. Cool. Finish with white frosting. Choc-O-Nut Topping is ideal for the square or oblong.

All you have to do—

To keep cocoa cakes brown on the outside: grease and "cocoa" the pans instead of grease and flour.

DARK DEVILS FOOD CAKE (🔑 Recipe)

Margaret Norrdin of our Staff says this cake is the "best ever" . . . especially for picnics.

	For Large Cake	*Small Cake*
Grease and flour	2 9″ layer pans *or* 13x9″ oblong pan	2 8″ layer pans *or* 9″ square pan
Sift together	2¼ cups *sifted* SOFTASILK *or* 2 cups *sifted* GOLD MEDAL Flour	1¾ cups *or* 1½ cups
	1¾ cups sugar	1⅓ cups
	⅓ tsp. baking powder	¼ tsp.
	1¾ tsp. soda	1¼ tsp.
	1 tsp. salt	¾ tsp.
	⅔ cup cocoa	½ cup
Add	⅔ cup soft shortening	½ cup
*Pour in a little over half of	1 cup water	¾ cup
	1 tsp. vanilla, if desired	¾ tsp.
Beat 2 min. Add remaining water and	3 eggs (½ to ⅔ cup)	2 eggs (⅓ to ½ c.)
Beat 2 min.		

**If the batter seems too thick, add more of the liquid at first. When using* GOLD MEDAL, *add all the liquid at once.*

Pour into prepared pans. Bake until cake tests done. Cool. For a striking color contrast, spread snowy white frosting between layers and over top and sides.

TEMPERATURE: 350° (mod. oven).

TIME: Bake layers 30 to 40 min., square or oblong 35 to 40 min.

MILK CHOCOLATE CAKE

Very fine-textured and soft.

Prepare 9″ or 8″ layer pans and use method as given in 🔑 recipe above. Use:

For 9″ Layers	*8″ Layers*
2 cups *sifted* SOFTASILK	1½ cups
1⅔ cups sugar	1¼ cups
4 tsp. baking powder	3 tsp.
1 tsp. salt	¾ tsp.
5 tbsp. cocoa	4 tbsp.
⅔ cup soft shortening	½ cup
1⅓ cups evaporated milk (diluted, half water)	1 cup
1⅓ tsp. vanilla	1 tsp.
3 eggs (½ to ⅔ cup)	2 eggs

Batter may appear "curdled" but do not worry. Bake and cool. Finish with:

MILK CHOCOLATE ICING

For 9″ Layers	*8″ Layers*
Melt together . . .	
5 tbsp. shortening	4 tbsp.
½ cup cocoa	6 tbsp.
Stir in . . .	
2⅔ cups *sifted* confectioners' sugar	2 cups
*7 tbsp. hot scalded milk	5 tbsp.
1⅓ tsp. vanilla	1 tsp.

Beat until thick enough to spread.

**Evaporated milk may be used.*

★ DUTCH COCOA CREAM CAKE

Follow recipe in opposite column for Milk Chocolate Cake. When cake is cool, split each layer into two layers.

For perfect cutting, use long, thin, sharp knife.

Spread sweetened whipped cream (1½ to 2 cups) between layers. Frost top and sides with Milk Chocolate Icing. Cake will keep in refrigerator 2 or 3 days.

They'll all "take" Dutch Cocoa Cream Cake.

POPULAR DEVILS FOOD CAKE (🔑 Recipe) *Moist . . . fluffy . . . a family favorite.*

	For Large Cake	*Small Cake*
Grease and flour	2 9″ layer pans *or* 13x9″ oblong pan	2 8″ layer pans *or* 9″ square pan
Cream together until fluffy	2/3 cup soft shortening	1/2 cup
	1 1/2 cups sugar	1 1/4 cups
Beat in thoroughly	3 eggs (1/2 to 2/3 cup)	2 eggs (1/3 to 1/2 c.)
Blend in	2 1/2 sq. chocolate (2 1/2 oz.), melted	2 sq. (2 oz.)
Sift together	2 1/4 cups *sifted* SOFTASILK *or* 2 1/8 cups *sifted* GOLD MEDAL Flour	1 3/4 cups *or* 1 5/8 cups
	1 tsp. soda	3/4 tsp.
	1 tsp. salt	3/4 tsp.
Stir in alternately with	1 1/4 cups buttermilk or sweet milk	1 cup

Pour into prepared pans. Bake until cake tests done. Cool. Finish with Chocolate Butter Icing or special icings given with Chocolate Peppermint Cake (*below*).

TEMPERATURE: 350° (mod. oven).

TIME: Bake layers 30 to 35 min., square or oblong 40 to 45 min.

EASY CHOCOMINT ICING

A bit sticky, but elegant to eat. Ideal for an oblong or square cake.

Use about 12 of the large chocolate peppermint patties for the frosting for Oblong Cake, 8 for the Square Cake. The minute the cake comes out of the oven, place the chocolate peppermints over top of cake. As they melt, spread over top.

Place chocolates on cake. Begin to spread.

And complete spreading to cover cake.

CHOCOLATE PEPPERMINT CAKE

Follow 🔑 recipe above—*except* add about 1 tsp. peppermint extract. Frost with Easy Chocomint Icing (*opposite*), or with a cooked white frosting with about 1/2 cup crushed peppermint stick candy folded into icing and some sprinkled over top.

★ CHOCOLATE JOY CAKE

A family favorite from Mrs. Samuel C. Gale, wife of our own Vice President.

Follow 🔑 recipe above for method—*except* combine chocolate and hot water first.

For Large Cake	*Small Cake*
1/2 cup hot water	1/3 cup
3 sq. chocolate (3 oz.), melted	2 sq. (2 oz.)
Stir until thick. Cool. Then use:	
1/2 cup soft shortening	1/3 cup
1 2/3 cups sugar	1 1/8 cups
3 eggs (1/2 to 2/3 cup)	2 eggs
cooled chocolate mixture	cooled choc.
2 1/4 cups *sifted* SOFTASILK *or* 2 1/8 cups *sifted* GOLD MEDAL Flour	1 1/2 cups *or* 1 3/8 cups
1/4 tsp. soda	1/4 tsp. (scant)
2 1/4 tsp. baking powder	1 1/2 tsp.
1 tsp. salt	1/2 tsp.
1 cup buttermilk	2/3 cup

Bake, cool, finish with Chocolate Joy Icing (*p. 168*). *In color picture, p. 119,* it is trimmed with sliced Brazil nuts.

NEW POPULAR DEVILS FOOD CAKE (🔑 Recipe) *The choice of many, many recipes that were tested.*

	For Large Cake	*Small Cake*
Grease and flour	2 9″ layer pans *or* 13x9″ oblong pan	2 8″ layer pans *or* 9″ square pan
Sift together	2⅜ cups *sifted* SOFTASILK *or* 2¼ cups *sifted* GOLD MEDAL Flour	1¾ cups *or* 1⅝ cups
	1⅞ cups sugar	1½ cups
	1 tsp. soda	¾ tsp.
	1 tsp. salt	¾ tsp.
Add	⅔ cup soft shortening	½ cup
*Pour in a little over half of	1¼ cups buttermilk	1 cup
Beat 2 min.		
Add remaining milk and	3 eggs (½ to ⅔ cup)	2 eggs (⅓ to ½ c.)
	2½ sq. chocolate (2½ oz.), melted	2 sq. (2 oz.)
Beat 2 min.		

**If the batter seems too thick, add more of the liquid at first. When using GOLD MEDAL, add all the liquid at once.*

Pour into prepared pans. Bake until cake tests done. Cool. Finish with Chocolate Butter Icing or special icings given with New Chocolate Peppermint Cake (*below*).

TEMPERATURE: 350° (mod. oven).
TIME: Bake layers 30 to 35 min., square or oblong 40 to 45 min.

★ **NEW CHOCOLATE PEPPERMINT CAKE**

Follow 🔑 recipe above—*except* add about 1 tsp. peppermint extract. Frost as for Chocolate Peppermint Cake (*p. 134*).

CREOLE DEVILS FOOD CAKE

A fluffy, very dark cake developed for SOFTASILK *by Mabel Martin of our Staff.*

Prepare pans, bake as in 🔑 recipe above.

For Large Cake	*Small Cake*
Stir until smooth and let cool . . .	
2½ sq. chocolate (2½ oz.), melted	2 sq. (2 oz.)
¾ cup hot coffee	½ cup
Sift together . . .	
2⅜ cups *sifted* SOFTASILK	1¾ cups
1⅞ cups sugar	1½ cups
1 tsp. soda	¾ tsp.
1 tsp. salt	¾ tsp.
1 tsp. ground cloves	¾ tsp.
Add . . .	
½ cup buttermilk	½ cup
⅔ cup soft shortening	½ cup
Beat 2 min. and add . . .	
3 eggs (½ to ⅔ cup)	2 eggs (⅓ to ½ c.)
chocolate mixture	choc. mix.
Beat 2 min.	

Bake, cool, and finish with white frosting.

Cut the pieces nice and big; they'll love it!

MARDI GRAS CAKE

Makes you think of New Orleans and its traditional and gay Mardi Gras season.

Make Creole Devils Food Cake (*opposite*) in layers. Spread White Mountain Frosting between cooled layers and over top and sides. Decorate the icing by dipping the tip of a teaspoon into melted chocolate and making indentations in the shape of circles here and there over entire surface.

PRIZE FUDGE CAKE (🔑 Recipe)

Little boys from eight to eighty go for this.

	For Large Cake	*Small Cake*
Grease and flour	2 9″ layer pans or 13x9″ oblong pan	2 8″ layer pans or 9″ square pan
Cream together (yes, only this little shortening)	1/4 cup soft shortening	3 tbsp.
	1 1/2 cups sugar	1 cup
Blend in	2 egg yolks	1 yolk
	4 sq. chocolate (4 oz.), melted	3 sq. (3 oz.)
Sift together	2 cups *sifted* SOFTASILK *or* 1 7/8 cups *sifted* GOLD MEDAL Flour	1 1/3 cups *or* 1 1/4 cups
	2 tsp. baking powder	1 1/4 tsp.
	1 tsp. salt	1/2 tsp.
Stir in alternately with	1 1/2 cups milk	1 cup
	1 tsp. vanilla	1/2 tsp.
Stir in	1 cup nuts, cut-up	2/3 cup
Fold in meringue of	2 egg whites (1/4 cup)	2 whites
	1/2 cup sugar	1/3 cup

Pour into prepared pans. The batter will be thin. Bake until cake tests done. Cool. Finish with Prize Fudge Frosting or other desired icing. Decorate with nuts.

TEMPERATURE: 350° (mod. oven).

TIME: Bake layers 30 to 40 min., square or oblong 35 to 45 min.

★ CHOCOLATE SPICE DE LUXE

Echo from Dixie—rich, moist, with subtle flavor.

Prepare pans, bake as in 🔑 recipe above.

For Large Cake	*Small Cake*
Cream together until fluffy . . .	
3/4 cup soft shortening	1/2 cup
1 1/2 cups sugar	1 cup
Blend in . . .	
3 egg yolks	2 yolks
3 sq. chocolate (3 oz.), melted	2 sq. (2 oz.)
Sift together . . .	
2 1/4 cups *sifted* SOFTASILK	1 1/2 cups
or 2 cups *sifted* GOLD MEDAL Flour	*or* 1 1/3 cups
2 1/2 tsp. baking powder	1 1/2 tsp.
1 tsp. salt	1/2 tsp.
3/4 tsp. cloves	1/2 tsp.
3/4 tsp. allspice	1/2 tsp.
3/4 tsp. cinnamon	1/2 tsp.
Stir in alternately with . . .	
1 cup milk	2/3 cup
Fold in . . .	
3 egg whites (3/8 cup), stiffly beaten	2 whites
2 tsp. citron, shaved	1 1/2 tsp.

Bake, cool. Frost with Lemon Butter Icing.

CHOCOLATE CAKE DE LUXE

Omit spices and citron in Chocolate Spice De Luxe. Use Chocolate De Luxe Icing.

Gently cut and fold in the egg whites or the meringue.

CHOCOLATE NOUGAT CAKE

Just like chewy chocolate candy.

Prepare pans and use method as given in 🔑 recipe above. Use:

For Large Cake	*Small Cake*
1/2 cup soft shortening	1/3 cup
1 1/3 cups sugar	7/8 cup
3 egg yolks	2 yolks
3 sq. chocolate (3 oz.), melted	2 sq. (2 oz.)
2 1/4 cups *sifted* SOFTASILK	1 1/2 cups
or 2 cups *sifted* GOLD MEDAL Flour	*or* 1 1/3 cups
2 tsp. baking powder	1 1/4 tsp.
1 tsp. salt	1/2 tsp.
1 1/3 cups milk	7/8 cup
3/4 cup nuts, cut-up	1/2 cup
3 egg whites (3/8 cup)	2 whites
2/3 cup sugar	1/2 cup

Frost as directed and pictured on p. 137. →

NEW FUDGE CAKE (🔑 Recipe) *Dark, delectably fudge-like, crunchy with nuts.*

	For Large Cake	*Small Cake*
Grease and flour	2 9″ layer pans *or* 13x9″ oblong pan	2 8″ layer pans *or* 9″ square pan
Sift together	2 cups *sifted* SOFTASILK *or* 1⅞ cups *sifted* GOLD MEDAL Flour	1⅓ cups *or* 1¼ cups
	2 cups sugar	1⅓ cups
	2 tsp. baking powder	1¼ tsp.
	¼ tsp. soda	¼ tsp.
	1 tsp. salt	½ tsp.
Add only this small amount	¼ cup soft shortening	3 tbsp.
*Pour in a little over half of	1½ cups milk	1 cup
	1 tsp. vanilla	½ tsp.
Beat 2 min. Add remaining milk and	2 eggs (⅓ to ½ cup)	1 egg (¼ to ⅓ c.)
	4 sq. chocolate (4 oz.), melted	3 sq. (3 oz.)
Beat 2 min. Stir in	1 cup nuts, cut-up	⅔ cup

Some of our home testers liked this cake best when made with GOLD MEDAL *Flour.*

**When using* GOLD MEDAL, *add all the liquid at once.*

Pour into prepared pans. Batter will be thin. Bake until cake tests done. Cool. Finish with Fudge Frosting.

TEMPERATURE: 350° (mod. oven).
TIME: Bake layers 30 to 35 min. square or oblong 35 to 45 min.

★ NEW CHOCO-NOUGAT CAKE

More chewy than the Fudge Cake above—more like nougat candy. It's a favorite.

Prepare pans, bake as in 🔑 recipe above.

For Large Cake	*Small Cake*
Sift together . . .	
2⅛ cups *sifted* SOFTASILK	1⅜ cups
or 2 cups *sifted* GOLD MEDAL Flour	*or* 1⅓ cups
2 cups sugar	1⅓ cups
3 tsp. baking powder	2 tsp.
1 tsp. salt	½ tsp.
Add . . .	
½ cup soft shortening	⅓ cup
***Pour in a little over half of . . .**	
1⅓ cups milk	⅞ cup
Beat 2 min. Add remaining milk and . . .	
3 eggs (½ to ⅔ cup)	2 eggs (⅓ to ½ c.)
3 sq. chocolate (3 oz.), melted	2 sq. (2 oz.)
1 tsp. red food coloring, if red color desired	⅔ tsp.
Beat 2 min. Stir in . . .	
1 cup nuts, cut-up	⅔ cup

Ice with Fluffy White Frosting. Decorate top with swirls of melted semi-sweet or unsweetened chocolate. See picture →

Add melted chocolate the last 2 min. of beating.

All you have to do—

For a cake studded with nuts: sprinkle some cut-up nuts over batter before baking.

Chocolate Nougat Cake with decorative icing.

SIMPLE CAKES WITH EASY TOPPINGS

And they're just as good as they look.

Applesauce Cake with Lacy Sugar Topping   Inexpensive Sponge with Broiled Icing   Light Yellow Cake with Choc-O-Nut Filling and Topping.

★ INEXPENSIVE SPONGE CAKE

Often called Mock Sponge or Butter Sponge or Hot Milk Sponge Cake. Contributed years ago by Lucile Brown of our General Office. Her mother used to say she could have it in the oven 7 minutes after she decided to make a cake.

	For Large Cake	*Small Cake*
Grease and flour	2 9″ layer pans *or* 13x9″ oblong pan	9″ square pan *or* 12 muffin cups (lined)
Beat with rotary beater until very light	4 eggs (⅔ to 1 cup)	2 eggs (⅓ to ½ c.)
Beat in	2 cups sugar ½ tsp. salt 2 tsp. flavoring	1 cup ¼ tsp. 1 tsp.
Beat in	2 tbsp. butter melted in 1 cup boiling hot milk	1 tbsp. ½ cup
Sift together and beat in (very quickly)	2 cups *sifted* SOFTASILK *or* 2 cups *sifted* GOLD MEDAL Flour 2 tsp. baking powder	1 cup *or* 1 cup 1 tsp.

Immediately pour into prepared pan. (Fill muffin cups ⅔ full.) Bake until cake tests done. Cool. Serve fresh with fruit; or top squares of cake with sweetened whipped cream and berries, peaches or bananas.

TEMPERATURE: 350° (mod. oven) for cake. 400° for cupcakes.

TIME: Bake 25 to 35 min. for cakes. Bake 18 to 20 min. for cupcakes.

Inexpensive Sponge Cake with fresh peaches and whipped cream.

JELLY ROLL JAMBOREE

Tired of jellies and jams? Try these fillings.

Clear Orange	Rich Orange
Clear Lemon	Rich Lemon
Pineapple	Chocolate Cream

To use these special fillings in a jelly roll... roll up a plain jelly roll right after baking. Let cool. Unroll. Spread with cooled filling and reroll.

STRAWBERRY CREAM ROLL

Less than an hour before serving, unroll the Jelly Roll cake. Spread with about 1 cup sweetened whipped cream. Sprinkle with 2 cups sliced fresh strawberries. Reroll. Chill. Serve in thick slices.

JELLY ROLL

Lots of fun to make and serve.

Grease and flour a 15½x10½″ jelly roll pan *or* line a pan with greased paper (waxed, plain, or aluminum foil) and turn up edges to make the proper size pan.

Beat with rotary beater until thick . . .
- 3 large eggs (⅔ cup)

Gradually beat in . . .
- 1 cup sugar

Beat in all at once . . .
- 5 tbsp. water
- 1 tsp. vanilla

Sift together and beat in all at once . . .
- 1 cup *sifted* GOLD MEDAL Flour *or* 1 cup *sifted* SOFTASILK
- 1 tsp. baking powder
- ¼ tsp. salt

Beat just until smooth. Pour into prepared pan. Bake *just* until cake tests done. Loosen edges and *immediately* turn upside down on a towel sprinkled with confectioners' sugar. If you have used paper, quickly and carefully pull it off. Spread cake at once with soft jelly or jam and roll up, beginning at short end. Wrap in the towel until cool (½ hr.). *See page 237.*

TEMPERATURE: 375° (quick mod. oven).

TIME: Bake 12 to 15 min.

CAUTION: Overbaking makes it difficult to remove the paper from the jelly roll.

CREAM CAKES The shortening is rich, rich cream.

SWEET CREAM CAKE (🔑 Recipe) *Easy and quick to make. Different, too!*

	For Large Cake	*Small Cake*
Grease and flour	2 9″ layer pans *or* 13x9″ oblong pan	2 8″ layer pans *or* 9″ square pan
Beat until very thick (about 5 min.)	3 eggs (½ to ⅔ cup)	2 eggs (⅓ to ½ c.)
Beat in gradually (rotary beater)	1⅓ cups sugar	1 cup
Sift together	2⅓ cups *sifted* SOFTASILK *or* 2¼ cups *sifted* GOLD MEDAL Flour	1¾ cups *or* 1⅔ cups
	3 tsp. baking powder	2 tsp.
	1 tsp. salt	¾ tsp.
Stir in alternately with	1⅓ cups rich cream (*30 to 35% butterfat*)	1 cup
	1½ tsp. vanilla	1 tsp.

Pour into prepared pans. Bake and cool. For a tempting sugary topping, sprinkle sugar and cinnamon over top of cake 3 min. before removing from oven.

TEMPERATURE: 350° (mod. oven).

TIME: Bake layers 25 to 30 min., square or oblong 40 to 45 min.

SPICE CREAM CAKE

Follow 🔑 recipe above—*except* add spices to the dry ingredients before sifting. Use:

For Large Cake	*Small Cake*
3 tsp. cinnamon	2 tsp.
1½ tsp. cloves	1 tsp.
1½ tsp. allspice	1 tsp.

Delicious with a cooked white frosting, with ½ cup chopped raisins, or dates, or figs, and ½ cup chopped nuts added to it.

★ WHIPPED CREAM CAKE

A superbly rich and moist eating quality.

Grease and flour 2 9″ layer pans.

Whip until stiff . . .
1½ cups rich cream
(*30 to 35% butterfat*)

Beat very thoroughly and fold in . . .
3 eggs (½ to ⅔ cup)

Sift together . . .
2¼ cups *sifted* SOFTASILK
or 2 cups *sifted* GOLD MEDAL Flour
1½ cups sugar
2 tsp. baking powder
½ tsp. salt

Fold in gently with a wire whip.

Blend in . . .
1½ tsp. vanilla

Pour into prepared pans. Bake. Cool. Serve uniced or with sugar topping.

TEMPERATURE: 350° (mod. oven).

TIME: Bake 30 to 35 min.

SOUR CREAM SPICE CAKE

Prepare oblong or square pan. Follow 🔑 recipe above for method, but use:

For 13x9″ Oblong	*9″ Square*
3 eggs (½ to ⅔ cup)	2 eggs (⅓ to ½ c.)
1½ cups sugar	1 cup
2½ cups *sifted* SOFTASILK	1⅔ cups
or 2¼ cups *sifted* GOLD MEDAL Flour	*or* 1½ cups
1½ tsp. baking powder	1 tsp.
¾ tsp. soda	½ tsp.
2 tsp. cinnamon	1⅓ tsp.
1 tsp. cloves	⅔ tsp.
1 tsp. allspice	⅔ tsp.
½ tsp. salt	⅓ tsp.
1½ cups sour cream (*30 to 35% butterfat*)	1 cup

Pour into prepared pans. Bake. Cool.

All you have to do—

To make a plain Sour Cream Cake: omit spices. Add vanilla and lemon extract for flavoring.

SOUR CREAM CUPCAKES

Vera Child of Seattle, Washington, remembers them as family favorites made by her mother, a wonderful cook.

Follow recipe for Sour Cream Spice Cake above and fold in at the last, about ½ cup *each* chopped nuts and raisins. Pour into muffin cups and bake (*see p. 123*).

BANANA CAKE (🔑 Recipe) *Looks good, smells better, tastes best.*

	For Large Cake	*Small Cake*
Grease and flour	2 9″ layer pans *or* 13x9″ oblong pan	2 8″ layer pans *or* 9″ square pan
Cream together until fluffy	½ cup soft shortening	⅜ cup
	1½ cups sugar	1⅛ cups
Beat in thoroughly	2 large eggs (½ cup)	2 eggs (⅓ cup)
Sift together	2¼ cups *sifted* SOFTASILK *or* 2 cups *sifted* GOLD MEDAL Flour	1¾ cups *or* 1½ cups
	¼ tsp. baking powder	¼ tsp. (scant)
	¾ tsp. soda	½ tsp.
	1 tsp. salt	¾ tsp.
Stir in alternately with	¼ cup buttermilk	3 tbsp.
	1 cup mashed ripe bananas (about 3)	¾ cup (about 2)
	½ cup chopped nuts, if desired	⅜ cup

Pour into prepared pans. Bake until cake tests done. Cool. Use whipped cream and sliced bananas for filling and spread whipped cream over top of cake. Place slices of banana upright around outer edge.

TEMPERATURE: 350° (mod. oven).

TIME: Bake layers 25 to 30 min., square or oblong 35 to 45 min.

MOCHA PRUNE CAKE

A spice cake deliciously moist and fruity. "Ideal for grange meetings!" says a former Staff member, Norma Ammann Shaffer.

Prepare pans and follow method as in 🔑 recipe above. Fold in prunes last. Use:

For Large Cake	*Small Cake*
½ cup soft shortening	⅜ cup
1½ cups sugar	1⅛ cups
3 large eggs (⅔ cup)	2 eggs (½ cup)
2¼ cups *sifted* SOFTASILK	1¾ cups
or 2 cups *sifted* GOLD MEDAL Flour	*or* 1½ cups
1 tsp. baking powder	¾ tsp.
1 tsp. soda	¾ tsp.
1 tsp. salt	¾ tsp.
1 tsp. cinnamon	¾ tsp.
1 tsp. nutmeg	¾ tsp.
1 tsp. allspice	¾ tsp.
1 cup buttermilk	¾ cup
1 cup cooked prunes, drained, chopped	¾ cup

Pour into prepared pans. Bake. Cool. Finish with Mocha Butter Icing (*p. 167*).

MOCHA FIG OR DATE CAKE

Substitute dates, or canned or stewed figs for prunes in Mocha Prune Cake.

★ RAISIN CAKE

Cakes with raisins or currants were favorites in the 17th and 18th centuries. Directions were to "hurle in a good quantity." Today's cake is lighter, fluffier, the raisins sweeter.

First, rinse seeded raisins in hot water, drain, and dry. Cut in fourths with scissors (so they will not sink to the bottom). Prepare pans and follow method as given in 🔑 recipe above. Use:

For Large Cake	*Small Cake*
¾ cup soft shortening	½ cup
1⅛ cups sugar	¾ cup
3 eggs (½ to ⅔ cup)	2 eggs (⅓ to ½ c.)
2 cups *sifted* GOLD MEDAL Flour	1⅓ cups
1¾ tsp. baking powder	1¼ tsp.
1 tsp. salt	½ tsp.
¾ cup milk	½ cup
¾ cup raisins, cut fine	½ cup

Pour into prepared pans. Bake. Cool. This cake is delicious uniced and served warm. Many like the White Fudge Raisin Frosting on the layers.

All you have to do—

For an old-fashioned loaf cake: follow recipe above for Raisin Cake—*except* add 4 tbsp. more flour to Large Cake; 3 tbsp. more to Small Cake. Bake in 9x5x3″ loaf pan 65 to 70 min. at 350° (mod. oven).

SPECIALTY CAKES Cakes of distinction.

★ OLD KENTUCKY NUT CAKE

The most delicious nut cake ever tested in our Kitchens! As given to us by a famous Kentuckian, Irene Dunne.

	For Large Cake	*Small Cake*
Grease and flour	2 9″ layer pans *or* 13x9″ oblong pan	2 8″ layer pans *or* 9″ square pan
Cream together until fluffy	$\frac{2}{3}$ cup soft shortening (half butter for flavor)	$\frac{1}{2}$ cup
	$1\frac{2}{3}$ cups sugar	$1\frac{1}{4}$ cups
Beat in thoroughly	3 eggs ($\frac{1}{2}$ to $\frac{2}{3}$ cup)	2 eggs ($\frac{1}{3}$ to $\frac{1}{2}$ c.)
Sift together	$2\frac{3}{4}$ cups *sifted* SOFTASILK *or* $2\frac{2}{3}$ cups *sifted* GOLD MEDAL Flour	$2\frac{1}{8}$ cups *or* 2 cups
	2 tsp. baking powder	$1\frac{1}{2}$ tsp.
	1 tsp. salt	$\frac{3}{4}$ tsp.
Stir in alternately with	1 cup milk	$\frac{3}{4}$ cup
	1 tsp. vanilla	$\frac{3}{4}$ tsp.
Fold in	$1\frac{1}{3}$ cups walnuts, cut-up	1 cup

Pour into prepared pans. Bake until cake tests done. Cool. Finish with Creamy Caramel Icing (*p. 131*), and garnish with walnut halves. *Color picture on p. 118.*

TEMPERATURE: 350° (mod. oven).

TIME: Bake layers 25 to 30 min., square or oblong 35 to 40 min.

POUND CAKE

Originally 1 lb. of each ingredient was used in the recipe. Now we use $\frac{1}{2}$ lb. of each. This is a very stiff batter—an electric mixer is a great help. Beating times are given for mixer. Beat a little longer by hand.

Grease and flour a 9x5x3″ loaf pan.

Cream thoroughly (1 min.) . . .
- 1 cup *soft* butter

Add gradually (10 min.) . . .
- 1 cup sugar

Beat in (30 sec.) . . .
- $\frac{1}{4}$ tsp. grated lemon rind
- 1 tbsp. lemon juice

Beat in one at a time ($1\frac{1}{2}$ min. each) . . .
- 4 large eggs (1 cup)

Sift together and beat in all at once . . .
- 2 cups *sifted* SOFTASILK *or* $1\frac{7}{8}$ cups *sifted* GOLD MEDAL Flour
- $\frac{1}{4}$ tsp. baking powder

Beat *just* until smooth (1 min.). Pour into prepared pan. Bake until cake tests done with a wooden pick. Cool. Slice thin and serve plain.

TEMPERATURE: 300° (slow oven).

TIME: Bake 75 to 90 min.

FRUIT CAKE BARS

Make Inexpensive Fruit Cake above in square pan. Cut into 24 bars. Trim with candied cherries, almonds, etc.

INEXPENSIVE FRUIT CAKE

Rosemary Meyer of our Staff likes this moist cake from the first World War . . . called "milkless, butterless, eggless cake."

Grease and flour a 9″ square pan or a 9x5x3″ loaf pan. Mix in saucepan . . .
- 1 cup brown sugar
- $1\frac{1}{4}$ cups water
- $\frac{1}{3}$ cup shortening
- 2 cups seeded raisins
- $\frac{1}{2}$ tsp. nutmeg
- 2 tsp. cinnamon
- $\frac{1}{2}$ tsp. cloves, if desired

Boil for 3 min. Cool. Then add a mixture of
- 1 tsp. soda
- 1 tsp. salt
- 2 tsp. water

Sift together and blend in . . .
- 2 cups *sifted* GOLD MEDAL Flour
- 1 tsp. baking powder

TEMPERATURE: 325° (slow mod. oven).

TIME: Bake square 55, loaf 75 min.

WHITE FRUIT CAKE

Mix, bake as for 🔑 recipe on p. 143 but use: 1 cup shortening, 2 cups sugar, 4 cups flour, 2 tsp. baking powder, 1 tsp. salt, 1 cup water, 8 egg whites (beaten stiff, folded in last). Add double amount fruit and nuts (blanched almonds) as in Golden Fruit Cake. Use only 1 lb. white raisins.

First, prepare fruits: Slice finely and cut up (¼ to ½″) citron, orange, and lemon peel. Cut other candied fruits larger. "Plump up" seedless raisins and currants (*see p. 24*); leave whole. Heat nuts and cut them up coarsely. To measure raisins, cut-up candied peel, candied cherries, etc.: ½ lb. = 1½ cups; ¼ lb. = ¾ cup.

FRUIT CAKE (🔑 Recipe for the Basic Batter)

Line with heavy wrapping paper and grease....	2 9x5x3″ loaf pans (or tube pan)
Cream together until fluffy.........	1 cup soft shortening 2 cups brown sugar
Beat in............................	4 large eggs (1 cup)
Sift together......................	3 cups *sifted* GOLD MEDAL Flour 1 tsp. baking powder 1 tsp. salt spices as given in recipes below
Stir in alternately with............	1 cup liquid (jelly, molasses, coffee, etc.)
Blend in...........................	candied fruit, nuts, etc.

Fill prepared pans almost full. Bake (cover with paper the last hr.) until wooden pick thrust in, comes out clean. Cool. Wrap in waxed paper. In old days, fruit cakes were wrapped in wine-dampened cloth to "keep" and mellow. Store in air-tight container in *cool* place. To glaze, *see p. 169.*

NOTE: For small cakes divide pan, with cardboard cut to fit, or use any small can or pudding mold.

TEMPERATURE: 300° (slow oven).

TIME: Bake 2½ to 3 hr. (½ hr. less for cakes of half size).

★ **GOLDEN FRUIT CAKE**

A holiday tradition in the home of Mae Chesnut of our Staff.

Follow 🔑 recipe above and add 1 tsp. cinnamon to dry ingredients. For liquid, use ½ cup milk and ½ cup light jelly. Add 1 tsp. vanilla. Blend in:

- 1 lb. white raisins
- ½ lb. citron
- ¼ lb. *each* candied cherries and pineapple
- ¼ lb. *each* candied orange and lemon peel
- ½ lb. nut meats

Southern Fruit Cake: Use 1½ times the fruit (fruit was formerly soaked in bourbon).

HOLIDAY FRUIT CAKE

From our good friend Jessie De Both of New York City.

Follow 🔑 recipe above—*except* use 6 eggs. Add to the dry ingredients:

- 1 tsp. *each* cinnamon and nutmeg
- ½ tsp. *each* mace and cloves
- ½ tsp. soda

Increase liquid . . . using ¾ cup strong coffee, ½ cup tart jelly, and ½ cup molasses. Blend in:

- 1 lb. seedless raisins
- ½ lb. *each* currants and dates
- 1 lb. mixed candied fruits
- ½ lb. nut meats
- grated rind, juice of 1 orange, 1 lemon

DARK FRUIT CAKE

Fewer fruits—least expensive.

Follow 🔑 recipe above. Add to the dry ingredients:

- 1 tsp. *each* cinnamon and mace
- ½ tsp. *each* nutmeg and allspice
- ¼ tsp. cloves

For liquid, use ½ cup fruit juice and ½ cup dark jelly beaten with fork. Blend in:

- 1½ lb. seeded raisins
- ½ lb. currants
- ½ lb. citron
- ½ lb. nut meats

BLACK FRUIT CAKE

Very dark and moist. Blacker when steamed.

Follow 🔑 recipe above—*except* use only 1 cup brown sugar and 3 eggs. Add to the dry ingredients:

- 1½ tsp. cinnamon
- ½ tsp. *each* nutmeg and allspice
- ½ tsp. soda

For liquid, use ½ cup molasses and ½ cup grape juice or coffee. Blend in:

- 1 lb. seeded raisins
- ½ lb. seedless raisins
- ½ lb. currants
- ¼ lb. citron
- ¼ lb. candied orange and lemon peel
- ½ lb. dates
- ½ lb. nut meats

EGG YOLK CAKES

An excellent use for leftover egg yolks.

GOLD CAKE (🗝 Recipe) *Fluffy . . . tender . . . a little like a sponge cake.*

	For Large Cake	*Small Cake*
Grease and flour	2 9″ layer pans *or* 13x9″ oblong pan	2 8″ layer pans *or* 9″ square pan
Cream together until fluffy	½ cup soft shortening (half butter for flavor)	⅜ cup
	1⅔ cups sugar	1¼ cups
Blend in	5 egg yolks (⅜ cup), well beaten	4 yolks (⅓ c.)
Sift together	2½ cups *sifted* SOFTASILK *or* 2⅓ cups *sifted* GOLD MEDAL Flour	1⅞ cups *or* 1¾ cups
	2½ tsp. baking powder	2 tsp.
	1 tsp. salt	¾ tsp.
Stir in alternately with	1 cup milk	¾ cup
	1 tsp. lemon extract	¾ tsp.
	½ tsp. vanilla	¼ tsp.

CAUTION: Beat eggs thick with rotary beater.

Pour into prepared pans. Bake until cake tests done. Cool. Delicious served with crushed strawberries or sliced peaches with whipped cream or White Butter Icing flavored with almond, lemon, or vanilla.

TEMPERATURE: 350° (mod. oven).

TIME: Bake layers 25 to 30 min., square or oblong 35 to 40 min.

★ LORD BALTIMORE CAKE

Named for one of the wealthiest gentlemen who first colonized America . . . George Calvert, Lord Baltimore.

Make 🗝 recipe above in layers. Spread *both* cooled layers with Fruit-Nut Filling below. Cover with a thin layer of Pink Frosting. Put layers together. Then cover top and sides with the Pink Frosting.

PINK FROSTING

For 9″ Layers	*8″ Layers*
Mix together and boil to 242°, or until an 8″ thread spins from spoon . . .	
2½ cups sugar	1⅞ cups
1 tbsp. light corn syrup	¾ tbsp.
¾ cup water	½ cup
¼ cup juice from cherries	¼ cup
Pour slowly, beating constantly, over . . .	
3 egg whites, beaten stiff	2 whites
Add . . .	
½ tsp. lemon extract	⅓ tsp.
½ tsp. grated orange rind	⅓ tsp.

Beat with spoon until mixture holds shape.

FRUIT-NUT FILLING

Take about ⅓ of frosting and mix in . . .

¼ cup *each*	3 tbsp. *each*
dried macaroon crumbs, toasted	
cut-up pecans, toasted	
cut-up almonds, blanched, toasted	
maraschino cherries, chopped	

NOTE: Toast almonds, pecans, and grated macaroon crumbs together.

BABY BALTIMORE CAKES

Cunning children of Lord and Lady Baltimore, . . . rich yellow coloring of Lord Baltimore and fruity, nutty filling of Lady Baltimore.

Follow 🗝 recipe for Large Cake above. Pour batter into paper-lined muffin cups (fill ⅔ full). Bake. Cool. Split cupcakes into 2 layers. Put together with filling and frosting for Lady Baltimore Cake (*p. 150*).

TEMPERATURE: 400° (mod. hot oven).

TIME: Bake 15 to 20 min.

AMOUNT: 15 to 20 cupcakes.

BERRY BASKET CAKE

Follow 🗝 recipe above—*except* use only ½ of recipe for Small Cake. Pour into one round 8 or 9″ layer pan. Make meringue and bake as in directions on p. 145.

★ FLUFFY GOLD CAKE (Key Recipe) *Soft and fluffy and bright yellow.*

	For Large Cake	Small Cake
Grease generously and flour (or line with paper and grease)	2 9″ layer pans *or* 13x9″ oblong pan	2 8″ layer pans *or* 9″ square pan
Sift together	2½ cups *sifted* SOFTASILK *or* 2⅓ cups *sifted* GOLD MEDAL Flour	1⅞ cups *or* 1¾ cups
	1⅔ cups sugar	1¼ cups
	4 tsp. baking powder	3 tsp.
	1 tsp. salt	¾ tsp.
Add	½ cup soft shortening	⅜ cup
*Pour in a little over half of	1¼ cups milk	1 cup
Beat 2 min.	1 tsp. lemon extract	¾ tsp.
	½ tsp. vanilla	¼ tsp.
Add remaining milk and Beat 2 min.	5 egg yolks (⅜ cup), unbeaten	4 yolks (⅓ c.), unbeaten

Pour into prepared pans. Bake until cake tests done. Cool. Finish with desired frosting. Ideal with White Butter Icing flavored with almond, lemon, or vanilla or cover with crushed berries.

**When using* GOLD MEDAL, *add all the liquid at once.*

TEMPERATURE: 350° (mod. oven).
TIME: Bake layers 25 to 35 min., square or oblong 40 to 45 min.

NEW LORD BALTIMORE CAKE

Follow key recipe above for *Large* or *Small* Cake in layers. See opposite page for complete filling and frosting directions.

NEW BERRY BASKET CAKE

A simple-to-make, stunning-to-serve dessert for afternoon or evening bridge.

Follow key recipe for *Small Cake* above—*except* use only ½ of recipe. Pour into one prepared round 8″ or 9″ layer pan.

Make a meringue as follows:

Beat together until foamy . . .
  2 egg whites
  ¼ tsp. cream of tartar
Gradually beat in . . .
  ½ cup sugar

Pile lightly and *evenly* over batter. Bake at 350° (mod. oven) about 45 min.

Cool 10 min. Then loosen sides from pan and invert on a folded towel on palm of hand, and place . . . right side up . . . on wire rack to finish cooling. Serve generously covered with sweetened berries and surrounded by ice cream balls. *See picture on opposite page.*

ROYAL HAWAIIAN CAKE

Gold and white triumph perfected by Irene Anderson of our Staff. The yolks are in the cake . . . the whites in the frosting.

Follow key recipe above in layers—*except,* in place of the egg yolks, use 3 egg yolks and 1 whole egg in *Large Cake*; 2 egg yolks and 1 whole egg in *Small Cake.*

Put cooled layers together with Pineapple Filling (p. 172). Spread about ½ cup over center of top layer. Frost sides and a 1½″ border on top with Fluffy White Frosting. Swirl icing on sides.

As elegant to eat as it is beautiful to look at.

EXQUISITE COCONUT CAKE

Layers of Rich White or Yellow Cake piled with luscious white frosting and sprinkled with snowy coconut . . . being cut for a party.

We used to call it the "Bride's Cake" . . . that ethereal structure of white tender cake all iced and decorated with snowy frosting. The dark fruit cake which maidens put under their pillows to dream on is traditional wedding cake. But nowadays it's the Bride's Cake that is the "Wedding Cake," and the fruit cake is the "Groom's Cake." It is sometimes given to guests in small white boxes to take home.

CHOOSE THE RECIPE

Plan to use Small Cake recipe of Silver White Cake (p. 149).

Assemble ingredients for twice the recipe...then for the single recipe. Use half almond, half vanilla flavoring.

Grease well, bottom and sides of 3 round layer pans: one 12″, one 9″, one 6″ in diameter.

Cut rounds of heavy paper for bottoms and strips 3″ wide for sides. Line and grease.

MAKE THE CAKE

Mix batter for twice the recipe, beating $2\frac{1}{2}$ min. *each* mixing time. Let stand while mixing batter for single recipe. Combine the two batters. Pour about $\frac{1}{2}$ of batter (7 cups) into 12″ pan and place in center of preheated oven, allowing space for cake to rise. Bake.
Pour $1\frac{3}{4}$ cups of remaining batter into 6″ pan, the rest into 9″ pan. Refrigerate these layers until 12″ cake is baked. Then bake them. Let cool 10 min. Remove paper. (Brown crust will come off easily.)

TEMPERATURE: 350° (mod. oven).

TIME: Bake 12″ layer 50 to 60 min.
Bake 9″ layer 35 to 45 min.
Bake 6″ layer 30 to 35 min.

MAKE THE FROSTING

While cake is still *slightly* warm, spread each layer with thin coating of White Butter Icing (to prevent crumbs getting into final frosting and help keep moist and fresh). *Do not* put layers together.

Choose an appropriate permanent foundation such as a mirror, crystal or silver cake plate, or a heavy, round cardboard covered with lace paper doilies.

Make 3 times the Large Recipe for Fluffy White Frosting. Place largest layer on its base, frost it; add the next layer, frost it, etc. Reserve about 2 cups frosting for decoration (add sifted confectioner's sugar to stiffen).

DECORATE THE CAKE

Pipe icing (delicately tinted if desired) around base of each layer and elsewhere as desired. Little icing flowers and other decorations appropriate for a wedding cake are available in stores. A small vase, all iced, with a few perfect rosebuds in it, or a miniature bride and groom, etc., may be placed on top of cake.

SERVE THE CAKE

The bride cuts the first piece and shares it with the groom. Then someone else cuts pieces for the guests. After the first few pieces are cut from the outer bottom layer so as not to destroy its appearance, the cake may be removed to the kitchen and the layers cut individually and served to the wedding guests.

SIMPLE EGG WHITE CAKES

CREAMING METHOD

Perennial favorites you'll make often.

DELICIOUS WHITE CAKE (🔑 Recipe) *Lovely to look at . . . luscious to eat.*

	For Large Cake	*Small Cake*
Grease generously and flour	2 9″ layer pans or 13x9″ oblong pan	2 8″ layer pans or 9″ square pan
Cream together until fluffy	⅔ cup soft shortening (half butter for flavor)	½ cup
	1¾ cups sugar	1⅓ cups
Sift together	3 cups *sifted* SOFTASILK *or* 2⅔ cups *sifted* GOLD MEDAL Flour	2¼ cups *or* 2 cups
	3½ tsp. baking powder	2½ tsp.
	¾ tsp. salt	½ tsp.
Stir in alternately with	1⅓ cups thin milk (half water)	1 cup
	2 tsp. flavoring	1½ tsp.
Fold in	4 egg whites (½ cup), stiffly beaten	3 whites (⅜ c).

Pour into prepared pans. Bake until cake tests done. Cool. Finish with desired filling and frosting. Elegant with Almond Cream Filling; a white frosting and melted chocolate poured over the edge (*see p. 151*); or with Fluffy White Frosting sprinkled with shredded fresh coconut.

TEMPERATURE: 350° (mod. oven).

TIME: Bake layers 30 to 35 min., square or oblong 35 to 45 min.

★ CHOCOLATE CHIP LAYER CAKE

With chips of dark chocolate to bite on, this cake has new taste and eye appeal. See p. 163.

Follow 🔑 recipe above using layer pans. Before pouring batter into pans, fold in carefully ⅔ cup *finely shaved* sweet or semi-sweet chocolate (3 sq.) for Large Cake; ½ cup (2 sq.) for Small Cake. Bake. Cool. Put layers together with Dark Chocolate Filling (*opposite page*). Finish with a glossy white frosting. Decorate top with curls of chocolate.

Sheet cakes can be frosted just on top.

DARK AND WHITE MARBLE CAKE

Follow 🔑 recipe above. Add chocolate, etc., to a third of the batter. See directions for Miracle Marble Cake (*opposite page*).

EASTER LAYER CAKE

The idea for this lovely springtime cake came from Dorothy Smith Raynor of Perry, Iowa.

Follow 🔑 recipe for Large Cake above—*except* use 3 8″ layer pans and divide batter into 3 parts. Use ⅓ batter for white layer. Color 2nd part pink with few drops red food coloring. Color 3rd part light lavender. Bake. Cool. Spread Rich Orange Filling between layers. Frost with Orange Butter Icing.

FLUFFY WHITE CAKE

Nice and high, fluffy and showy.

Follow 🔑 recipe above for method. Makes 2 thick 8″ layers (or square) or 2 thinner 9″ layers (or oblong). Use:

- ½ cup soft shortening (half butter)
- 1½ cups sugar

- 2½ cups *sifted* SOFTASILK *or* 2¼ cups *sifted* GOLD MEDAL Flour
- 2½ tsp. baking powder
- ½ tsp. salt

- 1 cup thin milk (half water)
- 1½ tsp. flavoring

4 egg whites (½ cup), stiffly beaten

Pour into prepared pans. Bake. Cool. For a special treat, finish with Date Cream Filling and a cooked white frosting with cut-up dates folded in.

SILVER WHITE CAKE (🔑 **Recipe**) *Full snowy, white layers. Marian Ralston (Mrs. Everett Ralston) made it in our film on New Method cakes, "400 years in 4 Minutes;" now makes it for her family in Rochester, Minnesota.*

	For Large Cake	*Small Cake*
Grease generously and flour	2 9″ layer pans or 13x9″ oblong pan	2 8″ layer pans or 9″ square pan
Sift together	2⅞ cups *sifted* SOFTASILK or 2⅔ cups *sifted* GOLD MEDAL Flour	2¼ cups or 2⅛ cups
	1⅞ cups sugar	1½ cups
	4½ tsp. baking powder	3½ tsp.
	1 tsp. salt	¾ tsp.
Add	⅔ cup soft shortening	½ cup
*Pour in a little over half of	1¼ cups milk	1 cup
	2 tsp. flavoring	1½ tsp.
Beat 2 min.		
Add remaining milk and	5 egg whites (⅔ cup), unbeaten	4 whites (½ c.) unbeaten
Beat 2 min.		

Pour into prepared pans. Bake until cake tests done. Cool. Finish with desired filling and frosting. Elegant with Almond Cream Filling; or a white frosting with melted chocolate poured over it *(see p. 151)*; or with Fluffy White Frosting sprinkled with shredded fresh coconut.

**When using* GOLD MEDAL, *add all the liquid at once.*

TEMPERATURE: 350° (mod. oven).

TIME: Bake layers 30 to 35 min., square or oblong 35 to 45 min.

NEW CHOCOLATE CHIP CAKE
Flecks of dark chocolate all through white cake. Picture on p. 163.

Follow 🔑 recipe above in layer pans. Before pouring batter into pans, fold in carefully ⅔ cup *finely shaved* sweet or semi-sweet chocolate (3 sq.) for Large Cake; ½ cup (2 sq.) for Small Cake. Bake. Cool. Put layers together with Dark Chocolate Filling. Finish with a glossy white frosting. Decorate top with curls of chocolate.

DARK CHOCOLATE FILLING

For 9″ Layers	*8″ Layers*
Mix together in saucepan . . .	
1 large egg yolk	1 yolk
3 tbsp. cream	2 tbsp.
Blend in	
½ cup sugar	⅜ cup
1 sq. chocolate (1 oz.), cut-up	¾ sq. (¾ oz.), cut-up
1 tbsp. butter	¾ tbsp

Cook over moderate heat only until bubbles appear around edge, stirring constantly. Remove from heat. Beat until thick.

All you have to do –

To make chocolate curls: Barely warm a bar of chocolate (*do not melt*). With razor blade, take off thin shavings from back or sides of chocolate. (They curl up.)

★ **TOASTED ALMOND CAKE**

Frost the large Silver White Cake with Browned Butter Icing. Decorate with split or slivered blanched almonds, toasted.

MIRACLE MARBLE CAKE

Follow 🔑 recipe above. Pour ⅔ of batter into pans. Beat into remaining batter a mixture of 1¼ sq. chocolate (1¼ oz.), melted, ¼ tsp. soda, and 2½ tbsp. warm water for Large Cake; 1 sq. chocolate, ⅛ tsp. soda, and 2 tbsp. warm water for Small Cake. Pour here and there over white batter. Cut through batter with knife several times for marbled effect. Bake. Cool. Frost with chocolate icing. *See picture on opposite page.*

Luscious cakes with special finishes.

RICH WHITE CAKE (Key Recipe) *The richest and most elegant of all. Favorite of Mary Fraser Morse (Mrs. Willard A. Morse of Minneapolis) whose mother used to make the best cakes we ever ate in our college days.*

	For Large Cake	*Small Cake*
Grease generously and flour (or line with paper and grease)	**2 9″ layer pans**	**2 8″ layer pans**
Cream together until fluffy	**1 cup soft shortening (half butter for flavor)**	**3/4 cup**
	2 cups sugar	**1½ cups**
Sift together	**3 cups *sifted* SOFTASILK**	**2¼ cups**
	4 tsp. baking powder	**3 tsp.**
	1 tsp. salt	**3/4 tsp.**
Stir in alternately with	**1⅓ cups thin milk (half water)**	**1 cup**
	2 tsp. flavoring	**1½ tsp.**
Fold in	**6 egg whites (3/4 cup), stiffly beaten**	**4 whites (½ c.)**

Pour into prepared pans. Bake until cake tests done. (This rich cake will shrink a little.) Cool. Finish with Pineapple Filling and Fluffy White Frosting with ½ cup *drained* crushed pineapple added.

TEMPERATURE: 350° (mod. oven).

TIME: Bake layers 30 to 35 min.

LADY BALTIMORE CAKE

Made famous long ago by cooks of the town and plantation mansions of South Carolina and Maryland. A Christmas delicacy there.

Make key recipe above in layers. Spread both cooled layers with Fruit-Nut Filling below. Cover with a thin layer of White Frosting. Put layers together. Then cover top and sides of cake with the remaining White Frosting.

WHITE FROSTING

For 9″ Layers	8″ Layers
Mix together and boil to 242°, or until an 8″ thread spins from spoon . . .	
2½ cups sugar	**1⅞ cups**
1 tbsp. light corn syrup	**3/4 tbsp.**
1 cup water	**3/4 cup**
Pour slowly, beating constantly, over . . .	
3 egg whites, beaten stiff	**2 whites**
Add . . .	
1 tsp. vanilla	**3/4 tsp.**

Continue beating with spoon until mixture is fluffy and will hold its shape.

FRUIT-NUT FILLING

Take about ⅓ of frosting and mix in . . .	
⅓ cup raisins, cut fine	**¼ cup**
⅓ cup figs, cut in strips	**¼ cup**
½ cup walnuts, chopped	**6 tbsp.**

Filling should be thick enough to stay on cake.

PINK AZALEA CAKE

Makes you feel the beauty of springtime in Virginia with all the pink azaleas in bloom.

Follow key recipe for Large Cake above preparing 2 or 3 pans for 2 thick or 3 thinner layers. Tint batter for one layer a delicate pink. Bake. Cool. Into ½ of Fluffy White Frosting fold cut-up maraschino cherries or strawberries and nuts. Put layers together with this filling between. Tint remaining frosting pink and frost top and sides of cake. (*See color picture on p. 118.*)

LINCOLN'S FAVORITE CAKE

Follow key recipe for Large Cake above. At the last, stir in 1 cup almonds, blanched and chopped fine. Bake in 2 9″ or 3 8″ layer pans. Cool. Finish with Tutti-Frutti Frosting between layers and on top and sides of cake.

★ STRAWBERRY FESTIVAL CAKE

For those very special springtime parties.

Follow key recipe above—*except* use coconut milk in place of sweet milk. Fold in 1 cup finely grated fresh coconut for Large Cake; ⅔ cup for Small Cake. Frost according to directions on opposite page.

RICH SILVER CAKE (🔑 Recipe) *Delicate . . . rich . . . fine-grained.*

	For Large Cake	*Small Cake*
Grease generously and flour (or line with paper and grease)	2 9″ layer pans	2 8″ layer pans
Sift together (*See CAUTION below*)	3⅓ cups *sifted* SOFTASILK	2½ cups
	2 cups sugar	1½ cups
	1 tsp. salt	¾ tsp.
	5 tsp. baking powder	3½ tsp.
Add	1 cup soft shortening	¾ cup
Pour in	1⅓ cups thin milk (half water)	1 cup
	2 tsp. flavoring	1½ tsp.
Beat 2 min.		
Add	6 egg whites (¾ cup), unbeaten	4 whites (½c.) unbeaten
Beat 2 min.		

Pour into prepared pans. *Batter may appear curdled.* Bake until cake tests done. Cool. Finish with desired frosting. Delicious with special fillings and icings below.

TEMPERATURE: 350° (mod. oven).

TIME: Bake 9″ layers 30 to 35 min., 8″ layers 25 to 30 min.

CAUTION: This cake rated exceptionally high (10) with testers who followed all directions accurately. Because it is extra rich, it pays to be extra careful (see p. 116 re. shortening and baking powder).

★ NEW COCONUT CREAM CAKE

A specialty of Mrs. James F. Mason of Los Gatos, California—the most hospitable and gracious of homemakers.

Follow 🔑 recipe for Large or Small Cake above. Cool. Make Custard Cream Filling (*recipe below*). Add about ½ cup coconut to ⅓ of the filling and spread between the layers. Coat top and sides of cake thinly with remaining filling. Sprinkle generously with coconut (about 1½ cups).

CUSTARD CREAM FILLING

For 9″ Layers	*8″ Layers*
Mix together in saucepan . . .	
½ cup sugar	⅓ cup
⅓ cup flour	¼ cup
½ tsp. salt	⅓ tsp.
Stir in . . .	
1⅓ cups rich milk	1 cup

Cook over low heat, stirring until it boils. Boil 1 min. Remove from heat. Pour a little of this mixture into . . .

1 large egg (¼ cup), slightly beaten	1 egg

Blend into hot mixture in saucepan. Bring to boiling point. Cool and stir in . . .

2 tbsp. soft butter	1½ tbsp.
1⅓ tsp. vanilla	1 tsp.

NEW PINK AZALEA CAKE

Follow 🔑 recipe for Large Cake above, preparing 2 or 3 pans for 2 thick or 3 thinner layers. Tint batter for one layer a delicate pink. Finish with pink filling and frosting, as for Pink Azalea Cake (*opposite*).

NEW STRAWBERRY FESTIVAL

With fresh coconut—a Maytime sonata.

Follow 🔑 recipe above—*except* use coconut milk in place of sweet milk. Fold in 1 cup finely grated fresh coconut for Large Cake; ⅔ cup for Small Cake. Bake. Cool. Finish with Fresh Strawberry Frosting (1 cup slightly crushed fresh strawberries folded into White Mountain Frosting). Decorate with whole berries (hulls on).

CHOCOLATE ALLEGRETTI CAKE

Using a teaspoon, drip melted chocolate (2 sq. unsweetened, and ½ tsp. butter melted with it) around edge of white frosted cake and let run down over sides in uneven lines.

WHITE WITH NUTS CAKES Old-time favorites.

MARASCHINO CHERRY CAKE (🔑 Recipe) *A lovely pink, high cake. Olga Stege of our Staff especially likes it for February parties.*

	For Large Cake	Small Cake
Grease and flour	2 9″ layer pans or 13x9″ oblong pan	2 8″ layer pans or 9″ square pan
Cream together until fluffy	2/3 cup soft shortening (half butter for flavor)	1/2 cup
	1 1/2 cups sugar	1 1/8 cups
Sift together	3 cups *sifted* SOFTASILK or 2 3/4 cups *sifted* GOLD MEDAL Flour	2 1/4 cups or 2 cups
	2 1/2 tsp. baking powder	2 tsp.
	1 tsp. salt	3/4 tsp.
Add alternately with	1/4 cup cherry juice	1/4 cup
	3/4 cup milk	1/2 cup
Stir in	1/2 cup chopped nuts	3/8 cup
	16 maraschino cherries, cut in eighths	12 cherries
Fold in	5 egg whites (2/3 cup), stiffly beaten	4 whites (1/2 c.)

Pour into prepared pans. Bake. Cool. Finish with cooked white frosting made with cherry juice in place of water. Decorate with red stemmed cherries.

TEMPERATURE: 350° (mod. oven).

TIME: Bake layers 30 to 35 min., square or oblong 30 to 35 min.

NUT LOAF CAKE

White, rich with nuts, delicious uniced.

Prepare 9x5x3″ loaf pan or 2 8″ layer pans. Follow 🔑 recipe above for method. Use:

1/2 cup soft shortening (half butter)
1 cup sugar
2 cups *sifted* SOFTASILK
or 1 3/4 cups *sifted* GOLD MEDAL Flour
2 tsp. baking powder
1/2 tsp. salt
1/2 cup thin milk (half water)
1/2 tsp. each vanilla and almond flavoring
2/3 cup nuts, cut-up
4 egg whites (1/2 cup), stiffly beaten

Pour into prepared pan. Bake. Cool.
TEMPERATURE: 350° (mod. oven).
TIME: Bake loaf 55 to 60 min., layers 25 to 30 min.

MAMMY'S PUFF CAKE

Elegant! From the Old South.

Prepare 2 9″ layer pans. Follow recipe for Nut Loaf Cake above. Substitute 30% whipping cream for milk and 2 tsp. lemon juice for the vanilla and almond. Increase the flour, sugar, and egg whites . . . using

2 1/4 cups *sifted* SOFTASILK
or 2 cups *sifted* GOLD MEDAL Flour
1 1/2 cups sugar
8 egg whites (1 cup), stiffly beaten

All you have to do–

To lessen the size of the "crack" typical of loaf cake: let batter stand in pan 20 minutes before baking.

★ POPPY SEED CAKE

Luscious! An old German recipe sent in years ago by Mrs. P. R. Aust of Minneapolis.

Soak 1/3 cup poppy seeds in 1/2 cup water for 2 hr. Drain off water. Add seeds to creamed mixture. Prepare 2 8″ layer pans. Follow 🔑 recipe above for method. Use:

3/4 cup soft shortening (half butter)
1 1/2 cups sugar
the drained poppy seeds
2 1/4 cups *sifted* SOFTASILK
or 2 cups *sifted* GOLD MEDAL Flour
2 tsp. baking powder
1/2 tsp. salt
1 cup water
4 egg whites (1/2 cup), stiffly beaten

Pour into prepared pans. Bake. Cool. Use Cream Filling between layers and finish with a cooked white frosting.

All you have to do–

To use the egg yolks:
bake a Gold Cake or Sponge Cake
make a Cream Filling for a cake
make Hollandaise Sauce for vegetables
make eggnogs for the children

NEW MARASCHINO CAKE (🔑 Recipe) *As pink and high as a summer cloud.*

	For Large Cake	Small Cake
Grease and flour	2 9″ layer pans or 13x9″ oblong pan	2 8″ layer pans or 9″ square pan
Sift together	3 cups *sifted* SOFTASILK or 2¾ cups *sifted* GOLD MEDAL Flour 1¾ cups sugar 4 tsp. baking powder 1 tsp. salt	2¼ cups or 2⅛ cups 1⅓ cups 3 tsp. ¾ tsp.
Add	⅔ cup soft shortening ⅓ cup juice from cherries ⅔ cup milk	½ cup ¼ cup ½ cup
Beat 2 min. Add	5 egg whites (⅔ cup), unbeaten	4 whites (½ c.) unbeaten
Beat 2 min. Fold in	½ cup chopped nuts 16 maraschino cherries, cut in eighths	⅜ cup 12 cherries

Pour into prepared pans. Bake. Cool. Finish with cooked white frosting made with cherry juice in place of water. Decorate with bright red cherries.

TEMPERATURE: 350° (mod. oven).

TIME: Bake 30 to 35 min. for layers, square or oblong 35 to 40 min.

★ NEW NUT LOAF CAKE

Fine textured. Yummy! Nice to have in the house for unexpected guests.

Prepare 9x5x3″ loaf pan or 2 8″ layer pans. Follow method in 🔑 recipe above. Use:

2 cups *sifted* SOFTASILK
1¼ cups sugar
1½ tsp. baking powder
1 tsp. salt
½ cup soft shortening
½ cup milk
1 tsp. vanilla
4 egg whites (½ cup)
½ cup cut-up nuts

TEMPERATURE: 350° (mod. oven).

TIME: Bake loaf 60 to 65 min., layers 30 to 35 min.

Pour into prepared pan. Bake. Cool. Loaf cakes are delicious uniced and actually mellow on standing.

ORANGE LOAF CAKE

Refreshing flavor, rich tasting, mellows on standing.

Follow recipe for New Nut Loaf Cake above—*except* substitute fresh or frozen orange juice for milk. Use 2 whole eggs in place of egg whites. Omit vanilla and nuts. Fold in 1 tbsp. grated orange rind.

> CAUTION: If you use a maraschino *type* cherry (*artificial coloring added*), omit the cherry juice, use all milk.

TUTTI-FRUTTI LOAF CAKE

"My children say, 'It is so pretty!'" reported Mrs. Russell V. Moe, one of our Minneapolis home testers.

Follow recipe for New Nut Loaf Cake opposite—*except* increase flour ¼ cup. Use only ¼ cup cut-up nuts and fold in at the last with a mixture of 1 cup cut-up candied fruit, as cherries, citron, orange rind, etc., mixed in 2 tbsp. extra flour.

Slice and serve warm. Delicious!

SPONGE CAKES How to keep the shadows out of Sunshine and Sponge Cakes.

Beat in sugar very gradually, a little at a time. With mixer, use medium speed.

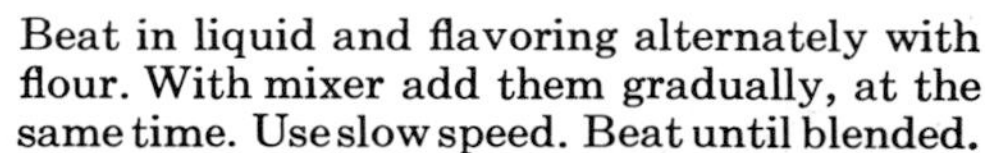

Beat egg yolks with rotary beater by hand or mixer (fast speed) until thick and lemon colored (5 to 10 min.).

Beat in liquid and flavoring alternately with flour. With mixer add them gradually, at the same time. Use slow speed. Beat until blended.

Beat egg whites with a wire whip or rotary beater until fine-grained, glossy, and just stiff enough to hold a peak (less than for Angel or Chiffon). Wire whip gives better volume.

Pour egg yolk mixture in thin stream over entire surface of beaten egg whites, carefully cutting and folding with whip or rubber scraper until completely blended.

Pour into ungreased tube-center pan. Pull knife gently through batter in widening circle, to break air bubbles. Bake until no imprint remains. Invert and let hang until cold.

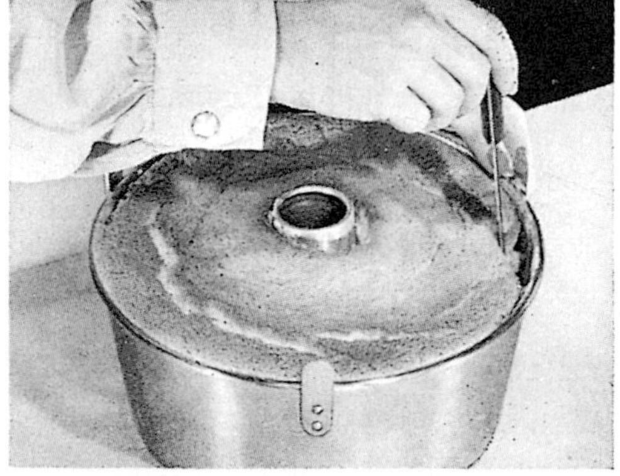

To loosen cake, plunge spatula down close against pan, then pull it out and continue thus around cake, and tube, and from bottom, if it's removable. Or shake sharply out of pan.

★ GLORIOUS SPONGE CAKE (🔑 Recipe) *The most delicious of all true sponge cakes.*

Set out but do not grease .... 10″ tube pan, 4″ deep

Beat until thick (at least 5 min.) .... 6 egg yolks ($\frac{3}{8}$ to $\frac{1}{2}$ cup)
Beat in gradually .... 1 cup sugar
Beat in .... 1 cup *sifted* SOFTASILK
(Yes, the same amount of either flour) *or* 1 cup *sifted* GOLD MEDAL Flour

alternately with ....
- $\frac{1}{4}$ cup cold water
- 1 tsp. lemon extract
- 1 tsp. grated lemon rind

In a *large* bowl, beat until stiff ....
- 6 egg whites ($\frac{3}{4}$ cup)
- $\frac{1}{2}$ tsp. cream of tartar
- $\frac{1}{2}$ tsp. salt

Gradually and gently cut and fold the egg yolk mixture into the beaten whites. Pour into *ungreased* pan. Bake. When cake tests done, invert and let hang until cold. Serve as is, or frost with a butter icing.

NOTE: Can use a 13x9″ oblong pan for the cakes below. Grease *bottom* of pan.
TEMPERATURE: 325° (slow mod. oven).
TIME: Bake tube cake 60 to 65 min., oblong 35 to 40 min.

SUNSHINE CAKE

Between a Sponge and an Angel Food.

Follow method and bake as in 🔑 recipe above—*except* beat only $\frac{1}{2}$ cup sugar into the yolks. Gradually beat remaining 1 cup into stiffly beaten egg whites. Use:

5 egg yolks ($\frac{1}{3}$ to $\frac{3}{8}$ cup)
$\frac{1}{2}$ cup sugar
1 cup *sifted* SOFTASILK
or 1 cup *sifted* GOLD MEDAL Flour
2 tbsp. cold water
$\frac{1}{2}$ tsp. vanilla
$\frac{1}{2}$ tsp. *each* almond and lemon extract
8 egg whites (1 cup)
$\frac{1}{2}$ tsp. cream of tartar
$\frac{1}{2}$ tsp. salt
1 cup sugar

FLUFFY SPONGE CAKE

A joy to the amateur. (With baking powder.)

Follow method and bake as in 🔑 recipe above—*except* add the baking powder and salt with the flour. Use:

6 egg yolks ($\frac{3}{8}$ to $\frac{1}{2}$ cup)
$1\frac{1}{2}$ cups sugar
$1\frac{1}{2}$ cups *sifted* SOFTASILK
or $1\frac{1}{2}$ cups *sifted* GOLD MEDAL Flour
1 tsp. baking powder
$\frac{1}{2}$ tsp. salt
6 tbsp. cold water
1 tsp. grated lemon rind
1 tsp. lemon extract
6 egg whites ($\frac{3}{4}$ cup)
$\frac{1}{2}$ tsp. cream of tartar

★ EGG YOLK SPONGE CAKE

From Mrs. Ludwig Rice, a homemaker for 23 years and one of our Minneapolis recipe testers.

Follow method and bake as in 🔑 recipe above—*except* add baking powder and salt. Sift with flour. (No egg whites.) Use:

11 egg yolks ($\frac{3}{4}$ cup)
1 whole egg ($\frac{1}{4}$ cup)
$1\frac{3}{4}$ cups sugar
2 cups *sifted* SOFTASILK
or 2 cups *sifted* GOLD MEDAL Flour
2 tsp. baking powder
$\frac{1}{2}$ tsp. salt
$\frac{1}{2}$ cup cold water
1 tbsp. grated orange rind
1 tbsp. strained orange juice
$\frac{1}{2}$ tsp. lemon extract

SUNSHINE FLOWER CAKE

Frost Sunshine or Sponge Cake with Orange Butter Icing and trim with gum drop flowers of assorted colors (cut and molded with fingers into shapes of flowers and leaves). Arrange in clusters over top and sides of cake to look like flowers scattered over it. (See *p. 242* for other dessert ideas.)

Special Ways to Serve Sponge Cake:

The Egg Yolk Sponge is ideal for an elegant Baked Alaska (DESSERTS, *p. 242*).

The Sunshine Cake baked in a 13x9″ oblong pan is perfect for Sunshine Rings (Wedding Rings) (DESSERTS, *p. 242*).

ANGEL FOOD CAKES How our "angels" get their wings.

Read recipe

Preheat oven. Yes *Pre*heat

Assemble ingredients

Collect utensils

Sift flour, measure sugar

Remember to take eggs out of refrigerator ahead of time

Beat eggs with wire whip for highest volume

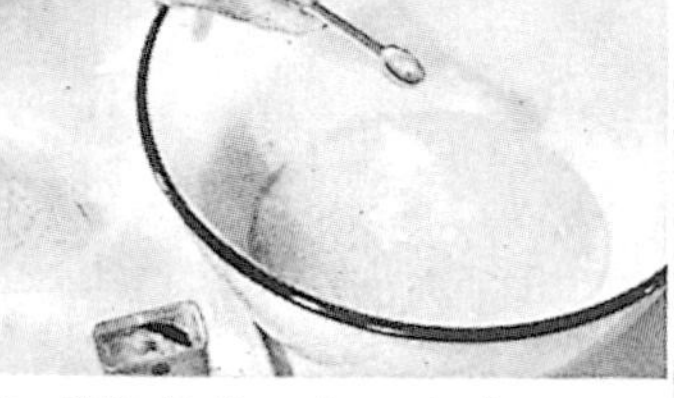

2 Sift (3 times) part of sugar with flour. Measure egg whites into *large* bowl. Add cream of tartar, salt, flavorings.

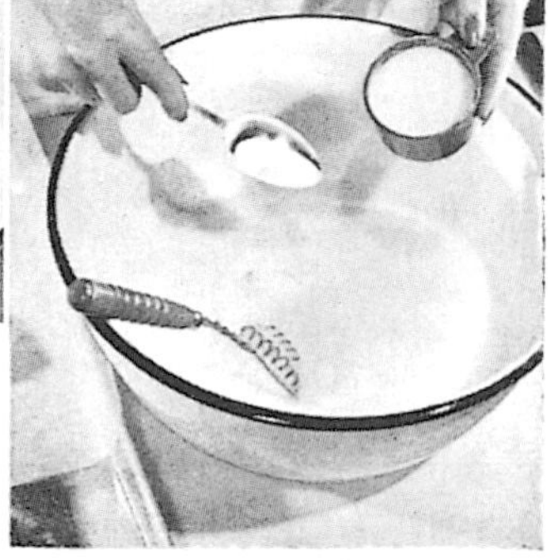

1 Separate eggs, drain off each white into saucer. Drop yolks into cup. Pour whites into measuring cup.

3 Beat whites until frothy, beat in remaining sugar (2 tbsp. at time), beating 10 sec. after each addition. (Medium speed on mixer.)

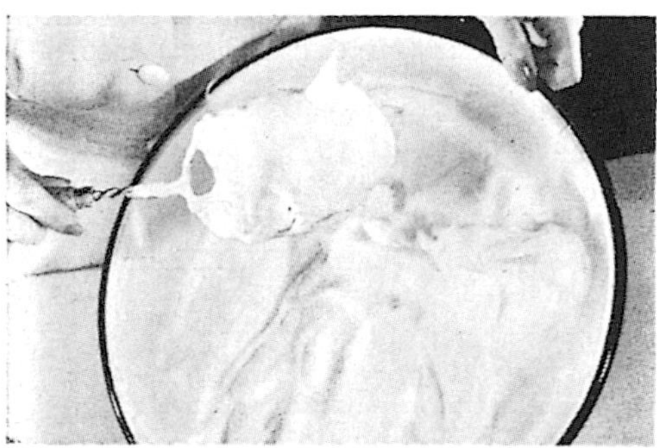

4 Continue beating until meringue is very *firm* and holds stiff *straight* peaks when wire whip is pulled up. (Use high speed on mixer.)

5 Sift flour-sugar mixture (3 tbsp. at a time) over meringue. Cut and fold in gently, with spatula, until it disappears each time.

7 Pull knife gently through batter . . . in widening circle, to break air bubbles.

6 Carefully push with rubber scraper into deep tube pan. Even up surface of batter.

8 Bake until no imprint remains when finger lightly touches top of cake.

ANGEL FOOD CAKE (🔑 Recipe) *Light as air . . . fluffy as a cloud.*

	Angel Food	★*Angel DeLuxe*
Set out but do not grease	10″ tube pan, 4″ deep	
Measure and sift together 3 times.....	*1 cup *sifted* SOFTASILK	1 cup
	$\frac{7}{8}$ cup sugar (granulated)	$1\frac{1}{2}$ cups (*sifted* confect'ners)
Measure into large mixing bowl.......	$1\frac{1}{2}$ cups egg whites (12)	$1\frac{1}{2}$ cups (12)
	$1\frac{1}{2}$ tsp. cream of tartar	$1\frac{1}{2}$ tsp.
	$\frac{1}{4}$ tsp. salt	$\frac{1}{3}$ tsp.
	$1\frac{1}{2}$ tsp. vanilla	$1\frac{1}{2}$ tsp.
	$\frac{1}{2}$ tsp. almond extract	$\frac{1}{2}$ tsp.
Beat with wire whip until foamy.		
Gradually add, 2 tbsp. at a time......	$\frac{3}{4}$ cup sugar (granulated)	1 cup (granulated)
Continue beating until meringue holds stiff peaks. Sift gradually ..	the flour-sugar mixture	
over................................	the meringue	

Fold in gently just until the flour-sugar mixture disappears. Push batter into ungreased tube center pan. Gently cut through batter with a knife. Bake. When cake tests done, invert. Let hang until cold.

**Or 1 cup sifted* GOLD MEDAL *Flour.*

TEMPERATURE: 375° (quick mod. oven).

TIME: Bake 30 to 35 min.

MARBLE ANGEL FOOD

Follow either 🔑 recipe above—*except* omit almond. Divide batter into 2 parts. To one half the batter, fold in 2 tbsp. *sifted* cocoa. Drop by spoonfuls into pan, alternating white and chocolate batter. Cut through batter several times.

CHOCOLATE ANGEL FOOD

Follow either 🔑 recipe above—*except* substitute $\frac{1}{4}$ cup cocoa for $\frac{1}{4}$ cup of the flour (sift together 3 times). Omit almond.

GOLD-SILVER ANGEL FOOD

For those special anniversaries.

Follow either 🔑 recipe above—*except* omit flavoring. Divide batter into 2 parts. Fold into one part, 4 well beaten egg yolks and 1 tsp. lemon extract. Fold 1 tsp. vanilla into the other part. Drop by spoonfuls into pan, alternating white and yellow batter. Cut through batter with knife . . . going around 5 or 6 times.

ALMOND CREAM ANGEL FOOD

Made for one of our early ads by Esther Bierman, then on our Staff, now Mrs. John Simon of Portland, Oregon.

For this and other special Angel Food Desserts, *see pp. 240–241.*

PEPPERMINT ANGEL FOOD

Have you ever seen a pale pink or delicate green angel? Well, we have.

Follow either 🔑 recipe above—and add 1 tsp. peppermint extract or few drops peppermint oil as flavoring. Add few drops of red or green coloring.

CHERRY ANGEL FOOD CAKE

Follow either 🔑 recipe above—*except* at the last, fold in $\frac{1}{2}$ cup chopped maraschino cherries drained on paper towel (or pineapple or other fruit). Add $\frac{1}{2}$ cup chopped nuts, if desired.

CHIFFON CAKES Once upon a time we had a secret . . .

Read recipe **Assemble ingredients**
Collect utensils **Preheat oven**
Sift flour and measure ingredients

2 Beat with spoon (or electric mixer) until smooth.

1 Sift flour, sugar, salt, baking powder into mixing bowl. Make a "well," add in order: oil, egg yolks, water, lemon rind, and flavoring.

3 Add cream of tartar to egg whites. Beat until they hold *very stiff* peaks. Do not underbeat.

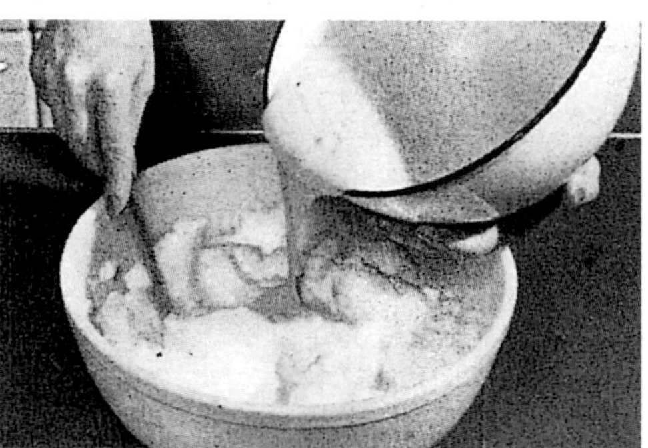

4 Pour egg yolk mixture in thin stream over entire surface of egg whites, gently cutting and folding in with rubber spatula.

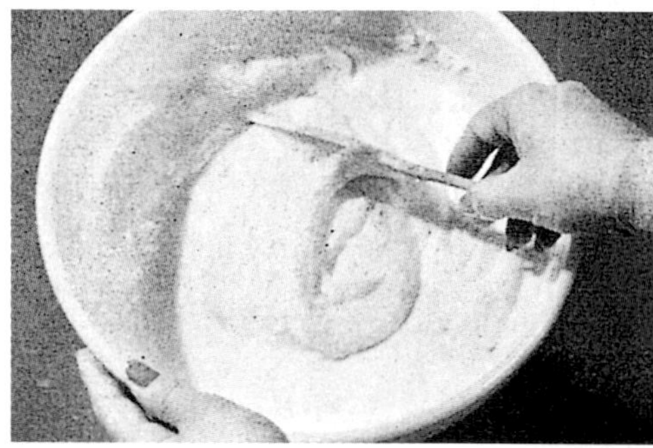

5 Fold gently . . . bringing scraper across *bottom* of bowl, up the side and over. Turn bowl and continue until completely blended.

6 Pour into ungreased pan. Bake until surface springs back when lightly touched. Invert pan immediately. Let hang until cold. Loosen with a spatula. Turn pan over and hit edge sharply on table to loosen.

7 Frost and trim cake as desired. This is the Peppermint Chip Chiffon, *p. 160*, with a cooked white frosting and crushed peppermint candy sprinkled over it. Chiffon cakes are delicious unfrosted.

★ CHIFFON CAKE (🔑 Recipe) *Light as angel food, rich as butter cake.*

	For Large Cake	*Small Cake*
Set out but do not grease	10″ tube pan, 4″ deep *or* 13x9″ oblong pan	9″ tube pan *or* 9x5x3″ loaf *or* 9″ square pan
Sift together into mixing bowl	2¼ cups *sifted* SOFTASILK **or* 2 cups *sifted* GOLD MEDAL Flour	1⅛ cups **or* 1 cup
	1½ cups sugar	¾ cup
	3 tsp. baking powder	1½ tsp.
	1 tsp. salt	½ tsp.
"Make a well" and add in order	½ cup cooking (salad) oil	¼ cup
	*5 egg yolks, unbeaten, (if you use SOFTASILK)	*2 yolks
	¾ cup cold water	⅜ cup
	2 tsp. vanilla	1 tsp.
	2 tsp. grated lemon rind	1 tsp.
Beat with a spoon until smooth.		
Then measure into large mixing bowl	1 cup egg whites (7 to 8)	½ cup (4)
	½ tsp. cream of tartar	¼ tsp.
	*7 egg yolks, unbeaten (if you use GOLD MEDAL Flour)	*3 egg yolks

Whip together until whites form very stiff peaks. Pour egg yolk mixture gradually over whipped whites, gently folding with rubber scraper just until blended. Pour into ungreased pan. Bake. When cake tests done, invert and let hang until cold.

TEMPERATURE and TIME:
Bake 10″ tube at 325° for 55 min., then at 350° for 10 to 15 min.
Bake 9″ tube at 325° for 50 to 55 min.
Bake oblong cake at 350° for 45 to 50 min.
Bake loaf cake at 325° for 50 to 55 min.
Bake square cake at 350° for 30 to 35 min.

All you have to do—

To make variations for Small Cake: use only half the amount of ingredients.

MAPLE PECAN CHIFFON

Follow 🔑 recipe for Large Cake above *except* omit vanilla and lemon rind. Sift only ¾ cup white sugar with the dry ingredients. Add ¾ cup brown sugar (no lumps) to the sifted dry ingredients. Use 2 tsp. maple flavoring. Gently fold in at the last 1 cup very finely chopped pecans.

BUTTERSCOTCH CHIFFON

A sun-tanned favorite.

Follow 🔑 recipe for Large Cake above *except* omit sugar and lemon rind. Add 2 cups brown sugar to sifted ingredients. Finish with Penuche Frosting.

PINEAPPLE CHIFFON

Follow 🔑 recipe for Large Cake above *except* use pineapple juice or syrup in place of water. Add to "well" ½ cup well drained *finely* crushed pineapple.

CHOCOLATE CHIP CHIFFON

Delicious chips all through.

Follow 🔑 recipe for Large Cake above *except* increase sugar to 1¾ cups and omit rind. At the last, sprinkle over batter and fold in carefully with a few strokes 3 sq. grated chocolate (3 oz.). Frost with Creamy Chocolate Icing, *p. 237.*

SPICE CHIFFON

Tantalizing combination of flavors.

Follow 🔑 recipe for Large Cake above *except* omit vanilla and lemon rind. Add to the dry ingredients 1 tsp. cinnamon, ½ tsp. *each* of nutmeg, allspice, and cloves. 2 tbsp. of caraway seeds may be added.

ORANGE CHIFFON

Follow 🔑 recipe for Large Cake above *except* omit vanilla and lemon rind. Add 3 tbsp. grated orange rind. All or part orange juice may be used in place of water. Finish with Orange Butter Icing.

CHIFFON CAKES

More Chiffon Cake variations.

BIT O' WALNUT CHIFFON

Follow recipe for Large Cake, p. 159 —*except* omit rind. At the last, sprinkle over batter . . . gently folding in with a few strokes . . . 1 cup very finely chopped walnuts. (If black walnut flavor is desired, use black walnuts or ½ tsp. black walnut extract.) Frost top and sides with Browned Butter Icing with toasted walnut halves.

HOLIDAY FRUIT CHIFFON

Follow recipe for Large Cake, p. 159 —*except* add 1 tsp. cinnamon to dry ingredients. At the last, sprinkle over batter . . . gently folding in with a few strokes . . . ¾ cup very finely chopped candied cherries, ½ cup very finely chopped pecans, ¼ cup very finely chopped citron.

COCOA CHIFFON

For Large Cake	*Small Cake*
Combine and let cool . . .	
¾ cup boiling water	**⅜ cup**
½ cup cocoa	**¼ cup**
Sift together . . .	
1¾ cups *sifted* SOFTASILK	**⅞ cup**
1¾ cups sugar	**⅞ cup**
3 tsp. baking powder	**1½ tsp.**
1 tsp. salt	**½ tsp.**
Make a "well" and add . . .	
½ cup cooking (salad) oil	**¼ cup**
7 egg yolks, unbeaten	**4 yolks**
cooled cocoa mixture	**cocoa mixture**
1 tsp. vanilla	**½ tsp.**

Beat until smooth. Then measure into mixing bowl and beat until very stiff . . .

1 cup egg whites (7 or 8)	**½ cup (4)**
½ tsp. cream of tartar	**¼ tsp.**

To combine, see directions in right hand column. Finish with Brown Beauty Icing (hobnail design, if desired). *See p. 168.* →

PEPPERMINT CHIP CHIFFON

Follow recipe for Large Cake, p. 159 —*except* omit lemon rind and use 1 tsp. peppermint extract in place of the vanilla. At the last, sprinkle over batter . . . gently folding in with a few strokes to give marbled effect . . . ½ tsp. red food coloring. To frost, *see picture, p. 158.*

CHERRY NUT CHIFFON

Follow recipe for Large Cake, p. 159—*except* omit rind, use only 1 tsp. vanilla. Use ¼ cup maraschino cherry juice and ½ cup water. At the last, sprinkle over batter . . . and fold in with a few strokes . . . ½ cup *each* very finely chopped nuts and well drained maraschino cherries.

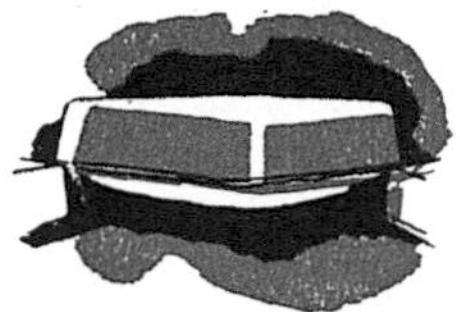

To cool a square or oblong cake . . . rest edges of pan on two other inverted pans.

When cold, loosen with spatula. Invert pan, hit sharply on table. Cake drops out.

★ BANANA CHIFFON

For Large Cake	*Small Cake*
Sift together . . .	
2¼ cups *sifted* SOFTASILK	**1⅛ cups**
1½ cups sugar	**¾ cup**
3 tsp. baking powder	**1½ tsp.**
1 tsp. salt	**½ tsp.**
Make a "well" and add . . .	
½ cup cooking (salad) oil	**¼ cup**
5 egg yolks, unbeaten	**2 yolks**
⅓ cup cold water	**2½ tbsp.**
1 cup mashed ripe bananas	**½ cup**
1 tsp. vanilla	**½ tsp.**

Beat until smooth. Then measure into large mixing bowl and beat till very stiff . . .

1 cup egg whites (7 or 8)	**½ cup (4)**
½ tsp. cream of tartar	**¼ tsp.**

Pour egg yolk mixture in thin stream over entire surface of egg whites, gently cutting and folding in with rubber spatula until completely blended. Pour into ungreased pan. Bake until cake tests done. Invert. Let hang until cold.

Frostings Dress the Cake

A BUTTER ICING is like a favorite cotton dress . . . simple and easy to put on . . . cooked white frostings like a perky street ensemble . . . and the extra touches of tinted coconut, toasted nuts, or allegretti are the gay accessories that make a costume "special." Your family will enjoy your "dressed-up" cakes the more because they look so pretty.

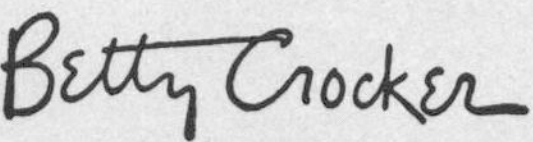

FROSTING FACTS AND FANCIES

For best results with cooked frostings, use a "candy" thermometer. To check its accuracy: at sea level—when water boils, the mercury reads 212°. Both our frosting and filling recipes have been developed in two amounts for large and small cakes. Each is generous for the size given. Any extra *filling* may be spread on top and sides of cake as well as between layers. "Extra" frosting may be stored in a covered container in the refrigerator for later use. See below for proper frosting amounts.

A Large Recipe frosts:

Between layers and on top and sides of 2 9″ layers.
Top and sides of a 10″ tube, 4″ deep.
Top and sides of a 13x9″ oblong.

ONE-HALF the Large Recipe frosts:

Top and sides only of 2 8″ layers.
Top only of a 13x9″ oblong.

A Small Recipe frosts:

Between layers, top and sides of 2 8″ layers.
Top and sides of a 9″ square.
Top and sides only of 2 9″ layers.
Top and sides of 10x5x3″ loaf.

ONE-HALF the Small Recipe frosts:

Top only of a 9″ square.

HOW TO FROST A 2-LAYER CAKE: Frost as soon as thoroughly cool. Brush away crumbs.

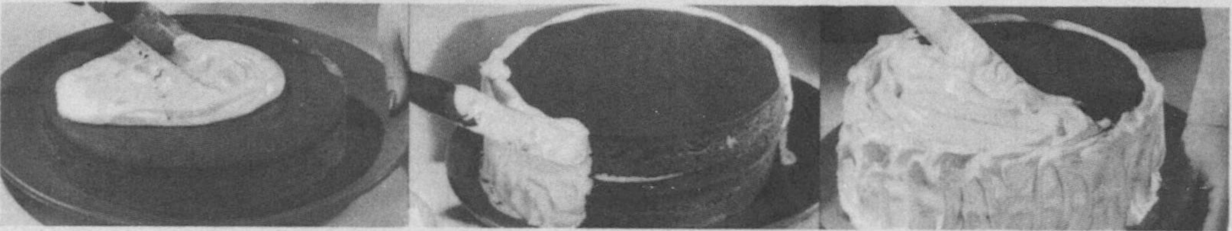

Place layer upside down on plate. Spread with filling or frosting. Let stand until set.

Place remaining layer right side up on top of filling. Frost top and sides with spatula.

Spread lightly and make attractive swirls, ridges, with outer ridge to shape up cake

HOW TO CUT A 2-LAYER BEAUTY TO GET MORE PIECES AND DAINTIER ONES: Use a thin, sharp knife. Insert the point of knife into the cake . . . keeping the point down and handle up, slice . . . pulling the knife toward you. If frosting sticks, dip knife in hot water.

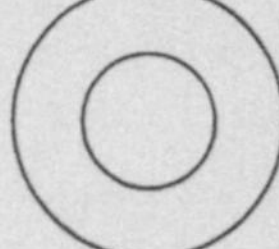
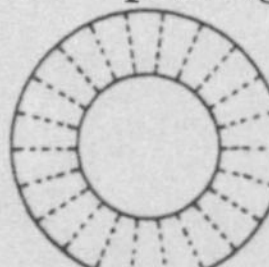
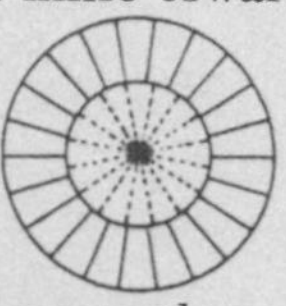
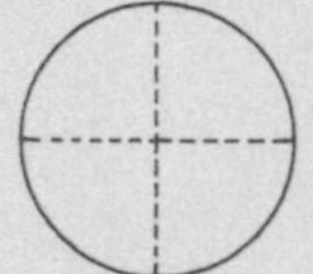

Cut around cake in a circle half way to the center. Cut pieces from outer circle. Cut pieces from inner circle. Makes 38 pieces. *or* Cut cake in 4 quarters. Then cut each quarter into slices. The 2 pieces closest to the middle of cake may be cut in half. 32 pieces.

HOW TO CUT A SHEET CAKE FOR A PARTY

Cut oblong cake in half lengthwise. Cut diagonally starting at one corner to make wedge shaped pieces. Then cut diagonally starting at opposite corner. Serves 22.

HOW TO QUICK-FROST CUPCAKES

Twirl the cupcake right in the frosting bowl

CHOCOLATE CHIP CAKE

Little surprise chunks of chocolate all through fluffy white layers . . . luscious dark chocolate filling . . . gleaming white frosting topped with festive curls of chocolate.

FROSTINGS AND FILLINGS

From the countless frosting and filling recipes and the ideas for trimming and decorating cakes which we have tested through the years, we have chosen for these pages those that have proved to be most popular and practical. We hope you will find just what you can use to best advantage in your cake-making.

January

Carnation — Garnet

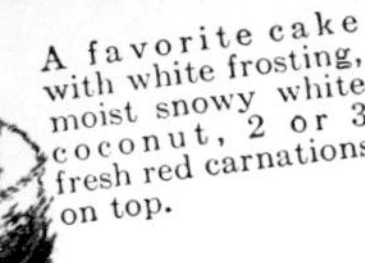

A favorite cake with white frosting, moist snowy white coconut, 2 or 3 fresh red carnations on top.

February

Primrose — Amethyst

The birthday child's best liked cake with white frosting and trimmed with cherries, cinnamon hearts, or peppermint candy.

March

Violet — Bloodstone

A cake baked in a tube pan (Angel or Chiffon) with delicately tinted icing and a bunch of fresh violets in a glass vase in the center hole.

April

Easter Lily — Diamond

The chosen cake baked in layers spread with luscious filling. Frost top and sides with a soft white frosting. Make little tinted swirls of frosting for candle holders.

May

Lily of the Valley — Emerald

A favorite cake frosted with a dark icing. Tie up tiny bouquets of lilies of the valley with emerald green ribbon and place around cake.

June

Rose — Moonstone

The special oblong cake with cooked white frosting—fresh strawberries folded in. Trim with whole berries (hulls left on) for color.

What month is your birth date?
What star shines on you?
Here are jewels and flowers
and birthday cakes, too!

July

Sweet Pea — Pearl

Frost a selected cake. Tie up little bunches of sweet peas with satin ribbon. Place around the cake and give to women guests.

August

Gladiolus — Sardonyx

Three layers of cake with filling and soft icing and individual flowers of assorted gladioli attractively arranged around cake.

September

Morning Glory — Sapphire

Cut layer cake in two. Place rounded edges together (butterfly fashion). Trim with white icing . . . sprinkle with blue sugar. Serve on blue plate. (Appropriate for twins' birthdays, too.)

October

Dahlia — Opal

The birthday child's favorite with Satiny Beige Frosting, toasted pecans and flaming red dahlias or autumn leaves around base.

November

Chrysanthemum — Topaz

A rich white layer cake with lemon filling between layers and over the top. Ice entire cake with a white cooked frosting. Sprinkle with grated lemon and orange rind.

December

Holly — Turquoise

Trim a white frosted cake (using pastry tube) with gay red musical notes and "Happy Birthday." Place red candles in red holders. Sprigs of holl[y] are appropriate.

Happy birthday to you!

A revolving musical cake plate that plays "Happy Birthday to You" adds to the joy of the birthday.

LINCOLN'S BIRTHDAY CAKE

Fill a jelly roll with red jelly or jam and roll in confectioners' sugar. Little axes of colored paper can be tucked here and there on top and sides of the roll.

LACY VALENTINE

Maxine Utke (Mrs. Chester H. Utke) of our Staff likes this cake on her Valentine Birthday.

Bake favorite white cake in layers. Cut each slightly to heart shape. Frost with a white icing. For pink trim, mix 1 cup moist shredded coconut with 8 minced red cherries. Sprinkle over top. Place red cinnamon hearts on sides. Serve on a dainty lace doily.

WASHINGTON'S BIRTHDAY

Frost a Maraschino Cherry Cake with a white icing and trim with clusters of the cherries. Use green gumdrops or strips of citron for leaves, and angelica for stems.

BLARNEY STONES

(for St. Patrick's Day)

Combine ½ cup butter, 1 egg yolk, 2½ cups *sifted* confectioners' sugar, 1 tsp. vanilla. Frost oblongs of sponge cake (baked in a sheet). Roll in chopped *salted* peanuts.

EASTER EGG CAKES

Bake any white cake in an oblong pan. Cut in 1½″ squares or oblongs. Brush with slightly beaten egg white and let dry. Roll each square in thick white icing until it looks oval. Then roll each in a different colored coconut.

MAY DAY BASKET

First made up for a party for our Staff.

Cover the sides of a 2-layer cake with cooked white icing. Hollow out the top a little and frost with green icing. Wind a wire handle with crepe paper and fasten into the two sides of the cake. Stick into the top of the cake, sweet peas, bachelor buttons, daisies, and lavender lace flowers.

MOTHER'S DAY CAKE

Given in our radio program years ago and featured every year by bakeries.

Cover top and sides of a rich white cake with cooked white frosting. Sprinkle lavishly with moist shredded coconut. Lay 2 or 3 fresh red roses on the top.

FATHER'S DAY CAKE

Establish tradition in your own family and make Dad *his* favorite cake . . . frosted as he likes it. Present with a kiss and hug.

FOURTH OF JULY CAKE

Frost a Peppermint Chip Chiffon Cake with white icing. Sprinkle top and sides with rather large chips of red peppermint candy. Outline a star with blue candles.

HALLOWE'EN CAKE

Make a Peanut Butter Cake and frost with Peanut Butter Fudge Frosting. Trace a witch on top, and spread a coating of melted chocolate inside the outline.

CHRISTMAS CANDLE CUPCAKES

They thrill the children—grownups, too.

Make the Last Minute Fruit Cake or the Inexpensive Fruit Cake as cupcakes. Frost with cooked white icing. Place a red candle in each cake, and decorate with small sprays of holly. Cut the red berries out of candied cherries, leaves from citron.

FESTIVE FROSTINGS Attractive finishes.

SNOW SCENE CAKE

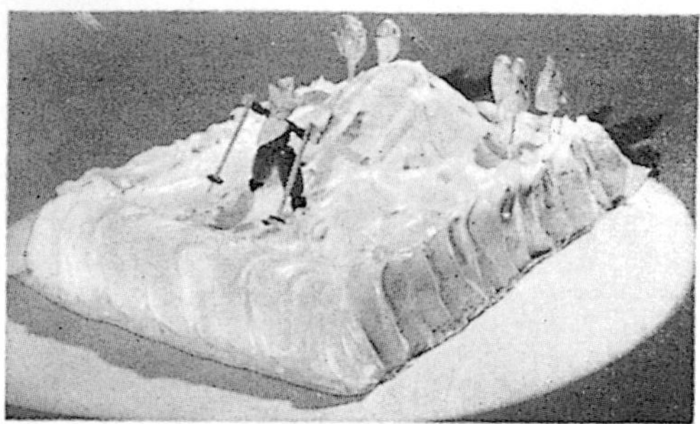

Originally designed for guests who came to the St. Paul Winter Carnival.

BOUQUET OF FLOWERS CAKE

Perfect for parties for the bride. (Notice the picture in color, pp. 118–119.)

Make 2 chiffon cakes; large size in 13x9″ oblong pan; small size in 9x5x3″ loaf pan. Place large cake upside-down on serving plate. Cover the top with Fluffy White Frosting (double the large recipe). Place smaller cake (upside-down) in the exact center. Frost top and sides.

Choose garden flowers or flowers in season, and use a free hand in decorating your cake. Flowers that hold up and are especially effective are hyacinths, bachelor buttons, baby roses, and stephanotis.

SPRIGGED CALICO CAKE

Frost top of an oblong cake with ¾ of Fluffy White Frosting. Blend 1 sq. unsweetened chocolate (1 oz.), melted and cooled, into remaining ¼. Frost sides and bring up over edge of cake to resemble scalloped edges of quilt. Pipe lines of chocolate frosting across the top to make squares. Sprinkle crushed peppermint candy in center of each square to make it resemble quilt pattern.

MERRY-GO-ROUND CAKE

A thrill for youngsters at a party.

Frost layer cake with Chocolate Butter Icing.

Select 8 pairs animal crackers.

Trim appropriately with colored frosting. Set in pairs around top of cake. Put a colored straw upright between each pair and a long peppermint candy stick in center. On top of poles rest a canopy made from colored art paper with scalloped edges.

COCONUT BALLS (Snowballs)

You'll never forget your first taste . . . they're heavenly!

Cut 2″ squares from white cake (or from the parts of white Angel Food removed when filling an Angel Food). Gently mold into rounded shape. Dip into and cover with Fluffy White Frosting. Roll in moist shredded coconut. See color picture on p. 213.

LITTLE CIRCUS CAKES

Ice tops of cupcakes in different colors. Outline faces with melted chocolate. Wrap frilled crepe paper around cakes for neck ruffs. Make circus characters . . . clowns, thin man, plump lady, etc.

JACK-O-LANTERN CUPCAKES

Frost chocolate cupcakes with orange colored icing, and on each draw a Jack-O-Lantern face with melted chocolate.

CLOWN CUPCAKES

Cut cone-shaped pieces out of tops of cupcakes. Turn cover upside-down and frost with chocolate icing . . to form peaked nats. Fill cavities of cupcakes with scoops of ice cream. Make eyes and nose with raisins. Set frosted hats on top of clown heads.

With confectioners' sugar—simplest of all. **FROSTINGS** **UNCOOKED**

WHITE BUTTER ICING (🔑 Recipe)

Use butter for extra richness and flavor.

	For Large Cake	*Small Cake*
Blend together	3 cups *sifted* confectioners' sugar	2 cups
	1/3 cup soft shortening	1/4 cup
Stir in until smooth	about 3 tbsp. cream	2 tbsp.
	1 1/2 tsp. vanilla	1 tsp.

CHOCOLATE BUTTER ICING

Follow 🔑 recipe above. Add 3 sq. unsweetened chocolate (3 oz.), melted, to blended mixture for Large Cake; 2 sq. (2 oz.) for Small Cake.

MOCHA BUTTER ICING

Follow 🔑 recipe above—*except* omit vanilla, and in place of the cream, use strong black coffee.

BROWNED BUTTER ICING

Follow 🔑 recipe above. Use all butter for shortening and brown it in a heavy skillet before blending with sugar.

ORANGE (or Lemon) ICING

Follow 🔑 recipe above—*except* omit vanilla, and in place of the cream, use orange (or lemon) juice. Add grated rind for extra flavor.

PINEAPPLE BUTTER ICING

Follow 🔑 recipe above—*except* omit cream and vanilla. Add 1/3 cup well drained crushed pineapple for Large Cake; 1/4 cup for Small Cake.

All you have to do—

For a very simple frosting: add to sifted confectioners' sugar enough hot cream to make easy to spread. Flavor as desired.

WHITE BUTTER YOLK ICING

The egg yolks add flavor and richness.

Blend together . . .

4 tbsp. soft shortening	3 tbsp.
1 large egg yolk	1 small
3 cups *sifted* confectioners' sugar	2 cups
about 3 tbsp. cream	2 tbsp.
1 1/2 tsp. vanilla	1 tsp.

CHOCOLATE: add 3 sq. unsweetened chocolate, melted, for Large Cake; 2 sq. for Small Cake.

ORANGE OR LEMON: Omit vanilla. Use orange or lemon juice in place of cream. Add grated rind for extra flavor.

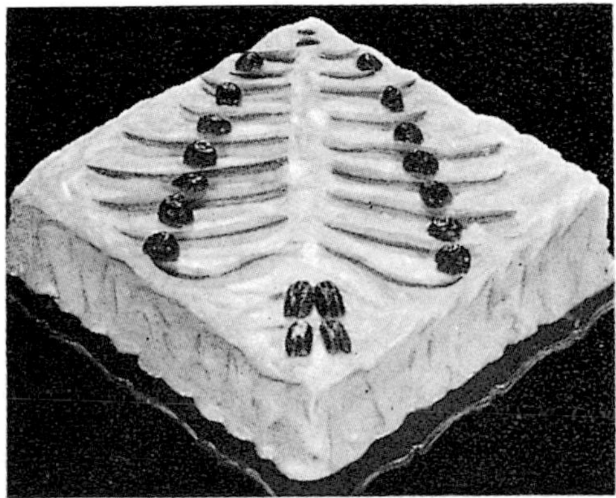

A quaint Christmas Tree Cake . . . full branches of green citron . . . red "balls" of candied cherries . . . sturdy trunk of pecans.

AS YOU LIKE IT FROSTING

To suit three different tastes.

Divide 🔑 recipe above into 3 parts. To first part, add 1 sq. unsweetened chocolate (1 oz.), melted. To second part, add grated rind of 1 orange, plus a few drops of orange food coloring. Leave third part plain.

Mark cake in thirds, and frost each third with one of the icings. Sprinkle chopped nuts over white section.

UNCOOKED FROSTINGS More easy icings, all chocolate favorites.

For hobnail effect, twist tip of spoon in icing.

BROWN BEAUTY ICING

Soft, dark, glossy, and moist.

For Large Cake	*Small Cake*
Place bowl in ice water, beat together until consistency to spread (3 to 5 min.).	
1⅓ cups *sifted* confectioners' sugar	1 cup
⅓ tsp. salt	¼ tsp.
3 or 4 egg yolks (or 1 large egg)	2 or 3 yolks (1 small)
4 tbsp. milk	3 tbsp.
4 tbsp. soft shortening	3 tbsp.
3 sq. chocolate (3 oz.), melted	2 sq. (2 oz.)
1 tsp. vanilla	¾ tsp.

CAUTION: Chocolate means *unsweetened* chocolate unless otherwise stated.

CHOCOLATE DE LUXE ICING

Fluffy, medium chocolate color. Developed by Ruth Kerker Smith, formerly of our Staff.

For Large Cake	*Small Cake*
Beat together until fluffy . . .	
2 cups *sifted* confectioners' sugar	1½ cups
⅓ tsp. salt	¼ tsp.
1 large egg	1 egg
⅓ cup soft shortening	¼ cup
2 sq. chocolate (2 oz.), melted	1½ sq. (1½ oz.)

Reserve some frosting, stir in nuts for glamor.

CREAMY CHOCOLATE ICING

One of easiest to handle, delish! (*See p. 237.*)

THIN CHOCOLATE ICING

For Boston Cream Pie, Cream Puffs, and such.

Melt together . . .
- 2 tbsp. shortening
- 2 sq. chocolate (2 oz.)

Blend in . . .
- 1 cup *sifted* confectioners' sugar
- 2 tbsp. boiling water

Beat until smooth but not stiff.

CHOCOLATE JOY ICING

A favorite dark icing like the Chocolate de Luxe only using cocoa and egg yolk.

For Large Cake	*Small Cake*
Sift together . . .	
2⅔ cups *sifted* confectioners' sugar	2 cups
⅓ tsp. salt	¼ tsp.
4 tbsp. cocoa	3 tbsp.
Add . . .	
1 large egg yolk	1 yolk
⅓ cup soft shortening	¼ cup
about 5 tbsp. hot water	3½ tbsp.

Beat until smooth and easy to spread.

All you have to do –

For Mocha Joy Icing: use only ½ the amount of cocoa and hot black coffee instead of water.

GLOSSY CHOCOLATE ICING

Like a cooked fudge frosting, but very dark and chocolatey. No eggs.

For Large Cake	*Small Cake*
Melt together . . .	
4 tbsp. shortening	3 tbsp.
4 sq. chocolate (4 oz.)	3 sq. (3 oz.)
Blend in . . .	
2⅔ cups *sifted* confectioners' sugar	2 cups
⅓ tsp. salt	¼ tsp.
about 6½ tbsp. milk	5 tbsp.
1¼ tsp. vanilla	1 tsp.

Beat until it becomes smooth and glossy and thick enough to spread. Stir in ½ cup chopped nuts, if desired.

BROWN SUGAR MERINGUE

13x9" oblong pan	*9" square pan*
A few minutes before cake is removed from oven, beat until stiff. . .	
2 egg whites	1 egg white
Gradually beat in . . .	
1 cup brown sugar	⅔ cup
3 tsp. lemon juice	2 tsp.
Spread on hot cake immediately.	
Sprinkle with . . .	
½ cup nuts, cut-up	⅓ cup

CHOC-O-NUT TOPPING

Some in the middle; some on the top.

13x9" oblong pan	*9" square pan*
Mix together . . .	
2 cups coconut, cut-up	1⅓ cups
6 tbsp. water	4 tbsp.
½ cup semi-sweet chocolate, melted	⅓ cup

Pour ½ of cake batter into prepared pan. Sprinkle with ½ of choc-o-nut mixture. Add remaining batter. Bake. As soon as cake is done, sprinkle with remaining choc-o-nut mixture. (See picture, *p. 138.*)

CREAMY WHITE ICING

Melt in saucepan . . .	
½ cup shortening (part butter)	6 tbsp.
Remove from heat. Blend in . . .	
2½ tbsp. flour	2 tbsp.
¼ tsp. salt	⅛ tsp.
Stir in slowly . . .	
½ cup milk	6 tbsp.
Bring to a boil, stirring constantly. Boil 1 min. Remove from heat. Stir in . . .	
about 3 cups *sifted* confectioners' sugar	2¼ cups
½ tsp. vanilla	⅓ tsp.

Beat until right consistency to spread. (Place pan in ice water while beating to set more quickly.)

CREAMY RAISIN OR NUT
Add about ½ cup cut-up raisins or nuts.

CREAMY ORANGE OR LEMON
Omit vanilla. In place of the milk, use orange or lemon juice. Add 1 extra tbsp. flour. Add grated rind for extra flavor.

CREAMY FUDGE
Add 1½ to 2 sq. melted chocolate with the sugar.

CREAMY BROWNED BUTTER
Use all butter. Brown it first.

BROILED ICING

Bubbles and browns under the broiler.

13x9" oblong pan	*9" square pan*
Mix together . . .	
6 tbsp. soft butter	¼ cup
¾ cup brown sugar	½ cup
4 tbsp. rich cream	3 tbsp.
½ cup nuts, cut-up	⅓ cup

Spread over top of warm cake. Place about 3" under broiler (low heat) until mixture browns. For extra goodness, add about 1 cup WHEATIES or moist shredded coconut. (*See picture on p. 138.*)

PEANUT BUTTER BROILED ICING

13x9" oblong pan	*9" square pan*
Mix together . . .	
⅔ cup brown sugar	½ cup
4 tbsp. soft butter	3 tbsp.
4 tbsp. cream	3 tbsp.
4 tbsp. peanut butter	3 tbsp.
Stir in . . .	
1 cup peanuts, chopped	¾ cup

Spread on cold cake, place under broiler (low heat) until mixture browns.

SIMPLE GLAZE

A shiny finish for fruit cakes—not sticky.

Combine and bring *just* to a rolling boil . . .
½ cup light corn syrup
¼ cup water

Remove from heat. Cool to lukewarm. Pour over cold cake before or after storing.

Fruit cakes are usually decorated after storing. Dip under side of candied fruits in cooked white frosting or sugar water syrup and press lightly into top surface. For candied fruit decorations, *see p. 28.*

For a Christmas "package," pipe ribbon and bow of colored icing over white frosted cake.

COOKED FROSTINGS

Queenly frostings—all pure white.

FLUFFY WHITE FROSTING (⚷ Recipe) *The favorite with many of us. Barbara Sampson, a former Staff member, now of New York, made the frosting for these pictures.*

For Large Cake	*Small Cake*
Mix thoroughly in saucepan . . .	
1 cup sugar	**3/4 cup**
1/3 cup water	**1/4 cup**
1/3 tsp. cream of tartar	**1/4 tsp.**

Boil slowly without stirring until syrup spins a 6 to 8″ thread (242°). Keep saucepan covered first 3 min. to prevent crystals from forming on sides of pan.

While syrup is cooking, beat until stiff enough to hold a point . . .	
2 egg whites (1/3 cup)	**2 whites (1/4 c.)**
Pour hot syrup very slowly in a thin stream into stiffly beaten egg whites, beating constantly. Add . . .	
1½ tsp. vanilla	**1 tsp.**

Beat until frosting holds its shape. Spread between layers and on top and sides.

> *For very special eating quality, carefully fold into Fluffy White Frosting at the last, 1 to 2 tbsp. very soft butter.*

All you have to do—

If cooked white frosting becomes sugary: beat in a little lemon juice.

WHITE MOUNTAIN FROSTING

Soft and luscious and easy to swirl.

Follow ⚷ recipe above for method. Use:

For Large Cake	*Small Cake*
2/3 cup sugar	**1/2 cup**
2 2/3 tbsp. water	**2 tbsp.**
1/3 cup light corn syrup	**1/4 cup**
2 egg whites (1/3 cup)	**2 whites (1/4 c.)**
1½ tsp. vanilla	**1 tsp.**

LEMON FROSTING

Follow any recipe above—*except* in place of the vanilla, use lemon juice and fold in a little grated lemon rind.

LIGHT CHOCOLATE FROSTING

Follow any recipe above. At the very last, fold in *carefully*, melted and cooled unsweetened chocolate. Use 2 sq. for the Large Cake; 1½ sq. for Small Cake.

MARSHMALLOW FROSTING

Follow any recipe above. At the last, fold in 6 to 8 quartered marshmallows.

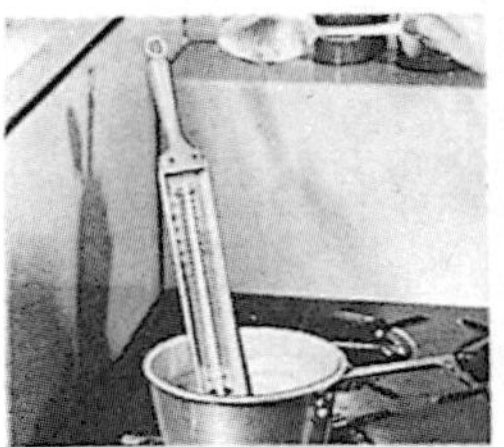

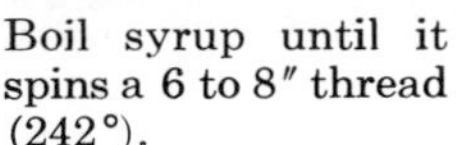

Boil syrup until it spins a 6 to 8″ thread (242°).

Pour very slowly into stiffly beaten egg whites.

Add vanilla and continue beating until frosting holds its shape.

COMFORT FROSTING

Like divinity candy, forms a crusty top.

Follow ⚷ recipe above for method. Use:

For Large Cake	*Small Cake*
2 cups sugar	**1½ cups**
1/2 cup water	**6 tbsp.**
2 tbsp. light corn syrup	**1½ tbsp.**
2 egg whites (1/3 cup)	**2 whites (1/4 c.)**
1½ tsp. vanilla	**1 tsp.**

All you have to do—

If cooked white frosting will not set: add *sifted* confectioners' sugar, a little at a time, until mixture is stiff enough.

PINEAPPLE FROSTING

Follow any recipe above—*except* in place of the water, use pineapple juice. Fold in a little grated lemon rind.

TUTTI-FRUTTI FROSTING

Follow any recipe above. At the very last, fold in nuts, candied cherries, dates and raisins (all chopped).

SATINY BEIGE FROSTING

Follow any recipe above—*except* use brown sugar in place of white sugar.

DOUBLE BOILER FROSTING (7-Minute)

For Large Cake	*Small Cake*
Combine in top of double boiler . . .	
2 egg whites (1/3 cup)	2 whites (1/4 c.)
1½ cups sugar	1 cup
1/4 tsp. cream of tartar	1/8 tsp.
1/3 cup water	1/4 cup

Place over boiling water and beat with rotary beater until mixture holds its shape. Fold in . . .

1½ tsp. vanilla	1 tsp.

WHITE WONDER FROSTING

A very soft icing. Easy with a mixer.

For Large Cake	*Small Cake*
Mix in top of double boiler . . .	
2 egg whites (1/3 cup)	2 whites (1/4 c.)
2/3 cup sugar	½ cup
3 tsp. light corn syrup	2 tsp.
1/8 tsp. cream of tartar	1/16 tsp.

Place over boiling water for 6 minutes, stirring with finger until you can no longer keep your finger in the mixture (150°). Remove from heat. Beat with rotary beater until icing will hold its shape. Fold in . . .

1½ tsp. vanilla	1 tsp.

SIMPLE VARIATIONS:

Fold in carefully at the very last . . . strips of raisins and walnut pieces *or* cut-up candied cherries and pecans *or* grated orange rind and Brazil nuts *or* chopped cooked dried fruit and slivered almonds.

PRIZE FUDGE FROSTING (🔑 Recipe) *Save the pan and spoon for the children.*

	For Large Cake	*Small Cake*
Combine and stir in saucepan.........	3 cups sugar	2¼ cups
	1 cup water	¾ cup
	2 tbsp. corn syrup	1½ tbsp.
	2 tbsp. butter	1½ tbsp.
	4 sq. unsweetened chocolate (4 oz.), cut-up	3 sq. (3 oz.)
Cook without stirring to a soft ball stage (234°), keeping covered the first three minutes. Remove from heat. Let stand until cool. Add..................................	1½ tsp. vanilla	1 tsp.

When fudge-type frostings become too *thick* to spread, add a little cream as needed. When too *thin*, add *sifted* confectioners' sugar.

Beat until thick enough to hold shape.

PEANUT BUTTER FUDGE

Follow 🔑 recipe above for method. Add peanut butter when mixture is cool. Use:

For Large Cake	*Small Cake*
1 cup sugar	¾ cup
1 cup brown sugar	¾ cup
2/3 cup top milk or cream	½ cup
1/3 cup peanut butter	¼ cup

All you have to do–

For White Fudge Frosting: omit the chocolate and use rich milk or sour cream in place of water in recipe for Prize Fudge Frosting. Fold in seeded raisins (about 1 cup, cut in strips), if desired.

PENUCHE FROSTING

For Large Cake	*Small Cake*
Mix together thoroughly . . .	
2 2/3 cups brown sugar	2 cups
2/3 cup milk	½ cup
2/3 cup shortening	½ cup
1/3 tsp. salt	¼ tsp.

Stir over low heat, then bring rapidly to a full boil, stirring constantly. Boil to 220° or exactly 1 min. Remove from heat. Beat until lukewarm and of right consistency to spread.

FILLINGS FROSTINGS Delicious cream fillings and fruity fillings.

CREAM FILLING (Key Recipe) *Smooth, rich, and creamy.*

	For Large Cake	*Small Cake*
Mix together in top of double boiler...	1/4 cup sugar	3 tbsp.
	1 tbsp. cornstarch	2 tsp.
	1/2 tsp. salt	1/3 tsp.
	1 cup rich milk or cream	3/4 cup
Bring to boil over direct heat, *stirring constantly*. Boil 1 min. Remove from heat. Pour a little over...	4 egg yolks, slightly beaten	3 yolks
Blend into hot mixture. Cook over boiling water, *stirring* until thick (2 min.). Remove from heat. Add...	1 1/2 tsp. vanilla	1 tsp.

NOTE: Chill until it sets.

ALMOND CREAM FILLING

Follow key recipe above—*except* use part almond flavoring. Cool. Add about 1/2 cup toasted chopped blanched almonds.

PINEAPPLE FILLING

Mix together in saucepan . . .

1/2 cup sugar	6 tbsp.
3 tbsp. cornstarch	2 tbsp.
1/2 tsp. salt	1/3 tsp.
3/4 cup pineapple juice	1/2 cup
3/4 to 1 cup crushed pineapple, well drained	1/2 to 3/4 cup
1 tbsp. butter	3/4 tbsp.
1 tsp. lemon juice	3/4 tsp.

Bring to a rolling boil and boil 1 min., stirring constantly. Chill before using.

CLEAR LEMON FILLING (Key Recipe)

Tangy flavor . . . just tart enough.

Mix together in saucepan . . .

1 cup sugar	3/4 cup
4 tbsp. cornstarch	3 tbsp.
1/2 tsp. salt	1/3 tsp.
1 cup water	3/4 cup
2 tbsp. grated lemon rind	1 1/2 tbsp.
1/2 cup lemon juice	6 tbsp.
2 tbsp. butter	1 1/2 tbsp.

Bring to a rolling boil and boil 1 min., stirring constantly. Chill before using.

RICH LEMON FILLING

Follow key recipe for Clear Lemon Filling above—*except* omit 1 tbsp. of the cornstarch. After the mixture has boiled 1 min., beat in . . .

4 egg yolks, slightly beaten	3 yolks

Return to heat and cook 1 more min., stirring constantly. Chill before using.

DATE OR FIG CREAM FILLING

Follow key recipe above—and fold in about 1/2 cup *each* cut-up dates or figs and toasted nuts.

CHOCOLATE CREAM FILLING

Follow key recipe above for method. Use:

1/2 cup sugar	6 tbsp.
2 tsp. cornstarch	1 1/2 tsp.
1/2 tsp. salt	1/3 tsp.
1 cup rich milk or cream	3/4 cup
2 sq. chocolate (2 oz.), cut-up	1 1/2 sq. (1 1/2 oz.)
4 egg yolks	3 yolks
1 tsp. vanilla	3/4 tsp.

CLEAR ORANGE FILLING (Key Recipe)

Full flavored and luscious.

Mix together in saucepan . . .

1 cup sugar	3/4 cup
4 tbsp. cornstarch	3 tbsp.
1/2 tsp. salt	1/3 tsp.
1 cup orange juice	3/4 cup
2 tbsp. grated orange rind	1 1/2 tbsp.
1 1/2 tbsp. lemon juice	1 tbsp.
2 tbsp. butter	1 1/2 tbsp.

Bring to a rolling boil and boil 1 min., stirring constantly. Chill before using.

RICH ORANGE FILLING

Follow key recipe for Clear Orange Filling above—*except* omit 1 tbsp. of the cornstarch. After the mixture has boiled 1 min., beat in . . .

4 egg yolks, slightly beaten	3 yolks

Return to heat and cook 1 more min., stirring constantly. Chill before using.

A Full Cooky Jar Makes a Home "Homey"

SOME of the sweetest memories of Home are bound up with Mother's Cooky Jar. Long after the spicy fragrance of her ginger cookies baking has faded into the years . . . the thought of that ample cooky jar on the shelf will bring back vividly the old-time peace . . . and comfort . . . and security of Home. Every Home should have a cooky jar!

Betty Crocker

Hidden Treasures for the Toddlers

"Tea-Off" with Cookies (*for tea*)

For Hungry Home-Comers

Lunch Box Surprises (*taste-thrillers all!*)

Put a "Lift" in Simple Desserts

Picnic Stars (*under any skies*)

Say "MERRY CHRISTMAS" with Cookies

- Holiday Fruit Cookies 180
- Berliner Kränser 206
- Poinsettias 196
- Zucker Hütchen 202
- Scotch Shortbread 203
- Hazelnut Bars 193
- Mandel Kager 206
- Lebkuchen 202
- Nurnberger 202
- Merry Christmas Cookies . . 201
- Spritz 207
- Jell-Meringue-Filbert Bars . . 192
- Almond Wreaths 207
- Finska Kakor 203
- Sandbakelser ("Sand Tarts") . 203
- Almond Crescents 205

Quick Cure for Homesickness *(send plenty to divvy up)*

- Date-and-Nut Squares . . 191
- Hermits 181
- Chocolate Chip Cookies . 184
- Filled Cookies 196
- Date-Apricot Bars 193
- Chocolate-Frosted Brownies 190
- Ginger Creams 183
- His Mother's Oatmeal Cookies 197

Fun for the Youngsters *("tricks or treats" for Hallowe'en)*

- Animal Cookies 201
- Wheaties Macaroons . . . 185
- Cookies with Faces 195
- Decorated Party Cookies . 195
- Jewelled Cookies 191
- Chocolate Cream Drops . . 182
- Chocolate Pinwheels . . . 194
- Gingerbread Boys 198

Beau-Catchers *(and Husband-Keepers)*

- Ginger Creams 183
- Chocolate-Frosted Brownies 190
- His Mother's Oatmeal . . 197
- Nut Sugar Cookies 194
- Date-Nut Refrigerator . . 186
- Date Bars. 193
- Chocolate Chip Cookies . 184
- Toffee-Nut Bars 192

Say It with Cookies *(for birthdays, sick friends, etc.)*

- Butter Fingers 205
- Walnut Squares 191
- Cinnamon Coffee Bars. . . 208
- Nut Bonbon Cookies . . . 208
- Coconut Cherry Cookies . 208
- Filled Cookies 196
- Almond Wreaths 207
- Orange-Chocolate Chip . . 184
- Rich Sugar Cookies. . . . 194
- Swedish Macaroon Tea Cakes 208

Where to find recipes for Cookies in color photograph, pp. 176 and 177

1. Place Card Cookies 195
2. Gingerbread Boys 198
3. Boy and Girl and Animal Cookies . 201
4. Date-Nut Squares (wrapped) . . . 191
5. Toffee-Nut Bars 192
6. Peanut Butter Cookies 204
7. Sugar Cookies. 194
8. Chocolate Chip Cookies 184
9. Hermits 181
10. Hatchets, Flowers, Hearts 195
11. Flower and Leaf-shaped Butter • Cookies. 195
12. Scotch Shortbread 203
13. Thumbprint Cookies 205
14. Coconut Macaroons 185
15. Chocolate Cream Drops 182
16. Date-Nut Squares 191
17. Butterscotch Cookies with Burnt Butter Icing 182
18. Brownies 190
19. Filled Cookies 196
20. Chocolate Refrigerator Cookies . . 186

COOKIES

Won't you come into our kitchen and join us in our "Cooky Shines?" That used to mean tea parties, but it's what we call our sessions of cooky baking. We have lots of fun trying out all the delicious cookies that come to us from many lands. I'd like to show you the cookies most popular with Staff members and friends who have shared their favorite recipes with us. You'll see many varieties in the color picture on the next page.

They're ever so easy to make! For we've worked out a new simplified method—a *double-quick* method! Takes less than half the usual mixing time! Would you like to know the secret? Then turn to the step-by-step pictures following. Imagine you are standing right beside one of our Staff while she makes cookies. Could anything be easier? There's no laborious creaming, no separate beating of eggs, only one bowl!

Now turn to the recipe pages. You'll find all the little pointers you would notice if you were right in our kitchen. There's a brand-new feature which I think will be a big help to you. We tell how to judge when the cookies are done. We've tried to include all the hints, shortcuts and tricks that save you time and work so you can delight your family with new treats each week.

The recipes are given in practical amounts for average sized families. Those for everyday cookies, and holiday cookies that keep well, make enough so you won't have to bake too often. Recipes for the richer, dainty cookies make enough for *special* occasions.

Cookies bring such a big reward in cheer and satisfaction! They make hospitality so easy! Invite your friends to join you for "Cooky Shines" in your kitchen and you'll be giving them happy memories they'll all cherish as long as they live.

Dave
Judy
To Son
from Mother

COOKIES LEARN THE "A-B-C's" HERE . . .

BEFORE YOU START

1 Select baking sheets (cooky sheets or pans) as indicated in each recipe. Heavy or double sheets (two sheets of the same size placed one on top of the other) prevent cookies from browning on the bottom too much and too quickly.

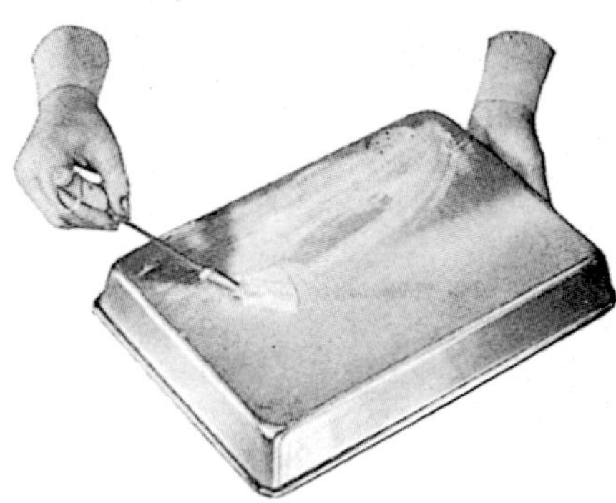

2 If pan with sides is used for cooky sheet, turn it upside-down and bake cookies on the bottom . . (insures even browning). Grease cool pans as indicated in recipes . . . with *unsalted* shortening.

3 Mix thoroughly the *softened* shortening, sugar, and eggs—also any molasses, syrup, or melted chocolate in the recipe.

4 Stir in the liquid and flavoring. (A few recipes indicate that liquid and flour mixture should be added alternately.)

. . . AND THE REST IS EASY! COOKIES

5 Sift together and stir in the flour, salt, and leavening (baking powder *or* cream of tartar and soda)—also any spices in the recipe. Then, mix in any fruit or nuts.

6 Chill dough, if indicated in recipe, to make it easy to handle. Then shape dough for different types of cookies as directed in the recipe. Place on prepared pans.

7 Bake. Place pan on rack in center of oven. If cooky tops do not brown properly, move to a higher rack for last few minutes. Pans should be narrower, shorter than oven (to leave a 1″ space for circulation of heat).

8 Look at cookies when minimum baking time is up. As soon as they are done (according to recipe), remove from oven. With a wide spatula, slip off baking sheet or out of pan onto wire rack to cool (as recipe directs).

Store cooled cookies properly to keep top eating quality. Keep crisp, thin cookies in can with loose cover.

Keep soft cookies in air-tight container (a covered earthen jar or a can with tight cover). Slices of apple or orange in jar help mellow and moisten cookies. Change fruit frequently.

Where to Find:

DROP COOKIES "Quickies" busy mothers love to make.

HOW TO MAKE DROP COOKIES (preliminary steps on pp. 178, 179)

1 It will save time in spacing dough, if you grease in symmetrical rows where you want to drop the dough. It will also save washing browned grease off a tin pan.

2 Drop dough by rounded or heaping teaspoonfuls, depending on size of cookies desired. With another teaspoon, push dough onto baking sheet . . . being careful to peak up the dough.

BROWN SUGAR DROPS (🗝 Recipe) *Soft, chewy. Wonderful brown sugar flavor.*

Mix together thoroughly................	1 cup soft shortening 2 cups brown sugar 2 eggs
Stir in.................................	½ cup sour milk or buttermilk
Sift together and stir in................	3½ cups *sifted* GOLD MEDAL Flour 1 tsp. soda 1 tsp. salt

Chill at least 1 hour. Drop rounded teaspoonfuls about 2″ apart on lightly greased baking sheet. Bake until set . . . just until, when touched lightly with finger, almost no imprint remains.

TEMPERATURE: 400° (mod. hot oven).

TIME: Bake 8 to 10 min.

AMOUNT: About 6 doz. 2½″ cookies.

★ HOLIDAY FRUIT COOKIES

Elegant. Richly studded with fruits and nuts. Butterscotch-flavored. Perfect for your loveliest hospitality.

Follow 🗝 recipe above—and mix into the dough 1½ cups broken pecans, 2 cups candied cherries, cut in halves, and 2 cups cut-up dates. Place a pecan half on each cooky. Make these rich cookies smaller . . . only 2″.

SALTED PEANUT COOKIES

These tempting peanut crunches are always a favorite both with children and grownups.

Follow 🗝 recipe above—*except*, in place of the 3½ cups flour, stir in 2 cups *sifted* flour, 2 cups rolled oats, 1 cup WHEATIES, 1 cup coarsely chopped salted peanuts (without husks). Bake until brown, 12 to 14 min.

To prevent drop cookies spreading . . . chill dough, peak it up, be sure oven temperature is correct.

BUSY-DAY NUT DROPS

Easy budget-savers. One of our home-testers calls these her "wash day" cookies.

Follow 🗝 recipe above—and mix into the dough 1 cup cut-up nuts.

BUSY-DAY COCONUT DROPS

Follow 🗝 recipe above—and mix into the dough 1 cup moist shredded coconut.

COFFEE-AND-SPICE DROPS (🔑 Recipe) *Intriguing flavors from the Far East.*

Mix together thoroughly	1 cup soft shortening 2 cups brown sugar 2 eggs
Stir in	½ cup cold coffee
Sift together and stir in	3½ cups *sifted* GOLD MEDAL Flour 1 tsp. soda 1 tsp. salt 1 tsp. nutmeg 1 tsp. cinnamon

Chill at least 1 hour. Drop rounded teaspoonfuls about 2″ apart on lightly greased baking sheet. Bake until set . . . just until, when touched lightly with finger, almost no imprint remains.

TEMPERATURE: 400° (mod. hot oven).

TIME: Bake 8 to 10 min.

AMOUNT: About 6 doz. 2½″ cookies.

★ HERMITS

Spicy, fruity, satisfying . . . contributed by Mrs. William G. Dorr, who worked with us in our test kitchen one summer. She says they were always first choice with her little girls.

Follow 🔑 recipe above—and mix into the dough 2½ cups halved seeded raisins and 1¼ cups broken nuts. Be careful not to overbake.

Wash them and spread out in a flat pan. Cover the pan and heat slowly in a moderate oven.
To get full flavor from seedless raisins, cut them in two with scissors after plumping.

MINCEMEAT COOKIES

Extra quick, no extra fruits needed . . . they are in the mincemeat.

Follow 🔑 recipe above—and mix into the dough 2 cups well drained mincemeat.

SPICED PRUNE DROPS

Follow 🔑 recipe above—and add ¼ tsp. cloves with other spices. Mix into dough 2 cups cut-up cooked prunes (pitted and well drained) and 1 cup broken nuts.

APPLESAUCE COOKIES

Yummy applesauce cake in cooky form.

Follow 🔑 recipe above—*except* add 1 tsp. cloves with other spices. Mix into the dough 2 cups well drained thick applesauce, 1 cup cut-up raisins, and ½ cup coarsely chopped nuts. Bake 9 to 12 min.

WHEATIES DROP COOKIES

Treats for young champions.

Mix together thoroughly . . .
- 1 cup soft shortening
- 1 cup sugar
- 2 eggs

Stir in . . .
- 1 cup sour milk

Sift together and stir in . . .
- 2 cups *sifted* GOLD MEDAL Flour
- ½ tsp. soda
- ½ tsp. salt
- 1 tsp. cinnamon
- ½ tsp. nutmeg
- ½ tsp. cloves

Stir in . . .
- ¾ cup coarsely chopped nuts
- 1 cup cut-up raisins

Fold in . . .
- 3 cups WHEATIES

Chill dough. Drop by teaspoonfuls about 2″ apart on lightly greased baking sheet. Bake until, when touched lightly with finger, *no* imprint remains.

TEMPERATURE: 400° (mod. hot oven).
TIME: Bake 10 to 12 min.
AMOUNT: About 5 doz. 2½″ cookies.

DROP COOKIES Some of grandmother's prize cooky favorites.

OLD-FASHIONED SOUR CREAM DROPS (🔑 Recipe) *Soft, tender, cream-rich.*

Mix together thoroughly	½ cup soft shortening 1½ cups sugar 2 eggs
Stir in	1 cup thick sour cream 1 tsp. vanilla
Sift together and stir in	2¾ cups *sifted* GOLD MEDAL Flour ½ tsp. soda ½ tsp. baking powder ½ tsp. salt

Chill at least 1 hour. Drop rounded teaspoonfuls about 2″ apart on ungreased baking sheet. Bake until delicately browned, just until, when touched lightly with finger, almost no imprint remains.

TEMPERATURE: 400° (mod. hot oven).

TIME: Bake 8 to 10 min.

AMOUNT: About 5 doz. 2½″ cookies.

★ BUTTERSCOTCH COOKIES WITH BURNT BUTTER ICING

Really delectable, especially with the unusual buttery icing. Mrs. R. C. Karstad of Nicollet, Minnesota, won a prize on them.

Follow 🔑 recipe above—*except* use brown sugar in place of granulated sugar. Mix into the dough ⅔ cup cut-up nuts. Spread cooled cookies with

BURNT BUTTER ICING

Melt 4 tbsp. butter until golden brown. Blend in 1 cup *sifted* confectioners' sugar and ½ tsp. vanilla. Stir in 1 to 2 tbsp. hot water until icing spreads smoothly.

AMOUNT: Icing for about 30 cookies.

COCONUT CREAM DROPS

Follow 🔑 recipe above—*except* mix into the dough 1 cup moist shredded coconut.

Use freshly soured cream for good flavor. Buy it from the dairy. Or sour it yourself by adding 1 tbsp. vinegar or lemon juice to 1 cup sweet cream.

To give iced cookies a professional air: place the same amount of icing (1 tsp.) on center of each. Then, with a spatula, spread the icing with circular motion in pretty swirls.

CHOCOLATE CREAM DROPS

Follow 🔑 recipe above—*except* stir into shortening mixture 2 sq. unsweetened chocolate (2 oz.), melted. Mix into the dough 1 cup cut-up nuts. Frost cooled cookies if desired with

CHOCOLATE ICING

Melt together over hot water 1 tbsp. butter and 1 sq. unsweetened chocolate (1 oz.). Stir in 3 tbsp. top milk and 1½ cups *sifted* confectioners' sugar. Thin with cream to make glossy and easy to spread.

AMOUNT: Icing for about 30 cookies.

FRUIT-AND-NUT DROPS

Follow 🔑 recipe above—*except* sift with dry ingredients 1 tsp. cinnamon, ½ tsp. cloves, ¼ tsp. nutmeg. Mix into the dough 1 cup cut-up dates (or raisins) and 1 cup cut-up nuts.

NOTE: The spices may be omitted.

★ GINGER CREAMS *Fluffy ginger cakes . . . topped with creamy white icing.*

They bring memories of a real farm home near Owatonna, Minnesota, where children trooped to the cooky jar after chores were done. Mildred Bennett (now Mrs. Axel Anderson), who was honored one year as national 4-H girl, brought us this recipe when she was a member of our Staff.

Mix together thoroughly . . . .
- ¼ cup soft shortening
- ½ cup sugar
- 1 small egg
- ½ cup molasses

Stir in . . . . 1 tsp. soda dissolved in ½ cup hot water

Sift together and stir in . . . .
- 2 cups *sifted* GOLD MEDAL Flour
- ½ tsp. salt
- 1 tsp. ginger
- ½ tsp. nutmeg
- ½ tsp. cloves
- ½ tsp. cinnamon

Chill dough. Drop rounded teaspoonfuls about 2″ apart on lightly greased baking sheet. Bake until set . . . just until, when touched lightly with finger, almost no imprint remains. While slightly warm, frost with Quick Cream Icing (*below.*)

TEMPERATURE: 400° (mod. hot oven).

TIME: Bake 7 to 8 min.

AMOUNT: About 4 doz. 2″ cookies.

QUICK CREAM ICING

Delicious, creamy-tasting topping . . . ideal for Ginger Creams and other festive cookies.

Blend together ¾ cup *sifted* confectioners' sugar, ¼ tsp. vanilla, and cream to make easy to spread (about 1 tbsp.).

OATMEAL DROP COOKIES

Chewy . . . with a hint of molasses.

We created this recipe in our test kitchen for the little daughter of a famous actress, and for all little children.

Mix together thoroughly . .
- ½ cup soft shortening
- 1¼ cups sugar
- 2 eggs
- 6 tbsp. molasses

Sift together and stir in . . .
- 1¾ cups *sifted* GOLD MEDAL Flour
- 1 tsp. soda
- 1 tsp. salt
- 1 tsp. cinnamon

Stir in . . .
- 2 cups rolled oats
- ½ cup cut-up nuts
- 1 cup cut-up raisins

Drop rounded teaspoonfuls about 2″ apart on lightly greased baking sheet. Bake until lightly browned.

TEMPERATURE: 400° (mod. hot oven).

TIME: Bake 8 to 10 min.

AMOUNT: About 5 doz. 2½″ cookies.

★ MONKEY-FACED COOKIES

You'll be amused by the droll faces.

In an antique shop, pasted on the underside of a drawer in an old table, a radio friend of Fultonville, New York, discovered this recipe written in faded ink in old-fashioned script: "for Elsa."

Mix together thoroughly . . .
- ½ cup soft shortening
- 1 cup brown sugar
- ½ cup molasses

Stir in . . .
- ½ cup sour milk
- 1 tsp. vinegar

Sift together and stir in . . .
- 2½ cups *sifted* GOLD MEDAL Flour
- 1 tsp. soda
- ½ tsp. salt
- ½ tsp. ginger
- ½ tsp. cinnamon

Drop rounded teaspoonfuls 2½″ apart on ungreased baking sheet. Place 3 raisins on each for eyes and mouth. Bake until set. Remove from sheet in 1 min. Faces take on droll expressions in baking.

TEMPERATURE: 375° (quick mod. oven).

TIME: Bake 10 to 12 min.

AMOUNT: About 4 doz. 2½″ cookies.

DROP COOKIES Easy to "jumble up" in a hurry!

SUGAR JUMBLES (Key Recipe) *Little sugar cakes of old-time goodness.*

Mix together thoroughly...
- ½ cup soft shortening (part butter)
- ½ cup sugar
- 1 egg
- 1 tsp. vanilla

Sift together and stir in...
- 1⅛ cups *sifted* GOLD MEDAL Flour
- ¼ tsp. soda
- ½ tsp. salt

Drop rounded teaspoonfuls about 2″ apart on lightly greased baking sheet. Bake until delicately browned . . . cookies should still be soft. Cool slightly . . . then remove from baking sheet.

TEMPERATURE: 375° (quick mod. oven).

TIME: Bake 8 to 10 min.

AMOUNT: About 3 doz. 2″ cookies.

COCONUT JUMBLES

Follow key recipe above—and mix into the dough 1 cup moist shredded coconut.

★ CHOCOLATE CHIP COOKIES

The glamorous Toll House *cookies . . . first introduced to American homemakers in 1939 through my series of radio talks on "Famous Foods from Famous Eating Places."*

Follow key recipe above—*except* in place of ½ cup sugar use ¾ cup (half brown, half white). Then mix into the dough ½ cup cut-up nuts and one 6-oz. package chocolate pieces (about 1¼ cups).

ORANGE-CHOCOLATE CHIP COOKIES

Follow recipe for Chocolate Chip cookies and add 1 tsp. grated orange rind to the shortening mixture.

3-IN-1 JUMBLES

Choco-nut . . . coco-nut . . . date-nut.

Follow key recipe above—and divide dough into three parts. *Choco-Nut:* To one part, add ½ sq. unsweetened chocolate (½ oz.), melted, and drop whole nutmeats (½ cup) into it . . . coating each thoroughly. *Coco-Nut:* To another part, add ½ cup moist shredded coconut. *Date-Nut:* Leave third part plain . . . and drop nut-stuffed dates (14) into it . . . coating each thoroughly. Each coated date and each coated nut makes a cooky.

GLAZED ORANGE JUMBLES

Double-orange flavor . . . sure to win favor.

Follow key recipe above—mix into dough 1½ tsp. grated orange rind and, if desired, 1 cup chopped nuts. Bake. While hot, dip tops of cookies in orange glaze (⅓ cup sugar, 3 tbsp. orange juice, 1 tsp. grated orange rind . . . heated together).

BRAZIL OR PECAN JUMBLES

Follow key recipe above—and stir into the dough 2 cups cut-up Brazil or other nuts.

OLD-TIME CINNAMON JUMBLES

Made with buttermilk . . . soft and cake-like. "So easy . . . that making them is a thrill for the girls in the Home Economics classes each year," according to Miss Sarah M. Knight of Buffalo, New York. And even her little sixth-graders report making them with great success in their own homes!

Mix together thoroughly . . .
- ½ cup soft shortening (part butter)
- 1 cup sugar
- 1 egg

Stir in . . .
- ¾ cup buttermilk
- 1 tsp. vanilla

Sift together and stir in . . .
- 2 cups *sifted* GOLD MEDAL Flour
- ½ tsp. soda
- ½ tsp. salt

Chill dough. Drop rounded teaspoonfuls about 2″ apart on lightly greased baking sheet. Sprinkle with mixture of sugar and cinnamon (¼ cup sugar and 1 tsp. cinnamon). Bake until set but not brown.

TEMPERATURE: 400° (mod. hot oven).

TIME: Bake 8 to 10 min.

AMOUNT: About 4 doz. 2″ cookies.

COCONUT MACAROONS (🔑 Recipe) *Moist, chewy, chock-full of coconut.*

Beat until fluffy (only ½ min.) .... **½ cup egg whites**

Stir in .... **1¼ cups sugar, ¼ tsp. salt, ½ tsp. vanilla**

Blend in .... **2½ cups moist shredded coconut**

Drop rounded teaspoonfuls 2″ apart on ungreased wrapping paper on baking sheet. Bake until set and delicately browned. (*Illustrated directions at bottom of page tell how to remove macaroons from paper easily.*) They spread during baking, so when they come from oven shape into mounds by gathering in edges with fingers.

TEMPERATURE: 325° (slow mod. oven).

TIME: Bake 15 to 18 min.

AMOUNT: About 2½ doz. 1½″ macaroons.

CHOCOLATE-COCONUT MACAROONS

Follow 🔑 recipe above—and add 2 sq. unsweetened chocolate (2 oz.), melted.

CHERRY-COCONUT MACAROONS

Follow 🔑 recipe above—and add ½ cup chopped candied cherries.

ALMOND MACAROONS

Soften with hands . . .
- **1 lb. almond paste (bought from bakery or made from recipe below)**

Work in . . .
- **2 cups sugar**
- **¼ tsp. salt**
- **4 tbsp. GOLD MEDAL Flour**
- **⅔ cup *sifted* confectioners' sugar**
- **⅔ cup egg whites, unbeaten**

Drop teaspoonfuls 2″ apart on ungreased wrapping paper on baking sheet. Pat tops lightly with fingers dipped in cold water. Bake until set and delicately browned. Remove from paper.

TEMPERATURE: 325° (slow mod. oven).

TIME: Bake 18 to 20 min.

AMOUNT: About 5 doz. 2″ macaroons.

ALMOND PASTE

Grind 2 cups blanched almonds, thoroughly dried (not toasted), through finest knife of food grinder. Then grind twice more. Mix in 1½ cups *sifted* confectioners' sugar. Blend in ¼ cup egg whites, unbeaten, and 2 tsp. almond extract. Mold into ball. Let age in tightly covered container in refrigerator at least 4 days.

WHEATIES-COC'N'T MACAROONS

Follow 🔑 recipe above—*except,* in place of 2½ cups coconut, use 2 cups WHEATIES and 1 cup coconut. Bake 12 to 15 min.

PEANUT MACAROONS *Thin, wafery.*

Beat until lemon-colored (5 min.) . . .
- **1 egg (large)**

Gradually beat in . . .
- **⅔ cup sugar**
- **1 tsp. water**

Mix together and gently fold in . . .
- **1 tbsp. GOLD MEDAL Flour**
- **⅓ tsp. salt**
- **⅓ tsp. baking powder**

Add and mix just enough to blend in . . .
- **1⅓ cups finely ground roasted peanuts (*1 cup shelled, brown husks removed*)**

Drop teaspoonfuls 2″ apart on ungreased wrapping paper on baking sheet. Bake until set and delicately browned. Remove from paper immediately.

TEMPERATURE: 325° (slow mod. oven).

TIME: Bake 14 to 15 min.

AMOUNT: About 3 doz. 2″ macaroons.

Remove paper with baked macaroons on it. Lay a wet towel on the hot baking sheet. Place paper of macaroons on towel and let stand 1 minute. Steam will loosen macaroons. Slip off with spatula. ➡

REFRIGERATOR COOKIES Mix when convenient . . .

HOW TO MAKE REFRIGERATOR COOKIES (preliminary steps on pp. 178, 179)

1 Press and mold with hands into a long roll, even and smooth, and as big around as you want your cookies to be.

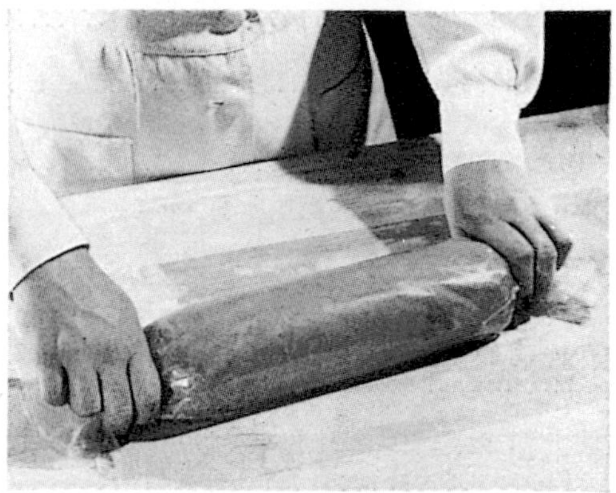

2 Wrap in waxed paper . . . twisting ends to hold the roll in shape. Or press into a waxed cardboard carton (*butter or ice cream carton*).

REFRIGERATOR COOKIES (🗝 Recipe) *Melt-in-the-mouth, rich, and crispy.*

Mix together thoroughly . . . .
- 1 cup soft shortening
- ½ cup sugar
- ½ cup brown sugar
- 2 eggs

Sift together and stir in . . . .
- 2¾ cups *sifted* GOLD MEDAL Flour
- ½ tsp. soda
- 1 tsp. salt
- *2 to 3 tsp. cinnamon

*Or use 1½ tsp. vanilla (add with eggs).

Mix thoroughly with hands. Press and mold into a long smooth roll about 2½″ in diameter. Wrap in waxed paper, and chill until stiff (several hours or overnight). With a thin, sharp knife, cut in thin slices ⅛″ to 1/16″ thick. Place slices a little apart on ungreased baking sheet. Bake until lightly browned.

TEMPERATURE: 400° (mod. hot oven).
TIME: Bake 6 to 8 min.
AMOUNT: About 6 doz. 2½″ cookies.

★ NUT REFRIGERATOR COOKIES

Nut-lovers really go for these cookies.

Follow 🗝 recipe above—and mix into dough ½ cup cut-up blanched almonds *or* black walnuts *or* other nuts.

DATE-NUT REFRIGERATOR COOKIES

Follow 🗝 recipe above—using both cinnamon and vanilla. Mix into dough ½ cup finely chopped nuts and ½ cup finely cut dates.

ORANGE-ALMOND REFRIGERATOR COOKIES

Follow 🗝 recipe above—but omit cinnamon. Stir 1 tbsp. grated orange rind into shortening mixture. Mix into dough ½ cup cut-up blanched almonds.

CHOCOLATE REFRIGERATOR COOKIES

Follow 🗝 recipe above—but omit the cinnamon. Blend 2 sq. unsweetened chocolate (2 oz.), melted and cooled, into the shortening mixture.

All you have to do—

For an elegant dessert: make a roll by arranging the chocolate or ginger cookies (*see p. 187*) side by side with sweetened whipped cream between. Spread whipped cream over top and sides of roll. Chill 6 to 8 hr. Slice diagonally for gaily striped servings.

3 Chill roll of dough until it is firm enough to slice easily. To speed up chilling, place in freezing compartment.

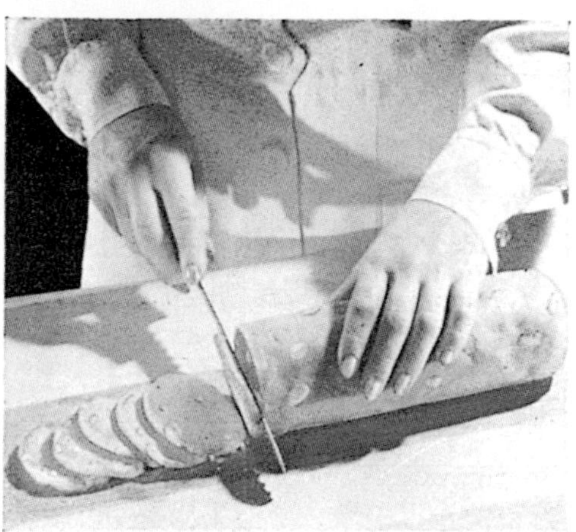

4 Slice with a thin knife, very sharp, to insure neat slices with uncrumbled edges. Return unused dough to refrigerator so it can remain stiff.

GINGER REFRIGERATOR COOKIES

Gingery favorites in jig-time!

Mix together thoroughly . . .
- **1 cup soft shortening**
- **1 cup sugar**
- **2 eggs**
- **½ cup dark molasses**

Sift together and stir in . . .
- **4½ cups *sifted* GOLD MEDAL Flour**
- **1 tsp. soda**
- **1 tsp. salt**
- **1 tbsp. ginger (3 tsp.)**

Mix thoroughly with hands. Press and mold into a long, smooth roll about 2½″ in diameter. Wrap in waxed paper, and chill until stiff (several hours or overnight). With thin, sharp knife, cut in thin slices ⅛″ to 1/16″ thick. Place slices a little apart on ungreased baking sheet. Bake until lightly browned.

TEMPERATURE: 400° (mod. hot oven).

TIME: Bake 8 to 10 min.

AMOUNT: About 9 doz. 2½″ cookies.

★ NEW NORTHLAND COOKIES

Crunchy, flavorful shortening-savers.

Languid days on the St. Lawrence; the pink, rocky cliffs and blue icebergs of Labrador; and afternoon tea on deck. Such are the memories these cookies bring to Ruth G. Anderson of our Staff who brought back the recipe after a cruise to the Northland.

Mix together thoroughly . . .
- **6 tbsp. soft shortening (part butter)**
- **1 cup brown sugar**

Stir in . . .
- **¼ cup cold water**

Sift together and stir in . . .
- **1¾ cups *sifted* GOLD MEDAL Flour**
- **1 tsp. soda**
- **½ tsp. salt**
- **½ tsp. cinnamon**

Mix in . . .
- **½ cup cut-up blanched almonds**

Mix thoroughly with hands. Press and mold into a long smooth roll about 2½″ in diameter. Wrap in waxed paper, and chill until stiff (several hours or overnight). With thin, sharp knife, cut in thin slices ⅛″ to 1/16″ thick. Place slices a little apart on ungreased baking sheet. Bake until lightly browned. Remove from pan immediately.

TEMPERATURE: 400° (mod. hot oven).

TIME: Bake 6 to 8 min.

AMOUNT: About 4 doz. 2½″ cookies.

REFRIGERATOR COOKIES

Snip off and bake . . . for unexpected guests.

★ PETTICOAT TAILS *Richly delicate and dainty.*

This recipe was brought from France to Scotland by Mary, Queen of Scots. The French name "Petits Gateaux Tailles" means—"little cakes cut off." But the name came to be pronounced as it sounded to the Scotch and English—"Petticoat Tails."

Mix together thoroughly ....
- **1 cup soft butter**
- **1 cup *sifted* confectioners' sugar**
- **1 tsp. flavoring (vanilla, almond, wintergreen or rose)**

Sift together and stir in ....
- **2½ cups *sifted* GOLD MEDAL Flour**
- **¼ tsp. salt**

Mix thoroughly with hands. Press and mold into a long, smooth roll about 2″ in diameter. Wrap in waxed paper, and chill until stiff (several hours or overnight). With thin, sharp knife, cut in thin slices ⅛″ to 1/16″ thick. Place slices a little apart on ungreased baking sheet. Bake until lightly browned.

TEMPERATURE: 400° (mod. hot oven).

TIME: Bake 8 to 10 min.

AMOUNT: About 6 doz. 2″ cookies.

OATMEAL REFRIGERATOR COOKIES *Nice and chewy, with a molasses-lemon tang.*

Voted the best oatmeal cooky ever tasted . . . when sent to our Recipe Contest by Mrs. J. A. Gmeinder of St. Paul, Minnesota. The distinguishing molasses-lemon flavor was an idea from Mrs. Richard Nugent, Brooklyn, New York.

Mix together thoroughly ....
- **½ cup soft shortening**
- **½ cup sugar**
- **½ cup brown sugar**
- **1 egg**
- **1½ tsp. grated lemon rind**
- **1½ tbsp. molasses**
- **½ tsp. vanilla**

Sift together and stir in ....
- **⅞ cup (¾ cup plus 2 tbsp.) *sifted* GOLD MEDAL Flour**
- **½ tsp. soda**
- **½ tsp. salt**

Mix in .... **1½ cups rolled oats**

Mix thoroughly with hands. Press and mold into a long, smooth roll about 2½″ in diameter. Wrap in waxed paper, and chill until stiff (several hours). With thin, sharp knife, cut in thin slices ⅛″ to 1/16″ thick. Place slices a little apart on ungreased baking sheet. Bake until lightly browned.

TEMPERATURE: 400° (mod. hot oven).

TIME: Bake 8 to 10 min.

AMOUNT: About 4 doz. 2½″ cookies.

All you have to do—

PRETTY FOR PARTIES

To make Petticoat Tails match your color scheme: tint the dough with a few drops of red food coloring and use rose flavoring for a pink party. Use wintergreen flavoring and a few drops of green coloring for a green party.

SNICKERDOODLES

Fun to say . . . to sniff . . . to eat!

Pat Roth of our Staff said, "It's one of my happy childhood memories. My mother would be baking when we came home from school and we would have Snickerdoodles hot out of the oven with a glass of milk."

Mix together thoroughly . . .
- **1 cup soft shortening**
- **1½ cups sugar**
- **2 eggs**

Sift together and stir in . . .
- **2¾ cups *sifted* GOLD MEDAL Flour**
- **2 tsp. cream of tartar**
- **1 tsp. soda**
- **½ tsp. salt**

Chill dough. Roll into balls the size of small walnuts. Roll in mixture of 2 tbsp. sugar and 2 tsp. cinnamon. Place about 2" apart on ungreased baking sheet. Bake until lightly browned . . . but still soft. (These cookies puff up at first . . . then flatten out with crinkled tops.)

TEMPERATURE: 400° (mod. hot oven).

TIME: Bake 8 to 10 min.

AMOUNT: About 5 doz. 2" cookies.

GOLD COOKIES

Really awfully good . . . and they use up those extra egg yolks!

Mix together thoroughly . . .
- **½ cup soft shortening**
- **1½ cups sugar**
- **4 egg yolks**

Stir in . . .
- **2 tbsp. milk**
- **1 tsp. vanilla**

Sift together and stir in . . .
- **1½ cups *sifted* GOLD MEDAL Flour**
- **½ tsp. baking powder**
- **¼ tsp. salt**

Chill dough. Roll into balls the size of walnuts . . . then roll balls in a mixture of ¾ cup finely chopped nuts and 2 tsp. cinnamon. Place 3" apart on ungreased baking sheet. Bake until golden brown . . . but still soft.

TEMPERATURE: 400° (mod. hot oven).

TIME: Bake 12 to 15 min.

AMOUNT: About 5 doz. 2" cookies.

★ MOLASSES CRINKLES

Thick, chewy, with crackled, sugary tops.

When served at Mrs. Fred Fredell's in St. Paul, Minnesota, they were so delicious I begged the recipe. Thanks to her, thousands of homes have enjoyed these spicy cookies.

Mix together thoroughly . . .
- **¾ cup soft shortening**
- **1 cup brown sugar**
- **1 egg**
- **¼ cup molasses**

Sift together and stir in . . .
- **2¼ cups *sifted* GOLD MEDAL Flour**
- **2 tsp. soda**
- **¼ tsp. salt**
- **½ tsp. cloves**
- **1 tsp. cinnamon**
- **1 tsp. ginger**

Chill dough. Roll into balls the size of large walnuts. Dip tops in sugar. Place, sugared-side-up, 3" apart on greased baking sheet. Sprinkle each cooky with 2 or 3 drops of water to produce a crackled surface. Bake just until set but not hard.

TEMPERATURE: 375° (quick mod. oven).

TIME: Bake 10 to 12 min.

AMOUNT: About 4 doz. 2½" cookies.

WASHBOARDS *Coconut-taffy bars.*

Mix together thoroughly . . .
- **1 cup soft shortening (half butter)**
- **2 cups brown sugar**
- **2 eggs**

Stir in . . .
- **¼ cup water**
- **1 tsp. vanilla**

Sift together and stir in . . .
- **4 cups *sifted* GOLD MEDAL Flour**
- **1½ tsp. baking powder**
- **½ tsp. soda**
- **¼ tsp. salt**

Mix in . . .
- **1 cup moist shredded coconut (cut up any long shreds)**

Chill dough 2 hr. Roll into balls the size of walnuts. Place 2" apart on ungreased baking sheet. With fingers, flatten each ball into a 1½"x2½" oblong ¼" thick. (And we *do* mean ¼ inch!) Press each cooky lengthwise with tines of floured fork in washboard effect. Bake until lightly browned.

TEMPERATURE: 400° (mod. hot oven).

TIME: Bake 8 to 10 min.

AMOUNT: About 5 doz. 2"x3" cookies.

BAR COOKIES Perennial favorites . . . cut in squares or bars.

HOW TO MAKE BAR COOKIES (preliminary steps on pp. 178, 179)

1 Spread dough in greased pan and bake as directed. **2** Cut into squares or bars when slightly cool. **3** Remove from the pan with a wide spatula.

BROWNIES (Key Recipe) *Chewy, fudgy squares . . . everyone loves them!*

Melt together over hot water	2 sq. unsweetened chocolate (2 oz.) 1/3 cup shortening
Beat in	1 cup sugar 2 eggs
Sift together and stir in	3/4 cup *sifted* GOLD MEDAL Flour 1/2 tsp. baking powder 1/2 tsp. salt
Mix in	1/2 cup broken nuts

Spread in well greased 8″ square pan (8x8x2″). Bake until top has dull crust. A slight imprint will be left when top is touched lightly with finger. Cool slightly . . . then cut into squares.

TEMPERATURE: 350° (mod. oven).
TIME: Bake 30 to 35 min.
AMOUNT: 16 2″ squares.

CHOCOLATE-FROSTED BROWNIES

Star of Marie Watson's delightful parties.

Follow key recipe above—and spread cooled bars or squares before cutting with

MARIE'S CHOCOLATE ICING

Melt over hot water 1 tbsp. butter and 1 sq. unsweetened chocolate (1 oz.). Blend in 1 1/2 tbsp. warm water. Stir and beat in about 1 cup *sifted* confectioners' sugar (until icing will spread easily).

DAINTY TEA BROWNIES

Picturesque . . . very thin. A highlight of the silver teas at a Minneapolis church.

Follow key recipe above—*except* chop nuts *finely* and spread dough in *two* well greased 13x9″ oblong pans. Sprinkle with 3/4 cup blanched and finely sliced green pistachio nuts. Bake 7 to 8 min. Cut immediately into squares or diamonds. Remove from pan while warm.

PLANTATION FRUIT BARS

Little sugar and shortening . . . but delicious. Sent to us by Mrs. Charles Willard of Chicago.

Mix together thoroughly . . .
- 1/4 cup soft shortening
- 1/2 cup sugar
- 1 egg
- 1/2 cup molasses

Stir in . . .
- 1/2 cup milk

Sift together and stir in . . .
- 2 cups *sifted* GOLD MEDAL Flour
- 1 1/2 tsp. baking powder
- 1/4 tsp. soda
- 1/2 tsp. salt

Mix in . . .
- 1 cup broken nuts
- 1 to 2 cups cut-up raisins or dates

Spread in greased 13x9″ oblong pan. Bake. Cool slightly . . . spread with Lemon Icing (*see next page*) and cut into bars.

TEMPERATURE: 350° (mod. oven).
TIME: Bake 25 to 30 min.
AMOUNT: 4 doz. 1″x2″ bars.

DATE-AND-NUT SQUARES

Chewy favorites with rich nutty flavor. Much like the Bishop's Bread served to circuit-riding preachers in days of Early America.

Beat until foamy . . .
2 eggs

Beat in . . .
½ cup sugar
½ tsp. vanilla

Sift together and stir in . . .
½ cup *sifted* GOLD MEDAL Flour
½ tsp. baking powder
½ tsp. salt

Mix in . . .
1 cup cut-up walnuts
2 cups finely cut-up dates

Spread in well greased 8″ square pan (8x8x2″). Bake until top has dull crust. Cut into squares while warm, cool, then remove from pan. If desired, dip in confectioners' sugar.

TEMPERATURE: 325° (slow mod. oven).
TIME: Bake 25 to 30 min.
AMOUNT: 16 2″ squares.

JEWELLED COOKIES

Glowing with gems of spicy gumdrops (red and green for Christmas holidays).

Beat until foamy . . .
2 eggs

Beat in . . .
1 cup sugar
1 tsp. vanilla

Sift together and stir in . . .
1 cup *sifted* GOLD MEDAL Flour
½ tsp. salt

Mix in . . .
½ cup cut-up toasted blanched almonds
½ cup cut-up gumdrops (¼″)

Spread in well greased and floured 9″ square pan (9x9x2″). Sprinkle extra cut-up gumdrops (about ½ cup) over top of batter. Bake until top has a dull crust. Cut into squares while warm, cool, then remove from pan. (Crust will crack.)

TEMPERATURE: 325° (slow mod. oven).
TIME: Bake 30 to 35 min.
AMOUNT: 16 2″ squares.

LEMON ICING (for Plantation Fruit Bars)

Gradually beat ½ cup *sifted* confectioners' sugar into 1 stiffly beaten egg white. Add dash of salt, ¼ tsp. lemon extract.

To sugar confection-like Date-and-Nut Squares (*left*) . . . dip in confectioners' sugar and shake.

★ WALNUT SQUARES

Almost candy . . . so rich and nutty.

Beat until foamy . . .
1 egg

Beat in . . .
1 cup brown sugar
½ tsp. vanilla

Sift together and stir in . . .
½ cup *sifted* GOLD MEDAL Flour
½ tsp. salt
⅛ tsp. soda

Mix in . . .
1 cup cut-up walnuts

Spread in well greased 8″ square pan (8x8x2″). Bake until top has a dull crust. Cut into squares while warm, cool, then remove from pan.

TEMPERATURE: 325° (slow mod. oven).
TIME: Bake 25 to 30 min.
AMOUNT: 16 2″ squares.

TUTTI-FRUTTI SURPRISES

Like moist fruit cake . . . full of good things.

Beat until foamy . . .
2 eggs

Gradually beat in . . .
1 cup *sifted* confectioners' sugar

Stir in . . .
3 tbsp. shortening, melted

Sift together and stir in . . .
¾ cup *sifted* GOLD MEDAL Flour
1½ tsp. baking powder
1 tsp. salt

Mix in . . .
1 cup cut-up nuts
1 cup cut-up dates
¾ cup cut-up candied fruit

Spread in well greased 8″ square pan (8x8x2″). Bake until top has a dull crust. Cut into squares while warm, cool, then remove from pan.

TEMPERATURE: 325° (slow mod. oven).
TIME: Bake 30 to 35 min.
AMOUNT: 16 2″ squares.

TOFFEE-NUT BARS (🔑 Recipe) *Almond-coconut topping on melt-in-the-mouth crust.*

BOTTOM LAYER

Mix together thoroughly	**½ cup soft shortening (half butter)** **½ cup brown sugar**
Stir in	**1 cup *sifted* GOLD MEDAL Flour**

Press and flatten with hand to cover bottom of ungreased 13x9″ oblong pan. Bake 10 min. Then spread with

TEMPERATURE: 350° (mod. oven).
TIME: Bake 10 min.

ALMOND-COCONUT TOPPING

Beat well	**2 eggs**
Stir in	**1 cup brown sugar** **1 tsp. vanilla**
Mix together and stir in	**2 tbsp. GOLD MEDAL Flour** **1 tsp. baking powder** **½ tsp. salt**
Mix in	**1 cup moist shredded coconut** **1 cup cut-up almonds (or other nuts)**

Return to oven and bake 25 min. more until topping is golden brown. Cool slightly . . . then cut into bars.

TEMPERATURE: 350° (mod. oven).
TIME: Bake 25 min.
AMOUNT: About 2½ doz. 1″x3″ bars.

Spread almond-coconut topping on bottom layer.

COCONUT-LEMON BARS

Follow 🔑 recipe above for Bottom Layer. Bake 10 min. Let stand a few minutes before spreading with

COCONUT-LEMON TOPPING

Beat well . . .
- **2 eggs**

Stir in . . .
- **1 cup brown sugar**
- **2 tbsp. lemon juice**
- **1 tsp. grated lemon rind**
- **½ tsp. salt**

Mix in . . .
- **1 cup moist shredded coconut**
- **1 cup cut-up walnuts**
- **½ cup cut-up raisins**

Return to oven and bake 25 min. more until topping is golden brown. Cool slightly . . . then cut into bars.

★ JELL-MERINGUE-FILBERT BARS

Specialty of Mrs. George Ludcke, Jr. (formerly Jeanette Campbell of our Staff).

Follow 🔑 recipe above for Bottom Layer—*except* use *sifted* confectioners' sugar in place of brown, and stir 2 egg yolks into the sugar and shortening mixture. Bake. Spread with ½ to ¾ cup softened jelly (currant, raspberry, or grape), then with

MERINGUE-FILBERT TOPPING

Beat until stiff . . .
- **2 egg whites**

Beat in gradually . . .
- **½ cup sugar**
- **¼ tsp. cinnamon**

Fold in . . .
- **1 cup ground filberts (unblanched)**

Return to oven and bake 25 min. more until topping is golden brown. Cool slightly . . . then cut into bars.

The fluffy meringue-filbert topping is piled on top of softened jelly spread over the crust.

FILLED BAR COOKIES (🗝 Recipe)

First, prepare desired filling (*see below*), and cool.

FOR CRUST

Mix together thoroughly	3/4 cup soft shortening (part butter) 1 cup brown sugar
Sift together and stir in	1 3/4 cups *sifted* GOLD MEDAL Flour 1/2 tsp. soda 1 tsp. salt
Stir in	1 1/2 cups rolled oats

Mix thoroughly. Place one-half of this crumb mixture in greased and floured 13x9" oblong pan. Press and flatten with hands to cover bottom of pan. Spread with cooled filling. Cover with remaining crumb mixture . . . patting lightly. Bake until lightly browned. While warm, cut into bars and remove from pan.

TEMPERATURE: 400° (mod. hot oven).
TIME: Bake 25 to 30 min.
AMOUNT: About 2 1/2 doz. 1 1/2"x2" bars.

DATE BARS (Matrimonial Cake)

These cookies won the first prize at the famous Minnesota State Fair one year . . . for Mrs. C. Arlt of St. Paul.

Follow 🗝 recipe above, using:

DATE FILLING

Mix together in saucepan . . .
- 3 cups cut-up dates
- 1/4 cup sugar
- 1 1/2 cups water

Cook over low heat, stirring constantly, until thickened (about 10 min.). Cool.

PRUNE-ORANGE BARS

Follow 🗝 recipe above using

PRUNE-ORANGE FILLING

Mix together in saucepan . . .
- 3 cups cut-up cooked prunes (drained)
- 1/2 cup sugar
- 1/2 cup orange juice
- 2 tbsp. lemon juice
- 2 tbsp. grated orange rind

Cook over low heat, stirring constantly, until thickened (about 10 min.). Cool.

DATE-APRICOT BARS

Follow 🗝 recipe above using

DATE-APRICOT FILLING

Mix together in saucepan . . .
- 1 cup cut-up dates
- 2 cups mashed cooked dried apricots (drained)
- 1/2 cup sugar
- 2 tbsp. of the apricot juice

Cook over low heat, stirring constantly, until thickened (about 5 min.). Cool.

Date Bars . . . perfect pals for good hot coffee or tea

★ HAZELNUT BARS *Crusty, macaroony.*

Old-time German party cookies that keep beautifully.

Beat in top of double boiler until stiff . . .
- 2 large egg whites

Beat in gradually . . .
- 1 cup sugar

Fold in . . .
- 1 tbsp. GOLD MEDAL Flour

Cook over boiling water 3 min., stirring constantly. Remove from over hot water.

Blend in . . .
- 1 tsp. vanilla
- 1 1/2 cups coarsely ground unblanched filberts (*hazelnuts*)

Spread dough smoothly 1/4" thick in ungreased paper-lined 13x9" oblong pan. With fingers, pat top gently with warm water. Bake until top looks dull. While warm, cut into bars 1 1/2"x2". Cool slightly, then turn paper over (bars and all). Dampen entire surface with cold water. When water penetrates paper, bars are easily removed. If desired, place two bars together with a butter icing between (*see Burnt Butter Icing, p. 182*).

TEMPERATURE: 350° (mod. oven).
TIME: Bake 15 to 20 min.
AMOUNT: 32 single bars, 1 1/2"x2".

ROLLED COOKIES Pat 'em, and roll 'em and sugar for tea.

HOW TO MAKE ROLLED COOKIES (preliminary steps on pp. 178, 179)

1 To prevent "sticking," slip a canvas cover over board, and stockinet over rolling pin. Rub flour into the covers.

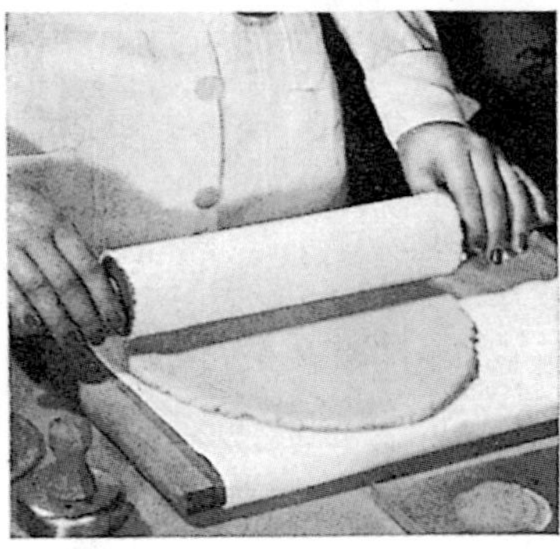

2 Roll lightly, small amount dough at a time . . . keeping the rest chilled. Roll very thin for crisp cookies.

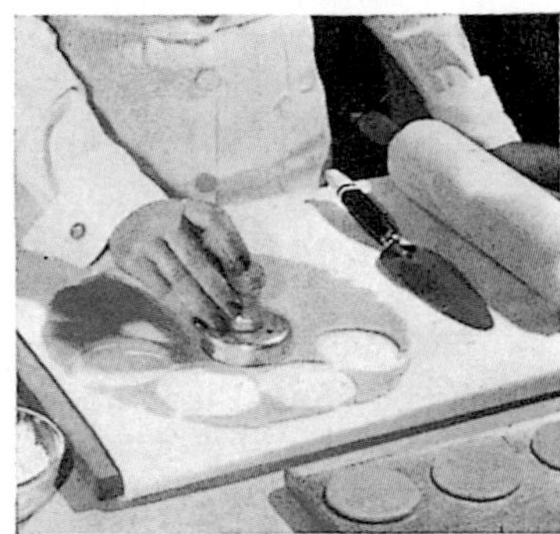

3 Cut as many cookies from each rolling as possible. Dip cooky cutter in flour, then shake it and cut.

Short cut: instead of rolling it, drop dough and flatten with glass. See page 204.

★ SUGAR COOKIES (🔑 Recipe) *Crispy, thin, flavorful.*

Mix together thoroughly	½ cup soft shortening (half butter) ¾ cup sugar 1 egg
Stir in	1 tbsp. milk or cream 1 tsp. flavoring (vanilla or lemon or a combination of the two)
Sift together and stir in	1¼ cups *sifted* GOLD MEDAL Flour ¼ tsp. baking powder ¼ tsp. salt

Chill dough. Roll very thin (1/16″). Cut into desired shapes. Place on lightly greased baking sheet, and sprinkle with sugar. Bake until delicately browned.

TEMPERATURE: 425° (hot oven).
TIME: Bake 5 to 7 min.
AMOUNT: About 5 doz. 2½″ cookies.

LEMON SUGAR COOKIES

Follow 🔑 recipe above—*except,* in place of vanilla, use 2 tsp. grated lemon rind and 1 tsp. lemon juice.

NUT SUGAR COOKIES

Follow 🔑 recipe above—and mix into the dough 1 cup finely chopped nuts.

RICH SUGAR COOKIES

Extra tender. . . a flavor favorite!

Follow 🔑 recipe above—*except* use ½ cup sugar in place of ¾ cup. Use 1 tsp. cream of tartar and ½ tsp. soda in place of the baking powder.

CARAWAY COOKIES

Follow 🔑 recipe above—*except* omit vanilla, sift ½ tsp. nutmeg with the dry ingredients, and mix 1 tsp. caraway seeds into the dough.

CHOCOLATE PINWHEELS

Fascinating whirls of dark and light . . . an unusual taste delight.

Follow 🔑 recipe above or recipe for Rich Sugar Cookies. Divide dough into 2 equal parts. Into 1 part, blend 1 sq. unsweetened chocolate (1 oz.), melted and cooled. Chill. Roll out white dough 9″x12″. Roll out chocolate dough same size and lay on top of white dough. Roll the double layer of dough gently until 3/16″ thick. Roll up tightly, beginning at wide side, into a roll 12″ long and 2″ in diameter. Chill. Slice ⅛″ thick. Place slices a little apart on lightly greased baking sheet. Bake.

TEMPERATURE: 350° (mod. oven).
TIME: Bake 10 to 12 min.
AMOUNT: About 5 doz. 2″ cookies.

BUTTER COOKIES (Key Recipe) *Crisp, with the true buttery flavor, but not sweet.*

Mix together thoroughly	1 cup soft butter ½ cup sugar 1 egg
Stir in	3 tsp. flavoring (vanilla, lemon, etc.)
Sift together and stir in	3 cups *sifted* GOLD MEDAL Flour ½ tsp. baking powder

Chill dough. Roll very thin (1/16″). Cut into desired shapes. Place on ungreased baking sheet. Press blanched almond or pecan half into top of each cooky. If glazed cooky is desired, brush mixture of 1 egg yolk and 2 tbsp. water over top of cookies before baking. Bake until they are delicately browned.

TEMPERATURE: 425° (hot oven).

TIME: Bake 5 to 7 min.

AMOUNT: About 7 doz. 2″ cookies.

COOKIES FOR PARTIES *Delightful for all sorts of special occasions.*

Follow Key recipe for Sugar Cookies on opposite page, or Key recipe for Butter Cookies above. Cut and decorate cookies for special occasions as follows:

HEART COOKIES
For special Valentines.

Cut with heart-shaped cutter. Brush lightly with a little beaten egg white. Then sprinkle with red sugar. Bake.

Cut round cookies. Place a tiny red candy heart in center of each. Bake.

Cut dough with two heart-shaped cutters, one smaller than the other. Lay a smaller heart on each of the larger ones and bake each pair as *one* cooky. When baked, ice the smaller heart with red or pink icing.

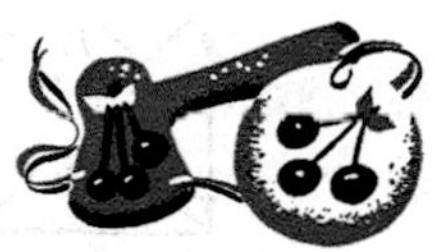

CHERRY AND HATCHET COOKIES
For George Washington's Birthday.

Cut small round cherries from red candied cherries and stick them on baked cookies in sprays of three, with little stems and leaves of green citron.

Cut cookies with hatchet-shaped cooky cutter. Or stick little candy hatchets on cookies.

PLACE CARDS OR FAVORS
For children's parties.

Roll dough ⅛″ thick. Cut into 2″x3″ oblong shapes. Bake. When cookies are cool, write names on them with melted chocolate or colored icing.

FLOWER COOKIES
For Easter, spring and summer parties.

Color dough pink or yellow. Cut cookies with little scalloped cutters, for petal effect. Brush with egg white and sprinkle with pink or yellow sugar before baking. Bits of candied orange peel or yellow gumdrops may be used for yellow centers.

Make flower and rosette shapes by forcing the dough through a cooky press.

DECORATING ICING

Into 1 cup *sifted* confectioners' sugar, stir just enough water (about 1 tbsp.) to make icing easy to force through pastry tube —yet hold its shape. Tint if desired with a few drops of food coloring. (Pile into pastry tube and squeeze.)

COOKIES WITH FACES
For Hallowe'en.

Follow recipe for soft molasses cookies such as Gingies on page 198. Tint the Decorating Icing (*above*) orange. Then force it through a pastry tube or paper cornucopia to make faces with eyes, nose, mouth, and hair.

ROLLED COOKIES Little taste-tempters in fascinating shapes.

FILLED COOKIES (🔑 Recipe) *Tender, creamy-white turnovers hold luscious fillings.*

Mix together thoroughly	½ cup soft shortening 1 cup sugar 2 eggs
Stir in	2 tbsp. thick cream 1 tsp. vanilla
Sift together and stir in	2½ cups *sifted* GOLD MEDAL Flour ¼ tsp. soda ½ tsp. salt

Chill dough. Roll very thin (1/16″). Cut 3″ rounds or squares. Place on lightly greased baking sheet. Place a rounded teaspoonful of desired cooled filling (*opposite page*) on each. Fold over like a turnover, pressing edges together with floured tines of a fork or tip of finger. Bake until delicately browned.

TEMPERATURE: 400° (mod. hot oven).

TIME: Bake 8 to 10 min.

AMOUNT: About 6 doz. 3″ cookies.

FILLED COOKIES IN FANCY SHAPES

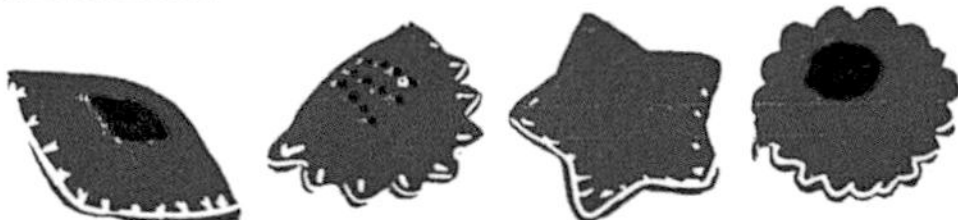

Follow 🔑 recipe above—but cut dough with scalloped round cooky cutter or with heart, diamond, or 2½″ cutter of any desired shape, cutting 2 alike for each filled cooky. To give a decorative effect, cut the center out of the top cooky with a tiny cutter of heart, star, or scalloped round shape. Place the bottom pieces on lightly greased baking sheet. Spread desired filling (*see opposite page*) on each . . . covering up to edge. Place on, the top pieces. Press edges together.

AMOUNT: 4 doz. 2½″ filled cookies.

Spread filling almost to the edges . . . when making filled cookies. To keep the filling in, press edges of filled cookies together with the fingers or with floured tines of a fork.

POINSETTIAS

A smart new favorite for the holidays.

Follow 🔑 recipe above—and roll chilled dough ⅛″ thick. Cut in 3″ squares. Place on lightly greased baking sheet. Cut with sharp knife from corners of each square almost to center (making 4 triangular sections in each square). In center, place 1 teaspoonful cooled Prune Filling (*opposite page*). Pick up corresponding corner of each triangular section, and fold over center filling. Press gently in center to hold 4 points together. (*See diagrams below.*)

AMOUNT: About 5 doz. poinsettia cookies.

FIG BARS

Plump with fruity filling.

Follow 🔑 recipe above—and roll one-half of dough ⅛″ thick. Cut into 4 long strips (3½″x12″). Spread ⅓ to ½ cup Fig Filling (*opposite page*) on each strip lengthwise, covering only ½ of strip except for a ¼″ edge. Lift this edge up and stick it to filling. Quickly flop the uncovered half of strip over the filling, folding it under at edge. Seal the 2 edges together securely. With sharp knife, cut into bars 2″ long. Place 1″ apart on lightly greased baking sheet.

AMOUNT: 2 doz. 2″ bars.

Filled cooky favorites.

RAISIN, FIG, *AND* DATE FILLING

Mix together in saucepan . . .
- ½ cup raisins, finely cut up
- ½ cup figs, finely cut up
- ½ cup dates, finely cut up
- ½ cup sugar
- ½ cup water
- 2 tbsp. lemon juice

Cook slowly, stirring constantly, until thickened (about 5 min.). Cool.

AMOUNT: Filling for 4 doz. filled cookies.

RAISIN, FIG, *OR* DATE FILLING

In recipe above for Raisin, Fig, *and* Date Filling, use 1½ cups raisins, *or* figs, *or* dates . . . in place of the combination of the three.

PINEAPPLE FILLING

Mix together in saucepan . . .
- 1 cup sugar
- 4 tbsp. GOLD MEDAL Flour

Stir in . . .
- 1½ cups well drained crushed pineapple (# 2 can)
- 4 tbsp. lemon juice
- 3 tbsp. butter
- ¼ tsp. nutmeg
- ¾ cup pineapple juice

Cook slowly, stirring constantly, until thickened (5 to 10 min.). Cool.

AMOUNT: Filling for 4 doz. filled cookies.

Clean sticky fruits from your food grinder quickly and easily by running a few small pieces of dry bread through it.

PRUNE FILLING

Mix together in saucepan . . .
- 1⅓ cups mashed cooked prunes (2 cups uncooked)
- ½ cup sugar
- 2 tbsp. lemon juice

Cook slowly, stirring constantly, until thickened (about 4 min.).

AMOUNT: Fills 5 doz. Poinsettias (*p. 196*).

★ HIS MOTHER'S OATMEAL COOKIES

Crispy, nutty-flavored cookies . . . sandwiched together with jelly or jam.

Nora M. Young of Cleveland, Ohio, won a prize in the "plain cooky class" on these. Wonderful for lunch box and cooky jar.

Mix together	2 cups *sifted* GOLD MEDAL Flour ½ tsp. salt 3 cups rolled oats
Cut in until mixture is well blended	1 cup shortening (part butter)
Stir in	1 tsp. soda dissolved in ⅓ cup milk (sweet or sour) 1½ cups brown sugar

Chill dough. Roll out ⅛″ thick. Cut into desired shapes. Place on ungreased baking sheet. Bake until lightly browned. When cool, and just before serving, put together in pairs with jelly or jam between.

TEMPERATURE: 375° (quick mod. oven).

TIME: Bake 10 to 12 min.

AMOUNT: About 4 doz. 2½″ double cookies.

ROLLED COOKIES Old-time goodies every home should know.

★ GINGIES (🔑 Recipe) *Soft and puffy . . . true old-fashioned ginger cookies.*

A happy tradition at the famous Girard College, Philadelphia, Pennsylvania. The boys hoard them . . . old grads long for them.

Mix together thoroughly
- **1/3 cup soft shortening**
- **1 cup brown sugar**
- **1½ cups dark molasses**

Stir in
- **½ cup cold water**

Sift together and stir in
- **6 cups *sifted* GOLD MEDAL Flour**
- **1 tsp. salt**
- **1 tsp. allspice**
- **1 tsp. ginger**
- **1 tsp. cloves**
- **1 tsp. cinnamon**

Stir in
- **2 tsp. soda dissolved in 3 tbsp. cold water**

Chill dough. Roll out very thick (½"). Cut with 2½" round cutter. Place far apart on lightly greased baking sheet. Bake until, when touched lightly with finger, no imprint remains.

TEMPERATURE: 350° (mod. oven).

TIME: Bake 15 to 18 min.

AMOUNT: 2⅔ doz. fat, puffy 2½" cookies.

FROSTED GINGIES

Follow 🔑 recipe above—and frost when cool with Simple White Icing (*recipe below*).

SIMPLE WHITE ICING

Blend together 1 cup *sifted* confectioners' sugar, ¼ tsp. salt, ½ tsp. vanilla, and enough milk or water to make easy to spread (about 1½ tbsp.). Part of icing may be colored by adding a drop or two of food coloring.

GINGERBREAD BOYS

Make holidays gayer than ever.

Follow 🔑 recipe above—and mix in 1 more cup *sifted* GOLD MEDAL Flour. Chill dough. Roll out very thick (½"). Grease cardboard gingerbread boy pattern, place on the dough, and cut around it with a sharp knife. Or use a gingerbread boy cutter. With a pancake turner, carefully transfer gingerbread boys to lightly greased baking sheet. Press raisins into dough for eyes, nose, mouth, and shoe and cuff buttons. Use bits of candied cherries or red gumdrops for coat buttons; strips of citron for tie. Bake. Cool slightly, then carefully remove from baking sheet. With white icing, make outlines for collar, cuffs, belt, and shoes.

AMOUNT: About 12 Gingerbread Boys.

★ STONE JAR MOLASSES COOKIES *Crisp and brown . . . without a bit of sugar.*

Heat to boiling point
- **1 cup molasses**

Remove from heat.

Stir in
- **½ cup shortening**
- **1 tsp. soda**

Sift together and stir in
- **2¼ cups *sifted* GOLD MEDAL Flour**
- **1¾ tsp. baking powder**
- **1 tsp. salt**
- **1½ tsp. ginger**

Chill dough. Roll out very thin (1/16"). Cut into desired shapes. Place on lightly greased baking sheet. Bake until set. (Overbaking gives a bitter taste.)

TEMPERATURE: 350° (mod. oven).

TIME: Bake 5 to 7 min.

AMOUNT: About 6 doz. 2½" cookies.

PATTERN FOR GINGERBREAD BOY

Trace on tissue paper. Then cut pattern from cardboard. Place greased pattern on dough. Cut around it with a sharp knife. Other cooky patterns can be made in same way.

To make "dancing" Gingerbread boys . . . bend the legs and arms into "action" positions when you place them on baking sheet (as shown in small figures above).

Packing cookies successfully for mailing

1 Select heavy box, line with waxed paper. Use plenty of filler (crushed wrapping or tissue paper, or unbuttered popcorn or Cheerios).

2 Wrap each cooky separately . . . in waxed paper. Or place cookies back-to-back in pairs . . . then wrap each pair.

3 Pad bottom of box with filler. Fit wrapped cookies into box closely, in layers.

4 Use filler between layers to prevent crushing of cookies.

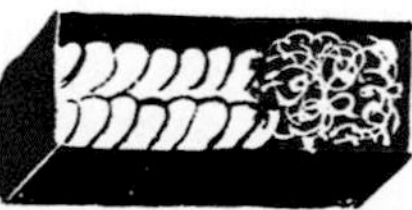

5 Cover with paper doily, add card, and pad top with crushed paper. Pack tightly so contents will not shake around.

6 Wrap box tightly with heavy paper and cord. Address plainly with permanent ink . . . covering address with Scotch tape or colorless nail polish. Mark the box plainly: "PERISHABLE."

MERRY CHRISTMAS COOKIES (Recipe) *Soft, cushiony cookies, dark or light.*

DARK DOUGH . . . *For animal shapes, toy shapes, and boy and girl figures.*

Mix together thoroughly . . . .
- 1/3 cup soft shortening
- 1/3 cup brown sugar
- 1 egg
- 2/3 cup molasses

Sift together and stir in . . . .
- 2 3/4 cups *sifted* GOLD MEDAL Flour
- 1 tsp. soda
- 1 tsp. salt
- 2 tsp. cinnamon
- 1 tsp. ginger

Chill dough. Roll out thick (1/4″). Cut into desired shapes. Place 1″ apart on lightly greased baking sheet. Bake until, when touched lightly with finger, no imprint remains. When cool, ice and decorate as desired.

TEMPERATURE: 375° (quick mod. oven).

TIME: Bake 8 to 10 min.

AMOUNT: About 5 doz. 2 1/2″ cookies.

LIGHT DOUGH

For bells, stockings, stars, wreaths, etc.

Follow recipe for Dark Dough above *except* substitute honey for molasses, and granulated sugar for brown. Use 1 tsp. lemon extract in place of spices.

TO HANG ON CHRISTMAS TREE

Just loop a piece of green string and press ends into the dough at the top of each cooky before baking. Bake with string-side *down* on pan.

TO DECORATE

Use recipe for Decorating Icing (p. 195) (thin the icing for spreading). For decorating ideas, see picture on preceding page. Sugar in coarse granules for decorating is available at bakery supply houses.

STARS

Cover with white icing. Sprinkle with sky blue sugar.

WREATHS

Cut with scalloped cutter . . . using smaller cutter for center. Cover with white icing. Sprinkle with green sugar and decorate with clusters of berries made of red icing—leaves of green icing—to give the realistic effect of holly wreaths.

BELLS

Outline with red icing. Make clapper of red icing. (A favorite with children.)

STOCKINGS

Sprinkle colored sugar on toes and heels before baking. Or mark heels and toes of baked cookies with icing of some contrasting color.

CHRISTMAS TREES

Spread with white icing . . . then sprinkle with green sugar. Decorate with silver dragées and tiny colored candies.

TOYS

(Drum, car, jack-in-the-box, etc.): Outline shapes with white or colored icing.

ANIMALS

(Reindeer, camel, dog, kitten, etc.): Pipe icing on animals to give effect of bridles, blankets, etc.

BOYS AND GIRLS

Pipe figures with an icing to give desired effects: eyes, noses, buttons, etc.

←NOTE: To find recipes of cookies in color photograph, see p. 206.

ROLLED COOKIES "Old country" Christmas treasures.

LEBKUCHEN (Recipe) *The famous old-time German Christmas Honey Cakes.*

Mix together and bring to a boil........ **½ cup honey**, **½ cup molasses**

Cool thoroughly.

Stir in........ **¾ cup brown sugar**, **1 egg**, **1 tbsp. lemon juice**, **1 tsp. grated lemon rind**

Sift together and stir in........ **2¾ cups *sifted* GOLD MEDAL Flour**, **½ tsp. soda**, **1 tsp. cinnamon**, **1 tsp. cloves**, **1 tsp. allspice**, **1 tsp. nutmeg**

Mix in........ **⅓ cup cut-up citron**, **⅓ cup chopped nuts**

Chill dough overnight. Roll small amount at a time, keeping rest chilled. Roll out ¼" thick and cut into oblongs 1½x2½". Place one inch apart on greased baking sheet. Bake until when touched lightly no imprint remains. While cookies bake, make Glazing Icing (*recipe below*). Brush it over cookies the minute they are out of oven. Then quickly remove from baking sheet. Cool and store to mellow.

TEMPERATURE: 400° (mod. hot oven).
TIME: Bake 10 to 12 min.
AMOUNT: About 6 doz. 2"x3" cookies.

GLAZING ICING

Boil together 1 cup sugar and ½ cup water until first indication of a thread appears (230°). Remove from heat. Stir in ¼ cup confectioners' sugar and brush hot icing thinly over cookies. (*When icing gets sugary, reheat slightly, adding a little water until clear again.*)

★ **NURNBERGER** *Round, light-colored honey cakes from the famed old City of Toys.*

Follow recipe above—*except* in place of honey and molasses use 1 cup honey; and reduce spices (using ¼ tsp. cloves, ½ tsp. allspice, and ½ tsp. nutmeg ... with 1 tsp. cinnamon).
Roll out the *chilled* dough ¼" thick. Cut into 2" rounds. Place on greased baking sheet. With fingers, round up cookies a bit toward center. Press in blanched almond halves around the edge like petals of a daisy. Use a round piece of citron for each center. Bake just until set. *Immediately* brush with Glazing Icing (*above*). Remove from baking sheet. Cool, and store to mellow.

AMOUNT: About 6 doz. 2½" cookies.

TO "MELLOW" COOKIES

... store in an airtight container for a few days. Add a cut orange or apple; but fruit molds, so change it frequently.

ZUCKER HÜTCHEN (Little Sugar Hats)
From the collection of Christmas recipes by the Kohler Woman's Club of Kohler, Wisconsin.

Mix together thoroughly . . .
- **6 tbsp. soft butter**
- **½ cup sugar**
- **1 egg yolk**

Stir in . . .
- **2 tbsp. milk**

Sift together and stir in
- **1⅜ cups *sifted* GOLD MEDAL Flour**
- **½ tsp. baking powder**
- **¼ tsp. salt**

Mix in . . .
- **¼ cup finely cut-up citron**

Chill dough. Roll thin (⅛"). Cut into 2" rounds. Heap 1 tsp. Meringue Frosting (*recipe below*) in center of each round to make it look like the crown of a hat. Place 1" apart on greased baking sheet. Bake until delicately browned.

TEMPERATURE: 350° (mod. oven).
TIME: Bake 10 to 12 min.
AMOUNT: About 4 doz. 2" cookies.

MERINGUE FROSTING

Beat 1 egg white until frothy. Beat in gradually 1½ cups *sifted* confectioners' sugar and beat until frosting holds its shape. Stir in ½ cup finely chopped blanched almonds.

SCOTCH SHORTBREAD

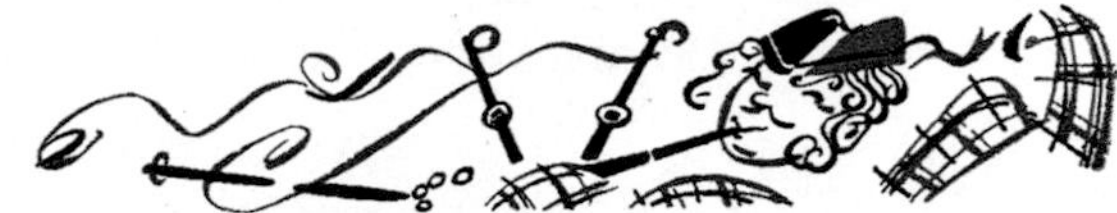

Old-time delicacy from Scotland . . . crisp, thick, buttery.

Mix together thoroughly . . . . **1 cup soft butter**
5/8 cup sugar (1/2 cup plus 2 tbsp.)

Stir in . . . . **2 1/2 cups *sifted* GOLD MEDAL Flour**

Mix thoroughly with hands. Chill dough. Roll out 1/3 to 1/2" thick. Cut into fancy shapes (small leaves, ovals, squares, etc.). Flute edges if desired by pinching between fingers as for pie crust. Place on ungreased baking sheet. Bake. (The tops do not brown during baking . . . nor does shape of the cookies change.)

TEMPERATURE: 300° (slow oven).

TIME: Bake 20 to 25 min.

AMOUNT: About 2 doz. 1"x1 1/2" cookies.

★ FINSKA KAKOR (Finnish Cakes)

Nut-studded butter strips from Finland.

Mix together thoroughly . . .
- **3/4 cup soft butter**
- **1/4 cup sugar**
- **1 tsp. almond extract**

Stir in . . .
- **2 cups *sifted* GOLD MEDAL Flour**

Mix thoroughly with hands. Chill dough. Roll out 1/4" thick. Cut into strips 2 1/2" long and 3/4" wide. Brush tops lightly with 1 egg white, slightly beaten. Sprinkle with mixture of 1 tbsp. sugar and 1/3 cup finely chopped blanched almonds. Carefully transfer (several strips at a time) to ungreased baking sheet. Bake just until cookies begin to turn a very delicate golden brown.

TEMPERATURE: 350° (mod. oven).

TIME: Bake 17 to 20 min.

AMOUNT: About 4 doz. 2 1/2"x3/4" cookies.

The ring of sleigh bells fills the air as everyone races to church on Christmas Day in Finland.

SANDBAKELSER (Sand Tarts)

Fragile almond-flavored shells of Swedish origin, made in copper molds of varied designs.

Put through fine knife of food grinder twice . . .
- ***1/3 cup blanched almonds**
- ***4 unblanched almonds**

Mix in thoroughly . . .
- **7/8 cup soft butter (1 cup minus 2 tbsp.)**
- **3/4 cup sugar**
- **1 small egg white, unbeaten**

Stir in . . .
- **1 3/4 cups *sifted* GOLD MEDAL Flour**

**In place of the almonds, you may use 1 tsp. vanilla and 1 tsp. almond extract.*

Chill dough. Press dough *into* Sandbakels molds (or tiny fluted tart forms) to coat inside. Place on ungreased baking sheet. Bake until very delicately browned. Tap molds on table to loosen cookies and turn them out of the molds.

TEMPERATURE: 350° (mod. oven).

TIME: Bake 12 to 15 min.

AMOUNT: About 3 doz. cookies.

MOLDED COOKIES Mold 'em fast with a fork or a glass!

HOW TO MAKE MOLDED COOKIES (preliminary steps on pp. 178, 179)

1 With hands, roll dough into balls or into long, pencil-thick rolls, as indicated in recipe.

2 Flatten balls of dough with bottom of a glass dipped in flour (or with a damp cloth around it), or with a fork—crisscross.

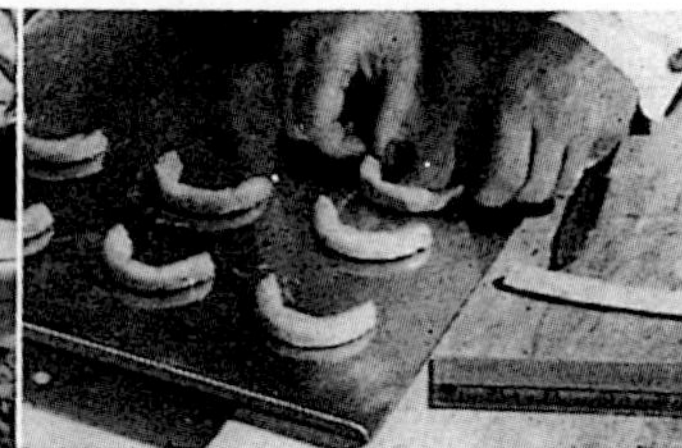

3 Cut pencil-thick strips . . . and shape as directed . . . as for Almond Crescents (p. 205) or Berliner Kranser (p. 206).

DATE-OATMEAL COOKIES

Mix together thoroughly
- **¾ cup soft shortening (half butter)**
- **1 cup brown sugar**
- **2 eggs**
- **3 tbsp. milk**
- **1 tsp. vanilla**

Sift together and stir in
- **2 cups *sifted* GOLD MEDAL Flour**
- **¾ tsp. soda**
- **1 tsp. salt**

Stir in
- **2 cups rolled oats**
- **1½ cups cut-up dates**
- **¾ cup chopped nuts**

Chill dough. Roll into balls size of large walnuts. Place 3″ apart on lightly greased baking sheet. Flatten (to ¼″) with bottom of glass dipped in flour. Bake until lightly browned.

TEMPERATURE: 375° (quick mod. oven).
TIME: Bake 10 to 12 min.
AMOUNT: About 4 doz. 2½″ cookies.

★ PEANUT BUTTER COOKIES (Key Recipe) *Perfect for the Children's Hour.*

Mix together thoroughly
- **½ cup soft shortening (half butter)**
- **½ cup peanut butter**
- **½ cup sugar**
- **½ cup brown sugar**
- **1 egg**

Sift together and stir in
- **1¼ cups *sifted* GOLD MEDAL Flour**
- **½ tsp. baking powder**
- **¾ tsp. soda**
- **¼ tsp. salt**

Chill dough. Roll into balls size of large walnuts. Place 3″ apart on lightly greased baking sheet. Flatten with fork dipped in flour . . . crisscross. Bake until set . . . but not hard.

TEMPERATURE: 375° (quick mod. oven).
TIME: Bake 10 to 12 min.
AMOUNT: About 3 doz. 2½″ cookies.

HONEY PEANUT BUTTER COOKIES

Follow key recipe above—*except* use only ¼ cup shortening, and in place of brown sugar use ½ cup honey.

THUMBPRINT COOKIES *Nut-rich . . . the thumb dents filled with sparkling jelly.*

I'm as delighted with this quaint addition to our cooky collection, from Ken MacKenzie, as is the collector of old glass when a friend presents her with some early thumbprint goblets.

Mix together thoroughly
- ½ cup soft shortening (half butter)
- ¼ cup brown sugar
- 1 egg yolk
- ½ tsp. vanilla

Sift together and stir in
- 1 cup *sifted* GOLD MEDAL Flour
- ¼ tsp. salt

Roll into 1″ balls. Dip in slightly beaten egg whites. Roll in finely chopped nuts (¾ cup). Place about 1″ apart on ungreased baking sheet. Bake 5 min. Remove from oven. Quickly press thumb gently on top of each cooky. Return to oven and bake 8 min. longer. Cool. Place in thumbprints a bit of chopped candied fruit, sparkling jelly, or tinted confectioners' sugar icing.

TEMPERATURE: 375° (quick mod. oven).
TIME: Bake 5 min., then 8 min.
AMOUNT: About 2 doz. 1½″ cookies.

★ ENGLISH TEA CAKES *Tender, flavorful tidbits with a sugary glaze.*

Mix together thoroughly
- ½ cup soft shortening (half butter)
- ¾ cup sugar
- 1 egg
- 3 tbsp. milk

Sift together and stir in
- 1¾ cups *sifted* GOLD MEDAL Flour
- 1½ tsp. baking powder
- ¼ tsp. salt

Mix in
- ½ cup finely cut sliced citron
- ½ cup currants or raisins, cut-up

Chill dough. Roll into balls the size of walnuts. Dip tops in slightly beaten egg white, then sugar. Place sugared-side-up 2″ apart on ungreased baking sheet. Bake until delicately browned. The balls flatten some in baking and become glazed.

TEMPERATURE: 400° (mod. hot oven).
TIME: Bake 12 to 15 min.
AMOUNT: About 3 doz. 1½″ cookies.

ALMOND CRESCENTS

Richly delicate, buttery. Party favorites.

Mix together thoroughly . . .
- 1 cup soft shortening (half butter)
- ⅓ cup sugar
- ⅔ cup ground blanched almonds

Sift together and work in . . .
- 1⅔ cups *sifted* GOLD MEDAL Flour
- ¼ tsp. salt

Chill dough. Roll with hands pencil-thick. Cut in 2½″ lengths. Form into crescents on ungreased baking sheet. Bake until set . . . not brown. Cool on pan. While slightly warm, carefully dip in 1 cup confectioners' sugar and 1 tsp. cinnamon mixed.

TEMPERATURE: 325° (slow mod. oven).
TIME: Bake 14 to 16 min.
AMOUNT: About 5 doz. 2½″ cookies.

LEMON SNOWDROPS

Refreshing, lemony . . . with snowy icing.

Follow recipe for English Tea Cakes above—*except* use 2 tbsp. lemon juice and 1 tbsp. water in place of the milk. Add 2 tsp. grated lemon rind. Omit citron and currants. Mix in ½ cup chopped nuts. Chill dough. Roll into balls and bake. Then roll in confectioners' sugar.

BUTTER FINGERS

Nut-flavored, rich buttery party cookies.

Follow recipe for Almond Crescents—*except* in place of almonds use black walnuts or other nuts, *chopped*. Cut into finger lengths and bake. While still warm, roll in confectioners' sugar. Cool, and roll in the sugar again.

MOLDED COOKIES Festive cookies for the holidays . . . ideal for Christmas boxes.

RUSSIAN TEA CAKES *Crunchy, sugared, nut-filled snowballs.*

This favorite with men came to us from a man. Carl Burkland, a radio executive of New York City, made them himself for me one Christmas season.

Mix together thoroughly . . . .
- **1 cup soft butter**
- **½ cup *sifted* confectioners' sugar**
- **1 tsp. vanilla**

Sift together and stir in . . . .
- **2¼ cups *sifted* GOLD MEDAL Flour**
- **¼ tsp. salt**

Mix in . . . . **¾ cup finely chopped nuts**

Chill dough. Roll into 1″ balls. Place 2½″ apart on ungreased baking sheet. Bake until set, but not brown. While still warm, roll in confectioners' sugar. Cool. Roll in sugar again.

TEMPERATURE: 400° (mod. hot oven).

TIME: Bake 10 to 12 min.

AMOUNT: About 4 doz. 1½″ cookies.

MANDEL KAGER (Almond Cookies)

These little cakes of intriguing flavor are always on hand for Norway's holiday festivities.

Mix together thoroughly . . .
- **1 cup soft shortening (part butter)**
- **½ cup sugar**
- **1 egg**

Sift together and stir in . . .
- **1⅔ cups *sifted* GOLD MEDAL Flour**
- **½ tsp. baking powder**
- **1 tbsp. cinnamon (3 tsp.)**
- **1 to 1½ tsp. ground cardamom**

Mix in . . .
- **½ cup chopped toasted almonds**

Chill dough. Roll into 1″ balls. Place on ungreased baking sheet. Flatten slightly. Brush tops with *egg glaze* (1 slightly beaten egg yolk mixed with 1 tbsp. water). Top each with a blanched almond half. Bake until golden brown.

TEMPERATURE: 375° (quick mod. oven).

TIME: Bake 10 to 12 min.

AMOUNT: About 3½ doz. 1½″ cookies.

Where to find recipes in color photograph, p. 200:

1. Sandbakelser . . 203
2. Spritz 207
3. Trees, Stars . . . 201
4. Nurnberger . . . 202
5. Almond Crescents 205
6. Lebkuchen 202
7. Shortbread 203
8. Berliner Kranser 206
9. Finska Kakor 203
10. Russian Tea Cakes 206

All you have to do—

To shape a Berliner Krans: form a circle and bring one end over and through.

If rich dough splits apart or seems crumbly, let it get slightly warm or work in a few drops of liquid until the dough sticks together.

BERLINER KRANSER (Berlin Wreaths)

Delicious and buttery, these gay little wreaths are made each holiday season in Norway.

Mix together thoroughly . . .
- **1½ cups soft shortening (half butter)**
- **1 cup sugar**
- **2 tsp. grated orange rind**
- **2 eggs**

Stir in . . .
- **4 cups *sifted* GOLD MEDAL Flour**

Chill dough. Break off small pieces and roll to pencil size about 6″ long and ¼″ thick. Form each piece into a circle, bringing one end over and through in a single knot. (*See sketch above.*) Leave ½″ end on each side. Place on ungreased baking sheet. Brush tops with *meringue* (made by beating 1 egg white until stiff, gradually beating in 2 tbsp. sugar). Press bits of red candied cherries on center of knot for holly berries. Add little jagged leaves cut out of green citron. Bake until set . . . but not brown.

TEMPERATURE: 400° (mod. hot oven).

TIME: Bake 10 to 12 min.

AMOUNT: About 6 doz. 2″ cookies.

HOW TO MAKE COOKIES WITH A PRESS

Force dough through a cooky press (or pastry tube). Follow directions accompanying cooky press. Hold the press upright, and force out the dough until it appears at the edge of the mold . . . then lift the press away. Dough should be pliable. If very warm, chill dough. (Crumbles if *too* cold.)

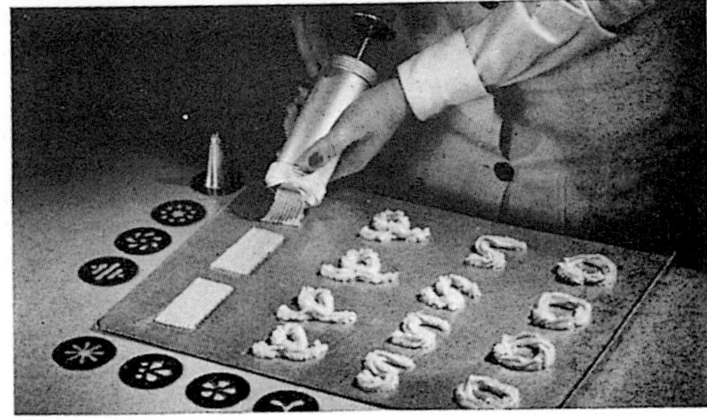

SPRITZ (🔑 Recipe) ("Spurted out of a press") *Crisp, fragile, buttery-tasting curlicues.*

Mix together thoroughly	1 cup soft butter 2/3 cup sugar 3 egg yolks 1 tsp. flavoring (almond or vanilla) or 4 tbsp. grated almonds
Work in with the hands	2 1/2 cups *sifted* GOLD MEDAL Flour

Force the dough through cooky press onto ungreased baking sheet in letter S's, rosettes, fluted bars, or other desired shapes. Bake until set . . . but not brown.

TEMPERATURE: 400° (mod. hot oven).
TIME: Bake 7 to 10 min.
AMOUNT: About 6 doz. cookies.

CHOCOLATE SPRITZ

Follow 🔑 recipe above—but blend into the shortening mixture 2 sq. unsweetened chocolate (2 oz.), melted.

Have baking sheet cold before forcing cooky dough through press onto it. If sheet is not cold, the fat in the dough will melt and the cookies will pull away from the sheet when the press is lifted.

BUTTER COOKIES

Follow 🔑 recipe for Butter Cookies on p. 195. Force pliable dough through cooky press onto ungreased baking sheet in form of flowers, wreaths, or any desired shapes.

Dough for press cookies may be rolled out and cut into desired shapes. For wreaths, cut with scalloped cooky cutter . . . then cut out center with a smaller sized cutter.

★ ALMOND WREATHS

Beautiful almond-topped garlands.

Mix together thoroughly . . .
- 1 cup soft shortening (mostly butter)
- 3/4 cup sifted confectioners' sugar
- 2 egg yolks
- 1 egg white
- 1 tsp. vanilla
- 1/4 tsp. salt

Sift together and work in with the hands . . .
- 2 cups *sifted* GOLD MEDAL Flour

Force the dough through cooky press onto ungreased baking sheet in shape of wreaths. Brush wreaths with slightly beaten egg white. Sprinkle with mixture of 2 tbsp. sugar, 1/4 tsp. cinnamon, and 1/4 cup very finely chopped blanched almonds. Bake until set but not brown.

TO DECORATE

Press bits of red or green candied cherry into top of wreaths to simulate a bow.

TEMPERATURE: 350° (mod. oven).

TIME: Bake 8 to 10 min.

AMOUNT: About 6 doz. cookies.

SPECIALTY COOKIES Fascinating specialties for tea-time.

SWEDISH MACAROON TEA CAKES

They look like tiny tarts. The rich cooky-type crust and the delicious macaroony filling are baked together.

Cream together thoroughly . . .
- **1 cup soft butter**
- **½ cup sugar**

Beat in . . .
- **1 egg**
- **1 tsp. vanilla**

Stir in . . .
- **2 cups *sifted* SOFTASILK Cake Flour or GOLD MEDAL Flour**

Drop a rounded teaspoonful of batter into each greased tiny muffin cup . . . pressing batter over bottom and up around sides (a coating ¼″ thick . . . leaving center hollow). Chill. Fill each hollow with

ALMOND MACAROON FILLING

Beat until light and foamy . . .
- **2 eggs**

Gradually beat in until well blended . . .
- **½ cup sugar**

Mix in . . .
- **1¼ cups blanched almonds, finely ground**
- **½ tsp. almond extract**

Bake until delicately browned and set.

TEMPERATURE: 325° (slow mod. oven).

TIME: Bake 25 to 30 min.

AMOUNT: 2 doz. tea cakes.

NUT BONBON COOKIES

Dainty rolls with a variety of fillings. Mrs. Mildred Jolly of Barberton, Ohio, sent us this delicious Slovak recipe.

Mix together with a fork . . .
- **½ lb. white cream cheese**
- **1 cup soft shortening (part butter)**

Mix in well with hands . . .
- **2 cups *sifted* GOLD MEDAL Flour**

Chill several hr. or overnight. Roll out ⅛″ thick on cloth-covered board which has been sprinkled generously with confectioners' sugar (dough will absorb 1 cup). Cut into bars 1″x3″. Place walnut half on each and roll up. Place, folded side down, on baking sheet. Bake. Sprinkle with confectioners' sugar.

NOTE: Prunes, raisins, maraschino cherries, pecans, finely shredded coconut may be substituted for walnuts.

TEMPERATURE: 375° (quick mod. oven).

TIME: Bake 15 to 17 min.

AMOUNT: 9 doz. cookies.

CINNAMON COFFEE BARS

Cake or cooky bars . . . "So quick and easy to make for a last minute dessert!" says Ramona Gerhard Sutton of Minneapolis, Minnesota, an accomplished cook as well as a most gifted musician.

Cream together thoroughly . . .
- **¼ cup soft shortening**
- **1 cup brown sugar**
- **1 egg**

Stir in . . .
- **½ cup hot coffee**

Sift together and stir in . . .
- **1½ cups *sifted* GOLD MEDAL Flour**
- **1 tsp. baking powder**
- **¼ tsp. soda**
- **¼ tsp. salt**
- **½ tsp. cinnamon**

Blend in . . .
- **½ cup seedless raisins**
- **¼ cup chopped nuts**

Spread in greased and floured 13x9″ oblong pan. Bake. Cut into bars. Frost while warm with thin coating of Quick Cream Icing (*p. 183*).

TEMPERATURE: 350° (mod. oven).

TIME: Bake 15 to 20 min.

AMOUNT: 2 doz. 1½″x3″ bars.

COCONUT CHERRY COOKIES

Luscious, macaroon-like, colorful. From Ruth Brand, Director, Dairy Council of the Twin Cities, St. Paul, Minnesota.

Mix together thoroughly . . .
- **1 cup soft shortening (half butter)**
- **1 cup sugar**
- **3 eggs**

Stir in . . .
- **½ cup sour cream**

Sift together and stir in . . .
- **3¼ cups *sifted* GOLD MEDAL Flour**
- **1 tsp. baking powder**
- **½ tsp. soda**
- **1½ tsp. salt**

Stir in . . .
- **½ cup chopped candied cherries**
- **¼ cup cut-up citron**
- **1 cup shredded coconut**
- **1 tsp. grated orange rind**
- **1½ tsp. lemon or almond extract**

Drop rounded teaspoonfuls about 2″ apart onto ungreased baking sheet. Bake.

TEMPERATURE: 400° (mod. hot oven).

TIME: Bake 10 to 12 min.

AMOUNT: 7 to 8 doz. 2″ cookies.

Consider Desserts The Grand Finale

WE LOOK FORWARD *to dessert. It is like the last act of a play . . . the happy ending we've anticipated from the first. This may be a gorgeous fanfare of triumph, or a homey, heart-satisfying scene. In the same way the dessert, in keeping with the meal preceding it, can be dramatic and spectacular, or a cozy old-time favorite beloved by generations.*

Betty Crocker

Quick Easy Desserts

Homey Baked Desserts for Oven Dinners

Simple Sweets for the Very Young

Old-Time Favorites

Company Desserts

Desserts for Large Parties

Holiday Desserts

Dessert and Coffee Entertaining

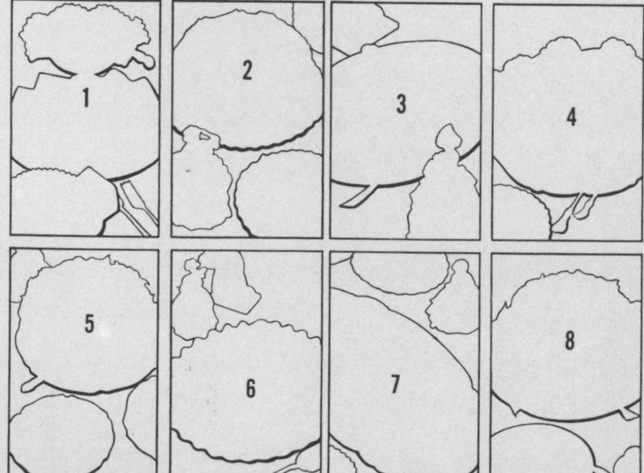

Where to find recipes for Desserts in color photograph, pp. 212, 213:

DESSERTS

Dessert originally meant food served after the table had been cleared or "deserted" of everything else . . . even the cloth removed. We find accounts of grand dinners served in the early days of our country describing the polished mahogany tables with candles in tall silver candelabra casting a mellow glow over the guests enjoying a "dessert" of fresh fruit. In Europe, "dessert" still means fruit served at the end of the meal. However, for them, this fruit course follows a "sweet" . . . that is, a pudding, pastry, soufflé, or an elaborate torte creation. We Americans have simply promoted the "sweet" to the place of honor at the end of the meal.

European visitors in our country are amazed at the array of "sweets" Americans have to choose from. In addition to those we have adopted from other nations, British steamed puddings, German and Austrian tortes, French meringues, and Italian soufflés, we have developed our own special favorites, including ice creams and our fruit shortcakes and cobblers.

This wide variety of truly delightful desserts makes it difficult to choose a selection for one chapter. It would have been easier to fill a whole cook book with dessert recipes. We have tried, however, to give you dessert favorites of each type. You will find some that are suitable for holiday dinners and parties . . . others for simple family meals where consideration must be given to what the children may eat. Then there are the elaborate distinctly party desserts for buffet suppers or dessert luncheons. Of course we have made it a point to include homey, old-time favorites, too!

With all these at your fingertips, we hope you will have fun serving desserts that will bring each meal to a satisfying and delightful finish.

FRUIT AND CHEESE DESSERTS To please the epicures and dieters.

FRESH FRUIT

The easiest of all desserts.

A bowl heaped with colorful fruit washed, dried, and chilled,—a variety to choose from . . . is both decorative and tempting. Cheese and crisp unsweetened crackers are natural affinities, or crisp rich cookies are pleasant accompaniments. Serving can be very simple: just an individual dessert plate, a suitable knife for cutting fruit and spreading soft cheese. Finger bowls are correct to save linens from stubborn fruit stains, but nowadays paper napkins are often used with fruit.

FRESH FRUITS IN SEASON

Combinations always popular.

Honeydew melon with lime or lemon, and mint leaves.

Cantaloupe filled with ice cream.

Peaches and raspberries, plain or with ice cream.

Brandy-flavored cherries and ice cream.

Strawberries, raspberries, blackberries, or blueberries with cream.

Sliced peaches and cream.

FOR CHEESE AND FRUIT PARTNERS

Concord grapes, smoked cheese, flaky crackers.

Red apples, New York or Gouda cheese (an apple slice, slice of cheese on a cracker).

Fresh pears, Bar-le-Duc (currant preserves), cream cheese, tiny hot buttered baking powder biscuits or salty crackers.

Fresh strawberries (with hulls) around a mound of cream cheese sweetened with confectioners' sugar, a hint of rum flavoring. Dip strawberries in cheese mixture.

Green gage or other plums stewed with strips of candied ginger, Brie cheese, and crackers.

Tart plums, thin slices caraway rye bread, Camembert cheese.

Tokay grapes, American Liederkranz, thin slices buttered pumpernickel bread.

SALADS SERVED AS DESSERTS

See "SALADS" for many delightful fruit combinations.

DESSERT CHEESES

Know your cheeses for variety.

Soft, sharp type: French Brie, American Liederkranz, American Camembert.

Soft, mild type: white spreading cream cheese, cottage cheese.

Semi-hard: American type Cheddar cheeses ranging from sharp New York cheese to mild brick cheese.

Blue or mold-ripened: American Roquefort, "Blue" cheeses, Gorgonzola.

Hard: Gouda, Edam, Pineapple, Swiss, Gruyère.

SIMPLE ACCOMPANIMENTS

Cracker assortment may be varied with thin slices buttered rye or pumpernickel bread, or thin fingers of buttered raisin or nut bread.

Butter wafers or flaky crackers may be spread lightly with melted butter, sprinkled with celery seed, paprika, or garlic salt ready to place under the broiler a few minutes before serving.

★ INFORMAL COMPANY DESSERT TRAY

Guests will be thrilled with this charming Hospitality Tray, an idea from Marye Dahnke of Kraft Foods Company.

Arrange sections of fresh cored (but not peeled) pears petal-fashion on lettuce or grape leaves. Surround with cored (but not peeled) apple rings. On outer edge of tray place alternate wedges of American Camembert and American Roquefort or Bleu cheeses.

Fruits are used in place of crackers: pears with American Roquefort or Bleu cheese, and apples with American Camembert.

SOUTHERN AMBROSIA

Pile shredded fresh coconut with sliced orange into sherbet glasses.

MEXICAN AMBROSIA

Heap snowy shredded coconut over slice of fresh or drained canned pineapple on each dessert plate.

FRUIT CUSTARD

Easy last-minute dessert, always pleases.

Place cut-up oranges, or bananas, or other fruit in sauce dishes. Pour cooled Soft Custard (*p. 219*) over fruit.

BAKED PEACHES, APRICOTS, OR PEARS

Place well drained canned peach, apricot or pear halves hollow-side-up in baking dish. Place bit of butter in each. Sprinkle with mace and grated lemon rind. Pour a little of the fruit juice around. Bake at 425° (hot oven) 12 min. Serve cold with cream, ice cream, or Zabaglione Sauce.

BAKED RHUBARB

Cut 2 lb. rhubarb in 1″ pieces (4 cups). Do not peel pink tender rhubarb. Place in baking dish. Sprinkle with 2 tbsp. water, 1 cup sugar, and ¼ tsp. nutmeg. Bake at 350° (mod. oven) 45 min.

RHUBARB SAUCE

Follow recipe for Baked Rhubarb—*except* use 1 cup water. Simmer in saucepan on top of stove 20 min.

BAKED PRUNE WHIP

Mix together . . .

- **1 cup cut-up prunes (cooked, drained, pitted)**
- **3 tbsp. confectioners' sugar**
- **⅛ tsp. salt**
- **1 tsp. lemon juice**

Carefully fold in. . .

- **3 egg whites, stiffly beaten**

Pour into buttered round 1-qt. casserole (6½″). Set in pan of water (1″ deep). Bake. Serve plain or with Soft Custard (*p. 219*) as a sauce.

TEMPERATURE: 350° (mod. oven).

TIME: Bake 30 to 35 min.

AMOUNT: 6 servings.

BAKED APPLES (🔑 Recipe)

Rome Beauties hold their shape in baking, as do Red Delicious.

Boil together 2 min. ½ cup sugar, 1 cup water. Core 6 apples and pare the upper halves. Place in 12 x 7½ x 2″ baking dish. Pour the syrup around apples. Bake until soft, basting occasionally with the syrup. Center cavity may be filled with chopped figs and almonds or orange marmalade, or cut-up dates and nuts. Serve warm or cold.

TEMPERATURE: 350° (mod. oven).

TIME: Bake 45 min. to 1 hr.

AMOUNT: 6 baked apples.

GLAZED BAKED APPLES

Follow 🔑 recipe above—*except* use 3 cups sugar to 1 cup water for the syrup.

FROSTED BAKED APPLES

Follow 🔑 recipe above—*except* roll each apple in melted butter, then in sugar and shredded coconut before baking. Surround with syrup—do not baste. Cover.

APPLESAUCE (The thick type)

As made by Mrs. Peter Larson of Webster, Wis.

Wash, pare, core, and slice about 8 tart apples. Place in saucepan. Add water (1 cup to 1 qt. apples). Simmer until apples are tender. Stir in ½ cup sugar, dash of salt, 1 tsp. lemon juice, ⅛ tsp. grated lemon rind, and ⅛ tsp. cinnamon or nutmeg. Taste, add more sugar, if desired. Cook 1 min. more. Serve cold. Elegant topped with whipped cream or ice cream.

STEWED APPLES

Follow recipe for Applesauce—*except* cut apples in eighths and place in a hot syrup of the sugar and water. Cook gently until apples are tender. Flavor to taste.

★ APPLE CRISP (Apple Crumble)

Place in buttered 10x6x2″ baking dish 4 cups sliced apples. Sprinkle with 1 tsp. cinnamon, 1 tsp. salt, ¼ cup water. Rub together ¾ cup *sifted* GOLD MEDAL Flour, 1 cup sugar, ⅓ cup butter. Drop mixture over apples. Bake. Serve warm with cream.

TEMPERATURE: 350° (mod. oven).

TIME: Bake 40 min.

AMOUNT: 6 servings.

GELATIN DESSERTS Light, refreshing chilled desserts.

Packages of fruit-flavored sweetened gelatin carry directions for making. *Plain unflavored gelatin* is softened in a little cold liquid, then dissolved in hot liquid . . . 1 envelope gelatin (1 tbsp.) sets 2 cups liquid; with acid fruit added, only 1¾ cups liquid. Fresh pineapple and its juice must be scalded before using in gelatin because of an enzyme action which prevents stiffening.

FRUIT GELATIN (🔑 Recipe)

Place in mixing bowl	**1 envelope unflavored gelatin (1 tbsp.)**
Soften in	**¼ cup cold water**
Stir in	**¾ cup boiling water** **½ cup sugar** **⅛ tsp. salt**
Stir until gelatin and sugar are dissolved. Cool. Then stir in	**1 cup fruit juice (drained from fruit) or ¾ cup juice if fruit is acid** **1 tbsp. lemon juice** **1 tsp. grated lemon or orange rind**
Chill until it begins to set. Add	**1 to 2 cups cut-up fruit (fresh or canned)**

Pour into oiled 1-qt. mold or 6 individual molds. Chill until set. Unmold. Serve with cream, whipped cream, or Soft Custard.

NOTE: Add fruit after mixture begins to set.

AMOUNT: 6 servings.

COFFEE JELLY

Follow 🔑 recipe above—*except,* in place of the boiling water and fruit juice, use hot strong coffee. Reduce sugar to ⅓ cup. Omit fruit, lemon juice, rind.

GRAPE JELLY

Follow 🔑 recipe above—*except,* in place of the boiling water and the fruit juice, use hot unsweetened grape juice.

WHIPPED GELATIN

For a frothy appearance, when gelatin is partially set, beat with rotary beater until light. Mold and chill.

COLORFUL GELATIN EASTER EGGS

Save egg shells where only the tip has been broken away when the egg was removed. Fill thoroughly dried shells with fruit-flavored gelatin in different colors. Set filled egg shells in muffin cups to chill until gelatin is firm. Break away shells. Serve in little nests of coconut on large chop plate.

All you have to do—

To unmold gelatin: loosen at edge. Let air in at side, turn quickly onto serving dish (hold serving dish on top, turn upside-down). If mold sticks, dip it *quickly* into hot water, then unmold.

★ SUMMER FRUIT COMPOTE

A colorful variety of fruits held together by soft jelly. Enjoyed at Ann Mulholland's home, Santa Barbara, California.

Follow 🔑 recipe above—*except* use *4 cups* mixed *fresh* fruits (strawberries, cherries, green grapes, melon balls, sliced peaches, etc.) and add 2 tbsp. cointreau or sherry flavoring. Serve in a large compote.

SNOW PUDDING (Lemon Sponge)

Soften . . .

1 envelope unflavored gelatin (1 tbsp.)

in . . .

¼ cup cold water

Stir in . . .

1 cup boiling water
¾ cup sugar
¼ cup lemon juice
1 tbsp. grated lemon rind

Strain, and cool. Stir occasionally. When it begins to set, beat with rotary beater until frothy. Beat in . . .

2 egg whites, stiffly beaten

Continue beating until mixture holds its shape. Pile into sherbet glasses. Chill. Serve with Soft Custard (*p. 219*) as sauce.

AMOUNT: 8 servings.

GRAPE SPONGE

Follow recipe for Snow Pudding above—*except,* in place of water, use hot grape juice; use only 2 tbsp. lemon juice; omit the lemon rind.

TAPIOCA CREAM (⚷ Recipe)

Elegant!

Mix in saucepan . . .
- 2 egg yolks, slightly beaten
- 2 cups milk
- 2 tbsp. sugar
- 2 tbsp. quick-cooking tapioca
- ¼ tsp. salt

Cook over low heat, stirring constantly, until mixture boils. Remove from heat. Cool.

Stir in . . .
- 1 tsp. vanilla

Fold in Meringue made with . . .
- 2 egg whites
- 4 tbsp. sugar

Spoon into sherbet glasses. Serve with cream. If desired, fold in fresh or drained canned fruit; or pour over fruit in sherbet glasses.

AMOUNT: 6 servings.

ORANGE CREAM TAPIOCA

Follow ⚷ recipe above—and add 1 tbsp. grated orange rind with the sugar. In place of vanilla, use 1 tbsp. lemon juice. Garnish with orange sections.

PEANUT BRITTLE TAPIOCA

Follow ⚷ recipe above. Fold in ¼ cup crushed peanut brittle.

★ **CHOCOLATE MARSHMALLOW CREAM**

Lovely, fluffy pudding.

Soften . . .
- 1 envelope unflavored gelatin (1 tbsp.)

in . . .
- ¼ cup milk

Heat together in saucepan . . .
- 2 cups milk
- ½ cup sugar
- 1 sq. unsweetened chocolate (1 oz.)

Beat with rotary beater. Remove from heat and beat in gelatin. Beat until smooth. Chill until mixture begins to set. Then stir in . . .
- ¼ lb. marshmallows (11-16), cut-up
- ¼ cup ground nuts, if desired

Fold in . . .
- 2 egg whites, beaten stiff
- 1 cup whipping cream, whipped stiff

Chill 4 hr. Serve in sherbet glasses.

AMOUNT: 8 servings.

FRUIT TAPIOCA (⚷ Recipe)

Refreshing!

Mix in saucepan .
- 2½ cups fruit juice and water
- ½ cup sugar
- ¼ cup quick cooking tapioca
- ¼ tsp. salt

Cook over low heat, stirring constantly, until mixture boils. Remove from heat. Cool.

Fold in . . .
- 1 cup drained cut-up fruit

Spoon into dessert dishes.

AMOUNT: 6 servings.

STRAWBERRY TAPIOCA

Follow ⚷ recipe directly above—using 2½ cups strawberry juice (sweetened berries crushed and with water added) and, for the fruit, 1 cup sliced strawberries. Omit vanilla and add 1 tbsp. lemon juice.

FIG TAPIOCA

Follow ⚷ recipe for Fruit Tapioca above, using all water in place of fruit juice and water, and for the fruit this *Fig Mixture:*

Cook together until thick . . .
- 1 cup water
- ¾ cup brown sugar
- 1 cup chopped figs

ORANGE MARSHMALLOW CREAM

Afternoon-out dessert contributed by Mrs. Earl Gammons of Washington, D. C.

Heat together in saucepan over low heat . . .
- 1 cup orange juice (with pulp)
- ¼ lb. marshmallows (11-16), cut-up

Stir until marshmallows are dissolved. Remove from heat. Cool. When partially set, fold in . . .
- ½ cup whipping cream, whipped stiff

Chill 4 hr. Serve in sherbet glasses. Garnish with fresh fruit or berries.

AMOUNT: 4 servings.

PINEAPPLE MARSHMALLOW CREAM

From "Homemaker of the Week," Mrs. J. Leo Clagett of Clarksburg, Maryland.

Follow recipe for Orange Marshmallow Cream above—*except,* in place of orange juice, use 1 cup crushed pineapple with ½ tbsp. lemon juice.

AMOUNT: 4 servings.

CUSTARD DESSERTS

Delightful ways to enjoy milk and eggs.

Some like them hot,
Some like them cold,
Spooned from the cup
Or turned out in a mold...

BAKED CUSTARD (🔑 Recipe)

Homey dessert enjoyed by tiny tots and grownups.

Beat slightly to mix . . . .
- **2 large eggs (or 4 egg yolks)**
- **⅓ cup sugar**
- **¼ tsp. salt**

Scald (crinkly film forms on top) . . . . **and pour into egg mixture**
- **2 cups milk**
- **nutmeg for flavoring**

Strain into 6 custard cups or a 1½-qt. casserole and set in pan of hot water (1″ up on cups). Sprinkle a little nutmeg over tops. Bake just until silver knife thrust into custard comes out clean. Immediately remove from heat. Serve cool or chilled in same cups on dessert plates.

NOTE: Add vanilla, if desired.

TEMPERATURE: 350° (mod. oven).

TIME: Bake 30 to 35 min.

AMOUNT: 6 servings.

MOLDED CUSTARD

Follow 🔑 recipe above—*except* use 3 eggs (or 6 egg yolks). Pour into buttered molds. Unmold onto serving dish.

BAKED CARAMEL CUSTARD

A hotel on the Bay of Naples served it on a silver platter under a glistening cover of spun caramelized sugar.

Caramelize (melt over low heat, stirring until brown) ½ cup sugar. Pour a little into each custard cup. Move cups about so that caramel will coat sides. When caramel is hard, fill cups with custard (follow recipe directly above for Molded Custard). When unmolded, melted caramel runs down sides forming a sauce.

MODERN RICE PUDDING

The good old taste, but quicker . . . easier.

Follow 🔑 recipe above—*except* increase sugar to ½ cup. Mix with . . .

- **2 cups cooked rice**
- **½ cup seedless raisins**

Pour into 1-qt. casserole (6½″) and set in pan of water (1″ deep). Sprinkle with nutmeg. Bake. Serve warm with cream.

TEMPERATURE: 350° (mod. oven).
TIME: Bake 1 hr. and 15 min.
AMOUNT: 6 servings.

All you have to do—

To make Old-Time Rice Pudding: bake it in slow oven 3 hr., stirring 3 times the first hour. Use ⅓ cup uncooked rice to 1 qt. milk, ⅓ cup sugar, ½ tsp. salt. . . nutmeg and grated lemon rind if desired.

All you have to do—

To make Custard Surprise: lift a spoonful of custard from center of individual baked custards, drop in a bit of jelly or jam; replace custard.

BAKED CHOCOLATE CUSTARD

Follow 🔑 recipe above—*except* add 1½ sq. unsweetened chocolate (1½ oz.) to milk before scalding. Before pouring into egg mixture, beat with rotary beater until smooth.

INDIAN PUDDING

The Puritan women learned to make it from the Indians. In New England, it always shared the old brick oven with Baked Beans.

Mix together . .
- **¼ cup corn meal (Indian meal)**
- **1 cup cold salted water (1 tsp. salt)**

Stir in . . .
- **2 cups scalded milk**

Bring to a boil and, stirring, boil 10 min.
Blend in a mixture of . . .
- **1 egg, well beaten**
- **¼ cup sugar**
- **½ cup molasses**
- **1 tbsp. butter**
- **1 tsp. cinnamon**
- **½ tsp. ginger**

Pour into buttered 1-qt. casserole (6½″).
Bake ½ hr. Stir in . . .
- **1 cup cold milk**

Bake 2 hr. It is soft, looks slightly curdled. Serve warm or cold with cream or ice cream.

TEMPERATURE: 300° (slow oven).
TIME: Bake 2½ hr.
AMOUNT: 6 servings.

SOFT CUSTARD (🔑 **Recipe**) *Delicate pudding or a sauce to dress up other desserts.*

Beat in top of 1-qt. double boiler....... 4 egg yolks (or 2 whole eggs)

Blend in.............................. 1/4 cup sugar, 1/4 tsp. salt, 1 tsp. vanilla

Pour in......................... 1 1/2 cups scalded milk

Cook over simmering (not boiling) water, stirring constantly. When custard coats silver spoon (thin coating), remove from heat. If custard should start to curdle, remove from heat and beat vigorously with rotary beater until smooth. Cool. Serve in sherbet glasses, topped with whipped cream; or use as a sauce over fruit, cake, or other desserts.

AMOUNT: 6 servings.

FLOATING ISLAND

Grandma called it "float," a company dessert presented in tall glass compote.

Follow 🔑 recipe above—*except* use 2 egg yolks and 1 whole egg instead of 4 egg yolks. Beat the 2 leftover egg whites stiff. Fold in gradually 4 tbsp. sugar. Drop this meringue as "islands" on custard in serving dish. Chill before serving.

STRAWBERRY FLOATING ISLAND

Pink "islands" on a sea of custard.

Follow recipe for Floating Island—and pour the custard over sweetened strawberries in bottom of serving dish. Fold 1/4 cup crushed sweetened strawberries into the meringue.

★ CARAMEL-COATED CUSTARD

Melt 1/2 cup confectioners' sugar in top of small (1-qt.) double boiler over direct heat. Stir constantly until medium brown. Stir in 2 tbsp. hot water. Remove from heat. Tip and turn boiler until caramel coats all sides. Chill.

Follow 🔑 recipe above—*except* use 6 egg yolks (or 3 eggs) to make custard firm enough to mold.

Pour into chilled caramel-coated boiler. Cover. Cook 45 min. over *simmering* water. Turn onto serving dish. The caramel runs down over sides forming a sauce.

CORNSTARCH CUSTARD

Mix together in saucepan . . .

- 1/4 cup sugar
- 2 tbsp. cornstarch
- 1/4 tsp. salt
- 1 egg (or 2 egg yolks)

Stir in gradually . . .

- 2 cups milk

Cook over low heat, stirring until mixture boils. Boil 1 min. Blend in . . .

- 1 tbsp. butter, if desired
- 1 1/2 tsp. vanilla

Chill. Serve in sherbet glasses with grape juice or any flavorful fruit juice.

AMOUNT: 6 servings.

CHOCOLATE PUDDING

Follow recipe for Cornstarch Custard above—*except* use 1/4 cup more sugar and add with the sugar 2 sq. unsweetened chocolate (2 oz.), shaved. Serve with cream.

CARAMEL PUDDING

Caramelize 1/2 cup sugar, add 1/2 cup boiling water. Stir, cook to a syrup. Use in place of half the sugar in Cornstarch Custard above. Pour the pudding over 2 marshmallows in each sherbet glass. Serve warm or cold, with cream, if desired.

PLAIN CORNSTARCH PUDDING

(Blanc Mange)

The French name means "White Food."

Follow recipe for Cornstarch Custard above—*except* use 1 tbsp. more cornstarch, omit egg, butter.

All you have to do—

To make a thick dessert sauce is: make Cornstarch Custard with only 1 tbsp. cornstarch. Call it French Cream.

BREAD CRUMB DESSERTS Odds and ends in delicious disguise.

OLD-FASHIONED BREAD PUDDING (Recipe) *Rich, crusty, raisin-filled.*

Heat to scalding .... **2 cups milk**
Pour over .... **4 cups coarse bread crumbs**
Cool and add ....
- **1/4 cup butter, melted**
- **1/2 cup sugar**
- **2 eggs, slightly beaten**
- **1/4 tsp. salt**
- **1/2 cup seeded raisins**
- **1 tsp. cinnamon or nutmeg**

Pour into buttered 1½-qt. casserole (7½″). Bake until silver knife inserted in pudding comes out clean. Serve warm, with or without Hard Sauce or cream.

TEMPERATURE: 350° (mod. oven).
TIME: Bake 40 to 45 min.
AMOUNT: 6 servings.

CUSTARD BREAD PUDDING

Follow recipe above—*except* increase milk to 4 cups; use only 2 cups bread crumbs. Omit raisins.

CHOCOLATE BREAD PUDDING

Follow recipe above—and melt 2 sq. unsweetened chocolate (2 oz.) in the milk. Flavor with vanilla or cinnamon. (Instead of chocolate, ⅔ cup cocoa may be blended with the sugar.)

All you have to do—

To make old-time QUEEN'S PUDDING: spread freshly baked bread pudding with tart jelly. Cover with meringue. Lightly brown in oven.

★ SPICED CRUMB PUDDING

Combine . . .
- **1 cup soft bread crumbs**
- **1 cup buttermilk**

Mix together thoroughly . . .
- **3 tbsp. butter**
- **1 cup brown sugar**
- **2 tbsp. molasses**

Stir in the bread mixture.

Sift together and stir in . . .
- **1/2 cup *sifted* GOLD MEDAL Flour**
- **1/2 tsp. salt**
- **1 tsp. soda**
- **1/2 tsp. cinnamon**
- **1/8 tsp. cloves**

Blend in . . .
- **1/2 cup raisins, cut-up**

Pour into greased 10x6x2″ baking dish. Bake. Serve hot with Satin Sauce.

TEMPERATURE: 350° (mod. oven).
TIME: Bake 20 to 25 min.
AMOUNT: 6 to 8 servings.

DANISH APPLE CAKE

Jean Hersholt's favorite for smörgasbords. Looks like pie. Refreshing fresh applesauce flavor with rich buttery crumbs.

Make 3 cups thick tart applesauce.

Sauté gently until evenly browned . . .
- **2 cups fine dry bread or zwieback crumbs in . . .**
- **3/4 cup butter or margarine**

Line bottom of *deep* 9″ pie pan with crumbs. Spread ⅓ of sauce over crumbs. Sprinkle with cinnamon. Add 2 more alternate layers sauce and cinnamon-sprinkled crumbs (crumbs on top). Bake. Serve hot or cold with whipped cream garnished with bits of jelly.

TEMPERATURE: 325° (slow mod. oven).
TIME: Bake 30 min.
AMOUNT: 10 servings.

QUICK BROWN BETTY

Delicious version of old favorite.

Mix together lightly in 10x6x2″ baking dish
- **3 cups chopped tart apples**
- **1½ cups coarse bread crumbs**
- **1/4 cup butter or margarine, melted**
- **1 cup brown sugar**

Sprinkle with . . .
- **1/2 tsp. cinnamon or nutmeg**

Pour over the top . . .
- **1/2 cup water**

Bake. Serve warm with cream or Hard Sauce.

TEMPERATURE: 325° (slow mod. oven).
TIME: Bake 45 to 50 min.
AMOUNT: 6 servings.

BLUSHING BETTY

Follow recipe directly above—*except* use diced unpeeled pink rhubarb instead of apples, white sugar instead of brown, omit water.

COTTAGE PUDDING (🔑 Recipe) *Fluffy, delicious, easy-to-make.*

Sift together into bowl ....
- **1¾ cups *sifted* GOLD MEDAL Flour**
- **2 tsp. baking powder**
- **½ tsp. salt**

Add ....
- **¼ cup soft shortening**
- **¾ cup sugar**
- **1 large egg**
- **¾ cup milk**
- **1 tsp. vanilla**

Beat with rotary beater or spoon until smooth. Pour into greased and floured 9″ sq. pan. Bake. Cut into 3″ squares. Serve warm with hot Vanilla, Lemon, Nutmeg, or Chocolate Sauce.

TEMPERATURE: 350° (mod. oven).

TIME: Bake 25 to 30 min.

AMOUNT: 9 servings.

VANILLA, LEMON, OR NUTMEG SAUCE

Mix together in saucepan . . .
- **1 cup sugar**
- **2 tbsp. cornstarch**

Stir in gradually . . .
- **2 cups boiling water**

Boil 1 min., stirring constantly. Stir in . . .
- **4 tbsp. butter**
- **2 tsp. vanilla or 2 tsp. lemon juice with 1 tbsp. grated lemon rind or 2 tsp. nutmeg**

Keep hot until time to serve.

THIN CHOCOLATE SAUCE

Follow recipe for Vanilla Sauce above—*except* add 2 sq. chocolate (2 oz.), cut-up, with the sugar. Use only 1 tsp. vanilla.

CINNAMON FLUFF

Mrs. Mary Putnam of Pine Bluff, Arkansas, describes her prize-winning dessert as "more delicate than cake."

Mix together thoroughly . . .
- **½ cup soft shortening**
- **⅔ cup sugar**
- **2 eggs**

Sift together . . .
- **1½ cups *sifted* GOLD MEDAL Flour**
- **2 *tbsp.* cinnamon**
- **1 tsp. baking powder**
- **1 tsp. soda**
- **½ tsp. salt**

Stir in alternately with . . .
- **1 cup sour milk**

Pour into greased and floured 9″ sq. pan. Rub together ½ cup sugar, 1 tbsp. butter, and 1 tbsp. cinnamon, and sprinkle over batter. Bake. Serve with cinnamon-flavored whipped cream or Lemon Sauce.

TEMPERATURE: 325° (slow mod. oven).

TIME: Bake 40 to 45 min.

AMOUNT: 9 servings.

★ GOLDEN COTTAGE PUDDING

Surprise! Guess what's in it! Moist, goozly!

Follow 🔑 recipe above—*except* increase shortening to ⅓ cup, sugar to 1 cup. In place of vanilla, use lemon extract. Blend in 1 cup finely shredded carrots, measured lightly. Bake 30 to 35 min. Serve hot with hot

GOLDEN SAUCE

Mix together in saucepan . . .
- **1 cup sugar**
- **4 tbsp. GOLD MEDAL Flour**

Stir in gradually . . .
- **1½ cups boiling water**

Boil 1 min. Remove from heat. Stir in . . .
- **3 tbsp. finely shredded carrot**
- **2 tbsp. lemon juice**
- **2 tbsp. orange juice**
- **4 tbsp. soft butter**

CHERRY CARNIVAL

Rich, luscious cherry favorite from Mrs. Jessie Smith of Galesburg, Illinois.

Follow 🔑 recipe above—*except* increase sugar to 1 cup, omit vanilla. Blend in 2 cups cut-up well drained pitted sour cherries (#2 can, save juice), and ½ cup cut-up nuts. Bake 30 to 40 min. Serve hot with hot

CLEAR RED SAUCE

Mix together in saucepan . . .
- **½ cup sugar**
- **2 tbsp. cornstarch**

Stir in gradually . . .
- **1 cup boiling water**
- **¾ cup juice from cherries or raspberries**

Boil 1 min., stirring constantly. Stir in . . .
- **¼ tsp. almond extract**
- **few drops red coloring, if desired**

Keep hot until time to serve.

PUDDING DESSERTS

Where pudding and sauce bake in same dish.

LEMON CAKE PUDDING (🔑 Recipe)

Made with lemon, lime, orange, or pineapple.

Sift together into mixing bowl........
- 1/4 cup *sifted* GOLD MEDAL Flour
- 1 cup sugar
- 1/4 tsp. salt

Stir in..............................
- 1 1/2 tsp. grated lemon rind (1 lemon)
- 1/4 cup lemon juice
- 2 egg yolks, well beaten
- 1 cup milk

Fold in..............................
- 2 egg whites, stiffly beaten

Pour into 1-qt. casserole (6 1/2″) or 6 custard cups. Set in pan of water (1″ deep). Bake. Serve warm or cold, with or without whipped cream.

TEMPERATURE: 350° (mod. oven).

TIME: Bake 50 min.

AMOUNT: 6 servings.

LIME CAKE PUDDING

Follow 🔑 recipe above—*except*, in place of lemon, use lime juice and rind.

ORANGE CAKE PUDDING

Follow 🔑 recipe above—*except*, in place of lemon, use orange juice and rind.

PINEAPPLE CAKE PUDDING

Follow 🔑 recipe above—*except* use only 1/2 cup milk, only 1 tbsp. lemon juice. Add 1/4 cup drained crushed pineapple and 1/4 cup pineapple juice.

For a refreshing warm weather dessert: serve these puddings cold.

LAST-MINUTE DATE RAPTURES

Delicate, luscious with fruit . . . fresh from the oven . . . they really are raptures.

Sift together into bowl . . .
- 1 cup *sifted* GOLD MEDAL Flour
- 1/2 tsp. baking powder
- 1/2 tsp. soda
- 1/2 tsp. salt

Add . . .
- 1/4 cup soft shortening
- 1/2 cup sugar
- 1 egg
- 1/3 cup buttermilk or sour milk
- 1 tbsp. grated orange rind

Beat with rotary beater until smooth.

Blend in . . .
- 1 cup cut-up dates

Pour into greased muffin cups (2/3 full). Bake.

TEMPERATURE: 350° (mod. oven).

TIME: Bake 25 to 30 min.

AMOUNT: 6 servings.

Serve hot. Pour over them

SWEETENED ORANGE JUICE

Mix together . . .
- 3/4 cup strained orange juice
- 1/4 cup sugar

No cooking; the juice soaks into cakes.

All you have to do—

To keep pudding sauce hot until time to serve: let stand over hot water.

HOT FUDGE PUDDING

We are grateful to Mrs. Oswin Keifer of Bostwick, Nebraska, for this rich tasting chocolate dessert . . . easy to make, inexpensive.

Sift together into bowl . . .
- 1 cup *sifted* GOLD MEDAL Flour
- 2 tsp. baking powder
- 1/4 tsp. salt
- 3/4 cup sugar
- 2 tbsp. cocoa

Stir in . . .
- 1/2 cup milk
- 2 tbsp. shortening, melted

Blend in . . .
- 1 cup chopped nuts

Spread in 9″ sq. pan.

Sprinkle with mixture of . . .
- 1 cup brown sugar
- 4 tbsp. cocoa

Pour over entire batter . . .
- 1 3/4 cups *hot* water

Bake. During baking, cake mixture rises to top and chocolate sauce settles to bottom. Invert square of pudding on dessert plates. Dip sauce from pan over each. Or the entire pudding can be inverted in a deep serving platter. Serve warm, with or without whipped cream.

TEMPERATURE: 350° (mod. oven).

TIME: Bake 45 min.

AMOUNT: 9 servings.

UPSIDE-DOWN CAKE (Recipe) *Handsome dessert to serve at table.*

First, prepare the pan:

Melt ⅓ cup butter in heavy 10" skillet or baking dish. Sprinkle ½ cup brown sugar evenly over butter. Arrange drained cooked fruit in attractive pattern on the butter-sugar coating.

Make the Cake Batter (*see right*) and pour it over fruit. Bake until wooden pick thrust into center of cake comes out clean. Immediately turn upside-down on serving plate. Do not remove pan for a few minutes. Brown sugar mixture will run down over cake instead of clinging to pan. Serve warm with plain or whipped cream.

CAKE BATTER

Beat until thick and lemon-colored (5 min.)
  2 eggs
Gradually beat in . . .
  ⅔ cup sugar
Beat in all at once . .
  6 tbsp. juice from fruit
  1 tsp. flavoring
Sift together and beat in all at once . . .
  1 cup *sifted* GOLD MEDAL Flour
    or SOFTASILK Cake Flour
  ⅓ tsp. baking powder
  ¼ tsp. salt

TEMPERATURE: 350° (mod. oven).

TIME: Bake 45 min.

PINEAPPLE UPSIDE-DOWN CAKE

Follow recipe above—using vanilla for flavoring. Arrange slices of pineapple over butter-sugar coating, and garnish with maraschino cherries and pecan halves as shown in picture below

★ PRUNE UPSIDE-DOWN CAKE

Follow recipe above—using lemon extract for flavoring. Arrange very large drained pitted cooked prunes (not sweetened) over butter-sugar coating. Garnish with walnut halves as shown in picture below.

PEACH OR APRICOT UPSIDE-DOWN CAKE

Follow recipe above—using lemon and vanilla for flavoring. Arrange drained canned peach or apricot halves hollow-side-down over butter-sugar coating with blanched almond in center of each. Sprinkle moist shredded coconut around fruit as in picture below.

All you have to do—

For a simpler Peach Upside-Down Cake: use sliced cooked peaches for the fruit.

Apple Pan Dowdy, an early apple cobbler; *Apple or Berry Slump,* the crust slumped down when the fruit cooked; *Apple or Berry Grunt,* made a gurgling noise as it steamed in the big kettle on the crane.

SHORTCAKE (Recipe) *The good old-time American dessert . . . still first choice.*

	Large Shortcake	*Small Shortcake*
Sift together	2 cups *sifted* GOLD MEDAL Flour	1 cup
	2 tbsp. sugar	1 tbsp.
	3 tsp. baking powder	1½ tsp.
	1 tsp. salt	½ tsp.
Cut in fine with pastry blender	6 tbsp. shortening	3 tbsp.
Stir in to make soft dough	⅔ to ¾ cup milk	⅓ to ½ cup

Knead lightly. Pat ½ of dough into well greased 8″ round layer pan. Dot with butter. Pat out other half on top. Bake. Split layers apart. Spoon sweetened fruit (not chilled) between and on top. Serve warm with whipped or plain cream.

TEMPERATURE: 450° (hot oven).

TIME: Bake 12 to 15 min.

AMOUNT: 6 servings. 3 servings.

All you have to do—

To make Individual Shortcakes: roll dough ½″ thick. Dot with butter. Fold over. Cut with 3″ cutter. Place a little apart on baking sheet.

STRAWBERRY OR RASPBERRY SHORTCAKE

Follow recipe above—using 1 to 1½ qt. berries. Crush slightly with back of spoon. Add ¾ to 1 cup sugar. Let stand at room temperature 30 min.

FRESH PEACH SHORTCAKE

Follow recipe above—using 1 qt. sliced peaches with 1 cup sugar.

★ STRAWBERRY LONG-CAKE

Luscious . . . makes strawberries go a long way.

Make Small Shortcake dough above—*except* increase sugar to 3 tbsp. and add 1 egg with the milk. Spread in 12x7½x2″ greased baking dish. Cover with 1 qt. sweetened strawberries and juice. Mix ¼ cup soft butter, ¼ cup sugar, 3 tbsp. flour. Drop here and there on fruit. Bake at 400° (mod. hot oven) 35 to 40 min. Serve warm with cream.

AMOUNT: 8 servings.

FRESH FRUIT COBBLER (Recipe) *"Cobble up" means put together in a hurry.*

Mix together in saucepan	⅔ to 1 cup sugar
	1 tbsp. cornstarch
Stir in gradually	1 cup boiling water
Bring to boil. Boil 1 min., stirring constantly, then add	3 cups fruit with any juice on them
Pour into 10x6x2″ baking dish.	
Dot with	½ tbsp. butter
Sprinkle with	½ tsp. cinnamon

Make Small Shortcake dough above—using ½ cup milk. Drop by spoonfuls onto fruit. Bake. Serve warm with the juice and cream.

TEMPERATURE: 400° (mod. hot oven).

TIME: Bake 30 min.

AMOUNT: 6 servings.

PEACH OR APRICOT COBBLER

Follow recipe directly above—using sliced peeled peaches or apricots with 1 cup sugar.

To make cobbler with canned fruit: Use 2½ cups canned fruit (#2 can), sweetened to taste. Use the juice in place of the sugar and water.

BLACKBERRY OR BOYSENBERRY COBBLER

Follow recipe directly above—using 3 cups berries with ¾ cup sugar.

FRESH CHERRY COBBLER

Follow recipe above—using sweet cherries. Add 3 drops almond extract.

FRUIT ROLL (🔑 Recipe) *Fruit rolled in fluffy biscuit blanket, baked in syrup.*

Place in 13 x 9″ oblong pan............. 1½ cups sugar, 2 cups water

Cook 5 min. Make Large Shortcake dough (*p. 224*). Roll ⅓″ thick into an oblong 6 x 12″. Spread with..... 3 cups cut-up fruit

Dot with............................ 1 tbsp. butter

Sprinkle with........................ ½ tsp. cinnamon

Roll up into a long roll. Pinch edge into roll to seal. Slice (1½″ thick) and quickly place slices cut-side-down in the pan of boiling syrup. Or lay entire roll in hot syrup. Bake immediately. Serve warm, with whipped cream.

TEMPERATURE: 450° (hot oven).

TIME: Bake 20 to 25 min.

AMOUNT: 8 servings.

NOTE: Cut with string or very sharp knife.

RHUBARB-AND-STRAWBERRY ROLL

Follow 🔑 recipe above—using 2 cups cut-up rhubarb (½″), 1 cup cut-up strawberries sprinkled with ½ cup sugar.

FRESH CHERRY ROLL

Follow 🔑 recipe above—using pitted sweet cherries for the fruit. Sour cherries should be sprinkled with ½ cup extra sugar.

CANNED FRUIT ROLL

Follow 🔑 recipe above—using 2 cups fruit or berries (#2 can). Drain fruit; use juice as part of syrup.

★ SOUTHERN PEACH SKILLET PIE

The recipe for this luscious, homey dessert was given me by a gracious, charming educator, Miss Wylle B. McNeal.

Make the Small Shortcake dough (*p. 224*). Roll or pat out dough ¼″ thick. Pat into heavy 8″ skillet, allowing some of dough to hang over edge. Add 6 fresh peaches, peeled and sliced.

Mix . . .
½ cup sugar
½ tsp. salt
¼ tsp. cinnamon

Sprinkle over fruit. Dot with . . .
1½ tbsp. butter

Fold hanging dough toward center, leaving a little space uncovered. Bake.

TEMPERATURE: 425° (hot oven).

TIME: Bake 25 min.

AMOUNT: 6 servings.

APPLE ROLL

Quick, easy apple dumplings.

Follow 🔑 recipe above—using 3 cups chopped tart juicy apples.

CINNAMON APPLE PUFFS

Streamlined version of Apple Roll.

Make half of syrup as in 🔑 recipe above. Add 6 apples, sliced. Make Small Shortcake dough (*p. 224*). Drop by spoonfuls over apples in 6 mounds. Make a dent in each mound. Drop in a little butter, sugar, and cinnamon, and bake. Serve warm with cream.

All you have to do—

To give festive color to Apple Roll or Puffs: use a few red cinnamon candies in place of cinnamon, or add ½ tsp. red food coloring to syrup.

MAGIC PEACH DESSERT

Melt about ½ cup currant jelly (⅔ of custard cup). Place a large custard cup upside-down in a round 8″ baking dish (cup and baking dish *must* be same height). Arrange 5 or 6 peeled whole peaches (fresh or canned) around cup. Pour hot jelly over peaches. Cover with Small Shortcake dough (*p. 224*). Press edge of dough to inside of baking dish to seal *airtight*. Bake at 400° (mod. hot oven) 30 min. Let stand 3 min.

Place large serving plate over casserole. Invert quickly. The peaches rest on juice-tinged pastry. The custard cup, as if by magic, holds all the sauce. Offer cream to dip over dessert with the sauce.

AMOUNT: 5 or 6 servings.

GINGERBREAD DESSERTS Popular today as in ancient Greece and Rome.

Early American colonists made gingerbread much as we do today. When Lafayette returned to America in 1784, he went to Fredricksburg to visit George Washington's mother. She served him mint julep with "spiced gingerbrede." Her recipe included "West India molasses," a "wine glass of brandy," and "the juice and rind of orange" in addition to the usual ingredients.

FAVORITE GINGERBREAD (🔑 Recipe) *Deliciously rich, black, and moist. Grandma knew it as "Fort Atkinson Gingerbread" in the popular old brown covered* GOLD MEDAL *Cook Book that was a treasure trove for brides in the 1870's.*

Mix together thoroughly	½ cup soft shortening 2 tbsp. sugar 1 egg
Blend in	1 cup dark New Orleans molasses 1 cup boiling water
Sift together and stir in (beating until smooth)	2¼ cups *sifted* GOLD MEDAL Flour 1 tsp. soda ½ tsp. salt 1 tsp. ginger 1 tsp. cinnamon

Pour into well greased and floured 9″ sq. pan. Bake. Cut into 3″ squares in pan. Keep hot and serve piping hot with sweetened whipped cream, or with applesauce, chocolate sauce, or any of the toppings given below.

TEMPERATURE: 325° (slow mod. oven).

TIME: Bake 45 to 50 min.

AMOUNT: 9 servings.

GINGERBREAD WITH APRICOT GLAZE

Mix 2½ cups cooked apricots with juice (#2 can), 1 cup sugar, ⅓ cup boiling water. Boil until thick and smooth like jam. Cool. Cover top of hot gingerbread with slices of banana. Pour apricot glaze over all.

HADDON HALL GINGERBREAD

Ideal for "dessert and coffee" party.

Soften white cream cheese with a little cream. Beat until fluffy. Split each serving of hot Gingerbread, drop cheese between layers. Top with dab of cheese, add

FLUFFY LEMON SAUCE

Mix together in saucepan . . .
- ½ cup sugar
- 2 tbsp. cornstarch
- ⅛ tsp. nutmeg

Stir in gradually . . .
- 1 cup boiling water

Boil 1 min., stirring constantly.

Stir in . . .
- 1 tbsp. butter
- 4 tbsp. lemon juice
- 2 tsp. grated lemon rind

Gradually blend into . . .
- 1 egg, well beaten

DE LUXE GINGERBREAD

(Old-Time Molasses Cake)

Sweet and dark, really cake-like. Perfected by Ruth Sweat when she was in charge of our early test kitchen.

Follow 🔑 recipe above—*except* use ½ cup sugar instead of 2 tbsp. sugar and ¾ cup dark molasses instead of 1 cup. Use 1 cup sour milk instead of water.

★ GINGERBREAD RING WITH APPLESAUCE

Glamour with old-time taste appeal.

Bake either Favorite or De Luxe Gingerbread in 9″ ring mold. Serve it hot and fragrant with bowl of fresh applesauce in center. Offer whipped cream or ice cream with Gingerbread and Applesauce.

FAVORITE OLD-TIME PUDDINGS

on a red fringed tablecloth with great grandmother's china.

New England Plum Pudding with Hard Sauce — Strawberry Shortcake
Squares of Favorite Gingerbread — Sauce — Plum Duff — Cherry Roll

STEAMED PUDDING DESSERTS The old-fashioned art of steaming.

1 (1) A steamer with holes in the bottom, and a tight fitting cover to hold in steam. (2) A deep kettle that holds water to last through the entire steaming, or a deep well cooker with wire frame to hold pudding mold.

2 (1) Tube center mold allows steam to quickly reach center of pudding. (2) Turk's head mold with spiral fluting. (3) Round can (coffee can, etc.) or bowl. (4) Individual molds, custard cups, or jelly glasses.

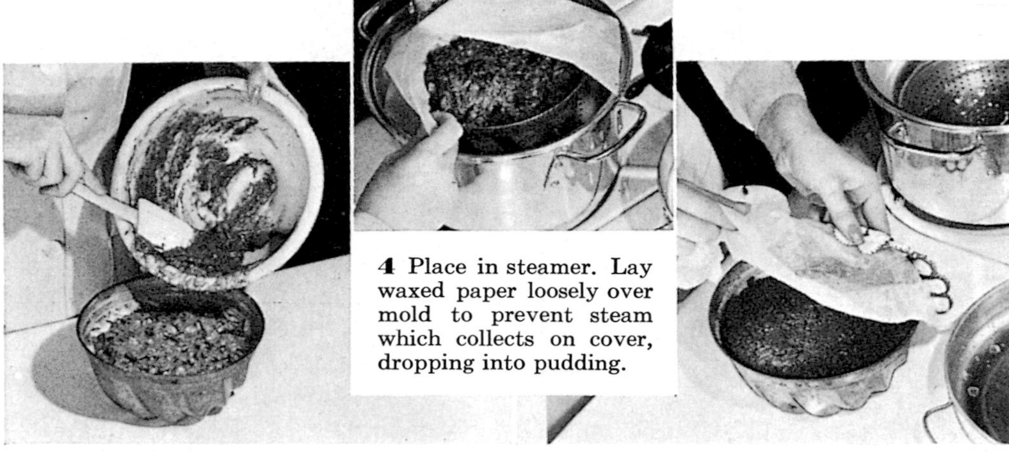

4 Place in steamer. Lay waxed paper loosely over mold to prevent steam which collects on cover, dropping into pudding.

3 Pour pudding batter into generously greased mold. Fill about ⅔ full.

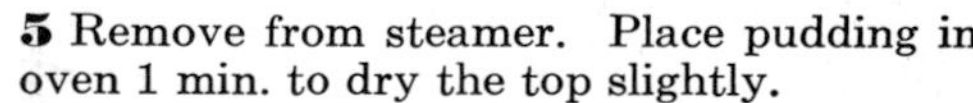

5 Remove from steamer. Place pudding in oven 1 min. to dry the top slightly.

6 Loosen at one side to let in air. Turn out on hot serving dish. The flaming pudding of old had heated brandy over it. A lighted match touched off the brandy.

7 The new way is to soak lumps of sugar in lemon or orange extract, place around pudding. Touch match to one lump and the pudding is encircled with bright flames as above.

An old Yorkshire tradition: "In as many homes as you eat plum pudding in the 12 days following Christmas, so many happy months will you have during the year."

Thrifty colonial homemakers evolved new variations. Modern methods and equipment have made puddings lighter, fluffier, and more delicious.

ENGLISH PLUM PUDDING

The best of all the real English recipes for plum pudding we ever tested.

Sift together . . .
- 1 cup *sifted* GOLD MEDAL Flour
- 1 tsp. soda
- 1 tsp. salt
- 1 tsp. cinnamon
- 1/4 tsp. nutmeg
- 3/4 tsp. mace

Mix in . . .
- 1 1/2 cups finely cut raisins (1/2 lb.)
- 1 1/2 cups currants (1/2 lb.), plumped
- 3/4 cup finely cut citron (1/4 lb.)
- 3/4 cup finely cut candied orange and lemon peel
- 1/2 cup chopped walnuts
- 1 1/2 cups coarse soft bread crumbs

Mix together and blend in . . .
- 2 cups ground suet (1/2 lb.)
- 1 cup brown sugar
- 3 eggs, beaten
- 6 tbsp. currant jelly
- 1/4 cup fruit juice (old recipes called for brandy or sherry)

Pour into a well greased 2-qt. mold (or 2 1-qt. molds). Steam. Serve piping hot with Hard Sauce (*below*).↘

TIME: Steam 6 hr.

AMOUNT: 16 servings.

NEW ENGLAND PLUM PUDDING

Suet Pudding, not as rich as earlier type.

Sift together . . .
- 1 3/4 cups *sifted* GOLD MEDAL Flour
- 1/2 tsp. soda
- 1 tsp. salt
- 1 tsp. cinnamon

Mix in . . .
- 1/2 cup cut-up seeded raisins
- 1/2 cup finely cut citron

Mix and blend in . . .
- 1/2 cup ground suet
- 1/2 cup sour milk or sweet milk
- 1/2 cup molasses

Pour into a well greased 1-qt. mold. Steam. Serve piping hot with Fluffy Hard Sauce (*see right*↗).

TIME: Steam 3 hr.

AMOUNT: 8 servings.

★ QUAKER PLUM PUDDING

This delectable pudding dated 1790 came down from "Friend Hannah." The most popular of all at many of our family dinners today.

Pour . . .
- 1 cup milk

over . . .
- 3 cups coarse soft bread crumbs

Blend in . . .
- 1/2 cup shortening, melted
- 1/2 cup molasses

Sift together . . .
- 1 cup *sifted* GOLD MEDAL Flour
- 1 tsp. soda
- 1 tsp. salt
- 2 tsp. cinnamon
- 1/4 tsp. *each* allspice and cloves

Stir into bread crumb mixture with . . .
- 1/2 cup cut-up seeded raisins
- 1/2 cup finely cut citron

Pour into a well greased 1-qt. mold. Steam. Serve piping hot with Sauce O'Velvet (*below*).

TIME: Steam 3 hr.

AMOUNT: 8 servings.

ORANGE MARMALADE PUDDING

From Mrs. Lura E. Lonquist of Stockton, California. A California version with delightful New World flavor.

Follow recipe for Quaker Plum Pudding above—*except*, in place of molasses and fruit, use 1 cup orange marmalade; omit spices. Serve with Foamy Sauce (*p. 230*).

HARD SAUCE

Cream until soft 1/2 cup butter. Blend in gradually 1 1/2 cups *sifted* confectioners' sugar and 2 tsp. vanilla.

FLUFFY HARD SAUCE

Mix 1 beaten egg white into Hard Sauce.

SAUCE O'VELVET

Cream until soft 1/2 cup butter. Blend in gradually 1 1/2 cups *sifted* confectioners' sugar. Mix in 2 beaten egg whites, 1/2 tsp. vanilla, and 1 tbsp. desired flavoring. (The old recipe called for sherry.)

DOWN EAST PUDDING (🗝 **Recipe**) *Economical, but delicious and satisfying.*

Pour	1 cup boiling water
over	1 cup cut-up raisins or cranberries 2 tbsp. shortening
Beat well	1 egg
Stir in	½ cup sugar ½ cup molasses
Blend in fruit mixture.	
Sift together and stir in	1½ cups *sifted* GOLD MEDAL Flour 1 tsp. salt 1 tsp. soda

Pour into well greased 1-qt. mold. Steam. Serve piping hot with Foamy Sauce (*below*) or any desired sauce.

TIME: Steam 2 hr.

AMOUNT: 8 servings.

FOAMY SAUCE

In top of double boiler, beat 1 egg. Blend in 1 cup *sifted* confectioners' sugar, ½ cup soft butter, and 1 tsp. vanilla. Keep over hot water until time to serve.

FIG PUDDING

From the famous old Beaumont Inn at Harrodsburg, Kentucky.

Follow 🗝 recipe above—*except*, in place of raisins, use cut-up figs; and use 1 cup sugar in place of molasses and sugar. Add 1 cup cut-up nuts.

DATE PUDDING

Follow 🗝 recipe above—*except*, in place of raisins, use cut-up dates; and use 1 cup brown sugar in place of molasses and sugar. Add ½ cup chopped nuts and 1 tsp. grated lemon rind.

★ PLUM DUFF (Dark)

Moist, fruity, yet delicate and light. From Mrs. E. A. Parker of San Francisco, California, who knows elegant food.

Beat well . . .
- 2 eggs

Blend in . . .
- 1 cup brown sugar
- ½ cup shortening, melted
- 2 cups well drained cut-up pitted cooked prunes

Sift together and stir in . . .
- 1 cup *sifted* GOLD MEDAL Flour
- ½ tsp. salt
- 1 tsp. soda

Pour into well greased 1-qt. mold. Steam. Serve hot with Creamy Sauce (*above*).

TIME: Steam 1 hr.

AMOUNT: 8 servings.

CREAMY SAUCE

Beat 1 egg until foamy. Blend in ⅓ cup melted butter, 1½ cups *sifted* confectioners' sugar, and 1 tsp. vanilla. Fold in 1 cup whipping cream, whipped stiff.

CHOCOLATE PUDDING

Many were tried, this one chosen . . . brought in by Dorothy Elliott of our own Staff.

Beat well with rotary beater . . .
- 1 egg
- 1 cup sugar
- 2 tbsp. soft butter
- 2 sq. unsweetened chocolate, melted

Sift together . . .
- 1¾ cups *sifted* GOLD MEDAL Flour
- 1 tsp. salt
- ¼ tsp. cream of tartar
- ¼ tsp. soda

Beat in alternately with . . .
- 1 cup milk

Pour into greased 1-qt. mold. Steam. Serve hot with Creamy Sauce (*above*).

TIME: Steam 2 hr.

AMOUNT: 8 servings.

SNOWBALLS

Beat together with rotary beater . . .
- 2 egg whites
- 1 cup sugar
- ½ cup soft shortening (part butter)
- 1 tsp. vanilla

Sift together . . .
- 2¼ cups *sifted* GOLD MEDAL Flour
- 3½ tsp. baking powder
- ½ tsp. salt

Beat in alternately with . . .
- 1 cup milk

Pour into 8 well greased cups. Steam. Serve hot with Clear Red Sauce (*p. 221*).

TIME: Steam 1 hr.

AMOUNT: 8 servings.

CREAM PUFFS (🔑 Recipe) *French-born delicacy . . . crisp, hollow.*

Heat to boiling point in saucepan . . .
- **1 cup water**
- **½ cup butter**

Stir in . . .
- **1 cup *sifted* GOLD MEDAL Flour**

Stir constantly over low heat until mixture leaves the pan and forms into a ball (about 1 min.). Remove from heat. Cool.

Beat in, 1 at a time . . .
- **4 eggs**

Beat mixture until smooth and velvety. Drop from spoon onto ungreased baking sheet (*see pictures below*). Bake until dry. Allow to cool slowly.

TEMPERATURE: 400° (mod. hot oven).
TIME: Bake 45 to 50 min.
AMOUNT: 8 large puffs.

1 Stir constantly until mixture leaves the pan and forms a ball. Cool. Beat in the eggs, one at a time. Beat until velvety.

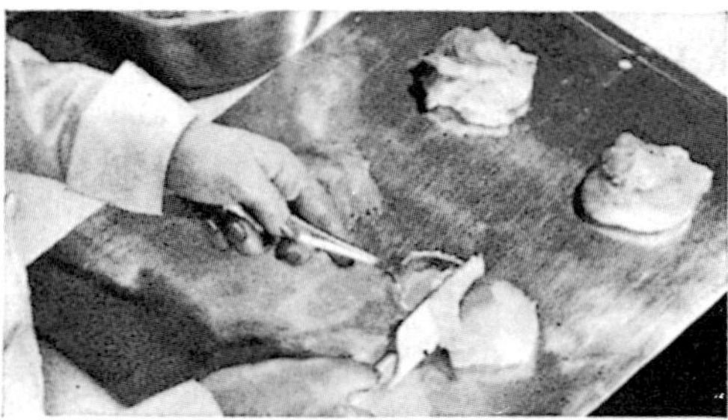

2 Drop from spoon onto baking sheet forming 8 mounds 3″ apart. Bake until puffed, golden brown, and dry. Allow to cool slowly, away from drafts.

3 Cut off tops with sharp knife. Scoop out any filaments of soft dough. Fill with sweetened whipped cream. Replace tops. Dust with confectioners' sugar. Serve cold.

CHOCOLATE ÉCLAIRS

Follow 🔑 recipe above—*except* put dough through pastry tube, or shape with spatula into fingers 4″ long and 1″ wide. Fill with Rich Custard Filling (*at right*), and frost with Thin Chocolate Icing.
AMOUNT: 12 eclairs.

★ FRUIT-FILLED CREAM PUFFS

Fold stiffly whipped cream into sweetened cut-up fresh fruit (strawberries, raspberries, sweet cherries, peaches, etc.). Use ¾ cup fruit, ¼ cup sugar, and ¾ cup whipping cream. Fill Cream Puffs with the mixture.

PETITS CHOUX (Midget Puffs)

Three on a plate . . . a dessert of distinction.

Follow 🔑 recipe above—*except* make 18 tiny puffs the size of a walnut. Bake 30 min. Fill with Rich Custard Filling (*above*). Frost with Thin Chocolate Icing.

CUSTARD-FILLED PUFFS

Fill Cream Puffs with

RICH CUSTARD FILLING

Mix together in saucepan . . .
- **½ cup sugar**
- **½ tsp. salt**
- **6 tbsp. GOLD MEDAL Flour**

Stir in . . .
- **2 cups top milk (or milk and cream)**

Cook over low heat, stirring until it boils. Boil 1 min. Remove from heat. Stir a little of this mixture into . . .
- **4 egg yolks (or 2 eggs), beaten**

Blend into hot mixture in saucepan. Bring to boiling point. Cool and blend in . . .
- **2 tsp. vanilla or other flavoring**

ICE CREAM PUFFS

Fill Cream Puffs with ice cream. Serve with appropriate sauce: chocolate sauce with peppermint ice cream, butterscotch sauce with burnt almond ice cream.

TORTE DESSERTS Special desserts of Old World elegance.

Torte is the old German name for a special type of rich dessert . . . compact and flat rather than high and fluffy. Made light with eggs, the bread crumbs or ground nuts take the place of flour.

★ DATE AND NUT TORTE

Beat thoroughly . . .
- **4 eggs**

Beat in gradually . . .
- **1 cup sugar**

Mix together and stir in . . .
- **1 cup fine dry bread crumbs**
- **1 tsp. baking powder**

Stir in . . .
- **2 cups finely cut pitted dates**
- **1 cup cut-up walnuts**

Spread in well greased 9″ sq. pan. Bake until set. Cut in oblongs 2x3″. Serve cool with whipped cream or ice cream.

TEMPERATURE: 350° (mod. oven).

TIME: Bake 35 min.

AMOUNT: 12 servings.

BLITZ TORTE (Lightning Cake)

Beautiful . . . the meringue top encrusted with sugar and toasted almonds.

Mix together thoroughly . . .
- **½ cup soft shortening**
- **¾ cup *sifted* confectioners' sugar**

Beat in . . .
- **4 egg yolks, well beaten**

Sift together and stir in . . .
- **1 cup *sifted* GOLD MEDAL Flour**
- **1 tsp. baking powder**
- **¼ tsp. salt**

Stir in . . .
- **3 tbsp. milk**

Spread batter in 2 greased and floured round 8″ layer pans.

For Meringue, beat until frothy . . .
- **4 egg whites**

Beat in gradually . . .
- **1 cup sugar (half confectioners')**

Spread half of meringue over batter in each pan. Sprinkle each with half of . . .
- **½ cup shaved blanched almonds**
- **2 tbsp. sugar**

Bake until cake tests "done" and meringue is set. Cool. Then remove from pans. Place one layer on serving plate *meringue-side-up*. Spread with Rich Custard Filling (*p. 231*). Place other layer on top *meringue-side-up*. If desired, pipe with sweetened whipped cream.

TEMPERATURE: 325° (slow mod. oven).

TIME: Bake 35 to 40 min.

AMOUNT: 12 servings.

CHEESE CAKE (Torte)

Epicures say it's the most elegant cheese cake ever tasted. First enjoyed at a buffet supper at the Bob Rypinski's in Pasadena. The recipe comes from Mrs. Rheba Holloway, Sterling Holloway's mother.

Cream well to soften . . .
- **8 3-oz. pkg. white cream cheese**

Beat until stiff . . .
- **4 egg whites**

Blend in . . .
- **1 cup sugar**

Combine with cheese. Add . . .
- **1 tsp. vanilla**

Pour into 8″ spring form pan 3″ deep, buttered and dusted with . . .
- **⅔ cup zwieback crumbs (4 rusks)**

Bake at 350° (mod. oven) 25 min.

Mix together and spread over top . . .
- **2 cups thick sour cream (fresh) (1 pt.)**
- **2 tbsp. sugar**
- **½ tsp. vanilla**

Sprinkle ⅓ cup toasted shaved blanched almonds on top. Bake 5 min. longer at 475° (very hot oven). Chill 2 hr. If desired, garnish with fresh fruits.

GRAHAM CRACKER TORTE

Mix together . . .
- **16 graham crackers, rolled fine**
- **½ cup butter or margarine, melted**
- **½ cup sugar**
- **¼ tsp. cinnamon**

Reserve ½ cup for topping. Pat remainder into deep 9″ pie pan. Bake at 300° (slow oven) 10 min. Pour cooled Vanilla Cream Pie Filling into the cooled crust.

Make Meringue of . . .
- **3 egg whites, beaten until stiff**
- **¼ tsp. cream of tartar**
- **½ cup sugar, beaten in gradually**

Spread meringue over cream filling. Sprinkle with remaining crumb mixture. Bake until delicately browned. Serve cool.

TEMPERATURE: 400° (mod. hot oven).

TIME: Bake 8 to 10 min.

AMOUNT: 8 servings.

CHOCOLATE VIENNA TORTE (Recipe) *Easy to make . . . like a Chocolate Chip Sponge Cake, but not as moist. Ideal with cream filling.*

Beat until thick and lemon-colored. . . .	6 egg yolks
Beat in half (½ cup) of.	1 cup sugar
Sift together and stir in.	¾ cup *sifted* GOLD MEDAL Flour 1 tsp. baking powder 1 tsp. salt
Beat until stiff (holds a point).	6 egg whites ½ tsp. cream of tartar
Beat in gradually the remaining sugar. Beat until very stiff and glossy.	
Gently fold in.	¾ cup grated unsweetened chocolate 1 tsp. vanilla

Carefully fold in egg yolk mixture. Pour into two round 9″ layer pans lined with greased paper. Bake until, when touched lightly with finger, no imprint remains. Turn out of pans and immediately remove paper. Cool. Put together with flavored sweetened whipped cream, and top with the cream. Garnish with flakes of dark chocolate.

TEMPERATURE: 350° (mod. oven).
TIME: Bake 25 to 30 min.
AMOUNT: 16 servings.

All you have to do—

To make Whipped Cream Filling: soften ½ tsp. gelatin in 1 tbsp. cream or milk and dissolve over hot water. Whip until stiff 1 cup cold whipping cream. Beat in ¼ cup *sifted* confectioners' sugar, the cooled gelatin, and 1 tsp. of desired flavoring.

CARAMEL ALMOND VIENNA TORTE

Caramelize (melt in heavy skillet over low heat, stirring until brown) ¾ cup sugar. Add and cook, stirring until lumps are dissolved, ½ cup hot water.

Follow recipe for Chocolate Vienna Torte above—*except* stir 2 tbsp. of caramel mixture into egg yolk mixture. Instead of chocolate, fold ¾ cup finely chopped *toasted* almonds into the egg white mixture. Put cooled layers together with Whipped Cream Filling. Cover with

CARAMEL TOPPING

Add to caramel syrup in skillet . . .
- ½ cup sugar
- ¼ cup butter
- ¼ tsp. salt
- ½ cup milk

Stir until smooth. Cook over mod. heat, stirring occasionally, until mixture reaches soft ball stage, 234°. Add . . .
- ¼ cup cream

Cook again to 234°. When partially cool, (no stirring), pour over top of torte letting it drip down sides here and there.

★ **PECAN TORTE** (Recipe)

Rich, nutty, flat . . . not cake-like. Found on a very old plantation along the Bayou Teche of Louisiana by Mrs. T. M. Dupes of Tescott, Kansas.

Beat until thick and lemon-colored . . .
- 6 egg yolks

Beat in gradually half of . . .
- 1½ cups sugar

Mix together . . .
- 2 tbsp. GOLD MEDAL Flour
- 2 tsp. baking powder
- ¼ tsp. salt

Blend into . . .
- 3 cups very *finely* chopped pecans

Beat until stiff (holds a point) . . .
- 6 egg whites

Beat in gradually the remaining sugar. Carefully fold in egg yolk mixture, then the nut mixture. Pour into two round 9″ layer pans lined with greased paper. Bake until, when touched lightly with finger, no imprint remains. Cool. Spread Whipped Cream Filling between layers and over top and sides of cake, and pipe with sweetened whipped cream. Garnish with chocolate curls and pecan halves.

TEMPERATURE: 350° (mod. oven).
TIME: Bake 25 to 30 min.
AMOUNT: 16 servings.

BRAZIL NUT TORTE

Follow recipe above—*except* use Brazil nuts instead of pecans.

BAKED MERINGUE DESSERTS Elegant special occasion desserts.

MERINGUE TORTE (Schaum Torte) (🔑 Recipe) *German for "Foam Cake."*

Beat until stiff (holds a point) . . .
6 egg whites (3/4 cup)
Gradually beat in half (1 cup) of . . .
2 cups sugar
Beat in a little at a time (adding alternately with the remaining sugar) . . .
1 1/2 tsp. lemon juice or vinegar

Beat until very stiff and glossy. Bake (*see below*) until delicately browned and crusty. Cool. Remove from pan. Serve filled with ice cream and fresh berries or cut-up fruit.
TEMPERATURE: 275° (very slow oven).
TIME: Bake layers 60 min., shells 40 min.
AMOUNT: 12 servings.

1 Beat until very stiff and glossy. For tinted meringues, add a few drops of pink, yellow, or green coloring.

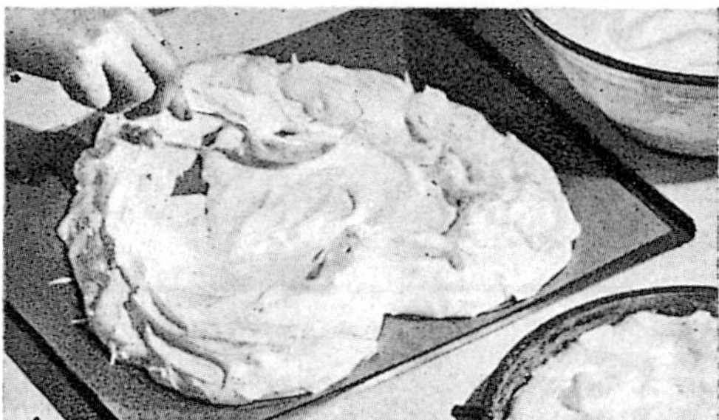

2 Spread in two 9″ round layer pans, lined with paper. For heart-shaped meringue, drop by spoonfuls in shape of heart drawn on paper (on baking sheet).

3 For an individual meringue shell, drop by small spoonfuls in a circle on brown paper on baking sheet, *or* heap into a high mound (hollow out top with back of spoon).

4 Add ice cream and sweetened fresh fruit to 1 layer, top with other layer. Decorate with sweetened whipped cream.

5 Fill individual meringue shells with ice cream. Top with fresh fruit, or hot chocolate, or butterscotch sauce.

★ ANGEL PIE (Lemon Schaum Torte) *The perfect finish for a hearty meal.*

Make 1/2 of 🔑 recipe above. Spread in a paper-lined 9″ round layer pan. Bake and cool. Whip until stiff 1 cup whipping cream. Spread half of it over Meringue Shell. Spread with cooled Lemon Custard Filling. Top with remaining whipped cream. Chill about 12 hr. before serving.

NOTE: Other fillings can be used: Orange, Pineapple, or Chocolate Fillings.

LEMON CUSTARD FILLING

Beat until thick and lemon-colored . . .
4 egg yolks
Gradually beat in . . .
1/2 cup sugar
Blend in . . .
4 tbsp. lemon juice
2 tbsp. grated lemon rind

Cook over hot water, stirring constantly, until thick (5 to 8 min.). Cool.

ANGEL SOUFFLÉ (🔑 Recipe) *Light, airy, enchanting. Served at a luncheon given by Mrs. Ray Brang of Minneapolis, Minnesota, who has contributed several fine recipes.*

	For Large Soufflé	Small Soufflé
Grease well (with butter)	10″ tube center pan (not removable bottom)	top of double boiler (2-qt.)
Beat together until stiff	9 egg whites	3 whites
	3/4 tsp. cream of tartar	1/4 tsp.
	1/4 tsp. salt	dash
Beat in gradually, a little at a time	9 tbsp. sugar	3 tbsp.
	3 tsp. vanilla or other flavoring	1 tsp.

Pour into prepared pan. Set large Soufflé in pan of water (1″ deep) and bake. Steam small Soufflé in double boiler. Do not lift cover. When time is up, keep in warm place a moment. Carefully turn out onto *hot* serving dish. If desired, spread with whipped cream or Egg Nog Sauce (*below*). Serve immediately. Pour crushed, sweetened berries (1 qt. for large Soufflé) over top and around Soufflé (*see pictures below*).

NOTE: These delicate Soufflés must be thoroughly cooked and kept hot until they are served, or they may fall.

TEMPERATURE: 275° (slow oven). Steam over boiling water.

TIME: Steam bake 1½ hr. Steam 1 hr.

AMOUNT: 12 servings. 4 servings.

★ **ORANGE SOUFFLÉ**

"I'm crazy about it! I want it for my wedding supper," says Beverly Prevey of our Staff.

Follow 🔑 recipe above—using orange extract for flavoring. At the last, fold in finely cut orange marmalade,—2 tbsp. for small Soufflé, 6 tbsp. for large. Garnish with shaved almonds and serve with

EGG NOG SAUCE

Beat until thick, lemon-colored 2 egg yolks
Beat in . . ½ cup *sifted* confectioners' sugar
2 tbsp. rum or sherry flavoring

Fold into ½ cup cream, whipped stiff.

VANILLA SOUFFLÉ (🔑 Recipe)

Served at smart French restaurants.

Melt in saucepan . . .
¼ cup butter
Mix in . . .
¼ cup *sifted* GOLD MEDAL Flour
¼ tsp. salt
¾ cup milk
Cook over low heat, stirring constantly, until thick and smooth. Remove from heat.
Beat until thick and lemon-colored . . .
3 egg yolks
Beat in gradually . . .
½ cup sugar
1 tsp. vanilla
Blend milk mixture into egg yolk mixture.
Beat until stiff . . .
3 egg whites
¼ tsp. cream of tartar

Carefully fold in egg yolk mixture. Pour into buttered 2-qt. baking dish. Set in pan of water (1″ deep). Steam bake until puffed up and delicately browned. Serve *immediately* on warm dessert plates. Top with flavored whipped cream sprinkled with toasted sliced almonds.

TEMPERATURE: 350° (mod. oven).
TIME: Steam bake about 45 min.
AMOUNT: 8 servings.

CHOCOLATE SOUFFLÉ

Follow 🔑 recipe for Vanilla Soufflé above —*except* add 2 sq. unsweetened chocolate (2 oz.), cut up, with the milk.

CHILLED CREAM DESSERTS Glamorous chilled desserts from Europe.

Bavarian, Velvet, or Spanish Cream . . . names applied to smooth, creamy molded desserts of gelatin and milk made delicate with whipped cream or fluffy egg whites.

CRÈME VANILLE (Vanilla Cream) (🗝 Recipe) *As elegant as its French name.*

Soften	1 envelope unflavored gelatin (1 tbsp.)
in	1/4 cup milk
Beat well in saucepan	4 egg yolks
Gradually beat in	1/2 cup sugar 1/4 tsp. salt
Blend in slowly	2 cups milk, scalded
Cook over *low* heat just until mixture boils. Remove from heat. Stir in softened gelatin. Cool. When partially set, beat with rotary beater and fold in	1 cup whipping cream, whipped stiff 1 tsp. vanilla

Pour into oiled 1-qt. mold, chill about 4 hr. Unmold on large serving dish. Garnish with sweetened whipped cream, fresh fruit (strawberries, peaches, etc.).

AMOUNT: 8 servings.

MOCHA BAVARIAN CREAM

Follow 🗝 recipe above—*except* omit vanilla and for milk, use *coffee-flavored milk*: Boil together 3 min., then strain. . . .

3/4 cup ground coffee
2 cups milk

Add extra milk, if necessary, to make 2 cups. Cook, cool, beat, and add cream as in 🗝 recipe. Garnish with candied cherries, nuts, or crushed peanut brittle.

CHOCOLATE BAVARIAN CREAM

Follow 🗝 recipe above—*except* increase sugar to 2/3 cup. Before scalding milk, stir in 2 sq. unsweetened chocolate (2 oz.), *shaved*. Beat with rotary beater.

MACAROON BAVARIAN CREAM

Follow 🗝 recipe above—and fold in 2/3 cup macaroon crumbs with the flavored whipped cream.

PINEAPPLE BAVARIAN CREAM (🗝 Recipe) *Soft, luscious, slices beautifully.*

Heat	1 cup pineapple juice
Soften	1 envelope unflavored gelatin (1 tbsp.)
in	2 tbsp. cold water
Stir into hot pineapple juice. Stir in	1/2 cup sugar 1/4 tsp. salt
Blend in	1 cup crushed pineapple 1 tbsp. lemon juice
Cool. Stir occasionally until mixture is partially set. Beat with rotary beater. Fold in	1 cup whipping cream, whipped stiff

Pour into oiled 1-qt. mold. Chill about 4 hr. Unmold on large serving dish. Garnish with colorful fresh fruits.

AMOUNT: 8 servings.

STRAWBERRY BAV'N CREAM

Follow 🗝 recipe above—*except*, in place of pineapple juice, use strawberry juice. Add the 1 cup crushed sweetened strawberries with the whipped cream.

RASPBERRY BAV'N CREAM

Follow recipe for Strawberry Bavarian Cream above—*except* use raspberry juice and crushed raspberries.

★ ORANGE CREAM

Flavored gelatin to accent the orange.

Mix together . . .

2 cups boiling water
1 pkg. orange-flavored gelatin
1/2 cup sugar
1 cup orange juice
3 tbsp. grated orange rind

Cool, and proceed as in 🗝 recipe. Fold in . . .

1 cup whipping cream, whipped stiff

CHOCOLATE ROLL (Recipe) *More delicate . . . more partyfied than Jelly Roll.*

Beat until stiff (hold a point)..........	6 egg whites ½ tsp. cream of tartar
Beat in gradually (until glossy)........	½ cup sugar
Beat until thick and lemon-colored....	6 egg yolks
Beat in..............................	½ cup sugar
Sift together and beat into yolk mixture..............................	4 tbsp. cocoa 4 tbsp. *sifted* GOLD MEDAL Flour ¼ tsp. salt
Stir in..............................	1 tsp. vanilla

Carefully fold into egg white mixture. Spread ½" thick in shallow 15½x10½" pan lined with well greased paper. Bake just until surface springs back when touched lightly with finger. *Immediately* turn upside-down onto towel sprinkled with confectioners' sugar. *Immediately* remove paper from cake, and roll up (beginning at side). To finish, see pictures.

NOTE: If a thick, shorter roll is desired (more circles of cake), begin to roll at end.

TEMPERATURE: 325° (slow mod. oven).

TIME: Bake 20 to 25 min.

AMOUNT: 12 to 16 servings.

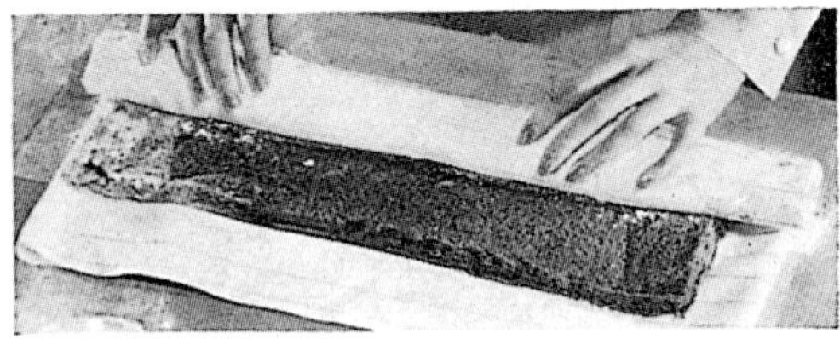

1 Roll the sugar-covered towel in with the cake to prevent cake sticking together.

2 Unroll, shortly before serving. Place cake on folds of waxed paper. Remove towel.

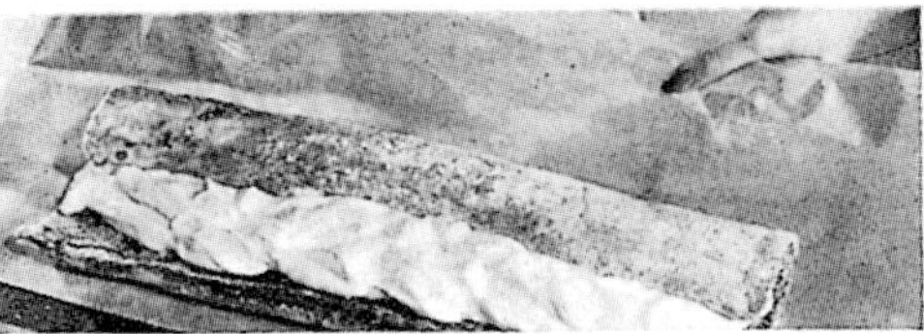

3 Fill with double Whipped Cream Filling (*p. 233*). Roll up carefully to keep in cream. Chill.

4 Serve thick slices with cool Chocolate Custard Sauce. Or frost as Cherry Tree Log.

CHOCOLATE CUSTARD SAUCE

Mix together . . .
- 2 tbsp. cornstarch
- ⅝ cup sugar (½ cup plus 2 tbsp.)
- ½ tsp. salt

Stir in . . .
- 2 cups milk

Bring to boil over low heat, stirring constantly. Boil 1 min. Add . . .
- 4 tbsp. butter
- 2 to 3 sq. unsweetened chocolate, grated

Boil, stirring until thick and smooth (about 2 min.). Cool.

★ CHERRY TREE LOG

For glamorous effect on a buffet table.

Spread Creamy Chocolate Icing on Chocolate Roll, pulling a spatula down length of roll to simulate bark of a log. Decorate with sprays of cherries (candied cherries) and cherry leaves (green peppermint gumdrops shaped with fingers). (See picture in color, *p. 213.*)

All you have to do—

To make Chocolate Roll ahead of time: make it at your leisure. Wrap and freeze it.

CREAMY CHOCOLATE ICING

Mix ¾ cup sugar and ¾ cup cream. Cook over low heat just until it boils. Pour slowly over 1¼ cups shaved chocolate in bowl (4 oz. German Sweet Chocolate and 3 sq. unsweetened chocolate (3 oz.)). Beat until chocolate is melted and mixture is smooth. If too thick for spreading, add a little cream.

REFRIGERATOR DESSERTS

Luscious party desserts in different forms.

SILHOUETTE PUDDING (🔑 Recipe)

Dramatic . . . delicious flavor combinations.

Use 30 *crisp thick 3″ cookies* (ginger or chocolate refrigerator cookies). Whip 2 cups whipping cream stiff and sweeten with 4 tbsp. confectioners' sugar. Spread a spoonful on a cooky. Place another cooky on top . . . continue until there is a pile of cookies with whipped cream between.

Lay pile lengthwise on serving platter. Add remaining cookies with cream and cover the roll evenly with remaining whipped cream. Chill at least 6 hr. To decorate **Fudge Cream Roll** (made with chocolate cookies): Garnish with walnut or pecan halves. Offer Quick Fudge Sauce.

★ **For Ginger Cream Roll** (made with ginger cookies): Garnish with bits of candied ginger. A bit of clear apricot jam on top is delicious.

CHOCOLATE REFRIGERATOR PUDDING

So rich, you can eat only a little.

Mix together in saucepan . . .
- **4 egg yolks, slightly beaten**
- **¼ cup milk**
- **¼ cup sugar**
- **1 tbsp. cornstarch**
- **2 sq. unsweetened chocolate (2 oz.), grated**

Cook slowly until mixture boils. Cool.

Cream together . . .
- **¼ cup soft butter**
- **1 cup *sifted* confectioners' sugar**

Blend into cooled mixture.

Fold in . . .
- **4 egg whites, stiffly beaten**

Split into halves . . .
- **1½ doz. ladyfingers (or 1x5″ strips of sponge cake)**

Line bottom and sides of lightly buttered 8″ round mold (3″ deep) with ladyfinger halves. Pour in chocolate mixture. Arrange remaining ladyfingers on top.

Chill in refrigerator 4 hr. (or overnight). Unmold onto serving plate. Decorate with sweetened whipped cream, if desired. Cut in small servings.

AMOUNT: 10 servings.

VANILLA STRAWBERRY ROLL

Follow 🔑 recipe above—using Vanilla Wafers. In place of whipped cream, use Strawberry Bavarian Cream (*p. 236*).

ENGLISH TRIFLE

Glamorous, elegant dessert from early days.

Make Soft Custard (*p. 219*) *except* add . . . 1 tbsp. cornstarch with the sugar; use for flavoring 1 tsp. lemon juice and 1 tsp. grated lemon rind (add after custard is cooked). Cool. Then assemble:
- **2 doz. ladyfingers**
- **⅓ cup raspberry jam**
- **⅓ cup sherry flavoring**
- **1 doz. macaroons**

Split the ladyfingers into halves. Stand them upright, close together around edge of 8″ round mold 3″ deep. Stick remaining ladyfinger halves together with raspberry jam. Cover bottom of dish with a layer of these, sprinkle with half of sherry. Pour in half of cooled custard. Add half of macaroon crumbs. Chill.

Add another layer of filled ladyfingers. Sprinkle with sherry flavoring. Add remaining custard and macaroon crumbs. Chill 4 hr. Decorate with sweetened whipped cream, blanched almonds, and bits of candied cherries and green citron.

AMOUNT: 12 servings.

RAINBOW DESSERT (Blöte Kage)

A dazzling dessert with fillings of rainbow colors served at exclusive hotels in Norway. The Norwegian name Blöte Kage means Soft Cake. It was brought to me by Mrs. Gladys Petch, formerly of Oslo, Norway, now of New York, Radio Consultant to the Norwegian Information Services.

Cut a high 10″ Sponge or Chiffon Cake into four 1″ layers. Put layers together with 3 different fillings:

On bottom layer, spread *Pineapple Filling.* Place second layer on top and spread with *Apricot Filling.*

Place third layer and spread with *Raspberry Filling.*

Add the fourth layer and cover top and sides of cake with sweetened whipped cream. Sprinkle with green pistachio nuts (blanched and shaved). Chill 3 hr. before serving. Arrange apricot halves, rounded-side-out, around base of cake. Add a few green leaves. Serve. See picture, *p. 213.*

WHIPPED CREAM FOR FILLING AND FROSTING

Whip until stiff 3 cups whipping cream. Beat in 6 tbsp. confectioners' sugar.

For *each* one of the 3 fillings, soften 2 tsp. gelatin in 1 tbsp. fruit juice. Dissolve over hot water. Stir into the fruit. Chill. When partially set, fold in 1 cup of the sweet whipped cream (1 cup for each).

PINEAPPLE FILLING

Use 1 cup drained crushed pineapple (#1 can). Tint with green food coloring.

APRICOT FILLING

Use 1 cup mashed apricot pulp (sweet).

RASPBERRY FILLING

Use 1 cup thick raspberry jam.

★ NORWEGIAN CHARLOTTE

Chosen as a thrilling dessert from a set of Scandinavian recipes by our true Swedish blonde, Margaret Lindquist Remington, now of St. Joseph, Missouri.

To Prepare Cake:

Cut a high 10″ Sponge or Chiffon Cake (Egg Yolk Sponge saves eggs) into four 1″ layers. With a sharp knife, cut out the center of the top 3 layers of cake, enlarging the hole in center until about 4″ across. Leave a 2″ wall of cake. *Do not cut through bottom layer.*

Fill the small hole in this layer with a piece of the cake. Fit it in tightly. Place the part of cake cut from center in a bowl with the cooled Rich Custard (↗). Stir together until smooth and blend in 2 cups whipping cream, whipped stiff, and 2 tsp. orange flower water. Chill.

To Finish Cake:

On bottom layer (but not over center), spread half of Almond Filling (↗); add next layer of cake and spread with Coconut Filling (→). Add third layer of cake and spread with rest of Almond Filling. Add the fourth layer. Fill center with chilled Rich Custard. Frost entire cake with Meringue Frosting (→), pulling up points for decorative effect (*p. 212*).

RICH CUSTARD (for center of cake)

Beat together . . .
- **6 egg yolks**
- **6 tbsp. sugar**
- **1 tbsp. cornstarch**
- **1½ cups rich milk**

Cook over low heat, stirring until it boils. Boil 1 min. Cool. Blend in 1½ tsp. vanilla.

ALMOND FILLING (for 2 layers)

Grind very fine . . .
- **1 cup blanched and dried almonds**

Rub to a paste with . . .
- **1½ tsp. almond extract**
- **½ tsp. green coloring**

Make a Meringue by beating until stiff . . .
- **4 egg whites**
- **4 tbsp. sugar**

Mix in half of this meringue and a little water, if necessary, to make easy to spread.

COCONUT FILLING (for 1 layer)

Mix the remaining meringue into . . .
- **1 cup moist shredded coconut**
- **1 tsp. rose water**

MERINGUE FROSTING (for top and sides)

Beat until stiff . . .
- **4 large egg whites (½ cup)**

Gradually beat in . . .
- **1 cup *sifted* confectioners' sugar**
- **2 tbsp. lemon juice**

Beat until stiff and very glossy.

CAKE DESSERTS Surprise desserts from Angel Foods.

HOW TO FILL ANGEL FOOD CAKES: First make a high 10″ Angel Food (see p. 157). Then read recipes on p. 241 and prepare the desired filling and frosting.

1 Place a high 10″ Angel Food Cake upside-down on plate or waxed paper. Slice entire top from cake about 1″ down. Lift off top and lay to one side.

2 Cut down into the cake 1″ from outer edge, and 1″ from middle hole, leaving a substantial "wall" of cake about 1″ thick, and a 1″ base at the bottom.

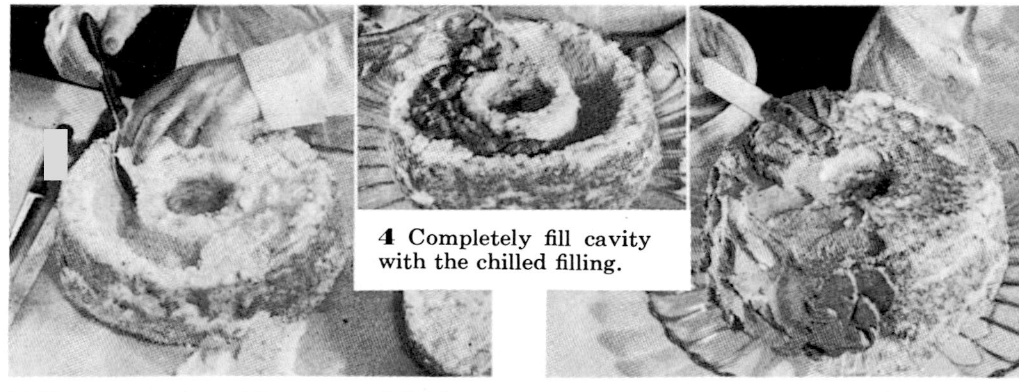

4 Completely fill cavity with the chilled filling.

3 Remove center with a curved knife or spoon, being careful to leave a "wall" of cake at bottom 1″ thick. Place on serving plate.

5 Replace top of cake and press gently. Cover top and sides with the remaining chilled cream mixture.

6 Decorate appropriately (*see recipes*) and chill until well set (4 hr. or more). Cut into generous pieces. Serves 12 to 16.

All you have to do –

To get the greatest volume when whipping cream: chill cream, bowl, and beater together

★ ANGEL FOOD WALDORF

Crunchy nuts in luscious creamy chocolate.

Prepare Angel Food Cake as above. Make:

CHOCOLATE WHIPPED CREAM

Mix together . . .
- 6 tbsp. sugar
- $\frac{1}{8}$ tsp. salt
- 6 tbsp. cocoa
- 3 cups whipping cream ($1\frac{1}{2}$ pt.)

Chill 1 hr. or more. Whip until stiff. Fold into about half of cream mixture . . .
- $\frac{1}{3}$ cup *cut-up* toasted almonds

Use this part to fill cake cavity. Replace top of cake and spread remaining cream mixture on top and sides of cake. Sprinkle with $\frac{1}{3}$ cup shaved toasted almonds. Chill 3 hr. or more before serving.

APRICOT ICE CREAM-FILLED ANGEL FOOD

Most beautiful, delicious, and unusual. From Adair McRae Roberts of Philadelphia.

Prepare Angel Food Cake for filling (*p. 240*). But first make the Apricot Purée and Apricot Ice Cream for the filling.

APRICOT PURÉE

Wash and soak several hr. . . .
- **¾ lb. dried apricots in . . .**
- **2 cups warm water**

Simmer until soft (30 min.). Stir in 4 tbsp. sugar, press through sieve. Cool.

APRICOT ICE CREAM

Into 1 qt. vanilla ice cream, blend 1 cup cold Apricot Purée (work quickly before ice cream melts). Place in refrigerator freezing tray until firm again (about 1 hr.).

Fill cake cavity with Apricot Ice Cream. Replace top of cake. Spread remaining Apricot Purée over top and sides.

Spread 1½ cups whipping cream, whipped stiff, and sweetened, over the apricot coating. Arrange 6 fresh apricot halves round-side-out, around base. Add a few fresh green leaves. Serve immediately.

ALMOND CREAM ANGEL FOOD

Split high 10″ Angel Food into 2 layers. Put layers together with Almond Cream Filling and frost cake with Fluffy White Icing. Decorate with daisies of toasted blanched almond halves for petals—and rounds of orange rind for the centers.

LUSCIOUS CHOCOLATE ALMOND DESSERT

Served at lovely dinner parties by Louise Strong Cosgrove of Minneapolis, Minnesota.

Split Chocolate Angel Food into 2 layers. Put layers together with Almond Cream Filling and frost with White Mountain Frosting. Cover with Chocolate Allegretti coating.

FRESH STRAWBERRY COCONUT ANGEL FOOD

Split high 10″ Angel Food into 2 layers. Put layers together with Strawberry Cream (*p. 242*). Frost cake with sweetened whipped cream (2 cups). Sprinkle with moist shredded coconut. Chill 1 hr. before serving.

ANGEL FOOD DELIGHT

Choice of an epicure, Judge Leslie L. Anderson, Minneapolis, Minnesota.

Prepare Angel Food Cake for filling (*p. 240*). Fill cake cavity with

FRUIT CREAM FILLING AND FROSTING

Whip until stiff . . .
- **3 cups whipping cream**

Beat in . . .
- **6 tbsp. confectioners' sugar**

Fold into a little less than half the cream . . .
- **¾ cup crushed pineapple, well drained**
- **1 cup fresh strawberries, cut in halves**
- **6 marshmallows, cut in quarters**

Replace top of cake and spread remaining cream on top and sides. Chill 4 to 8 hours.

★ CHOCOLATE PEPPERMINT ANGEL FOOD

Make green tinted peppermint-flavored Angel Food. Split into 2 layers. Put layers together and frost cake with

CHOCOLATE FILLING AND FROSTING

Cook over boiling water 5 min . . .
- **4 sq. unsweetened chocolate (4 oz.), shaved**
- **1 cup confectioners' sugar**
- **¼ tsp. salt**
- **⅔ cup milk, scalded**

Blend in . . .
- **2 envelopes unflavored gelatin (2 tbsp.) softened in ⅔ cup cold water**

Cool. When mixture begins to set, fold in . .
- **3 cups whipping cream, whipped stiff**

Decorate frosted cake with green mints. Chill 4 hr. before serving.

ANGEL FOOD À LA RUSSE

Serve large pieces of Angel Food Cake topped with Russian Sauce (*p. 355*).

ICE CREAM SANDWICHES

Place ice cream (any flavor desired) between 2 slices Angel Food. Pour Chocolate Sauce over. For 6, use 1 qt. ice cream, 12 slices cake, 1 cup Chocolate Sauce.

SINGED ANGEL WINGS

Brush cut sides of wedges of Angel Food with melted butter. Lightly brown both sides under broiler (about 1 min. each side). Serve with Orange Butter Sauce.

CAKE DESSERTS Some of our most elegant cake desserts.

STRAWBERRY DELIGHT

Split a 10″ Sunshine or Chiffon Cake into 2 layers. Put layers together with

STRAWBERRY CREAM

Mash lightly most of 1 pt. ripe strawberries. Add 2 tbsp. sugar. Blend in 1 tsp. gelatin soaked in 1 tbsp. water and dissolved over hot water. Chill. When partially set, fold in 1 cup sweetened whipped cream. Chill.

Cover top and sides of cake with sweetened whipped cream (whip 2 cups). Decorate with a few large berries.

FRENCH RIBBON CAKE

Split a loaf of Chiffon Cake (baked in a 10x5x3″ loaf pan) into 4 layers. Put layers together and frost cake with

CHOCOLATE FILLING AND FROSTING

Cream together ¾ cup soft butter and 1 cup *sifted* confectioners' sugar. Beat in 3 egg yolks, one at a time, and 3 sq. unsweetened chocolate (3 oz.), melted. Fold in 3 egg whites, beaten stiff.

Sprinkle sides of frosted cake with chopped nuts or decorate edge with blanched almond halves stuck into frosting. Chill in refrigerator several hours.
AMOUNT: 10 servings.

SUNSHINE RINGS (Wedding Rings)

Bake Sunshine Cake or Chiffon Cake in 13x9″ oblong pan. Cool. Cut into 16 strips ½″ wide and 12″ long. Bring ends of each strip together. Fasten with wooden pick. Place a scoop of vanilla ice cream in center of each ring on dessert plate. Top with Clear Orange Sauce.

BOSTON CREAM PIE

Make a one-egg cake, pp. 124, 125, in one round 9″ layer pan. Split into 2 thin layers. Put together with cooled Cream Filling (p. 172). Spread Thin Chocolate Icing over top. Serve like pie.

WASHINGTON PIE

From Civil War days when Washington, D.C. housewives could not get lard for pies. They made plain cakes, split and filled them with jelly from their cellars. Ever since, they have been called "Washington Pies."

Make Inexpensive Sponge Cake in a layer pan. Split into 2 layers, fill with jelly. Sprinkle confectioners' sugar on top.

★ ORANGE ALMOND DELIGHT

Split a 10″ Sponge or Chiffon Cake (orange-flavored) into 2 layers. Put layers together and frost cake with

ORANGE CUSTARD FILLING

Beat until thick and lemon-colored . . .
5 egg yolks

Blend in . . .
¼ cup sugar
¼ cup orange juice (strained)
2 tsp. grated orange rind

Cook over low heat, stirring constantly, until it begins to boil. Cool. Fold in 1 cup stiffly whipped cream with 1 tsp. lemon juice. Sprinkle frosted cake with sliced toasted almonds.

BAKED ALASKA

Bake half recipe Egg Yolk Sponge Cake in 10″ spring form pan which makes a cake with high sides and cavity in top. Shortly before serving, make a

SPECIAL MERINGUE

Beat 6 large egg whites with ½ tsp. cream of tartar until stiff. Beat in gradually 1 cup sugar. Continue beating hard until meringue is stiff and glossy.

Place cooled Sponge Cake on several thicknesses of wrapping paper on a wet board. Pile 2 qt. ice cream (preferably pink) into hollow in cake. *Completely* cover ice cream (and sides of cake) with a *thick* coating of the meringue. Place in *very* hot oven (500°) for 3 to 5 min. (just until meringue is delicately browned). Slip the dessert from board onto serving platter. Serve at once.
AMOUNT: 12 to 16 servings.

PEACH MELBA CHIFFON DESSERT

On each slice of Chiffon Cake, place (curved-side-up) ½ peach (cooked in thin sugar syrup and cooled). Pour over it a sauce of mashed fresh raspberries, sweetened and chilled.

PINEAPPLE BUTTERSCOTCH DESSERT

Pour over each generous piece of Sponge or Chiffon Cake 2 spoonfuls of Hot Butterscotch Sauce. Add topping of cold

PINEAPPLE CREAM

For 8 servings, whip 1 cup whipping cream. Fold in ½ cup drained crushed pineapple.

BAKED ALASKA

A dessert of beauty . . . and mystery.

FROZEN DESSERTS

Favorite for company dinners.

Luxury-loving Romans of Julius Caesar's day knew a kind of ice cream . . . snow from the high mountain passes, carried to Rome by fleet runners. There it was flavored with fruit juices and enjoyed as a rare delicacy. Centuries later, Marco Polo returned from Japan to Venice with a recipe for a kind of milk ice. Italians quickly introduced it to the rest of Europe. "Cream Ice" was so well liked by Charles I. of England that he pensioned the French chef who made it for him. Virginia cavaliers brought that idea to the new world. Generations later, Dolly Madison reversed the name and "Ice Cream" appeared on the White House menu.

HOW TO MAKE FREEZER ICE CREAM (in a crank freezer). The churning of the dasher prevents ice crystals from forming.

1 Chill the freezer can and mixture.

2 Place can in freezer tub. Put dasher in place. Fill can ⅔ full (allowing for expansion). Cover. Adjust crank.

3 Fill freezer tub ⅓ full of ice (crushed until it's like rock salt). Add remaining crushed ice alternately with layers of coarse salt.

4 Use 3 to 6 parts ice to 1 part salt for ice cream, ices, and sherbets. The larger amount of ice to salt (5 to 1) gives finer grained ice cream, but it freezes more slowly. Use 3 parts ice for mousses, etc. Pack solidly.

5 Let mixture stand in ice-packed freezer about 5 min. before turning crank. Turn slowly at first (5 to 10 min.), to insure smooth, fine grained ice cream. Then turn rapidly until crank turns with difficulty.

6 Draw off water. Wipe off and remove lid. Take out dasher. Plug opening in lid. Pack mixture down. Repack in ice and salt. Cover with heavy cloth. Let ripen several hr.

PHILADELPHIA ICE CREAM

(🔑 Recipe)

For crank freezer only, not adaptable to automatic refrigerator. Smooth . . . melts down to pure cream.

Mix together . . .
- **1 qt. cream, scalded**
- **¾ cup sugar**

Cool. Blend in . . .
- **1½ tbsp. vanilla**
- **⅛ tsp. salt**

Freeze in ice cream freezer using 5 parts ice to 1 of salt.

AMOUNT: 6 servings (1 qt.).

All you have to do–

To make other kinds in crank freezer:

Fresh Peach Ice Cream
Strawberry Ice Cream
Banana Ice Cream
Mocha Ice Cream
Chocolate Ice Cream
Orange Almond Ice Cream

Follow directions on opposite page, but use 🔑 recipe above for Philadelphia Ice Cream.

VARIETY WITH VANILLA ICE CREAM

Into 1 qt. of Vanilla Ice Cream, blend special flavor ingredients (*see below*). Work quickly to prevent melting. Then replace in freezer or freezing tray and allow to become firm again.

Chocolate Chip Ice Cream: Add 1 cup shaved or tiny bits of semi-sweet chocolate.

Lemon Ice Cream: Add 1 cup crushed lemon drops.

Peppermint Ice Cream: Add ½ cup crushed peppermint sticks.

★ **NUT CRUNCH ICE CREAM:** 1 cup Nut Crunch (*see below*).

NUT CRUNCH

Melt in saucepan ¼ cup butter. Blend in ⅓ cup brown sugar. Cook over low heat, stirring constantly to prevent scorching, to the "crack" stage (270°). Remove from heat. Stir in 1½ cups WHEATIES and ⅓ cup chopped nuts. Stir until well coated. Spread in thin layer on baking sheet to cool. Crumble (makes 2 cups).

HOW TO FREEZE ICE CREAM IN AUTOMATIC REFRIGERATORS

1 Use a stabilizer to prevent crystals from forming (some ingredient such as gelatin, eggs, flour, or cornstarch).

2 Set control for fast freezing. Pour ice cream mixture into refrigerator tray. Place in bottom of freezing compartment.

3 To make creamy ice cream: after first mixture has partially frozen (½ hr.), turn into chilled bowl, beat with cold rotary beater until smooth (not melted). Fold in whipped cream. Return to *cold* refrigerator tray. Freeze until firm, stirring occasionally. Time depends on formula, temperature, etc.

VANILLA ICE CREAM (🔑 Recipes) *Two types adapted to automatic refrigerators.*

	American Type	*French Type*
Scald	**1 cup rich milk**	**1 cup**
Gradually stir into a mixture of	**½ cup sugar** **⅛ tsp. salt** **1 tbsp. GOLD MEDAL Flour**	**½ cup** **⅛ tsp.** **3 egg yolks, beaten**
Cook over low heat, stirring, until it boils. Boil just 1 min. Cool. Pour into freezing tray. Freeze ½ hr.		
Whip until barely stiff	**1 cup whipping cream**	**1 cup**
Beat in	**1 tbsp. vanilla (3 tsp.)**	**1 tbsp.**

Turn the partially frozen mixture into a chilled bowl. Beat with rotary beater until smooth. Fold in whipped cream, return to cold tray, and freeze until firm, stirring well during first hour of freezing period.

TIME: Freeze 3 to 4 hr.

AMOUNT: 6 servings (1 qt.).

FRESH PEACH OR STRAWBERRY ICE CREAM

Follow either 🔑 recipe above—and, before freezing, blend in 1½ cups mashed fresh peaches or strawberries, sweetened with ½ to ¾ cup sugar.

NUT BRITTLE ICE CREAM

Follow either 🔑 recipe above—and, before freezing, fold in 1 cup crushed almond, pecan, or peanut brittle.

BANANA ICE CREAM

Follow either 🔑 recipe above—*except* omit vanilla and, before freezing, blend in 1½ cups mashed bananas (put through sieve) with 1 tbsp. lemon juice and 2 tbsp. sugar.

ORANGE ALMOND ICE CREAM

Follow either 🔑 recipe above—and, before freezing, blend in ½ cup chopped blanched almonds, ½ cup orange juice and pulp (1 orange), ½ tsp. grated orange rind.

PEPPERMINT ICE CREAM

Follow either 🔑 recipe above—*except*, in place of sugar, use ½ cup (¼ lb.) crushed peppermint stick candy. Add to milk.

PISTACHIO ICE CREAM

Follow either 🔑 recipe above—and, before freezing, blend in ½ cup chopped pistachio nuts or almonds, ½ tsp. almond extract, and a few drops of green coloring.

MOCHA ICE CREAM

(Coffee Ice Cream)

Follow either 🔑 recipe above—*except* scald the milk with 3 tbsp. ground coffee in it. Strain, and pour into sugar mixture.

★ CHOCOLATE ICE CREAM

Follow either 🔑 recipe above—*except*, before cooking, stir into milk 2 sq. unsweetened chocolate (2 oz.) melted with ¼ cup water. Stir until well blended.

NESSELRODE PUDDING

A guest paid a New York hotel $20 for this recipe. Years later she gave it to a friend, the mother of Mae Chesnut of our Staff.

Follow either 🔑 recipe above—*except* add 2 tbsp. cocoa with the sugar. With the whipped cream, fold in . . .

½ cup cut-up seeded raisins
¼ cup chopped toasted blanched almonds

FROZEN DESSERTS

Sherbet means water-ice with egg white added.

FRUIT SHERBET (🗝 Recipe) *Refreshing . . . slightly less rich than Ice Cream.*

	Cream Sherbet	*Milk Sherbet*
Mix together	¾ cup crushed fruit ¼ cup lemon juice ¾ cup sugar	¾ cup 2 tbsp. ¾ cup
Let stand until syrup forms (2 hr.).		
Soften	1 tsp. gelatin	1½ tsp.
in	2 tbsp. cold water	2 tbsp.
Dissolve in	¼ cup boiling water	¼ cup hot milk
Add to fruit mixture. Stir in slowly	—	1 cup milk
Pour into freezing tray, freeze (1 hr.).		
Whip until stiff	½ cup whipping cream	—
Fold in	1 egg yolk, beaten very light 1 egg white, beaten stiff	— 1 white

Beat the partially frozen mixture in a chilled bowl with a rotary beater until creamy and frothy. Fold in whipped cream mixture. Return to tray. Freeze until firm, stirring occasionally.

TIME: Freeze 3 to 4 hr.

AMOUNT: 6 servings (1 qt.).

PINEAPPLE SHERBET

Follow either 🗝 recipe above—using for the fruit, crushed pineapple.

STRAWBERRY OR RASPBERRY SHERBET

Follow either 🗝 recipe above—using crushed strawberries or raspberries.

LEMON CREAM SHERBET

Follow either 🗝 recipe above—using in all ¾ cup lemon juice with 2 tsp. grated lemon rind, 1 cup sugar, 1½ tsp. gelatin.

★ 3-IN-1 SHERBET

Follow either 🗝 recipe above—using ¼ cup *each* of pineapple, orange, and banana.

APRICOT SHERBET

Follow either 🗝 recipe above—using canned apricot pulp.

ORANGE CREAM SHERBET

Follow either 🗝 recipe above—using ¾ cup orange juice and pulp, and add 1½ tbsp. grated orange rind (1½ oranges).

FRUIT WATER SHERBET

Low calorie dessert . . . meat accompaniment.

Soften . . .
- 1 tsp. gelatin in . . .
- 2 tbsp. cold water

Mix in saucepan and stir over low heat . . .
- ¾ cup sugar
- 1½ cups water

Boil 5 min. Stir in gelatin. Cool. Stir in . .
- 4 tbsp. lemon juice
- 1 cup crushed fruit (orange, lemon, pineapple, or grape, pulp and juice)

Pour into freezing tray; freeze to a mush. Beat in chilled bowl with rotary beater until fluffy. Fold in . . .
- 1 egg white, beaten stiff

Return to tray. Freeze until firm, stirring occasionally.

TIME: Freeze 2 to 3 hr.
AMOUNT: 8 servings (1 qt.).

CRANBERRY ICE

Bright holiday ice . . . orange rind adds zest.

Makes a colorful holiday dessert with Pistachio Ice Cream (*see picture, p. 216*). Serve in avocado for holiday appetizer.

Cook until skins are broken (about 10 min.).
- 1 qt. cranberries (4 cups)
- 2 cups water

Rub through a sieve to make a smooth pulp. Stir in . . .
- 2 cups sugar
- ¼ cup lemon juice (1 lemon)
- 1 tsp. grated orange rind
- 2 cups cold water

Pour into freezing tray. Freeze until firm, stirring 2 or 3 times.

TIME: Freeze 2 to 3 hr.
AMOUNT: 8 servings (1 qt.).

"Mousse," French for moss or foam, describes the smooth, spongy quality. Parfait, meaning "perfect," is less cold and more creamy than ice cream. The name was first used with coffee parfait. Marlows use marshmallows instead of gelatin.

HOW TO FREEZE MOUSSE, PARFAIT, MARLOW (they do not require beating or turning)

IN AUTOMATIC REFRIGERATOR

It's very simple. Set control for fast freezing. Just pack mousse in freezing tray. Place in bottom of freezing compartment. Freeze until firm (3 to 4 hr.).

IN CRANK FREEZER

Fill mold or can full. Cover with waxed paper . . . binding it on tightly (with adhesive tape). Pack in equal amounts salt and ice. Draw off salt water before it reaches top of mold. Do not stir. Freeze until firm (3 to 4 hr.).

MOUSSE (🔑 Recipe)

Whip until stiff . . .
  2 cups whipping cream
Beat in . . .
  ½ cup confectioners' sugar
  ¼ tsp. salt
Soften . . .
  1 tsp. gelatin
in . . .
  1 tbsp. liquid (fruit juice or water) and dissolve over hot water. Stir into . . .
  1 cup fruit pulp or chocolate syrup or coffee (*see recipes below*)

Fold in whipped cream mixture. Turn into freezing tray, freeze until firm.
TIME: Freeze 3 to 4 hr.
AMOUNT: 6 servings (1 qt.).

PARFAIT (🔑 Recipe)

Boil together to a syrup (5 min.) . . .
  ½ cup sugar
  ¼ cup water
Beat syrup, pouring slowly, into . . .
  2 egg yolks, beaten until *very* light
Cook over hot water in double boiler, stirring until thick (15 min.). Cool. Blend in . . .
  1 tsp. flavoring
Fold in . . .
  1 cup whipping cream, whipped stiff
  2 egg whites, beaten stiff

Pour into freezing tray. Freeze until firm (no stirring necessary).
TIME: Freeze 3 to 4 hr.
AMOUNT: 6 servings (1 qt.).

STRAWBERRY OR RASPBERRY MOUSSE

Follow 🔑 recipe above—using slightly sweetened strawberries or raspberries, mashed, for the fruit pulp and 1 tbsp. of the juice to soften the gelatin.

PEPPERMINT MOUSSE

Follow 🔑 recipe above—using, in place of fruit pulp, 1 cup crushed peppermint stick candy (crush in cloth bag). Omit the sugar, gelatin and 1 tbsp. liquid.

EASY CHOCOLATE MOUSSE

From Mrs. Lewis Washburn Child of Minneapolis, Minnesota, who gave us several fine frozen dessert recipes.

Follow 🔑 recipe above—using 1 cup canned chocolate syrup (or 2 sq. unsweetened chocolate (2 oz.) and ½ cup sugar cooked with ¾ cup water). Use 1 tbsp. cold water to soften gelatin.

COFFEE MOUSSE

Follow 🔑 recipe above—using 1 cup strong coffee with ¼ cup extra sugar.

★ MOCHA (Coffee) PARFAIT

Follow 🔑 recipe above—using ¼ cup *strong* coffee in place of water, vanilla flavoring.

LEMON PARFAIT

Follow 🔑 recipe above—using 1 tsp. grated lemon rind for flavoring and beat 2 tbsp. lemon juice into the egg whites.

MAPLE PARFAIT

Della Child of Glencoe, Minnesota, made this for her nieces when they came to visit.

Follow 🔑 recipe above—*except*, in place of sugar and water syrup, use ½ cup heated maple syrup. Omit flavoring.

STRAWBERRY PARFAIT

Follow 🔑 recipe above—*except* omit yolks and blend in 1 cup mashed strawberries.

All you have to do–

To make Marlows: heat 1 cup fruit pulp and juice and 2 tbsp. lemon juice with ½ lb. marshmallows, cut-up. Chill. Fold in 1 cup cream whipped stiff. Freeze.

ELEGANT FRUIT DESSERTS Simple to make, spectacular and delicious.

"With these desserts, serve dainty cookies, macaroons, or unfrosted nut or pound cake," says Minette Crouch Teske (Mrs. Frederick Teske), who used to offer our service to Bakers.

LEMON SHERBET OR ICE WITH FROSTED GRAPES

A delight for epicures. Contributed by Bess Plummer of Minneapolis, Minnesota.

Unmold 1 qt. lemon ice (in a round carton) directly onto serving dish. Place large perfect berries or cherries (1 pt.) directly on the ice. Arrange around the mold, clusters of blue, green, and red grapes, frosted (*see below*) . . . also fresh peach halves and pear slices. Garnish with grape leaves and a few berries. If desired, pass Crème de Menthe to pour over the fruit and ice.

All you have to do–

To frost grapes: pick over and wash grapes, dividing into small bunches. Sprinkle with sugar. Place in defrosting (not freezing) tray of refrigerator 1 hr.

PORTIA'S PEARS

I first met this intriguing dessert at the home of Mrs. Chester MacMillan of Murray Hill, Excelsior, Minnesota.

Use a whole canned pear (small) for each serving. Fill center cavity of one half with 1 tbsp. cocoa. Place 2 halves together, fasten with wooden pick. Chill over night. Brush pears with pink coloring. Place in dessert dish on top of

SUNSHINE SAUCE (Creamy Egg Nog)

Whip until stiff . . .
1 cup whipping cream

Blend in . . .
½ cup *sifted* confectioners' sugar
2 egg yolks, very well beaten
2 tbsp. brandy flavoring

PEAR HELENE

First enjoyed at the luxurious Chateau Lake Louise in the Canadian Rockies.

Pare and core fresh pears. Poach halves in syrup (*see right above*). Chill. For each serving, arrange a pear half on a mound of vanilla ice cream in a deep dessert dish. If desired, sprinkle with crystallized violets. Pass Glossy Chocolate Sauce to pour over the ice cream and pear.

All you have to do–

For an elegant dessert: top poached fruits and ice cream with Zabaglione Sauce.

★ CRÈME BRULÉE (Burned Cream)

Served at a lovely luncheon by a delightful hostess, Elizabeth Case, co-author of "Cook's Away." This elegant dish was a feature of the famous hospitality of Thomas Jefferson's Virginia home, "Monticello." He brought the recipe from France in 1790.

Heat until it barely reaches boiling . . .
3 cups whipping cream

Blend in . . .
6 egg yolks, beaten until very thick

Cook over low heat, stirring constantly, until it thickens. Pour into 12x7½x2" baking dish. Cool. An hour before serving, sprinkle top with a thin layer of *sifted* brown sugar (⅓ cup). Set under hot broiler until sugar melts and forms glaze (about 1 min.). Chill. AMOUNT: 8 servings. Serve with sweetened fresh strawberries, raspberries, or peaches; or green gage plums, or pears gently poached in syrup. The Crème Brulée is spooned over the fruit in dessert dishes.

All you have to do–

To poach fruit: cook it gently (a single layer) just until tender in a thin sugar-and-water syrup. Do not stir. Dip syrup over fruit to glaze.

PEACH MELBA

Peel fresh peaches and poach halves in syrup (*see above*). Chill. Place a peach half on a mound of vanilla ice cream. Add sweetened mashed raspberries, chilled.

ELENA ZELAYETA'S FRESH FRUIT DESSERT

From Elena Zelayeta of San Francisco, California, whose courageous spirit is an inspiration to us all.

Around a pile of melon balls, arrange clusters of Bing cherries (stems on) alternating with small bunches of green grapes. Border with sliced peeled peaches. Lay bananas (cut in half, then split in two) over peaches like spokes in a wheel. Garnish with strawberries and mint leaves. Serve with Fresh Raspberry Sauce, then a swirl of creamy cheese (pkg. of white cream cheese softened with milk) spooned over each serving.

FRESH RASPBERRY SAUCE

Let 1 pt. raspberries stand 2 hr. with ½ to 1 cup sugar. Put through sieve.

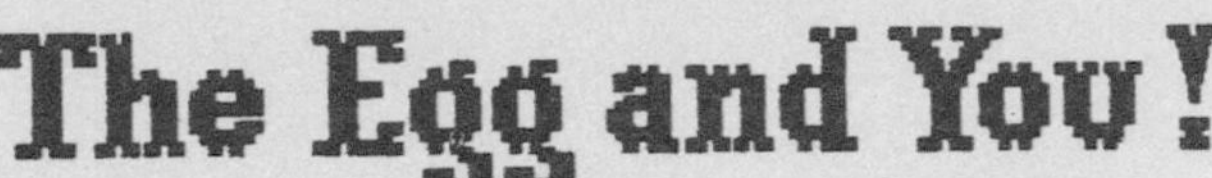

The Egg and You!

A FRESH EGG is a delicacy . . . not only in the morning but all 'round the clock. Eggs are so versatile, they can provide a tempting breakfast, a nourishing lunch, or a party supper. Every way you fix them, they have a different flavor. In fact, you'll find the egg and you can get together every day without boredom.

Betty Crocker

Good Morning

Luncheon Is Served

At the Picnic

Tea or Cocktail Hour

Meatless Supper

Evening Refreshments

Dinner

KNOW YOUR EGGS!

Federal and state regulations for grading eggs vary. Find out what your state regulations mean. Different grades are found in all sizes of eggs. Eggs for the breakfast table should be strictly fresh (top grade) of any size you prefer. For cooking (in meat loaves, custards, etc.), you may use smaller eggs and of lower grade. For baking (especially cakes), use large eggs (2 oz.) or their equivalent.

IF YOU MEASURE EGGS

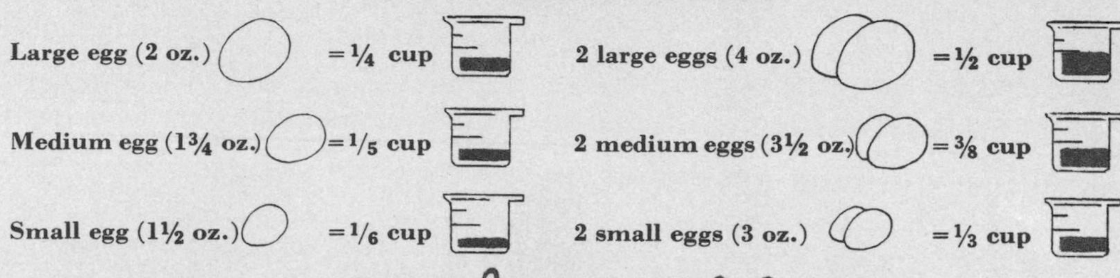

Large egg (2 oz.)	= 1/4 cup	2 large eggs (4 oz.)	= 1/2 cup
Medium egg (1 3/4 oz.)	= 1/5 cup	2 medium eggs (3 1/2 oz.)	= 3/8 cup
Small egg (1 1/2 oz.)	= 1/6 cup	2 small eggs (3 oz.)	= 1/3 cup

Are they fresh?

"Their shells should look dull . . .
Not shiny or bright;
But it makes no difference
If they're brown or they're white."

A fresh egg sinks when placed in cold water. Inside, the yolk is firm and upstanding; the white thick.

Chances that you are getting fresh eggs are greater if you buy from a stock that is refrigerated.

Keep Them Cool!

Place eggs immediately in refrigerator—in the humidity-controlled section if you have one. (Do not freeze!)

To Separate Yolks From Whites

It's much easier if the eggs are cold (yolks are less apt to break).

Leftover Egg Yolks

Store yolks (with water over them) in a tightly covered jar in refrigerator.

•

Use 2 egg yolks for 1 whole egg in soft and baked custards, salad dressings, cream pie fillings, etc.

•

Use 2 egg yolks plus 1 tbsp. water for 1 whole egg in yeast doughs, cookies, etc.

•

For salads, sandwich fillings, garnishes, etc., hard cook yolks by simmering in hot water 10 minutes.

Don't Wash Eggs!

The protective coating on the shell helps preserve them until ready to use. If eggs are dirty, wipe with a cloth, or rub off spots with a brush.

Leftover Egg Whites

Egg whites keep for weeks if stored in a tightly covered jar in the refrigerator.

•

Use them in making angel foods, white butter cakes, icings, meringues, frozen desserts, fruit whips, etc.

All you have to do— *For highest volume:* let egg whites stand at room temperature a while before beating.

EGGS

REMEMBER how you used to chant the old "One, Two, Buckle My Shoe" rhymes? Generations of children have learned to count by them. Well, here are some rhymes to learn for *egg* wisdom:

One, two—they're good for you! Humpty Dumpty (alias The Egg) is a many-sided food! Remember—Humpty Dumpty's always on call, bursting with vitamins for us all,—proteins and minerals, too, in his shell, what we all need to help keep us well.

Three, four—they taste like "more!" Nothing can match the wonderful flavor of fresh eggs properly cooked. For eggs that are delicate (done just *so*) . . . cook them over heat that's low!

Five, six—they're fun to fix! Eggs don't have to be "just eggs." The poached egg on a toasted English muffin with thinly sliced fried ham and hollandaise sauce becomes delicious "Eggs Benedict." Creamed eggs with a bright garnish of sieved hard-cooked egg yolks and parsley bouquets become "Eggs à la Goldenrod."

Seven, eight—they're mealtime bait! The recipes that follow are sure to lure the family to meals. And the pages will show you by word and picture tested methods to insure superbly cooked eggs and egg dishes in attractive variety for many a meal to come.

Nine, ten—here's how and when! There's more than one way to crack an egg . . . and cook it! There's a *best* way even to cook eggs in the shell. The pages that follow show you how to work egg wonders for many a day.

Eleven, twelve—dig and delve! Delve into the recipes and we feel sure you'll be inspired to try every one of them.

COOKED-IN-THE-SHELL EGGS Never let them boil!

You like them soft to start the day,
But hard, they make a garnish gay

1 Have eggs at room temperature to prevent "cracking" during cooking.

2 Start in cold or boiling water.

3 Cover eggs completely with water.

4 Choose large enough pan. Do not pile eggs on top of each other.

5 Time accurately, by clock or timer.

6 Cook at temperature below boiling.

Cold Water Start

Soft-Cooked Eggs
2 to 4 min. *off the heat*

Hard-Cooked Eggs
23 to 25 min. *off the heat*

1 Cover eggs in saucepan with cold water. Heat until water boils.

2 Remove from heat. Cover pan. Let stand *off heat* until eggs are cooked.

Boiling Water Start

Soft-Cooked Eggs
3 to 5 min.

Hard-Cooked Eggs
18 to 20 min.

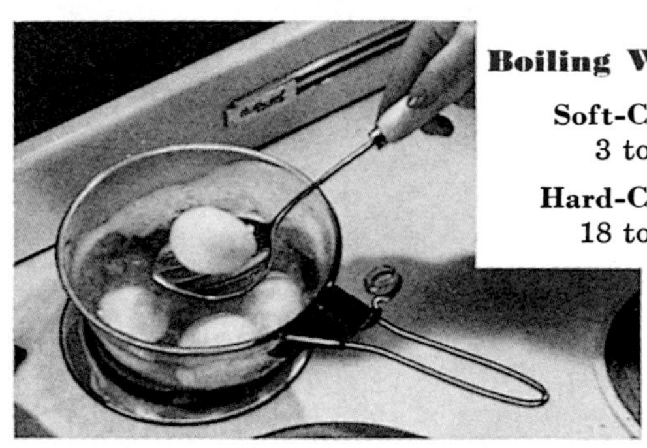

1 Bring water to a boil in saucepan. With a spoon, carefully lower eggs into the water to prevent cracking the shell.

2 Reduce heat. Keep water simmering until eggs are cooked. (Turn eggs several times... helps keep yolks centered.)

Cool eggs under cold water. This makes eggs easier to handle, eases shelling hard-cooked eggs, and immediately stops the cooking (overcooking causes the yolks to become darkened).

CODDLED EGGS *Super-delicate.*

Follow directions for cooking eggs with Boiling Water Start above—*except* cover pan tight, and remove from heat. Let stand until eggs are cooked.

Soft-Coddled Eggs: 4 to 6 min. *off heat.*

Hard-Coddled Eggs: 30 to 35 min. *off heat*

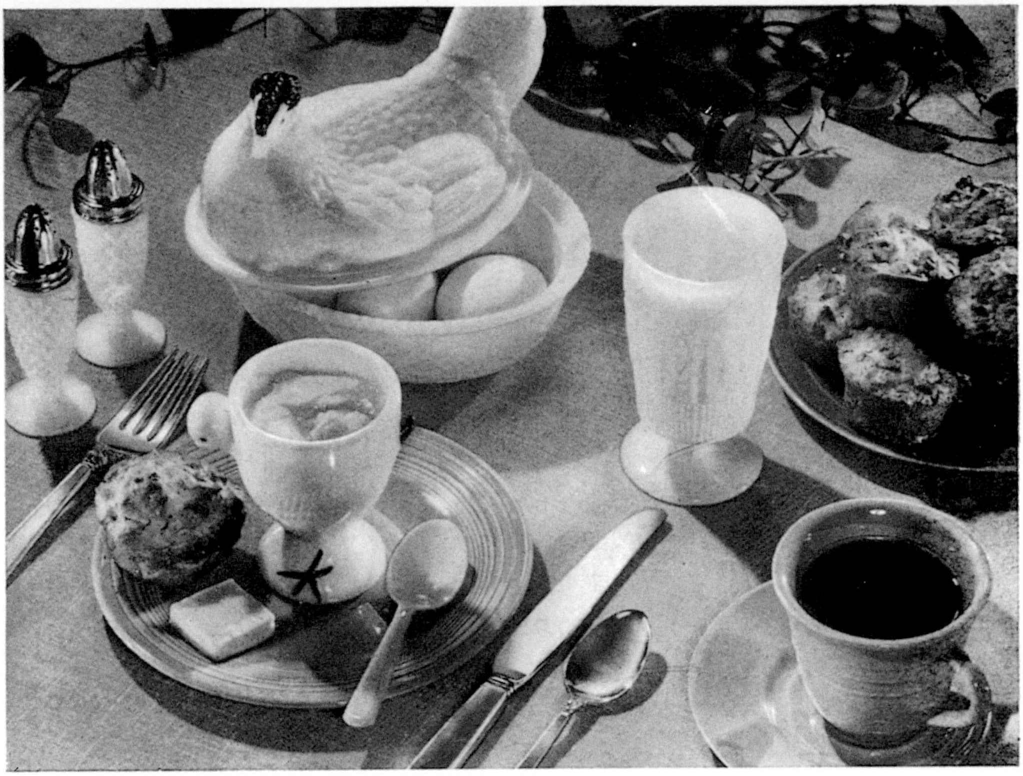

MILK GLASS HEN KEEPS EGGS WARM AND COZY

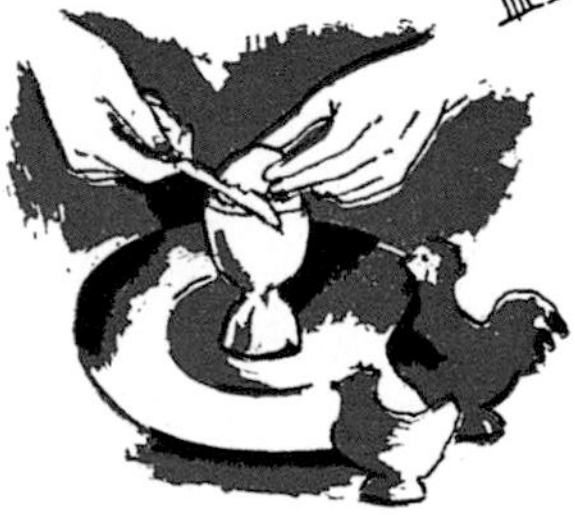

Crack egg sharply *at large end* when egg is to be eaten from shell, set in individual egg cup.

Crack egg sharply *in center* if to be turned into egg dish or cup.

Season with salt, pepper, and butter. "Use bone or ivory spoon," say the English.

Pull down top of egg slicer. Fine wires cut hard-cooked eggs. Use slices for gold-and-white garnish for salads, fish, etc.

Tap hard-cooked eggs to crackle. Roll between hands to loosen shells. Peel under cold water. Cut with sharp knife.

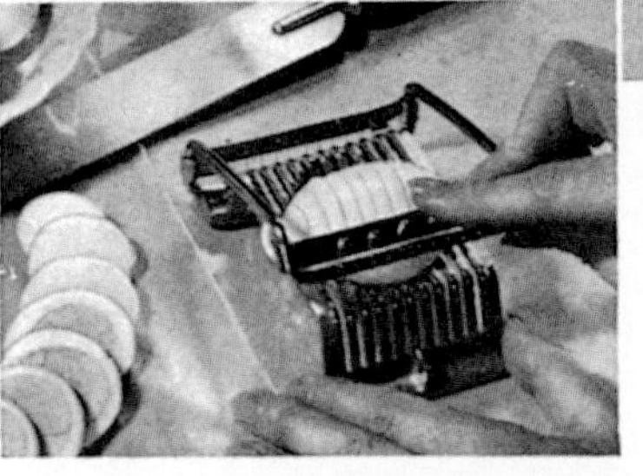

Press yolks and whites separately through coarse sieve. Use rows of white and yellow on canapés, to border meat loaves. Sprinkle over spinach, creamed eggs, etc.

WAYS WITH HARD-COOKED EGGS Versatile, Satisfying, Festive.

DEVILED EGGS (🗝 Recipe) *Mounds of savory yellow egg yolks in white frames. A stunning garnish and satisfying appetizer . . . food for picnics and parties.*

Cut in halves . . . 6 hard-cooked eggs

Slip out yolks. Mash with fork.

Add........ ½ tsp. salt
¼ tsp. pepper
½ tsp. dry mustard
about 3 tbsp. salad dressing or vinegar or cream (enough to moisten)

Refill whites with egg yolk mixture, heaping it up lightly. Use with salads, cold meat platters, etc.

To Carry Deviled Eggs To Picnics

Fit two halves together, wrap in waxed paper (twisting the ends).

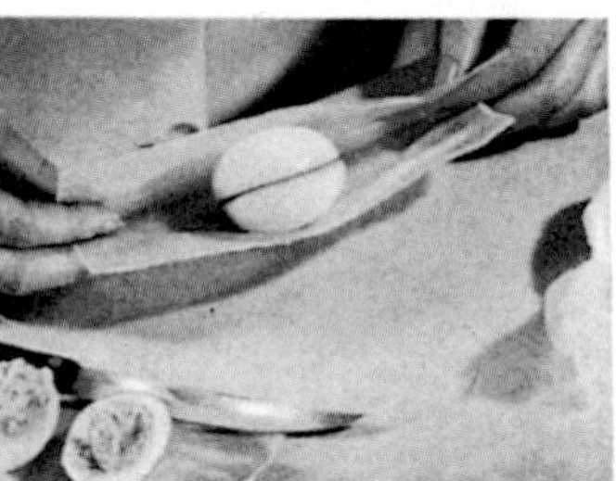

DEVILED EGGS DE LUXE

"Different" for appetizers, meat garnish, etc.

Follow 🗝 recipe above—*except* add to egg yolks with the seasonings 2 tbsp. of any of the following: finely minced parsley, chives, celery, or pimientos. Refill whites with this egg yolk mixture.

STUFFED EGGS FOR SPECIAL DISHES

Follow 🗝 recipe above—and add to mashed yolks 2 tbsp. minced cooked ham, crisp bacon, or frizzled dried beef; or flaked tuna, lobster, salmon, shrimp, or crabmeat; or mashed sardines or anchovies.

CREAMED EGGS (🗝 Recipe) *Offer endless possibilities for plain and fancy fare.*

Make.................................... *1 cup Medium White Sauce
Carefully fold in......................... 4 hard-cooked eggs, cut into quarters

Serve hot over hot buttered toast or biscuits, or in toast buttercups. Sprinkle with paprika and garnish with sprigs of parsley, crisp bacon, etc.

*QUICK VARIATION-DELICIOUS: Use seasoned canned Cream of Mushroom Soup (undiluted) in place of Medium White Sauce.

Deviled Egg Plate ready for the party.

CURRIED EGGS

Add ¼ tsp. curry powder with other seasonings when making Creamed Eggs.

CREAMED EGG SPECIALS

For luncheons, suppers, and parties.

Add to Creamed Eggs about 1 cup of:
Flaked Shrimp, Salmon, or Tuna
or Diced Cooked Chicken or Ham
or Frizzled Dried Beef
or Sautéed Mushrooms and Minced Pimiento

EGGS À LA GOLDENROD

Pretty gold and white main dish ready for luncheon.

Creamed Eggs with whites and some of yolks in the White Sauce, poured over buttered toast . . . . . . sieved yolks over top.

FRIED, BAKED EGGS Two favorite ways . . . for nights or days.

HOW TO FRY EGGS . . . SUNNY-SIDE-UP

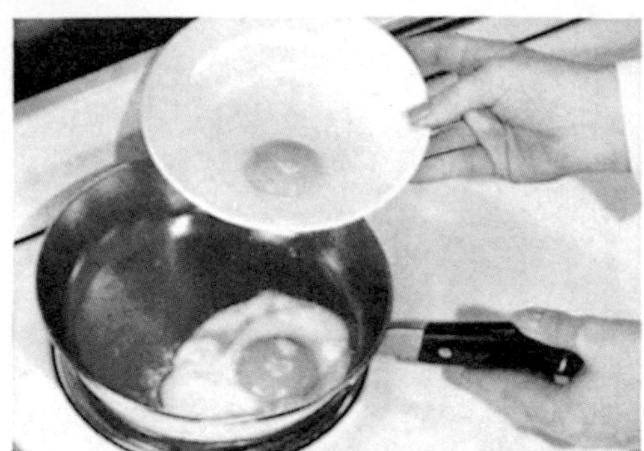

1 Heat a thin layer of butter or bacon fat in heavy skillet until moderately hot. Break eggs, one at a time, into saucer; slip into skillet. Immediately reduce heat to low.

2 Cook *slowly*, spooning fat over eggs until whites are set and a film forms over yolks (3 to 4 min.). Sprinkle with salt and pepper. Serve at once on warm plate.

FRIED EGGS . . . OVER

Fry eggs (*see above*)—*except* turn eggs over quickly when whites are set. Cook until done as desired.

POACHED-FRIED EGGS

They have lovely pink tops.

Fry eggs (*see above*)—*except* use just enough fat to coat skillet. Immediately add ½ tsp. water or cream for each egg. Cover tightly. Cook to firmness desired (5 to 6 min.).

Delicious Combination

Egg fried in butter . . . served on fried tomato slice. Curry Sauce.

BACON-OR-HAM AND EGGS

Fry bacon or ham in skillet; remove; keep warm. Then fry eggs in some of fat in pan. Serve immediately surrounded by hot bacon or ham, garnished with parsley, broiled peach or apricot halves, etc.

EGGS IN A FRAME

A Sunday evening treat.

Cut circle from slice of bread; then butter slice generously on both sides. Place in hot buttered skillet over low heat. Drop an egg into center. Cook slowly until egg is set and underside of bread is brown. Turn. Brown on other side. Season with salt and pepper.

BAKED OR SHIRRED EGGS

Break each egg into a greased 3″ shallow baking dish. Dot with butter. Sprinkle with salt and pepper. Add 1 tbsp. cream. Bake at 350° (mod. oven) until set (15 to 20 min.). Serve hot in the dish as an individual serving.

EGGS BAKED ON CORNED BEEF HASH

Spread warmed moist Corned Beef Hash in well greased shallow baking dish. With bottom of custard cup, make deep hollows in hash. Dot each with butter and break an egg into it. Season with salt and pepper; cover with 1 tbsp. cream. Bake at 400° (mod. hot oven) until eggs are set (15 to 20 min.). Serve immediately from the same dish.

EGGS BAKED IN BACON RINGS

Festive serving of Bacon and Eggs.

Follow directions opposite—*except* circle inside of each baking dish with a partially cooked bacon strip (not crisp) before breaking in egg.

HOW TO POACH EGGS

1 Fill greased skillet with hot water to cover eggs by 1″. Add salt (1 tsp. to 1 qt. water). Bring to boil; then reduce to simmering. Break each egg into a saucer and slip one at a time into the water. Slide egg toward side of pan to keep yolk in center.

2 Cover pan. Cook below simmering 3 to 5 min. Lift eggs from water, one at a time, with slotted spoon. Drain. Season with salt and pepper. Serve at once on hot buttered toast, split and toasted English Muffins, codfish cakes, or seasoned spinach, etc.

Poaching Eggs in Muffin Rings.

EGGS POACHED IN MILK

Poach eggs (*see above*)—*except* use milk in place of water (enough to barely cover eggs). Pour the hot milk over eggs on the hot toast.

Poaching Eggs in Egg Poacher

EGGS À LA REINE

Fit for a queen's luncheon or supper.

Place rounds of toast in baking dish. Cover with sliced mushrooms sautéed in butter . . . then with poached eggs. Pour over all, hot Cheese Sauce. Sprinkle with grated cheese and place in quick mod. oven (375°) until cheese is melted.

EGGS À LA LEE

As served in Old Virginia.

For each serving, cover hot toast round with thin slice of boiled ham. Top with hot poached egg. Pour hot Mushroom Sauce over all. Serve at once.

POACHED EGGS IN SPINACH NESTS

Arrange a nest of cooked garden spinach on each luncheon plate. Place in each a hot poached egg. Serve immediately.

POACHED EGGS ON HASH CAKES

They go together like ham 'n' eggs.

Prepare patties of hash. Top each with a poached egg. Serve hot with chili sauce.

EGGS POACHED IN A WHIRLPOOL

Stir simmering water in skillet briskly . . . slip egg into center of whirlpool. Cover pan. A number of eggs may be cooked at one time. Cut eggs apart.

EGGS BENEDICT

The original recipe was brought to Old New Orleans by the French.

For each serving, cover a round of split and toasted English Muffin (or toast) with a thin slice of fried ham (same size), or spread with deviled ham. Top each with a poached egg and cover with Hollandaise Sauce. Serve at once.

SCRAMBLED EGGS Quick, easy answer to a big Sunday breakfast.

SCRAMBLED EGGS (🔑 Recipe) *Moist, tender, and golden.*

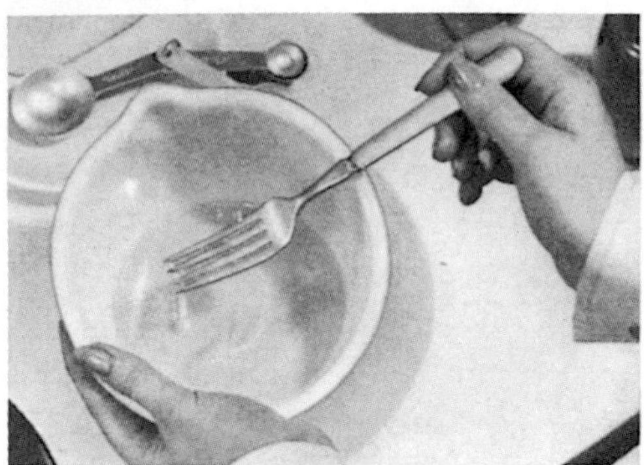

1 Place in bowl with egg 1 tbsp. milk or cream for each egg, a dash of salt, and pepper. Beat with fork. For gold-and-white effect, do not blend completely.

2 Heat butter or other fat (½ tbsp. for each egg) in mod. hot skillet. Pour in egg mixture and reduce heat to low. (Eggs should be scrambled slowly and gently.)

3 When mixture starts to set at bottom and sides, lift cooked portions with spatula, and turn gently so as to cook all portions evenly.

4 As soon as eggs are cooked through but are still moist and glossy (5 to 8 min.), quickly remove to hot platter and serve at once.

QUICK SCRAMBLED EGGS

Pour eggs directly into hot fat in skillet. Add salt and pepper to taste. Stir gently.

DELICATE SCRAMBLED EGGS

Made in double boiler without fat.

Follow 🔑 recipe above—*except* cook in top of double boiler over simmering—not boiling water, stirring occasionally, until eggs are thick and creamy.

SAVORY SCRAMBLED EGGS

Follow 🔑 recipe above—*except* add minced chives and parsley to egg mixture.

All you have to do–

To make Eggs à la Buckingham: pour scrambled eggs (slightly underdone) over toast covered with Medium White Sauce. Sprinkle with grated cheese. Put in oven to melt cheese.

SCRAMBLED EGGS WITH CHEESE

Follow 🔑 recipe above—*except*, for each egg, add 1 tbsp. grated American cheese, ¼ tsp. minced onion to egg mixture.

SCRAMBLED EGGS WITH MUSHROOMS

Follow 🔑 recipe above—*except* first sauté fresh sliced mushrooms (1 to 2 tbsp for each egg) in the hot fat.

SCRAMBLED EGGS WITH DRIED BEEF OR HAM

Follow 🔑 recipe above—*except* frizzle flaked pieces of dried beef or boiled ham in the hot fat before adding eggs.

FRENCH OMELET (🗝 **Recipe**) *Creamy, yet hearty.*

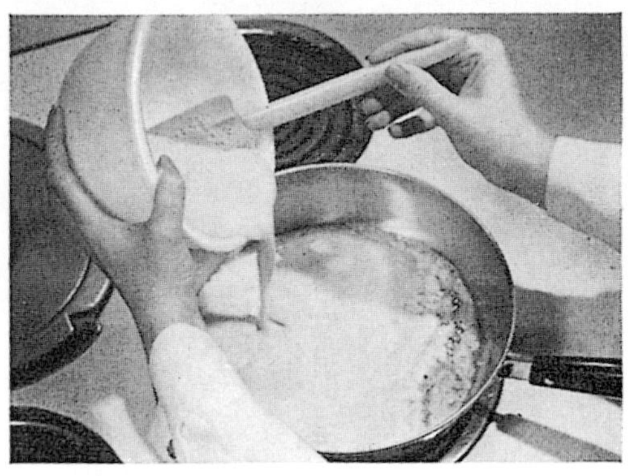

1 Beat eggs until fluffy. For each egg, beat in 1 tbsp. milk or cream, a dash of salt, pepper. Pour into sizzling butter (1 tsp. per egg) in skillet over *low* heat.

2 Cook slowly . . . keeping heat low. As undersurface becomes set, start lifting it slightly with spatula to let uncooked portion flow underneath and cook.

3 To add herbs, cheese, meat, etc., sprinkle ½ tbsp. per egg over top of eggs.

4 As soon as all of mixture seems set, fold or roll it; serve immediately.

OMELET AUX FINES HERBES
On every menu in France.

Follow 🗝 recipe above—sprinkling with ½ tbsp. *each* minced chives and parsley. Add a dash of other herbs (chervil, basil, thyme, sweet marjoram).

CHEESE OMELET

Follow 🗝 recipe above—adding grated American cheese.

MUSHROOM OMELET

Follow 🗝 recipe above—adding sautéed sliced mushrooms (2 to 4 tbsp. per egg).

TOMATO OMELET

Follow 🗝 recipe above—adding 2 tbsp. sautéed cut-up fresh tomatoes per egg.

INDIVIDUAL OMELETS (Roll-ups)
Clever egg maneuver from Mrs. Anthony Kennedy, Media, Pennsylvania.

Follow 🗝 recipe above—spreading 1 egg with 1 tbsp. milk over bottom of 10″ skillet. When egg is set, cut through center. Roll up each half (from end near you) as an individual omelet. Serve each with a small strip of crisp bacon.

JELLY OMELET

Follow 🗝 recipe above—*except,* just before folding, spread with jelly.

BACON OR HAM OMELET

Follow 🗝 recipe above—sprinkling with 2 tbsp. broken crisp cooked bacon or flakes of cooked ham per egg.

PUFFY OMELET (🔑 Recipe) *A lovely main dish . . . the cook's pride.*

2 Pour into sizzling butter (½ tbsp. per egg) in heavy skillet.

1 Beat egg whites until stiff. Beat egg yolks until thick and lemon-colored, beat in 1 tbsp. milk or cream per egg, . . . salt and pepper. Fold into the beaten whites.

3 Turn heat to low. Cook slowly until light brown underneath (about 10 min.). (Bubbles will still appear through uncooked puffy top and mixture will look moist.)

4 Place skillet in mod. oven (350°). Bake until light brown on top and until, when touched lightly with finger, no imprint remains (about 10 to 15 min.).

5 Make ½″ deep crease across omelet . . . half way between handle and opposite side. Slip spatula under, tip skillet to loosen omelet, and fold in half without breaking.

6 Roll omelet top-side-down onto hot platter.

7 Garnish with hot sauce and serve at once.

HELPS TO HOLD UP PUFFY OMELETS

Soft Bread Crumbs: Use ½ tbsp. for each egg. Soak crumbs in the milk.

Medium White Sauce: Use 4 tbsp. for each egg. Blend into beaten yolks.

Cream of Tartar: Beat in with egg whites (¼ tsp. for 4 whites).

FAVORITE SAUCES

Delicious with Puffy Omelet.

Cheese Sauce
Mushroom Sauce
Tomato Sauce
Creamed Chicken
Creamed Ham
Creamed Asparagus

Any of these may be made as variations of Medium White Sauce.

The Importance of Knowing Our Meats

MEAT *is like the star of the show . . . the center around which the rest of the meal revolves. All the other foods are chosen on the basis of how well they go with the meat selected. Meat is also the most expensive item in our food budget . . . which makes it doubly important that we present this star performer to the best advantage.*

Betty Crocker

Fish

For additional Meat, Fish, Poultry recipes (combination and casserole dishes, one-dish meals, etc.), see "SUPPER DISHES."

Poultry

Wild Game

HOW MUCH MEAT TO BUY

Boneless Meat (rolled roasts, tenderloins, ground meat, variety meats, etc.): Plan 1/4 to 1/2 lb. per serving, depending on your pocketbook and tastes.

Bone-in-the-Meat (roasts, steaks, chops, shanks, ribs, etc.): 1/3 to 1/2 lb. per serving is the least you can plan on. For hearty meat-eaters, plan on 1 lb. per serving.

THRIFTY BUYING AND PLANNING

Pet idea from Monica Clark, American Meat Institute, Chicago, who contributed so much good information and photographs for this chapter.

A larger cut of meat often saves money and shopping time

Have three fresh cooked meat meals (without leftovers)

Buy a whole fresh pork shoulder butt (5 to 7 lb.). Cut at home as shown.

1 Pork Roast

Cut with sharp knife into 2 pieces. The piece with bone is your smaller one-meal roast.

2 Pork Steaks

From remaining piece of meat, cut boneless 1/2″ steaks. Braise like pork chops.

3 Chop Suey

Cut remaining boneless piece into 1/2″ cubes for a meat-stretching dish, such as chop suey.

Buy a thick round-bone pot roast. Cut at home as shown.

1 Beef Stew

Cut a piece from the round end of the roast and cut meat into cubes for beef stew.

2 Pot Roast

Cut a piece from the center for a chunky pot roast.

3 Swiss Steak

With sharp knife (saucer under hand for safety), split remaining pieces into 2 Swiss Steaks.

Buy a full-cut leg of lamb. Ask meat dealer to cut off a few lamb steaks (as indicated), and to cut from shank leaving 1 lb. on bone.

1 Lamb Steaks

Broil the lamb steaks as you would chops.

2 Lamb Roast

Use the easy-to-carve center portion for your Sunday roast.

3 Stew or Casserole

Cut the meat from the shank into cubes for an Irish Stew or Lamb Curry or Shish Kabob (grilled on skewer).

Four Favorite Roasts, pp. 264, 265

We are indebted to Beth McLean, Martha Logan of Swift and Company, Chicago, for these stunning color pictures, the charts on cooking of meat, and much helpful advice as to the latest and best information on meats.

Roast Leg of Lamb with Carrot Flowers, black olive centers, in parsley bouquets.

Easter Baked Ham with Colored Eggs and Carrot Daffodils, watercress.

Standing Rib Roast of Beef, Fruit Cups in Orange Baskets set in parsley.

Rolled Shoulder of Veal Roast, Browned Potatoes, Stuffed Onions, Watercress.

MEATS

Meat has been the backbone of man's diet from the beginning of time. Wild fowl and fish were devoured with the deer and wild boar which the cave man brought from the hunt. The great feasts of medieval times were made up of meat and very little else. It is not strange that food in those times was referred to merely as "meat."

Less than fifty years ago in our own country even, any dinner or banquet worthy of the name included a separate fish course, a main course usually referred to as "the roast," and following that "roast" an "entree" or made-dish such as creamed sweetbreads or chicken patties.

Family and guests in a famous Washington mansion at the beginning of this century started Thanksgiving day with Porterhouse steak and codfish balls for breakfast. The dinner a few hours later began with oysters on the half shell, followed by cream of chicken soup. Next came fried smelts with tartar sauce. All this was a prelude to the roast turkey with cranberry sauce, mashed potatoes, baked squash, boiled onions, and parsnip fritters as "trimmin's." Following was chicken salad, then a venison pastry. The traditional mince pie and pumpkin pie shared honors as dessert with ice cream and hickory nut cake. Fruit and cheese topped off the meal. In the evening, a supper was served including cold roast turkey and scalloped oysters.

Today we are content with a serving of meat, fish, or poultry for dinner. Without one of the three, it is an unsatisfactory meal for most people . . . undoubtedly because they miss essential nutritional elements. All three give adequate amounts of high quality protein and B-complex vitamins. Oily fish also gives some Vitamin D, and fish roe is a good source of Vitamin A. Meat is particularly rich in iron and phosphorus for blood and bones. Shellfish and salt water fish contain more iodine than any other common food. In addition, the fat of these foods is a rich source of energy . . . and it also adds flavor and eating enjoyment. In this chapter you will find the best cooking methods for nutrition and eating satisfaction.

STORING MEATS To preserve quality.

"BUY MEAT WISELY . . . STORE IT CAREFULLY"

says Reba Staggs of the National Live Stock and Meat Board, Chicago, who contributed their good information to help us.

1 The lean and fat of all grades of meat have essentially the same nutritive value.

2 Select the grade best fitted to your pocketbook and the way you plan to cook it.

3 Insist on government-inspected meat. You can recognize it by this purple inspection stamp for wholesomeness on most fresh and cured meats. It is required for your protection on all meat shipped interstate.

U. S. Choice: Highest grade of beef, veal, lamb or mutton found in retail stores . . . is well marbled with fat and has a moderately thick fat covering.

U. S. Good: Has a fat covering somewhat thinner than the U. S. Choice.

U. S. Commercial and U. S. Utility: Lower grades with thin fat covering . . . for braising or cooking in liquid.

NOTE: Very little pork is branded by packers.

HOW TO STORE MEAT

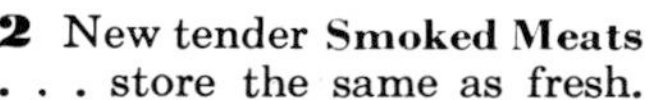

2 New tender **Smoked Meats** . . . store the same as fresh.

1 Fresh Meat: Remove wrapping. Cover loosely with waxed paper, leaving ends open. Store in coldest part of refrigerator in meat compartment or drip tray. Use within 2 or 3 days.

3 Ground Meat: Darkens on standing and spoils more quickly than whole cuts. Unwrap, cover loosely with waxed paper. Store as for fresh meat. Cook within 24 hr. If kept longer, wrap each serving and freeze.

5 Variety Meats: Store the same as ground meat.

4 Frozen Meat: Store in freezing unit. Do not unwrap. Keep meat frozen until ready to use. It should be used promptly after thawing. *Do not refreeze.*

6 Cooked Meat: Cover tightly in dish or with foil to prevent drying, store in coldest part of refrigerator. Do not cut, grind, or slice until ready to use.

7 Poultry: Keeps better whole than in pieces. *Drawn:* Wrap loosely in waxed paper. Store in coldest part of refrigerator.

8 Fresh Fish: Wrap completely or place in tightly covered dish. Keep in coldest part of refrigerator. Cook within 24 hr.

With dry heat. MEATS HOW TO COOK

A meat thermometer is the only sure test for the doneness of meat. The minutes per pound are only a guide. Size, shape, fat covering, and initial temperature of the roast influence the cooking period. The approximate minutes per pound given below are based on meat taken from the refrigerator. *Insert* meat thermometer *in center of thickest part of meat . . .* not touching bone *. . . nor resting in fat.*

ROASTING

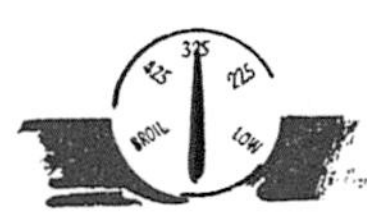

Place fat side up on rack in open pan in preheated oven (325°). Keep at this low temperature.

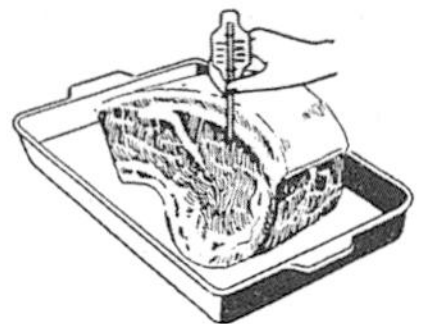

Do not add water.
Do not cover.
Do not baste.

CHART FOR ROASTING (Meat directly from refrigerator)

CUT OF MEAT	Approximate Min. per Lb. for 3 to 6 Lb. Roast	Total Time	Internal Temperature (Meat Thermometer)
Beef			
Standing ribs . . . rare	26 min.	1¾ hr.	140°F.
medium	30 min.	2 hr.	160°F.
well done	35 min.	2⅓ hr.	170°F.
Boned and rolled roasts . . . increase cooking time 5 to 10 min.			
Pork (Fresh)			
Leg	45 to 50 min.	3 hr.	185°F.
Rib and loin	35 to 40 min.	2⅔ hr.	185°F.
Shoulder, Picnic	40 min.	3 hr.	185°F.
Shoulder (boned and rolled)	55 min.	4 hr.	185°F.
Shoulder, butt	40 to 50 min.	3½ hr.	185°F.
Lamb			
Leg . . . medium	35 min.	2¼ hr.	175°F.
well done	40 min.	2¾ hr.	182°F.
Crown . . . well done	45 min.	3 hr.	182°F.
Shoulder . . . well done	35 min.	2¼ hr.	182°F.
Shoulder (boned and rolled)	40 min.	3 hr.	182°F.
Veal			
Leg	35 to 40 min.	2¾ hr.	180°F.
Loin	35 min.	2¼ hr.	180°F.
Shoulder	40 min.	2¾ hr.	180°F.
Boneless Shoulder Roll	55 min.	3½ to 4 hr.	180°F.

All you have to do—

To reheat without losing flavor: wrap roast in aluminum foil or parchment paper, heat in a slow moderate oven (325°) to an internal heat of 130°.

FROZEN ROASTS
(directly from freezer)

Increase cooking time 10 to 15 min. per lb.

HOW TO COOK MEATS With dry heat.

CHART FOR ROASTING CURED OR SMOKED PORK—325°
(Meat directly from refrigerator) (*See roasting directions, p. 267*)

CUT OF MEAT		Time per Lb.	Total Time	Internal Temperature (Meat Thermometer)
Ham	12 to 15 lb.	16 to 17 min.	3½ hr.	150°F.
	10 to 12 lb.	18 min.	3¼ hr.	150°F.
	Under 10 lb.	20 min.	3 hr.	150°F.
	Half Hams	22 min.	2½ hr.	150°F.
Shoulder (Picnic)				
	5 lb.	30 min.	about 3 hr.	170°F.
	8 lb.	25 min.	3¼ hr.	170°F.
Boneless Butt				
	2 lb.	45 min.	1½ hr.	170°F.
	4 lb.	35 min.	2¼ hr.	170°F.

All you have to do—

To finish baked ham: about 45 min. before baking time is up, remove from oven. Take off rind and score (cut fat surface into squares or diamonds). Stud each square with a whole clove. Ham *may* be spread with paste of 1 cup brown sugar, 1 tsp. dry mustard, and 2 or 3 tbsp. vinegar, honey, or syrup. Return to oven 45 min. Baste occasionally with fruit juice, cider, or juice from pickled peaches.

OVEN BROILING

Slash edges of fat to prevent curling.

Place meat 3 to 5 in. from heat. Broil to desired brownness. Season. Turn once, brown on other side. For cuts to broil, *see below.*

PAN-BROILING

Same cuts as for oven broiling. Use heavy skillet. It may be lightly rubbed with fat to prevent sticking. Place meat in hot skillet. Brown on 1 side, then on other. Reduce heat; occasionally turn meat and pour off fat. Season, serve.

Do *not* cover.

Do *not* add water.

CHART FOR BROILING (Meat directly from refrigerator)

CUT OF MEAT	Thickness	Minutes per Side: Rare	Medium	Well Done
Beef Steak (Rib, Club, Tenderloin (Fillet), Porterhouse, T-Bone, Sirloin)	1 in.	5 min.	6 min.	7 min.
	1½ in.	9 min.	10 min.	12 min.
	2 in.	16 min.	18 min.	20 min.
Lamb (Loin, Rib, or Shoulder Chops)	1 in.	Lamb is	6 min.	7 min.
	1½ in.	never served	9 min.	11 min.
	2 in.	rare	15 min.	17 min.
Cured Pork (Ham, Shoulder)				
Uncooked	1 in.			10 min.
Ready-to-eat	1 in.			5 min.

PAN-FRYING

Pan-broiling becomes pan-frying when the meat is first browned in hot fat, then slowly fried on both sides. "Minute steaks" (thin slices of round or chuck steak) are pan-fried. Sliced heart and slices of liver are usually dipped in flour, then pan-fried.

BRAISING

Season, dredge with flour if desired. Brown in a little hot fat in heavy kettle. Cover, cook slowly on stove or in mod. oven until tender in the meat juices, or add small amount of liquid (water, milk, cream, or stock). The juices are served as pan gravy or may be thickened for gravy. Time depends on cut and size of meat (1 to 3 hr.).

Stewing is to braise with enough water added to cover meat. Cut-up carrots, onions, potatoes, etc. may be added during last 20 to 30 min. The stock is thickened for gravy.

SIMMERING

Cover with water and cook gently. Add seasonings and keep kettle covered. Cook until meat is tender when tested with a fork (2 to 4 hr. depending on size and cut). Add vegetables, if desired, during last 20 to 30 min. of cooking.

CUTS OF MEAT FOR BRAISING

Beef: Pot roast (rump, heel of round, chuck, flank steak, short ribs, stewing beef shank, brisket, oxtails, liver, heart, round or chuck steak).

Lamb: Boneless rolled shoulder, shanks, riblets (neck slices), heart, shoulder chops, breast, or stewing meat.

Veal: Boneless rolled shoulder, loin or rib chops, Frenched cutlets, steak or cutlets, shank or breast.

Pork: Rib or loin chops, shoulder steak, spareribs, whole tenderloin and slices, heart, pork liver, cutlets.

CUTS OF MEAT FOR SIMMERING

Beef: Corned brisket, tongue, sweetbreads.

Lamb: Heart, tongue.

Veal: Heart, tongue, sweetbreads.

Pork: Shoulder, tongue, heart, spareribs.

This method also used in cooking meats for soups . . . brisket or plate, oxtails, hocks, etc.

To Follow Directions in many of the Meat Recipes

Bread: Dip meat into slightly beaten egg mixed with a little milk, then in fine dry bread or cracker crumbs. Cook.

Roll or Dip in Seasoned Flour: 1 to 2 tsp. salt and ¼ tsp. pepper to each cup flour. Other seasonings, such as celery salt, garlic salt, are often added.

Flatten: Pound meat with mallet or flat side of cleaver or edge of heavy saucer.

Season Meat: Sprinkle with salt and pepper to taste. Add other appropriate seasonings, such as celery salt, onion salt, garlic salt, herb powders, etc.

Certain herbs have an affinity for certain meats. We suggest:

For Beef: Basil, sweet marjoram, summer savory, thyme, rosemary.

For Pork: Thyme, sage, basil, rosemary, sweet marjoram, chives.

For Lamb: Sweet marjoram, mint, summer savory, rosemary, dill.

For Veal: Rosemary, summer savory, sage, thyme, basil, tarragon.

For Poultry: Chervil, sage, summer savory, tarragon, thyme, sweet marjoram.

For Fish: Fennel, sage, thyme, basil, chives, chervil, parsley, dill, marjoram.

POT ROAST

Roll a 4 to 5-lb. beef chuck in seasoned flour. Brown in hot fat. Then spread with . . .

½ cup horseradish

Add a little water. Cover kettle, cook slowly (*3 to 3½ hr.*). During last hr., add . . .

8 to 10 small onions
8 to 10 medium carrots
8 to 10 stalks celery
8 to 10 peeled potatoes
½ tsp. salt

Remove meat and vegetables to hot platter. Thicken juice for gravy. Serve hot.
AMOUNT: 8 servings.

BARBECUED BEEF

Unroll a rolled rump roast and spread with Barbecue Sauce and minced onion. Sprinkle with salt and pepper. Roll up again and tie; or fasten with skewers. Braise (*p. 269*). Serve hot slices between slices of buttered fresh bread.

NEW ENGLAND BOILED DINNER

Corned beef and cabbage . . . and other home-grown vegetables . . . cooked together.

Place in kettle a 4 to 5-lb. corned brisket of beef. Cover with cold water, add herbs and seasonings (*no salt*), simmer 5 min. (*p. 269*). Remove scum, cover; simmer until tender (3½ to 5 hr.). About 45 min. before beef is done, skim off excess fat. Add . . .

8 pared white turnips, cut in pieces
8 pared potatoes, cut in medium pieces
8 whole carrots

Cover, cook about 25 min. Then add . . .

1 green cabbage, quartered and cored

Cover, and cook until vegetables are tender (25 min.). Serve on hot platter . . . the vegetables around the corned beef. (Serve beets also, but cook separately.)
AMOUNT: 8 servings.

PLANKED STEAK

Glamorous, showy one-dish meal.

Broil on one side 1½" thick steak (rare, 9 min.). Place broiled-side-down on heated wooden plank. Around edge of plank, pipe . . .

border of mashed potatoes (brushed with beaten egg)

Return to broiler and broil until steak is done and potatoes browned.
Between steak and potatoes, arrange . . .

seasoned cooked vegetables of contrasting colors, suitable flavors (caulifloweretes, fried tomato, mushrooms, etc.)

FILLET OF BEEF

Season a tenderloin of beef (4 to 5 lb.). Place strips of bacon on top. Roast at 325° 20–25 min. per lb. (*see p. 267*). Place in long roll on hot platter . . . cutting in thick slices to serve. Serve with Thin Mushroom Sauce. *Serves 12.*

FILET MIGNON

Deliciously tender steaks from the tenderloin trimmed into neat rounds.

Wrap strip of bacon around edge of each fillet, fasten with wooden pick. Brush with butter or bacon fat. Broil (*p. 268*). Serve with sautéed mushrooms.

SWISS STEAK

Pound 6 tbsp. seasoned flour into sides 2-lb. round or flank steak (1½" thick). Brown in hot fat in heavy skillet. Add . . .

2 cups cooked tomatoes (#1 tall can)
1 onion, sliced
1 stalk celery, diced

Cover. Cook over low heat or in mod. oven (300°) until tender (2 to 2½ hr.) . . . uncovering last ½ hr. to cook down sauce to a rich thickness. Serve hot.

MOCK DUCK

Happy substitution for a holiday bird.

Use 5-lb. shoulder of lamb from forequarter . . . with foreleg on. Cut off 4″ below knee to form head and neck of duck. Have shoulder boned . . . and mold and sew it in shape of body of duck . . . leaving hollow for stuffing. The foreleg should stand up to give effect of neck and head. Split leg bone 1″ to form mouth. Use bits of bone for eyes. Remove a few stitches and fill hollow with Stuffing. Re-sew. Rub with fat. Roast. Serve hot . . . surrounded with small molds of mint or cranberry jelly on orange slices.

BRAISED LAMB SHANKS

Brown 4 lamb shanks (2 lb.) in 4 tbsp. hot fat. Add salt, pepper, 2 cups water. Cover, and simmer 1½ hr. (Or bake in mod. oven, 350°, 1½ hr.)

Add . . .

- **1 cup *each* cut-up carrots and potatoes**
- **½ cup *each* cut-up celery and onion**

Cook until tender (30 min. to 1 hr.). Thicken juice for gravy. Serve hot.

AMOUNT: 4 servings.

LAMB CURRY DE LUXE

Use lamb in making Meat Curry (*p. 276*) . . . and add, with the thickening, 1 cup chopped apple, ¼ cup minced celery, and, if desired, 1 tbsp. minced onion.

LAMB CROQUETTES

Use last bits of roast lamb in making Meat Croquettes (*p. 277*).

LAMB KABOBS

Marinating in French Dressing makes the lamb cubes-on-a-skewer extra tender.

Trim surplus fat and bone from lamb shoulder meat. Cut in 1½″ cubes; place from 3 to 4 on each skewer. Marinate in French Dressing in shallow pie plate 1 to 2 hr., turning occasionally. Drain. Broil. Serve hot.

LAMBIE PIES

One of the smart thrift ideas of Mrs. E. A. Anderson, Stonington, Connecticut.

Use leftover lamb in making individual meat pies. (See Savory Meat Pie, *p. 277*).

PICTURE PLATTER

*Roast Lamb surrounded by *Browned Stuffed Potatoes and Pear Halves filled with Green Mint Jelly. Gay watercress garnish.*

*Carve into each peeled raw potato a little cave large enough to insert onion. Place in roasting pan close to meat. When roast begins to brown, put a little butter on each potato; continue browning until tender. Garnish with minced parsley.

RULLE POLSE (Rolled Sausage)

Famous Norwegian recipe from Hatton, North Dakota. The Icelanders make it with mutton.

Place thin strips of salt pork on flank of veal or mutton. Sprinkle with minced onion, salt, pepper, and allspice. Roll up like a jelly roll. Sew with a string and tie tightly to hold in filling.

Place in kettle with sliced onion, celery tops, crushed bay leaves, and boiling water to cover. Simmer until meat is tender (about 2 hr.). Remove from water, place in loaf pan, and cover with clean cloth.

Press the meat by placing a heavy weight on it until cold. (For pressing, place a brick or flatiron in another loaf pan and set on top of cloth-covered meat.) Store in cool place. Serve cold . . . in slices.

CHINESE LAMB SUEY

Brown in 2 tbsp. hot fat, 1 lb. lamb (cut in narrow strips 2″ long and rolled in seasoned flour) with 1 small clove garlic, minced.

Add . . .

- **2 cups broccoli or green beans (cut in 1″ pieces)**
- **1 tsp. soy sauce**
- **1 cup Bouillon or lamb stock**

Cover, and simmer until vegetable is tender. Stir in 1 tbsp. cornstarch dissolved in ¼ cup cold water. Cook 5 min. Serve.

AMOUNT: 6 servings.

NOTE: The cornstarch gives the glaze typical of such Chinese meat dishes.

LAMB PRINTANIERE

A savory lamb stew with spring vegetables (*see p. 276*).

BREADED VEAL CUTLETS

Cut veal cutlet (½″ thick) into serving-sized pieces. Dip in seasoned flour. Then bread the pieces (*p. 269*). Pan-fry slowly in hot fat in heavy skillet until tender (about 15 min. on each side). Serve hot with hot Tomato Sauce.

BLANQUETTE OF VEAL

A French chef gave me this recipe . . . it's wonderful.

Dip veal steak (1″ thick) in seasoned flour. Brown in hot fat in heavy skillet. Add 1 tbsp. vinegar and a bit of water. Cover. Cook slowly until tender. Serve on hot platter with hot Mushroom Sauce.

VEAL PATTIES WITH TOMATO SAUCE

Pan-broil little cakes of seasoned ground veal. Serve with hot Tomato Sauce.

VEAL DAUBE

An example of the superb French cuisine of New Orleans. Our Staff said, "About the best seasoned meat we ever tasted!"

Rub a 4 to 5-lb. veal rump or shoulder roast with bacon fat . . . adding a bit of dried hot red pepper and tiny bit of garlic.

Sprinkle with . . .

- **1 tsp. salt**
- **⅛ tsp. *each* pepper, mace, cloves**
- **¼ tsp. allspice**

Rub well into the meat a mixture of . . .

- **½ tsp. *each* thyme and sage**
- **2 bay leaves, crushed**
- **¼ cup GOLD MEDAL Flour**

Brown in hot fat. Meanwhile, brown in hot fat in heavy kettle . . .

- **1 onion, minced**
- **4 carrots, sliced**
- **1 turnip, cut-up**
- **2 celery stalks, diced**
- **1 sweet red pepper, minced**

Add browned veal to browned vegetables with 1 cup boiling water. Cover, and cook slowly until tender (2 to 2½ hr.). Thicken juice for gravy. Serve hot.
AMOUNT: 8 servings.

STUFFED VEAL FILLETS

Nell Nichols, writer and epicure, was our guest the first time we served this delicious and partyfied meat dish in our Early American dining-room.

Flatten a 1″ thick, boned 2-lb. veal steak into a 6x10″ oblong ¾″ thick. Spread with ½ lb. sausage meat. Lay 6 shelled whole hard-cooked eggs end to end, pressing into sausage in a line down center.

Roll up steak like a long jelly roll. Tie securely with string. Brown in hot fat. Then pour over the roll 2 cups brown stock (Bouillon). Add 2 celery stalks with leaves, 2 cut-up carrots, a pinch *each* of thyme, onion salt, and black pepper. Cover and simmer gently in slow oven (300°) 1½ hr. Place on hot platter. Remove string. Thicken stock for gravy, and add ½ lb. sautéed sliced fresh mushrooms. Serve in 1″ thick slices with the hot mushroom gravy. *Serves 7.*

VEAL SUPREME

Popular at Sibley Tea House, near the home of an early Minnesota governor, at Mendota-on-the-Mississippi.

Savory mixture of browned cubes of veal steak simmered until tender with diluted tomato juice and appropriate seasonings (salt, pepper, onion, bay leaf, rosemary, and chervil) . . . then combined with a little sour cream, sautéed sliced mushrooms, diced celery, cooked noodles, and sliced canned water chestnuts . . . and baked 15 min. in a mod. oven.

VEAL CUTLETS MORNAY

Make same as Pork Cutlets Mornay (*p. 273*)—*except* use veal cutlets in place of pork.

VEAL PARMESAN

Remove white fibers from veal cutlets or serving-sized pieces of veal steak . . . and flatten. Sprinkle with salt, pepper, and paprika. Coat with grated Parmesan cheese. Sauté in hot chicken fat until lightly browned (3 min. on each side). Serve hot.

VEAL STEW

See recipe for Savory Stew (*p. 276*).

BRAISED PORK CHOPS (OR STEAK)

Chops from the loin are the choicest . . . those from ribs or shoulder most economical.

Brown seasoned pork chops (or steak) in a greased heavy skillet. Add a bit of water. Cover. Cook over low heat until tender (30 to 45 min.). Serve at once.

PORK CHOPS WITH APPLE RINGS

Cover browned seasoned pork chops with ¾" thick rings of tart raw apple. Sprinkle with a little brown sugar. Add a bit of water. Braise as above.

PORK CHOPS SUPREME

Top each browned seasoned pork chop with 1 thin onion slice and 1 thin lemon slice. Sprinkle with brown sugar. Add ½ cup catsup. Braise as above.

CURRIED PORK CHOPS WITH APRICOTS

Top each browned seasoned pork chop with an apricot half (round side up). Pour over them Curry-Onion Sauce (*below*). Top with sautéed mushrooms. Braise as above.

All you have to do–

To make Curry-Onion Sauce: add desired amount sautéed minced onion to Curry Sauce.

CABIN CASSEROLE

A heart-warming dish for a cold day.

Place in alternate layers in buttered casserole sliced onions and sliced tomatoes (green preferred) . . . using in all ½ cup of each for each chop and sprinkling each layer with salt and curry powder. On top, lay browned seasoned pork chops. Bake uncovered at 350° (mod. oven) 45 min. Then cover, and continue baking until tender (30 to 45 min. more). Serve hot.

PORK CUTLETS MORNAY

Flatten pork cutlets. Season and bread them. Braise until tender. Place on hot platter coated with Tomato Sauce. Cover with Sauce Mornay. Sprinkle with grated American cheese and paprika. Place under broiler until hot and bubbly. Serve at once.

BAKED SPARERIBS

Place spareribs on rack in shallow baking pan. Season with salt, pepper, and crushed bay leaf. Bake at 325° (slow mod. oven) until tender (about 1½ hr.). Serve.

SPARERIBS AND SAUERKRAUT

Choice of one of Hollywood's most exotic movie stars of all time.

Cut spareribs into 3 or 4-rib pieces. Brown in hot skillet (adding a little shortening if pan seems dry). Season with salt and pepper. Place on top of drained sauerkraut in large kettle. Add just enough water to cover kraut. Simmer until spareribs are tender (about 1 hr.). Then drain off liquor and serve hot . . . the spareribs arranged in attractive design on bed of sauerkraut on platter.

BARBECUED SPARERIBS

Place in bottom of heavy kettle a layer of small meaty spareribs. Cover with layer of sliced onions. Pour Barbecue Sauce (*below*) over top. Repeat layers. Cover. Bake at 325° (slow mod. oven) until meat is tender (2 to 2½ hr.). Uncover last ½ hr. Serve hot.

All you have to do–

For Barbecue Sauce: mix ½ cup catsup, 1½ tsp. salt, ¼ tsp. tabasco sauce, ⅛ tsp. chili powder, 1 cup water, ½ tsp. mustard, 1 tbsp. brown sugar.

BAKED STUFFED SPARERIBS

Ideal for a stag supper.

Season 2 matching sides of spareribs with salt and pepper. Place together with stuffing between. Tie securely with string to hold stuffing in. Lay on rack in uncovered roasting pan. Bake at 325° (slow mod. oven) until tender (about 2 hr.). Remove string, and serve hot on bed of sauerkraut . . . garnished with parsley.

For a Smart Touch: Add caraway seed to Applesauce served with Pork.

GROUND MEATS Meat-Stretchers.

HAMBURGERS OR BEEF PATTIES

Shape hamburger or ground beef gently into round cakes ($\frac{3}{4}$″ thick). Pan-broil until brown on each side, seasoning with salt and pepper. Cook until done.

HAMBURGERS DE LUXE

Minced onion may be added to meat. Serve the pan-broiled meat (*above*) in a split heated bun with slices of tomato and Bermuda onion or chili sauce and onion, etc.

NUTBURGERS (Mock Meat Patties)

Mix together 1$\frac{1}{2}$ cups ground pecans, 1 cup soft bread crumbs, 1 well beaten egg, 1 tsp. finely cut onion, 2 tbsp. finely cut parsley, 1$\frac{1}{2}$ tsp. salt, 1 cup milk. Chill 2 hr. Drop by heaping spoonfuls into hot fat in skillet, and brown (about 5 min.) on each side. Serve with hot Mushroom Sauce. *Serves 8.*

MEAT PATTIES WITH TOMATO SAUCE

Heat a spicy Tomato Sauce in same pan and pour over Meat Patties.

MEAT BALL PANCAKES

Quick-and-easy. Inexpensive. Good!

Blend together . . .

- **3 egg yolks, lightly beaten**
- **$\frac{1}{2}$ lb. ground beef**
- **$\frac{1}{4}$ tsp. baking powder**
- **$\frac{1}{2}$ tsp. salt**
- **dash of pepper**
- **1 tsp. lemon juice**
- **1 tbsp. minced parsley**
- **1 tbsp. grated onion**

Fold in . . .

- **3 egg whites, stiffly beaten**

Drop by spoonfuls onto greased hot griddle. When puffed and brown, turn and brown other side. Serve at once . . . with Mushroom Sauce or a creamed vegetable.

AMOUNT: 6 servings.

EMERGENCY STEAK

"T-Bone," family style. Strips of carrot may be inserted to resemble the bone.

Mix together . . .

- **1 lb. ground beef**
- **1 tbsp. minced onion**
- **$\frac{1}{2}$ cup milk**
- **1 tsp. salt**
- **$\frac{1}{4}$ tsp. pepper**
- **1 cup WHEATIES or $\frac{1}{4}$ cup dry bread crumbs**

Place on lightly greased pan, pat into shape of T-bone steak (1″ thick). Broil (*see p. 268*). Serve hot . . . immediately.

AMOUNT: 6 servings.

SCOTCH SCALLOPS

The Scotch recipe featured in a series of radio talks on "Menus of Allied Nations" in World War II.

Brown 1 lb. ground beef and 2 tbsp. minced onion in hot fat. Then mix, stirring very little, with $\frac{1}{2}$ cup milk, 1 tsp. salt, and $\frac{1}{4}$ tsp. pepper. Cover; simmer until meat is done (15 min.). Serve hot on platter . . . in border of fluffy mashed potatoes.

All you have to do –

To make ground meat go farther: mix it with WHEATIES, bread or cracker crumbs, cooked rice, or oatmeal . . . and milk to moisten.

BEEF ÉCLAT

Dressed-up version of the humble ground beef.

Brown 1 lb. ground round steak in 4 tbsp. butter in heavy skillet. Sprinkle with . . .

- **2 tbsp. lemon juice**
- **3 tbsp. GOLD MEDAL Flour**

Stir until smooth. Stir in and cook 5 min.

- **2 cups cream (or top milk)**

Blend in . . .

- **1 tsp. salt**
- **$\frac{1}{16}$ tsp. pepper**
- **2 cups sautéed sliced mushrooms**

Cook 5 min. more, stirring to loosen browned particles from pan. Pour into 1$\frac{1}{2}$-qt. casserole (7$\frac{1}{2}$″). Cover. Bake. Just before serving, stir in 1 tbsp. grated horseradish. Serve hot on toast or in toast "Buttercups" (*see p. 26*).

TEMPERATURE: 300° (slow oven).

TIME: Bake 1 hr.

AMOUNT: 6 servings.

MEAT LOAVES (Recipes) *Delicious hot or cold.*

	Fluffy Meat Loaf	Ham Loaf
	1 lb. ground beef (or veal)	ground smoked ham
	½ lb. ground lean pork	1 lb.
	2 cups bread crumbs	3 cups WHEATIES
Mix thoroughly.........................	1 egg, beaten	2 eggs, beaten
	1½ cups milk	1 cup
	4 tbsp. minced onion	——
	2 tsp. salt	1 tsp.
	¼ tsp. pepper	⅛ tsp.
	¼ tsp. dry mustard	——
	⅛ tsp. sage	——

Pack into greased 9x5x3″ loaf pan. Bake. Unmold. Serve hot . . . *or* serve cold. For Catsup-Topped Loaf, spread 3 tbsp. catsup over top before baking.

TEMPERATURE: 350° (mod. oven).
TIME: Bake 1½ hr.
AMOUNT: 8 servings.

BEEF LOAF

Follow recipe for Fluffy Meat Loaf above (using beef)—*except* use 1 tbsp. horseradish and 1 tbsp. catsup in place of mustard and sage.

INDIVIDUAL MEAT LOAVES

Jean Miller** (now Mrs. Robert Lynum of Seattle, Washington) **tested these when she was on our Staff.

Shape mixture for Fluffy Meat Loaf into individual loaves (1x2x3″). Place in greased shallow pan . . . with thin slices of onion on each. Pour Barbecue Sauce over all. Baste during baking. *8 ind. loaves.*

MEAT CRUST PIE

Mix together . . .
- 1 lb. ground beef
- 1 cup soft bread crumbs
- ½ cup milk
- 1 tbsp. chopped onion
- 1 tsp. Worcestershire sauce
- ¾ tsp. salt
- ⅛ tsp. pepper

Pack into 9″ pie pan to cover the bottom and sides. Press another pie pan on top. Bake at 350° (mod. oven) 7 min. Remove upper pan, bake 3 min. more. Turn into this hot meat shell . . .
- 2 cups heated and seasoned mixed vegetables (1 pkg. frozen)
- 1 cup cut-up fresh or cooked tomatoes (drained)

Garnish with green pepper rings (cooked 5 min.). Return to oven; bake 20 min.
AMOUNT: 6 servings.

PEANUT HAM LOAF

Follow recipe for Ham Loaf above—and add 4 tbsp. peanut butter.

PINEAPPLE-HAM LOAF

Line baking pan with pineapple slices. Pack Ham Loaf mixture on top. Pour a little pineapple juice over all. Rub top of loaf with paste of 2 tsp. brown sugar and 2 tsp. prepared mustard before baking.

All you have to do –

To make a Festive Meat Loaf: bake in a ring mold. Unmold on hot chop plate. Garnish with hot Broiled Peach or Apricot Halves (jelly in center), Cinnamon Apple Rings, or heated plums, etc.

SIX-LAYER DINNER

Tasty one-dish meal of 6 blended flavors.

Place in layers in greased 2-qt. casserole (8″) . . .
- 2 cups sliced raw potatoes
- 2 cups chopped celery
- 1 lb. ground beef
- 1 cup sliced raw onions (or less)
- 1 cup minced green pepper
- 2 cups cooked tomatoes (#1 tall can)

Season layers . . . using in all . . .
- 2 tsp. salt
- ¼ tsp. pepper

Garnish with green pepper slices. Bake.
TEMPERATURE: 350° (mod. oven).
TIME: Bake 2 hr.
AMOUNT: 6 servings.

MOCK CHICKEN LOAF

It's hard to tell it from the real thing.

Follow recipe for Chicken Loaf (*p. 286*)—*except* use veal and pork instead of chicken. Use canned chicken broth for flavor.

GROUND, CUT-UP MEATS Both homey and partyfied.

SAVORY STEW (⚷ Recipe)

Have 3 lb. stewing meat (beef, veal or lamb) cut in 1″ cubes. Roll in seasoned flour. Brown in 3 tbsp. hot fat in heavy kettle. Cover with boiling water, simmer 1½ hr. Add . . .

- **1 cup *each* cut-up carrots, turnips, celery**
- **1 cup whole tiny onions or cut-up onions**
- **4 cups cubed potatoes**
- **1 bay leaf**
- **2 tbsp. minced parsley**
- **½ tsp. thyme**

Simmer 30 min. Thicken liquid for gravy. If desired, cook Dumplings on meat (*p. 79*). Serve garnished with celery leaves.

AMOUNT: 8 servings.

FOR IRISH STEW: Use mutton or lamb with a bit of marjoram.

LAMB PRINTANIERE

(Lamb with spring vegetables.)

Follow ⚷ recipe above—using lamb. Use 1 cup peas in place of turnips. Add a pinch of crumbled rosemary or basil.

MEAT BIRDS (Roulades)

Spread 3x5″ pieces of beef, veal, or liver with Bread Stuffing. Roll up. Fasten with pick. Brown in hot fat. Braise. Serve hot.

MEAT CURRY

Roll in seasoned flour, brown in hot fat 1 lb. lamb or veal or beef shoulder (cut into ½″ pieces). Add . . .

- **4 cups boiling water**
- **2 tsp. salt**
- **¼ tsp. pepper**
- **3 cups diced celery**

Simmer 1 hr. Blend together and stir in . . .

- **4 tbsp. flour**
- **½ to 1 tsp. curry powder**
- **¼ cup water**
- **few drops gravy coloring**

Cook 10 min. Serve over fluffy rice.
AMOUNT: 6 servings.

MOCK DRUMSTICKS (City Chicken)

Season 1½″ cubes of veal, beef, and lamb with salt and pepper. Place on wooden skewers . . . arranging larger pieces at one end, and shaping to resemble chicken legs. Bread them (*see p. 269*) and braise until tender (45 min.). Thicken juice for gravy.

SWEDISH MEAT BALLS

For smorgasbords and simple family dinners.

Mix together lightly . . .

- **1 lb. finely ground beef**
- **½ cup fine dry bread crumbs**
- **1 egg**
- **⅔ cup milk**
- **2 tbsp. grated onion**
- **1 tsp. salt**
- **⅛ tsp. pepper**
- **⅛ tsp. nutmeg**

Gently form into small balls (1½″). Brown in hot fat. Add about ¼ cup hot water. Cover. Simmer 20 min. Serve hot . . . with slightly thickened pan gravy.

AMOUNT: 6 servings.

APPLESAUCE MEAT BALLS

So fluffy, moist, and flavorful. The choice for "father's" oven dinner.

Make same as Swedish Meat Balls above —*except* use ground pork in place of ¼ lb. of the beef, soft bread crumbs for dry, ½ cup unsweetened applesauce for the milk, and omit nutmeg. Form into 2″ balls. Brown in hot fat . . . place in baking dish and pour over them a mixture of ¼ cup catsup, ¼ cup water. Cover. Bake in mod. oven (350°) 1½ hr. Serve hot.

HUNGARIAN GOULASH

Old World favorite.

Cook 3 lb. onions, sliced, until yellow in ½ cup fat in kettle. Add and brown . . .

- **3 lb. veal shoulder (1″ cubes)**

Mix in . . .

- **4 tbsp. paprika**
- **1 bay leaf**
- **2 finely chopped cloves garlic**
- **2 qt. white stock (Consommé) or water**
- **2 finely chopped peeled tomatoes**
- **salt and pepper to taste**

Cover. Simmer until meat is tender (2 hr.). Remove bay leaf. Serve hot with Boiled Noodles.

AMOUNT: 8 servings.

CRISPY BROWNED HASH

(🔑 Recipe)

The secret is chopped, not ground, meat . . . and diced potatoes of the same size.

Combine equal quantities of *chopped* cooked roast (beef preferred) and diced cold cooked potatoes. Season with salt, pepper, and minced onion (also minced parsley, pimiento, or green pepper, if desired). Moisten with mild or leftover Brown Gravy. Spread evenly in a lightly greased hot skillet. Brown on one side over low heat. Fold over like an omelet. Turn onto hot platter. Serve hot.

FOR BAKED HASH: Follow 🔑 recipe above—*except* bake in greased casserole at 350° (mod. oven) until browned (30 min.).

FOR CREAMED HASH: Follow 🔑 recipe above—*except* add 1 cup milk mixed with 3 tbsp. flour for each cup of meat used. Cook gently until thickened and smooth (10 min.). Serve hot on toast triangles.

FOR RED FLANNEL HASH: Make hash with corned beef. Add chopped cooked beets.

SAVORY MEAT PIE

Glorifies leftover roast.

Sauté in hot fat desired amounts of diced celery and onion and minced green pepper. Combine in casserole with cut-up roast, equal amounts of diced cooked vegetables, and well seasoned gravy (add Medium White Sauce to leftover gravy to make amount needed).

Cover with Rich Biscuit dough (½ recipe fits 8″ dish) or English Pastry (*p. 315*) . . . cut slits in top. Or cover pie with cut-out Herb or Curry Biscuit dough. Bake at 425° (hot oven) until golden brown (about 25 min.). Serve hot.

HAM OR CHICKEN TIMBALES

Delicate . . . serve with hot Bechamel Sauce.

Mix together . . .

- **4 eggs, lightly beaten**
- **1¼ cups milk**
- **1 tsp. *each* salt and onion juice**
- **⅛ tsp. pepper**
- **¼ tsp. paprika**
- **1 cup chopped cooked ham or chicken**

Turn into buttered custard cups. Set in pan of water (1″ deep). Bake at 350° (mod. oven) until firm (about 25 min.). Unmold. *Serves 6.*

MEAT CROQUETTES

Leftover meat in sophisticated disguise.

Mix together . . .

- **1 cup *Thick* White Sauce**
- **1 tsp. *each* minced onion and parsley**
- **2 cups chopped cooked meat (roast beef, pork, veal, lamb, chicken, etc.)**

Chill. Shape into pyramids or cylinders. Roll in fine dry bread crumbs. Let dry (2 to 3 hr.). Dip in mixture of 1 egg, slightly beaten, and 2 tbsp. water. Again roll in fine dry bread crumbs. Let dry again (½ hr.). Fry in hot deep fat (400°) until delicately browned (1½ to 2 min.). Drain on absorbent paper in warm place. Keep hot in oven until time to serve. Serve hot with hot Mushroom or Tomato Sauce or any desired sauce.

AMOUNT: 8 pyramid croquettes (3″ high).

All you have to do—

For Croquettes of Distinction: add minced mint leaves with lamb; a dash of Worcestershire sauce with beef; diced celery, celery salt, or chopped sautéed mushrooms with veal or chicken.

MEAT SHORTCAKES

Split hot biscuits. Serve plenty of cut-up cooked meat or chicken in well seasoned gravy between and over top.

JELLIED MEATS

. . . veal, chicken, beef, or lamb in glamorous aspic setting.

Soften 2 envelopes gelatin (2 tbsp.) in 4 tbsp. cold water. Dissolve in 2½ cups hot meat stock. Cool until thickened. Add . . .

- **4 cups cut-up sliced cooked meat (simmered and cooked in stock)**
- **1 tsp. salt**

Pour into oiled 9x5x3″ loaf pan. Chill until set. Unmold on cold platter. Serve cold . . . garnished with parsley bouquets, radish roses, tomato wedges, lettuce.

AMOUNT: 10 servings.

HAM MOUSSE

Dainty pink main dish for parties.

Soften 1 envelope gelatin (1 tbsp.) in ½ cup cold water. Dissolve in ½ cup hot water. Combine with 3 cups finely ground cooked ham, 1 tsp. mustard, and dash of cayenne pepper. Fold in 1 cup whipping cream, stiffly whipped. Pour into oiled mold. Chill until set. Unmold on cold platter. Garnish with parsley or watercress. Serve cold with Epicurean Sauce.

WAYS TO COOK MEATS Sausages and Bacon.

PORK SAUSAGES *come in individual links of various sizes or as sausage meat in bulk.*

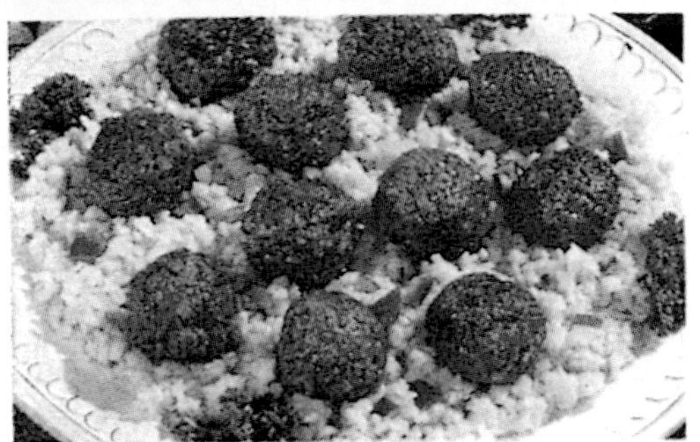

Pork Patties and Spanish Rice.

CORN SAUSAGE CASSEROLE

A favorite from Mrs. Paul Dowty, of Evanston, Illinois, remembered as "Your Housewife Friend" on the General Mills Radio Hour.

Mix together . . .

- **4 eggs, well beaten**
- **2½ cups cream style corn (#2 can)**
- **1 cup soft bread crumbs**
- **1 lb. sausage meat**
- **1 tsp. salt**
- **⅛ tsp. pepper**

Pour into greased round, deep 8″ casserole. Spread catsup over top. Bake in pan of water (1″ deep) at 350° (mod. oven) for 1 hr. *Serves 6.*

Pork Sausage Links (standard size): Place in frying pan, add a small amount of water. Cover and simmer 5 min. Drain and pan-fry slowly till browned. *Or* bake at 400° (mod. hot oven) for 20 to 30 min. using an open pan. Turn once to brown. Never prick. Delicious served with applesauce or chili sauce, on top of mashed sweet potatoes in a casserole, or tucked in acorn squash.

Country Style Pork Sausage (coarser ground pork in large links or coils): Simmer in small amount of water for 20 min. Then pan-fry, if desired. Use as above.

Pork Sausage Patties (same meat as in links but sold in bulk): Place patties in cold skillet. Cook over low heat 12 to 15 min. until brown. Turn with 2 forks. Pour off fat as it gathers. *Or* bake as for link sausage (see picture and recipe opposite for serving ideas).

Frankfurts are completely cooked when you buy them. Simply heat by simmering about 5 min. Serve with potato salad or sauerkraut, *or* slit frankfurt and fill with relish, cheese strips, mustard. Wrap in bacon slices, fasten with wooden pick and broil about 5 min. Turn often.

Bologna: Serve hot or cold. Delicious broiled with a coating of mustard and brown sugar.

Liverwurst (smoked or plain): Serve as cold cuts or lightly sautéed in butter. Most popular variety is Braunschweiger.

Salami (with garlic): Use "soft" type in sandwiches. Adds zest to Scalloped Potatoes.

Thuringer Sausage, Swedish Sausage: Serve hot.

BACON

Comes sliced, in packages or bulk (16 to 20 slices per lb.); or in slabs, which can be sliced as desired. Bacon squares are inexpensive.

Pan-Fry: Place separated slices in a cold skillet. Do not overcrowd. Do not drain off fat as it cooks over low heat. Turn to cook evenly. Drain on absorbent paper.

Broil: Place separated slices on broiling rack 3″ from heat. Turn, cook each side.

Bake: Place separate slices on wire rack in baking pan. Bake at 400° (mod. hot oven) until brown, about 10 min.

CANADIAN STYLE BACON

Boneless loin of pork, sugar cured and smoked. Very lean. In slices (22 to 26 slices per lb.); in larger pieces to bake or simmer.

Pan-Fry and **Broil** slices as for Bacon.

Simmer: Cover whole pieces with water. Cook slowly until tender.

Bake: Remove casing. Score fat and stud with cloves. Spread with brown sugar and mustard. Bake like ham. 1 lb. makes 4 servings.

Barbecue: Cover whole piece with Barbecue Sauce. Bake at 350° (mod. oven) until tender. Baste frequently.

LIVER (calf, lamb, beef, or pork) . . . *all rich in iron. Calf's liver is the most delicate, but young beef liver is often as tender. Unnecessary to scald liver except helpful when liver is to be ground. Remember over-cooking toughens liver.*

To Broil (calf, veal, or lamb): Slice ⅓ to ½″ thick; brush well with melted butter. Broil 10 to 20 min. (depending upon thickness), turning once.

To Pan-Fry (veal, beef, or lamb): Dip ⅓″ slices in flour, brown in hot fat. Season. Reduce heat. Cook over low heat 5 to 15 min. Turn once.

CALF'S LIVER SUPREME

Brown *very thin* slices of liver in bacon fat in skillet (rubbed with garlic). Cook 1½ min. on each side over low heat.

CREAMED LIVER

When pan-frying liver, *save* the brown and drippings in the pan. Next day add flour and milk to make a brown milk gravy. Add chopped leftover liver. Serve on toast.

LIVER AND SCRAMBLED EGGS

Chop pan-fried liver, and mix into scrambled eggs before cooking.

LIVER LOAF

Brown 1 lb. beef liver in hot fat. Put through food chopper with ½ lb. pork sausage. Add 1½ cups soft bread crumbs, 2 tbsp. minced onion, 1 tsp. Worcestershire sauce, 1 tbsp. lemon juice, 1 tsp. salt, ⅛ tsp. pepper, 1 tsp. celery salt, 2 eggs, ½ cup Bouillon. Top with 2 slices bacon. Bake in 9x5x3″ loaf pan 45 min. in mod. oven (350°).

To Braise (beef or pork liver): Cut into ½″ slices. Roll in seasoned flour. Brown in a small amount of hot fat. Add a very little water. Cover and cook slowly on top of range or in mod. oven (350°) for 1½ hr.

BRAISED LIVER WITH VEGETABLES

Braise liver (*see above*)—*except* brown with the liver chopped onions, carrots, and celery. Season. Place in greased casserole. Pour cooked tomatoes over all. Cover and cook. Bake 1½ hr. in mod. oven (350°).

MEXICAN LIVER

Brown floured and seasoned pieces of sliced liver in bacon fat with chopped onion and green pepper. Add equal amounts canned tomatoes and hot water. Add chili powder to taste. Simmer until liver is tender. Add cooked rice, and then half as much *each* of cooked peas and corn as of rice. Serve on hot crisp rounds of corn bread.

BAKED CALF'S LIVER

Remove the thin skin and tubes from a whole liver. Insert (lace) thin strips of fat through the surface of the whole liver. Season with salt, pepper, and onion slices. Add 2 cups water. Top with bacon strips. Cover. Bake 1¼ hr. in mod. oven (350°). Remove the liver. Make gravy of drippings in pan.

HEART (beef, lamb, veal, pork) . . . *delicious, nutritious, and economical.*

To Prepare: Trim off blood vessels and fat. Wash thoroughly by running water through it. Loosen and trim out small thread-like cords. Wipe with damp cloth.

	Braise or Simmer
Beef Heart	2½ hr.
Lamb Heart	1 hr.
Veal Heart	1½ hr.
Pork Heart	1½ hr.

HEART PATTIES: Grind cooked heart. Mix with seasoning, milk, eggs, bread crumbs, and grated onion. Shape into patties. Fry until brown in hot fat.

CHICKEN FRIED HEART

Slice heart in ¼″ thick pieces. Dip in seasoned flour. Brown on both sides in hot fat. Add a small amount of hot water. Cover and simmer 20 to 30 min.

STUFFED BEEF HEART

Fill cavity with well seasoned Bread Stuffing. Fasten with skewers and string. Roll in seasoned flour. Brown in hot fat. Add ½ cup hot water, cover tightly. Simmer until tender. Make gravy.

VARIETY MEATS Tongue, Sweetbreads, Kidneys.

TONGUE (beef, lamb, veal, or pork) . . . *always a favorite, hot or cold.*

To Cook: Wash thoroughly. Cover with hot salted water. Simmer until tender (1 to 1½ hr. per lb.). When just cool enough to handle, remove excess connective tissue, bones, and skin. Serve hot or cold.

BEEF TONGUE À LA JARDINIERE

Place 1 cooked beef tongue (about 3 lb.) in roaster. Pile around it . . . 2 cups *each* of diced carrots and celery and 1 cup diced onion. Pour 4 cups of liquor in which tongue was cooked over vegetables. Bake covered at 350° (mod. oven) about 30 min. Remove meat and vegetables to hot platter and keep hot in oven while making gravy in roaster. Pour some of gravy over meat and vegetables. Pass remainder at table. *Serves 6.*

SPICED TONGUE

An inviting summer-time supper dish. From Myrna Johnston, Food Editor of Better Homes and Gardens, who serves it at outdoor suppers in her own garden.

Add 1 lemon, sliced, 1 tsp. mixed pickling spices, and 2 tsp. salt to the hot water in which a 3-lb. beef tongue is to be simmered. Serve this pickled tongue either hot or cold with Easy Horseradish Sauce. See "SAUCES" for other interesting tongue accompaniments.

SWEETBREADS

A very special delicacy.

To Precook: Simmer 20 min. in boiling salted water to which lemon juice or vinegar has been added (1 tbsp. to 1 qt. water). Drain. Plunge in cold water. Remove membranes. Store covered in refrigerator.

PAN-FRIED SWEETBREADS

Dip cooked sweetbreads in melted butter or bacon fat. Pan-fry until brown (about 10 min.). Serve with Mushroom Sauce.

CREAMED SWEETBREADS

Serve in patty shells, on toast, or over rice. May be combined with leftover ham, chicken, veal, peas, mushrooms, or oysters.

BAKED SWEETBREADS AND MUSHROOMS

Elegant company luncheon dish. We served it frequently to guests.

Divide cooked sweetbreads into serving sized pieces. Roll in seasoned flour, and pan-fry in butter until light brown. Place in casserole. Sauté cut-up mushrooms and make thin White Sauce (top milk) in the pan. Bake at 350° (mod. oven) for 1 hr. Serve on rounds of toast or thin ham or Canadian Style Bacon slices garnished with watercress. Stunning with fresh red tomatoes and fresh green peas.

BRAINS

Prepare same as Sweetbreads. Especially good blended with scrambled eggs or spaghetti.

TRIPE

Honeycomb Tripe is considered most desirable. Muscular lining of stomach of beef creature. Sold fresh or pickled. (See Philadelphia Pepper Pot, *p. 368.*)

KIDNEY (beef, veal, lamb, or pork)

A real delicacy.

To Prepare: Wash. Remove outer membrane. Split through center lengthwise. Remove fat and white tissue. Soak in cold salted water 45 min. Precook (simmer) beef kidney 1 hr. and pork kidney 20 min.

Broiled Kidney (veal or lamb): Split open. Brush with melted butter. Broil 10 to 15 min. depending on size. Turn once. Season and sprinkle with lemon juice or a bit of mustard. Serve on buttered toast.

Broiled Kidney en Brochette: Thread pieces of kidney alternately with bacon on skewer and broil.

Breaded Kidneys: Dip lamb or veal kidney into egg. Roll in crumbs and pan-fry 15 min. in hot fat. Serve with Piquant Brown Sauce.

CHICKEN, TURKEY, DUCK, or GOOSE! *Associated with festive occasions. The special flavor, texture, and shape make them adaptable to many interesting dishes. They must be selected with care and expertly prepared to be at their supreme best. Kathryn B. Niles of the Poultry and Egg National Board in Chicago very kindly gave us their latest information and pictures.*

To Market, To Market . . . To Buy ? ? ? ? ? ?

HOW MUCH?

Allow ½ to ¾ lb. per person.

WHAT KIND?

For Broiling or Frying . . . Buy young chickens, "Broiler-Fryers" weighing 1½ to 4 lb. ready-to-cook weight. Use chickens under 2½ lb. cut in half for broiling. Quarter small chickens for frying. Disjoint and cut up larger chickens for frying, braising, or for any recipe designating young chicken.

For Roasting . . . Buy a plump young chicken, weighing 3 lb. or over, or a *Capon*, weighing over 5 lb.

For Stewing . . . Buy a "big fat hen" or stewing chicken, weighing 3½ to 5 or 6 lb.

HOW TO STORE UNCOOKED POULTRY

See p. 266 for "how to store poultry." Do not stuff the bird until just before roasting.

HOW TO STORE COOKED POULTRY

Refrigerate meat, stuffing, and gravy promptly after the meal. Wrap in waxed paper, aluminum foil, or parchment to prevent drying out and loss of flavor. Cover gravy. For later meals, heat only enough leftovers for the meal.

HOW TO DEFROST FROZEN POULTRY

Leave bird in its original moisture-proof wrapping and place on rack in refrigerator for 1 to 3 days, depending on size.

OR

Place unwrapped bird in pan under running cold water or out in room temperature for 2 to 4 hr., depending on size.
NOTE: Prompt cooking after defrosting is best. *Do Not Refreeze!*

WHAT STYLES ARE AVAILABLE?

1. **Ready-to-Cook** (Eviscerated): May or may not be pre-packaged; available whole, cut-up, and by the piece either fresh or frozen fresh; completely ready for cooking.

2. **Dressed** (formerly New York Dressed): Head and feet on, but not drawn. Your meat dealer will draw and cut it for you.

Fry, roast, or stew,
But whichever you do . . .
Long, slow cooking
Is the best cue for you!

Young, tender birds are cooked by dry heat. Less tender ones by moist heat.

WHAT TO DO WITH THE GIBLETS

Simmer the heart, gizzard, and neck in seasoned water until tender, 1 to 2 hr. Add the liver the last 5 to 15 min. Use meat and broth for gravy, soup, stuffing, etc.

WHAT KIND OF STUFFING?

The stuffing you select depends on the tastes of your family, as well as the type of bird. *See p. 362* for *Stuffing Tips and Recipes.*

For Chicken . . . The Celery variation of the Bread Stuffing.

For Turkey . . . The Sausage Stuffing gives special zest, and it bastes the inside.

For Goose . . . Use a dry (goose is fat), savory, tart dressing. Apple, raisins, or chestnuts may be added to Bread Stuffing.

For Duck . . . An orange stuffing is delicious. Make Bread Stuffing *except* use orange juice in place of water. Add orange rind.

BEFORE COOKING YOUR BROILER OR FRYER

Split in half lengthwise, by cutting through the ribs on both sides of backbone. Lift out backbone and neck in one piece. Finish dividing the front part, by splitting along one side of breast bone. Then break major joints by snapping the cartilage in each joint (this makes the broiled chicken easier to cook and manage on the plate).

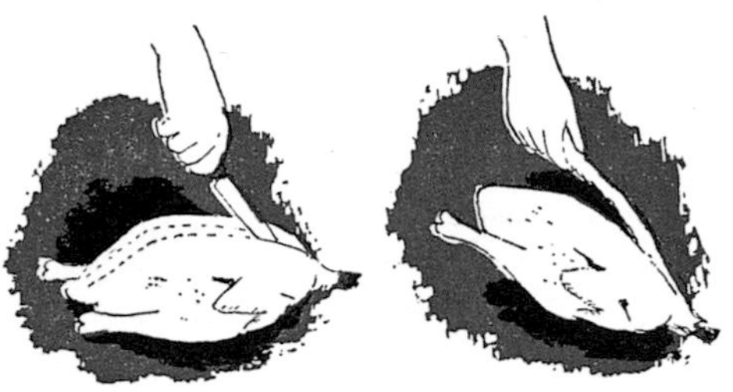

1 Split in half. **2** Lift out backbone.

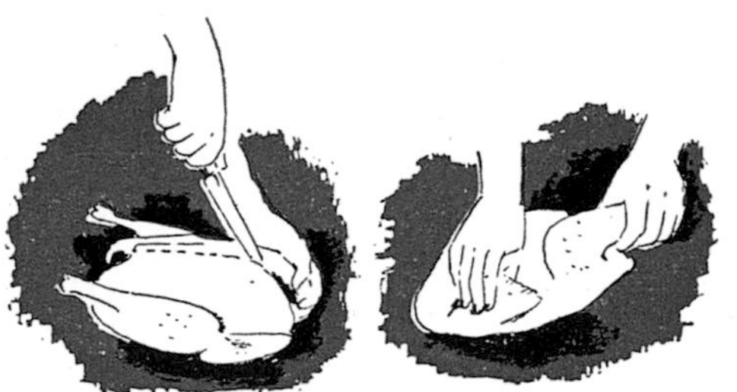

3 Split along one side. **4** Break major joints.

All you have to do—

If you want a boneless Fryer: remove all bones (have your meat dealer do it for you), leaving the meat all in one piece. Makes it easier to eat.

BROILED SQUAB

(domesticated 4 week-old pigeon)

Often served at formal parties.

Follow 🔑 recipe for Broiled Chicken above—*except* sprinkle a little lemon juice on the inside with the salt and pepper. One squab makes 1 generous or 2 small servings.

BROILED GUINEA HEN

Domesticated guinea hen with a slightly "gamey" flavor.

Follow 🔑 recipe for Broiled Chicken above. Allow ¾ to 1 lb. for each person.

NOTE: Squab and guinea may be fried, braised, or roasted. Follow directions given in the following pages.

BROILED CHICKEN (🔑 Recipe)

Crisp and brown on the outside; tender, juicy, and perfectly done inside.

Broiling Young, Tender Fryer

Brush or rub halves with fat (part butter) and sprinkle inside lightly with salt and pepper. Place skin side down in shallow pan 6″ from preheated broiler (5 to 15 min.). Broil slowly, about 20 min., then turn skin side up and broil 10 to 15 min. longer. Check for browning several times and brush with fat again if necessary.

OVEN COOKED FRYERS

Need less watching than under broiler.

Follow 🔑 recipe for Broiled Chicken above—*except* place in pan and cover tightly. Bake at 400° (mod. hot oven) until tender and nicely browned (45 to 60 min.). Brush with fat several times. Remove cover the last 20 min. to brown.

For Stuffed Oven Cooked Fryers: Fill halves with Stuffing (see *p. 362*). Place stuffing side down on greased pan. Roast as above . . . basting with 2 parts orange juice and 1 part butter.

BROILED DUCKLING

Something special!

Follow 🔑 recipe for Broiled Chicken—*except* allow about 5 more minutes of broiling on each side. For a rich brown color, brush skin side of duck with a mixture of 1 tbsp. honey or syrup and 1 tsp. gravy flavoring the last 2 min. of broiling.

NOTE: This same mixture may be used on Roast Duck.

Serve Giblet Gravy (see *p. 356*) with broiled poultry prepared in any of the delicious ways given on this page.

OR

Parboil giblets and brown with the chicken the last few minutes and serve with it.

The method of frying chicken varies with the section of the country . . . each has a special characteristic and each is delicious in its own way. Be sure to select the right type of "Fryer" depending on the method you use (see p. 281).

HOW TO PREPARE CHICKEN FOR FRYING

Cut in halves, quarters, or pieces.

Wash, dry well, and flour pieces by shaking several at a time in a paper bag containing . . .

1 cup GOLD MEDAL Flour
2 tsp. salt
¼ tsp. pepper
½ tsp. celery salt
1 tsp. paprika (if desired)

FRIED CHICKEN (Recipe)

Crisp and tender . . . according to the best Southern traditions.

Prepare *young, tender* Fryers as above. Place halves or quarters (in heavy deep skillet) in ½" hot fat (part butter) skin side down. Brown on both sides and cover tightly. Cook over very low heat until tender (35 to 40 min.). To crisp the crust . . . remove cover and cook 5 to 10 min. longer. Use the leftover flour plus extra, if needed, to make cream gravy (*p. 356*).

FRIED CHICKEN-MARYLAND STYLE

Sautéed Tomatoes and Fruit Fritters with it.

Prepare as for Fried Chicken including the making of the Cream Gravy. Arrange the Fried Chicken on a large platter. Pour over the gravy. Sprinkle with finely chopped chives and parsley. If desired, lay across top, crisply fried slices of lean Salt Pork (*p. 358*).

BRAISED CHICKEN (Recipe)

The fried chicken of the Middle West.

Prepare as for Fried Chicken—*except* use a Larger Fryer and cut in serving pieces. After browning, add 3 tbsp. water. Cover; cook over low heat on top of stove, or bake in a preheated oven . . . 325° (slow mod.) until tender (45 to 60 min.). In either case, remove cover the last 10 min. to crisp crust.

SMOTHERED CHICKEN

Seasoned perfectly and cooked in cream.

Prepare as for Braised Chicken—*except* sprinkle remaining seasoned flour over chicken. Pour over the browned chicken . . .

2 cups hot sweet or sour cream

Add more cream, if necessary, to half cover.

NOTE: Remove from oven as soon as tender. Cream will be less likely to separate.

All you have to do—

For an epicurean touch: drip a little white wine over the chicken while it is cooking (tenderizes and flavors it).

BARBECUED CHICKEN

A savory sauce for a "pick-up."

Prepare as for Braised Chicken—*except* pour Texas Barbecue Sauce (*p. 359*) over the browned chicken and finish cooking (*see above*).

CHICKEN FRIED IN BATTER

Encased in a delicious brown crust.

Cut Larger Fryer in serving sized pieces. Wash. Partially cook in boiling water, simmering 20 min. Drain. Sprinkle with a mixture of salt, celery salt, and pepper. Dip in Batter (*see p. 78*). Drop into deep fat at 360° (cube of bread browns in 60 sec.). Fry until rich golden brown and chicken is cooked through (5 to 7 min.). Serve immediately.

First of all . . .

Draw, singe, and remove pin feathers. (Use a candle for singeing; a tweezer or strawberry huller for pin feathers.)

Remove leg tendons (they spoil the quality of meat in the drumstick).

Cut off head, leaving as much neck as possible. Slit skin down back of neck and pull skin down . . . then cut off the neck.

Completely remove lungs and kidneys.

Cut out oil sac at base of tail (would give unpleasant taste).

Wash bird inside and outside. Dry well.

Rub *inside* with salt (1/8 tsp. per lb.).

Prepare stuffing (*see p. 362*). Stuff and truss.

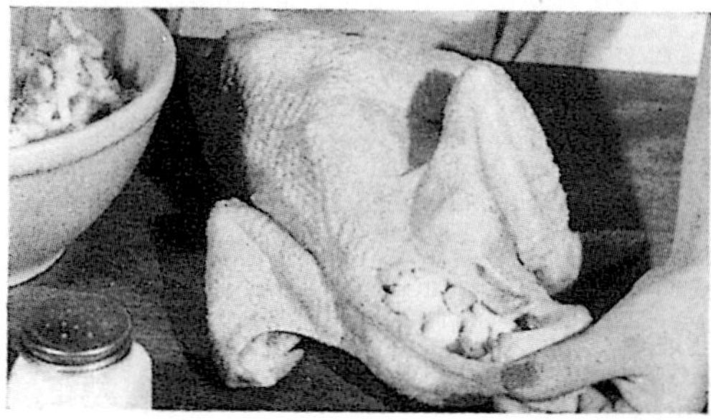

1 Fill neck cavity with stuffing.

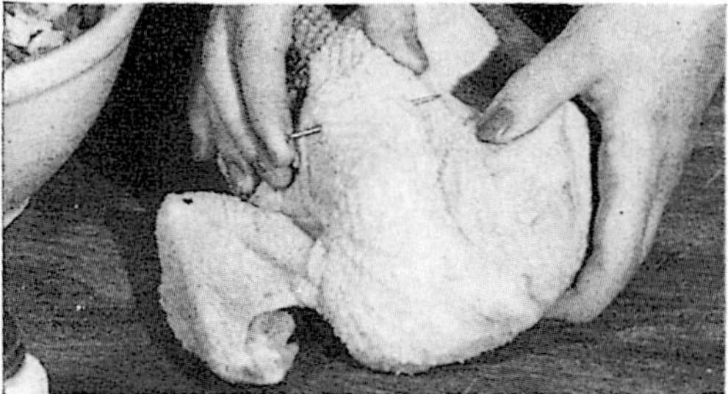

2 Fasten neck skin to back with skewer or pin. (A layer of stuffing may be inserted under skin of breast to protect breast.)

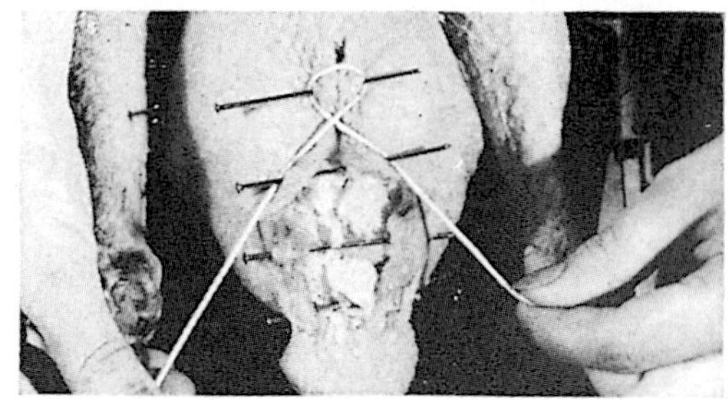

3 Stuff cavity well. *Do not pack.* (It will expand while cooking.) Fasten opening with skewer . . . then lace shut.

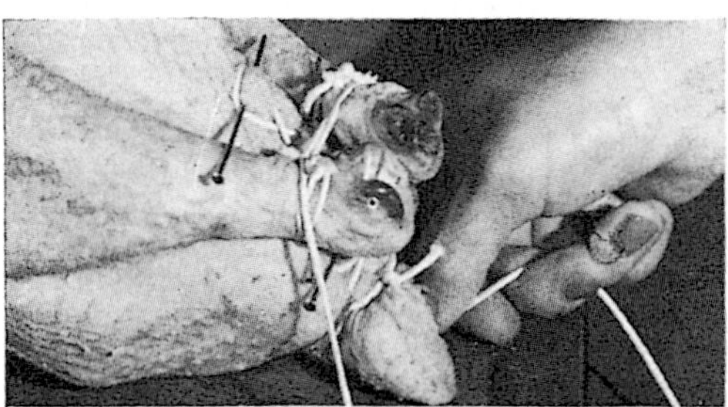

4 Tie leg ends to tail. Bring cord crisscross over back, around base of wings. Tie.

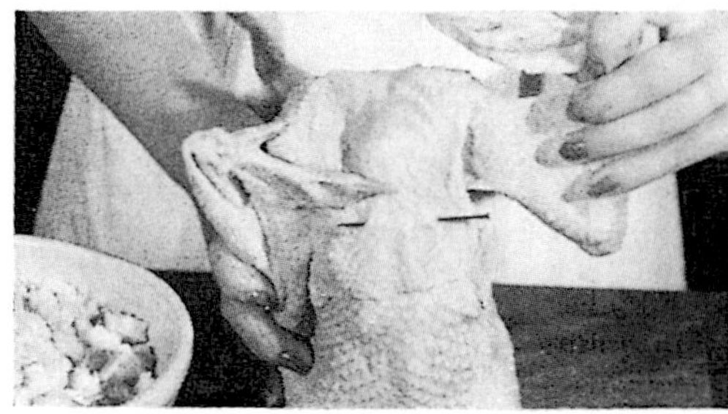

5 Lift wing tip up and over back for a natural brace when turned over.

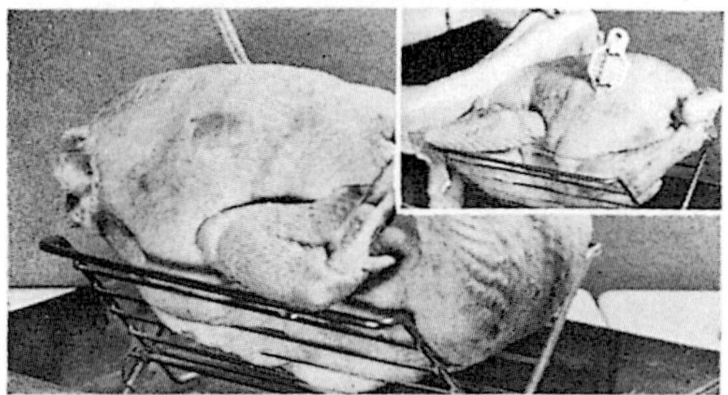

6 Brush entire bird with unsalted fat. Place on rack (breast side down, some cooks say, but large birds are difficult to turn later). Cover with cloth dipped in melted fat. Place in oven set at 300° or 325° (*see Chart, p. 285*). Keep cloth moistened in drippings.

When 3/4 done, carefully turn breast up.

If using a flat rack . . . tip bird so one side of breast rests on rack. When half done, turn to other side to roast evenly.

A smart new way to roast bird without watching is: cover with aluminum foil instead of cloth. Bird will brown . . . be tender and moist. Remove foil the last 20 min.

ROAST TURKEY

Traditional for the Holiday Feast.

If you want a turkey between 8 and 15 lb., ask for a hen turkey. If you want a turkey between 16 and 25 lb., it will be a tom turkey. Size is not an indication of age or tenderness.
Prepare and follow general directions for roasting (*see p. 284*).

HALF A TURKEY

Ideal for the small family.

Ready to serve.

Half turkey placed on dressing.

Roast as for whole turkey except skewer the skin on the breast to the meat on the breast bone (to prevent shrinkage and protect the breast meat). Tie leg above joint securely to tail. Roast, cavity down, until half done. Remove from oven, place stuffing, shaped to fill cavity, on heavy paper . . . then on rack in the pan. Replace turkey over stuffing, roast until done.

ROAST CHICKEN

Prepare and follow general directions for roasting (*see p. 284*).

ROAST GOOSE

Prepare and follow general directions for roasting (*see p. 284*)—*except:*

DO NOT brush with fat
DO NOT cover with cloth
DO NOT baste

Pour off fat as it accumulates in the pan.

If goose is very fat: parboil first 20 min.

ROAST DUCK

Follow directions above for Roast Goose. Some prefer no stuffing. Use a whole onion, a quartered apple, and a few celery stalks with leaves. Discard after roasting.

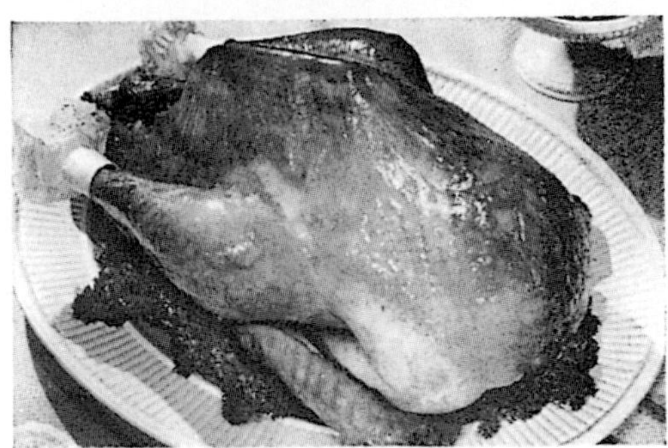

A handsome bird all ready to be served. (For carving directions, *see p. 292.*)

HOW CAN I TELL WHEN THE BIRD IS DONE?

Press fleshy part of drumstick. It is done if meat feels soft. Also move drumstick up and down. If it gives readily or breaks, it is done. Meat thermometer will register 180° when meat is done.

DON'TS IN ROASTING POULTRY

Don't add any water!
Don't season outside!
Don't prick skin!
Don't cover except with cloth or foil!
Don't overcook (becomes dry and stringy)!

CHART FOR ROASTING POULTRY

Ready-to-Cook Weight	Oven Temperature	Total Cooking Time
	TURKEY	
8 to 10 lb.	325°	3 to 3½ hr.
10 to 14 lb.	325°	3½ to 4 hr.
14 to 18 lb.	300°	4 to 4½ hr.
18 to 20 lb.	300°	4½ to 6 hr.
half turkey	325°	25 to 30 min. per lb.
	GOOSE	
8 to 12 lb.	300° to 325°	4 to 5 hr.
	DUCK	
4 to 6 lb.	300° to 325°	3½ to 4 hr.
	CHICKEN	
4 to 5 lb.	325°	2½ to 3 hr.
over 5 lb.	325°	3 to 4 hr.

Stuffed Weight of a bird is about the same as weight before it is drawn.

STEWED CHICKEN (🔑 Recipe)

For dishes made with cooked chicken.

Singe, clean, and cut up . . .
a stewing hen (4 to 5-lb.)
Place in kettle with just enough boiling water to cover, and add . . .
2 sprigs parsley
4 celery stalks with leaves
1 carrot, sliced
1 slice of onion (2 slices if older hen)
2 tsp. salt
1/8 tsp. pepper

Cover. Boil 5 min. Then simmer gently until tender (2 to 3 hr.). Add more water if necessary. Let cool in broth. Remove meat from bones in pieces as large as possible to use in chicken dishes (*below*).

CHICKEN PIE

Of the type served at Wayside Inn, South Sudbury, Massachusetts.

Follow 🔑 recipe for Stewed Chicken above. Make a gravy, using the same amounts as for Chicken Fricassee above.

Place the large pieces of boneless chicken in a 2-qt. casserole. Pour over them the boiling gravy to about 1″ of the top. Cover with Rich Biscuit dough using chicken fat for shortening, or use pastry for crust. Roll out about 1/4″ thick. Make slits in dough. Bake immediately at 450° (hot oven) for 15 min. *Serves 6 to 8.*

CHICKEN LOAF

Delicate, custardy consistency. Superb!

Sauté in 1 tbsp. butter . . .
1/4 lb. sliced mushrooms (4-oz. can)
Mix together and add . . .
1 1/2 cups soft bread crumbs
1 cup milk
1 cup chicken broth (well seasoned)
2 eggs
1/2 tsp. salt
1/4 tsp. paprika
1/4 cup finely cut pimiento
3 cups small pieces sliced cooked chicken

Pour into greased 9x5x3″ loaf pan. Set pan in water (1″ deep). Bake at 350° (mod. oven) for 55 to 60 min. Turn out onto platter. Serve hot, in slices, with Mushroom Sauce.

AMOUNT: 6 servings.

For Other Delicious Chicken Dishes, see "SUPPER DISHES."

CHICKEN FRICASSEE

Serve over fluffy mounds of boiled rice, egg noodles, or mashed potatoes.

Follow 🔑 recipe (*opposite*) for cooking Stewed Chicken *except* . . .

For White Fricassee . . . add about 1 cup milk.

For Brown Fricassee . . . brown in fat first. Do not cool or cut up chicken. Place the serving pieces on hot platter. Make gravy.

To Make Gravy: Stir into about 4 cups hot broth, a smooth paste of 1/2 cup flour and 1 cup milk or cold water. Cook, stirring until smooth and thickened. Season.

CHICKEN FRICASSEE WITH DUMPLINGS

A fricassee without dumplings is like a wedding without a bride.

Follow recipe for Chicken Fricassee above —*except* make Dumplings (*see p. 79*) before making the gravy. Arrange dumplings around the pieces of stewed chicken on hot platter. Serve hot . . . with gravy poured over chicken.

TURKEY OR CHICKEN CREAM PIE

Encore . . . leftovers take a bow!

Make English Pastry (*see p. 315*).
Pat into casserole to line sides. Fill with alternate layers of . . .

pieces of cold stuffing
small slices of cooked turkey or chicken
sautéed mushrooms

Pour a *generous* amount of leftover gravy over each layer (extend gravy with Medium White Sauce if necessary). (It takes 2 to 3 cups gravy to 1 cup meat, 1 cup stuffing.) Pat out remaining pastry to fit top. Cut slits in top. Place over filling. Brush pastry with slightly beaten egg. Bake at 425° (hot oven) for 25 to 30 min. Serve hot.

CHICKEN LIVERS AND MUSHROOMS

Delicious on toast or in an omelet.

Pan-fry livers and sliced mushrooms (5 to 15 min.) in fat (part butter). Season.

Game includes all wild animals and fowl used for food. The method of preparing it is determined by the amount of "gamey" or "wild" flavor you wish to retain. All freshly killed game is tough. Stored from 2 to 4 days in a cool, dry place, it becomes more tender, firm, and better flavored. Venison requires about two weeks to "ripen." All game tends to be less tender and very lean. Cook it with that in mind. To remove "wild" flavor, such as in ducks, soak in salt, soda, or onion water for about one hour.

PHEASANT AND PRAIRIE CHICKEN

Similar . . . however, pheasant is more plentiful. Wells Wilbor, star hunter of General Mills, says: "Add white wine when you cook it as it tends to be dry."

Prepare like Chicken (any method). Especially delicious "smothered" . . . using sour cream. If "roasted," use *Sausage Stuffing.*

POACHED PHEASANT

The epicurean way . . . as served at dinnertime by Mr. and Mrs. Edward Heum, formerly of Minneapolis, now of San Diego, California.

Poach sections of the breast of pheasant in hot butter in chafing dish at the table. Cook only until it loses its transparency (5 to 10 min.). The dark meat, legs, etc. can be served later in casserole.

QUAIL

Called Bob White and Partridge (the most delicate of all game). Mostly breast meat.

Split in halves and pan-broil breast-side-down in butter; or brush with butter and broil 10 to 20 min. Baste often; or place strips of bacon over each.

VENISON (Deer, Moose, Elk)

Jack Andrews of General Mills says: "It's an old wives' tale that venison must be cooked and cooked to remove wild taste and make it tender. My wife cooks it as she would a five dollar steak, and it's wonderful!"

Follow general directions for cooking Beef. It is usually well cooked. Most people feel that it is unappetizing when rare. Baste the roast with red wine for a special touch. Wild Plum Jelly is a natural with venison.

NOTE: If you like the "wild" flavor, cook a shorter time with simple seasonings. If you do not, increase cooking time and add more seasonings. *Never overcook! Venison becomes dry and unflavorful.*

All you have to do –

To remove down from ducks: brush with melted paraffin. Cool and peel off.

SQUIRREL AND RABBIT

Best in the fall and early winter.

Prepare like Chicken. When roasting, truss the forelegs back and the hind legs forward. Fasten bacon over the shoulders and back. Baste with a mixture of ¼ cup butter and ½ cup boiling water. Turn several times. The Stuffing is made as for Chicken. Garnish, when served, with lemon slices on watercress.

NOTE: Write to Betty Crocker for a folder of recipes for delicious Rabbit dishes.

ROAST WILD DUCK

Gourmets used to say: "Just heat the duck through. The red juice should follow every cut with the knife." Lewis Child, a crack-shot hunter, of Minneapolis, Minnesota, says they cook a large Mallard only about an hour in a hot oven . . . basting it with wine.

Most of our hunters and their families say:

Prepare as for Roast Duck, *p. 285*. Place quartered apples, sliced orange, slices of onion, and a few celery leaves in the cavity (discard after roasting), or fill with the suggested vegetable stuffing below.

To Roast . . . for a brown crispy crust, roast uncovered in 425° (hot oven). Baste several times with hot water at first, then with juices in pan or a wine, until moderately well done . . . tender and juicy (½ to 1 hr. depending on size and age of duck). If preferred, duck can be roasted longer in a moderate oven.

To Glaze . . . the last few minutes and just before serving, brush with a mixture of orange juice and currant jelly.

To Garnish . . . use slices of orange topped with currant jelly.

For Stuffed Wild Duck . . . the experts say to use a mixture of equal parts of chopped carrots, onion, and celery sautéed in butter, and surround Duck with the vegetables—the flavor is extended in them.

FISH and SHELLFISH

How to chart your fish course.

We are grateful to Heloise Parker Broeg, popular radio and television star, Director of WEEI Food Fair, Boston, for her help and information on fish and seafood cookery.

HOW TO BUY

Fresh Fish: Have clear, bulging eyes; elastic, firm flesh; reddish pink gills; are free from strong odor. Buy fish stored and displayed on crushed ice . . . just before using. (The fresher the better.)

Frozen Fish: Available the year 'round (in steaks and fillets). Thaw frozen fish just before cooking. Never refreeze. Prepare as fresh fish. Have flavor and texture of fresh-caught fish.

Amount to Buy
Whole or round fish 1 lb. per serving.
Dressed fish . . . . ½ lb. per serving.
Steaks, fillets, sticks ⅓ lb. per serving.
Shellfish . . . amount varies greatly according to the size portions desired. The meat dealer will help you select the amount.

Shellfish: Should be alive . . . such as crabs, lobster, turtles (move lively), clams, mussels, oysters (tight shells). Shrimp are not alive (headless), smell fresh, have green color, close fitting shell. Have soft-shelled crabs cleaned by dealer.

Shucked: Meat removed from shell of clams, oysters, and scallops. Must be refrigerated.

Cooked in Shell: Such as hard-shelled crabs, lobsters, shrimp. Must be refrigerated.

Cooked, Shell Removed: Such as lobster, crab, and shrimp. Must be refrigerated.

Canned: All shellfish are available. Some are smoked.

HOW TO IDENTIFY CUTS

Whole or Round
Exactly as caught.

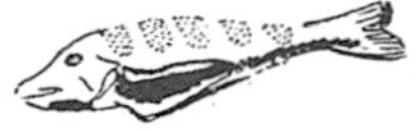
Drawn
Entrails removed.

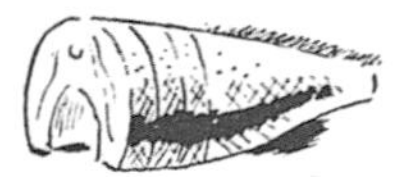
Dressed
Entrails, head, tail, fins removed.

Pan Dressed
Small sizes of dressed fish (such as crappie).

Fillets
Sides cut lengthwise. Usually boneless.

Butterfly Fillets
Double fillet held together by skin.

Steaks
Cross section slices of large dressed fish.

Sticks
Uniform pieces of fillets.

HOW TO COOK

Fat Fish: Have oil running through all the flesh and are generally best for broiling, baking, and planking. Examples:

Mackerel	**Barracuda**
Pompano	**Tuna**
Salmon	**Shad**
Lake Trout	**Sturgeon**
Rosefish	**Whitefish**
Herring	**Catfish**

HOW TO FILLET FRESH FISH

Cut down the back of fish from head to tail on either side of and close to backbone. Cut the flesh free from the rib bones. Skin fish (if desired), beginning at tail end. (Fish with scales are scaled before filleting.)

Lean Fish: Have a drier flesh with the oil stored mainly in the liver and are generally best for boiling and steaming. When baking, add strips of bacon; when broiling, baste with melted fat. *Examples:*

Bass	**Cod**
Haddock	**Buffalofish**
Pike	**Perch**
Carp	**Flounder**
Red Snapper	**Whiting**
Halibut	**Croaker**

Both types good for pan or deep fat frying.

All you have to do—

To scale and clean fresh fish: hold fish by the tail. Scrape with a blunt knife (or fish scraper) from tail to head in short, firm strokes. Slit underside, remove entrails. Wipe out well.

FISH and SHELLFISH

Seven standard methods of cooking fish.

Swimming is easy—no tough muscles. Cook fish briefly (done when it flakes easily with fork).

- Wash—Dry
- Never overcook
- Serve at once
- Enjoy often

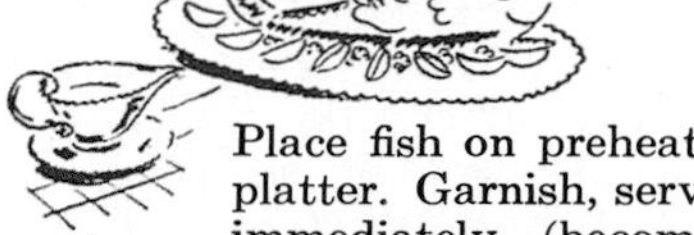

Place fish on preheated platter. Garnish, serve immediately (becomes soggy on standing).

OVEN METHODS

Baking . . . suitable for any size or cut.

Place fish in shallow baking dish on greased waxed or brown paper. Sprinkle with salt, pepper, melted butter. Bake. Serve with Egg Sauce, Anchovy Velouté Sauce, or Lemon Butter, etc.

TEMPERATURE: 400° (mod. hot oven).

TIME: Bake . . . 20 min. for fillets;
30 min. for steaks;
10 min. per lb. for whole fish.

Baked Fish with Stuffing:
For Whole Fish, fill cavity ⅔ full with Bread or Oyster Stuffing and sew shut. *For Fillets,* place stuffing between 2 pieces of fish and hold sides secure with wooden picks. Bake as above except longer.

Planking . . . elegant for whole fish.

Place fish on hot greased plank (hickory, oak, or ash 1½" thick) or on heatproof glass. Sprinkle with salt, pepper, and melted butter. Bake as above. When fish is almost done, arrange a border of hot mashed potatoes around it. Brown under broiler. Surround with hot vegetables. Garnish. Serve on plank at table.

Broiling . . . for small whole fish, fillets.

Place fish (skin side down) on a preheated greased broiler pan. Sprinkle with salt, pepper, and melted butter. Broil 2" under heat at 375° until fish tests done (10 to 12 min., longer for whole fish). Baste lean fish. Serve with appropriate sauce.

Smoked Fish . . . moist, tantalizing flavor.

Skillfully smoked fish are delicious plain or very simply prepared (boiled, steamed, baked). Most popular are salmon, whitefish, finnan haddie.

TOP OF STOVE METHODS

Pan-Frying . . . especially for small game fish.

Sprinkle fish with salt and pepper. Dip in flour, corn meal, or BISQUICK. Pan-fry in hot skillet with fat ⅛" deep (part butter gives superb flavor) over medium heat until golden brown. Turn carefully and brown other side (about 10 min. in all). Drain on absorbent paper. Serve hot.

Deep Fat Frying . . . perfect for fillets.

Heat fat in deep kettle until a cube of bread browns in 50 sec. (375°). Dip fish in milk or slightly beaten egg . . . then in bread or cracker crumbs, and immerse in hot fat. Fry quickly until golden brown (3 to 6 min.). Drain on absorbent paper. Serve with lemon and Tartar Sauce.

Boiling . . . for fillets, steaks, small fish.

Tie fish in cheesecloth. Lower into boiling water to which a sliced onion, carrot, several sprigs of parsley, 2 whole cloves, 1 bay leaf, 2 peppercorns, salt, and a little vinegar have been added. Simmer (6 to 10 min. per lb., depending on thickness). Serve with Caper Sauce, Egg Sauce, or Mousselaine Sauce. Or flake and use in salads, creamed, escalloped dishes, etc. *For Steamed Fish:* Place fish in cheesecloth or cooking parchment on perforated rack or in wire basket directly above boiling water. Cover pot tightly. Cook until done (10 to 15 min. per lb. depending on thickness). Remove skin and bones. Season and serve immediately with sauces as for boiled fish.

Salted Cured Fish

Cod, mackerel, etc. require removing excess salt. Soak overnight in cold water. (Or soak for 2 hr. . . . then simmer in fresh water for 30 min.) Cook as desired.

FISH and SHELLFISH

A "string" of good fish.

CRISPY FRIED FISH

Cover fish fillets . . . pike, smelt, flounder, etc. with buttermilk. Sprinkle with salt (allow 1 tsp. salt for each lb.). Let stand about ½ hr. Drain. Dip each fillet in BISQUICK. Pan-fry. Serve with lemon.

FILLETS ALMONDINE

Wonderful for fillets of sole, pike, whitefish.

Bake, broil, or pan-fry fish. Just before fish is done, add toasted, slivered, blanched almonds to butter. Pour over fish . . . season with salt and lemon juice. Serve immediately.

FISH À LA CREME

Delicately seasoned . . . baked in milk.

Place fish steaks (halibut, haddock, hake, etc.) in greased shallow baking dish. Scald milk (enough to cover) with bay leaf, parsley, and onion added. Strain. Pour over fish. Bake at 350° (mod. oven) until fish tests done (about 40 min.). Brown top under broiler and serve.

GOLDEN BROILED STEAKS

Use shad, salmon, gar, cod, buffalofish, etc.

Arrange fish steaks (cut ¾" thick) on greased broiler rack. Spread with part of mixture of grated onion, soft butter, lemon juice, salt, and pepper, and a little marjoram. Broil at 375° for 10 min. (2" under heat); turn and spread with remaining mixture. Broil until golden brown. Serve hot with parsley.

FILLETS FLORENTINE

A colorful way of serving boiled fish.

While boiling fish (trout, haddock, salmon, etc.), cook spinach, drain, chop, and season. Remove fish and thicken stock with flour. Add a little heavy cream, nutmeg, and lemon juice. Place cooked fish on bed of spinach (on heatproof glass) . . . cover with the sauce and sprinkle with grated Parmesan cheese. Place in very hot oven until cheese is delicately browned (about 5 min.). Serve hot.

All you have to do –

To serve a Scandinavian holiday menu: have boiled ludefisk (cod treated in lye) with drawn butter, garnished with lingonberry sauce . . . with boiled potatoes, lefse, rice pudding, and sandbakkels.

NOTE: For elegant main dishes, see "SUPPER DISHES."

SCALLOPED FISH OR SEAFOOD

Simple dish for flaked cooked fish.

Place flaked cooked fish or seafood in greased shallow casserole or scallop shells. Sprinkle with a little minced onion, minced green pepper, and lemon juice. Season. Cover with Medium White Sauce. Top with buttered crumbs. Bake at 400° (mod. hot oven) until browned on top (about 25 min.). Serve hot.

NOTE: Raw fillets (sole, haddock, fluke, etc.) may also be prepared this way. Bake 10 min. more.

FISH TURBOT (pike, trout, bass, etc.)

Elegant dish for leftover cooked fish.

Arrange alternate layers of flaked cooked fish with Medium White Sauce (seasoned with onion salt, minced parsley, lemon juice, mace, and 1 egg yolk to each cup of sauce). Cover with buttered cracker crumbs and bake at 400° (mod. hot oven) until browned on top (about 25 min.). Serve hot.

CODFISH BALLS

Favorite Sunday breakfast of New Englanders.

Cook together in boiling water . . .

- **1 cup codfish (soaked), shredded**
- **2 cups diced potatoes**

When potatoes are soft, drain, mash. Add . . .

- **1 egg, beaten**
- **salt and pepper**
- **1 tsp. butter**

Form into cakes. Dip in flour, fry in deep fat (*see p. 289*). Serve hot . . . garnished with parsley. *Serves 8.*

BAKED FISH LOAF

(Salmon, tuna, or other fish)

Combine 2 cups (13 oz. can) drained cooked salmon, tuna, or other fish, 2 cups Thin White Sauce, 2 cups soft bread crumbs, 2 eggs, and 1 tbsp. lemon juice. Bake in 9x5x3" greased loaf pan at 350° (mod. oven) for 35 to 45 min. Serve hot with Mushroom Sauce, if desired. *Serves 8.*

NOTE: Sliced mushrooms, minced pimiento, or green pepper (sautéed in butter) may be added.

All you have to do –

For variety: use flaked cooked fish or seafood in place of meat or cheese in:

CHEESE SOUFFLÉ   MEAT SHORTCAKE
MEAT CROQUETTES   MEAT TIMBALES

HOW TO COOK SHELLFISH

Plunge live hard-shelled crab or shrimp into boiling water, well seasoned with lemon, parsley, celery leaves, etc. (Use plain salted boiling water for lobster.) Bring to boil, then simmer:

Shrimp: 10 to 15 min. (shell turns pink).
Lobster: 10 min. per lb. for each.
Crab: about 20 min. (until red).

Drain. Let cool at room temperature.

TO SERVE LOBSTER

With sharp knife, split cooked lobster open from head to tail. Remove black vein, small sac back of head, and spongy lungs. Crack claws. Serve hot with melted butter, or chilled with mayonnaise. Or pry body meat and meat from claws loose with fork and use in hot dishes, salads, etc.

HOW TO CLEAN SHRIMP

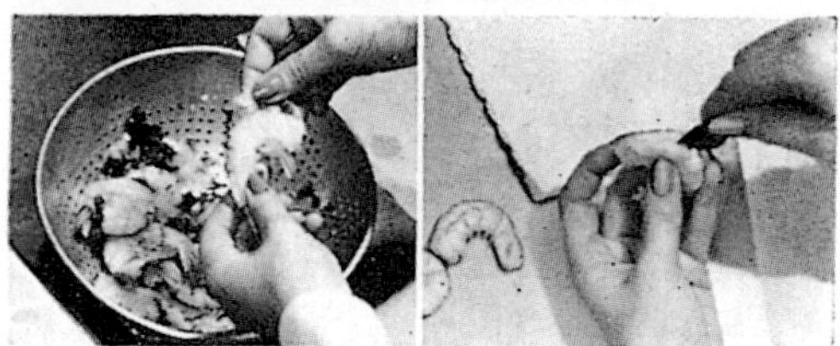

Peel off pink shells. Remove black vein.

To serve: see "APPETIZERS," "SUPPER DISHES."

TO SERVE CRAB

Break off claws and legs from cooked crab; crack; remove meat. Break off tail or "apron." Force shell apart. Discard spongy material. Remove meat with nut pick; or if Dungeness Crab, tap crab against inside of dish. *6 crabs yield about 1 cup meat for salads, hot dishes, etc.*

BROILED LIVE LOBSTER

Place lobster on back; kill by cutting through head with a sharp knife or plunge into boiling water for 5 min. Split open, etc. as directly above. Place lobster, top shell side up, on broiler rack 4″ from heat. Cut tail crosswise twice (to help prevent curling). Brush with melted butter. Broil 6 to 8 min., turn over, and brush again with melted butter. Broil 4 to 6 min. until meat and shell are pink (or stuff as below and broil). Serve with side dish of melted butter and lemon.

BAKED STUFFED LOBSTER

To prepare stuffing: sauté the red roe and green liver in butter. Add finely crushed crackers. Season with onion juice, salt, pepper, minced parsley, and a bit of basil, marjoram, tarragon, and thyme. Stuff cavity of cleaned lobster lightly. Bake at 450° (hot oven) for 12 to 15 min. Serve hot.

SCALLOPED OYSTERS

Into a greased *shallow* baking dish, place a layer of crumbs (half bread and half crackers) (1½ cups in all). Cover with a layer of oysters (1 pt. in all), minced parsley, and chopped celery. Season with salt, pepper, and dot with butter. Add one more layer of crumbs, oysters, etc. Pour over top 4 tbsp. *each* cream and oyster liquor. Cover. Bake at 350° (mod. oven) for 20 min. *Serves 4.*

STEAMED CLAMS

Scrub clams under cold running water. Place in kettle with 1 cup water and 1 tsp. salt. Cover and steam about 8 min. or until shell begins to open. Serve in shells with individual dishes of melted butter and lemon juice. Serve strained broth in bouillon cups. *½ peck serves 4.*

FRENCH FRIED SEAFOOD

Oysters, Shrimp, Clams, Scallops.

Roll the seafood in seasoned flour. Dip into egg, then into dry bread crumbs. Deep fat fry *(p. 289)*. Drain on paper. Serve with catsup or Tartar Sauce.

OLD-TIME FRIED CLAMS

Dip clams in Fritter Batter and deep fat fry *(p. 289)*.

All you have to do–

To cook soft-shelled crabs: season prepared crabs. Roll in crumbs . . . beaten egg . . . and crumbs. Deep fat fry, broil, or pan-fry lightly.

BAKED SEAFOOD IN SHELLS

Most delectable for a Friday night treat.

Combine cooked shrimp, crabmeat, and scallops. Sauté in butter 5 min. Season with salt and pepper. Combine with Sauce Velouté and pile in individual scallop shells or small ramekins. Top with additional sauce. Sprinkle with buttered crumbs and Parmesan cheese. Brown quickly under broiler.

CARVING MEAT How to Carve Meat and Poultry.

1. STANDING RIB ROAST

Have ribs at left of carver, rib ends toward him. Start at right outside edge. Slice toward ribs in ¼″ slices. When knife reaches rib, cut along full length of bone with knife tip.

2. PORTERHOUSE STEAK

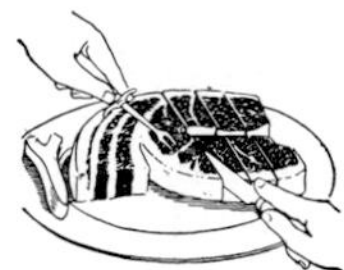

Have flank end at left of carver. With knife tip, cut around bone. Remove bone. With knife at right angle to platter, slice across full width of steak (1″ slices). Cut across flank end in the same way.

3. LOIN OF PORK

Turn rib side up. Run knife blade along close to back bone, removing bone. Place on platter with side from which bone was removed toward carver. Use ribs as a slicing guide. Start at right end of roast, cutting vertical slices.

4. LEG OF LAMB

Have shank end at right of carver (thinner part toward him). Cut 2 or 3 slices from this end. Turn roast on flat surface (shank pointing up). Cut down to leg bone as many slices as needed. Run knife along bone to release all.

5. WHOLE HAM

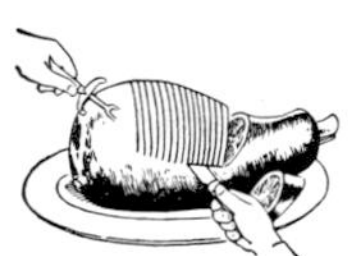

Have scored side up (shank at right of carver). Cut oval slices lengthwise. Turn ham so it rests on this cut surface. Cut out wedge-shaped piece 6″ from shank and then slice down to bone.

6. HALF HAM SHANK END

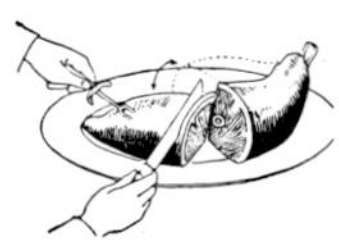

Remove meaty cushion in 1 piece, cutting close to bone straight to shank end. Lay cushion flat side down. Slice thin. Sever joint between shank and leg bone. Cut out leg bone. Slice boned meat.

7. CROWN ROAST (Pork or Lamb)

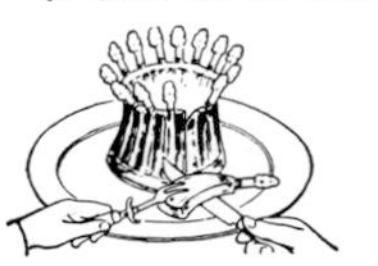

Slice by running knife close to bone of each rib down to platter. Remove each chop, one at a time.

8. TONGUE

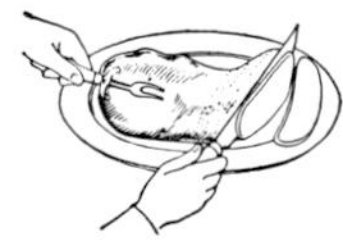

Have tip of trimmed, skinned tongue at right of carver. Slice at an angle from this part straight down so as to produce the largest slices.

9. TURKEY OR CHICKEN

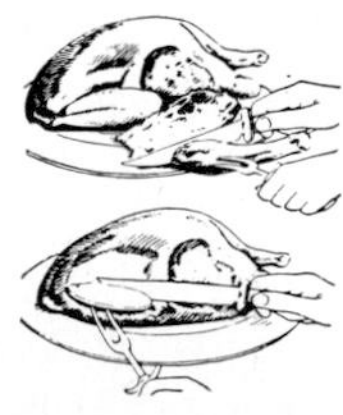

Have leg at right of carver. Cut leg from body, first bending it back with left hand. Sever and lift to plate. Sever thigh from drumstick. Slice meat from leg. Then with fork astride breast, cut down sharply on joint joining wing to body. Cut thin slices of breast where wing was, working up to breast bone.

10. DUCK OR GOOSE

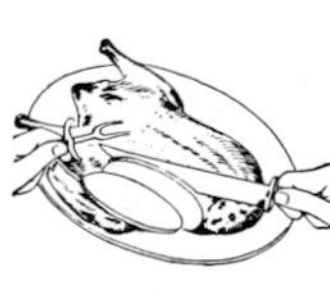

Since most of the meat is on the breast, some prefer slicing breast first. Insert knife just above wing joint parallel to breast bone. Push knife straight down. As it hits bone, turn it slightly to loosen meat. Do not carve slices too thick. An average duck will yield 4 slices on each side of the breast. A larger one, 5 to 6 slices. Remove leg (thigh joint is closer to the duck or goose back bone and harder to remove).

PIE... A Symbol of Good Eating in a Good Land

IF I WERE *to design a coat of arms for our country, a pie would be the main symbol. It would appear with a background of wild berry bushes,—and orchards. For pie is part of our history and tradition. By right of inheritance, adoption, and improvement, pies have become distinctively American. Every American home has its favorite pie.*

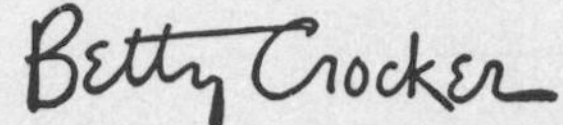

Pies for Spring

Pies for Summer

Pies for Autumn

Pies for Winter

Picnic Pies

Party and Special Occasion Pies

Pies from Famous Eating Places

Pies for Special Holidays

Christmas

St. Valentine's Day

Washington's Birthday

St. Patrick's Day

Hallowe'en

Thanksgiving

Old Family Favorites

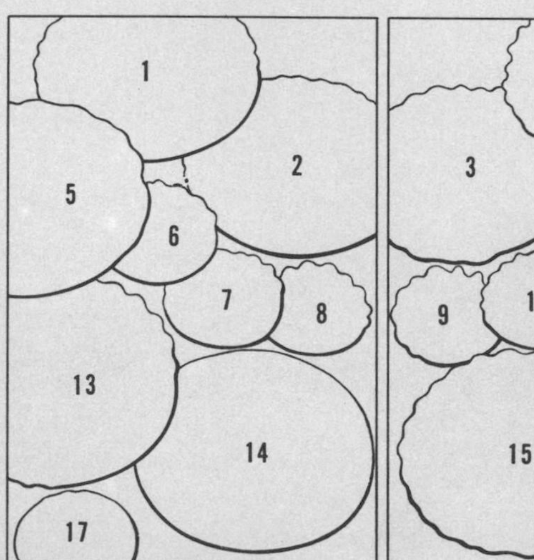

Where to find recipes for Pies in color photograph, pp. 296 and 297:

PIES AND PASTRIES

Pie is as American as the Fourth of July. Through those first lean and hungry years in New England and Virginia, courageous pioneer mothers contrived "pyes" out of the few simple foods at hand. They sliced the top off pumpkins, scooped out fiber and seeds, filled the pumpkins with milk, and set them to bake on the open hearth. Later, a greased pan sprinkled with rye meal was filled with pumpkin diluted with milk and spices. Still later, they added the pastry crust.

The "pyes" of old England were baked in a long deep dish called a coffin, and "pye receipts" up to Martha Washington's day directed colonial cooks to "first make your coffin." The first American pie pans were designed round to cut the corners, flat and shallow so pies would "go a long way." As orchards were planted and food became plentiful, pies gradually took on the "new world" look—large and richly crusted, lush with fruit and abundant fillings. Pies had become distinctively American, as glamorous and exciting as this thrilling new nation!

Step right up and take your choice! That's what we have tried to say in the colorful picture on the next two pages. It offers pies for every taste and for every occasion,—delectable fillings encased in crisp, flaky, melt-in-the-mouth pastry. Some are brand new pies. Others are "tried-and-true" favorites.

The old expression "easy as pie" has now come true, for our Staff has worked out new simplified methods. No guessing as to amount of water, no chilling of the pastry, no long, laborious preparation of fillings. For instance, there's a brand new method of making Lemon Pie Filling and other cream fillings that cuts the time from 20 minutes to 2 minutes. The recipes are adjusted to your family and needs, to fit a 9″ pie pan or an 8″ pan. These new ways with pies will save you time, work, and worry. They mean satisfying adventures in good eating.

EASY AS PIE..

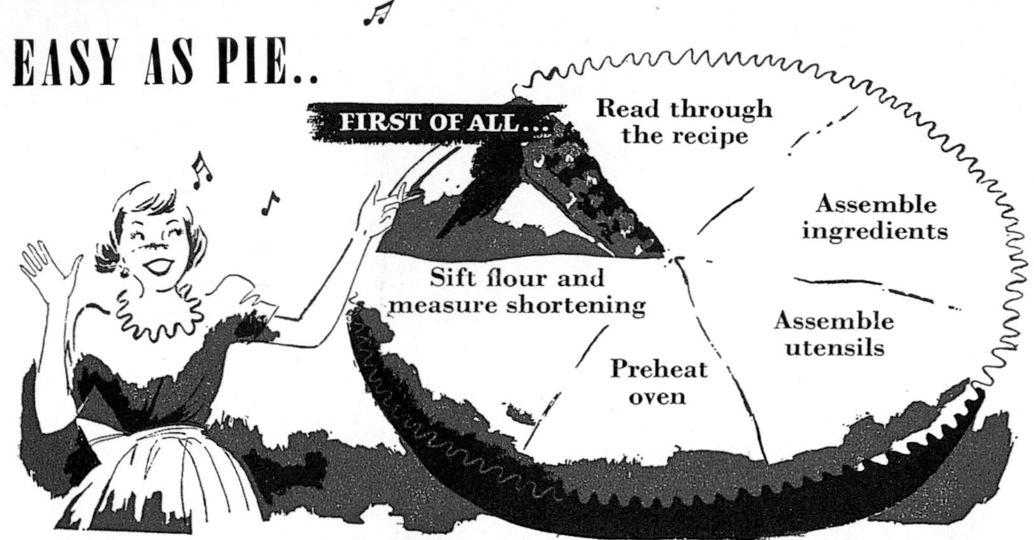

1 Measure the flour into the mixing bowl and mix the salt through it.

2 With pastry blender, cut in half the shortening finely . . . until mixture looks like meal. (This makes for tenderness.)

3 Cut in the remaining shortening coarsely . . . until particles are the size of giant peas. (This makes for flakiness.)

4 Sprinkle with the water, a tbsp. at a time . . . mixing lightly with fork until all the flour is moistened.

5 Gather dough together with the fingers so it cleans the bowl.

6 Press into a ball. Then roll out, or keep in waxed paper in refrigerator until needed.

PASTRY FOR TWO-CRUST PIES

(The pictures #1 through #6 show you just how!)

	For 9″ Pie	*For 8″ Pie*
Mix together	**2 cups *sifted* GOLD MEDAL Flour**	**1½ cups**
	1 tsp. salt	**¾ tsp.**
Cut in	***⅔ cup shortening**	***½ cup**
Sprinkle with	**4 tbsp. water**	**3 tbsp.**

**When using hydrogenated shortenings, add about 2 tbsp. more.*

Gather dough together and press into a ball. Proceed as directed for any two-crust pies *or* for two pie shells.

TEMPERATURE: See each recipe.

TIME: See each recipe.

For easy Stir-N-Roll Pastry, see p. 434.

PIE PAN POINTERS

The pies in this book are perfected for modern deep pie pans (1¼″ deep). If measured from inside rim to outside rim, standard pans are 8″ and 9″ across. If measured from inside to inside of rim, they will measure ½″ less (7½″ and 8½″).

For well baked, browned *under*crust, choose pie pans of heat resistant glass or enamelware. Shiny metal does not bake the undercrust as well because it deflects the heat. Blackened tin pans or aluminum pans with satiny finish give good results.

An 8″ pie cuts into 5 or 6 pieces.

A 9″ pie cuts into 7 or 8 pieces.

FOR TWO-CRUST PIES Follow steps on pp. 4 and 5—then

1 Divide dough about in half. Round up larger part on lightly floured cloth-covered board . . . the rolling pin covered with stockinette. Flour rubbed into covers keeps dough from sticking . . . yet is not taken up by dough.

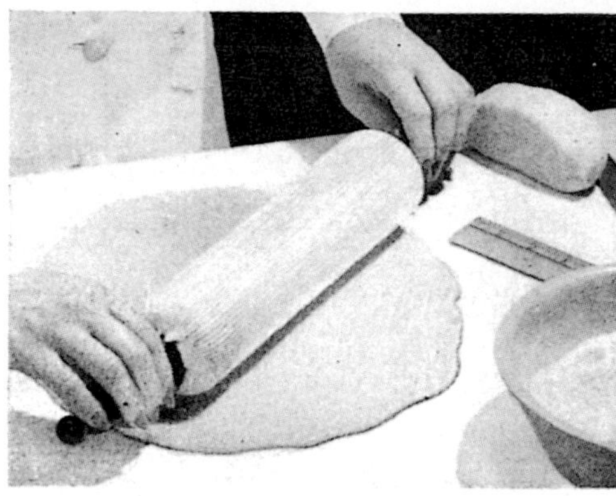

2 Flatten with hand, roll out not quite 1/8″ thick. Work quickly and roll lightly, being careful not to add extra flour as that makes pastry tough. Keep rounding edge of pastry. If it breaks apart, pinch broken edges together.

3 Keep pastry circular and roll it about 1″ larger around than the pie pan to line pan and allow for the depth.

4 Fold pastry in half. Quickly transfer to pan. Unfold, and pat and fit pastry down into pan. Avoid stretching.

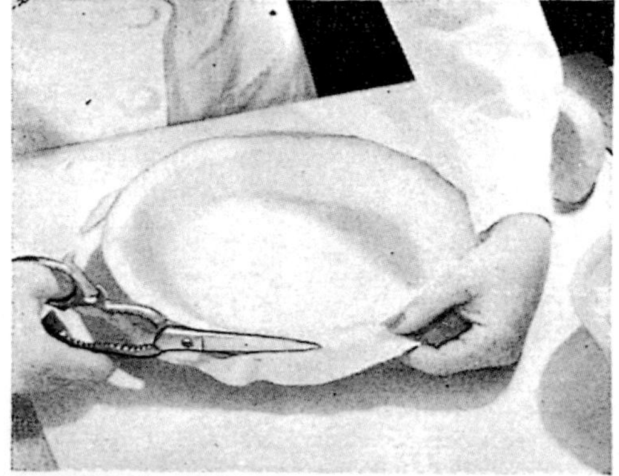

5 Trim off overhanging edges with scissors. Recent experiments prove it unnecessary to chill the pastry, so let it stand on the table.

6 Roll out other part of dough for top crust a *little thinner* than for bottom crust . . . large enough to extend 1″ beyond edge of pan.

7 Prepare any desired filling, and place in the pastry-lined pan.

8 To "dot with butter," distribute tiny bits of butter over top of filling.

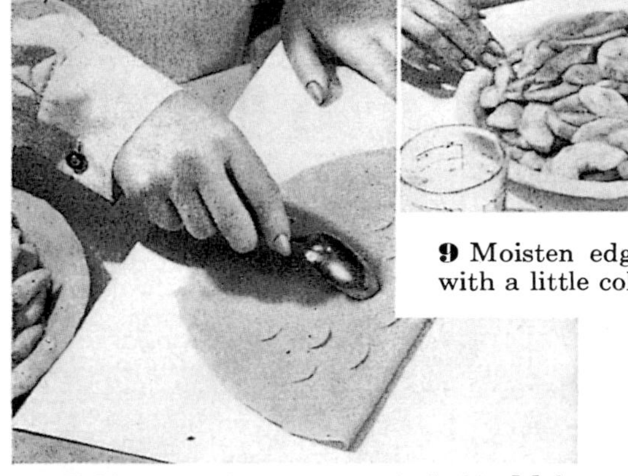

9 Moisten edge of pastry with a little cold water.

10 Fold pastry for top crust in half. Make several slits near center to allow steam to escape or top crust will puff up leaving a hollow space underneath.

11 Carefully place folded pastry evenly on top of filling. Unfold. There should be ½″ rim of pastry beyond edge of pan. Trim off any extra edges.

12 Fold the extra edge of top pastry under edge of lower pastry. Seal thoroughly by pressing together on edge of pan.

13 Build up fluted edge. Form crimped fluting between thumbs and forefingers. (*See pictures on page 307.*) Bake as directed.

NOTE: Store leftover fruit pie by covering it with waxed paper. Let stand on cupboard shelf.

FRESH FRUIT PIES A is for Apple . . . America's first choice in Pie.

APPLE PIE (🔑 Recipe) *From about 1630, Apple Pie was served almost daily in New England . . . when the newly planted orchards were bearing fruit.*

Pick the right apples if you want a prize apple pie. Select tart, juicy apples. The first apples of the season (Greenings and Duchess) make fine *Green* Apple Pie. Jonathans and Wealthies are ideal for pie. Winesaps and Roman Beauties are also good, but need a little lemon juice for tartness (1 tbsp. for 9″ pie).

Peel apples, quarter them, take out cores, and slice them thin (¼″ thick). If apples are dry, sprinkle with a little water. Use the smaller or larger amount of the sugar according to sweetness of apples and desired taste.

Make Pastry for Two-Crust Pie of desired size. Line pie pan. (*See pp. 298–301.*)

For the Filling	*For 9″ Pie*	*For 8″ Pie*
Mix together	**¾ to 1 cup sugar**	**½ to ¾ cup**
	1 tsp. cinnamon or nutmeg	**¾ tsp.**
Mix lightly through	**6 to 7 cups sliced apples**	**4 to 5 cups**
Heap up in pastry-lined pan.		
Dot with	**1⅓ tbsp. butter**	**1 tbsp.**

Cover with top crust. Bake until crust is nicely browned and apples are cooked through (*test with fork*). Serve warm or cold . . . may be topped with cream, whipped cream, or ice cream.

TEMPERATURE: 425° (hot oven).

TIME: Bake 50 to 60 min.

GREEN APPLE PIE

When "trees in apple orchards with fruit are bending down." Even 16th century English cook books refer to "pyes of greene apples."

Follow 🔑 recipe above—*except* use about ½ cup more sugar for tart green apples and only ½ tsp. nutmeg (or cinnamon). If apples are extra juicy, mix about 2 tbsp. flour with the sugar to thicken the juice.

DEEP DISH APPLE PIE

Lots of apples . . . no bottom crust.

Follow 🔑 recipe above—*except* use about double amount of filling. Bake in individual casseroles 2″ deep or an 8″ or 9″ round baking dish 2″ deep. Line sides but not bottom with pastry, having it come up over edge of pan to seal to top crust. Add filling, sprinkle with 1 to 2 tbsp. water, and cover with top crust. Bake at 425° (hot oven) 45 to 50 min.

All you have to do –

To save time and work . . . also vitamins and minerals: use unpeeled apples in pie. Adds color and flavor.

★ CHEESE CRUST APPLE PIE

"Apple pie without cheese is like a kiss without a squeeze." Here's an intriguing way to serve the cheese.

Follow 🔑 recipe above—*except,* when you roll out top crust, sprinkle with grated sharp yellow American cheese (not packaged grated cheese). Dot with butter. Use:

For 9″ Pie	*For 8″ Pie*
⅓ cup grated cheese	**¼ cup**
1⅓ tbsp. butter	**1 tbsp.**

Roll up like jelly roll, fold ends into center; fold again in middle, and roll out. Finish pie as usual. Serve warm.

FRENCH APPLE PIE

From a famous Hollywood tea room.

Make Pastry for One-Crust Pie. Line pie pan. (*See p. 310.*) Add filling as in 🔑 recipe above using minimum amount of sugar. Sprinkle with Crumb Topping:

For 9″ Pie	*For 8″ Pie*
Cream . . .	
½ cup butter	**6 tbsp.**
½ cup brown sugar	**6 tbsp.**
Cut in . . .	
1 cup GOLD MEDAL Flour	**¾ cup**

Serve warm with cream or ice cream.

CANNED BERRY PIE (🔑 Recipe) *Overflowing with bright, sparkly fruit and juice.*

Canned berry pies require less fruit than those made with fresh berries because the fruit has been precooked. Choose any canned berries. To determine amount of sugar needed, look on label to see whether the fruit was packed in syrup. Use minimum sugar for fruit packed in syrup, maximum sugar for water-packed fruit.

With different fruits and sometimes with different brands of the same fruit, the proportion of fruit and juice varies. The larger and more solid the berries, the more there are in the can and the less juice. It takes a #2 can for the 2½ cups of berries and juice. A #1 tall can gives about 2 cups (amount needed for 8″ pies).

Make Pastry for Two-Crust Pie of desired size. Line pie pan. (*See pp. 298–301.*)

For the Filling	*For 9″ Pie*	*For 8″ Pie*
Mix together in saucepan	¾ to 1 cup sugar	⅔ to ¾ cup
	4 tbsp. GOLD MEDAL Flour	3 tbsp.
	½ tsp. cinnamon	⅓ tsp.
Stir in	2½ cups berries and juice	2 cups
Cook over moderate heat, stirring constantly, until mixture thickens and boils. Pour into pastry-lined pan.		
Dot with	1⅓ tbsp. butter	1 tbsp.

Quickly cover with top crust. Bake until nicely browned and until juice begins to bubble through slits in crust. Serve slightly warm, not hot.

TEMPERATURE: 425° (hot oven).

TIME: Bake 30 to 40 min.

NOTE: For mild flavored fruits, such as most blueberries, add lemon juice,—1½ tbsp. for 9″ pie, 1 tbsp. for 8″ pie.

All you have to do—

To prevent edge of crust from becoming too brown: cover with a strip of wet cloth before baking. Remove the strip after baking.

CANNED CHERRY PIE

Brings you June in January.

Follow 🔑 recipe above—*except* use pitted sour red pie cherries and juice. In place of cinnamon, use ¼ tsp. almond extract. A few drops of red food coloring give a lively red color to the filling. Some of our Staff like ¼ tsp. cinnamon used with the almond flavoring.

No draining of fruit—no separate measuring of fruit and juice.

All you have to do—

To save precooking fruit and juice before putting into pastry-lined pan: mix tapioca with sugar, spice, and fruit. Use 2 tbsp. tapioca for 9″, 1½ tbsp. for 8″ pie, (no flour), and bake pie 5 min. longer.

CANNED PEACH OR APRICOT PIE

Follow 🔑 recipe above—*except* use sliced peaches or apricots and juice in place of berries and juice.

LEFTOVER FRUIT AND JUICE are a delicious addition *in* beverages, gelatin puddings, fruit cobblers, sherbets, tapioca, and rice puddings—*to* sauces for puddings or special fruit salad dressings.

FRESH FRUIT PIES Delicious treats from the berry patch.

FRESH BERRY PIE (🔑 Recipe) *With thick, fruity juice bubbling through the crust.*

Select ripe, juicy berries—blueberries, blackberries, raspberries, strawberries, loganberries, or boysenberries, etc. Berries picked at the height of the season are more flavorful, require less sugar, and make the most delicious pies.

1 Wash berries, drain well.

2 Then, pick them over.

3 Remove stems and hulls.

Use the smaller or larger amount of sugar according to the sweetness of the fruit. Very tart fruit may require even more sugar (up to 1½ cups for 1 qt.).

Make Pastry for Two-Crust Pie of desired size. Line pie pan. (*See pp. 298-301.*)

For the Filling	*For 9" Pie*	*For 8" Pie*
	⅞ to 1 cup sugar	⅔ to ¾ cup
Mix together	5 tbsp. GOLD MEDAL Flour	4 tbsp.
	½ tsp. cinnamon	⅓ tsp.
Mix lightly through	4 cups fresh berries	3 cups
Pour berries into pastry-lined pie pan.		
Dot with	1⅓ tbsp. butter	1 tbsp.

If fruit is dry, sprinkle 2 tbsp. water over it. Cover with top crust. Bake until crust is nicely browned and juice begins to bubble through slits in crust. Serve slightly warm, not hot.

TEMPERATURE: 425° (hot oven).

TIME: Bake 35 to 45 min.

★ BLUEBERRY PIE

Follow 🔑 recipe above—using:

For 9" Pie	*For 8" Pie*
⅞ cup sugar	⅔ cup

For tart flavor, add 1 tbsp. lemon juice.

FRESH CHERRY PIE

Follow 🔑 recipe above—*except* use pitted sour pie cherries in place of berries . . . also increase sugar, add almond extract. Use:

For 9" Pie	*For 8" Pie*
1⅓ cups sugar	1 cup
4 drops almond extract	3 drops

Cover with lattice top or cutouts (*see* →).

RASPBERRY OR BLACKBERRY PIE

Follow 🔑 recipe above—using:

For 9" Pie	*For 8" Pie*
⅞ cup sugar	⅔ cup

STRAWBERRY PIE

Follow 🔑 recipe above—using:

For 9" Pie	*For 8" Pie*
1 cup sugar	¾ cup

Very large berries should be halved.

LOGANBERRY OR BOYSENBERRY PIE

Follow 🔑 recipe above—using:

For 9" Pie	*For 8" Pie*
1 cup sugar	¾ cup

FRESH CHERRY PIE

Gay with pastry hatchets and a garland of cherry leaves.

Festive ending to a Washington's birthday dinner. For other special occasions, use cutouts of pumpkins for Hallowe'en, bells for New Year's Day, etc.

FRESH FRUIT PIES Some are old and some are new—try them, do!

FRESH RHUBARB PIE (🔑 Recipe) *Tart, refreshing, spring-time delight.*

For mild flavor, choose early pink rhubarb. If tender and pink, do not peel. Cut into 1″ pieces (1 lb. makes 2 cups). Amount of sugar depends on tartness of rhubarb. Early rhubarb requires less sugar. Make your pie shallow.

Make Pastry for Two-Crust Pie of desired size. Line pie pan. (*See pp. 298–301.*)

For the Filling	*For 9″ Pie*	*For 8″ Pie*
Mix together	1⅓ to 2 cups sugar 6 tbsp. GOLD MEDAL Flour	1 to 1½ cups 4½ tbsp.
Mix lightly through	4 cups cut-up rhubarb	3 cups
Pour into pastry-lined pie pan.		
Dot with	1⅓ tbsp. butter	1 tbsp.

Cover with top crust. Sprinkle with sugar. Bake until crust is nicely browned and juice begins to bubble through slits. Serve slightly warm.

TEMPERATURE: 425° (hot oven).

TIME: Bake 40 to 50 min.

STRAWBERRY-RHUBARB PIE

Old-time favorite.

Follow 🔑 recipe above—*except* substitute fresh strawberries for half the rhubarb. Use the minimum amount of sugar.

All you have to do–

Keep fresh rhubarb fresh and crisp in wet towel in refrigerator. Save time by cutting up several stalks at once.

BLUEBERRY-RHUBARB PIE

An inspiration of Mrs. Sherman Child, Minneapolis, Minnesota.

Follow 🔑 recipe above—*except* substitute fresh blueberries for half the rhubarb. Use the minimum amount of sugar.

PINEAPPLE-RHUBARB PIE

Happy partners in pie. Merriam Paulson of our Staff says, "It's wonderful!"

Follow 🔑 recipe above—*except* substitute about 1 cup drained crushed pineapple for about 1 cup of the rhubarb. Use the minimum amount of sugar.

All you have to do–

If you use sweetened fresh frozen fruit: use only half the amount of sugar.

★ RHUBARB CUSTARD PIE

Something special . . . the tart flavor of fresh rhubarb modified by sweet custard.

Fill pastry-lined pie pan (*see pp. 298–301*) with rhubarb custard filling. Use:

For 9″ Pie	*For 8″ Pie*
Beat slightly . . .	
3 eggs	2 (large)
Add . . .	
2⅔ tbsp. milk	2 tbsp.
Mix together and stir in . . .	
2 cups sugar	1½ cups
4 tbsp. GOLD MEDAL Flour	3 tbsp.
¾ tsp. nutmeg	½ tsp.
Mix in . . .	
4 cups cut-up pink rhubarb	3 cups
Dot filling in pan with . . .	
1 tbsp. butter	¾ tbsp.

Cover with lattice top. Bake until nicely browned. Serve slightly warm.

TEMPERATURE: 400° (mod. hot oven).

TIME: Bake 50 to 60 min.

PEACH OR APRICOT PIE

Juicy with golden fruit. Mary McNaughton, now Mrs. Lou Taylor of Wausau, Wisconsin, when on our Staff did a lot of testing on these fresh fruit pies.

Follow 🔑 recipe for Fresh Berry Pie (*see p. 304*)—*except* use sliced firm peaches or apricots instead of berries, and use 1 tbsp. less flour. Use ⅞ cup sugar for the 9″ pie, ⅔ cup for the 8″ pie. Serve slightly warm, not hot.

BEAUTY TOUCHES FOR PIES

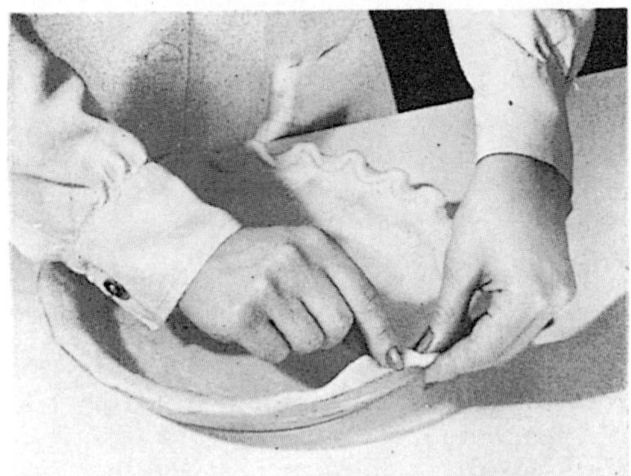

1 For a rippled fluting, pull rim, held by right thumb and forefinger, *down and over* toward you a little . . . hold back the rim with the other hand. Then place thumb and finger (hold about ½″ apart) of left hand where those of right hand were and repeat.

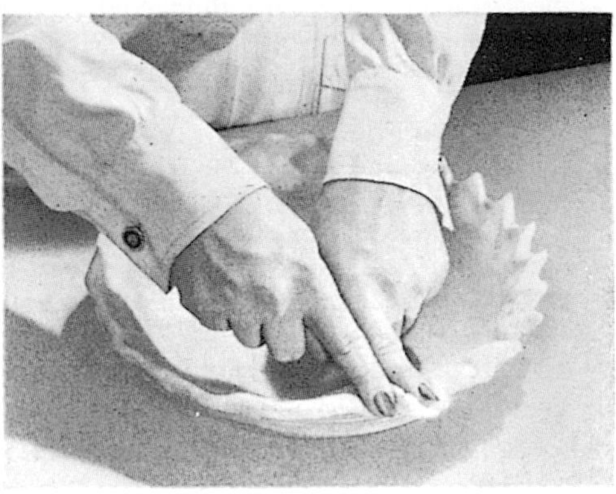

2 For shell edge fluting, place left forefinger diagonally across rim of pastry. Place right forefinger in same position about ¼″ apart. Slightly push right finger toward left one and pull toward center. Place left finger where right finger was and repeat.

3 For a shiny and sugary top crust, just before baking, brush top crust lightly with milk or water, then sprinkle with granulated sugar. For glazed top, brush with mixture of ½ whole egg or 1 egg yolk and ½ tbsp. water.

4 For pastry cutouts to decorate pies, cut pastry for top into appropriate shapes. Brush with water and sprinkle with colored sugar. Place on filling and bake. Or bake on pan and place on pie filling in baked shell.

5 For interwoven lattice top for fruit pies, weave ½″ strips of pastry (cut with pastry wheel) crisscross on waxed paper. Then chill.

6 Flip quickly over top of filling. Seal and finish edge. Insert shows finished pie . . . Berry Pie with gay lattice top.

AUTUMN FRUIT PIES *When autumn leaves are falling.*

★ GRAPE PIE

Prize of the harvest season . . . sweet, tart, juicy, fragrant with rich purple grapes. One of the many culinary secrets and recipes contributed by an ideal homemaker, Mrs. Philip Gearty of Minneapolis, Minnesota.

Make Pastry for Two-Crust Pie of desired size. Line pie pan. (*See pp. 298–301.*)

For the Filling	*For 9″ Pie*	*For 8″ Pie*
Remove and save skins from	**5⅓ cups Concord grapes**	**4 cups**
Put pulp into saucepan without water and bring to a rolling boil. While hot, rub through strainer to remove seeds. Mix strained pulp with skins.		
Mix together (and mix lightly through grapes)	**1⅓ cups sugar**	**1 cup**
	4 tbsp. GOLD MEDAL Flour	**3 tbsp.**
Sprinkle with	**1⅓ tsp. lemon juice**	**1 tsp.**
	dash of salt	**dash**
Pour grapes into pastry-lined pan.		
Dot with	**1⅓ tbsp. butter**	**1 tbsp.**

Cover with top crust. Bake until crust is nicely browned and juice begins to bubble through slits in crust. Serve cool or slightly warm, not hot.

TEMPERATURE: 425° (hot oven).

TIME: Bake 35 to 45 min.

GREEN TOMATO PIE

Old-time autumn favorite.

Fill pastry-lined pan (*see pp. 298–301*) with green tomato filling:

	For 9″ Pie	*For 8″ Pie*
Mix together . . .		
	1⅓ cups sugar	**1 cup**
	6⅔ tbsp. GOLD MEDAL Flour	**5 tbsp.**
	1⅓ tsp. salt	**1 tsp.**
	1⅓ tsp. nutmeg or cinnamon	**1 tsp.**
Mix lightly through . . .		
	4 cups green tomato slices (cut in quarters)	**3 cups**
	4 tbsp. lemon juice (or 1⅓ tbsp. mild vinegar)	**3 tbsp. (or 1 tbsp.)**
	1⅓ tsp. grated lemon rind	**1 tsp.**
Dot the filling (in the pan) with . . .		
	1⅓ tbsp. butter	**1 tbsp.**

Cover with top crust. Bake until nicely browned. Serve slightly warm.

TEMPERATURE: 425° (hot oven).

TIME: Bake 35 to 45 min.

SIMPLE LATTICE TOP: Roll pastry for top exact size of pan. Cut into ½″ strips. Lay half of them across filling 1″ apart. Then cross with the other strips.

EARLY AMERICAN PEAR PIE

Delicately spiced and baked to a luscious glaze. Pear Pie vied in popularity with apple pie during the early days of our country.

Fill pastry-lined pie pan (*see pp. 298–301*) with pear filling:

	For 9″ Pie	*For 8″ Pie*
Pare and slice firm pears . . .		
Mix together . . .		
	¾ cup sugar	**½ cup**
	1 tsp. nutmeg or cinnamon	**¾ tsp.**
	2 tbsp. GOLD MEDAL Flour	**1½ tbsp.**
Mix lightly through . . .		
	6 cups sliced pears	**4½ cups**
Dot the filling (in the pan) with . . .		
	1⅓ tbsp. butter	**1 tbsp.**

Cover with top crust. Bake until nicely browned. Serve cool. If desired, garnish with cheese, whipped cream, or ice cream.

TEMPERATURE: 425° (hot oven).

TIME: Bake 35 to 45 min.

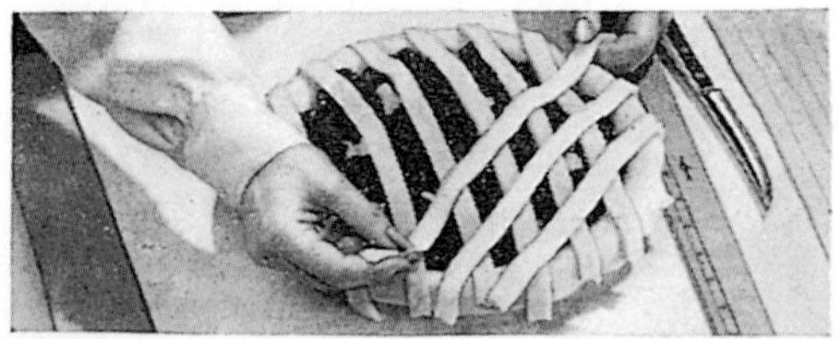

CRANBERRY PIE (🔑 Recipe) *From down Cape Cod way.*

Make Pastry for Two-Crust Pie of desired size. Line pie pan (*See pp. 298-301*). Use minimum or maximum amount of sugar according to tartness desired.

For the Filling	*For 9″ Pie*	*For 8″ Pie*
Mix together in saucepan............	1½ to 2 cups sugar	1 to 1½ cups
	4 tbsp. GOLD MEDAL Flour	3 tbsp.
	⅓ tsp. salt	¼ tsp.
Add................................	2¾ cups halved cranberries	2 cups
	½ cup water	⅓ cup
Bring slowly to a boil, and boil gently 5 min., stirring constantly. Remove from heat and blend in.......	½ tsp. almond extract	⅓ tsp.

Pour into pastry-lined pie pan. Cover with top crust. Bake until crust is nicely browned. Serve slightly warm.

TEMPERATURE: 425° (hot oven).

TIME: Bake 30 to 40 min.

MOCK CHERRY PIE

Follow 🔑 recipe above for method. Use:

Filling for 9″ Pie	*For 8″ Pie*
1 to 1½ cups sugar	¾ to 1 cup
4 tbsp. GOLD MEDAL Flour	3 tbsp.
⅓ tsp. salt	¼ tsp.
2¾ cups halved cranberries	2 cups
1 cup seeded raisins	¾ cup
1 cup water	¾ cup
½ tsp. almond extract	⅓ tsp.

RAISIN PIE

Called "Funeral Pie" by the Pennsylvania Dutch because it was always served when relatives and neighbors gathered from far and near to pay their "last respects."

Fill pastry-lined pie pan (*see pp. 298–301*) with hot raisin filling:

For 9″ Pie	*For 8″ Pie*
Cook covered until tender (about 5 min.)...	
2 cups seeded raisins	1½ cups
2 cups boiling water	1½ cups
Stir in mixture of ...	
½ cup sugar	⅓ cup
2 tbsp. flour	1½ tbsp.
Cook over low heat, stirring constantly, until boiling. Boil 1 min. Remove from heat. Stir in ...	
½ cup chopped nuts	⅓ cup
2 tsp. grated lemon rind	1½ tsp.
3 tbsp. lemon juice	2¼ tbsp.

Cover with top crust. Bake until nicely browned. Serve slightly warm.

TEMPERATURE: 425° (hot oven).

TIME: Bake 30 to 40 min.

OLD-FASHIONED MINCE PIE

One of the earliest pies—meat and fruit minced for a rich hearty filling.

Fill pastry-lined pie pan (*see pp. 298–301*) with mincemeat. Use:

For 9″ Pie	*For 8″ Pie*
3⅓ cups mincemeat	2½ cups

NOTE: To make mincemeat extra fruity, mix in a little chopped apple.

Cover with top crust. Bake until nicely browned. Serve warm.

TEMPERATURE: 425° (hot oven).

TIME: Bake 30 to 40 min.

★ MINCE PIE WITH BLACKBERRY SAUCE

"Different" . . . and elegant. Another prize-winning recipe . . . this one contributed by Miss Gertrude Mihm of Edwall, Washington.

Follow recipe for Old-Fashioned Mince Pie above—*except* substitute well drained canned blackberries for ½ the mincemeat in the filling. Serve warm with:

HOT BLACKBERRY SAUCE

Mix together in saucepan . . .
- 1 tbsp. sugar
- 1 tbsp. cornstarch

Blend in . . .
- 1 cup blackberry juice (drained from canned berries)

Cook until smooth and thickened, stirring constantly. Remove from heat. Add . . .
- 1 tbsp. butter
- ⅛ tsp. salt
- 2 tbsp. lemon juice

PASTRY PIES No pastry to hide what's baked inside.

HOW-TO-MAKE A ONE-CRUST PIE when filling and crust are baked together.

(Pictures on making pastry on pp. 298–301 show just how!)

For Plain Pastry	*For 9″ Pie*	*For 8″ Pie*
Mix together	1 cup *sifted* GOLD MEDAL Flour ½ tsp. salt	1 cup ½ tsp.
Cut in with pastry blender	*⅓ cup shortening	*⅓ cup
Sprinkle with	2 tbsp. water	2 tbsp.

Gather dough together and press firmly into a ball. Roll out into a circle 1″ larger than pan all around (*see p. 300*). Then follow method below. For temperature and time, see each recipe.

**Use almost one tablespoon extra if hydrogenated shortening is used.*

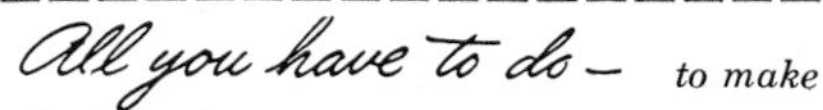

to make

Orange Pastry for Orange, Lemon, etc. Pies: Use orange juice in place of water in above recipe, add ½ tsp. grated orange rind.

Nut Pastry for Cream Pies: Add ¼ cup ground nuts to the flour. Bake as pie shells (*p.* 315).

1 Fit pastry loosely into pan. Avoid stretching to prevent shrinking.

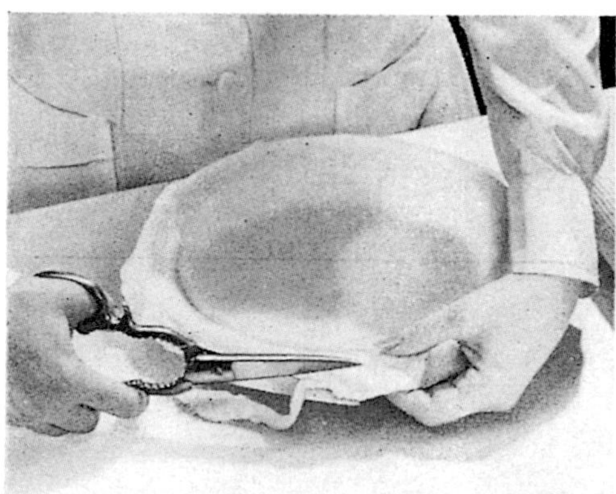

2 Trim off ragged edges with scissors . . . leaving ½″ overhanging edge of pan.

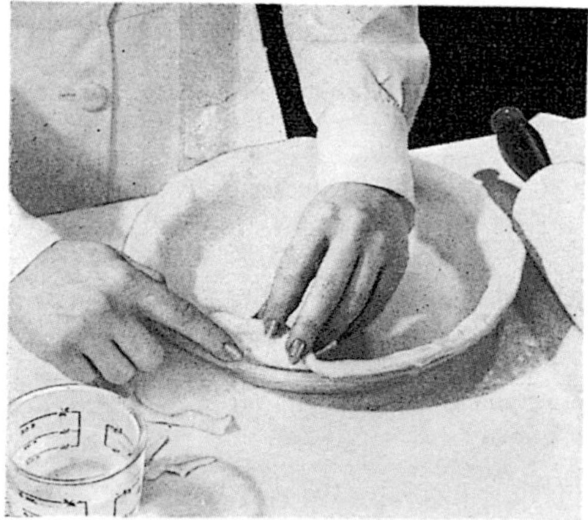

3 Fold extra pastry back and under, and build up a high fluted edge to hold a generous amount of filling. (Do not prick pastry!)

4 Pour most of filling into pastry-lined pan. To prevent spilling, place pan on rack in oven. Pour in remaining filling.

NOTE: Store any leftover pie of custard type in refrigerator.

CUSTARD PIE (🔑 **Recipe**) *Rich, satiny smooth custard baked right in the crust.*

Make Pastry for One-Crust Pie. Line pie pan. (*See p. 310.*) Build up high fluted edge.

For the Filling	*For 9″ Pie*	*For 8″ Pie*
Beat slightly with rotary beater........	**4 eggs (or 8 egg yolks)**	**3 eggs (or 6 yolks)**
Then beat in........................	**2/3 cup sugar**	**1/2 cup**
	1/2 tsp. salt	**1/3 tsp.**
	1/4 tsp. nutmeg	**1/4 tsp.**
	***2 2/3 cups scalding hot milk**	***2 cups**
	1 tsp. vanilla, if desired	**3/4 tsp.**

Pour into pastry-lined pie pan. Bake just until a silver knife inserted into *side* of filling comes out clean. The center may still look a bit soft but will set later. *Caution:* Too long baking makes custard "watery." Serve slightly warm or cold.

**Use part cream for an extra rich pie.*

TEMPERATURE: 450° (hot oven) for 15 min., then 350° (mod. oven) to finish.

TIME: Bake 25 to 30 min.

NOTE: Can be baked at 425° for same time.

All you have to do –

To prevent soggy crust on custard pie—

Bake the custard alone—
The crust by itself,
And your custard pies
Won't stay on the shelf.

★ **SLIP-SLIDE CUSTARD PIE**

Certain-sure of a crisp undercrust every time.

Follow 🔑 recipe above—*except* bake crust and filling separately. Pour filling directly into ungreased pie pan of *same* size as the one in which the crust is baked. Set pan in shallow pan of hot water. Bake just until a silver knife inserted into side of filling comes out clean. The center may still look a bit soft but will set later. When lukewarm, slip the baked filling into cooled baked pie shell (*p. 315*). Allow to settle a few minutes before serving.

TEMPERATURE: 350° (mod. oven).

TIME: Bake custard 30 to 35 min.

COCONUT CUSTARD PIE

Follow 🔑 recipe above—*except* omit nutmeg, stir into custard moist shredded coconut (1 cup for 9″ pie, 3/4 cup for 8″ pie). Sprinkle a little coconut over top. Bake.

FUDGE-TOPPED CUSTARD PIE

Follow 🔑 recipe above. Just before serving, spread evenly over the cooled custard filling:

FUDGE TOPPING: Mix together 1/2 cup *sifted* confectioners' sugar, 1/8 tsp. salt, and 2 tbsp. cream. Blend in 1 sq. unsweetened chocolate (1 oz.), melted, and 2 tbsp. melted butter.

SWEET CREAM PIE

Scald 2 cups 30% cream. Mix 2 tbsp. flour, 4 tbsp. sugar, 1/4 tsp. salt, and blend in thoroughly 2 egg whites (stirred with a fork) and 1 tsp. vanilla. Blend in the hot cream. Pour into pastry-lined 8″ pie pan. Bake as for Custard Pie above.

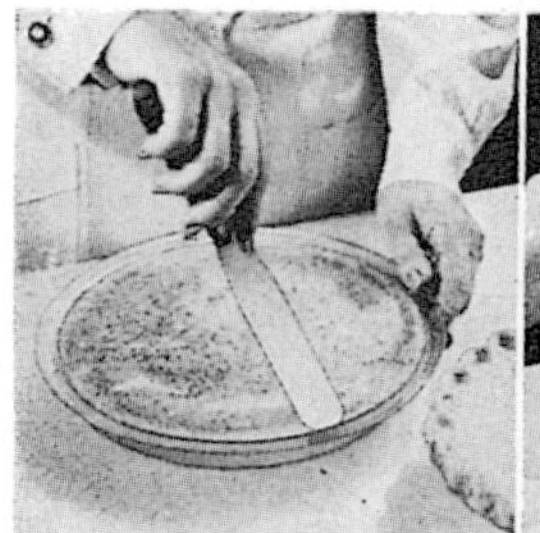

1 Loosen custard around edge of pan.

2 Shake pan gently to loosen completely.

3 Slip custard into shell, let settle.

4 The custard looks baked in the crust.

CUSTARD-TYPE PIES Early American pies brought up-to-date.

PUMPKIN PIE (🔑 Recipe) *The essence of golden pumpkin . . . flavorful with spices.*

Pumpkins, or "pompions," were a standby of the early New England settlements. An old verse goes:

"For pottage, and puddings, and custards, and pies,
Our pumpkins and parsnips are common supplies.
We have pumpkins at morning and pumpkins at noon;
If it were not for pumpkins, we should be undoon."

Make Pastry for One-Crust Pie. Line pie pan. (*See p. 310.*) Build up high fluted edge.

For the Filling	*For 9" Pie*	*For 8" Pie*
Beat together with rotary beater......	**1¾ cups mashed cooked pumpkin**	**1¼ cups**
	½ tsp. salt	**⅓ tsp.**
	1¾ cups milk	**1¼ cups**
	2 large eggs (½ cup) *or* 4 yolks	**2 eggs (⅓ cup) *or* 3 yolks**
	⅔ cup brown sugar	**½ cup**
	2 tbsp. sugar	**1½ tbsp.**
	1¼ tsp. cinnamon	**1 tsp.**
	½ tsp. ginger	**⅓ tsp.**
	½ tsp. nutmeg	**⅓ tsp.**
	¼ tsp. cloves	**¼ tsp.**

Pour into pastry-lined pie pan. (For crispness, have bottom pastry little thicker than ⅛".) Bake just until a silver knife inserted into side of filling comes out clean. The center may still look soft but will set later. Serve slightly warm or cold.

NOTE: This is a rich brown spicy pie. For lighter color and milder flavor, use all white sugar and omit cloves.

TEMPERATURE: 425° (hot oven).

TIME: Bake 45 to 55 min.

PUMPKIN PIE WITH WHIPPED CREAM

Follow 🔑 recipe above. Just before serving, cover cooled pie with a thin layer of sweetened whipped cream and sprinkle chopped nuts over the top.

GINGER CREAM: A gourmet's touch. Use ½ tsp. ginger with ½ cup whipping cream and 1 tbsp. sugar.

Pumpkins of pastry to set off the pie.

★ PUMPKIN PIE WITH CREAM AND POOLS OF HONEY

A delectable combination.

Follow 🔑 recipe above. Just before serving, top cooled pie with mounds of stiffly whipped cream, one for each serving. Make a little hollow in top of each mound of cream. Place a spoonful of honey in each to top the piece of pie.

SOUTHERN SWEET POTATO PIE

Follow recipe for New England Squash Pie opposite—*except* use mashed cooked sweet potatoes in place of squash. Strain.

NEW ENGLAND SQUASH PIE

Follow 🔑 recipe above for method. Use:

Filling for 9" Pie	*For 8" Pie*
1¾ cups strained mashed squash	**1¼ cups**
1 tsp. salt	**¾ tsp.**
1½ cups milk	**1⅛ cups**
2 large eggs (½ cup)	**2 eggs (⅓ cup)**
1 cup sugar	**¾ cup**
1 tsp. cinnamon	**¾ tsp.**
½ tsp. nutmeg	**⅓ tsp.**
½ tsp. ginger	**⅓ tsp.**
1 tbsp. melted butter	**¾ tbsp.**

SOUR CREAM PIE (🔑 Recipe)

From covered wagon days. A favorite of men everywhere for its rich spicy custard.

Make Pastry for One-Crust Pie of desired size. Line pie pan. (*See p. 310.*)

For the Filling	*For 9″ Pie*	*For 8″ Pie*
Beat until very light and fluffy	**3 eggs**	**2 (large)**
Mix together and blend in	**1⅓ tbsp. GOLD MEDAL Flour**	**1 tbsp.**
	⅔ cup sugar	**½ cup**
	½ tsp. salt	**⅓ tsp.**
	2½ tsp. cinnamon	**2 tsp.**
	⅔ tsp. cloves	**½ tsp.**
Fold in	**1⅓ cups thick sour cream**	**1 cup**
	1⅓ cups seeded raisins	**1 cup**

Pour into pastry-lined pie pan. Bake until a silver knife thrust into side of filling comes out clean.

TEMPERATURE: 350° (mod. oven).

TIME: Bake 50 to 60 min.

CHESS PIE

One of the interesting pastry delicacies from early England.

Follow 🔑 recipe above—*except*, in place of whole eggs, use egg yolks; in place of spices, use about 1 tsp. vanilla; sweet cream in place of sour; and add cut-up dates and walnuts with the raisins.

For 9″ Pie	*For 8″ Pie*
1 cup cut-up dates	**¾ cup**
1 cup cut-up walnuts	**¾ cup**

★ PECAN PIE

Traditional recipe from Tidewater Virginia. The choice among all desserts served at world renowned Williamsburg Inn in restored colonial Williamsburg.

Make Pastry for One-Crust Pie of desired size. Line pie pan. (*See p. 310.*)

Filling for 9″ Pie	*For 8″ Pie*
Beat together with rotary beater . . .	
3 eggs	**2 (large)**
⅔ cup sugar	**½ cup**
⅓ tsp. salt	**¼ tsp.**
⅓ cup butter, melted	**¼ cup**
1 cup dark corn syrup	**¾ cup**
Mix in . . .	
1 cup pecan halves	**¾ cup**

Pour into pastry-lined pan. Bake until set and pastry is nicely browned. Cool. Serve cold or slightly warm.

TEMPERATURE: 375° (quick mod. oven).

TIME: Bake 40 to 50 min.

PRUNE CREAM PIE

Delicious and homey-tasting. This prize-winning recipe was sent to us by a prize homemaker, Mrs. W. K. Robbins of Baytown, Texas.

Make Pastry for One-Crust Pie of desired size. Line pie pan. (*See p. 310.*)

Filling for 9″ Pie	*For 8″ Pie*
Beat slightly . . .	
3 eggs	**2 (large)**
Mix together and blend in thoroughly . . .	
4 tbsp. GOLD MEDAL Flour	**3 tbsp.**
1 cup sugar	**¾ cup**
½ tsp. salt	**⅓ tsp.**
⅛ tsp. cinnamon	**dash**
Stir in . . .	
1 cup milk	**¾ cup**
½ cup prune juice	**⅓ cup**
1 tsp. vanilla	**¾ tsp.**
1 cup cut-up cooked prunes	**¾ cup**

Pour into pastry-lined pie pan, distributing prunes evenly. Bake until a silver knife thrust into side of filling comes out clean. Cool. Just before serving, spread with sweetened whipped cream, if desired.

TEMPERATURE: 375° (quick mod. oven).

TIME: Bake 50 to 60 min.

FRUIT-AND-CREAM PIES De luxe version of berries and cream.

BERRIES-AND-CREAM PIE (**🔑 Recipe**) *Rich sweet cream over fresh ripe berries . . . baked together . . . perfectly delicious. Mrs. Edward A. Cook of Wayzata, Minnesota, learned this old-time trick with berries from her husband's mother who brought it from New York state. Edam Cheese was always served with it.*

Make Pastry for One-Crust Pie of desired size. Line pie pan. (*See p. 310.*)

For the Filling	*For 9″ Pie*	*For 8″ Pie*
Place in pastry-lined pan............	4 cups fresh berries	3 cups
Mix together and pour over berries....	2/3 cup sugar	1/2 cup
	4 tbsp. GOLD MEDAL Flour	3 tbsp.
	1/4 tsp. salt	1/4 tsp.
	1/2 tsp. cinnamon	1/3 tsp.
	1 cup cream (30%)	3/4 cup

Bake until crust is nicely browned and filling set. Serve slightly warm.

TEMPERATURE: 400° (mod. hot oven).
TIME: Bake 35 to 45 min.

★ **BLACKBERRIES-AND-CREAM PIE**

One of the most exotic and interesting of all.

Follow 🔑 recipe above using Blackberries.

BLUEBERRIES-AND-CREAM PIE

The Indians would have loved this!

Follow 🔑 recipe above using Blueberries.

RASPBERRIES-AND-CREAM PIE

A new idea for the raspberry festival.

Follow 🔑 recipe above using Raspberries.

PEACHES-AND-CREAM PIE

Just as luscious as it sounds.

Follow 🔑 recipe above—*except,* in place of berries, use peeled ripe, juicy peach halves. Use:

For 9″ Pie	*For 8″ Pie*
7 or 8 peach halves	6 peach halves

Arrange peach halves rounded-side-up in pastry-lined pan. Pour cream mixture over them, and bake.

A luscious fragrant treat ready for homecomers.

Pour cream-sugar-spice mixture over berries.

COUNTRY APPLE PIE

Rich and spicy . . . as from a country kitchen.

Make Pastry for One-Crust Pie. Line pie pan. (*See p. 310.*) Prepare thinly sliced pared apples.

For 9″ Pie	*For 8″ Pie*
Place in pastry-lined pan . . .	
5 cups sliced apples	3 3/4 cups
Mix together and pour over apples . . .	
3/4 cup sugar	1/2 cup
4 tbsp. GOLD MEDAL Flour	3 tbsp.
1/4 tsp. salt	1/4 tsp.
1/2 tsp. cinnamon	1/3 tsp.
1 cup cream (30%)	3/4 cup

Sprinkle 1 tbsp. sugar and 1/4 tsp. cinnamon mixed together over top of pie. Bake at 400° (mod. hot oven) 50 to 60 min.

HOW TO MAKE A PASTRY SHELL for a pie in which filling is piled into the baked shell.

Flaky Pastry, or Orange or Nut Pastry are "special" for pie shells, top crusts. *To Make Flaky Pastry,* roll Plain Pastry (*see p. 310*) ⅛″ thick. Then:

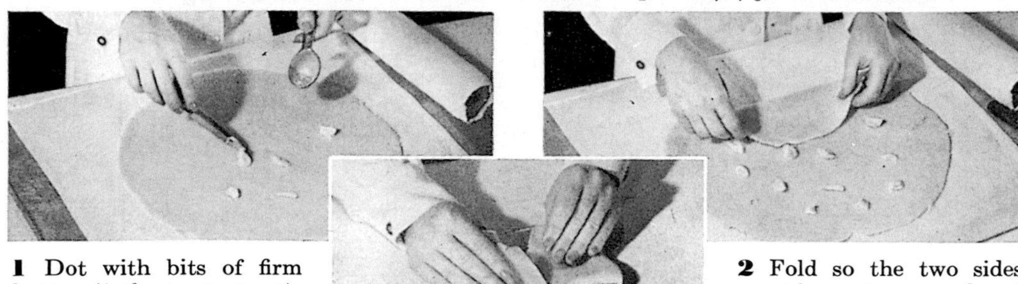

1 Dot with bits of firm butter (1 tbsp. per crust). Too hard or soft butter breaks through.

2 Fold so the two sides meet in center . . . and seal by pressing the side edges of pastry with fingers.

3 Fold ends to center and seal. Roll out, fit into pan. (Warm pan, moistened rim prevents shrinking.)

4 Prick pastry to prevent puffing during baking. (If pastry persists in puffing up, quickly reach in oven, prick again in two places.) Bake at 475° (very hot oven) 8 min.

5 Finish the pie according to each recipe. *For meringue pies,* pour in filling and top with meringue. See directions for Meringue (*p. 316*). For *chiffon pies,* pile in filling and chill.

SIMPLIFIED PUFF PASTRY

Extra-rich . . . extra-flaky . . . for cases or patty shells to hold creamed chicken, etc.

Make plain Pastry (*see p. 299*). Roll out, dot with ⅓ cup *butter.* Roll up like jelly roll. Roll out into rectangle. Fold and seal (*see above*). Wrap in waxed paper and chill.

For *Pastry Cases,* roll out ⅛″ thick, fit onto *backs* of tart pans. Place on baking sheet, chill again. Bake at 425° (hot oven) 20 to 30 min.—covering with brown paper after 15 min. to prevent excessive browning.

For *Patty Shells,* roll pastry almost ¼″ thick. Cut with biscuit cutter. Place 2 narrow rings (of same size) on top of each round. Stick them together with water. Bake as above . . . 30 to 40 min.

ENGLISH PASTRY

Easy, unusually tender, wonderful for Meat Pies.

Sift together . . .
- **2 cups *sifted* GOLD MEDAL Flour**
- **2 tsp. baking powder**
- **1 tsp. salt**

Mix well and stir into flour mixture . . .
- **⅔ cup shortening**
- **½ cup hot water**
- **1 tbsp. lemon juice**
- **1 egg yolk, unbeaten**

Chill. Pat out ¾ of pastry as lining in 2-qt. casserole (8″). Fill. Cover with rest of pastry. Bake at 425° (hot oven) 25 min.

GINGER COOKY CRUST

For Pumpkin Chiffon and Black Bottom Pie.

Mix ¼ cup butter, melted, into 1¼ cups fine gingersnap crumbs (crush 18). Pat and press into 9″ pie pan. Bake at 325° (slow mod. oven) 10 min. Cool, fill.

MERINGUE PIES With a little care, they'll be heavenly fare.

FOR PERFECT MERINGUE ON PIES

*In *meringue* pies (such as Lemon Meringue), a meringue is piled on top of the pie filling, and the pie with meringue baked according to directions below. In *chiffon* pies, an *unbaked* meringue is combined with the pie filling, and the pie is chilled.

MERINGUE

For 9″ Pie	*For 8″ Pie*
3 egg whites	**2 egg whites**
1/4 tsp. cream of tartar	**1/4 tsp.**
6 tbsp. sugar	**4 tbsp.**
1/2 tsp. flavoring (if desired)	**1/3 tsp.**

**Read paragraph above.*

TEMPERATURE: 400° (mod. hot oven).

TIME: Bake 8 to 10 min.

NOTE: This makes a very light, fluffy meringue . . . *easy to cut through.* Remember, too long baking and incomplete blending-in of sugar causes "weeping!" Stirring the cooked filling may cause *it* to "weep" (water appears under meringue).

Favorite meringue pies are given on p. 317. Others often topped with meringue are Chocolate Cream, Coconut Cream, Butterscotch Pie, etc.; although our Staff prefers whipped cream topping for these.

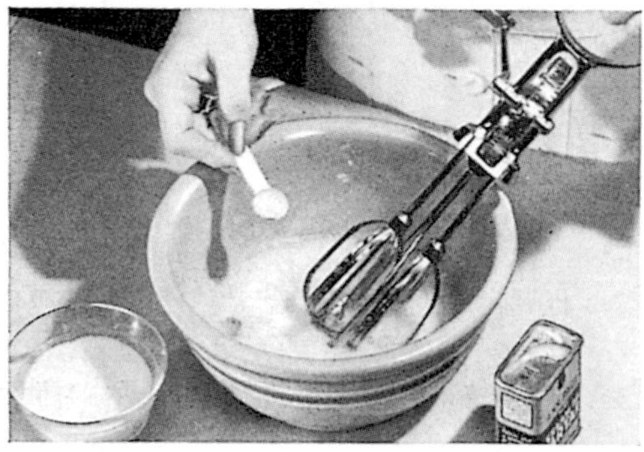

1 Beat whites with cream of tartar 'til frothy.

2 Gradually beat in sugar, a little at a time.

3 Continue beating until stiff and glossy.

4 Pile meringue onto pie filling, being careful to seal the meringue onto edge of crust to prevent shrinking. If the filling is exposed to the heat (not entirely covered), it may "weep."

5 Swirl or pull up points for decorative top. Bake until delicately browned. Cool gradually in a slightly warm place, away from drafts. A chill may make the meringue fall.

LEMON MERINGUE PIE (Recipe) *Robert Taylor's favorite . . . his mother's recipe, featured in our radio cooking school with an interview from this famous star. Its tangy refreshing flavor makes it our favorite lemon pie, too.*

Make Pastry Shell of desired size (*see p. 315*).

For the Filling	*For 9" Pie*	*For 8" Pie*
Mix in saucepan	1½ cups sugar	1⅛ cups
	5⅓ tbsp. (⅓ cup) cornstarch	4 tbsp.
Stir in gradually	1½ cups water	1⅛ cups
Cook over moderate heat, stirring constantly, until mixture thickens and boils. Boil 1 min. Slowly stir half the hot mixture into	3 egg yolks, slightly beaten	2 (large)
Then beat into hot mixture in saucepan. Boil 1 min. longer, stirring constantly. Remove from heat. Continue stirring until smooth. Blend in	3 tbsp. butter	2¼ tbsp.
	4 tbsp. lemon juice	3 tbsp.
	1⅓ tbsp. grated lemon rind	1 tbsp.

Pour into baked pie shell. Cover with Meringue (*p. 316*). Bake until a delicate brown. Serve as soon as cool.

TEMPERATURE: 400° (mod. hot oven).

TIME: Bake 8 to 10 min.

ORANGE MERINGUE PIE
Chosen in preference to every other orange pie.

Follow recipe above for method. Use:

Filling for 9" Pie	*For 8" Pie*
1 cup sugar	¾ cup
3 tbsp. cornstarch	2¼ tbsp.
½ cup water	⅓ cup
1 cup orange juice (unstrained)	¾ cup
3 egg yolks, slightly beaten	2 (large)
3 tbsp. butter	2 tbsp.
1 tbsp. lemon juice	¾ tbsp.
1 tbsp. grated orange rind	¾ tbsp.

STRAWBERRY MERINGUE PIE
Luscious! The meringue is the crust. Introduced by Gladys Black, University of Omaha, at a Home Economics dinner for executives.

Beat until stiff . . .
3 egg whites
½ tsp. baking powder
Beat in gradually . . .
1 cup sugar
Fold in . . .
10 sq. (2") soda crackers, rolled fine
½ cup cut-up pecans

Spread in well buttered 9" pie pan. Bake at 300° (slow oven) 30 min. Cool. Fill with 1 qt. unsweetened strawberries and top with sweetened whipped cream (whip ½ cup cream). Chill several hours.

All you have to do—

To save time: use frozen or bottled fruit juices.

To keep the pleasant pungent flavor of fresh lemon or orange: grate just the thin colored rind (fine grater).

★ **LIME MERINGUE PIE**
The idea for this pie with its cool sea green filling was brought from Florida by Jean Hall of our Staff.

Follow recipe above—*except,* in place of lemon, use lime and leave out the butter. Add a few drops of green food coloring to intensify the color . . . just a delicate lime green.

PINEAPPLE MERINGUE PIE
Follow recipe above for method, but blend in pineapple at the last. Use:

Filling for 9" Pie	*For 8" Pie*
1 cup sugar	¾ cup
4 tbsp. cornstarch	3 tbsp.
½ cup water	⅓ cup
1 cup pineapple juice	¾ cup
3 egg yolks, slightly beaten	2 (large)
3 tbsp. butter	2 tbsp.
1 tbsp. lemon juice	¾ tbsp.
1⅓ tsp. grated lemon rind	1 tsp.
1¼ cups well drained crushed pineapple	1 cup

CREAM PIES Delicious, delovely . . . the gourmet's delight.

VANILLA CREAM PIE (🔑 Recipe) *Velvety smooth filling. Flavor perfect.*

Make Pastry Shell (with high fluted edge) of desired size (*see p. 315*).

For the Filling	*For 9″ Pie*	*For 8″ Pie*
Mix in saucepan	**2/3 cup sugar** **1/2 tsp. salt** **2 1/2 tbsp. cornstarch** **1 tbsp. GOLD MEDAL Flour**	**1/2 cup** **1/3 tsp.** **2 tbsp.** **3/4 tbsp.**
Stir in gradually	**3 cups milk**	**2 1/4 cups**
Cook over moderate heat, stirring constantly, until mixture thickens and boils. Boil 1 min. Remove from heat. Slowly stir half the mixture into	**3 egg yolks, slightly beaten**	**2 (large)**
Then blend into hot mixture in saucepan. Boil 1 min. more, stirring constantly. Remove from heat.		
Blend in	**1 tbsp. butter** **1 1/2 tsp. vanilla**	**3/4 tbsp.** **1 tsp.**

Cool . . . stirring occasionally. Pour into cooled baked pie shell. Chill thoroughly (2 hr.). If desired, top with sweetened whipped cream. Or sprinkle with shaved nuts, toasted coconut, or fresh berries. Take chilled pie out of refrigerator 20 min. before serving.

NOTE: If adding Meringue (*see p. 316*), filling and crust need not be cooled. Cool finished pie at room temperature (2 hr.).

For Whipped Cream Topping: Beat 1/2 cup cream stiff, beat in 1 tbsp. confectioners' sugar and 1/4 tsp. vanilla.

All you have to do –

To save egg whites until needed for frostings, white cakes, meringues, etc.: keep in tightly covered jar in refrigerator.

★ ALMOND CREAM PIE

Crunchy toasted almonds; smooth, soft creamy custard in crispy pastry . . . made famous by Mrs. Inez Norton Crawford of the lovely Boulevard Twins, Minneapolis, Minnesota.

Follow 🔑 recipe above—*except,* in place of vanilla, use 1/2 tsp. almond extract and add 1/2 cup toasted slivered blanched almonds to the cooled filling. Sprinkle a few toasted slivered almonds over whipped cream topping.

CHOCOLATE CREAM PIE

Smooth, rich . . . the kind to rave about.

Follow 🔑 recipe above—*except* increase sugar and add cut-up unsweetened chocolate with the milk. Use:

For 9″ Pie	*For 8″ Pie*
1 1/2 cups sugar	**1 1/8 cups**
3 sq. chocolate (3 oz.)	**2 1/4 sq.**

If desired, top with sweetened whipped cream or meringue.

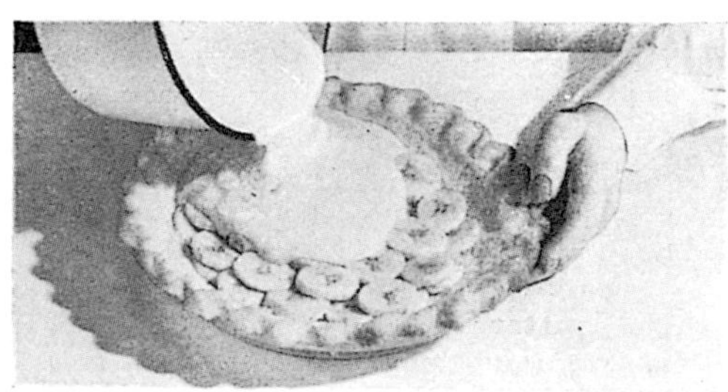

BANANA CREAM PIE

De luxe version.

Follow 🔑 recipe above—*except* arrange a layer of sliced bananas 1/2″ deep in pastry shell before pouring in cooled filling. Use:

For 9″ Pie	*For 8″ Pie*
3 large bananas	**2 bananas**

If whipped cream topping is used, garnish with a ring of sliced bananas.

COCONUT CREAM PIE

Always popular.

Follow 🔑 recipe above—*except* fold in 3/4 cup moist shredded coconut just before filling pastry shell. Sprinkle whipped cream or meringue topping with 1/4 cup shredded coconut (toasted, if desired).

BUTTERSCOTCH PIE *Glossy smooth . . . with the true butterscotchy flavor.*

Make Pastry Shell of desired size (*see p. 315*).

For the Filling	*For 9″ Pie*	*For 8″ Pie*
Melt in skillet over low heat.	6 tbsp. butter	4½ tbsp.
When butter is golden brown, add.	1 cup brown sugar (dark)	¾ cup
Boil until foamy (2 to 3 min.), stirring constantly. Stir in. . . . . Remove from heat.	1 cup boiling water	¾ cup
Mix in saucepan.	3 tbsp. cornstarch	2¼ tbsp.
	2 tbsp. GOLD MEDAL Flour	1½ tbsp.
	½ tsp. salt	⅓ tsp.
Stir in gradually until smooth.	1⅔ cups milk	1¼ cups
Stir in the brown sugar mixture.		
Cook over low heat, stirring constantly, until boiling. Boil 1 min. Remove from heat. Stir half of it into. .	3 egg yolks, slightly beaten	2 (large)
Then blend into hot mixture. Boil 1 min. longer. Remove from heat. Blend in.	1 tsp. vanilla	¾ tsp.

Cool, stirring occasionally. Pour into cooled baked pie shell. Chill. Top with sweetened whipped cream and decorate with toasted nuts. Serve cold.

NOTE: If topped with Meringue, filling and pie shell need not be cooled. Cool finished pie at room temperature 2 hr.

★ **CHOCOLATE MARVEL PIE**

Make Pastry Shell of desired size (*p. 315*).

Filling for 9″ Pie	*For 8″ Pie*
Melt and blend together over hot water . . .	
1 6-oz. pkg. semi-sweet chocolate pieces	¾ pkg.
2 tbsp. sugar	1½ tbsp.
3 tbsp. milk	2¼ tbsp.
Cool. Beat in, one at a time . . .	
4 egg yolks	3
1 tsp. vanilla	¾ tsp.
Beat until stiff . . .	
4 egg whites	3
Fold in chocolate mixture	

Pour into cooled baked pie shell. Chill. Garnish.

To make eyes stop, look, and glisten!

Garnish with whipped cream in this attractive design.

LEMON FLUFF PIE

Forerunner of delicate chiffon pies . . . can be served cold (unbaked) or warm (baked).

Make Pastry Shell of desired size (*p. 315*).

Filling for 9″ Pie	*For 8″ Pie*
Mix together in saucepan . . .	
3 egg yolks	2 (large)
½ cup sugar	⅓ cup
3 tbsp. water	2 tbsp.
3 tbsp. lemon juice	2 tbsp.
2 tsp. grated lemon rind	1⅓ tsp.

Cook over low heat, stirring constantly, until boiling. Remove from heat. Immediately fold gently into a Meringue (for method, *see p. 316*) of . . .

3 egg whites	2 (large)
¼ tsp. cream of tartar	¼ tsp.
½ cup sugar	⅓ cup

Pile into baked pie shell. Chill. Serve cold. Or, if preferred, bake at 400° (mod. hot oven) until delicately browned (about 5 min.). Serve immediately.

All you have to do–

To make the crust of a chilled pie taste its best: take it out of refrigerator 20 min. before serving.

CHIFFON PIES Light as sea foam. Enchanting flavors.

CREAM CHIFFON PIE (🔑 Recipe) *Luscious, fluffy, delicate.*

Make Pastry Shell (with high fluted edge) of desired size (*see p. 315*).

For the Filling	*For 9" Pie*	*For 8" Pie*
Soften	1 tbsp. gelatin (1 envelope)	2 tsp.
in	¼ cup cold water	3 tbsp.
Mix in saucepan	½ cup sugar ½ tsp. salt 1¼ cups milk	⅓ cup ⅓ tsp. 1 cup minus 1 tbsp.
Cook over low heat, stirring constantly until scalded. Remove from heat. Slowly stir half the mixture into	3 egg yolks, slightly beaten	2 (large)
Blend into hot mixture in saucepan.		
Cook over low heat, stirring until it begins to boil. Immediately remove from heat. Stir in softened gelatin. *Cool.* When mixture is partially set, beat with rotary beater until smooth.		
Blend in	1 tsp. vanilla	¾ tsp.
Gently fold in	½ cup whipping cream whipped until stiff	⅓ cup
Carefully fold into a Meringue of (for method, *see p. 316*)	3 egg whites ¼ tsp. cream of tartar ½ cup sugar	2 (large) ¼ tsp. 6 tbsp.

Pile into cooled baked pie shell. Chill until set (about 2 hr.). *Top with sweetened whipped cream and sprinkle with shavings of dark chocolate; or top *servings* with sweetened fruit. Serve cold.

**Take out of the refrigerator 20 min. before serving time.*

COFFEE CHIFFON PIE

Follow 🔑 recipe above—*except* use hot coffee beverage instead of milk.

CHOCOLATE CHIFFON PIE

First enjoyed at a patio supper at Mrs. Arch Vernon's home in Brentwood, California.

Follow 🔑 recipe above—*except* use hot water instead of milk, add cut-up chocolate to sugar before cooking (for 9" pie, use 2 sq. chocolate; 8" pie, 1½ sq.). Spread sweetened whipped cream over top.

CARAMEL NUT CHIFFON PIE

From Betty Sumner Retherford, formerly of Salmagundi Tea Room, Boston, Massachusetts.

Follow 🔑 recipe above—*except* caramelize the sugar (stir in heavy skillet until melted and brown). Add salt and milk (brittle sugar will dissolve). Use half brown sugar in Meringue. Fold in ½ cup cut-up toasted pecans.

EGG NOG CHIFFON PIE

"I just love it!" says Mabel Ross of our Staff whenever this pie is mentioned.

Follow 🔑 recipe above—*except* use 2 tsp. rum flavoring instead of vanilla, and sprinkle ¼ tsp. nutmeg over top.

★ BLACK BOTTOM PIE

Famous at the Hollywood Brown Derby.

Make Ginger Cooky Crust for 9" pie (*see p. 315*). Follow 🔑 recipe above for Filling *except* for 9" pie add 1¼ tbsp. cornstarch with sugar; increase milk to 2 cups; use 4 egg yolks. Before adding gelatin, take out *1 cup* of this custard mixture and add to it 1½ sq. unsweetened chocolate, melted. Beat well, pour into cooled crust. Chill.

Stir the gelatin into the remaining hot custard. Cool. Blend in 1 tbsp. rum flavoring and fold into the Meringue as in the 🔑 recipe. Use 4 egg whites. Chill. Spread the whipped cream on top. Sprinkle with shaved chocolate (1½ sq.).

WHITE CHRISTMAS PIE

Pure white heavenly concoction created by Ruby Livedalen Peterson of our Staff . . . from an idea brought by Dixie Willson of Mason City, Iowa.

Make Pastry Shell (with high fluted edge) of desired size (*see p. 315*).

For the Filling	*For 9" Pie*	*For 8" Pie*
Soften	1 tbsp. gelatin	2 tsp.
in	¼ cup cold water	3 tbsp.
Mix together in saucepan	½ cup sugar	6 tbsp.
	4 tbsp. GOLD MEDAL Flour	3 tbsp.
	½ tsp. salt	⅓ tsp.
Stir in gradually	1½ cups milk	1⅛ cups
Cook over low heat, stirring until it boils. Boil 1 min. Remove from heat. Stir in softened gelatin. Cool. When partially set, beat with rotary beater until smooth. Blend in	¾ tsp. vanilla	½ tsp.
	¼ tsp. almond extract	¼ tsp.
Gently fold in	½ cup whipping cream whipped until stiff	⅓ cup
Carefully fold into a Meringue of (for method, *see p. 316*)	3 egg whites (⅜ cup)	2 (large)
	¼ tsp. cream of tartar	¼ tsp.
	½ cup sugar	6 tbsp.
Fold in	1 cup moist shredded coconut	¾ cup

Pile into cooled baked pie shell. Sprinkle with moist shredded coconut. Chill until set (about 2 hr.). Serve cold.

NOTE: Take chilled pies out of refrigerator 20 min. before serving.

PUMPKIN CHIFFON PIE

Make Ginger Cooky Crust (*see p. 315*).

Filling for 9" Pie	*For 8" Pie*
Blend . . .	
1 tbsp. gelatin	2 tsp.
¼ cup cold water	3 tbsp.
Mix together in saucepan . . .	
¾ cup brown sugar	6 tbsp.
½ tsp. salt	⅓ tsp.
2 tsp. cinnamon	1½ tsp.
½ tsp. ginger	⅓ tsp.
½ tsp. allspice	⅓ tsp.
1⅓ cups mashed cooked pumpkin	1 cup
3 large egg yolks	3 (med.)
½ cup milk	⅓ cup

Cook over low heat, stirring until it boils. Boil 1 min. Remove from heat. Stir in softened gelatin. Cool. When partially set, beat until smooth. Carefully fold into a Meringue (as for Strawberry Chiffon Pie *opposite*). Pile into Ginger Cooky Crust. Chill until set (2 hr.). Garnish with whipped cream and bits of candied ginger.

RASPBERRY CHIFFON PIE

Follow recipe for Strawberry Chiffon Pie—*except* use raspberries and raspberry gelatin.

STRAWBERRY CHIFFON PIE

Make Pastry Shell of desired size (*p. 315*).

Filling for 9" Pie	*For 8" Pie*
Mix together in saucepan . . .	
3 large egg yolks	3 (medium)
6 tbsp. sugar	4½ tbsp.
¼ tsp. salt	¼ tsp.
2 tsp. lemon juice	1½ tsp.
1 cup crushed strawberries	¾ cup
Cook over low heat, stirring until it boils. Remove from heat. Stir in mixture of . . .	
2 tbsp. hot strawberry juice	1½ tbsp.
4 tbsp. strawberry-flavored gelatin	3 tbsp.
Cool. When partially set, beat with rotary beater and blend in . . .	
½ cup cream, whipped	⅓ cup
Carefully fold into a Meringue of . . .	
3 large egg whites (½ cup)	3 (medium)
¼ tsp. cream of tartar	¼ tsp.
6 tbsp. sugar	4 tbsp.

Pile into cooled baked pie shell. Chill until set (about 2 hr.). Serve cold . . . decorate top with halves of large berries.

CHIFFON PIES

A cool, refreshing finish to hot weather dinners.

LEMON CHIFFON PIE (Recipe) *Piquantly flavored . . . light and delicate.*

Make Pastry Shell (with high fluted edge) of desired size (*see p. 315*).

For the Filling	*For 9″ Pie*	*For 8″ Pie*
Mix together in saucepan............	3 large egg yolks 6 tbsp. sugar 1/4 tsp. salt	3 (medium) 4 1/2 tbsp. 1/4 tsp.
Then add............................	1/4 cup lemon juice, unstrained	3 tbsp.
Cook over low heat, stirring mixture until it boils. Remove from heat.		
Stir..................................	1/2 cup boiling water	1/3 cup
into..............................	4 tbsp. lemon-flavored gelatin	3 tbsp.
	1 tbsp. grated lemon rind	3/4 tbsp.
Then, with rotary beater, beat in the hot custard. Cool. When mixture is partially set, beat until smooth.		
Carefully fold into a Meringue of.... (for method, *see p. 316*)	3 large egg whites (1/2 cup) 1/4 tsp. cream of tartar 6 tbsp. sugar	3 (medium) 1/4 tsp. 4 1/2 tbsp.

Pile into cooled baked pie shell. Chill until set (about 2 hr.). Serve cold.

LIME CHIFFON PIE

Gives visions of cool green seas.

Follow recipe for Lemon Chiffon Pie above—*except* use lime juice and grated lime rind in place of lemon. Add a little green food coloring to intensify the color.

★ PINEAPPLE CHIFFON PIE

Follow recipe for Orange Chiffon Pie below—*except* use lemon rind in place of orange rind; drained canned crushed pineapple in place of orange juice; hot pineapple juice in place of hot orange juice.

ORANGE CHIFFON PIE (Recipe) *Adds extra zest and sparkle to your menu.*

Make Pastry Shell (with high fluted edge) of desired size (*see p. 315*).

For the Filling	*For 9″ Pie*	*For 8″ Pie*
Mix together in saucepan............	3 large egg yolks 6 tbsp. sugar 1/4 tsp. salt	3 (medium) 4 1/2 tbsp. 1/4 tsp.
Then add.....................	3 tbsp. orange juice and 1 tbsp. lemon juice, unstrained	2 1/4 tbsp. 3/4 tbsp.
Cook over low heat, stirring mixture until it boils. Remove from heat.		
Stir..................................	1/2 cup hot orange juice	1/3 cup
into..............................	4 tbsp. lemon-flavored gelatin	3 tbsp.
Then with rotary beater, beat in the hot custard. Cool. When mixture is partially set, beat until smooth.	1 tsp. grated orange rind	3/4 tsp.
Carefully fold in a Meringue of...... (for method, *see p. 316*)	3 large egg whites (1/2 cup) 1/4 tsp. cream of tartar 6 tbsp. sugar	3 (medium) 1/4 tsp. 4 1/2 tbsp.

Pile into cooled baked pie shell. Chill. Garnish with orange sections. Serve cold.

LITTLE PASTRIES

in sumptuous array . . . whirl the tray . . . take your pick!

Berry Basket Tarts of Glazed Strawberry, Grape, Blueberry.
Fluted Tarts of Peach, Lemon Fluff, Chocolate, Glazed Raspberry, Coconut.
Individual Pies of Pumpkin, Cherry, Lemon Meringue, French Strawberry.

FRENCH FRUIT PIES Elegant . . . yet homey as can be.

★ FRENCH GLACÉ STRAWBERRY PIE (Recipe) *An exciting and sparkling combination,—flaky pastry, cream cheese, and ripe red berries.*

Make Pastry Shell of desired size (*see p. 315*).

For the Filling	*For 9″ Pie*	*For 8″ Pie*
Wash, drain, and hull	1 qt. strawberries	3 cups
Spread over bottom of cooled baked pie shell	3-oz. pkg. white cream cheese (softened)	3/4 of pkg.
Cover with half the berries (the choicest). Mash and strain remaining berries until juice is extracted. If necessary, add a little water to make	1 1/2 cups juice	1 1/8 cups
Bring juice to boiling and gradually stir in mixture of	1 cup sugar 3 tbsp. cornstarch	3/4 cup 2 1/4 tbsp.

Cook over low heat, stirring constantly, until boiling. Boil 1 min. Cool. Pour over berries in the pie shell. Chill about 2 hr. Just before serving, decorate with whipped cream (piped on with pastry tube).

FRENCH GLACÉ RASPBERRY PIE

Follow recipe above—*except* use fresh raspberries in place of strawberries, and add 1/2 cup water to the berries to be mashed to form plenty of juice. Bring these berries and water to boiling. Then press through a fine sieve to extract all the juice.

FRENCH GLACÉ BLACKBERRY PIE

Follow recipe above—*except* use fresh blackberries in place of strawberries, and add extra water to the berries to be mashed (as for the raspberry pie).

FRENCH GLACÉ CHERRY PIE

Follow recipe above—*except,* in place of strawberries, use sweet cherries, pitted. Instead of mashing half the cherries, bring them to a boil with water (1 cup water for 9″ pie, 3/4 cup for 8″ pie). Boil 5 min. Gradually stir in a mixture of:

For 9″ Pie	*For 8″ Pie*
2/3 cup sugar	1/2 cup
2 2/3 tbsp. cornstarch	2 tbsp.

Boil 1 min. longer, stirring occasionally. Remove from heat. Blend in lemon juice (about 1 tbsp.). Cool and pour over cherries and cheese in pie shell.

FRUIT BASKET PIE (Recipe) *Colorful fresh fruit in a "basket" of pastry.*

Make Pastry Shell of desired size (*see p. 315*).

Select ripe, juicy strawberries, raspberries, sliced peaches or other fruits in season. Wash, drain, pick over, and hull berries; or pare and slice fresh peaches or other fruit.

For the Filling	*For 9″ Pie*	*For 8″ Pie*
Sweeten to taste . . . then chill	4 to 5 cups fruit	3 to 4 cups

Pile into cooled baked pie shell and drop spoonfuls of sweetened whipped cream around edge or in center so that some of the fruit shows. Serve immediately.

★ APPLE DUMPLINGS (🗝 Recipe) *Packages of luscious fruit encrusted with sugar.*

"Apple, Apple Dumpling,
My first choice,"
Cry all the husbands
With one voice.

"Apple for the Filling,
Sugar and spice,—
Wrap it up in pastry,—
Count me twice!"

Make Pastry (*see pp. 298, 299*) for number of dumplings desired. (Pastry for two-crust 9″ pie makes 6 dumplings, for 8″ pie 4 dumplings.) Roll out pastry a little less than ⅛″ thick, and cut into 7″ squares. Pare and core a medium-sized, tart, juicy apple for each dumpling. Then prepare a syrup. Use:

	For 6 Dumplings	*For 4 Dumplings*
Boil together for 3 min . . .		
	1 cup sugar	**⅔ cup**
	2 cups water	**1½ cups**
	3 tbsp. butter	**2 tbsp.**
	¼ tsp. cinnamon	**¼ tsp.**
Fill cavities of apples with mixture of . . .		
	½ cup sugar	**⅓ cup**
	1½ tsp. cinnamon	**1 tsp.**
Dot with . . .		
	1 tbsp. butter	**2 tsp.**

1 Place apple on each square of pastry. Fill core cavity with sugar and cinnamon mixture . . . dot with butter.

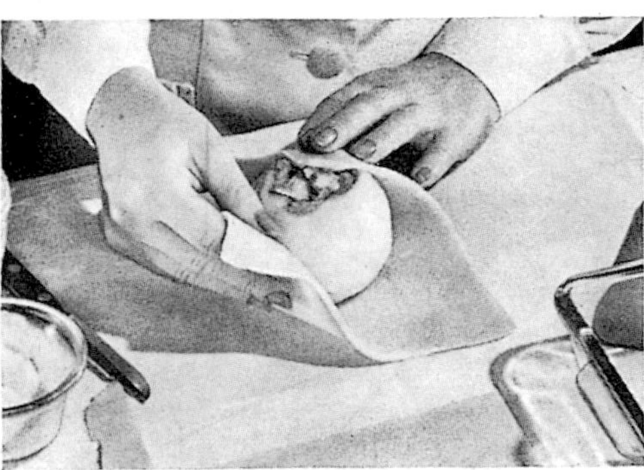

2 Bring opposite points of pastry up over the apple. Overlap, moisten, and seal.

3 Lift carefully, place a little apart in baking dish. Pour hot syrup *around* dumplings.

Bake immediately until crust is nicely browned and apples are cooked through (*test with fork*). Serve warm with the syrup and with cream or whipped cream.

TEMPERATURE: 425° (hot oven).

TIME: Bake 40 to 45 min.

PEACH DUMPLINGS

Follow 🗝 recipe above—*except* use 8 pared fresh peaches instead of 6 apples and smaller squares of pastry to fit. Cut a segment out of each peach. Remove the pit. Fill the hollow with jam or jelly (or the sugar, cinnamon and butter, as for Apple Dumplings). Replace segment. Wrap in pastry. Bake. (Good juicy peaches do not require the syrup.) Serve warm with cream or whipped cream.

APPLE TURNOVERS

Make Flaky Pastry (*see p. 315*). Roll out ⅛″ thick, cut into 5″ squares. Place drained cooked apple slices in center of each. Sprinkle with sugar, cinnamon, and lemon juice. Dot with butter. Moisten edges with cold water. Fold into triangle and seal well. Cut slits in top. Brush with milk, sprinkle with sugar. Bake at 475° (very hot oven) until delicately browned (15 to 20 min.).

INDIVIDUAL PIES

Tiny pies, just as their name implies . . . are of a size to serve one person. They are practical for brides or others concerned with "cooking for two." For picnics or for large groups, they save time in serving. Any pies may be baked in individual pie pans.

TARTS

Since long ago, tiny pastries have been popular for festive occasions. They are a fascinating addition to the tea table or to dinners and luncheons. They appear with top crust cut out in fancy design or no top crust . . . filled with fruit, jam, or any pie filling.

PASTRY FOR LITTLE PASTRIES (Two-Crust)

**8 Individual Pies (4″ diam.) or 12 Tarts (3½″ diam.):*	**6 Individual Pies or 8 Tarts:*	**3 Individual Pies or 4 Tarts:*
2 cups *sifted* GOLD MEDAL Flour	1½ cups	1 cup
1 tsp. salt	¾ tsp.	½ tsp.
⅔ cup shortening	½ cup	⅓ cup
4 tbsp. water	3 tbsp.	2 tbsp.

**From the above ingredients, you will get twice the number of Individual Pie and Tart Shells.*

Mix and handle as for any pie crust.
Butter may be added to make Flaky Pastry (*see p. 315*).

1 Fit pastry into individual pie pans. Fill with desired filling, cover with pastry with slits or cut-out design, and bake as for same type large pie *except* about 10 min. less time.

2 Fit pastry into fluted tart pans or muffin cups; or cut (2 pieces alike) into squares, crescents, or diamonds for fancy tarts. Fill. Cover and bake as for individual pies.

3 Fit pastry over backs of individual pie pans, fluted tart pans, or muffin cups. Prick to prevent puffing. Lay pans upside-down on a baking sheet. Bake at 475° (very hot oven) 8 to 10 min.

Ruth Davis, now Mrs. Bruce Silcox of Alexandria, Virginia, made beautiful little holiday tarts with pastry cutouts on top when she was on our Staff.

LEFTOVER PASTRY DAINTIES

Roll out trimmings from pie crust. Sprinkle with grated cheese, or with sugar and cinnamon, mixed. Cut into fancy shapes. Bake as for tarts. Serve with salads, tea.

FILLINGS FOR LITTLE PASTRIES

Choose any desired pie filling for individual pies and tarts.

For 8 Individual Pies (4″) or 12 Tarts (3½″):	*For 6 Individual Pies or 9 Tarts:*	*For 3 Individual Pies or 4 Tarts:*
Use filling for 9″ pie.	Use filling for 8″ pie.	Use ½ the filling for 8″ pie.

½ cup filling is enough for 1 individual pie. ⅓ cup filling is enough for 1 tart.

POPULAR FILLINGS FOR INDIVIDUAL PIES

Fill baked individual pie or tart shells with any pie filling, such as:

Lemon Fluff
Chocolate Marvel
Lemon Meringue and variations
Vanilla Cream and variations
Pumpkin and variations
Chiffon Pie fillings
Fresh Berry fillings

These tiny pies can be topped with meringue, with sweetened whipped cream, nuts, etc., or with pastry cutouts.

★ FAVORITE COCONUT TARTS

A delectable use for extra egg yolks.

Make 8 Tart Shells (*see p. 326*).

Mix in saucepan . . .
1 cup sugar
2 tbsp. cornstarch
½ tsp. salt

Stir in gradually
1 cup boiling water

Cook over low heat, stirring constantly, until boiling. Boil 1 min. Remove from heat. Stir a little of the hot mixture into

3 egg yolks, slightly beaten

Then beat into hot mixture in saucepan. Cook 1 min. longer, stirring constantly. Remove from heat, continue beating until smooth.

Stir in . . .
4 tbsp. butter
1 tsp. vanilla
2 tsp. lemon juice
1 cup moist shredded coconut
¼ cup cut-up filberts

Pour into baked tart shells.

Sprinkle over top . . .
¼ cup coconut

Bake at 350° (mod. oven) 20 min. Serve cool or slightly warm.

QUICK GLACÉ FRUIT TARTS

Melt currant or other bright jelly. Drop fresh berries, grapes, halved peaches or other fruits into the melted jelly to coat them with a glaze; or brush or spoon the jelly over the fruit. Pile into baked tart shells. Serve immediately.

SIMPLIFIED TARTS

Do not require tart pans.

Roll Flaky Pastry ⅛″ thick. Cut with cooky cutter into 3″ rounds. Place on ungreased baking sheet. Prick with fork. Bake at 475° (very hot oven) until delicately browned, 8 to 10 min. Top with softened cream cheese, then with sweetened or glazed fruit; or top with chocolate or other cream pie filling, then with whipped cream, nuts, etc.

JOSEPHINES

Like Napoleons, but daintier and not so rich.

Make Flaky Pastry (*see p. 315*). Roll it ⅛″ thick and cut into 2x3″ oblongs (*makes 12*). Place on baking sheet, prick. Bake at 475° (very hot oven) until delicately browned (8 to 10 min.).

Just before serving, spread tops of *half* the oblongs with Quick Cream Icing, then sprinkle with chopped nuts. Put oblongs together in pairs with chilled Vanilla Cream Filling (*p. 318*) between. Half the filling for 8″ pie is enough for 6 Josephines.

Simple Tarts for Dessert Luncheons.

BANBURY TARTS

Specialty of the famous Banbury Cross region near London. A favorite with Charles II.

Make Flaky Pastry (*see p. 315*). Cut in 4″ squares.

For the Filling:

Wash in warm water . . .

- ½ cup seeded raisins

Chop raisins and stir in . . .

- ½ cup sugar
- 1½ tbsp. fine cracker crumbs
- 1 egg yolk
- ½ tbsp. butter, melted
- dash of salt
- 1 tbsp. lemon juice
- 1 tbsp. grated lemon rind
- 2 tbsp. chopped walnuts

Spread filling over half of each square. Moisten edges, fold into triangles, and seal. Prick tops. Bake at 450° (hot oven) until delicately browned (12 to 15 min.).

ALMOND TARTS

One of the good recipes brought to us from England by Nan Parker Parkes . . . called Almond "Cheese" Tarts in England, meaning a rich, smooth, thick mixture.

Make 8 baked Tart Shells (*see p. 326*).

For the Filling:

Beat . . .

- 1 egg

Stir in . . .

- ½ cup sugar
- 2 tbsp. soft butter
- 1 cup ground dried blanched almonds
- 1 tsp. almond extract

Drop into each tart shell 1 tsp. raspberry jam. Fill ⅔ full with the almond filling. Bake at 425° (hot oven) until set (12 to 15 min.). Serve warm.

PLUM OR CHERRY TARTS

Make 8 baked Tart Shells (*see p. 326*).

For the Filling:

Cook together until tender (5 min.) . . .

- 2 cups *fresh* pitted plums or cherries
- 1 cup boiling water

Drain off juice. Stir in mixture of . . .

- 1 cup sugar
- 2 tbsp. cornstarch

Add the fruit and cook 10 min. Stir in . . .

- 1 tbsp. butter
- ½ tbsp. cinnamon

Chill and pour into baked tart shells.

COVENTRY TARTLETS

Cooks used to stand in the tavern doorways in old Coventry crying their goodies hot from the oven to the passerby.

Make 8 baked fluted Tart Shells (*p. 326*).

For the Filling:

Blend together (mash with a fork) . . .

- ½ lb. soft sharp flavored cheese (Old English type, warmed)
- ¼ cup butter
- ½ cup sugar
- 2 egg yolks
- ¼ tsp. nutmeg
- 1 tbsp. orange juice

Fill tart shells ⅔ full. Bake at 425° (hot oven) until puffed and golden brown (12 to 15 min.). Top each tart with a teaspoon of currant jelly. Serve warm.

★ CARAMEL TARTS

Smooth and rich with the real caramel flavor. Elegant! Mrs. Will A. Foster sent us one from Hollywood. We developed this recipe.

Make 8 baked fluted Tart Shells (*p. 326*).

For the Filling:

Melt in small heavy skillet over low heat, stirring constantly, until medium brown . . .

- ⅔ cup sugar

Immediately blend in and stir until smooth

- ⅓ cup butter
- ¼ cup hot water

Mix together in saucepan . . .

- ⅓ cup sugar
- ½ tsp. salt
- 2 tbsp. GOLD MEDAL Flour
- 1 tbsp. cornstarch

Stir in gradually . . .

- 1 cup hot water

Cook over low heat, stirring until mixture boils. Blend in caramel mixture. Beat a little of this mixture into . . .

- 2 egg yolks, slightly beaten

Beat into the hot mixture in saucepan. Stir over low heat until mixture boils again. Boil 1 min. Cool. Just before serving, fill cooled baked tart shells only half full. Garnish with pecans.

DE LUXE VARIATION: Place vanilla ice cream in the bottom of each tart shell; spoon the caramel filling over it. Use one pint ice cream for 8 tarts.

GOOSEBERRY TARTS

Follow recipe for Plum or Cherry Tarts opposite—*except* use stemmed and tailed gooseberries and omit cinnamon.

A Salad a Day

SALADS are refreshing, lovely . . . like coming upon a woodland spring, clear and cool. Beauty will be the reward of your understanding touch. And health benefits will abundantly bless your table through the precious vitamins and minerals of crisp, sparkling salad ingredients. Salads are the delightful way to ensure those prescribed raw vegetables and fruits every day.

Betty Crocker

Appetizer Salads

Dinner or With-the-Meal Salads

Main Dish Salads

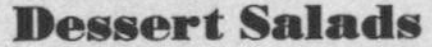

Dessert Salads

Party Salads

Salad Dressings

SALAD ETIQUETTE

Q *May salad be on the table at the beginning of a meal?*

A. Yes, if it is served as a first course. This simplifies serving and is a boon to the hostess without help. If salad is to be eaten with the main course, it is better to serve or pass it after the dinner plates are served.

Q. *Where should individual salads be placed?*

A. First course salads should be in the center of each place . . . on a large plate for formal serving. Main course salads should be placed at left of dinner plate . . . or, if table is crowded, directly above forks and the bread-and-butter plate omitted.

Q. *Should one eat the salad green?*

A. Yes, it is part of the salad and is intended to be eaten.

Q. *Where does the salad fork appear in the table setting?*

A. This depends on when in the meal the salad is served. If for the first course, the fork is at the extreme left. If with the main course or following it, the fork is inside the dinner fork just at left of the dinner plate.

Q. *Is a salad fork always necessary?*

A. A dinner salad may be eaten with the same fork as the main course.

Q. *How should I serve a bowl of mixed salad or a platter of salad?*

A. It may be passed; but the individual servings should be easy to remove. Or the hostess may serve it onto salad plates and pass them around the table.

Q. *Should dressing always be passed?*

A. Some salads are served without dressing so that their beauty of arrangement will not be marred; these require the passing of dressing.

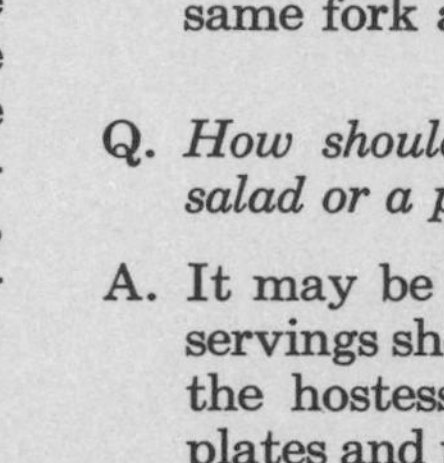

Special Salad Accompaniments

CHEESE STRAWS Roll grated sharp cheese into pastry or biscuit dough. Cut into strips. Bake at 475° (very hot oven) until lightly browned.

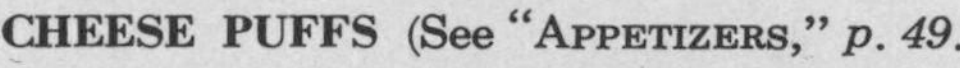

CHEESE PUFFS (See "APPETIZERS," *p. 49.*)

CRACKERS WITH SAVORY CHEESE SPREADS (See "APPETIZERS," *p. 49.*)

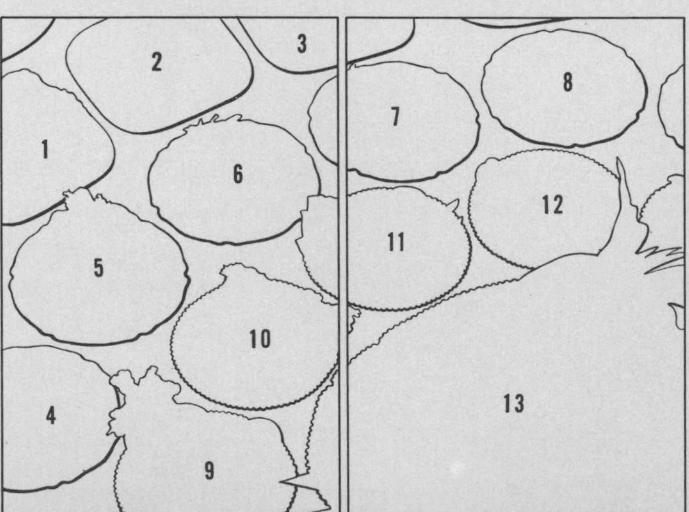

Where to find recipes for Salads in color photograph pp. 332 and 333:

SALADS

Here is a Custom from Ancient Days. "Roman emperors," we read, "dined on dressed lettuce, and ordered served on plates of gold, radishes so thin that the gold gleamed through." From Italy and early Greece, the custom of mixing greens with oils and herbs traveled to Spain and France where the people lovingly adopted it. When Catharine of Aragon went to England as the bride of Henry the Eighth, it was necessary for the royal household to send abroad to get greens to please her accustomed taste. In time, the French and Spaniards introduced salads to America.

Salads have become increasingly popular throughout the years until now they occupy a place of prominence in our menus. They appear in dinners and luncheons . . . and as smart party refreshments. They are important for balanced meals.

Choose the Right Salad. Salads may be classified according to the place they occupy in a meal: *Appetizer Salads* . . . served as a first course. *Dinner or With-the-Meal Salads* . . . served as an accompaniment to or just after the meat course. *Main Dish or Salad Plates* . . . served as the main course for luncheons or suppers or as the main dish at parties. *Dessert Salads* . . . served as the dessert course and often accompanied by cheese and crackers.

Just as an artist combines colors on a canvas to make a beautiful painting, a culinary artist combines ingredients of varying forms and colors to make a salad that is a picture.

Once you have mastered the making of the few basic types of salad, there is no end to the varieties you can serve. For almost any fruits or vegetables may be combined with salad greens. We have included suggestions for many of the most popular combinations. On the following pages, too, are little hints for attaining the refreshing salads that help make a luncheon or dinner or special party a memorable affair.

SECRETS OF SALADS Handy arrangement and special rules help.

A SALAD CENTER

For speed and ease in making salads, arrange a salad center with all the makings and seasonings and all the utensils together. The ideal spot is near the refrigerator . . . with cupboard for ingredients and equipment and counter for mixing nearby.

Nice to have at Salad Center:

Ingredients

Salad Oil	Garlic Buds
Vinegars	Onion
Dry Mustard	Chives (in flower pot)
Sugar	Celery Seeds
Salt	Herbs (*see below*)
Pepper	Curry Powder
Paprika	Chili Sauce

Equipment

Salad Bowls	Measuring Spoons
Wooden Salad Fork and Spoon	Measuring Cups
Small Sharp Knife	Can Opener
Scissors	Cutting Board
Bottle or Jar with Tight Cover	Gelatin Molds
Rotary Beater	Grater
	Sieve
	Colander

HERBS ADD THE GOURMET TOUCH

Dried herbs are available packaged in jars. Tarragon, sweet basil, chervil, and rosemary are first choice for salads. Learn to develop extra zest in salads with a dash of dill, or mustard, or curry powder, poppy seeds, etc.

SECRETS

that will make your dreams of perfect salads come true

1 CHOOSING COMBINATIONS

Strive for CONTRAST of texture, color, form, and flavor when selecting greens, fruits, or vegetables to combine in salads. Put them together as an artist combines colors on a canvas. Plan the salad as part of the nutritional balance of the meal.

2 THE IMPORTANCE OF THE DRESSING

Use a light, delicate dressing on a salad that accompanies a substantial meal . . . a more substantial dressing on a salad that forms the main dish.

The oil in the dressing may be olive oil or any mild vegetable oil. Choose a mild cider or wine vinegar. An herb vinegar (tarragon, basil, or garlic) gives an interesting flavor.

Lemon juice is sometimes used in place of vinegar. If vinegar is sharp, use less or dilute with water.

3 TOSS INGREDIENTS LIGHTLY

. . . do not bruise or crush the greens. And use the minimum of dressing. Too much dressing makes a salad limp.

4 THE CASUAL LOOK IS THE RIGHT LOOK

Simple, casual . . . but not messy. Avoid a "fixed" appearance in salads.

5 CHOOSE YOUR SERVICE

Serve salads from a large bowl or deep platter. Or arrange them on individual plates or in little salad bowls.

6 THE PLATE A FRAME

Use a large enough plate when arranging salads. Don't let any part of salad extend over edge of plate.

7 COLD . . . CRISP . . . COLD

Take salads and salad dressings from refrigerator just before they are to be eaten. Chill plates or bowls before using.

FRENCH DRESSING (Recipe)

The dressing for simple green salads.

Beat together with rotary beater or shake well in tightly covered jar . . .

1 tbsp. sugar
1 tsp. salt
1 tsp. paprika
1 tsp. mustard
¼ tsp. pepper
¼ cup mild vinegar or lemon juice
¾ cup salad oil
few drops onion juice or clove garlic

Keep in covered jar in refrigerator. Shake again to mix again before using.

AMOUNT: 1 cup dressing.

PIQUANT FRENCH DRESSING

The favorite of all with our Staff.

Follow recipe above—*except* increase sugar to ¼ cup and add 1 tsp. *each* celery seed and grated onion. Let 2 cloves garlic, cut crosswise, stand in dressing 1 hr.

HONEY FRUIT DRESSING

Perfect for citrus fruits.

Follow recipe above using lemon juice —*except* increase sugar to ⅓ cup. Add ⅓ cup strained honey and 1 tsp. celery seed.

VINAIGRETTE DRESSING

For vegetables cold or hot.

Follow recipe above—and add 6 green olives, chopped fine; 2 small dill pickles, chopped fine; 1 tbsp. minced chives; 1 tbsp. minced pimiento; 2 hard-cooked eggs, chopped fine. Mix. Chill.

ROQUEFORT DRESSING

Sophisticated touch for simple greens or greens-and-vegetable salads.

For 6 servings: Mash 4 tbsp. Roquefort cheese with ⅛ tsp. Worcestershire sauce. Blend in ½ cup French Dressing.

LORENZO DRESSING

For 6 servings: To ½ cup French Dressing, add 1 tbsp. chili sauce.

WATERCRESS DRESSING

Elegant with pear salads.

For 6 servings: To ½ cup French Dressing, add 2 tbsp. *each* minced watercress and chili sauce.

LIME HONEY DRESSING

Delicious with fruit.

Add . . .
2 to 3 tbsp. lime juice (or lemon)
to . . .
½ cup honey
Stir in . . .
2 eggs, well beaten

Mix together thoroughly. Cook over simmering hot water until thickened (mixture becomes clear), stirring constantly. Cool.

Fold in . . .
½ cup heavy cream, whipped stiff

AMOUNT: 1½ cups dressing.

RUBY RED DRESSING

On oranges and citrus things,
It makes a feast that's fit for kings.

Beat with fork until smooth . . .
½ cup currant jelly
Add . . .
4 tbsp. salad oil
2 tbsp. lemon juice
dash of salt
few drops onion juice

Continue beating until smooth.

AMOUNT: About ½ cup dressing.

CHIFFONADE DRESSING

For 6 servings: To ½ cup French Dressing, add 1 tbsp. shredded ripe olives, 1 tbsp. shredded green pepper, 1 hard-cooked egg (white sieved, yolk mashed), and 1 tbsp. finely cut chives.

SWEET FRENCH DRESSING

For 6 servings: To ½ cup French Dressing or Piquant French Dressing, add 2 tbsp. lemon juice (or half lemon juice and half other fruit juice) and 2 tbsp. *sifted* confectioners' sugar or honey.

Starting to make dressing.

MAYONNAISE (🔑 Recipe)

The foundation of a myriad of intriguing salad dressings.

Beat together with rotary beater . . .
- 1 egg yolk
- 1 tsp. mustard
- 1 tsp. confectioners' sugar
- 1/4 tsp. salt
- dash of cayenne pepper
- 1 tbsp. lemon juice or vinegar

Continue beating while adding, at first drop by drop, gradually increasing amount as mixture thickens until all is used . . .
- 1 cup salad oil

Slowly add . . .
- 1 more tbsp. lemon juice or vinegar

Beat well. Chill before serving. When using, modify as desired with heavy or whipped cream.

AMOUNT: 1½ cups dressing.

FRUIT SALAD MAYONNAISE

For 6 servings: Into ½ cup Mayonnaise, fold ¼ cup heavy cream, whipped stiff.

PRINCESS MAYONNAISE

A dainty pink dressing for fruits.

For 6 servings: Into ½ cup Mayonnaise, blend 1 tbsp. maraschino syrup and 4 chopped maraschino cherries. Mix well. Fold in ¼ cup heavy cream, whipped stiff.

TOMATO-CUCUMBER MAYONNAISE

Excellent on seafood salads.

For 6 servings: To 1 cup Mayonnaise, add ½ cup *each* drained diced tomato and cucumber, 1 tsp. minced onion, salt.

THOUSAND ISLAND DRESSING

Popularly used on just wedges of lettuce.

For 6 servings: Mix together ½ cup Mayonnaise; 1 tbsp. chili sauce; 1 tbsp. chopped stuffed olives; 1 tsp. minced chives; 1 hard-cooked egg, chopped; ¼ tsp. paprika, and additional salt and pepper to taste.

RUSSIAN DRESSING

With salad greens alone, it makes a perfect dinner salad.

For 6 servings: To ½ cup Mayonnaise, add 1½ tbsp. chili sauce and a few drops of onion juice. An additional tsp. lemon juice may be added, if desired.

COOKED MAYONNAISE

Uses those "extra" egg yolks.

Mix together in saucepan . . .
- 1/3 cup GOLD MEDAL Flour
- 1 tsp. sugar
- 1 tsp. salt
- 1 tsp. dry mustard

Add gradually . . .
- 3/4 cup water
- 1/4 cup mild vinegar or lemon juice

Cook over low heat, stirring constantly, until mixture boils. Boil 1 min. Remove from heat. Pour into bowl. Beat in with rotary beater . . .
- 4 egg yolks (or 2 whole eggs)

Continue beating . . . adding a little at a time . . .
- 1 cup salad oil

Chill before serving. When using, modify as desired with heavy or whipped cream.

AMOUNT: 2 cups dressing.

COOKED SALAD DRESSING

Also called "boiled" dressing.

Mix together in saucepan . . .
- 1/2 cup *sifted* GOLD MEDAL Flour
- 1/2 cup sugar
- 2 tsp. salt
- 2 tsp. dry mustard
- 1/8 tsp. paprika

Blend in gradually . . .
- 1 cup water
- 3/4 cup mild vinegar or lemon juice

Cook over direct low heat, stirring constantly, until mixture thickens and boils. Boil 1 min. Remove from heat. Beat in with rotary beater until smooth . . .
- 4 egg yolks (or 2 whole eggs)
- 1 tbsp. butter

Cool. When using, modify as desired with heavy sweet cream or sour cream.

AMOUNT: 2½ cups dressing.

SOUR CREAM MAYONNAISE

Ideal with mixed chopped garden vegetables: cucumber, tomato, tender spinach, or lettuce and carrots.

For 6 servings: To ¼ cup Mayonnaise, Cooked Mayonnaise, or Cooked Salad Dressing, add ¼ cup plain or whipped sour cream, 2 tsp. minced chives, and a dash of coarse black pepper.

PROMPT ATTENTION NEEDED

As soon as salad greens are delivered from market or gathered from the garden, trim off inedible leaves. Store unwashed in tightly covered receptacle in refrigerator and wash as needed (to avoid "rusting").

WASHING SALAD GREENS
when ready to use

HEAD LETTUCE

Cut out core. Hold cavity under cold running water until leaves are easily separated by water and fingers.

LEAF LETTUCE, ENDIVE, SPINACH, ETC.

Swish in water, wash each leaf separately, lift out. Lukewarm water is better than cold to remove sand.

DRYING SALAD GREENS
before making salad

Shake or pat gently in clean towel or absorbent paper.

KEEPING SALAD GREENS COLD
after washing . . until ready to use

Place in hydrator (or in plastic bag or cloth) in refrigerator.

A Variety of *Salad Greens* gives interest to salads

Lettuce, several types: Head, Boston, Great Lakes, Bronze, Oak Leaf, Mignonette.

Other greens: Chicory, Endive, Escarole, Dandelion Greens, Romaine, Spinach, Nasturtium Leaves, Watercress, Mint and Cabbage.

Use one alone or combine several.

MIXED GREEN SALADS For every day in the year.

HOW-TO-MAKE THE EASIEST, QUICKEST GREEN SALAD

1 For a faint whisper of garlic flavor, rub chilled bowl with garlic bud.

2 Pluck apart and break up crisp salad greens and place in bowl.

3 Add attractive sized pieces (to retain their identity) of vegetables, fruits, seafoods, etc.

4 Just before serving, add dressing . . . only enough to make leaves of greens glisten.

6 Add juicy tomato sections at the last.

5 Gently toss ingredients so that every piece is coated with dressing

7 Serve in large bowl or in individual bowls or on individual salad plates.

THERE CAN ALWAYS BE A SALAD

A glance in your refrigerator, cupboard, or garden will convince you that you always have ingredients available. Follow the general plan on opposite page, using whatever you happen to have on hand.

Commonly used with salad greens (*p. 337*) in mixed green salads, are the following:

RAW VEGETABLES: Thinly sliced radishes. Thinly sliced cucumbers. Diced celery. Tomato slices or sections. Thinly sliced carrots or thin carrot strips. Little new onions. Finely cut chives. Minced parsley. Rings of green or red pepper. Strips of pimiento. Flowerets of cauliflower. Wafer-thin slices of turnips. Shredded cabbage. Finely shredded baby beets. Shredded raw parsnips. Sliced raw mushrooms.

AMOUNTS FOR GREEN SALADS

For 6	*For 3*
1 head lettuce (or equivalent of other salad greens)	½ head
½ cucumber, thinly sliced	¼
6 radishes, thinly sliced	3
2 stalks celery, diced	1 stalk
3 ripe tomatoes, sectioned	1 (large)

COOKED VEGETABLES: Peas. Green beans. Lima beans. Beets. Asparagus tips. Artichoke hearts. Broccoli. Cauliflower flowerets. Hearts of palm.

BITS OF FRUIT: Grapefruit or orange sections. Little seedless green grapes. Tokay grapes. Melon balls or cubes (honeydew, cantaloupe, watermelon). Pomegranate seeds. Apple. Plum. Peach. Pear. Cherries. Avocado.

GARNISH: Remember that a bit of color contrast steps up appetite appeal. Add shiny black or green olives, gay radish roses, strips of red pimiento, or a sprig of dark green mint or watercress. Bits of colorful fruit such as slices of bright orange can also serve as garnish.

WESTERN WAY SALAD

A connoisseur's salad, made for our Staff by a delightful visitor, famous home economist Essie L. Elliott of California.

Place 3 qt. salad greens in large bowl. Add ⅓ cup each salad oil, grated dry cheese and crumbled blue cheese. Salt and pepper to taste. Break one raw egg over greens. Squeeze juice from 2 lemons over egg. Toss well. Dribble 2 tbsp. oil with garlic steeped in it over 1 pt. crisp croutons (bread cubes browned), and add just before serving. *Serves 8.*

CHEF'S SALAD

Julienne strips of meat with mixed greens make a hearty main dish salad. Served in many smart restaurants.

Follow recipe for Mixed Green Salad (*opposite page*) and add 1 cup match-like strips of cold baked ham and chicken or other meat (slices cut ¼″ wide, 3″ long). Just before serving, toss with Mayonnaise. Place ½ cup meat strips over the top. Garnish with quartered hard-cooked egg, radishes, and sliced olives or pickles.

SEAFOOD, CHEESE, OR EGGS

Any of these added to a salad of mixed greens makes of it a "meal-in-one-dish" for luncheon or supper.

Follow recipe for Mixed Green Salad (*opposite page*) and add, just before tossing together with Mayonnaise, boned seafood in large pieces (crab, lobster, shrimp, tuna, salmon, anchovy, or sardines, etc.); *or* strips of American cheese; *or* coarsely cut-up or sliced hard-cooked eggs.

SEASONAL SALAD BOWLS

Winter: Carrot Curls, Golden Orange Slices, Spinach, Lettuce and Celery Leaves.
Autumn: Red Apple Slices, Diced Green Celery, Lettuce Hearts, Sprigs of Parsley.
Summer: Caulifloweret*s*, Tomato Sections, Sprigs of Mint, Head Lettuce.
Spring: Radishes, Bermuda Onion Rings, Cucumber, Endive, Nasturtium Leaves.
Holiday Season: Green Grapes, Pomegranate Seeds, Cucumber, Watercress, Endive.

A GARDENFUL OF VEGETABLE SALAD FAVORITES

Serve on salad greens with desired dressing.

Asparagus tips sprinkled with grated cheese on thick tomato slices.

Thin slices of cooked beets sprinkled with finely cut fresh mint leaves, julienne strips of celery.

Grated raw carrots mixed with seedless raisins in lettuce cups.

Halves of peeled chilled tomatoes sprinkled with chopped parsley or chives. Basil in the dressing.

Cut-up cooked asparagus and sliced hard-cooked eggs in tomato aspic.

Shredded carrots and diced celery sprinkled with lemon juice, chopped nuts, and mayonnaise . . . mixed.

Raw cauliflowerets, shredded raw carrots, toasted almonds.

Sprigs of young spinach leaves sprinkled with bits of crisp bacon, sieved hard-cooked egg.

Overlapping beet and cucumber and raw onion slices.

Chopped mixture of diced cucumber, tomato, and celery, with minced onion and green pepper.

Small tomatoes stuffed with cottage cheese and chives or toasted almonds.

Tomato slices topped with egg salad (cut-up hard-cooked eggs, diced celery, grated onion, mayonnaise). Parsley garnish.

SOME FRUIT SALAD FAVORITES

Avocado cubes and melon balls.

Balls of cantaloupe, watermelon or honeydew in combination.

Fresh or canned peach halves . . . filled with cream cheese balls or with cut-up celery and nuts.

Pistachio nuts in cream cheese balls on apricot halves.

Pineapple spears spread with cream cheese and garnished with strawberries.

Pineapple slices topped with cream cheese mixed with cut-up dates and mayonnaise.

Pear halves stuck with salted almonds or salted peanuts.

Cantaloupe balls, Bing cherries, sweet green or Tokay grapes.

Cantaloupe balls, diced orange and pear.

Banana slices around apricot halves.

Pineapple cubes, banana slices, orange sections, cut-up dates.

Equal parts of diced pineapple, sweet green grapes, sliced bananas, and strawberries or raspberries.

Sweet green grapes or cherries in hollow of pear halves.

Pitted fresh cherries stuffed with cream cheese and nuts.

Orange sections, banana slices, halved and seeded Tokay or whole seedless green grapes, nuts.

Banana slices rolled in chopped peanuts, orange slices.

Pear or peach halves with mayonnaise and minced celery or cream cheese ball in hollows. Sprinkling of paprika or chopped pistachios or toasted almonds.

PLATTER OF CONTRASTING ROWS OF SALAD VEGETABLES

Arrange desired cut-up vegetables (cold and crisp) in rows . . . with an eye to color and pattern. (Tomato slices, cucumber slices, latticed carrots, asparagus stalks, etc.)

PLATTER OF SALAD GREENS

Cooling shades of dark and light.

Arrange a variety of different salad greens on a platter, such as: curly endive around the outside, inner leaves of lettuce next, then watercress sprigs, and in the center artichoke hearts. Sprinkle sliced shallots and finely minced St. Mary's herbs over all. Pass French Dressing.

STAR SALAD

Alternate wedges of lettuce and tomato in effective star design on large round chop plate. Garnish of lacy watercress or crispy endive.

INDIVIDUAL SALADS IN LETTUCE CUPS

Prepare enough lettuce cups to serve number desired. Fill with any desired combination of chilled vegetables mixed with just enough French Dressing to make glisten. Place on platter or tray and chill again. Serve on individual salad plates, or pass platter or tray for each guest to serve himself.

FLOWER ARRANGEMENT FOR SALAD BOWL →

A "center" of Bing cherries, "petals" of peach slices and honeydew or cantaloupe wedges, "leaves" of lettuce all around. Lemon wedges floating in French Dressing . . . to be passed separately.

SALAD BAR

"As pretty as a bouquet of vari-colored flowers. Perfect for a buffet supper or a big crowd!" said Eileen Kueffner of our staff (now Mrs. William Kueffner of Red Wing, Minn).

Marinate by tossing separately with ½ tbsp. French Dressing (each in separate bowl) and letting stand in refrigerator about 1 hr. . .

- **1 cup finely shredded cabbage**
- **1 cup chopped radishes**
- **1 cup watercress sprigs**
- **1 cup coarsely grated carrots**
- **1 cup cut-up fringed cucumber slices**

Pile up each vegetable high in a triangle . . . the point at center of plate and radiating out to edge. 2 or 3 pieces of cardboard held at angles to each other keep vegetables separate until placed. Serve cold . . . pass French Dressing. *Serves 8.*

RUSSIAN SALAD

Follow recipe for Salad Bar above—and divide sections with lines of chopped parsley, chopped green pepper, chopped pimiento or pimiento strips. Garnish each section differently,—with small pieces of smoked salmon, finely chopped hard-cooked egg white, hard-cooked egg yolks forced through a strainer, small pieces of chicken or ham or anchovies, etc. Serve with Russian Dressing.

All you have to do—

To prevent a last-minute rush when you entertain: prepare ahead of time, cover, and store in the refrigerator most of the ingredients. Then, just before serving, drain ingredients well; quickly combine or arrange salad. At last minute, add dressing.

GRAPEFRUIT-ORANGE SALAD

"This is one of our winter favorites!" says Mrs. George D. Cammack of Minneapolis, a lovely mother and perfect homemaker.

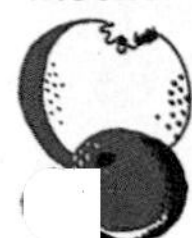

Arrange grapefruit and orange sections alternately on salad greens. Garnish with watercress. Serve with Ruby Red Dressing.

GRAPEFRUIT-CHERRY SALAD

Put sections of grapefruit together with softened cream cheese between. Top with a few large Royal Ann or Bing cherries. Place in lettuce cup. Serve with Sweet French Dressing.

GRAPEFRUIT-AND-POMEGRANATE SALAD

Lay sections of grapefruit with other fruit on salad greens. Sprinkle with pomegranate seeds. Serve with one of the sweet French Dressings.

ORANGE-AND-BERMUDA ONION SALAD

Arrange sections of orange on salad greens. Garnish with rings of Bermuda onion, watercress, and chopped fresh mint. Serve with Piquant French Dressing.

AVOCADO-GRAPEFRUIT-ORANGE SALAD

Place thin slices of peeled avocado between sections of grapefruit and orange on crisp lettuce leaves. Serve with Honey Fruit Dressing.

AVOCADO-GRAPEFRUIT-TOMATO SALAD

Place sections of tomato (curled like petals of a red flower) on lettuce leaf. Arrange around the tomato, sections of grapefruit and slices of orange. Insert thin slices of avocado here and there to look like green leaves. Serve with Piquant French Dressing.

All you have to do—

To keep fruit from discoloring: slice apples, bananas, peaches, pears, etc., with stainless steel knife last possible moment. Sprinkle with lemon or pineapple juice; or combine quickly with some cut-up citrus fruit. Store in refrigerator. Drain.

WALDORF SALAD

Lightly mix diced apple (red skin on) with half as much diced celery and a few broken nuts. Toss with Mayonnaise or Cooked Salad Dressing (combined with cream). Serve in lettuce cups. Garnish each with a maraschino cherry.

CANTALOUPE RING SALAD

Place ¾″ thick cantaloupe ring (rind removed) on bed of salad greens. Fill center with seasonal fruits (melon balls, sweet green grapes, cherries, strips of pear, blackberries, etc.). Serve with Sweet French Dressing.

MELON BOAT SALAD

Place boat-shaped section of cantaloupe (rind removed) on bed of salad greens. Fill boat with seasonal fruits (cherries, blackberries, strips of pear, watermelon or honeydew balls, seedless green grapes, etc.). Garnish ends of boat with tiny garden flowers. Serve with one of the sweet French dressings.

MELON BALL SALAD

With ball cutter, cut balls from boat-shaped sections of cantaloupe. Refill hollows in boat with watermelon or honeydew melon balls. Serve with Honey Fruit Dressing.

CHERRY-CANTALOUPE SALAD

Fill Bing cherries (stones removed) with softened cream cheese. Chill. Arrange in lettuce cup with equal number of cantaloupe balls. Serve with Sweet French Dressing. Garnish with sprig of mint.

STUFFED PEACH, APRICOT OR PEAR SALAD

Place peeled peach, apricot, or pear half in lettuce cup. Place in hollow of fruit small mound of cream cheese and minced celery mixed with Mayonnaise. Sprinkle with chopped pistachios or toasted almonds. Serve with Mayonnaise.

VEGETABLE SALADS Economical. For everyday and party meals.

CABBAGE SALAD (Recipe) *Probably the earliest in America!*

Soak in ice water (for milder flavor)......2½ cups *finely* shredded cabbage
Drain, wrap in towel, chill to crisp.
Sprinkle with............................1 tsp. salt
Moisten with............................Cooked Salad Dressing or Mayonnaise modified with cream

Toss lightly with fork to blend. Serve immediately in lettuce cups. *Serves 4.*

CABBAGE-RED APPLE SALAD

An autumn favorite in New York state.

Follow recipe above—and add to the cabbage 1 cup cut-up red apple (not pared) and ½ cup cut-up celery. Garnish with red cherries or walnuts. *Serves 6.*

CABBAGE-BANANA SALAD

Follow recipe above—and add to the cabbage 1 cup cut-up apple, ½ cup cut-up banana, ¼ cup cut-up salted peanuts. *Serves 6.*

CABBAGE-PINEAPPLE SALAD

Follow recipe above—and add to the cabbage 1½ cups well drained cut-up pineapple, 1 cup cut-up unpared red apple, and 8 marshmallows cut in quarters. *Serves 10.*

CABBAGE SALAD BOWL

"A decorative touch for your party!" says Mrs. Raymond R. Henry of Minneapolis, wonderful cook and delightful hostess.

Slice section off top of very large red or green cabbage. Hollow out center with sharp knife . . . leaving a 1″ wall of outer leaves. Notch down 2″ from top with broad petals to make look like a fancy bowl. Fill to top with Cabbage-Pineapple or other salad.

JACK-O-LANTERN SALAD BOWL

For Hallowe'en entertaining.

Cut Jack-O-Lantern face in hollowed-out pumpkin. Line with cabbage leaves. Fill with Cabbage-Pineapple Salad or other salad for Hallowe'en entertaining. (Cabbage leaves prevent salad from falling through slits.)

OLD-FASHIONED COLE SLAW

Mild flavored . . . easy to fix.

Follow recipe above—*except,* in place of half the shredded cabbage, use finely cut celery; add 1 tbsp. sugar, 1 tsp. scraped onion, 1 tbsp. vinegar, 6 tbsp. cream; use only 1 tbsp. mustardy salad dressing.

CABBAGE-PIMIENTO SALAD

Follow recipe above—and add to the cabbage ¼ cup minced green pepper, ¼ cup minced pimiento, 2 tbsp. minced onion, and ½ cup cut-up celery. Garnish with strips of green pepper and a sprinkling of celery seed. *Serves 6.*

NEW NETHERLANDS COLE SLAW

First introduced to America by the Holland Dutch when they settled in New York in 1624. They called it "Koolslaa." It was their "great sallad dressed with vinegar."

Heat to boiling in saucepan . . .
- **¼ cup mild vinegar**
- **1 tbsp. sugar**
- **1 tsp. salt**
- **¼ tsp. pepper**
- **½ tsp. mustard**
- **1 tbsp. butter**

Add some of hot mixture to . . .
- **1 egg, slightly beaten**

Then stir into the hot vinegar in saucepan. Cook until mixture thickens and boils. Remove from heat.

Beat in . . .
- **2 tbsp. cream**

Pour while hot over . . .
- **3 cups finely shredded cabbage**

Chill, and serve cold. *Serves 6.*

POTATO SALAD (🔑 Recipe)

A good potato salad is the mark of a good cook.

Place in bowl . . .
- 3 cups cubed cold boiled potatoes
- 1 tbsp. finely chopped onion

Sprinkle with . . .
- ½ tsp. salt
- dash of pepper

Mix lightly with . . .
- ¼ cup French Dressing

Chill an hour or two. Toss lightly with . . .
- ¾ cup Cooked Salad Dressing or Mayonnaise

Blend in carefully . . .
- 2 large cut-up hard-cooked eggs

Mix in a little minced pimiento and parsley for color. Add extra seasoning and dressing to taste. Serve in bowl or on platter surrounded with salad greens, tomato sections, slices of hard-cooked eggs, cucumber sticks, etc. Garnish with paprika. *Serves 6.*

SPECIAL POTATO SALAD

We like this the best of any potato salad we've ever tried.

Follow 🔑 recipe above—and add to potatoes 6 sliced radishes, ½ cup diced celery, and ½ cucumber, cubed.

MEAT-AND-POTATO SALAD

A meal in one dish. Wonderful for porch parties in hot weather.

Follow recipe for Special Potato Salad and add strips of cooked lean meat (beef, ham, veal, or chicken, etc.).

BEAN SALAD

A former member of our Staff, Jane Christiansen, now Mrs. Charles Kuoni, Jr. of Chicago, likes to serve this at impromptu luncheons in her suburban home.

Mix together . . .
- 2 cups drained cooked kidney beans
- ¼ cup diced celery
- 3 chopped pickles (dill or sweet)
- 1 small onion, minced

Add . . .
- 2 hard-cooked eggs, sliced
- ½ tsp. salt
- ⅛ tsp. pepper

Mix lightly with . . .
- about ¼ cup Mayonnaise

Chill thoroughly. Serve on salad greens. Garnish with grated cheese. *Serves 6.*

HOT GERMAN POTATO SALAD

An old family recipe from G. A. (Dick) Heinrich of Minneapolis. Often called "Dutch" potato salad. With baked spareribs, it's perfect for a stag supper.

Boil 6 medium-sized potatoes in their skins until tender. Peel and slice thinly into bowl. Fry 6 slices bacon until crisp.

Cook in ⅓ cup of the bacon fat in the skillet until yellow . . .
- ¾ cup chopped or thinly sliced onion

Mix in . . .
- 2 tbsp. GOLD MEDAL Flour
- 1 to 2 tbsp. sugar as desired
- 1½ tsp. salt
- ½ tsp. celery seed, if desired
- dash of pepper

Stir in gradually . . .
- ¾ cup water
- ½ cup vinegar

Cook, stirring until mixture boils. Boil 1 min. Pour over the potatoes. Add the crisp bacon, broken into pieces (save some for garnishing). Cover, and let stand until ready to serve. Heat over hot water. Serve in large bowl garnished with pieces of the crisp bacon and minced parsley or chives. *Serves 6.*

VITAMIN SALAD

Glowing with health-giving ingredients.

Mix together . . .
- 2 cups grated raw carrots
- 2 tbsp. lemon juice
- 1 cup diced celery
- ¼ cup finely chopped nuts

Toss lightly with . . .
- Cooked Salad Dressing

Serve very cold on crisp salad greens. *Serves 6.*

WINTER SUNSHINE SALAD

It brightens midwinter meals. "Even raw parsnips are good this way!" says Eleanor Combs Halderman, well known Home Economist of Minneapolis, who herself spreads sunshine.

Toss together with French Dressing . . .
- 2 coarsely grated parsnips
- 3 carrots, cut in strips
- grated rind and sections of 1 orange
- ¾ cup finely diced celery
- ½ tsp. salt
- 1 tsp. grated onion, if desired

Serve cold in lettuce cups. *Serves 6.*

MEAT AND SEAFOOD SALADS Main dish of special occasion meals.

CHICKEN SALAD (🔑 Recipe) *An All-American favorite.*

Toss together . . .
2 cups cut-up cold cooked chicken (large chunks)
1 cup cut-up celery (½" pieces)
1 tbsp. lemon juice
salt and pepper to taste
Mix in . . .
Mayonnaise (½ cup)
Carefully fold in . .
2 or 3 cut-up hard-cooked eggs

Chill thoroughly. Arrange a mound in each lettuce cup and garnish with olives or little sweet pickles and parsley. *Serves 6.*

Tomato Flower Cups: Cut tomatoes almost through into 6 sections so they will open like flowers. Fill with Chicken Salad. Garnish with sieved hard-cooked eggs.

CHICKEN-FRUIT PARTY SALAD

Follow 🔑 recipe above—*except* omit hard-cooked eggs. Add 1 cup sweet green grapes, halved, or drained cut-up pineapple and ½ cup salted almonds.

CHICKEN AND BACON-OR-ALMOND SALAD

Follow 🔑 recipe above—*except* add ½ cup finely broken crisp bacon or salted almonds, halved.

All you have to do—

For a different service for entertaining: serve chicken or seafood salad in peeled avocado halves or on drained round slices of canned pineapple on crisp lettuce. Garnish with sprigs of watercress. Dainty finger sandwiches of rye or brown bread make a pleasing accompaniment.

SEAFOOD SALAD

Delicious made with crabmeat, shrimp, lobster, tuna, or salmon.

Mix together lightly in order . . .
1 cup flaked seafood
1 tsp. lemon juice
1 tsp. finely minced onion
salt and paprika to taste
1 cup diced celery
1 cup lettuce hearts in small pieces

Chill thoroughly. Just before serving, drain and toss together with Mayonnaise to moisten. Serve on crisp lettuce. Garnish with tomato sections, wedges of lemon, and slices of hard-cooked egg. *Serves 4.*

CHICKEN-CRANBERRY SALAD

Recommended as "something special" by Janet Crawford of the National Cranberry Association, Hanson, Massachusetts.

Follow 🔑 recipe above—*except* omit hard-cooked eggs and substitute 1 cup cubed cranberry jelly for 1 cup of the chicken.

MOCK CHICKEN SALAD

A delicious and economical substitution for the real thing . . . when chicken is high and veal not so expensive.

Follow 🔑 recipe above—*except,* in place of the chicken, use cut-up cooked veal.

MIROTON OF SEAFOOD

An impressive main dish for the buffet tab'e . . and for years a favorite at our big community cooking schools.

Marinate by tossing separately with 2 tbsp. French Dressing (each in separate bowl) and letting stand in refrigerator about 1 hr . . .
2 cups cubed cold boiled potatoes
2 cups flaked tuna, salmon, crabmeat, shrimp, or lobster
Mix together lightly with . . .
3 tbsp. capers or chopped crisp pickles
Mayonnaise (to moisten)

Heap up in a high mound on serving platter. Sprinkle top with paprika and finely chopped parsley. Garnish with a crown of hard-cooked eggs (*see opposite page*). Surround with crisp lettuce cups. Place sections of tomatoes and shiny black olives in lettuce to be served with each portion. *Serves 6 to 8.*

APPETIZER SALADS

For a dramatic first course.

Plum tomato (its center sprinkled with sieved hard-cooked egg yolk), a deviled egg half (sprinkled with finely cut chives) at either side . . . on salad greens. Garnish of shiny ripe olives.

Artichoke hearts, diced celery, tomato sections, and anchovies, Piquant French Dressing . . . in lettuce cup. Garnish of strips of green pickles, large green olives.

Avocado half, stuffed with crabmeat, highly seasoned Mayonnaise . . . in lettuce cup. Garnish of sieved hard-cooked egg, watercress, radish roses, large ripe olives.

Avocado half, drenched with lemon juice, seed cavity filled with a little Mayonnaise (thinned with lemon juice). Then a spoonful of lemon or cranberry ice. Serve on a bed of watercress.

PINEAPPLE FRUIT PLATE

Helen Holloway Hallbert of our Staff, co-founder with her husband of a famous line of salad dressings, often serves this salad at her supper parties.

Cut top from fresh pineapple, cut pineapple in two crosswise, and scoop out inside; cut pineapple in cubes, removing core. Toss pineapple cubes together with other fresh fruits (halved Tokay or sweet green grapes, Bing cherries, orange sections, cut-up sweet plums, apricot halves, pear sticks, etc.) and Sweet French Dressing. Refill pineapple shell with the fruit salad mixture. Serve on large chop plate surrounded by sprigs of watercress or endive or by lettuce cups filled, if desired, with additional fruit.

A CROWN OF HARD-COOKED EGGS

Decorative touch for seafood salads.

Cut each hard-cooked egg lengthwise into quarters . . . dipping back of each into partially set gelatin to help it stick. Press each section into the mound of salad. The circle of eggs looks like a jewelled crown.

BOUQUET OF SALADS

With hot rolls, beverage, and dessert, a plate luncheon . . . as served at a famous eating place in Silver Springs, Maryland.

Circle 4 small servings of individual salads in lettuce cups on each dinner-sized plate. Fill center with sprigs of watercress, top with a fresh flower. Plan a variety of salads that will harmonize: (1) appetizer salad: tomato mixture; (2) hearty salad: chicken or seafood; (3) green vegetable salad: avocado, asparagus, or tossed garden; (4) dessert salad: fruit or fruit aspic.

PALACE COURT SALAD

A luncheon specialty at the Palace Hotel in San Francisco, California.

Arrange a mound of finely shredded lettuce on salad plate. On top, place a thick large tomato slice. On tomato, place one large cooked artichoke heart (or 3 small ones). Cover this with pieces of cooked crab, shrimp, or chicken. Garnish around edge of lettuce with sieved hard-cooked egg. Serve with Russian Dressing.

HOT CRABMEAT SALAD

Unusual, elegant . . . from a very clever cateress, Mrs. O. Schultz of Minneapolis.

Make a White Sauce of . . .

- **½ cup butter**
- **⅔ cup *sifted* GOLD MEDAL Flour**
- **2⅔ cups milk**

Cook about 10 min. Then blend in . . .

- **2 cups flaked crabmeat**
- **1 large bunch celery, diced**
- **⅓ green pepper, minced**
- **1 large pimiento, minced**
- **⅓ cup blanched almonds, quartered**
- **4 hard-cooked eggs, cut-up**
- **2 tsp. salt**

Pour into buttered 12x7½x2″ baking dish. Sprinkle with buttered fine dry bread crumbs. Bake at 350° (mod. oven) 35 min. Serve hot in crisp lettuce cups topped with Mayonnaise (with chopped sweet pickles added). *Serves 8.*

MOLDED SALADS Perfect for advance preparation.

HOW-TO-MAKE A MOLDED SALAD For example: STRAWBERRY SALAD GLACE

First, prepare the gelatin: Pour 2 cups hot water over 1 pkg. raspberry (or strawberry) flavored gelatin. Stir well to completely dissolve the gelatin.

Prepare the garnish: Shape into 12 balls, two 3-oz. pkg. cream cheese (softened with cream). Roll in ½ cup finely chopped nuts.

1 Brush mold with salad oil as the surest way to prevent gelatin sticking unusually hard to mold. Or rinse with cold water.

2 Place cheese balls evenly spaced in 10″ ring mold.

3 Cover with layer of lightly sugared strawberries (or use raspberries with strawberry gelatin for Raspberry Salad Glacé).

4 Pour the cooled raspberry (or strawberry) flavored gelatin over the cheese balls and strawberries. Chill until the gelatin is set.

5 Unmold on large serving plate: tip to let in air at one side; loosen with spatula thrust in around edge; turn upside-down onto plate.

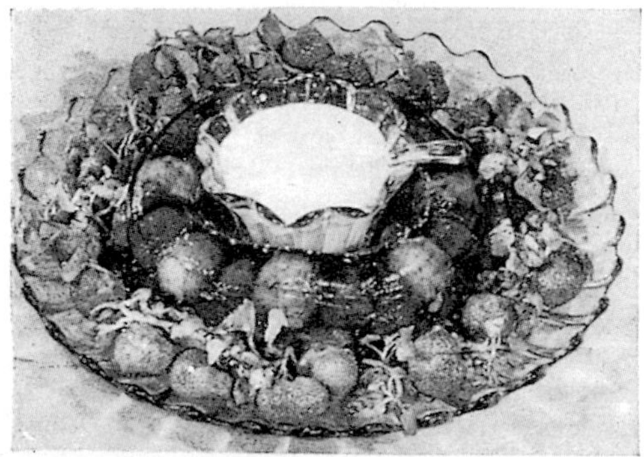

6 Garnish with watercress sprigs or lettuce frills and large perfect berries. (For a special dessert, fill center with pineapple sherbet.)

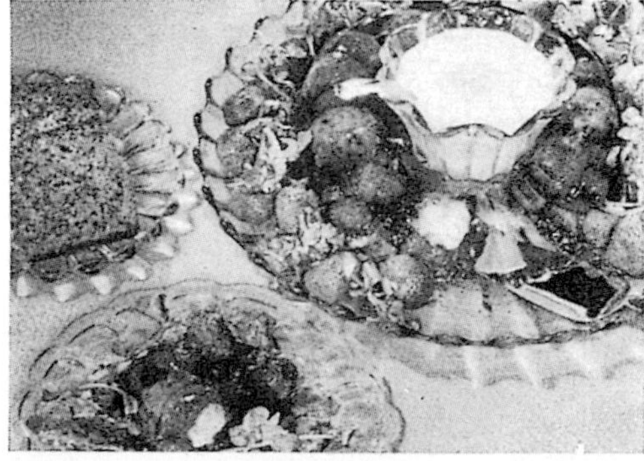

7 Serve on individual plates . . . topped with Mayonnaise to which whipped cream has been added or with Sweet French Dressing.

MOLDED GELATIN SALAD (🔑 **Recipe**) *Made with flavored gelatin. Choose flavor to make an interesting combination with the fruits or vegetables, etc. you add.*

Prepare according to directions on pkg.	**1 pkg. flavored gelatin**
Add	**2 tbsp. lemon juice (or vinegar)**
Chill, and when partially set, add	**1½ to 2½ cups well drained and cut-up fresh or canned fruit, vegetables, or seafood, etc.**

When partially set again, pour into a ring mold (8″ in diameter and 2½″ deep) *or* 8 to 10 individual molds. Chill until firm. Unmold on large chop plate or individual salad plates. Garnish with crisp lettuce, curly endive, or lacy watercress.

NOTE: Serve with appropriate dressing: Mayonnaise with whipped cream for mild salads . . . or Tomato-Cucumber Mayonnaise for vegetable and seafood salads. *Serves 8 to 10.*

JELLIED FRUIT MEDLEYS

Follow 🔑 recipe above using any flavored gelatin desired, omit lemon juice, and add whole or cut-up fruit:

Grapefruit or orange sections with strawberries . . . orange gelatin.

Pears or pineapple with sweet cherries . . . lemon gelatin.

Pears with sweet green grapes or apricots . . . lime gelatin.

Diced honeydew melon with cherries . . . lime gelatin.

JELLIED VEGETABLE-FRUIT SALADS

Follow 🔑 recipe above using lemon-flavored gelatin and adding combinations of cut-up vegetables and fruits:

Complexion Salad: 1½ cups grated raw carrots, 1¼ cups well drained canned crushed pineapple.

Hartley Salad: 1¼ cups *each* thin cucumber slices and well drained diced canned pineapple.

Carrot-Grape Salad: 1¼ cups *each* finely diced raw carrots and halved sweet green grapes.

CHICKEN-ALMOND SALAD MOLD

Delicate and partyfied. Insures chicken salad with no last-minute preparations.

Follow 🔑 recipe above using lemon-flavored gelatin—and add 1 cup diced cooked chicken; ½ cup Mayonnaise; 1 tsp. salt; ⅓ cup toasted slivered almonds; and ½ cup halved sweet green grapes.

PERFECTION SALAD

Molded version of an old church supper favorite of the Gay Nineties.

Follow 🔑 recipe above using lemon-flavored gelatin—and add 1 tsp. salt, 1 cup *finely* shredded cabbage, 1 cup finely diced celery, 2 finely chopped pimientos, and 6 chopped sweet pickles.

MOLDED GARDEN SALAD

Delicately refreshing.

Follow 🔑 recipe above using lemon-flavored gelatin—and add 1 tsp. salt, ¼ cup finely sliced green onions, ½ cup diced cucumber, ½ cup *each* thinly sliced radishes, celery, and raw cauliflowerets.

STUFFED TOMATO-MINT SALAD

Adds a sparkling touch to a roast lamb dinner.

Cut off ends of tomatoes; scoop out most of pulp. Turn tomatoes upside-down, let drain in refrigerator.

Follow 🔑 recipe above using mint-flavored gelatin, omit lemon juice, and add 1 cup diced celery and 1 cup diced cucumber. Fill tomato cups with the mixture, and chill. Top with watercress.

SEAFOOD SALAD MOLD

Follow 🔑 recipe above using lemon-flavored gelatin—and add 1 extra tbsp. lemon juice; ½ tsp. prepared mustard; dash of salt; paprika; 1 cup drained flaked tuna, salmon, lobster, crabmeat, or shrimp; and ½ cup thinly sliced celery.

GELATIN SALADS Chosen for glamour and good eating.

TOMATO ASPIC (🔑 Recipe) *Colorful, piquant, refreshing*

Soften .... 2 envelopes unflavored gelatin (2 tbsp.)
in .... ½ cup cold water

Meanwhile, simmer together 15 min..
- 2 cups tomato juice
- 1 tsp. salt
- 1 tsp. confectioners' sugar
- dash of cayenne pepper
- dash of celery salt
- 1 bay leaf
- 1 cut-up small onion
- a few celery leaves

Strain, and add softened gelatin and 1 tbsp. lemon juice, stirring until dissolved. Cool, then pour into individual oiled molds. Chill until firm (about 2 hr.).

NOTE: Double the recipe fills 9″ ring mold. *Serves 12.*
Unmold on salad greens and serve with Mayonnaise. *Serves 6 to 8.*

CHICKEN-TOMATO ASPIC

Follow 🔑 recipe above—and add 1 cup diced cooked chicken before chilling.

SEAFOOD IN TOMATO ASPIC

Make double the 🔑 recipe above in ring mold. Serve bowl of Seafood Salad (*double recipe on p. 346*) in center. Garnish with hard-cooked egg and stuffed olives.

HOLIDAY TOMATO ASPIC

Follow 🔑 recipe above—add 1 cup diced celery and ½ cup chopped bread-and-butter pickles before pouring into mold.

FESTIVE SALAD MOLD

First made for a guest luncheon in our Early American dining-room one hot midsummer day by Marion Knowlton of our Staff (now Mrs. C. W. Loomer of Madison, Wisconsin).

Make double the 🔑 recipe above in ring mold. Press 10 deviled egg halves stuffed-side-down around bottom of mold. Place slices of stuffed olives between eggs. Cover with the slightly thickened Tomato Aspic. Chill until firm. Unmold on crisp lettuce on chop plate. Serve with Thousand Island Dressing.

Cheese Mold with Fruit.

CRANBERRY-APPLE SALAD

Cranberries and salad in one!

Cook gently until skins break 2 cups cranberries in 1 cup water. Rub through sieve. To pulp, add . . .
- **1 cup sugar**

Boil slowly 5 min. Take off heat. Soften . . .
- **1 envelope unflavored gelatin in**
- **2 tbsp. cold water**

and blend into hot cranberry mixture. Let cool until mixture begins to thicken. Add . . .
- **¼ cup chopped roasted peanuts**
- **½ cup diced apples**
- **½ cup diced celery**

Pour into oiled molds and chill. When stiff, unmold and serve on salad greens with Mayonnaise or Cooked Salad Dressing mixed with whipped cream. *Serves 8.*

CRANBERRY-GRAPE SALAD

For holiday entertaining. Delicious with tiny hot rolls for parties.

Follow recipe directly above—*except*, in place of the peanuts, apples, and celery, use walnuts, Tokay grapes (seeded and quartered), and diced canned pineapple.

CHEESE MOLD WITH FRUIT

Soften 2 envelopes unflavored gelatin in ½ cup cold water. Dissolve over hot water. Cream together with little milk to soften . . .
- **4 pkg. white cream cheese (12 oz.)**
- **1 cup shredded mild American cheese**
- **1 tsp. salt**
- **½ tsp. paprika**

Add the gelatin. Fold in 2 cups cream, whipped. Pour into oiled 9″ ring mold. Chill until set. Unmold on greens. Garnish with fruits.

The woman who knows her sauces is a Culinary Artist

*O*NE WAY *to become known as an artist with foods is to be clever with sauces. The ingenious use of sauces has helped make French cooking famous the world over. It is a skill every woman who aspires to turning out exceptionally delicious food should develop.*

Betty Crocker

For Ice Cream and Ice Cream Desserts

For Waffles and Pancakes

For Angel Food, Sponge and Chiffon Cake Desserts

For Elegant Fruit Desserts

For Refrigerator Desserts

For Fruit Shortcakes and Dumplings

For Cottage Puddings

For Steamed Puddings

For Vegetables

For Meats (Beef, Pork, Lamb, and Veal)

For Fish

For Ham

For Eggs

For Meat Loaves, Meat Balls, Croquettes, Hash

Stuffing for Fish, Meat, and Poultry

Gravy and White Sauces

SAUCES

Sauces for meat and game were such an important part of medieval feasts that every palace and wealthy home had a *saucier* whose sole business it was to preside over that part of the menu. Old paintings of banquets of those days show this saucier at work with his two assistants at an elaborately equipped side table.

Today we have sauces for vegetables and desserts as well as meat, fish, and poultry. Modern chefs classify them all as "pick-ups" . . . their term for a finishing touch that literally lifts a dish up . . . glamorizes and gives it distinction.

This "picking-up" is accomplished by contrasts. First, a color contrast to make a dish *look* tempting. Like crushed strawberries served over white ice cream. Then when we taste this dessert, the strawberry flavor and texture add a great deal to our enjoyment of the ice cream.

A sauce does not need to be complicated and tricky. A little lemon added to the salt and pepper used in seasoning a baked fish becomes a sauce. It's as simple as that. The important point is learning to combine flavors.

A world famous chef has advised women to be daring and experiment with herbs and other seasonings. Better yet, you can have a wonderful time trying sauces others have found add to the enjoyment of desserts, vegetables, and meats. In these pages we have tried to give you a wide variety of the best known tried and true sauces. We know you will have fun serving them . . . and that your family will be very proud of your new skill.

DESSERT SAUCES You never tasted any better ones anywhere!

FOR ICE CREAM, ELEGANT FRUIT, AND FROZEN DESSERTS

Several Dessert Sauces are included with the desserts they usually accompany. (See p. 351.)

BUTTERSCOTCH SAUCE

True butterscotch flavor, super-smooth.

Mix in saucepan . . .
- **3/4 cup sugar**
- **1/2 cup light corn syrup**
- **1/4 tsp. salt**
- **1/4 cup butter**
- **1/2 cup cream**

Cook over low heat, stirring, to soft ball stage (234°). Stir in additional . . .
- **1/2 cup cream**

Cook to thick, smooth consistency (228°). Remove from heat. Stir in . . .
- **1/2 tsp. vanilla**

Serve hot or cold.
AMOUNT: 2 cups.

CARAMEL SAUCE

Melt over hot (not boiling) water . . .
- **1/2 lb. vanilla caramels (about 36)**

Stir in gradually . . .
- **4 tbsp. water**

Stir to blend well. Serve hot or cold.
AMOUNT: 1 cup.

TOFFEE SAUCE

Follow recipe above for Caramel Sauce—*except* use rum-and-butter toffee.

ORANGE BUTTER SAUCE

Cream together . . .
- **1/4 cup soft butter**
- **3/4 cup sugar**

Stir in . . .
- **2 egg yolks or 1 egg, beaten**
- **1 1/2 tsp. grated orange rind**
- **1/3 cup orange juice**
- **1/3 cup milk**

Cook over *hot* water 10 to 15 min. Cool.
AMOUNT: 1 1/2 cups.

CLEAR ORANGE SAUCE

Mix in saucepan 1 cup sugar, 1/4 tsp. salt, 2 tbsp. cornstarch, and 1 tbsp. flour. Stir in 1 1/4 cups orange juice, 1/4 cup lemon juice, 1/2 cup water. Cook over low heat, stirring until it boils. Boil 3 min. Remove from heat, mix in 1 tbsp. butter, 1 tsp. *each* grated orange and lemon rind. Serve warm.
AMOUNT: 2 cups.

HOT BITTERSWEET SAUCE

This is a thick, rich sauce.

Melt in saucepan, stirring over low heat until smooth . . .
- **1/4 cup butter**
- **1 1/2 sq. unsweetened chocolate (1 1/2 oz.), shaved fine**

Stir in . . .
- **1/4 cup cocoa**
- **3/4 cup sugar**
- **1/4 cup cream**
- **1/8 tsp. salt**

Bring slowly *just to* a boil. Do *not* stir. Remove from heat. Blend in . . .
- **1 tsp. vanilla**

Serve warm.
AMOUNT: 1 1/2 cups.

QUICK FUDGE SAUCE

Melt over boiling water . . .
- **2 1/4-lb. bars semi-sweet chocolate**

Stir in a tbsp. at a time . . .
- **3 tbsp. cream**

Stir until smooth and glossy. Remove from heat. Thin to desired consistency with . . .
- **1 to 4 tbsp. water**

AMOUNT: 1 1/2 cups.

GLOSSY CHOCOLATE SAUCE

Melt in saucepan over low heat . . .
- **2 sq. unsweetened chocolate (2 oz.)**

Mix in and heat slowly, stirring constantly . . .
- **1 cup light corn syrup**

Remove from heat and stir in . . .
- **1/2 tsp. vanilla**
- **1 tbsp. butter**

AMOUNT: 1 cup.

THIN CHOCOLATE SAUCE

(See "DESSERTS," p. 221.)

ZABAGLIONE SAUCE

Beat until thick and lemon-colored . . .
- **4 egg yolks**

Beat in thoroughly . . .
- **1/4 cup sugar**
- **1/4 tsp. salt**

Place over *hot* (not boiling) water. Cook, beating constantly, 5 min. Remove from heat. Blend in . . .
- **1/4 cup sherry flavoring**

Serve hot or cold. AMOUNT: 2 cups.

FOR ANGEL FOOD, SPONGE, AND CHIFFON CAKES (See pp. 154-160.)

BANANA WHIP

Clever mothers find that children love this topping on sponge cake.

Beat until light and fluffy and then chill . . .
- 1 ripe banana, sliced
- 1 unbeaten egg white
- 1/3 cup sugar
- dash of salt
- 1/2 tsp. vanilla
- 1/2 tsp. lemon juice

AMOUNT: 1 1/3 cups.

CHOCOLATE FLUFF

Mix together in chilled bowl, beat until stiff . . .
- 2 cups whipping cream
- 1 cup *sifted* confectioners' sugar
- 1/2 cup cocoa
- 1/8 tsp. salt

AMOUNT: 4 cups.

RUSSIAN SAUCE

(Orange Fluff Topping)

Mix together well in top of double boiler . . .
- 3 egg yolks
- 1/2 cup sugar
- 1/3 to 1/2 cup orange juice (1 large orange)

Cook over hot water, stirring constantly, until it thickens (about 15 min.). Stir in . . .
- 1 tbsp. grated orange rind

Cool. Fold in . . .
- 1 cup whipping cream, whipped stiff
- 1/2 cup toasted, chopped, blanched almonds or fresh grated coconut

AMOUNT: 4 cups.

PEANUT CRUNCH TOPPING

Fold . . .
- 1/2 cup finely crushed peanut brittle

Into . . .
- 1 cup whipping cream, whipped stiff

AMOUNT: 3 cups.

FOR SHORTCAKES (See p. 224 for others.)

FRESH MINT FOAMY SAUCE

Adds zest to fruit shortcakes.

Cream together . . .
- 1/4 cup soft butter
- 1 cup *sifted* confectioners' sugar

Blend in . . .
- 1 egg, well beaten
- 1/4 cup fruit juice

Beat until fluffy. Mix together . . .
- 2 tbsp. minced fresh mint leaves
- 1 tbsp. sugar

Let stand an hr. or more. Just before serving, blend the mint leaves into sauce.
AMOUNT: 2 cups.

RASPBERRY SAUCE

Elegant topping for Raspberry Shortcake.

Melt in saucepan . . .
- 1/2 cup butter

Stir in . . .
- 1 cup sugar
- 1 cup fresh raspberries, mashed

Blend in . . .
- 1 tbsp. cornstarch, dissolved in 1 tbsp. cold water

Cool. Fold in . . .
- 1 egg white, stiffly beaten

AMOUNT: 6 servings.

FOR STEAMED PUDDINGS (See pp. 229, 230 for others.)

AMBER SAUCE

Very sweet and butterscotchy.

Mix in saucepan . . .
- 1 cup brown sugar
- 1/2 cup corn syrup
- 1/4 cup soft butter
- 1/2 cup cream

Cook over low heat, stirring to blend well (5 min.). Serve warm.
AMOUNT: 2 cups.

All you have to do—

To color Hard Sauce: add a few drops of desired food coloring.

SATIN SAUCE

Beat until foamy in saucepan . . .
- 1 egg
- 1 tbsp. water

Stir in . . .
- 3/4 cup sugar
- 1/4 tsp. salt

Cook over low heat 1 min., stirring constantly. Remove from heat and stir in . . .
- 2 tbsp. lemon juice
- 1 tsp. vanilla

Serve hot.

AMOUNT: 1 1/2 cups.

GRAVY SAUCES Good gravy . . . sign of a good cook.

THIN, THICK, OR MEDIUM GRAVY?

It is just a matter of taste.

**The Correct Amount of Thickening to Use*

For 1 cup thin gravy.......... 1 tbsp. flour
For 1 cup medium gravy....... 2 tbsp. flour
For 1 cup thick gravy.......... 3 tbsp. flour

CAUTION: Gravy thickens on standing. If it becomes too thick, add a little hot water and reheat, stirring constantly.

All you have to do—

If the drippings or meat stock are not brown enough to give a rich brown color to the gravy: Add a little gravy coloring . . . or brown the flour first: spread in thin layer on a dry shallow pan over low heat, stirring occasionally.

GRAVY-WISE

- If there is less than a cup of meat stock (juice) in the pan, add extra liquid to make 1 cup, or the amount wanted.
- Water is the liquid usually added.
- Milk is added instead of water to make cream gravy with chicken, pork, or ham.
- Potato water or water drained from cooked mild vegetables may be used for part or all of the liquid.
- Bouillon cubes may be added to increase flavor, or dissolved in water to increase stock.
- Remember gravy contains some of the precious vitamins and minerals from the meat. Bread and gravy is a nutritious dish we can profitably enjoy.

METHOD I How to Make Gravy When There Is Plenty of Meat Juice (Stock) in the Pan

As with stews, pot roasts, etc.

**See "Correct Amount of Thickening for Thin, Medium, or Thick Gravy"* (above).

Blend double amount of water to flour (2 tbsp. cold water to 1 tbsp. flour, etc.) to a *smooth* paste with rotary beater or by shaking in a covered glass jar.

Remove meat, keep hot. Add liquid to stock to make amount of gravy desired, scraping brown from pan into liquid. Boil.

Gradually stir in flour paste. Cook, stirring until it thickens. Season to taste. Cook over low heat about 10 min. (stirring occasionally to blend flavors).

METHOD II How to Make Gravy When There Is Enough Fat but Little Meat Juice in Pan

As with steaks, chops, rib roasts, etc.

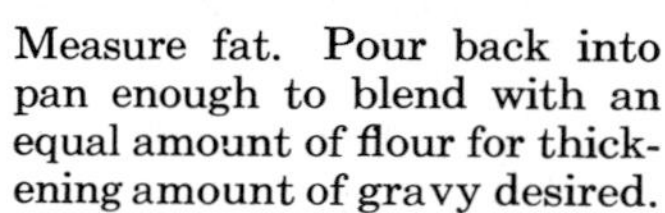

Measure fat. Pour back into pan enough to blend with an equal amount of flour for thickening amount of gravy desired.

Blend flour into fat in pan over *low* heat . . . making a paste (roux). Stir until mixture bubbles.

Stir in liquid (off heat); then cook over *low* heat, stirring until thick and smooth. Season with salt, pepper, onion, etc.

PAN GRAVY

Add very little boiling water, just enough to dissolve browned juices and fat. Stir well. Season. Serve over meat.

MUSHROOM GRAVY

Add ½ cup sautéed sliced mushrooms to 1 cup of gravy.

GIBLET GRAVY

Place cleaned giblets (liver, heart, and gizzard of chicken or turkey) in saucepan. Cover with boiling water. Simmer until liver is tender. Remove liver and simmer until gizzard is tender. Cool. Chop giblets. Use stock in making gravy. Stir in the chopped giblets.

WHITE SAUCE (🔑 Recipe) *A base for creamed dishes and many sauces.*

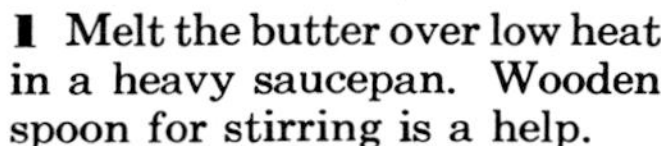

1 Melt the butter over low heat in a heavy saucepan. Wooden spoon for stirring is a help.

2 Blend in flour, seasonings. Cook over low heat, stirring until mixture is smooth, bubbly.

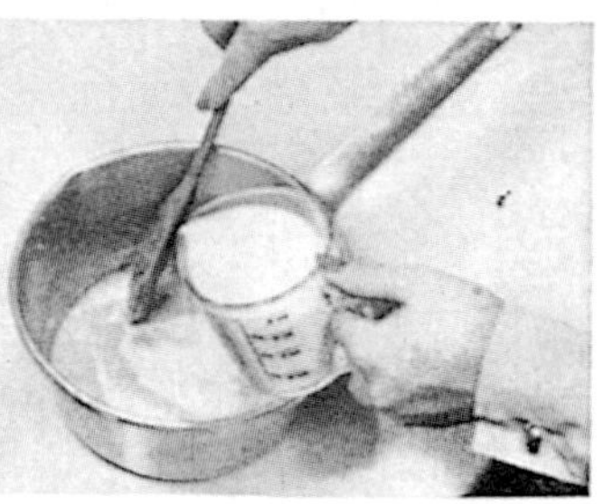

3 Remove from heat. Stir in milk. Bring to boil; boil 1 min., stirring constantly.

INGREDIENTS FOR WHITE SAUCE

Thin Sauce	*Medium Sauce*	*Thick Sauce*
1 tbsp. butter	2 to 3 tbsp.	4 tbsp.
1 tbsp. flour	2 to 3 tbsp.	4 tbsp.
¼ tsp. salt	¼ tsp.	¼ tsp.
⅛ tsp. pepper	⅛ tsp.	⅛ tsp.
1 cup milk	1 cup	1 cup

4 Cook until thickened (for best flavor cook 10 min.).

SHORT CUT TO WHITE SAUCE *Keep a roux (Butter Paste) in a jar in refrigerator.*

Blend to a smooth paste equal amounts of soft butter and flour . . . .

	Butter Paste	*Milk*
For Thin Sauce	1½ tbsp.	1 cup
For Medium Sauce	3 tbsp.	1 cup
For Thick Sauce	4½ tbsp.	1 cup

Heat to scalding the liquid (milk, meat or fish stock, or other liquid).
Blend in Butter Paste (*above*).
Add salt, pepper, and desired seasoning.
Stir constantly until mixture boils.
Boil 1 min. Remove from heat.

NOTE: If sauce is too thick, stir in more milk. Other liquids (meat broths, fish stock, etc.) may take place of part of milk.

CAPER SAUCE

For lamb or fish.

Follow 🔑 recipe above—and stir into the sauce ¼ cup capers. For richer sauce, add capers to Velouté Sauce (*p. 358*).

CHEESE SAUCE

For vegetable, rice, macaroni, and egg dishes.

Follow 🔑 recipe above—adding ¼ tsp. dry mustard with the seasonings. Blend in ½ cup nippy American cheese (cut-up or grated). Stir until cheese is melted.

EGG SAUCE

A pleasant addition to salmon and other fish.

Follow 🔑 recipe above—and carefully stir in 2 diced hard-cooked eggs. Season.

MOCK HOLLANDAISE SAUCE

Easier to make, less expensive than "regular" Hollandaise.

Follow 🔑 recipe above—and after removing from heat, beat in 2 egg yolks, slightly beaten. Gradually beat in 2 tbsp. melted butter, 3 tbsp. lemon juice. Serve at once.

WHITE SAUCES *Many famous sauces from the same family.*

CURRY SAUCE

Combines perfectly with chicken, lamb, shrimp, and rice.

Follow recipe for White Sauce (*p. 357*)—add ½ tsp. curry powder with seasonings.

PIQUANT SAUCE

For tongue, beef, veal, or fish.

Follow recipe for Medium White Sauce—*except* use 1 cup cooked tomato juice in place of milk. Add 1 tsp. grated onion, 3 tbsp. finely chopped sour pickle, and 1 tsp. minced parsley.

SAUCE MORNAY

Chefs glamorize meats, hash, eggs with it.

Follow recipe for Thick White Sauce (*p. 357*). Add 1 cup cream and ⅛ tsp. cayenne pepper. Heat, stirring constantly. Stir in 1 cup cut-up sharp American cheese, Parmesan, or Swiss cheese.

SHRIMP OR LOBSTER SAUCE

Ideal with codfish soufflé and other special fish dishes.

Follow recipe for Medium White Sauce and carefully stir into the sauce ½ to 1 cup cooked shrimps or pieces of cooked lobster.

MUSHROOM SAUCE

A general favorite with many supper dishes.

Follow recipe for White Sauce (*p. 357*)—*except* sauté 1 cup sliced mushrooms and 1 tsp. grated onion in the butter 5 min. before adding flour.

SALT PORK GRAVY

A New England classic. Serve over boiled potatoes with thin slices of salt pork fried to a crisp golden brown.

Slice ¼ lb. salt pork thin. Simmer in water to cover 20 min. to remove excess salt. Roll slices in flour and sauté over low heat. Drain off drippings. Make double recipe Medium White Sauce (*p. 357*), using salt pork drippings instead of butter. Omit salt. *Serves 4.*

All you have to do—

To make Bacon Gravy: substitute bacon drippings for the salt pork drippings.

SAUCE VERTE (Green Sauce)

For clam croquettes and other seafood dishes.

Follow recipe for Medium White Sauce (*p. 357*). Add ¼ tsp. celery salt, 1 tsp. onion juice, 1 tbsp. lemon juice. Blend in ¾ cup finely chopped cooked spinach.

VELOUTÉ SAUCE (Velvet Sauce) (Recipe) *An elegant white sauce cousin.*

Melt over low heat	**2 tbsp. butter**
Stir in until well blended	**2 tbsp. flour**
Remove from heat. Gradually stir in	**1 cup chicken or veal or fish stock**
Return to heat. Cook, stirring constantly, until thick and smooth.	
Blend in	**salt to taste** **dash of white pepper** **⅛ tsp. nutmeg**

Serve hot with croquettes, baked fish, etc.

AMOUNT: 1 cup.

ALLEMANDE SAUCE

Adds glamour to leftovers such as chicken, ham patties, croquettes, or meat loaves.

Follow recipe above. Stir into sauce 1 slightly beaten egg yolk, 1 tsp. lemon juice, and 2 tbsp. cream.

ANCHOVY VELOUTÉ SAUCE

For boiled or baked fish.

Follow recipe above—*except* blend 1½ tsp. anchovy paste into the flour and butter paste. Omit salt, and use fish stock instead of veal or chicken stock. Just before serving add 1 tbsp. finely chopped parsley.

BÉCHAMEL SAUCE

Named for Louis de Béchamel, steward to King Louis XIV of France.

Follow recipe above—and blend in ½ tsp. salt, ⅛ tsp. pepper, ¼ tsp. paprika. Then fold in ½ cup cream.

NORMANDY SAUCE

For fish mousse, timbales, or soufflé.

Follow recipe above—using fish stock. Beat a little hot sauce into 2 egg yolks, and beat into remaining sauce. Blend in . . .

1 tbsp. lemon juice
salt, pepper, and cayenne to taste

BROWN SAUCE (Sauce Espagnole) (🔑 **Recipe**) *White sauce with a deep sun tan.*

Heat in small heavy skillet over low heat until browned	2 tbsp. butter or drippings
Add and sauté until light brown	½ slice onion
Remove onion. Stir in until well blended	2 tbsp. flour
Cook over low heat, stirring constantly, until flour is a deep mahogany brown.	
Remove from heat. Gradually stir in	1 cup beef stock
Cook over low heat, stirring constantly, until thickened. Stir in	salt and pepper to taste

Strain, if desired.

AMOUNT: 1 cup.

OLIVE SAUCE

Good with steak, salmon loaf, cheese soufflé.

Follow 🔑 recipe above—adding 12 sliced pitted green or ripe olives.

DILL SAUCE

Choice for lamb or veal.

Follow 🔑 recipe above—and add 2 tbsp. vinegar and dill to taste.

TOMATO SAUCE

For meat loaves, fish croquettes, etc

Follow 🔑 recipe above—*except* brown flour lightly. Use 1 cup tomato juice in place of beef stock. Add 1 tsp. sugar; more onion, minced green pepper may be added.

TEXAS BARBECUE SAUCE

A zesty sauce to pour over the "ribs" during the last 45 min. of baking.

Mix together and simmer 15 min. . . .

- ½ cup finely chopped onion (1 med.-sized)
- 2 tbsp. brown sugar
- 1 tbsp. paprika
- 1 tsp. salt
- 1 tsp. dry mustard
- ¼ tsp. chili powder
- ⅛ tsp. cayenne pepper
- 2 tbsp. Worcestershire sauce
- ¼ cup vinegar
- 1 cup tomato juice
- ¼ cup catsup
- ½ cup water

AMOUNT: Sufficient for 3 lb. ribs.

SPANISH BROWN SAUCE

For hamburgers or spaghetti.

Follow 🔑 recipe above—adding to the melted butter 2 tbsp. minced onion, 2 tbsp. minced green pepper, and ¼ cup chopped mushrooms. Simmer 5 min. before adding flour. Use ½ cup tomato juice in place of half the stock. Do not strain.

MUSHROOM BROWN SAUCE

Follow 🔑 recipe above—adding 1 cup sliced mushrooms to the butter or drippings; brown slowly before adding flour. Stir in a few drops Worcestershire sauce.

MEXICAN SAUCE

A truly "hot sauce" to give zest to fish, meat, or omelets.

Follow 🔑 recipe above—and add ½ tsp. gravy coloring, ½ cup tomato catsup, 1 tbsp. *each* minced onion and green pepper sautéed in butter. Season to taste with salt, paprika, and celery salt.

EASY BARBECUE SAUCE

For barbecued ribs, wieners, or meat loaf.

Mix together and cook over low heat 5 min. . . .

- ¼ cup chopped onion
- 4 tbsp. sugar
- ⅛ tsp. pepper
- ¼ cup catsup
- 3 tbsp. vinegar
- 1 tsp. Worcestershire sauce

PIQUANT BROWN SAUCE

For tongue, beef, veal, or fish.

Simmer together 5 min.: ½ tbsp. *each* minced onion and chopped capers, 2 tbsp. vinegar, ½ tsp. sugar, dash of paprika and salt. Add to Brown Sauce (*follow 🔑 recipe above*). Then add 2 tbsp. thick chili sauce or chopped sweet pickle.

HOLLANDAISE SAUCES Basic sauces every cook should know.

HOLLANDAISE SAUCE (🔑 Recipe) *The aristocrat of sauces.*

Melt in top of double boiler over hot (not boiling) water	½ cup butter
Gradually stir in (stirring constantly)	4 egg yolks, well beaten
Gradually stir in	¾ cup boiling water
Cook over hot water until mixture begins to thicken. Be careful not to cook too long or hard as Hollandaise separates easily. Remove from heat and add	few grains cayenne pepper ¼ tsp. salt 2 tbsp. lemon juice

Cover and place over hot water until serving time (should not stand too long). If sauce starts to curdle, beat vigorously with rotary beater until smooth and creamy. Serve with fish dishes and broccoli, asparagus, or cauliflower, etc.

NOTE: For Mock Hollandaise, see p. 357.

AMOUNT: 1 cup.

CUCUMBER HOLLANDAISE

Serve with fish and shellfish.

Follow 🔑 recipe above—and add 1 cup drained chopped cucumber.

BÉARNAISE SAUCE

A popular sauce for baked, broiled, or cooked fish.

Follow 🔑 recipe above—and add 1 tsp. *each* minced parsley and fresh tarragon, and ½ tsp. tarragon vinegar.

MOCK HOLLANDAISE (see *p. 357*)

MUSTARD HOLLANDAISE

A real "pepper-upper" for any fish.

Follow 🔑 recipe above—and add 1 tbsp. dry mustard with salt and pepper. Substitute 1½ tbsp. tarragon vinegar for lemon juice.

MOUSSELAINE SAUCE

Elegant with boiled fish, eggs, artichokes, broccoli, cauliflower, etc.

Follow 🔑 recipe above—and when ready to serve, blend in stiffly whipped cream (whip ¼ cup). Serve warm.

TARTAR SAUCE

A favorite accompaniment for fried or broiled fish, scallops, shrimp, etc., or a dressing for fish salads.

Just before serving, combine . . .
- 1 cup mayonnaise
- 1 tbsp. chopped capers
- 1 tbsp. chopped olives
- 1 tbsp. minced parsley
- 1 tbsp. chopped pickles

AMOUNT: 1¼ cups.

MAITRE D'HOTEL BUTTER

Spread on steak or fish before serving.

Blend together 3 tbsp. soft butter, 1 tbsp. lemon juice, 1 tbsp. minced parsley, ½ tsp. salt, ⅛ tsp. pepper.
AMOUNT: 6 servings.

EPICUREAN SAUCE

Creamy, zestful sauce . . . especially delicious with ham, hot or cold.

Mix in bowl . . .
- 1 tbsp. tarragon vinegar
- 2 tbsp. grated horseradish
- 1 tsp. English mustard (dry)
- ½ tsp. salt
- few grains cayenne pepper

Blend in . . .
- ½ cup whipping cream, whipped stiff
- 3 tbsp. mayonnaise

AMOUNT: 10 servings.

EASY HORSERADISH SAUCE

Always welcome with tongue or ham.

Blend together . . .
- ½ cup whipping cream, whipped stiff
- 2⅔ tbsp. well drained horseradish
- 1⅓ tbsp. Cooked Salad Dressing

RAISIN SAUCE

A perennial favorite for baked ham.

Blend together in saucepan . . .
2 tbsp. butter, melted
2 tbsp. flour
Remove from heat, and blend in slowly . . .
2 cups apple cider
½ cup seedless raisins

Cook until mixture boils, stirring constantly; then boil 1 min. Remove from heat. Serve hot.

AMOUNT: 2 cups.

ORANGE SAUCE

See Clear Orange Sauce (p. 354) for ham.

ORANGE-CURRANT SAUCE

For roast duck, lamb, ham, or chicken.

Empty into bowl and break up with fork...
1 glass red currant jelly (½ cup)
Add . . .
grated rind of 1 orange
⅛ tsp. *each* salt and cayenne pepper
1 tbsp. prepared mustard dissolved in juice of 2 oranges

Beat well. Serve hot or cold.

WHOLE CRANBERRY SAUCE

Boil together 5 min. . . .
2 cups water
2 cups sugar
Add . . .
4 cups cranberries

Boil together without stirring until all skins pop (about 5 min.). Cool.

AMOUNT: 4½ cups.

MOLDED CRANBERRY SAUCE

Boil Cranberry Sauce above until thick and cranberries are clear (15 min.). Pour into oiled mold and chill.

CRANBERRY-ORANGE RELISH

Put through food chopper . . .
rind and pulp of 1 large orange
4 cups cranberries
Mix in and let stand several hours . . .
2 cups sugar

PAN-FRIED BANANAS

From a good friend, Ina S. Lindman of the United Fruit Company, New York City.

Peel 6 all-yellow or green-tipped bananas. (Leave whole or cut across into halves.)
Fry slowly in . . .
¼ cup melted butter or margarine
until tender, easily pierced with fork.

Turn bananas to brown evenly. Sprinkle lightly with salt. Serve hot as a vegetable.

MINT SAUCE

A perennial favorite for roast lamb.

Dissolve . . .
1½ tbsp. confectioners' sugar
In . . .
3 tbsp. hot water
Cool and blend in . . .
⅓ cup finely minced mint leaves
½ cup very mild wine vinegar

Let stand ½ hr. before serving. Serve cool.

AMOUNT: 1 cup.

SPICED PEARS

Delicious with veal, lamb, or chicken.

Combine and boil 20 min. . . .
1⅓ cups sugar
⅓ cup water
⅔ cup vinegar
1½ sticks cinnamon
12 whole cloves
Add . . .
6 winter cooking pears, carefully pared

Cook until tender, 35 to 40 min. Stick 1 or 2 cloves in each pear. If desired, add red or green coloring to tint pears.

CINNAMON APPLES

Delicious and colorful with roast pork.

Core and pare medium or small firm tart apples. Cook until tender in a syrup made with 2 cups sugar, 1 cup water, ⅓ cup red cinnamon candies ("red hots"), and a drop or two of red coloring. Chill, and serve around meat or as a salad.

APPLE RINGS

Cut cored, pared apples in ½″ rings or slices and cook in red syrup as for Cinnamon Apples. Use as a garnish for meat.

BROILED FRUITS

For attractive garnishes around meats.

Drain canned pear, peach, or apricot halves; pineapple circles, or green gage plums. Place on absorbent paper to absorb excess juice. Then place under broiler a few minutes. Fill centers of pears or peaches with red or green jelly.

TART APPLESAUCE

First choice with roast pork or duck.

Follow recipe for Applesauce (see "DESSERTS," p. 215) . . . using minimum amount of sugar.

STUFFING TIPS

Day-old bread is best for stuffing. Cut off crusts. Pull into ¼″ or ½″ crumbs.

A 1-lb. loaf of bread makes 8 cups loosely packed crumbs (2 qt.).

Plan a cup of stuffing for each pound of bird as purchased.

Make dry or moist stuffing as desired.

Pack stuffing loosely into bird. Packing too tightly makes it heavy and soggy.

If the family has divided tastes about texture and seasoning of stuffing, pack some of one kind in body cavity and some of other in the crop.

Shape leftover dressing into balls and bake separately on a pan during last 30 to 45 min. of roasting time. Baste occasionally.

It saves time to stuff the bird a day ahead. Cool stuffing. Fill cavity and truss the bird. Store at once in a cold place.

BREAD STUFFING (🔑 Recipe)

	1 qt. for 4-lb. chicken	*3 qt. for 12-lb. turkey*
First, prepare coarse or fine crumbs as desired	**4 cups (1 qt.)**	**12 cups (3 qt.)**
Melt in large heavy skillet	***⅓ cup fat**	**1 cup**
Add and cook until yellow (stirring occasionally)	**¼ cup finely minced onion**	**¾ cup**
Stir in some of bread crumbs. Heat, stirring to prevent excessive browning. Turn into deep bowl. Mix in lightly	**½ cup chopped celery (stalks and leaves)**	**1½ cups**
	2 tsp. salt	**2 tbsp.**
	¼ tsp. pepper	**1 tsp.**
	1 tsp. crumbled dried herbs (suit to taste; use sage, thyme, etc.)	**1 tbsp.**
	poultry seasoning (to taste)	
	remaining crumbs	

For dry stuffing, add little or no liquid. For moist stuffing, mix in lightly with fork just enough hot water to moisten dry crumbs. Cool and place stuffing in bird.

**Use butter, poultry fat, margarine, vegetable shortening, or fresh bacon fat.*

SAUSAGE STUFFING

Special flavor zest with Thanksgiving turkey.

Follow 🔑 recipe above—*except* omit salt, and add fresh pork sausage, crumbled and browned over low heat. Use ⅓ lb. sausage for 1 qt. stuffing, 1 lb. for 3 qt. Use the sausage fat in place of part of other fat in stuffing.

CHESTNUT STUFFING

The old-time holiday treat with turkey.

Follow 🔑 recipe above. Add chopped boiled chestnuts (1 cup for 1 qt. stuffing, 3 cups for 3 qt.).

OYSTER STUFFING

Follow 🔑 recipe above—using butter for fat. Add oysters, chopped and drained (1 cup for 1 qt. stuffing, 3 cups for 3 qt.).

CELERY STUFFING

Ideal for fish.

Follow 🔑 recipe above for 1 qt. stuffing—increasing chopped celery to 1½ cups. Omit sage, poultry seasoning, add 1 tbsp. lemon juice, 1 tbsp. minced parsley.

MUSHROOM-WILD RICE STUFFING

Elegant with roast pork or braised veal.

Melt in heavy skillet ½ cup butter or other fat. Add and cook for 5 min. 1 lb. sliced fresh mushrooms (or 1 8-oz. can). Remove mushrooms. Add ½ cup chopped onion, ½ cup minced parsley, 1 cup chopped celery. When onions turn yellow, add ⅓ cup water, 4 cups cooked wild rice, 1½ tsp. salt, ⅛ tsp. pepper. Add another ⅓ cup water and the cooked mushrooms. Simmer 15 min. Serve in roast. Serves 8.

Soups for Satisfaction

FEW FOODS can warm the cockles of the heart and produce such completely blissful satisfaction as a bowl of steaming, fragrant, flavorful soup.

Betty Crocker

Clear Dinner Soups

Meat and Vegetable Soups

National Soups

Elegant Cream Soups

GARNISHES

For Thin Clear Soups

Thin lemon slices
Minced parsley or chives
Stuffed olive slices
Thin cooked mushroom slices
Avocado cubes
Custard cubes
Egg Rivels

For Cream Soups

Whipped cream dusted with paprika
Minced parsley or chives
Pimiento strips or bits
Croutons and grated cheese
Slivered salted almonds
Buttered popcorn or KIX

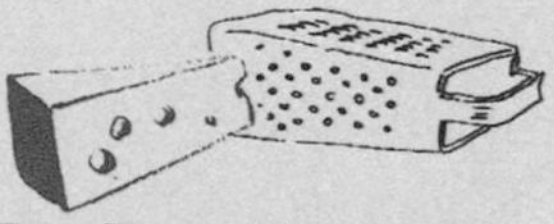

For Hearty Soups

Crisp cooked diced bacon
Frankfurt slices or smoked sausages
Buttered croutons
Toasted slices of French bread, grated cheese
Crumbled Blue cheese

SERVE HOT SOUPS IN HOT DISHES

At formal dinners, soup plates and soup spoons are high style for any type of soup.

Thin soups in bouillon cups with bouillon spoons or teaspoons.

Cream soups and chowders in cream soup cups or pottery bowls with either bouillon or soup spoons.

Hearty one-dish meal soups in pottery bowls or earthenware casseroles with soup spoons.

Rye Bread with Potage St. Germaine

Italian Bread Sticks with Minestrone

Hard-Crusted French Rolls with Onion Soup au Gratin

Buttered Toast with Clam Chowder

Assorted Plain Rolls with Navy Bean Soup

Easy way to thicken soup: Stir a roux (paste) of melted butter and flour into hot soup (only 1 tbsp. flour with 1 or 2 tbsp. butter for 1 qt. of soup).

SOME SPECIAL SOUP ACCOMPANIMENTS

SAVORY CRACKERS: Brush crackers with soft butter; sprinkle with poppy seed, celery seed, onion salt, or paprika. Heat in mod. oven (350°).

CHEESE PAPRIKA TOAST: Sprinkle toasted bread strips or triangles with grated American cheese and paprika. Place under broiler or in mod. oven (350°) until cheese is melted.

ROYAL CUSTARD: Make custard with 1 egg and 2 egg yolks and ½ cup Consommé or Bouillon, salt, and a pinch *each* of cayenne pepper and nutmeg. Pour ½″ deep into shallow pan. Set in pan of water (1″ deep). Bake 20 min. in mod. oven (350°). Cool and cut into fancy shapes or cubes. Drop into hot clear soup.

EGG RIVELS: Work 1 egg into 1 cup GOLD MEDAL Flour and ¼ tsp. salt, sifted together, until mixture looks like corn meal. Drop into boiling soup. Cover, cook gently 10 min.

BUTTER RIVELS: Use ⅓ cup butter instead of egg. Work until mixture is completely blended. Shape into ½″ balls. Drop into boiling soup. Cover, cook gently 10 min. Rivels will separate, look like rice.

SOUPS

Soup is as old as the art of cooking. In fact, it goes back to ages before cooking was an art at all—the days when the aborigines threw whatever flesh food they had into a kettle to cook over an open fire. Later, ingenious souls discovered, perhaps by accident, that a few herbs made the food taste better. The French *pot au feu* is a survival of these primitive soups. It's the soup always simmering on the stove, into which the French housewife throws herbs, vegetable tag ends, and meat bones. All the flavors are extracted and blended during the long slow cooking while the kettle smiles and chuckles, but *never* laughs outright in a full rollicking boil.

La Soupe is the name given the evening meal in parts of rural France today. The time for enjoying the steaming, savory contents of that smiling, simmering kettle. We have taken the word *supper* from this. But we have left behind the soup that made the meal.

Each nation has its own special soups, rich in chunks of meat, hearty with vegetables and barley, rice or macaroni. Such soups have long been celebrated in song and story. Some even as cures for various ailments, like the soup called "*Restaurant*" which was popular in 16th Century France. People believed it had "restorative" powers. A chef printed the name over his door to tell all that he was serving it. In time, "*restaurant*" came to mean a place where all kinds of foods were served.

Today, soup serves a double purpose. It stimulates the appetite and provides wholesome nourishment. We choose our soup with an eye on the rest of the meal. If this is to be rich and hearty, we decide on a thin clear soup with an aroma and flavor that will flag the appetite to attention. With less hearty food to follow, the soup can be richer . . . perhaps one of our delicious cream soups that help us maintain our daily milk quota. And, of course, there are still many grand soups that are meals in themselves. You will find them all here.

STOCK FOR SOUP

Stock is to soup what flour is to cake.

Good soup stock depends on long slow cooking to extract every bit of flavor. A beef shin for brown stock and a veal knuckle for white stock are preferred because they are especially flavorful. Use about two-thirds meat, one-third bone. Browning the beef in the marrow fat gives color and additional flavor.

STOCK FOR SOUP *Your kitchen will be warm and cozy, and smell so good.*

	Brown Stock (Bouillon)	White Stock (Consommé)
Scrape marrow from..................	1 to 2 lb. marrow bones, cracked	
Melt in large kettle over low heat.		
Add and brown in the marrow fat half of (Do not brown the meat for White Stock. Add all the meat with water at once.)	4 lb. shin of beef, cut in small pieces	5 lb. veal knuckle or chicken with bones (or $2\frac{1}{2}$ lb. each)
Add remaining meat and..............	3 qt. cold water	3 qt.
Cover and bring slowly to boil. Remove scum.		
Add..................................	3 sprigs parsley, minced	2 sprigs
	1/4 tsp. thyme	1/4 tsp.
	1/4 tsp. marjoram	———
	1 small bay leaf	1/2 leaf
	1/2 cup diced carrots	1/3 cup
	1/2 cup chopped onion	1/3 cup
	1/2 cup diced celery (with leaves)	1/2 cup
	10 peppercorns	6
	5 cloves	2
	1 tbsp. salt	1 tbsp.

Cover and simmer gently 4 hr. Remove scum occasionally. Strain and cool quickly. Store in covered jars in refrigerator. The layer of fat on top will help preserve the stock, but it must be skimmed off before heating stock for use in soups and sauces. Clarify stock for use as Bouillon or Consommé (*see* NOTE *at right*).

NOTE: To clarify stock: for each qt., beat together 1 egg white and 1 tbsp. cold water. Add with pieces of broken egg shell, stirring until stock boils. Boil 2 min. Let stand off heat 20 min. Strain through double cheesecloth.
AMOUNT: $2\frac{1}{2}$ qt.

CHICKEN STOCK (Broth)

Place in kettle . . .

5 lb. hen or stewing chicken, cut-up
3 qt. cold water

Cover and bring slowly to boil. Remove scum.
Add . . .

1/3 cup diced carrots
1/3 cup *each* chopped celery and onion
1 sprig minced parsley
2 tsp. salt

Cover and simmer gently 3 hr., removing scum occasionally. Strain, chill, remove fat and strain again as in recipe above.

For 1 cup Bouillon: (1) use canned bouillon, (2) dissolve 2 bouillon cubes in 1 cup hot water, or (3) dissolve 1 tsp. bouillon concentrate in 1 cup hot water.

TOMATO BOUILLON

Heat together equal amounts Bouillon and tomato juice with 3 or 4 whole cloves in it. Garnish with lemon slices.

JELLIED BOUILLON (or Consommé)

Thoroughly chill homemade Bouillon or Consommé (it will jell). The canned will usually jell if chilled overnight. To make it go further, heat 1 can bouillon or consommé with slice of onion, 1/2 tsp. celery salt. Strain, add $1\frac{1}{4}$ tsp. gelatin (softened in 1 tbsp. cold water). Add 1 cup water, 1/8 tsp. salt, 1 tbsp. lemon juice. Chill. Break up slightly with fork and pile in bouillon cups. Top with lemon slice.

OLD-TIME VEGETABLE SOUP

Add 3 cups finely diced vegetables (celery, onions, carrots or turnips, cabbage, or any desired combination) to 1½ qt. (6 cups) Brown Stock. Cook about 30 min. *Serves 6.*

VEGETABLE NOODLE SOUP

To Vegetable Soup above—add 1½ cups noodles and cook with the vegetables for the last 15 min.

CHICKEN NOODLE SOUP

To 1 qt. Chicken Broth, add 1 cup noodles and cook 10 to 15 min.

All you have to do—

For clear noodle soups: cook the noodles separately, drain, and add them (hot) when serving soup.

HOLIDAY TOMATO SOUP

Cook together in 4 tbsp. butter until tender...
- **¼ cup *each* diced onion, carrot, celery**

Blend in . . .
- **4 tbsp. GOLD MEDAL Flour**
- **½ tsp. peppercorns**
- **1 bay leaf**
- **3 cloves**
- **¼ tsp. crumbled thyme**

Cook 3 min., stirring occasionally, then add...
- **2½ cups cooked tomatoes (#2 can)**

Cover and simmer over low heat 1 hr., stirring occasionally. Rub through sieve, add . . .
- **1 qt. (4 cups) Brown Stock (Bouillon)**

Bring to boil. Salt and pepper to taste. Serve immediately.

AMOUNT: 6 servings.

ONION SOUP AU GRATIN

As served at boulevard cafés in France.

Brown in 2 tbsp. butter until tender . . .
- **4 large onions, sliced very thin. Add . . .**
- **1 qt. (4 cups) Brown Stock (Bouillon)**
- **1 tsp. Worcestershire sauce**
- **½ tsp. salt**
- **⅛ tsp. pepper**

Bring to boiling point and place in large or individual casseroles. Arrange over top of soup . . .
- **2 French rolls, sliced and toasted**

Sprinkle with ½ cup grated Parmesan cheese. Place under broiler to brown. Serve immediately.

AMOUNT: 6 servings.

CONSOMMÉ JULIENNE

To each serving of Consommé, add 1 tbsp. finely shredded vegetables (carrots, beans, leeks, celery, onions). Cook 5 min.

CONSOMMÉ ANGLAISE

To each serving of Consommé, add 1 tbsp. finely chopped cooked chicken and 1 tbsp. chopped toasted blanched almonds.

PEARL SOUP

Delightful "before dinner" soup served in the home of Caroline Crosby, of Minneapolis.

Bring 1 qt. (4 cups) Consommé to a boil and add ¼ cup quick-cooking tapioca. Cook 10 min. Stir in 1 well beaten egg yolk, 1 cup rich milk. Bring to boil, season to taste with salt and serve. *Serves 8.*

SPICY TOMATO SOUP

Often served as "first course" at guest luncheons by our Staff. Mrs. W. H. Bussey of Minneapolis served it at a lovely luncheon.

Place in kettle . . .
- **1½ qt. (6 cups) tomato juice**
- **1¼ cups tomato puree (#1 can)**
- **3 tbsp. sugar**
- **5 cloves and a dash of ground cloves**
- **1 slice onion**
- **2 cups Brown Stock (Bouillon)**
- **1¼ tsp. salt**
- **1 bay leaf**
- **⅛ tsp. mixed herbs (marjoram, thyme)**

Bring to boil, stirring occasionally. Simmer 5 min. Serve with lemon slice. *Serves 8.*

ITALIAN MINESTRONE

There's a version for every town in Italy.

Cook together in kettle (3 to 4 hr.) . . .
- **1 cup dried white beans, soaked (*p. 370*)**
- **1½ qt. (6 cups) liquid (Brown Stock which the water beans were soaked in)**

Skim. Cook in skillet in 2 tbsp. olive oil . . .
- **1 large onion, chopped**
- **1 clove garlic, minced fine**
- **3 sprigs parsley, minced**
- **3 large carrots, finely diced**
- **3 stalks celery, diced (with leaves)**
- **1 cup finely shredded cabbage**
- **1 cup diced raw potatoes**

Cover, simmer 30 min., stirring often. Add beans and . . .
- **1 cup cooked macaroni in ½" pieces**
- **1 tbsp. salt ¼ tsp. pepper**
- **1 cup cooked tomatoes**

Simmer together 15 min. Serve.

AMOUNT: 10 servings.

PHILADELPHIA PEPPER POT

Venders in old Philadelphia used to call—

"Peppery pot, piping hot,
All hot, all hot,
Pepper pot, pepper pot,
Makes back strong,
Makes live long,
All hot pepper pot!"

Place in kettle . . .

- 1½ qt. (6 cups) White Stock (Consommé)
- ½ lb. honeycomb tripe, cooked, rinsed, and diced
- ⅔ cup minced onion
- ½ sweet red pepper, minced
- 1½ tbsp. minced parsley
- ⅛ tsp. thyme
- 1 tsp. marjoram
- ½ bay leaf
- 6 whole allspice, peppercorns, cloves
- 1½ tsp. salt

Cover, and simmer about 30 min. Add . . .

- 1 cup diced raw potato
- 2½ cups cooked veal, cut in ½" cubes

Simmer until potatoes are done (20 min.). Stir in paste of 2 tbsp. melted butter, 2 tbsp. flour.

Bring to boil and serve.

AMOUNT: 6 servings.

AMERICAN POTAGE

A quick, savory, meat-and-vegetable soup.

Brown in a little hot fat in a heavy kettle . . .

- 1 lb. ground beef

Simmer ½ hr. in 1 qt. (4 cups) hot water

Then add . . .

- 1 cup *each* finely cut-up carrots, celery, onion, and potato
- 2 to 4 cups more boiling water
- salt and pepper to taste

Cover and simmer 30 min. or until vegetables are tender. Serve immediately.

AMOUNT: 6 servings.

EASY CHICKEN GUMBO

Tastes like the old-time Creole favorite.

Simmer in 3 tbsp. butter in kettle until soft

- ¼ cup chopped green pepper
- 1½ cups canned okra, cut in ½" pieces
- ¼ cup chopped onion

Stir in . . .

- 1 qt. (4 cups) Consommé or Chicken Stock
- 2½ cups cooked tomatoes (#2 can)
- 1 small piece bay leaf

Boil gently 15 min. Season to taste. Add . . .

- 1 tbsp. minced parsley
- 1 cup finely diced cooked chicken

AMOUNT: 6 servings.

SCOTCH BROTH

Appreciated equally by the epicure seeking interesting foods and the mother of a family in need of economical, hearty, one-dish meals. Broadcast as a Home Defense meal.

Soak overnight in 5 cups water . . .

- ½ cup *each* barley and dried yellow peas

Combine and simmer 1 hr. . . .

- 1 to 2 lb. mutton (1 lb. lean meat)
- 5 cups water
- 5 tsp. salt

Then add the soaked barley, peas and water . . .

- 3 leeks (or 2 small onions), diced
- 1 turnip, diced
- 2 medium carrots, diced
- 1 small cabbage, cut in pieces

Bring to boil and simmer 1 hr. Then add . . .

- 1 grated carrot
- ¾ cup minced parsley
- ⅛ tsp. pepper
- 2 tbsp. butter

Simmer 15 min. Serve piping hot.

AMOUNT: 8 servings.

OXTAIL SOUP

Brown well in a little hot fat in kettle . . .

- 1½ lb. oxtail, cut into 2" pieces

Add . . .

- 1½ qt. water
- 1 tbsp. salt (3 tsp.)

Simmer covered about 3¼ hr. Remove meat from bones. Return meat to soup. Add . . .

- ½ cup diced onion
- ¾ cup diced raw carrot
- ½ cup diced raw celery
- 2 tbsp. white rice

Cover, simmer 30 min. Skim off fat. Add . . .

- 1 cup cooked tomatoes

Heat and serve.

AMOUNT: 6 servings.

CHICKEN OR TURKEY SOUP

Curtain call of the holiday bird.

Remove meat from carcass of chicken, turkey, or duck and set aside. Crack bones. Place in kettle, add skin, several stalks of celery, 1 carrot, 1 onion, 6 peppercorns, tip of 1 bay leaf, 4 cloves. Cover with water. Simmer 2 hr. Cool slightly, strain. Return meat to stock. Chill, skim off fat. Add salt to taste. Simmer 15 min.

SHRIMP OR CRAB GUMBO

Follow recipe for Easy Chicken Gumbo opposite—using shrimp or crabmeat in place of chicken. Add ½ tsp. file powder.

"Of soup and love, the first is best!" said Thomas Fuller back in 1732.

POTAGE DE FROMAGE

The French is literally "soup of cheese." Eugene Burgess of our company who enjoys making it for his friends, showed us how.

Place in alternate layers in a deep kettle . . .
- 18 slices zwieback or 9 slices well dried-out toast
- 3/4 lb. well aged sharp cheese, shaved thin

Pour 1½ qt. hot Brown or White Stock over toast and cheese. Place in a slow oven (325°) about 20 min., just until cheese at the top begins to brown lightly.

Combine . . .
- 2 small eggs, beaten slightly with fork (just enough to break up the yolks)
- 3 tbsp. brandy flavoring

Stir very slowly into hot soup (eggs will cook, giving a curdled appearance). Serve at once in individual casseroles or in large soup plates. The liquid will be almost entirely absorbed by the toast, making the soup very thick.

AMOUNT: 6 servings.

MULLIGATAWNY SOUP

East Indian curry soup—popular in England.

Sauté in 1/4 cup butter in deep kettle or Dutch oven . . .
- 1 medium onion, peeled and sliced
- 1 medium carrot, diced
- 1 stalk celery, diced
- 1 green pepper, seeded and diced
- 1 medium apple, pared, cored, and sliced
- 1 cup cut-up cooked chicken

Stir frequently until onions are tender.

Stir in gradually . . .
- 1/3 cup GOLD MEDAL Flour
- 1 tsp. curry powder
- 1/8 tsp mace
- 2 whole cloves
- 1 sprig parsley
- 2 cups White Stock (Consommé)
- 1 cup cooked tomatoes
- salt and pepper to taste

Simmer covered ½ hr., then serve.

AMOUNT: 6 servings.

PETITE MARMITE

French for "small porridge bowls," the little casserole-like dishes in which this flavorful soup is served. "C'est quelque chose! C'est trés bon!" says our friend, Ed Sylvestre, with gusto.

Caramelize . . .
- 1½ tbsp. sugar

Add . . .
- 1½ qt. Brown or White Stock (Bouillon or Consommé)
- 1½ tbsp. butter
- 3/4 cup cooked diced carrots
- 1/2 cup cooked diced onions
- 3/4 cup cooked cut-up string beans

Bring to boiling point and pour into a casserole or individual casseroles.

Toast or brown in butter . . .
- 3 cups bread cubes (4 slices 1/2" thick)

Float cubed bread on top of soup. Sprinkle over all . . .
- 3/4 cup grated cheese

Place in a hot oven for 10 min. to melt cheese. Serve at once.

AMOUNT: 6 servings.

BORSCH

Russian beet soup with especially fine flavor. Also a native of Poland. Can be served hot or cold, so that it's good for cold or hot weather.

Combine with 1½ qt. (6 cups) Brown Stock (Bouillon) . . .
- 2 tbsp. tomato paste
- 6 raw beets, grated
- 3 egg whites, beaten stiff but not dry

Cook over *low* heat, beating constantly until soup comes to boil. Remove from heat. Let stand 10 min. Drain through damp cheesecloth. Do not squeeze. Reheat soup.

Stir in . . .
- 2 tbsp. lemon juice
- 1 tbsp. grated lemon rind
- 1/2 cup dill pickle juice

Pour piping hot soup into soup dishes.

Combine and drop as garnish on soup . . .
- 1/2 cup sour cream
- 1 tbsp. fresh dill seeds or minced parsley

Serve immediately.

AMOUNT: 6 servings.

BEAN AND PEA SOUPS A ham bone with beans or peas.

Quick-cooking dried peas and beans do not *require* overnight soaking. Some people, however, believe even those are *better* for soaking. Others prefer the old-fashioned type. If you prefer to soak beans or peas, measure the amount of water specified in these recipes. Leave the beans or peas in it overnight. Next morning add the remaining ingredients. *No draining is necessary*. 2 cups peas or beans = 1 lb.

BASIC RECIPE for...	**Split Pea Soup**	**Navy Bean Soup**
Place together in kettle (soaked overnight, *see above*)	**2 cups dried split peas**	**2 cups navy beans**
	3 qt. cold water	**3 qt.**
Then add	**1 ham bone or small shank end of ham**	**1 ham bone, etc.**
	1 large onion, minced	**1 onion, minced**
	———	**½ tsp. sugar**
	3 stalks celery (with tops), chopped fine	**2 stalks**
	1 sprig of parsley	———
Bring slowly to boiling point. Cover and simmer 4 to 5 hr. until beans or peas are tender and the liquid partially cooked down. For smooth soup, rub through a coarse sieve. Some prefer leaving some of the beans or peas whole.		
Skim off excess fat. Thicken, if desired, with	**3 tbsp. butter**	———
	3 tbsp. flour	———
Dilute as desired with additional	**milk or water**	**milk or water**
Season to taste with	**salt and pepper**	**salt and pepper**

Serve hot.

AMOUNT: 8 servings.

POTAGE ST. GERMAINE

"Wonderful soup, so rich and green."

Follow recipe for Split Pea Soup above. Garnish with thin slices of Bologna sausage. Serve with rye bread.

SWEDISH PEA SOUP

Place in kettle 2 cups dried split yellow peas, 2 qt. water; soak overnight. Add 2 tbsp. salt. Simmer 2 to 3 hr. (until peas are soft). At same time, cook 4 lb. pork (inexpensive cut with some bone) in 3 qt. cold water. Bring to boil. Simmer 2 to 3 hr. until meat is tender. Skim off excess fat. Add the cooked peas (undrained). Bring to boil. Serve with flakes of the meat in soup.

BLACK BEAN SOUP

From away down south in Dixie.

Follow recipe for Split Pea Soup above—*except* use black turtle beans in place of split peas. Garnish with a thin slice of lemon and a thin slice of hard-cooked egg on each portion.

LENTIL SOUP

Follow recipe for Split Pea Soup above—*except* use lentils in place of dried peas. Just before serving, add 1 tbsp. vinegar.

MONGOLE SOUP

Follow recipe for Split Pea Soup above—*except* dilute with strained cooked tomatoes in place of milk or water.

LENTEN PEA SOUP

Place in kettle 2 qt. water, 2 cups dried split green peas (1 lb.), 3 cups coarsely cut celery, 1 cup coarsely cut carrots, ½ cup minced onion, ¼ tsp. thyme, 1 tsp. salt, ⅛ tsp. pepper, dash of cayenne, and 1 bay leaf. Bring to boil and boil 20 min. Cover, simmer 1 hr. Press through sieve. Add 1 tbsp. butter. Season to taste. Bring to boil. Serve. *Serves 8.*

SEAFOOD CHOWDER (Recipe)

New England contribution to the international soup pot. The "makins" for Clam Chowder were always available in early New England. Everybody or his neighbor had a cow, raised potatoes and onions, and could get "quahogs" for the digging.

Cook slowly in kettle until fat begins to fry out ... 4 tbsp. finely cut salt pork or bacon

Add and cook over *low* heat until yellow ... 4 tbsp. minced onion

Add ... liquor from 2 7-oz. cans minced or whole clams, lobster, or other seafood; 2 cups finely diced potatoes; ½ cup boiling water

Cook until potatoes are tender, 10 min. (If potatoes are cooked, omit water.)

Just before serving, add ... clams or other seafood from 2 7-oz. cans; 2 cups milk; 1 tsp. salt; ⅛ tsp. pepper

Heat to boiling, stirring occasionally. Serve immediately.

NOTE: Butter may be used in place of pork or bacon.

AMOUNT: 6 servings.

MANHATTAN CLAM CHOWDER

The New Yorker's version . . . not historical.

Follow recipe above—using bacon. Use cooked tomatoes (#2 can) for the milk. Add ⅓ cup diced celery, 1 cup diced carrots with clam liquor. Add ¼ tsp. thyme, and 2 tsp. minced parsley.

VEGETABLE CHOWDER

Follow recipe above—and add 2 tbsp. minced green pepper with the onion. Add ¼ cup *each* diced carrots and celery, and ½ cup peas with the potato in 1 cup boiling water. Add soda crackers, broken, and 1 tbsp. butter just before serving.

CHICKEN AND CORN CHOWDER

Norman E. Dewes of our company enjoyed this chowder so much in Lancaster, Pennsylvania, that he begged the recipe for us.

Place the neck, wings, back pieces, and giblets of a fat hen in a kettle with . . .

- 1½ qt. boiling water
- 1 onion, sliced
- 3 stalks of celery (with leaves), chopped fine
- 1 carrot, diced
- 1 tbsp. salt

Cover and simmer until tender (about 1½ hr.). Slip meat from bones, cut it up fine, and return to broth. Add . . .

- 2 cups cream style corn (#1 tall can)

Simmer 10 min., then add . . .

- 2 hard-cooked eggs, chopped fine

Drop Rivels (*p. 364*) into soup, simmer 10 min.

AMOUNT: 6 servings.

CORN CHOWDER

Follow recipe above—*except* use only 2 tbsp. onion, omit liquor from seafood. Use 1 cup boiling water with potato and add 1 cup finely cut celery and carrots. In place of clams or other seafood, use 2 cups cream style corn (#1 tall can).

POTATO SOUP

The homey, old-fashioned kind.

Sauté gently in 2 tbsp. butter . . .

- 1 tbsp. grated carrot
- 1 tbsp. scraped onion

Stir in . . .

- 1 tsp. salt
- ¼ tsp. celery salt
- ⅛ tsp. pepper
- 2 cups hot milk
- 1 cup mashed or boiled potatoes put through a coarse sieve

Cook 20 min., stirring occasionally.

AMOUNT: 6 servings.

CREAM SOUPS Basis for a light dinner, or a main dish for lunch.

CREAM OF VEGETABLE SOUP (🔑 Recipe) *Delicious, nutritious, delicate.*

Melt over *low* heat in heavy saucepan . .	3 tbsp. butter
Blend in..............................	2 tbsp. flour 1 tsp. salt 1/8 tsp. pepper
Remove from heat and stir in..........	4 cups milk, or use part Consommé or Chicken Broth (1 to 2 cups)
Bring to boil. Boil 1 min., stirring constantly, then add..............	*1 cup cooked puréed vegetables (celery, spinach, asparagus, or peas) 1 tsp. grated onion

Cook 10 min. over boiling water. Serve hot with a swirl of whipped cream dusted with paprika, or minced parsley, or chives, or other colorful garnish.

**Use leftover cooked vegetables; or cook fresh vegetables in a little water (use celery leaves with stalks). Push through sieve.*

AMOUNT: 6 servings.

CREAM OF CORN SOUP

As served at the perfect dinners in the home of Mary Saunders Bulkely of Minneapolis, the City of Lakes, in Minnesota.

Heat 2½ cups cream style corn (#2 can) to boiling point. Put through coarse sieve. Follow 🔑 recipe above—using rich milk or part cream, and the puréed corn for the cup of puréed vegetable.

CREAM OF MUSHROOM SOUP

Rich, flavorful—ideal for special luncheons.

Follow 🔑 recipe above—using 2 cups rich milk and 2 cups Chicken Broth. Use 1 cup sautéed finely chopped mushrooms (the fresh preferred) in place of vegetable purée. Add paprika and onion salt.

CREAM OF PIMIENTO SOUP

Holiday luncheon or "before dinner" soup.

Follow 🔑 recipe above (using half Consommé)—*except* use only ½ cup puréed pimiento in place of 1 cup other vegetable. Add the grated onion, a dash of cayenne, and 1 or 2 drops tabasco sauce. Garnish with parsley.

CREAM OF SQUASH SOUP

Wonderful for children's autumn lunches.

Follow 🔑 recipe above—*except* use ¼ cup mashed cooked squash in place of 1 cup other vegetable.

CREAM OF CELERY DE LUXE

A favorite cream soup with many.

Follow 🔑 recipe above—using 2 cups rich milk, 2 cups Chicken Broth with 1 cup puréed celery.

CREAM OF CHICKEN SOUP

Follow 🔑 recipe above—using 3 cups Chicken Broth and 1 cup top milk or cream. Blend in ½ cup shredded cooked chicken in place of puréed vegetables. Sprinkle each serving with minced chives.

CREAM OF TOMATO SOUP

Always a favorite. No curdling, this way.

Follow 🔑 recipe above—*except* first stir 2 cups strained cooked tomatoes into the butter-flour mixture. Cook 5 min. and add ¼ tsp. soda with the salt and pepper. Add the milk, bring to boil, and serve.

WHOLE TOMATO SOUP

A meal-saver when unexpected guests drop in. A favorite with everyone . . . can be mixed up in a minute. Children love it.

Combine in saucepan . . .

1 cup cooked tomatoes (pulp and juice) (canned or cook cut-up fresh tomatoes 10 min.)
1/8 tsp. soda

Bring to boil and stir well to break up tomatoes. Add and heat, stirring constantly. . .

2 cups rich milk

Do not allow to boil. **Season to taste with salt, pepper, and 1 tbsp. butter, if desired.**

Serve piping hot.

AMOUNT: 4 servings.

CREAM OF SPINACH DE LUXE

As served to us in a little hotel midst the scenic grandeurs of Norway.

Follow 🔑 recipe above—using 2 cups rich milk, 2 cups Consommé with 1 cup puréed spinach (fresh spinach preferred).

CLAM BISQUE (⚷ Recipe)

Unusually delicious and so easy to make.

Mix together and simmer 3 min. . . .
- the liquor drained from a 7½-oz. can of minced clams
- 1 cup water
- 1 to 2 tsp. salt
- ⅛ tsp. pepper
- ⅛ tsp. celery salt
- 1 tsp. grated onion
- 2 tsp. finely minced parsley

Add . . .
- 2 cups milk

Stir in a paste (roux) of . . .
- 2 tbsp. butter, melted
- 1 tbsp. flour

Boil 1 min., stirring constantly, then place over boiling water until time to serve. Stir in . . .
- the minced clams (rinse out can with bit of water, add it for flavor)

Serve garnished with minced parsley.

AMOUNT: 8 servings.

OYSTER BISQUE

Follow ⚷ recipe above—*except*, in place of clams and clam liquor, use ½ pt. oysters and liquor from oysters. Rinse them with water; add it with liquor. In place of celery salt, use 2 tbsp. minced celery. Chop the oysters and add when time to serve.

CRAB, LOBSTER, OR SHRIMP BISQUE

Follow ⚷ recipe above—*except*, in place of clams and clam liquor, use 7½-oz. can of crabmeat, lobster, or shrimp (cutting in fine pieces) and liquor from seafood.

OYSTER STEW

Old-time favorite for sleighride parties.

Heat to scalding . . .
- 1 pt. milk
- ½ cup cream

Just before serving, melt in saucepan . . .
- ¼ cup butter

Add . . .
- 1 pt. oysters (with the liquor)

Cook gently *just* until oyster edges curl. Add to scalded milk and cream. Season with
- 1 tsp. salt
- dash of pepper

Serve immediately . . . offer oyster crackers.

AMOUNT: 6 servings.

CREAM OF CUCUMBER SOUP

Sophisticated, delicately flavored . . . to help make your reputation as a hostess.

Pare 3 large cucumbers, cut in lengthwise strips, and scrape out seeds. Dice strips. Sauté the cucumber gently 10 min. with . . .
- ½ diced small onion
- 4 tbsp. butter

Add . . .
- 3½ cups Chicken Broth

Cover and simmer 25 min. Rub mixture through sieve, and add . . .
- 1 cup cream

Beat together and bring to boil. Blend in slowly just before serving . . .
- 2 egg yolks
- ¼ cup cream

Season with salt and pepper to taste. Serve garnished with sliced radishes.

AMOUNT: 8 servings.

VICHYSSOISE (Chilled)

The faint flavor of nutmeg gives this soup special distinction when served by Gertrude McGee of Minneapolis, Minnesota.

Brown lightly in 2 tbsp. butter . . .
- 2 leeks or small onions, cut-up

Add, simmer 35 min., stirring occasionally . . .
- 2 cups Chicken Broth
- 4 cups thinly sliced potato
- ½ tsp. salt

Press through fine sieve and add . . .
- 1 cup milk
- 1 cup cream
- ⅛ tsp. pepper
- 1 tsp. salt
- ¼ tsp. nutmeg

Bring to boil. Strain and add . . .
- ½ cup scalded cream

Cool and chill several hr. Serve cold . . . garnished with finely chopped chives.

AMOUNT: 6 servings.

QUICK SOUPS Streamliners with the good old-time flavor.

HELPS TO QUICK SOUPS

There are two types of canned soups: (1) the condensed which should be diluted with water (2) the kind to be served "as is." In preparing, follow directions on the can. The dehydrated soups that come in packages are a convenience in several ways. Follow directions on the packages.

For use of bouillon cubes and bouillon concentrates, *see p. 366.*

MOCK TURTLE SOUP DE LUXE

Superb flavor, attractive to serve.

Simmer together for 10 min. . . .

- **2½ cups condensed Mock Turtle Soup (2 #1 cans)**
- **1½ cups cold water**
- **1 bouillon cube**
- **4 whole cloves**

Add and reheat . . .

- **¼ cup cream**
- **½ tsp. Worcestershire sauce**

Press 2 hard-cooked eggs through a sieve and divide between 6 soup bowls. Pour the hot soup over this. Garnish each serving with a lemon slice and a whole clove. If desired, add 1 tsp. sherry flavoring to each bowlful.

QUICK CRAB BISQUE

Fruit salad and rolls are all that's needed to make this a super-delicious meal.

Sauté about a cup of crabmeat in butter and season to taste with salt and cayenne pepper. Blend into 3 cups Cream of Pea Soup. Heat thoroughly, serve at once. *Serves 6.*

TUNA-VEGETABLE CHOWDER

Thick main dish soup. Cooks in the time it takes to make a salad and set the table.

Add about 1 cup flaked drained canned tuna to 3 cups Vegetable Noodle Soup, and 1 cup top milk or cream. Simmer 10 min. Serve hot. *Serves 6.*

LOBSTER SUPREME

Combine equal amounts condensed Cream of Asparagus and Cream of Mushroom Soup. Add light cream to make desired consistency. Then add desired amount flaked canned lobster meat. Heat but do not boil. Add sherry flavoring, if desired. Serve hot.

CREAM OF CHICKEN SOUP

Chilled, it tastes like Vichyssoise.

Combine equal amounts of condensed Cream of Chicken Soup and rich milk. Bring to boil. Season with salt and pepper. Serve hot or chilled, garnished with minced chives.

CURRIED CHICKEN SOUP

To hot Cream of Chicken Soup above, add curry powder (1 tsp. per cup). Serve hot or chilled, garnished with sprigs of watercress.

QUICK MONGOLE SOUP

Rich, delicious blend of flavors.

Combine equal amounts of condensed Pea Soup and Tomato Soup. Add top milk to give desired consistency. Heat and flavor to taste with salt and paprika. To each serving, a tbsp. sherry flavoring may be added. Sprinkle with grated cheese.

CREAM OF AVOCADO SOUP

A delicate, distinctive luncheon soup.

Blend a coarsely grated pared and seeded avocado into about 2 cups of Cream of Chicken Soup. Season to taste and add a dash of nutmeg, if desired. Heat and serve at once.

TOMATO-CELERY SOUP

Heat together equal amounts of condensed Tomato Soup and Celery Soup. Blend in an equal amount of top milk or soup stock, or half of each. Add minced parsley or chives. Season to taste. Serve hot.

CABBAGE PATCH SOUP

Different and delicious.

Boil together uncovered 3 min., stirring occasionally . . .

- **3 cups chopped cabbage**
- **¼ cup diced onion**
- **1 tsp. salt**
- **4 cups Split Pea Soup**

Add . . .

- **1 can condensed Tomato Soup**
- **⅛ tsp. pepper**

Reheat and serve at once.

AMOUNT: 6 servings.

MADRILENE

Heat together equal amounts Consommé or Bouillon, Chicken Broth, and tomato juice. Garnish with lemon slice, serve.

A Happily Chosen Main Dish Makes The Meal

FOR a cozy fireside supper . . . bridge luncheon . . . club gathering . . . neighborhood buffet . . . or the homey evening meal with the family. Prepare one delicious main dish—and it's easy to complete the menu.

Betty Crocker

Homey Hospitality

Gourmet Specialties

Cozy Family Dishes

To Celebrate the Holidays

Simple Serving for Large Groups

For Meatless Days

True One-Dish Meals

For Elegant Buffet Suppers

Economy Dishes (low in meat)

Hurry-Up Specialties

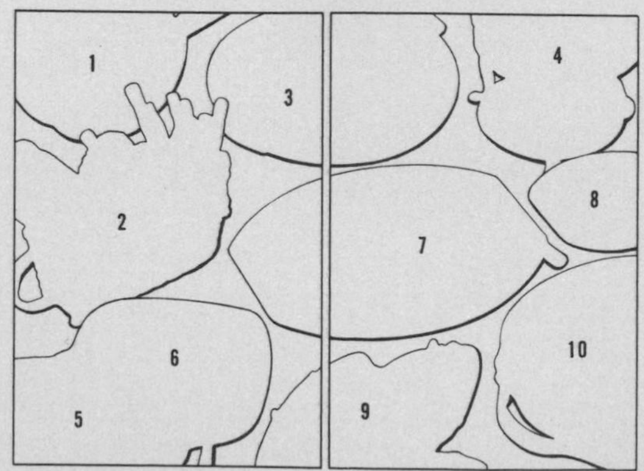

Where to find recipes for Supper Dishes in color photograph, pp. 378, 379

1. Tossed Green Salad.
2. French Bread. Bread Sticks.
3. Spaghetti with Meat Balls 385
4. Welsh Rarebit 393
5. Fluffy Boiled Rice 387
6. Sub-Gum 388
7. Sausages, Tomato Slices with Anchovy Fillets, Toast . . . for Welsh Rarebit.
8. Individual Serving of Welsh Rarebit.
9. Assorted Sweet Pickles.
10. Hot Tamale Pie 391

SUPPER AND LUNCHEON DISHES

SOME SUNDAY EVENING

Welsh Rarebit
with
Tomato Slices, Anchovies, and Gherkins
Chilled Pears Chocolate Cupcakes
Coffee Milk Tea

FOR GOURMET GUESTS

Avocado with Lemon Ice
Pompano en Papillote
Green Salad French Bread
Baked Alaska
Coffee Milk

A ONE-DISH MEAL

Hot Tamale Pie
Crisp Vegetable Salad Crusty Rolls
Fresh Fruit Butterscotch Cookies
Coffee Milk

FOR MEATLESS DAYS

Cheese Soufflé with Mushroom Sauce
Tomato-Lettuce Salad Crusty Currant Buns
Fresh Strawberry Shortcake
Coffee Milk

COZY FAMILY SUPPER

Ring of Plenty
with
Creamed Tuna and Peas in Center
Wheaties Muffins Garden Salad
Baked Pink Rhubarb Crisp Sugar Cookies
Coffee Milk

LAST-MINUTE FARE

Lumberjack Macaroni
Individual Lettuce Cups filled with
Chopped Fresh Vegetable Salad
Popovers
Fruit Sauce Chocolate-Frosted Brownies
Coffee Milk

HOMEY HOSPITALITY

Spicy Tomato Cocktail
Veal Paprika over
Noodles with Almonds and Poppy Seeds
Jelly Hot Rolls Pickles
Corn-on-the-Cob
Salad of Melon Balls, Sweet Green Grapes,
and Bing Cherries
Ginger Cream Roll
Coffee Milk

AN ELEGANT BUFFET

Curried Shrimp in Green Rice Ring
Herb Bread
Lettuce Cups holding Bits of Bright Red
Tomato, Pale Green Cucumber, Radish Discs,
and Little Green Onions
with French Dressing
Lemon Parfait with Crushed Raspberries
Angel Food de Luxe
Coffee Other Beverages

MACARONI SUPPER DISHES A food with a history.

There are many romantic stories about the origin of Macaroni. Some say that Marco Polo discovered it in the 13th century on one of his exploring expeditions to China. Others say that it was the Germans who first imported macaroni to Europe from China . . . and taught the Italians the art of making it. At any rate, it had become so popular in Italy by the 13th century that Emperor Frederick II. coined the name "macaroni" from "marcus," meaning "divine dish." Its introduction into the United States has been traced back to the 16th century, the time of the exploits of Spanish explorers. But it really became an important food in our country with the influx of Italians following the Civil War. The finest macaroni products are made from durum semolina.

BOILED MACARONI, SPAGHETTI, AND NOODLES

They may be used interchangeably in soups, in place of potato, and in a casserole.

1 For 8 or 9-oz. (1 pkg.) macaroni or spaghetti, or 5 or 6-oz. (1 pkg.) noodles, add 1 tbsp. salt to 3 qt. rapidly boiling water in *deep* kettle.

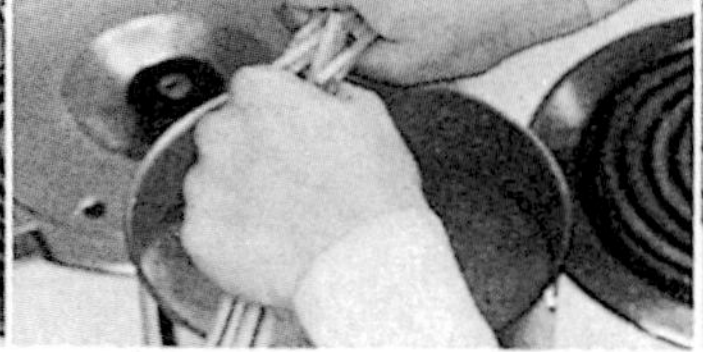

2 Break macaroni or spaghetti, or noodles into pieces of desired length (1½" to 2½") and drop in gradually to let the water keep boiling.

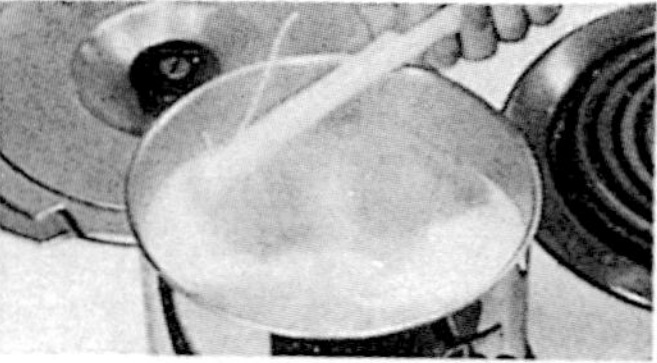

3 If sticks are left whole, place one end in water and as sticks soften, gradually coil them around in kettle until the whole length submerges.

4 Cook, uncovered, at fast boil, stirring occasionally with long fork to prevent sticking.

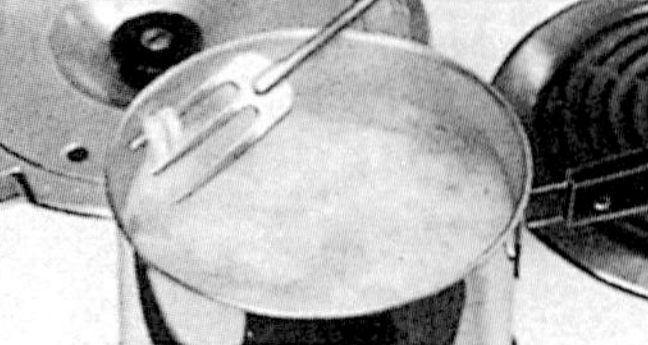

5 Cook just until tender (9 to 12 min.). Test by cutting piece with fork against kettle.

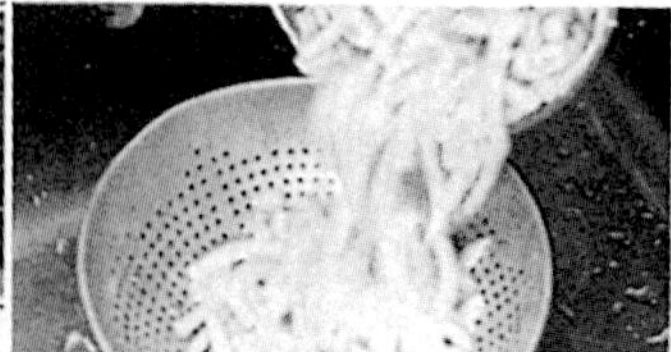

6 Drain quickly in colander. No rinsing necessary if to be reheated with sauce, etc.

A HELPFUL GUIDE

1 cup uncooked macaroni, or spaghetti	=4 oz.
1 cup broken spaghetti	=5 oz.
1 cup noodles, broken	=2½ oz.

MORE FOR LESS

Macaroni and Spaghetti double in bulk in cooking. Noodles swell scarcely at all (only about one-fourth).

HOMEMADE NOODLES

Beat until very light . . .
- **3 egg yolks**
- **1 whole egg**

Beat in . . .
- **3 tbsp. cold water**
- **1 tsp. salt**

Stir in and work in with hands . . .
- **2 cups *sifted* GOLD MEDAL Flour**

Divide dough into 3 parts. Roll out each piece as *thin as possible* (paper thin) on lightly floured cloth-covered board. Place between 2 towels until dough is partially dry (like chamois skin). Roll up dough as for jelly roll. With a thin sharp knife cut into strips of desired width (⅛" for fine noodles, up to ½" for broad noodles). Shake out the strips and allow to dry before using or storing. *6 cups or 10 oz.*

PIONEER MACARONI AND CHEESE (Recipe) *The simplest kind of dish.*

Place in alternating layers in buttered 12x7½x2″ baking dish...
- Boiled Macaroni (8 oz. uncooked) (*p. 380*)
- dots of butter (2 tbsp. in all)
- 1¼ cups cut-up sharp cheese (½″ cubes) (⅓ lb.)
- salt (¾ tsp. in all)
- pepper (¼ tsp. in all)
- 2 cups milk

Sprinkle with... paprika

Bake until golden brown on top. Serve hot from baking dish . . . garnished, if desired, with parsley sprigs, pimiento strips, pepper rings, etc.

TEMPERATURE: 350° (mod. oven).

TIME: Bake 40 min.

AMOUNT: 6 to 8 servings.

CREAMY MACARONI 'N CHEESE

Follow recipe above—*except* use 2 cups Medium White Sauce in place of the milk and seasonings.

EARLY AMERICAN MACARONI

Follow recipe above—*except* dissolve 2 bouillon cubes in the hot milk.

MACARONES CON JOCOQUI

Macaroni with sour cream.

Follow recipe above—*except,* in place of the milk, use 2½ cups sour or sweet cream. Bake 30 min.

MACARONI-TOMATO CASSEROLE

Follow recipe above—*except,* in place of the milk, use 2½ cups well seasoned cooked tomatoes. Bake 45 min. (until liquid is absorbed).

MACARONI WITH FRIED TOMATOES

Mrs. William P. Duerre, of Lake City, Minnesota, often serves this delicious and picturesque dish in her charming home near the shores of Lake Pepin.

Dip firm tomato slices (¼″ thick) into slightly beaten egg . . . then into fine cracker crumbs. Sprinkle with salt and pepper. Brown in melted butter. Remove slices and keep warm while making 2 cups Medium White Sauce in same skillet. Mix hot drained Boiled Macaroni (8 oz. uncooked) (*p. 380*) with the hot white sauce, ⅓ cup cut-up sharp cheese, and 1 tsp. salt. Heap onto hot platter, sprinkle with paprika. Surround with the pan-fried tomatoes. Add little parsley bouquets. Serve immediately.

MACARONI À LA CREME

A radio friend of Delta, Colorado, won a prize on this one-dish meal in our recipe contest.

Follow recipe above—*except* use only 4 oz. macaroni . . . boiling with it 2 finely minced large onions and 1 cup finely diced celery. In place of milk and seasonings, use 2 cups hot Medium White Sauce and ½ cup undiluted canned tomato soup. Pour into a 2-qt. casserole (8″), sprinkle with partially cooked diced bacon (2 slices) and grated cheese. Bake 20 min.

All you have to do—

To dress up leftover macaroni dishes: fill scooped-out unpeeled fresh tomatoes with mixture, and bake in mod. oven 30 min.

★ LUMBERJACK MACARONI

Mr. James Ford Bell, founder of General Mills, world traveler and epicure, actually made this dish for us himself in our test kitchen. It's one of his favorites.

Spread out on hot large platter . . .
- Boiled Macaroni (8 oz. uncooked) (*p. 380*)

Sprinkle with . . .
- 2 cups grated American cheese (½ lb.)
- 2 to 4 tbsp. Worcestershire sauce or more ("Do not be sparing!" says Mr. Bell.)
- ¼ cup chili sauce
- salt and pepper to taste

Pour over all . . .
- ¾ cup piping hot melted butter

Mix with 2 forks until sauce is creamy. Serve at once on hot plates.

AMOUNT: 6 servings.

★ **RING OF PLENTY (🔑 Recipe)** *A tonic for budget troubles . . . yet it reflects bounty. The clever idea for this custardy one-dish meal was brought to us by Mrs. Frank J. Ebsen of Wisconsin Rapids, Wisconsin.*

Boil and drain (*see p. 380*).............	**8 oz. macaroni**
Combine with........................	**2 cups hot milk** **4 tbsp. butter** **2 cups shredded American cheese (½ lb.)** **2 cups soft bread crumbs** **2 eggs, well beaten** **2 tbsp.** ***each*** **minced parsley, minced onion, and chopped pimiento** **2 tsp. salt** **¼ tsp. pepper**

Pour into well greased 10″ ring mold, set in pan of water (1″ deep). Bake until set. Unmold on hot platter; fill center with creamed seafood, chicken, or vegetable.

TEMPERATURE: 350° (mod. oven).

TIME: Bake 30 to 35 min.

AMOUNT: 8 servings.

MACARONI LOAF

Follow 🔑 recipe for Ring of Plenty above —*except* use half the amount of each ingredient and bake in 9x5x3″ loaf pan. Unmold. Serve hot with a hot sauce (Mushroom, Tomato, Seafood, etc.) or with creamed chicken, seafood, or vegetables. *Serves 6.*

MACARONI MOUSSE

Deliciously delicate loaf. Popular luncheon dish at tea rooms, bridge clubs, etc.

Pour . . .

1½ cups top milk, scalded

over . . .

1½ cups soft bread crumbs

Add . . .

4 tbsp. butter
1 finely minced pimiento
1 tbsp. minced parsley
1 tsp. onion juice
1 tsp. salt
1 cup shredded American cheese (¼ lb.)
3 egg yolks, well beaten

Combine with hot drained Boiled Macaroni (2 oz. uncooked) (*p. 380*). Fold in . . .

3 egg whites, stiffly beaten

Pour into 9x5x3″ loaf pan lined with buttered paper Set in pan of water (1″ deep). Bake . . . keeping covered with paper first 20 min. Unmold on hot platter and serve hot with hot Mushroom Sauce.

TEMPERATURE: 350° (mod. oven).

TIME: Bake 1 hr.

AMOUNT: 6 servings.

All you have to do—

To Make a Casserole of Plenty: make half the recipe of Ring of Plenty and bake in a 1½-qt. casserole (7½″).

CHICKEN TETRAZZINI

A simplified version of this elegant dish. Perfect for buffet suppers. Often served by Genevieve Callahan and Lou Richardson of San Francisco in their apartment on Russian Hill where guests enjoy two charming hostesses, sprightly conversation, and the glorious view of bay and bridges.

Cook until brown and crisp . . .

2 slices bacon, finely cut

Add and brown lightly in the bacon fat . . .

⅓ cup minced onion
½ cup minced green pepper

Add . . .

2 cups shredded American cheese (½ lb.)
¼ cup cut-up pimiento
¼ cup toasted shaved almonds
1¾ cups cooked peas
2 cups cut-up cooked chicken

Mix lightly with hot drained Boiled Macaroni (8 oz. uncooked) (*p. 380*). Heat . . . using chicken broth to moisten. Serve hot on chop plate garnished with tomato slices, parsley, and ripe olives.

AMOUNT: 8 servings.

Flavorful Meat Sauces add Zest!

Make sauce as directed in each recipe and pour over hot drained Boiled Macaroni (8 oz. uncooked) (*p. 380*) on hot platter. Sprinkle with grated sharp American or Parmesan cheese. Serve immediately. *Serves 6 to 8.*

HOME FRONT MACARONI

Developed by our Staff in the days of rationing to make a little meat go a long way.

Cook until yellow in 1 tsp. hot fat . . .
1 cup minced onion
Add and cook until brown . . .
½ lb. bulk sausage or well seasoned ground beef
Add and simmer 45 min. . . .
2½ cups cooked tomatoes (#2 can)
1 cup diced celery
¾ cup minced green pepper
1 tsp. Worcestershire sauce
2 tsp. salt
½ tsp. pepper

In Restaurants in Florence, Italy

According to Margaret Spader of our Staff, "a pat of parsley butter is always placed on each individual serving of a macaroni or spaghetti dish the last thing. As the butter melts, it combines with the hot sauce to give a delicious blend of flavors."

MONDAY MACARONI

Sunday leftovers in an easy and delicious dish for Monday's dinner.

Cook until yellow in 2 tbsp. hot butter and 1 tbsp. hot olive oil . . .
2 minced onions
Add and cook 5 min. . . .
1 cup finely chopped cooked meat
Add and let simmer 15 min. . . .
1 small can tomato purée or soup
2 tsp. minced parsley
bit of bay leaf
Add . . .
1 cup cooked vegetable
1 cup meat stock

★ YANKEE DOODLE MACARONI

About the time of our Revolutionary War, there was a group of young dandies in London who were called "Macaronis." They were the fops of that period, and adopted the title of "Macaroni" because it signified elegance. So when Yankee Doodle called his feather "Macaroni," he was assuring himself that it was elegant.

Cook until onions are yellow in 3 tbsp. hot fat . . .
2 cups minced onion
2 minced cloves of garlic
¾ cup sliced mushrooms, if desired
Add and cook until brown . . .
1 lb. ground beef
Add and boil gently until thickened (about 45 min.) . . .
3½ cups cooked tomatoes (#2½ can)
1 tbsp. minced parsley
1 tbsp. salt
⅛ tsp. pepper

ITALIAN MACARONI

The Italian serves macaroni or spaghetti with chicken and chicken livers in many delightful dishes. This is one of the most practical.

Cook until yellow in 2 tbsp. hot butter . . .
4 tbsp. minced onion
Add and cook slowly 10 min. . . .
¾ lb. beef or chicken liver, chopped
1 tbsp. minced parsley
2 tsp. salt
⅛ tsp. pepper
dash of garlic salt
few drops Worcestershire sauce
Add and let simmer 20 min. . . .
2 cups sieved tomatoes (purée)

SPAGHETTI SUPPER DISHES There's a sauce for every taste.

Spaghetti, favorite food of Italy, differs from macaroni only in shape . . . the tubes being much tinier. Travelers in Europe bring back memories of fascinating glimpses of great racks of spaghetti drying in the hot sun on the sandy shores of the Mediterranean between Naples and Amalfi. "They look almost like vineyards," one traveler said, ". . . row after row of wooden posts . . . only with skeins of spaghetti wound 'round and 'round them."

MEATLESS ITALIAN SPAGHETTI

Simple. Satisfying. Men like to make it. It doesn't take too much time . . . just mix and stir, add, taste, and add a bit of something else if desired.

Prepare	**desired sauce (*see below*)**
Pour over	**hot drained Boiled Spaghetti (8 oz. uncooked) (*p. 380*) on hot platter**
Sprinkle with	**grated Parmesan or Roman Italian cheese**

Serve immediately.

AMOUNT: 6 to 8 servings.

MARINARA SAUCE (🔑 Recipe)

Simmer about 1 hr. in heavy skillet . . .

- **1/4 cup olive oil**
- **1 clove garlic, minced**
- **2 tbsp. minced parsley**
- **1 tsp. salt**
- **1/4 tsp. pepper**
- **3 1/2 cups cooked tomatoes (#2 1/2 can)**
- **1 green pepper, minced**
- **dash of red pepper**

MILD TOMATO SAUCE

Follow 🔑 recipe above—*except* omit green pepper and red pepper, and add 1/3 cup minced onion, 1/3 cup finely cut celery, 1 bay leaf, and 1 tsp. sugar.

SPICY TOMATO SAUCE

Follow method for Marinara Sauce. Use:

- **1/3 cup olive oil**
- **1 cup minced onion**
- **1/2 cup minced leeks or green onions**
- **2 tbsp. minced parsley**
- **1 tsp. salt**
- **1/4 tsp. pepper**
- **8 drops tabasco sauce**
- **1 tsp. Worcestershire sauce**
- **2 cups catsup**

★ SPAGHETTI VALHALLA

Sprinkle 2 cups grated sharp cheese over hot drained Boiled Spaghetti (8 oz. uncooked) in 12x7 1/2x2" baking dish. On top, place alternately 1 lb. little pork sausages (parboiled 10 min., then browned) and 12 tomato slices. Season with salt and pepper. Pour 1/2 cup water over top. Bake at 350° (mod. oven) 35 min. *Serves 6.*

TOMATO AND CELERY SAUCE

Cook together 15 min. . . .

- **2 cups cooked tomatoes (#1 tall can)**
- **1 onion, sliced**
- **1/2 cup finely cut celery**

and rub through sieve.

In saucepan, melt . . .

- **2 tbsp. butter**

Blend in . . .

- **2 tbsp. flour**
- **1/4 tsp. salt**
- **1/8 tsp. pepper**

Remove from heat and stir in the hot tomato juice. Cook until thick.

CONCORDIA SPAGHETTI

The absence of meat does not lessen the satisfying appeal of this pretty red-and-green-topped supper dish. First made in our kitchen by Ruth Hitzhusen (now Mrs. Milton Hult of Chicago) when she was on our Staff.

Stir . . .

- **1/2 cup shredded American cheese**
- **1/4 cup minced green pepper**
- **1/4 cup minced pimiento**
- **3 hard-cooked eggs, chopped**

into . . .

- **2 cups Medium White Sauce**

Mix gently with . . .

- **hot drained Boiled Spaghetti (4 oz. uncooked) (*p. 380*)**

Pour into buttered 1-qt. casserole (6 1/2"). Bake until golden brown on top. Serve hot from casserole . . . the top sprinkled with sliced stuffed olives (1/4 cup).

TEMPERATURE: 350° (mod. oven).

TIME: Bake 30 min.

AMOUNT: 6 servings.

★ HOLIDAY SPAGHETTI

From a famous movie star whose wife often serves it at their informal supper parties.

Cook until onions are yellow in 3 tbsp. hot drippings . . .

- 1 cup minced onion
- ¾ cup minced green pepper
- 1 cup sliced mushrooms

Add and cook until browned . . .

- 1 lb. ground beef

Then add and heat . . .

- 2 tsp. salt
- 1 tsp. sugar
- 3½ cups cooked tomatoes (#2½ can)
- hot drained Boiled Spaghetti (8 oz. uncooked) (*p. 380*)

Pour into well greased 2-qt. casserole (8″). Sprinkle with grated sharp cheese. Bake. Serve hot . . . garnished with crisp bacon and parsley bouquets.

TEMPERATURE: 350° (mod. oven).

TIME: Bake 30 min.

AMOUNT: 8 servings.

SPAGHETTI ORIENTAL

Cook until browned in 1 tsp. hot drippings . . .

- ½ lb. ground beef
- ½ lb. ground pork

Add and cook 10 min. . . .

- 1 small onion, minced
- 1 cup diced celery
- 1½ cups drained Chinese vegetables (sprouts, sweet peppers, mushrooms, bamboo shoots, and water chestnuts) (#2 can) or a mixture of chopped green peppers, mushrooms, and cooked kidney beans

Then mix with hot drained Boiled Spaghetti (4 oz. uncooked) (*p. 380*).

Add and simmer 30 min. . . .

- 2 cups tomato soup
- ½ cup water or liquor drained from Chinese vegetables
- ¾ cup shredded sharp cheese
- 1½ tsp. salt

Or place in buttered 1½-qt. casserole (7½″) and bake. Serve hot.

TEMPERATURE: 350° (mod. oven).

TIME: Bake 45 min.

AMOUNT: 6 servings.

SPAGHETTI WITH MEAT BALLS

Mix and form into 1½″ balls . . .

- ¾ lb. ground beef
- ¼ lb. ground pork
- 1 cup fine dry bread crumbs
- ½ cup grated Parmesan cheese
- 1 tbsp. minced parsley
- 2 small cloves garlic, cut fine
- ½ cup milk
- 2 eggs, beaten
- 1½ tsp. salt
- ⅛ tsp. pepper

Pan-fry until browned in 4 tbsp. hot fat . . .

- 1 cup minced onion
- the meat balls

Blend in . . .

- 2 tbsp. flour

Then add and simmer about 1 hr. . . .

- 5 cups cooked tomatoes (2 #2 cans)
- 6 tbsp. minced parsley
- 6 tbsp. minced green pepper
- 2½ tsp. salt
- ¼ tsp. pepper
- 3 tsp. sugar
- 2 small bay leaves, crumbled
- 1 tsp. Worcestershire sauce

Serve hot over hot drained Boiled Spaghetti (8 oz. uncooked) (*p. 380*) on hot platter. Sprinkle with grated sharp cheese.

AMOUNT: 6 servings.

Every Italian dinner table—has its little sugar bowl-like dish of finely grated cheese.

SPAGHETTI, ITALIAN STYLE

From that sunny land across the sea.

Cook until browned in 2 tbsp. hot olive oil . . .

- 1 lb. ground beef or beef and pork

Add and simmer slowly ½ to 1 hr. (long cooking improves flavor) . . .

- 3½ cups cooked tomatoes (#2½ can)
- 2 cloves garlic, finely cut
- 1 bay leaf, crumbled
- 1 tsp. salt
- ⅛ tsp. black pepper

Pour over hot drained Boiled Spaghetti (1 lb. uncooked) (*p. 380*) on hot platter. Sprinkle with grated Parmesan cheese.

AMOUNT: 12 servings.

Noodles, the German version of macaroni, are made of a similar dough enriched with eggs, or egg yolks. They are usually in the form of long, flat ribbons . . . or sometimes letters of the alphabet.

NOODLES WITH BROWNED CRUMBS

Handed down from the early German settlers of Pennsylvania who brought this recipe with them from the old country.

Heat 4 tbsp. butter in heavy skillet.
Add and leave over low heat, stirring frequently, until lightly browned . . .
1 cup fine dry bread crumbs

Add drained hot Boiled Noodles (5 to 6 oz. uncooked) (*p. 380*) . . . gently mixing crumbs through noodles. Heap on hot platter. Sprinkle with minced parsley. Serve piping hot . . . with pot roast and gravy, wieners and sauerkraut, or baked pork chops and gravy, etc.

AMOUNT: 8 to 10 servings.

NOODLE RING

"My boys loved this filled with creamed chicken for Sunday supper for their friends!" says Mildred Stewart Sumner of our Staff.

Mix together gently . . .
3 eggs, lightly beaten
1 tsp. salt
1/8 tsp. pepper
3/4 cup milk
1 tbsp. butter, melted
drained hot Boiled Noodles (10 to 12 oz. uncooked) (*p. 380*)

Place in well buttered 10″ ring mold. Set in pan of water (1″ deep). Bake until silver knife plunged into center comes out clean. Unmold; fill center with hot creamed chicken, seafood, etc. Serve immediately.

TEMPERATURE: 350° (mod. oven).

TIME: Bake 45 min.

AMOUNT: 6 to 8 servings.

★ SCALLOPED SALMON, ALMONDS, AND NOODLES

For years a delightful specialty in a famous tea room in Minneapolis.

Gently mix flaked salmon, toasted cut-up almonds, salt, and pepper with drained hot boiled noodles. Place in buttered casserole. Cover with Medium White Sauce. Sprinkle with WHEATIES. Bake at 350° (mod. oven) 20 min. Serve hot.

NOODLES WITH ALMONDS AND POPPY SEEDS

Often served with Veal Paprika as the main dish of "a supper to remember" by Ruth M. Skinner of Chicago.

Stir over low heat until lightly browned in 1 tsp. butter, melted, in heavy skillet . . .
1/2 cup blanched almonds, cut-up
Add and stir gently until heated through . . .
3 tbsp. butter
drained hot Boiled Noodles (5 to 6 oz. uncooked) (*p. 380*)
2 tsp. poppy seeds

Arrange around edge of serving platter and pour seafood or meat in gravy in center. Garnish with parsley bouquets.

AMOUNT: 6 to 8 servings.

SAVORY NOODLE GOULASH

Called her "30 minute dinner" by Mrs. Elmer Anderson of Nekoosa, Wisconsin.

Cook until browned in 1 tbsp. hot fat . . .
3/4 lb. ground pork, beef, and veal (or 3/4 lb. pork or beef alone)
Add and cook 10 min. . . .
2 small onions, minced
2 cups diced celery
Gently mix in . . .
drained hot Boiled Noodles (5 to 6 oz. uncooked) (*p. 380*)
2 cups cooked tomatoes (#1 tall can)
3/4 cup shredded cheese
1 tsp. salt
dash of pepper

Simmer 30 min. Or place in buttered 2-qt. casserole (8″) and bake. Serve hot.

TEMPERATURE: 350° (mod. oven).

TIME: Bake 45 min.

AMOUNT: 8 servings.

NOODLES ROMANOFF

Mix together gently . . .
1 cup cottage cheese
1 cup sour cream
2 cups drained hot Boiled Noodles (5 to 6 oz. uncooked) (*p. 380*)

Season with minced onion, garlic, a little Worcestershire sauce, a dash of tabasco sauce, 1/2 tsp. salt. Place in greased 2-qt. casserole (8″). Sprinkle with grated cheese Bake at 350° (mod. oven) 40 min. Serve hot. *Serves 6.*

Rice is sometimes called "the food of the ages" . . . for it is as old as history. Twenty-eight hundred years before Christ, a Chinese emperor, Chin Nung, established a ceremonial custom of serving it. From Asia to Europe to America, rice cultivation has spread until rice rivals wheat as the world's most important food.

BOILED RICE . . . WHITE OR BROWN *1 cup cooks to 3 cups.*

First of all, wash 1 cup rice in sieve under cold water or in several waters in bowl, rubbing between hands and rinsing until water is not cloudy.

1 Drop washed rice gradually into 2 qt. boiling (*keep it boiling*) salted water (1 tbsp. salt).

2 Boil rapidly (lift to prevent "sticking") until tender (15 to 25 min.). Test by pinching.

3 Drain; run boiling water through to separate kernels.

4 Cover with cloth, set over boiling water until fluffy.

To make rice extra white, add 2 tbsp. lemon juice to water before boiling it.

HOW TO USE BOILED RICE: (1) in soups; (2) in place of potatoes; or (3) in a main dish. (*See following pages.*)

CURRIED RICE

With creamed shrimp, chicken, or ham, it's a highlight at buffet suppers.

Cook 1 tbsp. minced onion in 2 tbsp. butter until yellow. Gently stir in 3 cups fluffy Boiled Rice, ¼ tsp. salt, ¼ tsp. pepper, 1 tsp. curry powder. Serve hot with any meat or seafood cooked in a sauce. *Serves 6 to 8.*

BROWNED RICE (Risotto)

Distinctive and piquant flavor. Harold Hansen of Kentfield, California, likes to cook this for outdoor suppers, enjoyed by family and guests in the shadows of Mt. Tamalpais.

Cook until yellow in 4 tbsp. butter in heavy skillet, 1 cup drained washed rice. Stir in 4 cups Chicken Broth or Consommé (flavored with onion or garlic, herbs, salt, and paprika). Mr. Hansen adds diced Italian mushrooms (to taste) soaked overnight. Cover. Simmer without stirring until rice is dry, flaky (25 min.). Serve hot as a meat accompaniment. *Serves 6.*

★ GREEN RICE

One of the grand contributions of Abbie Reed Boutell (Mrs. R. E.) when she was one of our Staff. "Guests at our home in the country like it extra well with baked ham," she says.

Prepare . . .
3 cups fluffy Boiled Rice
Carefully stir in . . .
2 eggs, well beaten
1 cup milk
¼ cup butter
¼ cup grated sharp cheese
½ tbsp. grated onion
⅓ cup minced parsley
⅔ cup minced spinach
1 tsp. Worcestershire sauce
1¼ tsp. salt

Pour into greased and floured 2-qt. casserole (8″). Bake at 325° (slow mod. oven) about 45 min. Serve hot with meat, fish, or vegetable. *Serves 8.*

Curries from the Far East

Serve these and other favorites (*below*) over mounds or in nests of hot fluffy Boiled Rice (*p. 387*). Each recipe serves 6.

BEEF CURRY

Margarett Bradt Southmayd of Vesta, Minnesota, a friend who has given encouragement through the years, suggests this dish for church and community gatherings.

Frizzle in 2 tbsp. butter until edges curl . . .
¼ lb. cut-up dried beef
Add . . .
½ tsp. curry powder
5 cups Medium White Sauce (no salt in white sauce)

Heat to boiling.

CHICKEN CURRY

For a glamorous buffet . . . an East Indian dish.

7 little dishes of relishes around the platter of chicken and bowl of fluffy rice: sieved hard-cooked eggs, India relish, chopped salted peanuts, chutney, pickled onions, grated fresh coconut, crumbled crisp bacon, sautéed bananas.

Stew chicken until tender in water with celery tops, onion, and carrots. Remove tough skin, flour the nicest pieces, such as legs and breasts (divided into 2 or 3 pieces). Brown them in butter and set aside to serve on a platter or in the gravy. To pan, add freshly chopped garlic, onion, and tart apple . . . cooking until tender. Mix in salt, pepper, flour, curry powder . . . add milk and chicken broth to make a creamy gravy. Cook, stirring until thickened. Take rest of chicken from bones and add to gravy. Cook 30 min. to blend flavors.

To Serve: each guest goes around table, places a quarter of sautéed banana on his plate, on top of it a mound of rice, and spoons curried chicken on rice,—then sprinkles a little of each relish over top.

SUB-GUM

m leftovers.

Brown in 1 tbsp. fat in hot skillet . . .
½ cup sliced mushrooms
2 cups cubed leftover roast pork or veal
Add, cover, and simmer 30 min. . . .
2 cups diced celery
1½ cups *well seasoned* leftover gravy
1 tsp. salt
dash of pepper
Add and heat . . .
2½ cups bean sprouts (#2 can), drained

★ CURRIED SHRIMP

Especially elegant in a ring of Green Rice.

Just before serving, blend . . .
1½ tsp. lemon juice or sherry flavoring
2 cups cooked shrimp (14 oz.)
into . . .
3 cups hot Curry Sauce

> CAUTION: *When using uncooked (green) shrimp, cook in the sauce only until pink (10 min.).*

CREOLE SHRIMP

Prize recipe from Mrs. R. E. Smith of Redgate Plantation, Jeanerette, Louisiana.

Cook in 2 tbsp. butter until yellow . . .
½ cup minced onion
Blend in . . .
2 tbsp. flour
1 bay leaf, crushed
¼ cup diced celery
1 tsp. minced parsley
½ cup minced green pepper
dash of cayenne
¼ tsp. pepper sauce
½ tsp. salt
1 6¼-oz. can tomato paste
3 cups water
Cook slowly, stirring occasionally, until thickened (30 min.). Stir in . . .
2 cups cooked shrimp (14 oz.)

CURRIED LAMB OR VEAL

Simplified curry made with leftover meat.

Make Special Curry Sauce by blending 3 tbsp. minced onion and 1 tsp. curry powder into the fat when making each cup of meat gravy. Add browned cooked meat cut in small pieces.

★ FRENCH PILAU

Old-time masterpiece from South Carolina.

Place in one kettle . . .
- a stewed 4- to 5-lb. chicken (cut in serving pieces)
- just enough broth to reheat chicken (about 1½ cups)

Place in another kettle . . .
- about 6 cups chicken broth
- 1 cup washed uncooked rice

Boil slowly until rice is tender (*p. 387*). Drain. Save broth for chicken. Mix into rice . . .
- 1 cup Sultana (white) raisins
- ½ cup toasted split blanched almonds
- ½ tsp. curry powder
- 1 tsp. salt
- ⅛ tsp. pepper

Place in large serving bowl. Place chicken, with well seasoned broth, in soup tureen or deep dish. Serve rice in shallow soup dish. Ladle pieces of hot chicken with broth over rice.

AMOUNT: 8 servings.

TUNA-STUFFED EGGS ON RICE

Spoon into a greased 12x7½x2″ baking dish 3 cups fluffy Boiled Rice (*p. 387*). Place Tuna-Stuffed Eggs (add flaked tuna to yolk mixture when making Deviled Eggs) in slight depressions in the rice. Sprinkle with sieved hard-cooked egg yolk. Cover. Heat in slow mod. oven 15 min. Serve hot with hot Curry Sauce.

AMOUNT: 6 servings.

SPANISH RICE

Easy-to-prepare, homey supper dish.

Cook until yellow in 4 tbsp. hot butter . . .
- 1 onion, minced
- 1 green pepper, minced
- ¼ cup diced celery

Add and cook slowly 15 min. . . .
- 2 cups cooked tomatoes (#1 tall can)
- 2 tsp. salt
- ⅛ tsp. pepper

Gently stir in hot drained Boiled Rice (1 cup uncooked) (*p. 387*) and cook 5 min. longer. Serve hot . . . sprinkled with grated cheese or crumbled crisp bacon.

AMOUNT: 8 servings.

TEXAS HASH

One of the popular supper dishes served by Janette Kelley at her hundred year old home in Marine-on-the-St. Croix, Minnesota. The recipe was given to her by a Texas friend.

Cook in 3 tbsp. fat until onions are yellow . . .
- 3 large onions, sliced
- 1 large green pepper, minced

Add and fry until mixture falls apart . . .
- 1 lb. ground beef

Stir in . . .
- 2 cups cooked tomatoes (#1 tall can)
- 1 cup washed uncooked rice (or 2 cups uncooked noodles)
- 1 tsp. chili powder
- 2 tsp. salt
- ⅛ tsp. pepper

Pour into greased 2-qt. casserole (8″). Cover, and bake . . . removing cover last 15 min. Serve hot.

TEMPERATURE: 350° (mod. oven).

TIME: Bake 1 hr.

AMOUNT: 6 servings.

All you have to do—

To make a Rice Ring: lightly press 2 cups fluffy Boiled Rice (⅔ cup uncooked) (*p. 387*) into well greased 10″ ring mold. Keep hot until time to serve. Unmold on hot platter and fill center with creamed seafood or chicken and mushrooms. Serve hot. *Serves 8 to 10.*

AMERICAN CHOP SUEY

Chinese favorite . . . United States style.

Brown in hot fat . . .
- ½ to 1 lb. lean pork or veal, cut in small pieces
- 1 onion, sliced

Add . . .
- 2 cups cut-up celery
- 1 small green pepper, minced
- ¾ cup washed uncooked rice
- 5 cups meat stock (or 10 bouillon cubes dissolved in 5 cups boiling water)
- 1 to 2 tsp. salt
- ⅛ tsp. pepper
- 1 to 2 tbsp. chop suey sauce

Cover, simmer 40 min. Uncover last 10 min. Serve hot . . . in shallow bowls.

AMOUNT: 6 servings.

WILD RICE SUPPER DISHES Choice of epicures.

Wild rice does not resemble cultivated rice, either white or brown. It is the seed of a shallow water grass . . . still harvested by Indians in the marshes of Minnesota. Its grains are long, spindly, grayish in color. A special delicacy with wild duck or pheasant . . . or as stuffing for pork . . . or as in dishes below.

BOILED WILD RICE *1 cup uncooked wild rice equals 3 cups cooked.*

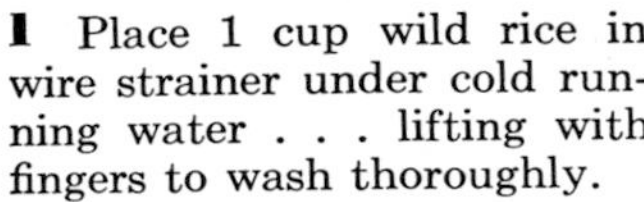

1 Place 1 cup wild rice in wire strainer under cold running water . . . lifting with fingers to wash thoroughly.

2 Soak 1 hr. in warm water to cover . . . to soften the bran coating (most of water will be absorbed).

3 Place with 2 cups boiling water, 4 tbsp. butter, 2 tsp. salt in top of double boiler. Cover, cook (about 2 hr.).

FLUFFY DRY WILD RICE *Our thanks to Lelia McClelland, Minneapolis for this method.*

Cover with cold water. Bring *just to* boil. Drain. Repeat 3 times. Add salt to fourth water, boil until soft. Drain. Cover with towel, let stand in sieve over hot water.

★KAEDJERE

American Indian version of a fish-and-rice dish from far-away India.

Lightly toss together with fork . . .
- **1 cup hot drained Boiled Wild Rice**
- **1 cup tuna (7-oz. can), flaked**
- **½ cup sautéed sliced mushrooms**
- **2 tbsp. minced green pepper**
- **2 tbsp. minced pimiento**
- **whites of 2 hard-cooked eggs, diced**

Gently blend in . . .
- **2 cups Curry Sauce**

Pour into buttered 12x7½x2″ baking dish. Sprinkle with sieved yolks of 2 hard-cooked eggs. Bake. Just before serving, dribble melted butter over top. Sprinkle with split salted almonds.

TEMPERATURE: 350° (mod. oven).
TIME: Bake 30 min.
AMOUNT: 6 servings.

WILD RICE-TUNA RING

Glamorous. Delectable.

Lightly pack into buttered ring mold:
- **layer of cooked wild rice**
- **layer of tuna (large chunks)**
- **another layer of cooked wild rice**

Dot with butter. Set mold in pan of water (1″ deep). Bake at 325° 15 min. Unmold. Serve with sautéed sliced mushrooms. Garnish with pimiento strips.

OYSTERS, HOLIDAY STYLE

A Christmas Eve favorite. And a tasty, sophisticated dish for any fall and winter supper. Perfected by Marguerite Truesdale (Mrs. Clark Truesdale of Glencoe, Minnesota) when she was a member of our Staff.

Brown lightly in 4 tbsp. hot butter . . .
- **½ cup minced onion**
- **2 cups chopped celery**

Stir in . . .
- **3 tbsp. GOLD MEDAL Flour**
- **½ cup milk**
- **3 cups hot drained Boiled Wild Rice**
- **½ tsp. salt**
- **¼ tsp. sage**
- **⅛ tsp. *each* thyme and pepper**

Place in 12x7½x2″ baking dish.

Dip into 4 tbsp. butter, melted . . .
- **1 pt. well drained small oysters**

Sprinkle with . . .
- **¼ cup cracker or dry bread crumbs**

Arrange over top of rice. Sprinkle with any crumbs and butter remaining from coating oysters. Place just low enough under broiler to keep crumbs from burning. Broil just until oysters curl (10 min.). Serve hot . . . with hot Mushroom Sauce.

AMOUNT: 6 to 8 servings.

Christmas Eve Supper: Oysters, Holiday Style. Crusty Rolls. Fruit Salad Bowl. Fruit Cake. Demitasse. Other Beverage.

HOT TAMALE PIE

Picturesque dish from Old Mexico.

Cook in 1 tbsp. butter until golden brown . . .

1 medium-sized onion, minced
1 green pepper, minced

Remove from skillet. Add and brown . . .

¾ lb. ground pork
¾ lb. ground beef

Add and simmer 20 min. . . .

the browned onion and pepper
2 cups cooked tomatoes (# 1 tall can)
2 to 3 tsp. chili powder
2 tsp. salt
½ tsp. pepper
½ cup ripe olives, sliced

Line bottom and sides of 2-qt. casserole (8″) with Corn Meal Mush (*below*). Pour in hot meat mixture. Top with remaining Corn Meal Mush. Bake. Serve hot.

TEMPERATURE: 375° (quick mod. oven).

TIME: Bake 1 hr.

AMOUNT: 8 servings.

All you have to do –

TO MAKE CORN MEAL MUSH: mix 1 cup cold water with 1 cup corn meal. Stir in 3 cups boiling water, 1 tsp. salt. Cook, stirring constantly, until mixture boils. Cover, cook over boiling water 30 min., stirring occasionally.

MUSHROOM POLENTA

Mrs. Frank D. Larrabee of Hollywood, California, worked out this recipe from what the Italian-speaking cook at the Excelsior Hotel in Rome conveyed to her.

Blend into hot Corn Meal Mush (*above*) . . .

4 egg yolks, beaten
¼ cup cream
¾ cup grated Parmesan cheese (1 box) or 1 cup American cheese (¼ lb.)

Pour into greased 12x7½x2″ baking dish. When cold and firm, cut into ¾″ cubes. Place the corn meal cubes in layers in 1½-qt. casserole (7½″) . . . alternating the layers with hot medium Mushroom Sauce (3 cups) made with sautéed fresh or dried mushrooms. Sprinkle with grated cheese (2 tbsp.). Bake. Serve hot.

Mrs. Larrabee sometimes serves the Mushroom Sauce over the Polenta instead of putting it into the dish.

TEMPERATURE: 350° (mod. oven).

TIME: Bake 25 min.

AMOUNT: 8 servings.

PHILADELPHIA SCRAPPLE

Meat-filled and meat-flavored crispy fried mush from Pennsylvania Dutch cookery.

Simmer until meat is very tender (2 hr.) . . .

2 lb. lean boneless pork
2 qt. boiling salted water (2 tsp. salt)

With fork, shred the cooked pork into fine pieces. Bring to boiling 1 qt. of the stock.

Mix together . . .

1½ cups corn meal
2 cups cold water

Stir into boiling stock

Cook, stirring until thick. Add . . .

¼ tsp. pepper
¼ tsp. savory and sage, mixed
salt to taste

Stir the meat into stock and cook 5 min. Pour into buttered 9x5x3″ loaf pan. Chill, —then slice, and fry as for Fried Corn Meal Mush (*below*). Serve hot . . . plain or with butter and syrup.

AMOUNT: 8 servings.

FRIED CORN MEAL MUSH

Pack Corn Meal Mush (*see left*) into greased bread loaf pan. Cover. Chill until firm. Slice ½″ thick. Brown on each side (for crispness, first dip slices in flour). Serve hot . . . with maple syrup or jelly, to accompany bacon, ham, sausages, etc.

FRIED CORN-SAUSAGE MUSH

Add to Corn Meal Mush before chilling it, cooked sausages cut into little pieces (or pieces of crisp bacon).

★CHICKEN SPOON BREAD

Custardy, soufflé-like main dish from the South.

Combine carefully . . .

hot Corn Meal Mush (*see left above*)
3 egg yolks, well beaten
1½ tsp. salt
1 tsp. baking powder
2 tbsp. shortening
1 cup cut-up cooked chicken

Fold in . . .

3 egg whites, stiffly beaten

Pour into greased 2-qt. casserole (8″). Bake at 325° (slow mod. oven) 1 hr. Serve hot with Creamed Chicken or Mushrooms.

AMOUNT: 8 servings.

CHEESE SUPPER DISHES Always high and puffy.

CHEESE SOUFFLÉ (🗝 Recipe) *Flavorful and tempting.*

Make *Thick* White Sauce (4 tbsp. butter, 4 tbsp. flour to 1 cup milk), adding ¼ tsp. mustard and a dash of cayenne pepper with the salt and pepper.

Stir into the hot white sauce . . .
1 cup shredded sharp cheese (¼ lb.)
Remove from heat; stir in . . .
3 egg yolks, well beaten
Beat until stiff . . .
3 egg whites with
¼ tsp. cream of tartar
Fold in . . . . .
the cheese mixture

Pour into ungreased 1½-qt. casserole (7½″). For High Hat Soufflé, make groove 1″ from edge. Set casserole in pan of water (1″ deep). Bake until puffed and golden brown. Serve immediately . . . with crisp bacon or Mushroom or Shrimp Sauce.
TEMPERATURE: 350° (mod. oven).
TIME: Bake 50 to 60 min.
AMOUNT: 4 servings.

1 Stir cheese into sauce.

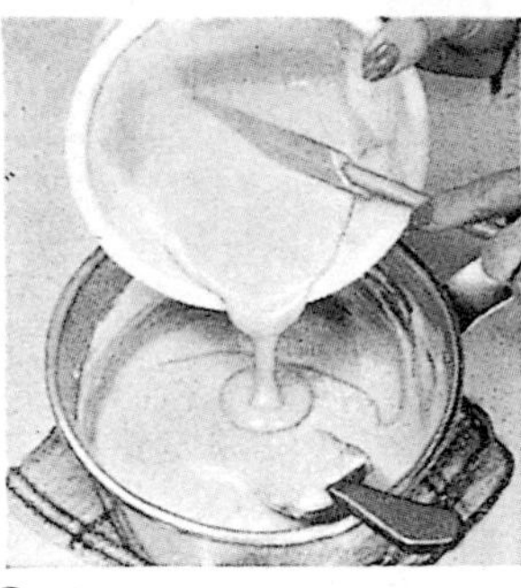
2 Stir in beaten egg yolks.

3 Fold into beaten whites.

4 Draw line around dish.

★ TOMATO-CHEESE SOUFFLÉ

A favorite at our guest luncheons served with creamed chicken or shrimp.

Follow 🗝 recipe above—*except* use tomato juice in place of the milk.

CHEESE-AND-CORN SOUFFLÉ

Follow 🗝 recipe above—*except* add, with seasonings, ¾ tsp. mustard and, with cheese, 1 cup drained cooked whole kernel corn and ½ cup soft bread crumbs.

INDIVIDUAL CHEESE SOUFFLÉS

For Individual Cheese Soufflés, pour into custard cups. Bake 20 to 25 min.

CHEESE-AND-HAM SOUFFLÉ

Follow 🗝 recipe above—and add, with the cheese, ½ cup ground cooked ham.

MUSHROOM-CHEESE SOUFFLÉ

Follow 🗝 recipe above—and fold 1 cup sautéed finely cut mushrooms into the Cheese Soufflé mixture at the last. Delicious with any Seafood Sauce.

All you have to do—

FOR SECOND SERVINGS
Bake Cheese Soufflé in two 5″ to 6″ casseroles . . . placing one in the oven 10 min. after the other. Bake only 30 to 35 min.

High, puffy Cheese Soufflé. Always serve immediately.

WELSH RAREBIT (Welsh Rabbit)

The story goes that long ago in Wales the peasants, not allowed to hunt on the estates of noblemen, served melted cheese as a substitute for rabbit, popular prize of the hunt. It became a famous dish at Ye Olde Cheshire Inn, meeting place of England's illustrious penmen. There rare wits from Ben Jonson to Charles Dickens conversed copiously while enjoying this specialty of the house.

Melt over hot, *not boiling*, water....... 4 cups sliced nippy American cheese (1 lb.)
(Never allow cheese to reach boiling point.)

Gradually stir in.......................
- **¾ cup cream**
- **½ tsp. dry mustard**
- **½ tsp. Worcestershire sauce**
- **¼ tsp. salt**
- **dash of pepper**

Serve at once on crisp crackers or toast, with pickles or relish on side. Serves 6.

All you have to do— *To make Welsh Rarebit de Luxe:* use ginger ale in place of cream.

All you have to do— *To make Quick Welsh Rarebit:* add cut-up cheese to Medium White Sauce.

WELSH RAREBIT WITH KIDNEY BEANS

Hollywood supper party favorite in the home of Joan Crawford, three-time academy award winner of the movies.

Melt in a chafing dish or top of double boiler over hot water 2 cups diced American cheese (½ lb.). Stir in 2½ cups heated cooked kidney beans with liquid (#2 can) and ½ cup diced green peppers. Keep hot. Serve on crisp toast or crackers.

★ CHEESE FONDUE

A simplified soufflé . . . from a culinary artist, Marion Miller, whose mother used to plan it for the Minneapolis Woman's Club luncheons.

Melt in skillet . . .
3 tbsp. butter

Add and stir until lightly browned . . .
3 cups bread cubes (5 slices)

Place bread cubes in greased 1-qt. casserole (6½″) in alternate layers with . . .
1 cup shredded sharp American cheese (¼ lb.)

Mix and pour over bread and cheese . . .
1 large egg, beaten
1 cup milk
½ tsp. salt
1/16 tsp. pepper
⅛ tsp. dry mustard

Sprinkle with paprika. Set casserole in pan of water (1″ deep). Bake. Serve hot.

TEMPERATURE: 350° (mod. oven).

TIME: Bake 40 min.

AMOUNT: 4 servings.

RUM TUM TIDDY (Pink Bunny)

Often served in the Boston Athletic Club. Inez-Muriel McLaughlin formerly of our Staff (now Mrs. Byron McLaughlin) says, "This is a nice easy Sunday supper dish for busy mothers."

Heat 1¼ cups condensed tomato soup (or seasoned cooked tomatoes). Place over hot water and stir in 2 cups shredded American cheese (½ lb.). Remove from heat and blend in 1 egg, slightly beaten, ¼ tsp. dry mustard, ¼ tsp. Worcestershire sauce. Serve hot on toast points or crackers. Garnish with green pickles. Serves 4 to 6.

NOTE: ½ cup minced onion cooked in butter may be added, if desired.

BRER RABBIT WITH CORN

Satisfying, quick party dish. Ideal for after skating on a cold night.

Cook in 3 tbsp. butter in top of double boiler over direct heat until soft (5 min.) . . .
½ cup minced green pepper
1 cup minced onion

Stir in . . .
3 tbsp. flour

Remove from heat. Slowly stir in . . .
1 cup cooked tomatoes or tomato juice
½ tsp. salt
⅛ tsp. *each* pepper and cayenne pepper
1¼ cups cooked whole kernel corn
1⅓ cups grated sharp cheese

Cook over hot water 15 min., stirring occasionally. Serve hot on crackers or toast.

SEAFOOD SUPPER DISHES Treats from the deep.

SEAFOOD À LA NEWBURG

Delicious with shrimp, lobster, crabmeat, etc.

Mix together carefully . . .

- 2 cups hot Medium White Sauce
- 2 egg yolks, beaten

Just before serving, stir in . . .

- 1 tbsp. sherry flavoring or lemon juice
- 2 cups drained cooked seafood, in large pieces

Serve hot over hot Rich Biscuits or toast points or in patty shells. Garnish with parsley and pimiento strips.

AMOUNT: 6 to 8 servings.

DEVILED CRABMEAT

So easy and quick . . . once served on half hour's notice to wives of officers of our Company in Minneapolis from nearby Ferndale on a shopping trip just before Christmas.

Combine . . .

- 1½ cups milk
- 1½ cups soft bread crumbs

Gently stir in . . .

- 2 cups flaked cooked crabmeat (2 7-oz. cans)
- whites of 5 hard-cooked eggs, finely sliced

Blend in . . .

- yolks of 5 hard cooked eggs, mashed
- 1½ tsp. salt
- ⅓ tsp. dry mustard
- ⅛ tsp. cayenne pepper
- ½ cup butter, melted

Pour into buttered 10x6x2″ baking dish. Sprinkle with WHEATIES or buttered crumbs. Bake. Serve hot.

TEMPERATURE: 450° (hot oven).

TIME: Bake 15 min.

AMOUNT: 6 servings.

MOCK CHICKEN PIE

A wonderful substitute for the real thing.

Combine gently . . .

- 2 cups hot Medium White Sauce
- 1 cup tuna (7-oz. can), in large pieces
- 2 cups cooked cut-up carrots
- 1 cup cooked peas, drained

Season with salt and pepper. Pour into greased 2-qt. casserole (8″). Heat in oven until mixture bubbles . . . then cover immediately with Rich Biscuit Dough (½ recipe). Bake at once. Serve hot.

TEMPERATURE: 450° (hot oven).

TIME: Bake 25 min.

AMOUNT: 6 servings.

"A perfectly grand dish for women's luncheons!" according to a former member of our Staff, Ruby Nelson (Mrs. Charles W. Turner of Delmar, New York), who first made it in our test kitchen.

Arrange in alternate layers in buttered 1½-qt. casserole (7½″) . . .

- 2 cups tuna (2 7-oz. cans), in large pieces
- 2 cups crushed cheese crackers
- 3 cups Medium White Sauce
- ¾ cup sliced ripe olives

Finish with a sprinkling of the crushed cheese crackers. Bake. Serve hot.

TEMPERATURE: 350° (mod. oven).

TIME: Bake 35 min.

AMOUNT: 6 servings.

TUNA-POTATO CHIP CASSEROLE

Follow recipe for Tuna Supreme above—*except,* in place of cheese crackers, use slightly crumbled potato chips; and, in place of olives, use sautéed mushrooms.

SALMON AU GRATIN

For an impromptu supper.

Place alternate layers of flaked salmon and Medium White Sauce in buttered casserole. Sprinkle with grated cheese . . . then with WHEATIES. Dot with butter. Bake at 350° (mod. oven) 20 to 25 min.

CHOW MEIN LOAF

Main dish of a prize-winning party menu.

First, make 3 cups Medium White Sauce.

Combine gently . . .

- 1¼ cups of the hot Medium White Sauce
- 2 egg yolks, well beaten
- 1 cup tuna (7-oz. can), flaked
- ½ cup toasted split blanched almonds
- 2 cups chow mein noodles (4 oz.)

Fold in . . .

- 2 egg whites, stiffly beaten

Pour into well greased 9x5x3″ loaf pan. Bake. Unmold on hot platter and serve with remaining 1¾ cups Medium White Sauce to which 2 tbsp. capers or chopped crisp pickles have been added.

TEMPERATURE: 350° (mod. oven).

TIME: Bake 30 min.

AMOUNT: 8 servings.

CELLINI PIE

Delicious. Sophisticated. Different.

Line individual baking dishes with English Pastry. Sprinkle with minced onion and garlic. In each, place thin slices of cheese, tomato slices dipped in flour, and on top minced anchovies or anchovy paste. Add a little heavy cream. Bake at 400° (mod. hot oven) 30 min. Serve hot.

All you have to do · *To bring out full flavor of canned mushrooms:* sauté canned mushrooms with the mushroom liquor in butter until liquor evaporates.

SALMON MOUSSE

A handsome dainty pink mold to tempt the appetite on warm nights. Perfect for buffets on lawn or porch.

Soften . . .
- **2 envelopes gelatin (2 tbsp.) in**
- **½ cup cold water**

Dissolve over hot water. Add . . .
- **½ cup lemon juice**
- **¾ tsp. salt**
- **⅛ tsp. paprika**

and pour over . . .
- **2 cups flaked salmon (1-lb. can)**

Fold in . . .
- **2 cups whipping cream, whipped**

Pour into 9x5x3″ loaf pan lined with paper. Chill thoroughly. Unmold on cold platter. Serve with Fresh Tomato and Cucumber Mayonnaise.

AMOUNT: 8 to 10 servings.

CODFISH SOUFFLÉ

With Lobster Sauce, a delectable dish.

Separate into tiny pieces, leave in cold water 3 hr. (change water 3 times) . . .
- **1 cup flaked codfish**

Boil the freshened codfish with . . .
- **2 cups cut-up raw potatoes**

When potatoes are done, drain, mash, and beat until creamy. Beat in . . .
- **1 tbsp. butter**
- **½ cup milk or cream**
- **½ tsp. salt**
- **⅛ tsp. pepper**
- **4 egg yolks, well beaten**

Fold in . . .
- **4 egg whites, stiffly beaten**

Pour into 12 buttered muffin cups, set in pan of water (1″ deep). Bake until set. Serve at once with hot Lobster Sauce.

TEMPERATURE: 350° (mod. oven).

TIME: Bake 30 min.

AMOUNT: 12 servings.

★ POMPANO EN PAPILLOTE

(Pompano in Paper Case) Reflects the glamor of old New Orleans. Worked out by Esther MacMillan of our Staff after she enjoyed it in its famous setting. When Barrett Kiesling of Metro-Goldwyn-Mayer had luncheon with us he said, "It's even better than what they served me in New Orleans."

Boil pompano or white trout (2½ lb. for 6 servings) until firm in water with salt, bay leaves, onions in it. Prepare *Mushroom-Shrimp Sauce:* Make 3 cups thick Medium White Sauce with equal parts fish stock and milk . . . seasoning with celery salt, onion salt, bouillon cube, and sherry flavoring. Add 1½ cups sautéed sliced mushrooms (¾ lb.) and 1 cup quartered cooked shrimp (7-oz. can).

For each serving, cut a 10x6″ oval out of parchment or heavy wrapping paper; butter both sides of paper. On half of oval, place 3 tbsp. Mushroom-Shrimp Sauce. Add 2 pieces boned cooked fish. Cover with more sauce. Fold other half of paper over. Close and seal by folding the 2 edges together (a double fold). Place on baking sheet. Bake. Cut slits in paper on top . . . and serve hot on supper plate.

TEMPERATURE: 350° (mod. oven).

TIME: Bake 20 min.

CLAM SOUFFLÉ

"This makes 'fasting' during Lent a pleasure!" was the comment when this dish was tested. We are indebted for the recipe to Mrs. John A. Hadley, now of Camden, Maine.

Combine and let stand 10 min. . . .
- **1½ cups minced clams (2 7-oz. cans)**
- **2 cups soft bread crumbs**
- **1 cup liquor from clams**

Add butter, milk, seasonings, eggs, as for Codfish Soufflé (*see left*), but add a little more salt and some onion juice. Bake in greased paper-lined 9x5x3″ loaf pan. Unmold. Serve at once with hot Sauce Verte.

TEMPERATURE: 350° (mod. oven).

TIME: Bake 40 min.

AMOUNT: 6 servings.

CHICKEN SUPPER DISHES For family or party fare.

HOT CHICKEN MOUSSE

Dainty, delicately flavored,—elegant main dish for wedding suppers and other festive affairs.

Put through fine knife of food chopper 3 times or pound until very fine . . .
raw breast of 2-lb. chicken (1/2 cup)

Stew and put through fine knife of chopper . . .
remaining chicken (1 cup), cooked

Heat together . . .
1/2 cup cream
1/2 cup milk
1 cup soft bread crumbs

Add and beat to mix well . . .
1 3/4 tsp. salt
dash *each* of pepper and paprika
the raw and cooked chicken

Fold in . . .
5 egg whites, stiffly beaten

Pour into 9x5x3" loaf pan lined with buttered paper, and set in pan of water (1" deep). Bake until firm . . . covering with greased paper first 30 min. to prevent browning. Serve immediately with hot Mushroom Sauce. Garnish with pimiento strips and parsley bouquets.

TEMPERATURE: 350° (mod. oven).
TIME: Bake 1 1/2 hr.
AMOUNT: 6 servings.

SCALLOPED CHICKEN

Marjorie Child Husted says, "When I was in college, I used to prepare this simple dish for my mother's guests at Sunday suppers. It's easy and delicious."

Into greased 1 1/2-qt. casserole (7 1/2"), place in alternate layers until all is used . . .
2 1/2 cups finely cut cooked chicken
2 1/2 cups rich chicken gravy
1 cup fine dry bread crumbs

Dot with butter. Bake. Serve hot.

TEMPERATURE: 350° (mod. oven).
TIME: Bake 20 to 30 min.
AMOUNT: 6 servings.

CHICKEN AND BROCCOLI

3-tiered delicacy.

On thin slice of cooked ham in each individual ramekin, place a slice of cooked breast of chicken. On top, place a tender green serving of lacy broccoli (cooked). Cover with Cheese Sauce. Place under broiler until sauce is bubbly and slightly brown on top. Serve immediately.

★ SCALLOPED CHICKEN SUPREME

Contributed by Ethel M. Hughes, former member of our Staff. Elegant enough for loveliest parties, yet not too fussy for a special treat for just the family.

Pour 1 cup chicken broth over . . .
2 cups Boiled Rice (2/3 cup uncooked) (*p. 387*).

Make 3 cups Creamy Chicken Gravy (*p. 397*), using 3 cups cooked chicken (5 1/2 lb. chicken). Place in alternate layers in greased 12x7 1/2x2" baking dish rice and chicken in gravy (2 layers of each) . . . sprinkling over each layer . . .
toasted slivered almonds (1/2 cup in all)
minced pimiento (2 tbsp. in all)
sautéed sliced mushrooms (1 cup in all)

Top with buttered bread crumbs or WHEATIES. Bake. Serve hot.

TEMPERATURE: 350° (mod. oven).
TIME: Bake 45 min.
AMOUNT: 8 servings.

15-MINUTE SPECIAL

Cover slices of buttered toast with sliced cooked chicken. Cover chicken with thin slices of tomato. Season with salt and pepper. Top with thin slices of cheese. Broil until cheese is melted. Serve hot with Mushroom Sauce.

CHICKEN CHOW MEIN

For a Large Group: Chicken Chow Mein, Poppyseed Rolls, Tossed Salad, Orange Sherbet, Little Almond Cakes, Tea.

Brown lightly in 2 tbsp. hot butter . . .
4 tbsp. minced onion
1 cup whole button mushrooms

Add and simmer 15 min. . . .
1 1/2 cups shredded cooked chicken
1 cup diced celery
1 1/2 cups meat stock or water
2 tbsp. soy sauce
1 tbsp. sugar

Blend and stir into meat mixture . . .
1 1/2 tbsp. cornstarch
3 tbsp. cold water

Cook until slightly thickened and clear. Serve hot over hot chow mein noodles.

AMOUNT: 4 servings.

CREAMED CHICKEN (🔑 Recipe) *Helps master many delicious dinners.*

Melt .... 6 tbsp. butter or chicken fat

Blend in .... 6 tbsp. GOLD MEDAL Flour, 1 tsp. salt, 1/8 tsp. pepper

and cook over low heat until bubbling.

Remove from heat and stir in .... 1½ cups well seasoned chicken broth, 1 cup cream or top milk

Bring to a boil and boil 1 min., stirring constantly. Stir in gently .... 1 cup cut-up cooked chicken

Just before serving, add if desired...... 2 tbsp. sherry flavoring

Serve hot in patty shells, pastry cases, biscuit rings, or timbale cases; or over toast points, noodles, fluffy rice, etc.

AMOUNT: 6 servings.

CHICKEN À LA KING

Follow 🔑 recipe above and, at the last, add 1 cup sautéed sliced mushrooms, ½ cup slivered green pepper, and ¼ cup slivered pimiento. Southerners substitute cooked ham for half the chicken.

All you have to do—

For fine flavor: add celery tops, cut-up carrots, and parsley to water when stewing chicken for broth.

CHICKEN VERSAILLES

The hot dish chosen for our special guest luncheons by Gertrude Jaeger (Mrs. Douglas T.), now of Birmingham, Michigan, when she was on our Staff.

Spread thin Pancakes (4″ in diameter) with well seasoned Creamed Chicken and Mushrooms. Roll up. Serve hot with more creamed chicken over top of rolls.

RING AROUND THE CHICKEN

Enthusiastically received when served at a special luncheon for Katherine Fisher and Dorothy Marsh of Good Housekeeping magazine.

Sift together into bowl . . .
- 1½ cups *sifted* GOLD MEDAL Flour
- 3 tsp. baking powder
- ¾ tsp. salt
- ½ to ¾ tsp. poultry seasoning

Cut in finely . . .
- ¼ cup shortening

Add, mixing well . . .
- ½ cup plus 2 tbsp. milk

Spoon into an 8″ ring mold. Bake. Unmold on hot platter. Serve hot with hot Creamed Chicken (*above*) in center.

TEMPERATURE: 450° (hot oven).
TIME: Bake 15 min.
AMOUNT: 6 servings.

CREAMY CHICKEN GRAVY

Follow 🔑 recipe above—*except,* in place of 1½ cups chicken broth, use 2 cups, omit chicken and sherry flavoring, and add seasonings, such as celery salt, poultry seasoning. *Makes 3 cups gravy.*

CHICKEN TERRAPIN

Served at "A Shower for Hermina" at the colonial home of the Director of our Staff overlooking beautiful Lake Harriet . . . just before Hermina Kure (Mrs. Harry Frederick) left our Staff.

Follow recipe for Chicken à la King (*opposite*)—and add 1 cup cooked fresh peas, 1 hard-cooked egg, cubed. Lemon juice may be used instead of sherry flavoring.

★ SOUTHERN CHICKEN UPSIDE-DOWN DINNER

Tender corn bread baked over meat. Savory, satisfying, a dinner-time treat!

Make double amount of 🔑 recipe above.

Sift together into bowl . . .
- 1 cup *sifted* GOLD MEDAL Flour
- 1 cup corn meal
- 2 tbsp. sugar
- 2 tsp. baking powder
- ¾ tsp. salt
- ½ tsp. soda

Cut in finely . . .
- 3 tbsp. shortening

Add, stirring just enough to blend . . .
- 1 cup buttermilk or sour milk

Spread over ⅔ of hot Creamed Chicken (*above*) in 10″ skillet or 2-qt. casserole (8″). Bake. Serve hot, upside-down, cut into wedges, with rest of chicken mixture over it.

TEMPERATURE: 400° (mod. hot oven).
TIME: Bake 25 min.
AMOUNT: 6 servings.

SPECIAL MEAT SUPPER DISHES Epicurean ways with old familiars.

CHILI CON CARNE

Zesty "south of the border" specialty.

Cook until browned in 3 tbsp. hot butter or drippings . . .
1 lb. ground beef
1¼ cups minced onion
Add and cook 10 min. . . .
2½ cups cooked kidney beans (#2 can)
1⅓ cups condensed tomato soup
Make into a paste and blend in . . .
1½ to 2 tbsp. chili powder
1 tbsp. flour
3 tbsp. water
1 tsp. salt

Cook over low heat, stirring frequently, 45 min. Serve hot . . . with crackers or hot Fried Corn Meal Mush.
AMOUNT: 8 servings.

ASPARAGUS—HAM AU GRATIN

A spring-time favorite of Florence C. Boran of our Staff.

Arrange cooked asparagus stalks on bed of cheese-sprinkled soft bread crumbs in casserole. Cover with Creamed Ham. Top with more of the crumbs. Bake at 350° (mod. oven) until lightly browned.

★ SWEETBREADS ON HAM ROUNDS

Mrs. Albert C. Loring, the originator of this delicious dish, often serves it at luncheons in her Minneapolis home.

Cut 2 lb. boiled sweetbreads into 1″ pieces.
Sauté in butter 1 lb. mushrooms, sliced.
Frizzle in 2 tbsp. butter . . .
¼ lb. dried beef, minced
Blend in . . .
2 tbsp. flour
Remove from heat and stir in . . .
2½ tbsp. sherry flavoring
1 tsp. Worcestershire sauce
3½ cups cream
Bring to boil over low heat, stirring constantly. Boil 1 min. Combine with . . .
the cooked sweetbreads
the sautéed sliced mushrooms

Place in buttered 12x7½x2″ baking dish. Bake. Serve hot on broiled ham rounds.
TEMPERATURE: 350° (mod. oven).
TIME: Bake 30 min.
AMOUNT: 10 to 12 servings.

CREOLE WIENERS

A new way of serving "hot dogs."

Pan-broil in heavy skillet until half done . . .
8 thin slices bacon, cut in ½″ squares
Drain off most of fat. Add and fry, stirring constantly, until golden brown . . .
3 cups minced onions
Stir in . . .
2½ cups cooked tomatoes (#2 can)
¾ tsp. salt
⅛ tsp. pepper
Place on top . . .
8 to 10 wieners (1 lb.)

Cover, and simmer gently, stirring occasionally, 45 min. Remove cover, and boil hard 5 to 10 min. to reduce liquid. Serve hot . . . a wiener and a spoonful of the hot sauce in each buttered bun.
AMOUNT: 10 wiener-filled buns.

NEW ENGLAND BEAN POT STEW

Made by thrifty old-time housewives not wanting to waste the oven heat on washday.

Place chunks of meat, large cubes of raw potatoes, cut-up onions, salt, and pepper in bean pot. Bake for several hours.

BEEF AND CORN CASSEROLE

A delicious Sunday supper dish from Isabel McGovern, formerly of our Staff, now Home Service Director, Minneapolis Gas Company.

Cook in 1 tbsp. fat until tender . . .
¼ cup chopped onion
¼ cup chopped green pepper
Add and cook until beef frizzles at edges . . .
¼ lb. cut-up dried beef
1 cup sliced mushrooms
Meanwhile, blend together . . .
2 cups Medium White Sauce
2 egg yolks, beaten
1 tsp. prepared mustard
salt and pepper to taste
Combine with dried beef mixture. Add . . .
2 cups kernel corn (#2 can), drained
Pour into greased 1½-qt. casserole (7½″).
Sprinkle with . . .
½ cup grated sharp cheese (⅛ lb.)
¼ tsp. paprika

Bake. Serve hot.
TEMPERATURE: 350° (mod. oven).
TIME: Bake 30 min.
AMOUNT: 6 to 8 servings.

HAM-AND-EGG PIE

"This is our family favorite for Easter!" wrote Mrs. Luman P. Cranz of Ira, Ohio, when she sent us the recipe. With creamed asparagus, a pineapple-banana-orange salad, and Hot Cross Buns, it makes a delicious early spring luncheon.

Line deep 8″ pie pan with Pastry (*make Pastry for Two-Crust Pie*). In bottom, arrange . . .

1 cup cut-up cooked ham (½ lb.)

Pour over the ham a mixture of . . .

6 eggs, slightly beaten
6 tbsp. top milk or cream
1 tbsp. minced chives or parsley
½ tsp. salt
¼ tsp. pepper

Cover with top crust. Bake until nicely browned. Serve hot.

TEMPERATURE: 425° (hot oven).
TIME: Bake 20 to 25 min.
AMOUNT: 6 servings.

SCALLOPED POTATOES–HAM

Leftover ham in a dish that is an old-time, all-time favorite.

Arrange in alternate layers in buttered 1½-qt. casserole (7½″) . . .

thinly sliced potatoes (3 cups in all) (sprinkle 1 tsp. flour over each layer)
minced onion (½ cup in all)
flaked cooked ham slices (1½ cups in all)

Season layers with salt, pepper, and dry mustard. Heat in oven 15 min.
Then pour over the top . . .

2 to 2½ cups *hot* milk (to *just* cover)

Sprinkle with paprika. Cover and bake until potatoes are tender, removing cover last ½ hr.

TEMPERATURE: 325° (slow mod. oven).
TIME: Bake 1 hr.
AMOUNT: 6 servings.

★ VEAL PAPRIKA

A gourmet dish of distinction . . . sent us by Mrs. W. H. Stutzman, Kirkwood, Missouri.

Roll individual servings of veal steak (2 lb. cut ½″ thick) in seasoned flour. Brown in hot fat in skillet rubbed with garlic. Season with salt, pepper, and 1 tbsp. paprika. Add 1 cup hot water, cover, simmer 1½ hr. Arrange meat on hot platter around hot boiled noodles. Into gravy left in pan, stir 1 cup cream, heat, and pour over noodles. Sprinkle with paprika and toasted almonds. *Serves 6.*

RED CINNAMON APPLES WITH TINY PORK SAUSAGES

Beautifully colored apples with little sausages sticking out at perky angles. Marian South (now Mrs. Russell K. Johnson of Davenport, Iowa) perfected the recipe as a Christmas Eve Supper specialty when she was on our Staff.

Boil together 5 min. . . .

1 cup sugar
½ cup water
⅓ cup small red cinnamon candies

Place peeled-side-down in the hot syrup and cook 5 min. . . .

6 cored firm apples (peeling removed from top halves)

Meanwhile, brown in skillet . . .

18 little pork sausages

Remove apples from syrup and place peeled-side-up in individual custard or muffin cups or in 1 large baking pan. Place 3 browned sausages in center of each apple. Pour red cinnamon syrup over all. Bake until tender. Serve hot in leafy green wreaths of watercress or lettuce . . . accompanied by fluffy rice with hot Cheese Sauce.

TEMPERATURE: 350° (mod. oven).
TIME: Bake 30 min.
AMOUNT: 6 servings.

SPRINGTIME SKILLET DINNER

Mrs. Claude Stuart of Florin, California, originator of this dish, wrote: "It takes less time than regular stew . . . and tastes much better." Serve it with a crisp salad, hot rolls, fresh berries, spice cake for a Purse-String Supper.

Brown in 2 tbsp. fat in 10″ skillet . . .

1 cut-up clove garlic

Remove garlic. Then add . . .

1 cup finely diced onion
½ lb. ground beef

Cook until browned, stirring. Add . . .

½ cup uncooked rice
5 to 6 cups water

Simmer uncovered over low heat 40 min. Add . . .

1 cup finely diced carrots
1 cup finely diced potatoes

Continue simmering until tender (20 min.). Season with . . .

1 to 2 tsp. soy sauce
1 tbsp. salt
⅛ tsp. pepper

Serve hot . . . garnished with parsley.

AMOUNT: 6 servings.

BOSTON BAKED BEANS

Really "Indian" Baked Beans, as they were originated by the Indians 3 centuries ago . . . baked in earthen pots as we bake them today. In early New England, they were traditional Saturday night fare.

Soak overnight in cold water . . .

1 qt. navy or pea beans

Simmer in same water until tender (2 to 3 hr.). Drain, and save liquor. Place in 2-qt. bean pot in layers . . .

the drained cooked beans
1 lb. salt pork (scalded, rind scraped)
2 slices onion

Combine . . .

⅓ cup molasses
2 tsp. salt
⅓ tsp. pepper
½ tsp. dry mustard

Pour over beans. Add just enough bean liquor to cover beans. Cover pot. Bake. Remove cover last half of baking, draw pork to top, add a little boiling water if beans seem dry. Serve hot with steaming hot Brown Bread.

TEMPERATURE: 300° (slow oven).

TIME: Bake 8 hr.

AMOUNT: 10 servings.

LIMA BEANS AU GOURMET

Soak 2 cups dried lima beans overnight in 1 qt. salted water (1 tsp. salt). Drain, and cook until tender (1½ hr.) in 1 qt. salted water. Drain. Mix with . . .

2 slices bacon, diced and crisped
½ cup sliced mushrooms, sautéed
2 tbsp. Worcestershire sauce
2 tsp. curry powder
1 blade mace, crumbled
8 whole cloves
1 drop tabasco sauce
1 can condensed pepperpot or tomato soup plus water to make 2 cups

Bake in 2-qt. casserole (8″). Serve hot.

TEMPERATURE: 350° (mod. oven).

TIME: Bake 30 min.

AMOUNT: 6 servings.

SPEEDY BAKED BEANS

Sauté until bacon is crisp and onion yellow

4 strips bacon, diced
1 large onion, minced

Stir in . . .

2 cans Baked Beans (with Pork) (#1 tall)
1 tsp. prepared mustard
¼ cup chili sauce

Pour into greased 1½-qt. casserole (7½″). Bake uncovered until beans are brown and bubbly. Serve hot.

TEMPERATURE: 350° (mod. oven).

TIME: Bake 45 min.

AMOUNT: 6 servings

VEGETARIAN BAKED BEANS

This discovery of Adah E. M. Anderson of Knollwood, Hopkins, Minnesota, shows how tasty baked beans can be without meat.

Sauté until yellow in 4 tbsp. butter . . .

1 large onion, minced

Stir in . . .

2 cans Vegetarian Baked Beans (#1 Tall)
¼ cup dark molasses
⅓ cup catsup

Bake as for Speedy Baked Beans above.

★ SPECIAL BAKED BEANS

Mrs. Nels I. Matson of Seattle, Washington, wrote, "This was given my husband by a man very fond of real baked beans. He carried the recipe in his pocket and offered it to all lovers of baked beans."

Soak overnight in cold water . . .

2 cups navy beans

In morning, drain. Save the bean liquor. Put through medium knife of food grinder . . .

½ lb. salt pork (scalded, rind removed)
6 sprigs parsley
1 large onion
1 clove garlic
1 green pepper
2 sweet red peppers

Mix above ingredients through beans with . . .

2 tbsp. maple syrup
6 tbsp. catsup

Cover with fresh water. Simmer 2 hr. Put into 2-qt. bean pot . . . add just enough bean liquid to cover beans. Cover pot. Bake. Uncover last half of baking. Serve hot . . . with hot Brown Bread.

TEMPERATURE: 300° (slow oven).

TIME: Bake covered 2½ hr., remove cover and bake 1½ hr. longer.

AMOUNT: 6 servings.

BROILED TURKEY AND CHEESE SANDWICHES

For after the holiday feast.

Make up sandwiches of toasted-on-one-side bread (buttered on untoasted side) and slices of roast turkey. Cover each sandwich with a thin slice of cheese. Place under broiler until cheese is melted. Serve hot with hot mushroom sauce (thickened mushroom soup) over them.

HOT FRENCH TOASTED SANDWICHES

Make up chicken, turkey, or ham sandwiches. Dip into beaten egg (or mixture of 1 beaten egg and ½ cup milk). Brown on both sides in butter in hot heavy skillet. Or bake on greased baking sheet at 400° (mod. hot oven)
Serve piping hot.

SHRIMP COCKTAIL SANDWICHES

Ideal for a hot weather one-dish

In center of each dinner plate, place a tiny glass of Special Cocktail Sauce (chili sauce and a drop of tabasco sauce with mayonnaise).

Place 4 triangles of buttered white bread on the plate . . . radiating out from the small dish like the spokes of a wheel. Place 3 large cooked or canned shrimps on lettuce on each triangle. Between the triangles, place wedges of tomatoes and tiny lettuce leaves and olives. Place half a deviled egg on each plate with the lettuce. Eat with cocktail fork or salad fork . . . dipping shrimps into cocktail sauce.

★ BROILED CRABMEAT OR SHRIMP SANDWICHES

Season mashed yolks of 4 hard-cooked eggs with 1 tsp. salt, ⅛ tsp. pepper, ¼ tsp. mustard, 1 tsp. minced chives. Blend in 2 tbsp. butter, melted, 1 raw egg yolk, ¼ cup thick cream, 1 cup flaked crabmeat or shrimp (7-oz. can), and chopped whites of 4 hard-cooked eggs.
Spread over *un*toasted side of 8 slices toasted-on-one-side bread. Sprinkle with paprika and a little grated cheese, if desired. Place (on baking sheet) under broiler until mixture is delicately browned. Serve immediately.
AMOUNT: 8 servings.

CHEESE SANDWICH LOAF

Glamorous but substantial party fare.

Prepare 4 fillings by mixing ingredients for each with enough salad dressing to make easy to spread:

RED FILLING
- **4 slices boiled ham, minced**
- **3 slices crisp bacon, crumbled**
- **1 pimiento, minced**

YELLOW FILLING
- **mashed yolks of 3 hard-cooked eggs, seasoned with salt and pepper**

WHITE FILLING
- **half a 3-oz. pkg. cream cheese**
- **½ cucumber, grated**

GREEN FILLING
- **4 small sweet pickles, minced**
- **6 sprigs watercress or parsley, minced**

Remove crusts and cut lengthwise into 5 equal long slices (*see picture, p. 26*) . . .
- **1 loaf sandwich bread**

Butter each slice and spread with a filling in order given above . . . and place one on top the other in the form of the whole loaf.

Soften 3 3-oz. pkg. cream cheese with sweet cream and spread on outside of loaf as you would ice a cake. Decorate with sliced stuffed olives and toasted almonds.

Wrap the loaf in a damp cloth and chill in refrigerator 3 hr. or more. Serve cold garnished with lettuce, olives, etc. . . . in full slices or half slices.

SPECIAL CLUB SANDWICH LOAF

Make same as Cheese Sandwich Loaf above—*except* cut loaf into 4 slices and use following fillings: (1) sliced chicken and lettuce (2) sliced tomatoes (3) crisp broiled bacon and lettuce. Coat with *thick* mild mayonnaise modified with *stiffly* whipped cream and with coarsely cut-up hard-cooked eggs mixed in.

TOMATO CLUB SANDWICH

Place 2 slices fresh tomato on one thin piece of hot toast. Cover with second piece of toast. Lay 1 strip crisp bacon and 3 slices green pickle on top. Cover with third piece of toast. Pour hot Cheese Sauce over it. Serve immediately.

★ TOASTED PIMIENTO BARS

With a refreshing fruit salad—a satisfying meal. Delicious, too, with fruit punch.

Cut 3 slices day-old bread 1″ thick. Then cut each slice into strips 1″ wide.

For 9 bars, melt over hot water . . .
- **6 tbsp. butter**
- **1 lb. pimiento cheese or 1 lb. sharp cheese with 2 tbsp. minced pimiento** (*thin with cream if necessary*)

Dip bread strips into the melted cheese mixture (covering all sides evenly). Place in rows on baking sheet. Place under broiler . . . and broil at mod. heat with oven door open until cheese is melted and strips are well browned on all sides, turning often. Garnish and serve at once.

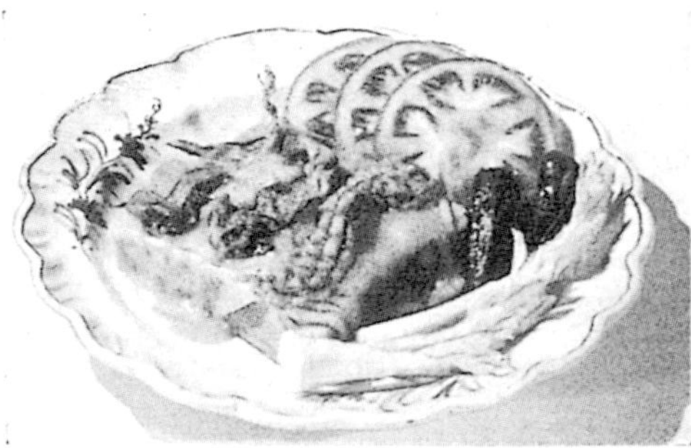

OPEN CHEESE-BACON SANDWICHES

Combine . . .
- **2 eggs, well beaten**
- **2 cups shredded sharp cheese (½ lb.)**
- **1 tsp. Worcestershire sauce**
- **½ tsp. salt**
- **¼ tsp. paprika**

Spread on *un*toasted side of . . . 6 slices bread (toasted on one side)

Top each with . . . 2 half-strips bacon

Place under broiler until cheese melts and bacon is crisp. Serve hot.

AMOUNT: 6 sandwiches.

CHEESE DREAMS

Invented by boarding school girls as a chafing dish specialty . . . now universally popular as a main dish for light suppers and luncheons.

For each serving, place slices of American cheese between 2 slices of bread. Spread butter over outside of both slices. Brown lightly on both sides in heavy skillet over low heat. Serve immediately.

OPEN GRILLED CHEESE SANDWICHES

Kathryn Soth (Mrs. William H. Wisdom of Des Moines, Iowa), formerly of our Staff, likes to make these to serve with coffee or tea for impromptu refreshments.

Cover lightly buttered untoasted side of bread slices (toasted on one side) with slices of American cheese. Place under broiler until cheese melts. Sprinkle with paprika, garnish with parsley and crisp pickles. Serve at once.

All you have to do—

To make Cheese Wafflettes: make *thin* cheese sandwiches. (Don't let cheese touch edges!) Bake in hot waffle iron until golden brown (2 min.). Serve hot . . . with crisp bacon and vegetable salad.

CHEESE SANDWICH CASSEROLE

Crispy, golden outside . . . melting, tender inside. Like glorified cheese sandwiches.

Arrange in greased baking dish . . .
- **6 slices bread**

Cover with . . .
- **6 thick slices sharp cheese (⅛″ thick)**

Top with . . .
- **6 more slices bread to make "sandwiches"**

Pour over all, a mixture of . . .
- **4 egg yolks (or 2 eggs), beaten**
- **2½ cups milk**
- **1 tsp. salt**
- **⅛ tsp. pepper**
- **¼ tsp. dry mustard**

Chill in refrigerator so milk mixture will soften bread. Bake until partially dried and golden brown on top. Serve hot . . . with creamed vegetable (asparagus, etc.).

TEMPERATURE: 350° (mod. oven).

TIME: Bake 1 hr.

AMOUNT: 6 servings.

Vegetables...a source of Color, Beauty, and Health

THE "VEGETABLE KINGDOM" *is worth exploring. It offers mineral and vitamin riches galore. And you will find in it the Humble and Haughty, the Strong and the Mild . . . the Brilliant and Pale. They need recognition, however, to keep them from hiding their light under a bushel. Let's enjoy all the wealth, beauty, and color of this wonderful kingdom.*

Betty Crocker

FROZEN VEGETABLES **Check the wide variety now available.**

Good brands keep the color, flavor, and tenderness of garden fresh vegetables. Nutritional losses are slight because they are picked at the peak of quality and frozen immediately.

Keep frozen until time to cook. If vegetables begin to thaw and soften, cook at once.

Most varieties come in 12-oz. pkg. (1½ to 2 cups).

FROM STORE TO RANGE Buying, Storing, and Cooking.

FRESH VEGETABLES To get your money's worth in nutrition and flavor.

I. Buy Wisely

Go to market in person whenever possible.
To keep posted on best buys of season.
To select vegetables free from blemishes and signs of decay.
Buy only enough for one or two days.

II. Store Carefully

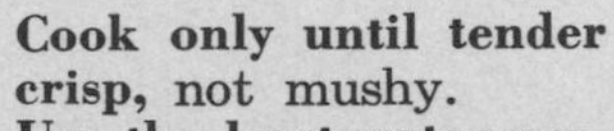

Perishables (lettuce, celery, tomatoes, etc.). Keep in food bags, a crisper, or damp cloth in refrigerator.

Less Perishables (potatoes, onions, beets, turnips, etc.). Keep in a cool, dry, well ventilated place (a vegetable or refrigerator bin).

Pod Vegetables (peas, beans). Keep *unshelled* in refrigerator until just before cooking to insure garden-fresh flavor.

III. Prepare Properly

Wash thoroughly just before cooking. Cook in skins if possible or, if vegetables must be pared (potatoes, etc.), pare *very thin*. Precious vitamins and minerals next to the skin are lost in thick parings.

IV. Cook Correctly

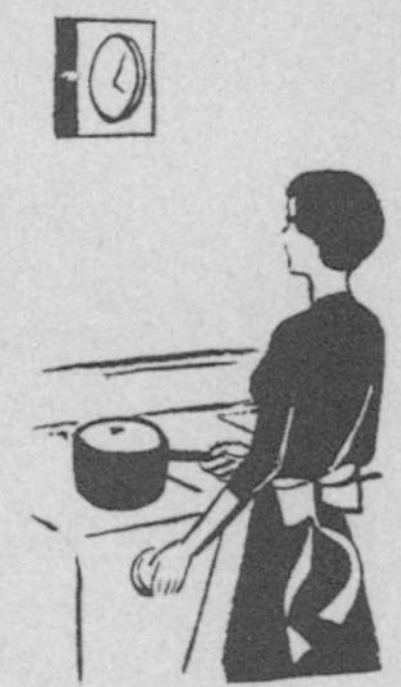

Cook only until tender crisp, not mushy.
Use the least water possible (see chart). Drowning in too much water ruins vegetables.
Keep track of vegetables while cooking. They differ so in size and age, it is impossible to give the exact time.
Save water in which vegetables were cooked. It contains precious minerals and vitamins.

CANNED AND GLASSED VEGETABLES Always read descriptive labels on cans or jars.

I. What Grade to Buy

All grades have the same nutritive value. Let your guide be your budget and the way you intend to cook the vegetables.

II. Leftover Canned Vegetables

Leave unused vegetables in opened can or jar. Cover and keep in refrigerator.

III. What Size to Buy

Sometimes larger cans are the best buy. Approximate contents are:

no. 1 can (tall)	2 cups
no. 2 can	2½ cups
no. 2½ can	3½ cups
no. 10 can	13 cups

PLEASING COMBINATIONS IN PLATE DINNERS in color photograph (*p. 406*).

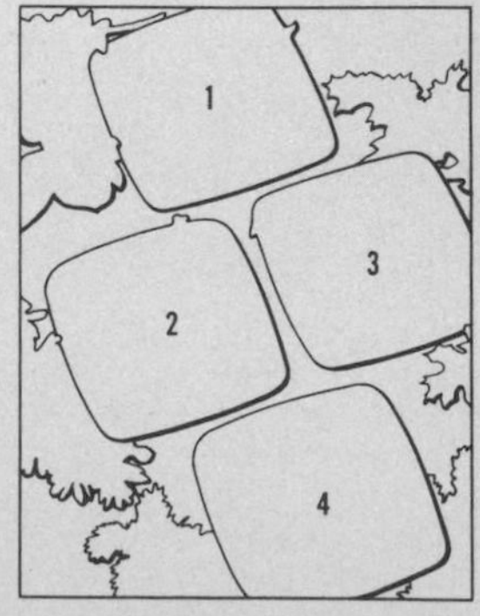

Spring 1. Fresh Fish Fillet, Parsley New Potatoes, Peas and New Onions in Cream, Garnish of Lemon, Carrot Curls, and Green Pickles, Tomato-Cucumber Salad.

Summer 2. Fried Chicken, Whipped Potatoes, Fresh Corn on Cob, Zucchini, Garnish of Pickled Peach, Celery Hearts.

Autumn 3. Broiled Ham Steak, Candied Yams, Green Beans Almondine, Garnish of Radish Roses and Cauliflowerets on Watercress.

Winter 4. Broiled Porterhouse Steak, Twice Baked and Stuffed Potato, Braised Pascal Celery, Fried Onion Rings, Garnish of Javanese Tomato with Watercress.

VEGETABLES

Vegetables have family trees that go back to the dawn of history. Even long before the Christian era, the Greeks and Romans were eating peas and spinach. In the early days of our own country, vegetables were "garden sauce" or just "sass" to go with meat. Beets and carrots sometimes were referred to as "long sauce," while onions and potatoes were "short sauce." A vendor who sold vegetables from door to door was a "sauce man."

We no longer depend on a sauce man plus our own kitchen gardens for vegetables. Thanks to modern agriculture, we not only have bigger, juicier vegetables than our grandmothers or the old Greeks and Romans ever knew, but because of modern transportation and refrigeration, we enjoy vegetables from all over the country the year around.

These fine, handsome vegetables add a bright note to our meals. Just think how drab and monotonous our food would be without the cheery gold of carrots, the refreshing green of peas and beans, or the rich reds of beets and tomatoes! We've learned to cook them, too, so they will keep their bright colors. For vegetables are like people. By treating them with sympathy and understanding, they give us their best in color, nutrients, and flavor. Indifferent treatment, however, makes them drab and lifeless, their precious minerals and vitamins lost. Like people whose fine talents are wasted.

Fortunately there's more than one way to cook vegetables so they will look bright, taste delicious, and reward us with their full bounty of health-giving minerals and vitamins. You'll find all these methods in these pages . . . making it possible for you and your families to enjoy vegetables in all sorts of interesting ways. There are both top-of-the-stove and oven methods to fit in with the rest of the meal you may be planning. So pick your pets from among fresh, canned, or frozen vegetables . . . and see how many delightful ways there are for serving them.

PLATE DINNERS

With eye appeal . . . appetite appeal.

A variety of colors and forms . . . complementary flavors and contrasting textures.

PLATE DINNERS

It's smart to serve vegetables on the same plate with the meat. The green, red, or yellow vegetables set off the brown meat and white potatoes. Each plate becomes a picture to tempt reluctant appetites.

In Grandma's day, a flotilla of little boat-shaped vegetable dishes used to surround each dinner plate. Now we try to set up our food to be "tasted" first with the eyes . . . and we like to save dishwashing.

GIVE EYE AND APPETITE APPEAL TO EACH PLATE

Look for Color: Always try to use a colorful vegetable with white, brown, or less vivid food. Add olives, pickles, jelly, or parsley for a bit of eye-catching accent.

Harmonize Flavors: Choose vegetable flavors that complement your other foods.

Watch that Shape: When serving 2 or 3 vegetables, choose those of different shapes. Avoid all "longies" (stalks, etc.) or all "roundies" (whole onions).

Contrast Textures: Serve a crisp food with a soft food. Never all crisp or all soft.

CHOOSING VEGETABLES TO GO WITH MEAT

Keep in mind that meat of delicate flavor is overwhelmed by a vegetable of strong flavor, while a meat of more definite flavor can take a more highly flavored vegetable, such as indicated below.

Meats Comparatively Strong in Flavor, high in calories with bulky, low calorie vegetables (3 to 6%) of definite flavor:

BEEF Broccoli, cabbage, cauliflower, celery, green beans, tomatoes, beets, mushrooms, eggplant, white turnips, parsnips, kohlrabi.

PORK Cabbage, cauliflower, celery, spinach and other greens, tomatoes, summer squash.

HAM Asparagus, broccoli, Brussels sprouts, celery, green beans, cabbage, cauliflower, spinach and other greens, zucchini.

FISH Tomatoes, peas, green beans, asparagus, cucumbers, celery.

Grandma had sound ideas about foods that taste good together. Her roast lamb with peas, roast pork with apple sauce, turkey with creamed onions or mashed rutabagas... carried out modern principles of nutritional and flavor balance.

Meats Comparatively Mild in Flavor, low in calories with vegetables of milder flavor and higher in calories (9 to 15%):

LAMB Artichokes (French), carrots, peas, winter squash, creamed cauliflower, yellow turnips.

VEAL Artichokes (French), beets, creamed asparagus, fried eggplant, succotash, winter squash, creamed mushrooms.

CHICKEN Fresh young green corn, green lima beans, fresh peas, sweet potatoes.

TURKEY Creamed onions, mashed rutabagas, Hubbard squash, sweet potatoes, Brussels sprouts, beets.

SERVING VEGETABLES FOR HEALTH

Vegetables are so important to a well balanced diet that nutritionists have awarded them *two places* on their chart of the "*SEVEN BASIC FOOD GROUPS.*"

Dr. Robert I. Rizer of Minneapolis says, "To reduce, I ate lots of meat, several servings of vegetables, fruit for dessert. Properly cooked vegetables are delicious."

Group One

Green and Yellow Vegetables . . .

Some raw, some cooked, frozen, or canned	1 serving a day

Group Three

Potatoes and other vegetables and fruits (raw, dry, frozen, canned)	2 or more servings a day

COOKING VEGETABLES Vegetables need never be monotonous.

PRESSURE COOKING

Speedy modern method using steam under pressure. Keeps the bright color, natural flavor, and vitamin values of vegetables to the highest degree. Vegetables cook in about ⅓ the boiling time. Refer to pressure saucepan instruction book for specific directions.

STEAMING

Preserves color and the nutritional value of vegetables to a very high degree. Place vegetables in perforated compartment of a steamer or deep well cooker. Cover. Steam *over* rapidly boiling water. Steaming takes 5 to 15 min. longer than boiling in most cases.

BAKING

Directly on rack in oven or in casserole. Preserves food value of vegetables to medium degree. *See Chart, pp. 410 to 414,* for baking time and temperature for the different vegetables.

BOILING

Cook covered in the smallest possible amount of boiling salted water (*see pictures on p. 409*). *See Chart, pp. 410 to 414,* for preparation, baking time and temperature for the different vegetables.

OVEN-STEAMING

Grand with oven meals. Vegetables are pared, left whole or cut, seasoned, and baked covered in a small amount of water. When part of an oven dinner, use the same temperature. Otherwise, use moderate temperature. Bake for *three* times the boiling time.

BRAISING (Panning)

Shred, dice, or slice thin such vegetables as carrots, celery, cabbage, etc. Place a little oil or butter (2 tbsp.) in skillet. Add 3 to 4 cups vegetables, 1 to 2 tbsp. water, season, and cover tight. Stir occasionally. Takes from 4 to 15 min.

BROILING

Use tender raw vegetables. Or reheat cooked vegetables this way. Time ranges from 5 to 10 min.

FRYING*

Gives special flavor, crispness. Raw or cooked vegetables can be *Pan-Fried* with a little fat in skillet, *Shallow-Fried* in 1″ to 2″ fat. *French Fried.* In fat deep enough to float food. 360° for raw vegetables, 390° for cooked vegetables.

COOKING CANNED VEGETABLES

To preserve their fresh flavor and food value, heat as follows:

Peas, Green Limas, Green Beans, Carrots, etc.: drain liquid into saucepan. Boil down to ½ the amount. Add vegetables, heat. Season with salt, pepper, butter.

Tomatoes, Cream-Style Corn, Squash, Pumpkin: heat contents of can or jar, season to taste, and serve.

COOKING FROZEN VEGETABLES

Accurate cooking time and amounts of water are most important.

Do not thaw before cooking. Cook in as little rapidly boiling salted water as possible for time indicated on the package. Follow package directions explicitly.

All you have to do—

To parboil vegetables: partially cook them half the regular time.

***Prevent* Mass Execution of Vitamins and Minerals and Killing of Flavor!**

Prepare just before time to cook.

Cook vegetables in their skins as often as possible.

Cook only as much as needed for one meal.

When boiling vegetables, conserve their *bright color, pleasing texture, garden fresh flavor,* and *mineral and vitamin wealth* by following this general strategy:

1 Start vegetables in boiling salted water. Use smallest possible amount (¼″ deep in heavy saucepan, 1″ deep in lighter weight pan). Drowning them in too much water makes them drab and uninteresting, leeches out vitamins and minerals.

2 Bring vegetables to boil quickly. Turn down heat, simmer (continuous heat destroys vitamins). The shorter the time in water, the more attractive and valuable they are. *Caution:* Do not add soda! It destroys vitamins and minerals, makes vegetables soggy.

3 Cover tightly to avoid exposure to air. Don't stir in air. "Air raids" are fatal to Vitamin C.

4 Cook vegetables just until tender, not mushy. They'll taste and look better, retain more of their minerals and vitamins.

5 Use the water in which vegetables are cooked for gravy, sauces, soups. It contains vitamins and minerals dissolved in it.

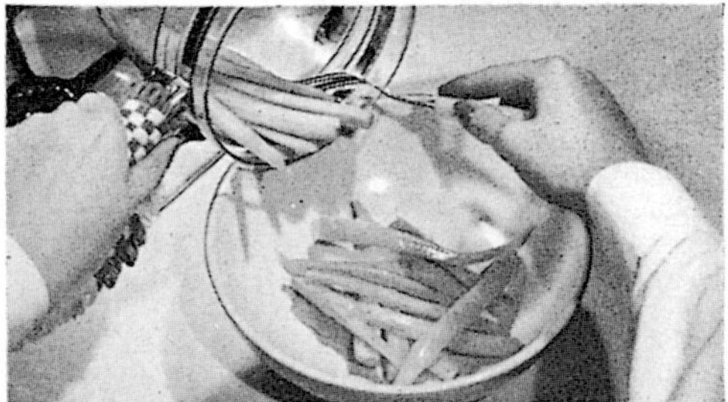

6 Serve as soon as they are cooked. Better keep the family waiting than allow the miner als and vitamins to escape.

CHART FOR MOST POPULAR WAYS OF COOKING VEGETABLES

MILD FLAVORED VEGETABLES

Cook Covered in a Small Amount of Boiling *Salted* Water—¼″ deep in heaviest saucepans . . . up to 1″ deep in the lighter weight pans.

VEGETABLE	Amount for 4	PREPARATION	POPULAR WAYS TO SERVE	COOKING TIME
ARTICHOKES (French, Globe)	Four	Trim stems leaving ½″. Remove outside lower leaves. Cut off thorny leaf tips. Tie leaves to keep in shape.	One per person on a separate plate with main course. Offer melted butter and lemon, or Hollandaise Sauce.	**Boil** 45 to 60 min. Add a slice of lemon to the water.
ARTICHOKES (Jerusalem)	1 lb.	Pare thin. Leave whole, slice, or dice.	Buttered (with lemon juice and minced parsley). Creamed, French Fried, or Baked.	**Boil** 15 to 35 min. **Bake** at 350° 30 to 60 min.
ASPARAGUS	2 lb.	Snap off tough ends. Remove scales if sandy or tough.	Buttered. Or with White Sauce or Hollandaise Sauce. Garnish with chopped hard-cooked eggs or grated cheese.	**Boil** (whole) 15 to 20 min.; (tips) 12 to 15 min.
BEANS Green or Wax	1 lb.	Cut off ends. Remove any strings. Leave whole or cut French style into crosswise slices or lengthwise strips (*see p. 416*).	Buttered (with such herbs as basil, marjoram, or thyme). Or serve in milk with butter; or creamed. Garnish with sliced toasted almonds or crisp bacon bits.	**Boil** (whole) 15 to 30 min.; (cut) 10 to 20 min.
GREEN LIMA BEANS	3 lb. or 1 pt. shelled	Cut off outer rim or rounded side of pods. Shell like peas.	Buttered (with such herbs as savory). Or serve in milk with butter . . . or in mixed casseroles.	**Boil** 20 to 30 min.
BEETS (For Beet Greens, see GREENS)	2 lb.	Don't skin or "bleed them white." Leave whole with 1″ stem. Boil until tender, drain. Run cold water over them and slip off skins and root ends. For quick cooking, pare . . . dice, or slice.	Buttered (with such herbs as basil, savory, coriander, or caraway). Baked. Sautéed, Pickled.	**Boil** (whole, young) 30 to 60 min.; (cut) 10 to 20 min. **Bake** at 350° 40 to 60 min.
CARROTS	1 lb.	Brush or pare thin. Leave whole or cut into "coins" (round slices), strips, or cubes.	Buttered (with such herbs as basil, savory, thyme, or mint). Creamed. Sautéed. Mashed.	**Boil** (whole) 20 to 30 min.; (cut) 6 to 15 min. **Bake** at 350° 35 to 45 min.

CELERY White (bleached) Green (Pascal)	**1 bunch**	Remove coarse strings, discoloration. Cut off leaves, trim roots. Cut into serving-sized pieces.	Buttered. Creamed. Braised. Use in soups, stews, chop suey.	**Boil** 15 to 20 min.
CORN (Green)	**8 ears**	Remove husks, silk, blemishes *just before cooking*. If necessary to husk corn ahead of time, cover with damp towel. The natural sugars in corn begin to change to starch within ½ hr. after picking.	On cob, with butter. Cut from cob—in milk and butter; or sautéed; in fritters; in soufflé; scalloped.	**Boil** 5 to 6 min. in *unsalted* water or skim milk to cover.
CUCUMBER	**One**	Pare, if desired. Cut into lengthwise quarters, thick slices, or cubes.	Buttered. Creamed. Sautéed.	**Boil** 15 min.
EGGPLANT	**One**	Pare and cut into slices or cubes. Do not pare and cook whole.	Dipped in crumbs or batter, and sautéed. Scalloped (creamed).	**Boil** 10 to 15 min. **Sauté** 10 to 15 min.
MUSHROOMS	**1 lb.**	Pare only if skins are coarse. To slice whole mushrooms, cut parallel with stems.	Sautéed. Broiled. Creamed. In scalloped dishes, sauces, or soup.	**Sauté or Broil** 5 to 8 min.
PARSNIPS	**1½ lb.**	Pare. Cut in halves, quarters, or slices. Remove core if tough.	Buttered. Sautéed. Baked.	**Boil** 7 to 15 min. **Bake** at 350° 30 to 45 min.
PEAS	**2 lb.**	Shell *just* before cooking.	Buttered (with such herbs as basil, mint, savory, thyme, or tarragon). In cream. Creamed.	**Boil** 8 to 20 min.
PEPPERS (Green)	**Four**	Remove stems, seeds, membrane. Wash inside and out.	Whole . . . stuffed and baked. Cut in slivers or rings. Sautéed.	**Bake** at 350° 25 to 30 min. (first parboiled whole 5 min.).
POTATOES (White)	**2 lb.**	Leave skins on whenever possible, or pare thin. Leave whole, or cut in large pieces or slices.	Buttered. Baked. Creamed. Fried. Scalloped. Mashed. In oven meals, bake at the right temperature for other foods being baked at the same time. At 350° bake 1½ hr.	**Boil** (whole) 30 to 35 min.; (cut) 20 to 25 min. **Bake** at 400° 1 hr.
PUMPKIN		Seed, pare, cut in 2″ pieces.	Mashed. Used for pie filling mostly.	**Boil** 25 to 30 min.

CHART FOR COOKING Mild Flavored Vegetables (*Continued*) VEGETABLES

	PREPARATION	POPULAR WAYS TO SERVE	COOKING TIME
RADISHES	Wash, trim stems, leave whole.	Creamed. With Chopped Chives. With Grated Cheese. With Sour Cream.	**Boil** 15 to 20 min.
SQUASH 2 lb. (Summer: Yellow, Crookneck, Zucchini, Cymling or White Scalloped, etc.)	Remove stem end. Remove large seeds, coarse fiber, if any. Leave whole, slice, or dice. Paring not necessary.	Buttered (with marjoram). Baked. Mashed.	**Boil** (whole) 30 to 60 min.; (cut) 10 to 15 min. **Bake** at 350° (whole) 30 to 60 min.
SQUASH (Winter) 2 to 3 lb.	Hubbard: Pare, if desired. Remove seeds and fibers. Cut into convenient pieces. Acorn: Wash, do not pare.	Baked. Buttered. Mashed. Baked whole or halves.	**Boil** 25 to 30 min. **Bake** at 350° 40 to 60 min.
TOMATOES 1 lb.	Peel, if desired. Leave whole, or cut in slices or quarters.	Stewed with such herbs as basil, sage, tarragon, or marjoram. Baked. Sautéed. In soups and sauces.	**Boil** 10 min. **Bake** at 350° 20 min. **Broil** 15 min.
1½ to 2 lb. **SWEET POTATOES**	Boil without paring. When tender, drain and slip off skins.	Baked. Glazed. Mashed. Sautéed.	**Boil** 30 to 35 min. **Bake** (large) at 350° 50 to 60 min.

GREENS

Cook in just the water that clings to the leaves. Cover for best nutrition. (Cooking uncovered gives fresher green color.)

Vegetable / Amount for 4	PREPARATION	POPULAR WAYS TO SERVE	COOKING TIME
1½ to 2 lb. **BEET GREENS, DANDELIONS, SWISS CHARD, SPINACH, KALE**	Wash in several waters (lukewarm at first). Be sure to lift greens from each water so sand sinks to bottom of pan. Or use a spray. Remove imperfect leaves, root ends (except for beets).	Season, butter . . . or chop and season . . . or serve with lemon or vinegar, garnished with hard-cooked egg slices.	**Boil** (young) 10 to 15 min.; (older) 20 to 30 min.

*TIP: Save the green leaves from young beets, turnips, and cauliflower. Cook them as greens.

STRONG FLAVORED VEGETABLES

For milder flavor, cook uncovered in salted water to cover. If head vegetables, broccoli, Brussels sprouts, cauliflower, cabbage, etc. seem sandy or buggy, soak in cold water ½ hr. before cooking, then wash thoroughly.

Vegetable	Amount for 4	PREPARATION	POPULAR WAYS TO SERVE	COOKING TIME
BROCCOLI	2½ lb.	Remove leaves, tough stalk parts. Split lengthwise ½″ thick.	Buttered. With Hollandaise. With grated cheese. Creamed.	**Boil** 15 to 20 min.
BRUSSELS SPROUTS	1 lb.	Remove discolored parts, part of stem.	Buttered. Creamed. With Hollandaise. With Cheese Sauce.	**Boil** 10 to 25 min.
CABBAGE	1 to 2 lb.	Remove wilted outside leaves. Shred or cut in sections.	Buttered (with caraway or mint). Creamed.	**Boil** (2″ wedges) 8 to 12 min.; (shredded) 5 to 8 min.
CHINESE CABBAGE Also called Celery Cabbage	1 to 2 lb.	Shred.	Buttered or with light cream.	**Boil or Sauté** 4 to 5 min.
CAULIFLOWER*	3 lb.	Remove outer leaves and stalks. Leave whole, cutting out center core; or separate into flowerets.	Buttered. Creamed. With Hollandaise. With grated cheese. With bacon fat and crisp bits of bacon.	**Boil** (whole) 15 to 18 min.; (flowerets) 8 to 10 min.
KOHLRABI	Six	Remove leaves. Pare. Cut into slices, slivers, or quarters.	Buttered (with marjoram). Creamed. Sautéed.	**Boil** 25 to 40 min.
ONIONS	1½ lb.	Peel, leave whole, slice, or quarter.	Buttered. Baked. Creamed. Sautéed.	**Boil** 10 to 35 min. **Bake** at 350° 50 to 60 min.
RUTABAGAS	2 lb.	Wash, pare. Cut in 2″ pieces.	Mashed. Cut-up, in soups.	**Boil** 30 to 40 min.
TURNIPS	2 lb.	Wash, pare, cut in 1″ pieces, or slice.	Mashed. Cut-up, in soups.	**Boil** 15 to 20 min.

BUTTERED VEGETABLES

Most frequently used method of serving.

Add butter, salt, pepper, and other desired seasoning to hot cooked vegetables, drained. Use 1 to 3 tbsp. butter to 2 cups vegetables. Meat drippings are good with some vegetables (corn, beans, etc.).

GLORIFIED BUTTERS FOR VEGETABLES

Pass Glorified Butter in a small pitcher.

To ¼ cup butter heated to golden brown

For	*Add*
Horseradish Butter	1 tbsp. horseradish
Scallion Butter	2 tbsp. sliced scallions
Cheese Butter	2 tbsp. grated Swiss or Parmesan cheese
Celery Butter	1 tsp. celery seed
Garlic Butter	1 small garlic bud. peeled and cut in 2 (remove before serving)
Lemon Butter	2 tbsp. lemon juice 1 tsp. grated lemon rind
Lemon Chive Butter	1 tbsp. minced chives in lemon butter
Maitre d' Hotel Butter	see "SAUCES"
Browned Butter (Beurre Noir)	brown butter until dark, add 2 tbsp. lemon juice or vinegar

HERBS AND BUTTER

Herbs add aroma and intriguing flavors.

Add a pinch (¼ tsp.) minced or powdered herbs (fresh or dry) to vegetables just before serving. (*See suggestions under individual vegetables.*)

AU BEURRE

French for "with browned buttered crumbs."

Melt 2 tbsp. butter. Stir in 1 cup fine dry bread crumbs until lightly browned.

With Cheese Crumbs: Melt ½ cup grated cheese in browned crumbs.

VEGETABLE POTPOURRI

A colorful vegetable medley.

Combine and cook until tender (about 20 min.) 1½ cups finely cut-up cabbage, 1 cup chopped carrots, ½ cup *each* chopped onions and celery, ¾ tsp. salt, 2 tbsp. salad oil, ½ cup boiling water. *Serves 4.*

CREAMED VEGETABLES

Makes them go further and adds a sauce. Use one vegetable or two or three in combination.

For 6 servings, add 1 cup hot Medium White Sauce to 2 cups hot cooked vegetables, drained. Serve plain, on toast or hot biscuits, or in a rice or noodle ring.

SCALLOPED VEGETABLES

Originally baked in scallop shells.

Place Creamed Vegetables in greased casserole, or arrange vegetables and White Sauce in alternate layers. Top with buttered bread crumbs. Bake until browned, 20 min. at 350° (mod. oven).

VEGETABLES AU GRATIN

French for "with crumbs." To Americans, it usually indicates the addition of cheese to Scalloped Vegetables and crumbs on top.

All you have to do—
To "personalize" scalloped vegetables: bake in scallop shells or ramekins.

SURPRISE PANCAKES

You'd never guess . . . vegetables in disguise!

Put through fine blade of food grinder . . .
- **½ medium-sized onion**
- **2 medium-sized potatoes**
- **3 carrots**
- **2 cups fresh spinach**
- **¼ of 1 lettuce head**

Blend in . . .
- **2 eggs, well beaten**

Sift together and stir into vegetables . . .
- **1 cup *sifted* GOLD MEDAL Flour**
- **1 tsp. baking powder**
- **½ tsp. salt (and ⅛ tsp. pepper, if desired)**

Mix well and drop by spoonfuls into hot fat in skillet. Flatten to about ½" thick. Sauté on both sides until golden brown. Serve plain, or with Cheese Sauce.
AMOUNT: 12 pancakes.

STUFFING FOR VEGETABLES

For artichokes, onions, or squash.

Mix together 1½ cups soft bread crumbs, ¾ cup grated Parmesan cheese, ½ tsp. salt, ¼ tsp. pepper, 3 tbsp. minced parsley, and ¼ cup hot bouillon.

See CHART (*p. 410*) for Preparation, Cooking Time, Serving Hints.

ARTICHOKES (French or Globe) *Aristocrats of the dinner table.*

Graceful Artichoke Eating

Pluck off leaf. Dip base in sauce. Scrape soft pulp from base with teeth. Discard the rest. With knife and fork, remove and discard the "choke." Dip cut-up "hearts" in sauce. Eat.

STUFFED ARTICHOKES ITALIAN

Hold artichokes under water. Pull leaves apart. Tuck bits of Stuffing (*p. 414*) between the leaves. Place in saucepan. Drizzle with 1 tbsp. salad oil. Add water 1″ deep, 1 sliced peeled garlic clove, 2 tsp. salt. Cook until leaves pull apart easily.

ASPARAGUS *Charles Lamb thought this "vegetable orchid" inspired gentle thoughts.*

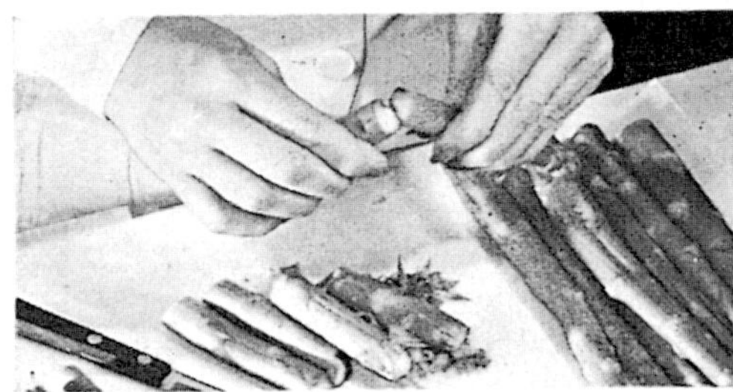

Snap off tough ends, remove any tough scales.

Cook stalks upright in water in deep saucepan.

ASPARAGUS AND ALMONDS

Alternate layers of drained cooked asparagus with Cheese Sauce and toasted blanched almonds (chopped), in a casserole. Bake 20 min. at 350° (mod. oven).

ASPARAGUS IN AMBUSH

Roll cooked stalks of asparagus in thin slices of ham or dried beef. Broil. Serve with Cheese or White Sauce.

ASPARAGUS IN RINGS

Thrust individual servings of cooked asparagus through large lemon, orange, or green pepper rings. Arrange on chop plate like the spokes of a wheel with a bowl of Hollandaise Sauce for the hub.

All you have to do—

To make a few stalks of leftover asparagus go further: cut them up and heat in a Medium White Sauce.

BEANS (Green Limas) *They change their names when they are larger. These kidney-shaped beans are "butter" or "baby limas" when small. But the larger varieties are "potato" or "Ford-hook." A real delicacy served with milk, butter and seasoning.*

SPICY LIMA BEANS

A grand way to serve canned limas.

Add 1 can condensed pepper pot or tomato soup to 3 cups cooked lima beans. Heat. *Serves 6.*

SUCCOTASH

Combine equal amounts hot cooked or canned whole grain corn with hot cooked or canned green limas. Add butter, a little top milk or cream, season to taste. Heat.

LIMAS IN BOLOGNA BOWLS

A different and easy supper dish.

Sauté ¼″ slices unskinned bologna until edges curl. Fill with hot cooked limas.

LIMAS IN SQUASH NESTS

See directions and picture on p. 425.

CREOLE LIMAS

Prepare like Creole Beans (*p. 416*).

Tip: Lima Beans combine deliciously with: Celery, Carrots, Tomatoes.

See CHART (*p. 410*) for Preparation, Cooking Time, Serving Hints.

BEANS (Green or Wax) *Young pods are now stringless.*

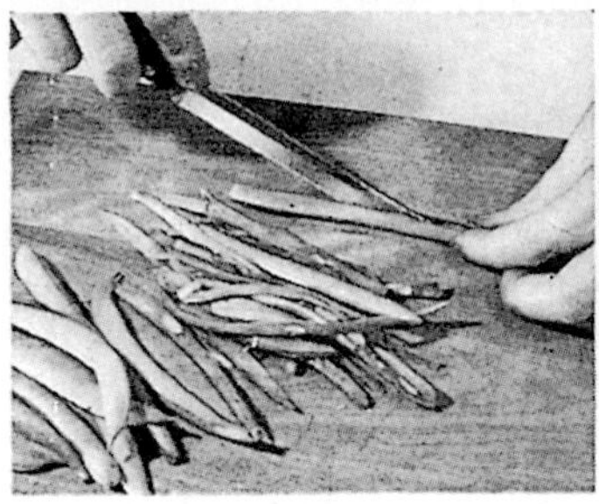

To "French" beans, cut in two strips. Then cut each strip in two narrow strips.

Shred raw beets on coarse shredder.

SWEET-SOUR BEANS

Brown until crisp 2 strips bacon.
Cook in the bacon fat until yellow . . .
- **1 cup minced onion**

Stir in . . .
- **1 tbsp. flour**

Add and bring to boil . . .
- **¾ cup vegetable liquid**
- **¼ cup vinegar**
- **2 tbsp. sugar**
- **1 tsp. salt**
- **¼ tsp. pepper**

Stir in . . .
- **2 cups cooked green or wax beans**

Stir gently until heated through. Serve with the crisp bacon sprinkled over top.
AMOUNT: 4 servings.

CREOLE BEANS

Cook in 2 tbsp. fat until tender . . .
- **1 cup thinly sliced onion**
- **⅔ cup chopped green pepper**
- **⅔ cup diced celery**

Mix in . . .
- **2 cups diced fresh or drained canned tomatoes**
- **2 cups cut-up beans (cooked or uncooked)**
- **1½ tsp. salt**
- **¼ tsp. pepper**

Cook until cooked beans are heated through or until uncooked beans are tender.
AMOUNT: 6 servings.

BEETS *A 2-in-1 specialty . . . tops and roots are nutritious and "eatable."*

HARVARD BEETS

A specialty of the Yale Club.

Heat together . . .
- **3 cups diced cooked beets**
- **1 cup liquid (beet juice and water)**

Mix together and stir in . . .
- **3 tbsp. flour**
- **2 tbsp. sugar**
- **1 tsp. salt**
- **dash of pepper**
- **⅓ cup vinegar**

Cook, stirring constantly, until smoothly blended and thickened.
AMOUNT: 6 servings.

BEETS WITH ORANGE SAUCE

To 3 cups sliced cooked beets, add a mixture of 2 tbsp. flour, ¼ cup sugar, ½ cup orange juice, and 2 tbsp. butter. Bake in covered pan 15 min. at 350° (mod. oven). Serve with Roast Pork, Duck, etc. *Serves 6.*

CHRYSANTHEMUM BEETS

Shred raw beets on coarse shredder. Cook 8 to 10 min. Serve buttered and seasoned in fluffy mass.

BEET RELISH

Irene Laviske Spack, when on our Staff, showed us this delicacy from Poland.

Season ground raw beets with sugar, vinegar, and lots of horseradish.

ZIPPY BEETS

Cook 3 cups shredded beets. Add ⅓ cup cream, 2½ tsp. horseradish, 1 tsp. salt.

QUICK BEET PICKLES

Bring to boil ½ cup vinegar, ½ cup liquid from a #2 can of baby beets, 2 tbsp. sugar, 2 cloves, ½ tsp. salt, 3 pepper-corns, and ¼ bay leaf. Pour over beets. Chill.

See CHART (*p. 413*) for Preparation, Cooking Time, Serving Hints.

BRUSSELS SPROUTS ("Tom Thumb Cabbage") *Originated in Brussels, Belgium.*

BRUSSELS SPROUTS PIQUANT

Place 1 qt. cooked sprouts in casserole with Tomato Sauce. Sprinkle with ¼ cup grated American cheese. Bake 15 min. at 350° (mod. oven). *Serves 6.*

Combine deliciously with Brussels Sprouts: Onions, Peas, Beans, Celery

Elizabeth Lyman, now of Hotpoint, Inc., Chicago, formerly of our Staff, says

All you have to do—

"*To add a distinctive touch to Creamed Brussels Sprouts:* sprinkle with a little nutmeg. If desired, add a little diced crisp bacon or a few chopped toasted almonds."

CABBAGE White . . . Savoy . . . Red . . . all take the same preparation.

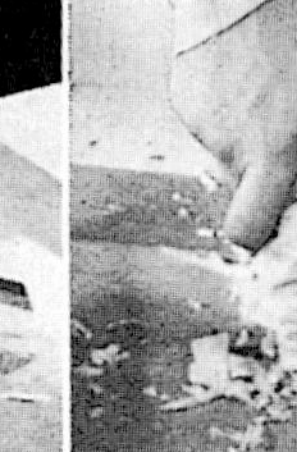

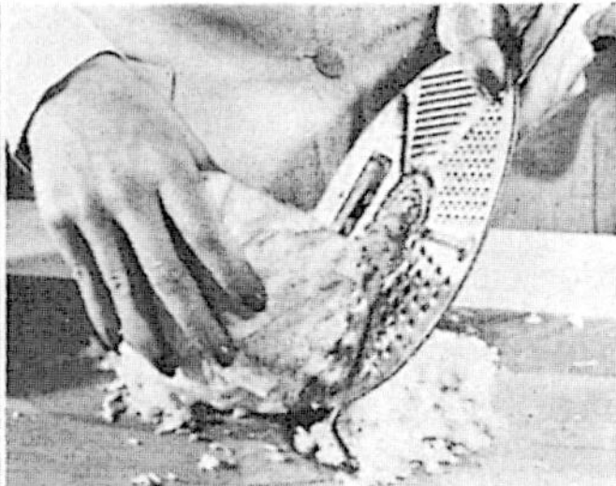

1 For "coarsely shredded" cabbage, use a knife.

2 For "medium shredded," use blade of shredder.

3 For "finely shredded," use the coarse shredder.

CABBAGE AND APPLES DE LUXE

Thanks to Mrs. Frederick H. K. Schaaf of Minneapolis, Minnesota, for this unusual dish.

Pour boiling water over cabbage in colander.
- 12 cups finely shredded red cabbage

Cook together 5 min. with
- 1 cup water
- 3 apples, cut into very thin ⅛″ slices
- ½ cup brown sugar
- 2 tbsp. butter
- 2 tsp. grated onion
- ½ tsp. salt
- dash of pepper

Mix in . . .
- ½ cup mild vinegar (dilute with water)
- ½ cup gingersnap pieces

Stir over heat until gingersnaps are dissolved and mixture is hot.

AMOUNT: 8 servings.

HOT CABBAGE-BACON SLAW

Add 1 cup heated Cooked Salad Dressing (thinned with sour cream) to ½ head cabbage, shredded. Heat 3 min. Just before serving, add 6 chopped crisp bacon slices. *Serves 6.*

SAUERKRAUT

Cabbage in brine.

Now usually purchased in bulk or in cans.

CABBAGE BUNDLES

Cook cabbage leaves one inside the other. Wrap around hot frankfurters brushed with mustard. Ideal for a vegetable plate. *Or* roll partially cooked cabbage leaves around seasoned hamburger, and braise.

GOLDEN CABBAGE

Cook 8 cups shredded cabbage until tender. Drain. Stir in 1 egg, beaten, 2 tbsp. butter, 1 tbsp. lemon juice. *Serves 6.*

CAULIFLOWER *An edible nosegay . . . white buds surrounded by a leafy green frill.*

Serve raw flowerets on the relish tray.

THRIFT TIP

Cook pared stalks cut into small pieces until tender (about 20 min.). Chop fine. Season, and serve with whole cauliflower or use for another meal. Cook the tender leaves with the flowerets.

BLUSHING CAULIFLOWER

Serve cooked flowerets in Tomato Sauce.

CAULIFLOWER AU BEURRE NOIR

With browned, buttered crumbs—very popular. *See page 414.*

FRESH VEGETABLES Carrots, Celeriac, and Celtuce.

See CHART (*p. 410*) for Preparation, Cooking Time, Serving Hints.

CARROTS *They don't make your hair curl, but do help protect your health. Formerly raised as fodder . . . now a colorful addition to our meals.*

SAVORY CARROTS

Brown 2 tbsp. melted butter and 3 tbsp. flour. Stir in 3 cups cooked carrot cubes or strips and ¾ cup carrot cooking water. Season. Stir over heat until sauce is

CARROTS AMBROSIA

They're truly glazed beauties.

Glaze 12 whole small cooked carrots with butter and sugar as in recipe below. Add 2 oranges, sliced, and heat thoroughly. *Serves 4.*

MINT-GLAZED CARROTS

Delicious served with buttered peas!

Simmer 2 cups cooked carrot strips with ¼ cup each of butter and sugar until soft and glazed. Add 1 tbsp. Mint Sauce. Serve carrots with the glazing syrup. *Serves 4.*

CARROT AND CELERY SOUFFLÉ

Delicious with roast chicken or baked ham.

Mix with 1 cup Thick White Sauce . . .

2 egg yolks, slightly beaten
1 cup grated raw carrots
½ cup cooked diced celery
⅛ tsp. paprika
1 tbsp. minced parsley

Fold in . . .

2 egg whites, well beaten

Pour into buttered 1-qt. casserole (6½″). Set in pan of water (1″ deep). Bake 40 to 50 min. in mod. oven (350°).

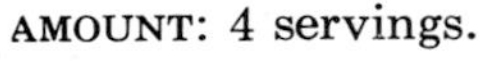
AMOUNT: 4 servings.

To make cooked carrots particularly appealing: serve whole, buttered or glazed, etc. with a sprig of green parsley thrust in the end (look like fresh carrots).

FRENCH CARROTS

Sprinkle 2 tsp. sugar over parboiled carrot strips. Simmer in butter until tender.

FLEMISH CARROTS

Stir together 2 cups hot cooked carrot slices, 2 tbsp. butter, ½ tsp. sugar, ⅛ tsp. nutmeg. Add 1 cup cream combined with 1 egg yolk. Stir constantly until slightly thickened. Serve sprinkled with minced parsley. *Serves 4.*

GOLD AND SILVER COINS

Cook together ¼″ thick carrot slices and slices of small parboiled onions (3 times more carrots). Season.

CARROT AND CELERY STICKS

Cook equal amounts slivered carrots and 1″ pieces celery.

SCALLOPED CARROTS, ONIONS, AND CELERY

Add 1 cup each of partially cooked sliced or diced carrots, diced celery, and sliced mild onions to 2 cups Medium White Sauce. Place in 10x6x2″ baking dish. Top with buttered bread crumbs. Heat in mod. oven.

CARROT CAPERS

Delight children with a golden heap of grated raw carrots. Sprinkle with lemon juice. Serve on a frilly leaf of lettuce.

Mix grated raw carrots with fluffy mashed potato.

Sprinkle grated raw carrots with ginger, salt, pepper, and enough water to moisten. Bake 30 min. in mod. oven.

CELERIAC (Celery Root) *A type of celery with root similar to a turnip.*

Prepared like any other root vegetable. Can be sliced or cubed. Boils in 20 to 25 min. Serve buttered, creamed, or with Hollandaise or Cheese Sauce.

CELTUCE *Derives its name from its flavor combination of celery and lettuce.*

Buy as you would lettuce; cook and serve as you would cabbage.

See CHART (p. 411) for Preparation, Cooking Time, Serving Hints.

CELERY

Grew wild for centuries . . . old cook books called it "smallage." A holiday delicacy until recent years, now available and popular at all seasons.

FRENCH BRAISED CELERY

Place in casserole . . .
- 2 cups 1″ celery pieces
- 4 sprigs parsley
- 4 onion slices
- ½ cup bouillon

Sprinkle with . . .
- 1 tsp. salt
- ¼ tsp. pepper
- 2 bacon strips, cut into pieces

Cover and bake at 375° (quick mod. oven) 30 min. Sprinkle with buttered bread crumbs and bake uncovered for 10 min. or until crumbs are browned.
AMOUNT: 4 servings.

Thrift Tips

Serve celery hearts as a relish or salad.

Save small branches and leaves to use in soups, stews, bread stuffings, and salads, and as garnishes.

Dry leaves in paper bag, then crumble fine. Use as celery seasoning.

Combine a little hot cooked celery with other hot cooked vegetables, such as carrots, string beans, peas, or tomatoes to make them go further.

CORN

Fresh young corn is at its best cooked within an hour after picking.

1 To retain fullest flavor in corn which has stood several hours, remove silk but not all of husks.

2 Cut off stem ends.

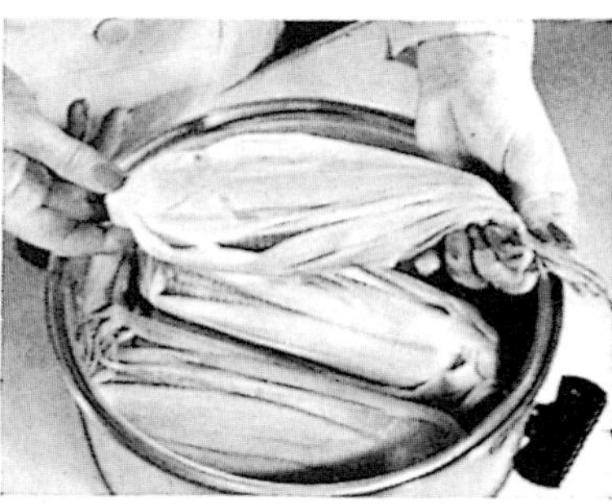

3 Place in kettle with boiling water to cover or on barbecue grill. Cook until tender (10 to 15 min.).

CORN SAUTÉ (With Peppers)

Cook chopped green peppers in butter for 5 min. Add cooked whole kernel corn. Salt and cook until lightly browned.

CORN (Southern Style)

From "Marie," one of the best cooks I ever met, who puts her own sunny nature and deep sympathy into good things she makes. This is one of the special recipes from her native Texas.

Choose 8 ears of corn with large kernels. Cut corn from cobs by first cutting down through kernels, then scraping the pulp from the cob with back of knife (this frees pulp from shells). Add corn to 6 tbsp. melted butter in large skillet. Stir in 2 tbsp. flour, 2 tbsp. sugar, 1 tsp. salt, ½ cup top milk, and cook covered for 10 min. Add ½ cup cream just before serving. *Serves 6.*

CORN-TOMATO CASSEROLE

Combine and place in greased casserole 2½ cups *each* cooked whole kernel corn and tomatoes, 1 chopped small green pepper, ½ cup coarse cracker crumbs, 1½ tsp. salt, dash of pepper, 1 tsp. sugar, and 2 tbsp. melted butter. Sprinkle with grated American cheese, additional cracker crumbs, and dot with butter. Bake in mod. hot oven for 30 min. *Serves 8.*

CORN PATTIES (Mock Oysters)

Blend together 2 egg yolks, well beaten; ½ tsp. salt; dash of pepper; 1½ cups cooked fresh corn, cut from cob; 2 tsp. cream; 1 tsp. butter; and 2 tsp. flour. Fold in 2 egg whites, stiffly beaten. Drop by teaspoonfuls onto a *hot greased* griddle. Cook until brown on each side. Serve hot, as meat accompaniment. *Makes 24 patties.*

DASHEEN (Taro) Raised and used mostly in the South. Colors range from violet to a cream shade. Boil in skins 20 to 35 min. Serve like potatoes, but do not mash.

See CHART (*pp. 411-413*) for Preparation, Cooking Time, Serving Hints.

EGGPLANT *Distinctively royal with its purple color and delicate flavor.*

STUFFED EGGPLANT (Scalloped)

Brought to us by Emily Child of Minneapolis.

Cut thick slice off side of medium-sized eggplant. Cook in boiling salted water until tender (15 min.). Scoop out pulp leaving shell 1/4″ thick. Cook 1/2 cup chopped onion and 3/4 cup sliced mushrooms in 4 tbsp. butter. Blend in 4 tbsp. flour and 2 cups milk. Cook, stirring constantly, until it boils. Boil 1 min. Add cut-up eggplant pulp (about 2 1/2 cups). Season. Pour into shell or into 10x6x2″ baking dish. Top with buttered bread or cracker crumbs. Bake 20 min. in mod. hot oven. (*See picture, p. 420.*) *Serves 6.*

EGGPLANT SANDWICHES

Place a slice of cheese between 2 eggplant slices (1/8″ thick). Dip sandwiches in beaten egg and cracker crumbs and sauté the same as Fried Eggplant.

ITALIAN EGGPLANT

Delicious, satisfying one-dish meal. . . according to Mildred Kranz, gracious hostess in our department.

Place in separate layers in 2-qt. casserole (8″) cooked noodles and cut-up tomatoes (2 cups each), 1 cup thin slices green pepper. Sprinkle each layer with a little flour, salt, and pepper. Cover with cut-up eggplant slices. Pour over top beef broth or bouillon (1/2 cup). Sprinkle with grated sharp cheese and more flour, salt, and pepper. Dot with butter. Top with WHEATIES or cracker crumbs. Bake about 1 hr. in mod. oven. *Serves 6.*

FRIED EGGPLANT

Pare eggplant and slice 1/4″ thick. Dip in beaten egg, then cracker crumbs. Sauté in fat in hot skillet until tender and brown on both sides. Sprinkle with salt and pepper while cooking.

GREENS *Includes Chicory, Collards, Dandelions, Escarole, Kale, Lamb's Lettuce, Endive, Mustard, Sorrel, Spinach, Swiss Chard, Beet and Turnip Tops.*

SPINACH (French Method)

Makes most anyone enjoy spinach.

Cook spinach. Drain. Chop while in strainer. Blend in *Thick* White Sauce (seasoned with nutmeg and onion) just to hold spinach together (1 tbsp. per cup).

MOLDED GREENS

Combine seasoned chopped cooked greens with crisp bacon bits. Pack into individual molds. Keep warm in oven. Unmold, and serve with lemon and hard-cooked egg slices.

ONIONS (Dry) *They come as "boilers," "picklers," or "sticks."*

STUFFED (Baked) ONIONS

Cook large onions in boiling salted water until slightly tender (15 min.). Drain. Cool. Cut thin slices from root end. Hollow out centers, leaving 1/2″ shell. Chop centers and combine with Mushroom or Cheese Sauce, or a creamed meat mixture. Use to fill onion shells. Top with buttered crumbs. Bake 1 hr. in mod. hot oven.

SPECIAL ONIONS

Insert 2 whole cloves into each parboiled small onion. Cover with Medium White Sauce made with Chicken Broth. Bake at 350° (mod. oven) until bubbling.

BROILED ONIONS

Pour cream over cooked onions. Sprinkle with grated cheese. Broil until it melts.

FRIED ONION RINGS

Slice large onions crosswise (1/4″ thick). Separate into rings. Dip in slightly beaten egg, then in flour. Fry in 1/4″ hot fat to delicate brown. Drain. Salt lightly. Serve.

FRENCH FRIED ONION RINGS

Perfectly prepared . . . beautifully served . . . at delightful Colonial Inn, Minneapolis.

Dip onion rings in Fritter Batter; fry (*see p. 78*).

TWO DRAMATIC VEGETABLE PLATTERS FOR DINNER PARTIES

← Cauliflower surrounded by Shredded Beets in Spinach Nests, Glazed Onions; Stuffed Eggplant on bed of Celery Cabbage, Glazed Carrots with Parsley Tops.

See CHART (*p. 411*) for Preparation, Cooking Time, Serving Hints.

PEAS *The most popular and most used of all cooked vegetables.*

Caution: Shell peas just before cooking. Do not wash.

How to Cook Fresh Peas by French Method to Give Most Delicious Flavor

1 Line saucepan with large wet lettuce leaves.

2 When peas are tender, discard lettuce.

PEAS, FRENCH STYLE

A favorite vegetable with Pat Warner Williams of Minneapolis, the beautiful brunette hostess in our department for several years.

Line heavy saucepan with 3 or 4 large wet outside leaves of lettuce. Place 2 lb. peas (shelled) in lettuce. Add 1 tsp. sugar, 2 to 4 tbsp water (the larger amount for larger peas). Cover pan tight. Cook until tender (about 20 min.). Season, add a little butter and milk (or cream) to any juice left, and serve. *Serves 4.*

Flavor Accents. Chopped mint, as in Mint-Glazed Carrots and Peas, *p. 418.*

PEAS IN PODS

Another French idea.

For extra-delicious flavor, add some new young pods when cooking peas. Serve with peas.

SPRING FAVORITES

Twosome: New potatoes with peas.
Little new onions with peas.

Threesome: New potatoes, little new onions, and peas together.

Green and Gold: Fresh peas with young, tender carrot strips.

PEPPERS (Sweet Green) *Do not confuse with the "hot" variety called Chili peppers.*

STUFFED GREEN PEPPERS

Cut a thin slice from the stem end of each pepper. Wash outside and inside. Remove all seeds and membrane. Place peppers in a kettle with salted water (1 cup water and 1½ tsp. salt for 6 peppers). Cover, and boil 5 min. Drain, reserving liquid. Lightly fill peppers with desired stuffing. Bake 20 min. in mod. oven.

All you have to do — *To keep peppers in shape while baking:* put in muffin pans or individual baking cups.

HAM-AND-CORN STUFFING FOR PEPPERS

Combine 1 cup Medium White Sauce, 1 cup cooked whole kernel corn, 2 cups ground cooked ham, and ¼ tsp. dry mustard. Fill loosely 6 parboiled green peppers. Sprinkle with ½ cup buttered bread or cracker crumbs. Bake 20 min. in mod. oven.

HASH-AND-TOMATO STUFFING

Blend together canned hash and canned tomato soup to make a stuffing of the right consistency. Fill peppers as directed above, and bake.

See CHART (*p. 411*) for Preparation, Cooking Time, Serving Hints.

POTATOES (White)

Native of America. Called "Irish potatoes" because they once sustained people during a famine in Ireland. Potatoes with their Vitamin C saved the sailors of old from dying of scurvy on long voyages. In Civil War days, the women packed potatoes in barrels of brine, and sent them to prison camps to save lives of the undernourished prisoners.

WELL COOKED POTATOES—*the test of an expert cook.*

"Mealy" potatoes are best for baking, boiling, and frying. "Waxy" potatoes are best for salads, scalloping, and creaming. Boil new potatoes in their skins.

1. Cook in jackets (saves minerals and vitamins).
2. If you do pare them, keep parings thin (minerals lie close to the skin).
3. Pare just before cooking. Do not soak potatoes (minerals and vitamins escape).
4. Cook in *boiling salted* water. Keep it boiling to prevent losses and sogginess.
5. Drain potatoes (saving potato water for soups, sauces, yeast breads); shake over heat to dry them.
6. Cover with a cloth while they stand to prevent getting soggy (it absorbs steam).

FLUFFY MASHED POTATOES

Cook potatoes until tender, not mushy. Drain. Shake potatoes in kettle over heat until dry. Mash thoroughly. Season with salt and pepper. Add butter and heated milk (½ cup to 8 potatoes). Whip into potatoes, beating until fluffy.

All you have to do— *To keep Mashed Potatoes hot:* Cover, and place pan in skillet of hot water. To keep fluffy, add a bit of baking powder.

POTATO CAKES

Shape cold Mashed Potatoes into 3″ cakes ¾″ thick. Roll in flour. Sauté in hot fat until golden brown.

BAKED POTATOES

Choose baking potatoes of same size. Rub the skins with fat. Bake until potatoes "squeeze" soft (see Chart, p. 411). Cut crisscross gash on potato top. Squeeze until potato pops up through opening. Season, and butter.

THREE MEN IN A BOAT

Children love this dramatized food.

Hollow out part of baked potato. Fill with creamed dried beef and peas. Cut a sail from a firm piece of cheese. Stick it on with a wooden pick. Three mushroom caps on edge of potato are the "men."

DUCHESS POTATOES

Make Fluffy Mashed Potatoes (*opposite*) and beat in beaten eggs (2 eggs for 3 cups potatoes). Spoon into mounds, or with pastry bag and tube form rosettes on a greased baking sheet, or pipe in a border around planked meat or fish. Brush with top milk. Brown in hot oven (425°).

POTATO PUFF

Make Fluffy Mashed Potatoes (*opposite*) and beat in 2 egg yolks, well beaten. Then fold in the 2 egg whites, stiffly beaten. Pile into greased casserole. Bake at 350° (mod. oven) 30 min. until puffed and brown.

TWICE-BAKED POTATOES

Cut Baked Potatoes in halves lengthwise. Scoop out potato and follow recipe for Fluffy Mashed Potatoes. Refill potato shells heaping full. Brown in hot oven.

SPECIAL STUFFED POTATOES

Follow directions above for Twice-Baked Potatoes—*except* mix in for *each* potato:

2 tbsp. bits of cooked ham or tuna, 1 tbsp. minced onion, 1 tsp. minced parsley *or*

2 tbsp. sour cream, 2 tbsp. crisp bacon bits, 1 tbsp. minced onion, dash nutmeg *or*

2 tbsp. cottage cheese, 2 tbsp. crisp bacon bits or cooked ham, etc., 1 tbsp. chives

DENVER POTATOES

Cut pared potatoes in halves lengthwise; trim to stand evenly. Make a 1″ cavity in each; fill with 1 tsp. butter. Sprinkle with salt and paprika. Place in baking dish with water (½″ deep). Bake at 450° (hot oven) for 30 min. or until tender.

FRANCONIA POTATOES
(Browned)

Place pared parboiled potatoes in pan in which beef or pork is roasting. To baste, turn them over in the fat in the pan several times. Bake until tender and browned (about 40 min.).

COTTAGE FRIED POTATOES

Slice cooked potatoes thin. Sauté in hot fat in skillet until underside is brown. Season well. Cover a few min. to steam. Turn to brown other side.

LYONNAISE POTATOES

Follow recipe for Cottage Fried Potatoes above—adding sautéed onion slices to the potatoes before frying.

HASHED BROWNED POTATOES

Combine 3 cups chopped cooked potatoes with 3 tbsp. flour, 1 tbsp. minced onion, ¼ cup top milk, 1 tsp. salt, ⅛ tsp. pepper. Heat 3 tbsp. fat in heavy skillet. Pack potatoes in firmly. Brown over low heat on underside (20 min.). Fold half over like an omelet. *Serves 4.*

SHIRRED POTATOES

Especially delicious when there's no gravy.

Combine 3 cups shredded raw potatoes and 2 cups *Thin* White Sauce in buttered casserole. Sprinkle with ½ tsp. salt; dot with 1 tbsp. butter. Bake 30 min. at 350° (mod. oven), then reduce to 300° (slow oven) and bake 2½ hr. longer. *Serves 6.*

AU GRATIN POTATOES

Pour hot Cheese Sauce with mustard in it over layers of hot diced boiled potatoes in casserole. Top with grated cheese. Bake in mod. oven 20 min.

CREAMED POTATOES

Pour Thin or Medium White Sauce over hot sliced or diced boiled potatoes or small new potatoes. Heat. Sprinkle with minced parsley or chives, and serve.

Savory, economical "meat-and-potato" dish.

DUTCH POTATOES

Core 6 pared medium potatoes. Draw a wiener through each. Place in baking pan with 4 tbsp. drippings. Add 1 cup milk. Bake at 350° (mod. oven) 1 hr. *Serves 6.*

FRIED RAW POTATOES

Pan-fry thin raw potato and a few onion slices in fat in hot skillet 10 min., covered. When brown, season, turn them, and fry uncovered, turning occasionally.

FRENCH FRIED POTATOES

Cut pared potatoes into ⅜″ lengthwise strips, balls, thin slices, cubes, or curls. Soak 20 min. to 1 hr. in ice water; drain, and dry thoroughly. Fry a few at a time in a frying basket in deep fat at 370° until slightly brown. Drain on paper. Just before serving, put back in basket and fry at 390° until crisp and brown. Drain on paper, sprinkle with salt, and serve immediately.

POTATO PANCAKES

Grate 2 cups raw potatoes into ¼ cup milk. Drain off milk and add 1 egg, well beaten, and 2 tbsp. flour. Season with salt, pepper. Add 1 tbsp. minced onion. Drop by spoonfuls onto well greased pan. Brown on both sides.

SCALLOPED POTATOES

Place a layer of thin raw potato slices (6 potatoes) in greased casserole. Sprinkle with 1 tbsp. flour, salt, and pepper. Dot with butter. Continue . . . making 3 layers. Pour in milk to barely cover. Bake at 350° (mod. oven) until tender (1 hr.). *Serves 6. WITH FRANKS:* Add ¼″ frankfurt slices (6 franks) with potato layers.

See CHART (pp. 411, 412) for Preparation, Cooking Time, Serving Hints.

PUMPKIN

Used as pie filling. Seed, pare, cut in 2″ pieces; boil 25 to 30 min. Mash.

RADISHES

Usually eaten raw . . . but for variety's sake, try them cooked.

Cut large radishes in half, boil 15 to 20 min. Serve creamed, or with chopped chives, grated cheese.

SALSIFY (Oyster Plant)

Looks like parsnips, tastes like oysters. The old name was "Johnny Go to Bed at Noon" because the big blossoms close at noon.

Prepare like parsnips. Plunge into cold water with lemon juice or vinegar to prevent discoloration.

It has a delicate flavor, is delicious cut-up and creamed.

SQUASH (Summer)

Includes Yellow Crookneck, White Scalloped, Zucchini, Vegetable Marrow, and Cymlings, "Patty Pans." For cooking, see p. 412. Acorn Squash is best baked.

How to Bake a Meal in an Acorn Squash.

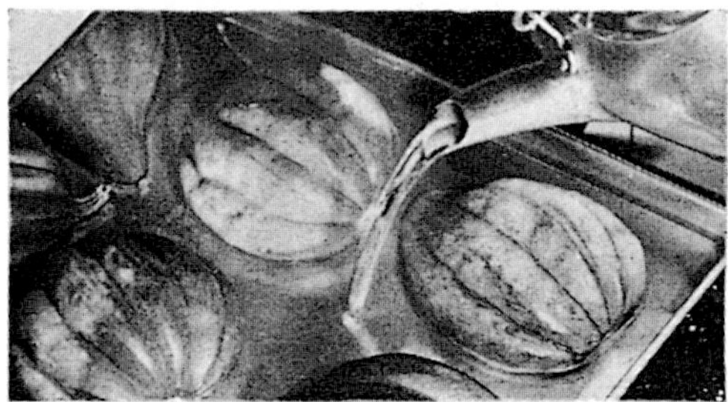

1 Place Acorn Squash halves cut-side down in pan. Pour in boiling water to ¼″ depth. Bake at 400° (mod. hot oven) 25 min

2 Turn squash cut-side up with fork. Fill centers with partially cooked sausage patties. Bake until tender (25 min.).

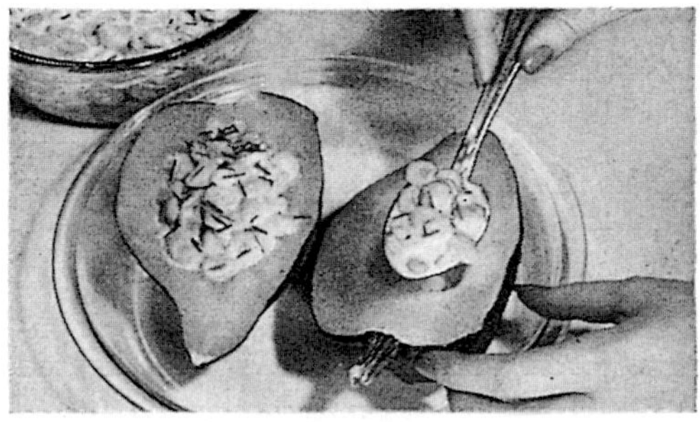

3 Or bake squash without stuffing, add butter and seasoning. For something different, fill with cooked seasoned lima beans mixed with sour cream and chives. Smart idea from Eloise Davison of New York City.

SCALLOPED SUMMER SQUASH

Cut large Crooknecks in halves lengthwise, remove seeds and fiber. Hollow out some of pulp. Dice unpared squash (other half). Cook 10 min. in a little water. Mix with salt, butter, a little onion juice, and a generous sprinkling of pepper. Heap in hollowed-out squash half. Bake 1 hr. at 350° (mod. oven).

PANNED ZUCCHINI

Slice tender Zucchini. Cut slices in quarters. Cook in very little water . . . adding a little oil or butter to water. Cover, cook until tender, then season.

SQUASH (Winter)

Includes Hubbard and Acorn. North American Indians called it "askutasquash." They termed it one of their "three sisters" . . . the others being corn and beans.

GLAZED SQUASH

Cut squash into 3″ squares. Pare and parboil 30 min. Drain. Place in shallow baking pan. Drizzle over pieces a Glazing Syrup (heat together ½ cup sugar, ½ cup brown sugar, ½ cup water and 2 tbsp. butter). Bake, basting with syrup until glazed, at 350° (mod. oven) 30 min.

To open or cut Winter Squash apart easily: place in a mod. hot oven (400°) until heated through. Cool, pare.

FRESH VEGETABLES Sweet Potatoes, Tomatoes, and Turnips.

See CHART (*pp. 412, 413*) for Preparation, Cooking Time, Serving Hints.

SWEET POTATOES:

The flesh of Jersey Sweets is dry, pale yellow; of Southern Yams is moist, orange-colored, sweeter. Order the type you prefer. Cooking methods are alike.

BAKED SWEET POTATOES

Follow directions for baking (*p. 412*). To bake quickly (30 min.), parboil sweet potatoes first about 20 min.

SWEET POTATO RING

Stunning and delicious for dinner parties. Enjoyed at the home of Mrs. Joseph Kennedy, Evanston, Illinois.

Boil and mash 3 lb. sweet potatoes. Blend in 3 well beaten egg yolks, 2 tbsp. melted butter, 1 tsp. salt, and 1 cup milk. Fold in 3 well beaten egg whites.

Butter a ring mold well. Place walnut halves around in it. Sprinkle with brown sugar. Cover with sweet potato mixture. Bake at 350° (mod. oven) 45 min. Turn upside-down on platter. Let stand 5 min. Remove pan. Fill ring with buttered peas or green limas.

GLAZED SWEET POTATOES

Add equal amounts of brown sugar and butter to cooked sweet potato halves or slices. Simmer or broil until browned.

CANDIED SWEET POTATOES

Slice 6 pared cooked sweet potatoes. Place in greased casserole. Add a syrup made of 1 cup brown sugar, ¼ cup water, ¼ cup butter, ½ tsp. salt. Bake at 350° (mod. oven) 45 min., basting occasionally.

SWEET POTATO APPLES

Delicious, different, spectacular for dinner parties as made by Oline Halsness, now Mrs. Patrick Casey of Minneapolis, Minnesota.

Shape seasoned mashed baked Jersey sweet potatoes around a marshmallow to form an apple. Place a clove in 1 end for a stem. Brush with beaten egg yolk mixed with water, then paprika. Place on greased pan. Heat 12 min. in mod. oven (350°).

TOMATOES

Formerly called "love apples" . . . pronounced "tomay-to" or "tomah-to."

STEWED TOMATOES

Simmer together 10 min. 2½ cups canned tomatoes, 1 tsp. minced onion, ½ tbsp. sugar, 2 tbsp. butter, ⅛ tsp. pepper, and 2 tbsp. flour or ½ cup soft bread cubes.

JAVANESE TOMATOES

Delicious with beef or pork. They retain a fresh tomato flavor and hold their shape.

Peel 8 small tomatoes carefully. Place in casserole. Sprinkle with salt and savory. Cover. Bake at 400° (mod. hot oven) 30 min. until tender. Remove from oven. Add 2 tbsp. butter and let it melt over tomatoes. Serve.

TOMATOES VINAIGRETTE

Favorite of Virginia Van Nostrand of our Staff.

Place sliced tomatoes in bowl. Add layers of minced onion and minced parsley. Pour French Dressing over them. Chill ½ hr.

SAUTÉED TOMATOES

Dip ¼" tomato slices into seasoned flour, then into beaten egg, then cracker crumbs. Sauté on both sides in hot butter. Remove tomato slices. Make Medium White Sauce in the pan. Serve over tomatoes.

BROILED TOMATOES

Top tomato halves with butter and seasoning. Broil under low heat until heated through.

STUFFED TOMATOES

Scoop out centers of 6 tomatoes. Fill with tomato pulp mixed with soft bread crumbs, grated American cheese, crisp bacon bits, grated onion, salt, and pepper. Top with buttered crumbs and additional cheese, if desired. Bake at 350° (mod. oven) 30 min.

TURNIPS WHITE and YELLOW

Called "neeps" by the early English and used as medicine. Yellow turnips, known as rutabagas, are stronger in flavor than the white. They are cooked and served in the same way.

MASHED TURNIPS OR RUTABAGAS

Cook like Fluffy Mashed Potatoes (*p. 423*).

TO MAKE THE FLAVOR MILDER:

1. Combine with equal amounts of mashed potatoes.
2. Fold in whipped cream.

MINUTES SAVED *can easily grow into that extra hour or two a day so many busy women want and need . . . just as saving a penny here and there in a little savings bank grows into dollars. Homemakers all over the country have shared with us their favorite time-savers and other short cuts. They are tucked into the pages of the book here and there . . . and we are passing many of them on to you on these pages.*

Betty Crocker

SOME SHORT CUTS IN FOODS MAY BE BOUGHT
. . . *We List a Few*

APPETIZER FOODS

JUICES: Canned . . . all kinds: tangerine, apricot, cranberry, sauerkraut, tomato.

Frozen, concentrated, or ready-to-serve: orange, grape, orange and grape fruit. (May be used in all recipes requiring fruit juice.)

SOUPS
Canned . many varieties.
Packaged . several kinds.

SEAFOODS: Canned . . . all varieties; some smoked.

Frozen . . . many kinds; some ready to serve.

MEAT, FISH, POULTRY

MEAT: Canned meat balls, hamburgers, ham with sauce, wieners in sauce, beef tongue.

MAIN DISH: Canned beef stew, Ravioli, chow mein, chop suey, corned beef hash, roast beef hash, chili con carne, creamed dried beef, beef and gravy, noodles and giblets, noodles and chicken.

POULTRY: Canned pheasant, turkey, chicken breasts, chicken fricassee, chicken à la king.

FISH: Canned halibut, trout, breaded shrimp, fish balls, deviled crab.

POTATOES (White and Sweet)

Canned . . . whole boiled, French fried, shoestring, and sweet potatoes.

Frozen . . . potato patties, candied sweet potatoes, French fries.

Packaged . . . dehydrated potatoes . . . mashed potatoes.

MACARONI AND SPAGHETTI, RICE AND BEANS

CANNED MACARONI, with cheese, and with tomato sauce, Spanish rice, cooked rice.

Frozen . . . spicy tomato sauces.

PACKAGED SPAGHETTI . . . may contain a glass jar of concentrated meat or mushroom sauce and grated cheese.

PRECOOKED BEANS.

GRAVY AND STUFFINGS

Canned beef gravy ready to heat and serve.

Dehydrated and concentrated gravy flavoring and coloring . . . require water only.

Dehydrated . . . seasoned stuffings . . . simply add water.

VEGETABLES

Canned . . . a tremendous variety; some in combination and some packed in layers.

Frozen vegetables . . . including mushrooms, corn on the cob, squash.

SALADS

FRUIT SALAD

Canned . . . all varieties; interesting combinations.
Frozen assortments that taste like fresh.

SPECIAL

Fresh greens in cellophane packages.
Prepared gelatin salad.

VEGETABLE SALAD

Canned . . . all kinds.
Frozen . . . most varieties.

BREADS, ROLLS, AND BISCUITS

Brown 'n Serve Rolls are prebaked, ready to be browned in the oven.

FROZEN rolls, blueberry muffins, English muffins are available in many shops.

CANNED BREADS: date-nut, brown bread.

BAKING POWDER BISCUITS (cut out . . . ready to bake).

YEAST ROLL AND BREAD MIXES, partly prepared muffin, biscuit, and pancake mixes are on most markets.

PIES

PIES AND PASTRY:

Frozen . . . baked and unbaked.

PIE CRUST MIXES:

Partly prepared . . . in packages.

PIE FILLINGS:

Dehydrated, such as apple. Canned berry fillings. Packaged . . . many flavors requiring only liquid.

TOPPINGS:

Canned . . . in variety for ice cream.

PUDDINGS, CAKES, COOKIES

PUDDINGS:

Packaged . . . many flavors. Tapioca.
Canned . . . plum, date, nut, etc.

CAKES:

Frozen . . . baked.
Packaged . . . as mixes.

BROWNIES:

Packaged . . . as mixes.

COOKIES:

Packaged . . . as mixes.

MENUS CHOSEN FROM PREPARED OR PARTIALLY PREPARED FOODS

Each menu has coffee for adults, milk for children

HOLIDAY MENU

Chilled Cranberry Juice
Hot Sliced Turkey Candied Sweet Potatoes
Buttered Baby Lima Beans
Brown 'n Serve Butter Fluff Rolls
Celery, Olives, Radishes Pickled Peaches
Steamed Pudding
Nuts Candies

* * *

Clam Bouillon Celery Crackers
Spaghetti with Vienna Sausages
Green Salad with French Dressing
Hot GingerCake with Whipped Cream
Instant Coffee

EVERYDAY MENU

Corned Beef Hash Chili Sauce
Buttered Green Beans
Baking Powder Biscuits Apple Jelly
Combination Fruit Salad
Cheese Crackers

* * *

Vegetable Noodle Soup
Crackers Rolls or Bread
Green Salad
Crustquick Pie with Chocolate Cream Filling
Coffee

KEEP A WELL STOCKED EMERGENCY SHELF

To stretch menus and add festive touches for unexpected guests or when too busy for shopping and cooking.

Very little time?

Some stores have a wide selection of hot cooked meats and main dishes, salads, desserts, etc., ready for you to take home and serve.

No time at all?

Larger cities have special eating places or preparation centers that will deliver complete hot meals right to your home for immediate serving.

Shortcut products that you buy and like and buy again will become standard grocery items. Those that do not meet standards of quality and cost will soon disappear.

Let your head save your heels. **SHORT CUTS**

Have a plan for your time and work. Map out a general schedule for every day in the week. Set a certain day each week to include at least one of the special tasks that must be done once a week.

Take time to plan meals for a week or several days at a time. Plan when you're hungry and appetite will help you. Keep at hand a few menus, simple to prepare but delicious to eat, for busy days.

Market only once or twice for the week. Keep your meal patterns in mind, filling them in with available, seasonal foods.

Have logical and orderly arrangement in your kitchen. **(See pictures pp. 430, 431.)**

Establish convenient work centers. Have a cleaning center around the sink . . . with space for utensils and supplies for dishwashing and cleaning vegetables; and a baking center (*see p. 2*); a salad center (*p. 334*); a cooking-and-serving center around the stove with enough space on or near it for cooking equipment, seasonings, and flour, also space to keep dishes warm.

Shelves of different widths

File between shelves   Dividers for drawers

If you have too few shelves (with waste space between), remove built-in shelves. Fit in boards of various widths to hold different types of dishes. Install upright partitions to file cake, pie pans, etc. Add racks to cupboard doors for small articles used often, dividers in deep and shallow drawers, etc. Keep on lower shelves, and forward, things used most often . . . on higher shelves, and toward the back, things used least often.

Keep utensils and equipment in good working order. Discard gadgets that add work.

Learn good work habits. For example, assemble materials before starting to bake. Keep table cleared and cooking dishes washed as you go along.

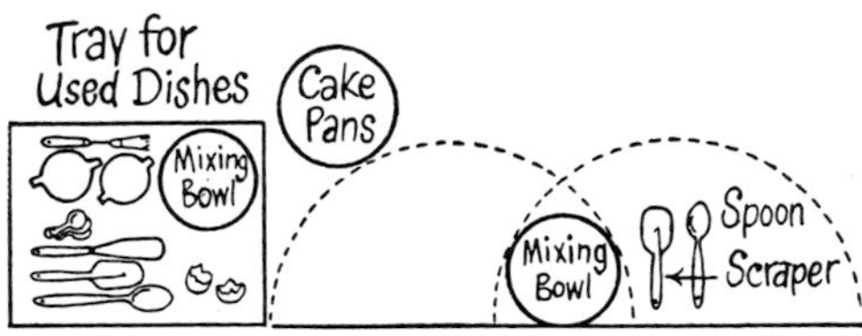

Prepare for tomorrow while cooking today. Make gelatin salads, cream sauces, salad dressings ahead of time.

Prepare some dishes for last-minute mixing or baking. Make refrigerator doughs for cookies and rolls to be baked on short notice; prepare meat loaf and casserole dishes ahead of time ready for baking; make gravies and sauces for meat pies.

Perfect your homemaking skills. Practice each task until it goes smoothly and easily. Thus develop techniques in

meal-planning	home-beautifying
cooking	nursing
marketing	bed-making
sewing	cleaning
dishwashing	laundering

Organize the family to cooperate.

Train the children to help with different jobs. Very young children can set and clear the table. Older ones can cook.

SHORT CUTS Make every motion count.

Planning your work
To save precious time,
Pays dividends . . .
Without costing a dime.

NOTE: *See tips, short cuts in every chapter.*

Keep a blackboard in your kitchen for grocery lists, menus, messages to your family, and reminders.

Save time... Insure sanitation.

Rinse dishes with boiling water, leave on rack to dry. Wipe glasses, silver. Some prefer to wash dishes only once a day. Saves soap, time. Rinse and stack, then cover.

To make coffee, measure all water at once. Have a mark on coffee pot to show correct amount. Measure coffee with one motion in marked cup.

Think ahead for efficiency

Right after using, ***fill cooking pans with*** hot water. Exception: use cold water for cereal, egg, milk dishes.

Keep spices on a tray or in a box. Lift out of cupboard all at one time.

One clean-up process instead of several

Before washing the breakfast dishes, do any necessary baking or advance meal preparation. Then wash all at once.

To boil potatoes in less time: remove a strip of skin from one side. Boil, then rest of skin peels off easily. *To bake potatoes* in half the time: boil first for 15 min.

Combine jobs to save time and energy

Bake cake or cookies while washing dishes or cooking dinner; peel potatoes while meat is browning; cook some foods to be served 2 or 3 times . . . beef for roast, hash, pie.

Do messy tasks, such as paring potatoes, on paper to be disposed of easily. Have a paper bag at working area for scraps.

Daily care saves time and equipment

Eliminate cleaning of broiler by placing aluminum foil over rack to catch drippings. Daily care of stove saves special cleaning.

Easy and fun . . . have family "make their own" lunch or Sunday supper: Take meat, cheese, leftovers, from refrigerator; set out bread, relishes.

Bake and cook ahead

Bake and prepare large amount of foods at a time and freeze according to directions with freezer.

After grating soft cheese, immediately rub hard crust of bread over grater to clean it. Clean grater with stiff brush.

Precaution saves clean-up work

Prevent splashing when whipping cream by placing waxed paper with a hole for beater over top of bowl. Tie a paper sack over food grinder to catch crumbs, nuts, etc. when grinding.

Keep all cleaning supplies and equipment in a basket and carry from room to room while cleaning.

Make work easy. **SHORT CUTS**

If you're tired from overwork,
Household chores you're bound to shirk.
Read these pointers tried and true
And discover what to do

Wear comfortable clothes and properly fitted shoes while working around the house.

For personal outlook

Eat proper food for health and vitality. Every morning before breakfast, comb hair, apply make-up, a dash of cologne, and perhaps some simple earrings. Does wonders for your morale.

While children are napping, do something refreshing. Write, knit, or listen to pleasant music.

Your mind can accomplish things while your hands are busy

Do head work while dusting, sweeping, washing dishes, paring potatoes, etc. Plan family recreation, the garden, etc.

Have sink, work table, counter tops, etc. at a height that is comfortable, to eliminate strain . . . if dishpan is too low, set it on a box.

Prevent unnecessary fatigue

Use a dust mop and a long-handled dust pan. Use self-wringing mop (no stooping).

If you feel tired, lie down on the floor on your back, put your hands above your head, close your eyes, and relax for 3 to 5 min.

Exercise, sunshine, fresh air are part of health

Get outdoors every day. Take a walk, do some gardening, take the children for an outing, or pay your neighbor a short visit.

If you have just a moment, sit down, put your feet up on a chair, close your eyes and just relax your muscles. Let your arms, hands, and head fall limp.

Good posture prevents fatigue

When standing, keep erect posture . . . do not slump or bend over tasks (poor posture is more tiring). Remember sitting uses much less energy than standing.

Alternate sitting down tasks and standing up tasks. Don't be on your feet too long at one time.

Check up on yourself

If after following all these rules for proper rest, exercise, diet, you are still tired and depressed, have a medical check-up and follow doctor's orders.

Harbor pleasant thoughts while working. It will make every task lighter and pleasanter.

Refresh your spirits

"Recreation" means "re-create" . . . for enthusiasm and courage. Garden, paint pictures, pursue any hobby, look through a magazine for home planning ideas, read a good book, or attend club meetings.

Notice humorous and interesting incidents to relate at dinner-time, etc.

SHORT CUTS Quick tricks with breads and desserts.

BISQUICK, an All-Purpose Mix: With this package on the shelf, the busy homemaker, the modern business woman, or the impromptu hostess is prepared to meet any mealtime emergency with complete assurance and success. BISQUICK will make 100 different bakings.

The package contains six top quality ingredients, including pure vegetable shortening, blended together more expertly than possible by hand.

To make any of the 12 basic popular bakings below, more easily and swiftly than ever before, just follow directions on the BISQUICK package.

JUST ADD LIQUID TO BISQUICK FOR

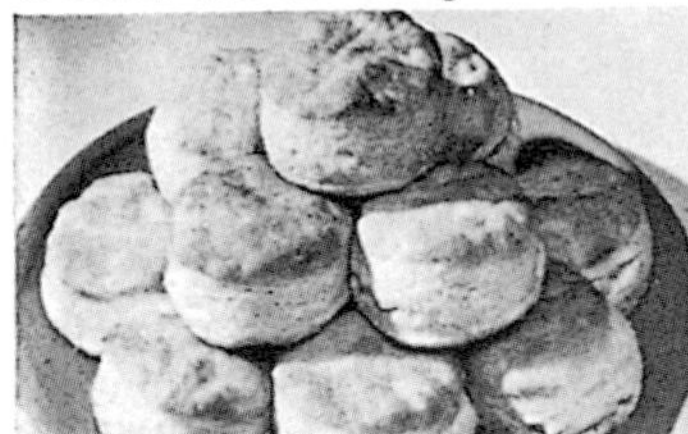
Fluffy Rolled Biscuits

Tender Drop Biscuits

Delicious Fruit Shortcakes

Melt-in-Your-Mouth Dumplings

Luscious Fruit Cobbler

Crusty Meat Pie

ADD ONLY A FEW EXTRA INGREDIENTS FOR

Crispy Waffles

Tender Pancakes

Golden Muffins

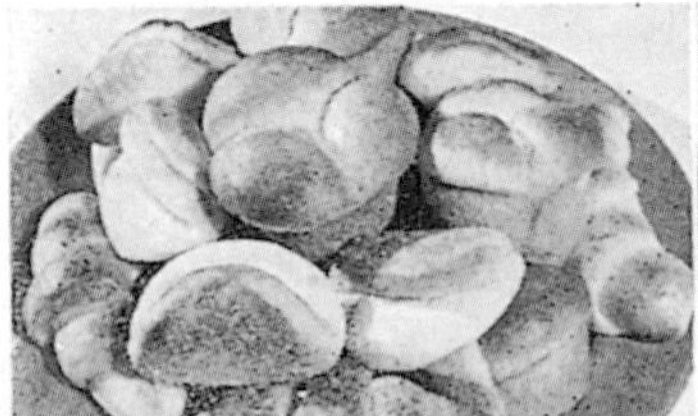
Light Yeast Rolls

Crumb-Topped Coffee Cake

Cookies in No Time

Quick, easy ways to pastry and pies. **SHORT CUTS**

CRUSTQUICK (Betty Crocker Pie Crust Mix) . . . **for speed in making perfect, flaky pastry.**

Contains GOLD MEDAL Flour and salt skillfully blended with a shortening extra-good for pastry. Anyone can make flaky, melt-in-your-mouth pastry with CRUSTQUICK.

Just add water. No guesswork. The exact amount is given in the directions on the package. Each box of CRUSTQUICK is ample for 2-crust 9″ pie.

YOUR FAVORITE PIES

Look for these time-saving recipes on your package of CRUSTQUICK:

APPLE PIE

QUICK LEMON MERINGUE PIE

FRESH FRUIT PIES (all fresh berries, pitted cherries, apricots, and peaches)

CANNED FRUIT PIES (berries, cherries, apricots, or sliced peaches)

CRUSTQUICK Will Make Any Kind of Pie

For any desired Pie Filling and for attractive Pie Finishes, see "PIES."

All you have to do—

To make quick-easy chocolate, butterscotch, or cream pie fillings: use prepared pudding mixes. Place in baked CRUSTQUICK shell. When cool, spread with whipped cream and serve.

SHORTCUT CREAMY LEMON MERINGUE PIE

Popular uncooked filling.

Mix together . . .

2 egg yolks
$\frac{1}{4}$ tsp. salt
few drops almond extract
$1\frac{1}{3}$ cups (15 oz. can) *sweetened condensed milk* (not evaporated)

Stir in . . .

$\frac{1}{2}$ cup lemon juice

Pour into cooled 8″ baked CRUSTQUICK shell. Add 2-egg white Meringue.

QUICK ORANGE MERINGUE PIE

Made with frozen orange juice.

Follow method in Lemon Meringue Pie recipe on CRUSTQUICK package, but use:

1 cup sugar
4 tbsp. cornstarch
$1\frac{1}{3}$ cups hot orange juice (instead of hot water). The orange juice is frozen concentrated orange juice diluted as directed on the can.
2 egg yolks
2 tbsp. butter

Omit grated rind.

For Meringue, use only 2 egg whites, 4 tbsp. sugar, and $\frac{1}{4}$ tsp. cream of tartar.

QUICK GRAPE JUICE PIE

Made with bottled or frozen grape juice.

Follow method in Lemon Meringue Pie recipe on CRUSTQUICK package, but use:

$\frac{3}{4}$ cup sugar
4 tbsp. cornstarch
$1\frac{1}{3}$ cups hot grape juice (instead of hot water). Grape juice is frozen concentrated juice diluted as directed on can.
2 egg yolks
2 tbsp. butter
2 tsp. lemon juice added with butter

Fold 2 stiffly beaten egg whites (with $\frac{1}{4}$ tsp. cream of tartar beaten in) into cooled filling. Top with thin coating of whipped cream.

SHORT CUTS

Quick easy way to luscious cakes.

BETTY CROCKER CAKE MIX uses:
3 ingredients **6 utensils**

TYPICAL "BUTTER-TYPE" CAKE uses:
8 ingredients **15 utensils**

Made of premium-quality SOFTASILK Cake Flour and special cake-mix shortening.

No compromise on quality. No dried eggs in this mix. This means longer shelf-life for the mix. Fresh eggs in the cake mean consistently better eating quality cakes.

What type of frosting????

Investigate "FROSTING" chapter for clues and hints and many likely choices.

For a super-speedy frosting: buy one of the "shortcut" frostings at your grocer's.

DEVILS FOOD CAKE

With a dark, moist, fudgy eating quality.

Follow directions on package of BETTY CROCKER DEVILS FOOD CAKE MIX. See "FROSTINGS" or "Chocolate Cake" pages for attractive ways to finish and serve.

GINGERCAKE AND COOKIES

Spicy, rich, tender, and light . . . as a 9" square cake or 18 medium cup cakes or 36 cookies.

Follow directions on package of BETTY CROCKER GINGERCAKE AND COOKY MIX. Serve piping hot as a dessert with any meal. A grand accompaniment to fruit salad, cottage cheese, etc. See package insert and "DESSERTS" for delicious ways to serve.

YELLOW, SPICE, OR WHITE CAKE

Many types of cakes and their variations found in the Cake chapter may be made with our Cake Mixes with just simple additions.

YELLOW CAKE: For full, fluffy, delicate layers, follow directions on package of BETTY CROCKER PARTYCAKE MIX. Finish as desired; or see "Whole Egg Cakes."

SPICE CAKE: Follow directions on package of BETTY CROCKER PARTYCAKE MIX. Delicious with Browned Butter Icing and toasted pecan halves.

WHITE CAKE: For a snowy white, melt-in-mouth cake, follow directions on package of BETTY CROCKER PARTYCAKE MIX. Luscious with Cream Filling, cooked white frosting generously covered with coconut.

Index

INDEX (cont.)

ALPHABETICAL INDEX BY CHAPTERS

BREADS, YEAST (cont.)

BREADS, YEAST (cont.)

CAKES (cont)

CAKES (cont.)

DESSERTS (cont.)

DESSERTS (cont.)

EGGS 249–260

FILLINGS 172

FROSTINGS 161–172

MEATS, FISH (cont.)

MEATS, FISH (cont.)

PIES 293–328

PIES (cont.)

PIES (cont.)

SALADS

SALAD DRESSINGS

SPECIALTIES

WHEN USING GOLD MEDAL "SELF-RISING" FLOUR

with recipes in this book

Omit baking powder, soda, and salt. Or write to Betty Crocker, General Mills, Inc., Minneapolis, Minnesota, for detailed "Self-Rising" adjustments. Do not use GOLD MEDAL "Self-Rising" Flour in yeast bakings unless the recipes call for yeast.

Some Changes Should Be Made . . .

WHEN BAKING CAKES AT HIGH ALTITUDES

BAKING TEMPERATURE

At all altitudes over 3,500 feet, increase baking temperature 25°.

GOLD MEDAL *"Kitchen-tested"* FLOUR
SOFTASILK CAKE FLOUR

At 3,500 feet add 1 tbsp. flour and then add 1 tbsp. for each 1,500 foot increase in elevation above 3,500 feet.

EGGS

Use maximum amount of egg called for in recipe. If part of egg is needed to make full measure, add egg white . . . not yolk.

SUGAR

Do not reduce at any altitude.

LEAVENING

If recipe calls for both baking powder and soda, make suggested changes in both ingredients (see table below). Measure accurately, and, above 2,000 feet, use only the amount of *baking powder* and/or *baking soda* shown in adjustment table. When sea level recipe calls for:

Sea Level	*2000–3500 ft.	*3500–5000 ft.	*5000–6500 ft.	*6500–8000 ft.	*Over 8000 ft.
1 tsp.	¾– ⅔	⅔–½	½–⅓	⅓–¼	¼
1½ tsp.	1¼–1	1 –¾	¾–⅔	⅔–½	½
2 tsp.	1¾–1½	1½–1¼	1¼–1	1 –¾	¾
2½ tsp.	2 –1¾	1¾–1½	1½–1¼	1¼–1	1
3 tsp.	2¼–2	2 –1½	1½–1¼	1¼–1	1
3½ tsp.	3 –2½	2½–2	2 –1½	1½–1	1
4 tsp.	3 –2½	2½–2	2 –1½	1½–1	1

*Use larger amount of leavening at lower altitudes within each given range and smaller amount of leavening at higher altitudes.

SPECIAL HINTS

Grease and flour cake pans thoroughly. Use a high grade vegetable shortening. Measure accurately and bake exactly as directed. In Angel Food and Sponge Cakes: beat egg whites only to a soft peak. Fold in dry ingredients lightly and quickly (use as few strokes as possible). Use proper adjustments for flour, eggs, leavening.

NOTES

NOTES

NOTES

NOTES